The Jurisdiction of the International Criminal Court

Victor Tsilonis

The Jurisdiction of the International Criminal Court

Second Edition

Springer

Victor Tsilonis
International Criminal Court Bar Association (ICCBA)
The Hague, The Netherlands

ISBN 978-3-031-46137-8 ISBN 978-3-031-46138-5 (eBook)
https://doi.org/10.1007/978-3-031-46138-5

This Springer imprint is published by the registered company Springer Nature Switzerland AG
The registered company address is: Gewerbestrasse 11, 6330 Cham, Switzerland

Paper in this product is recyclable.

To Avgi, Joan and Themistocles for this memorable journey

'One swallow may not a summer make
but still may bring more swallows'
'The Swallow and the Eagle', Konstantinos Melissas (original with the author)
contra

'Where is everybody?'
Enrico Fermi

Foreword of the First Edition

Politics and History as 'Extralegal' Interpretative Factors of Legal Provisions

The subject of the present monograph is the preconditions for the exercise of jurisdiction of the International Criminal Court (ICC). In the Rome Statute of the ICCI (ICCRSt), the Court's jurisdiction revolves around the commission of international crimes, i.e. war crimes, crimes against humanity, genocide and most recently, the crime of aggression. It is apparent that the interpretation of those multifaceted terms, as well as other similar notions also contained in the ICCRSt (e.g. 'conflict', 'attack' and 'immunities'), constitutes a fundamental criterion regarding whether or not the Court will eventually intervene. However, when interpreting such general concepts, it is reasonable to include considerations of 'extralegal' character, and, especially, the way that the interests of great geostrategic forces are served. Hence, the quest for the concepts' true meaning in certain cases cannot be fulfilled solely via purely dogmatic legal approaches, and also involves a wider approach, with an emphasis on those political and historical factors that decisively impact the rendering of decisions by the International Criminal Court. Otherwise, the interpretation of these legal concepts will be incomplete and exclude from the research's scope the deeper reasons behind the preference for one interpretive approach over the other.

It is precisely this broader interpretative approach, *the 'holistic' approach*, as the author calls it, that constitutes, in my opinion, the great comparative advantage of this monograph in comparison with others. Certainly, this 'holistic' approach somewhat restricts the scope of a purely dogmatic legal approach. However, International Law and relationships between States have always had, since Thucydides' times and the Melian Dialogue with the Athenian superpower of that era, an intense dimension of power relations, where ordinarily the strongest party prevails. And this, of course, cannot be disregarded in the interpretation of international law's legal provisions, especially when the perceptions of 'the law of the strongest' are in direct opposition to basic principles of human rights and social justice.

In a wider context, one could speak at this point about a clash between, on the one hand, legal positivism, which is usually characterised by formalism and strict adherence to the applicable legal rules for the sake of legal certainty (e.g. Hans Kelsen) and, on the other hand, natural law, idealism and leniency, and ultimately 'equitable law' and 'the spirit of the law' (cf. Matthew 23, 23–24), as safety valves for the protection of substantive justice and human rights (e.g. Rudolf Stammler).

This confrontation moves, ultimately, between the dipole *de lege lata* and *de lege ferenda*. In other words, on the one hand, between what has been legally enacted to apply, what is precisely defined by a legal provision on a particular issue at a given time according to theory and jurisprudence (*de lege lata*) and, on the other hand, what ought to apply based on the more appropriate legal interpretation, the legislator's will, the teleological and ultimately optimal interpretation that sufficiently takes into account not only the black letter of the law but also the 'extralegal' elements, including societal developments and changes, business practices, public morals, political correlations, the 'average' person's behaviour and so on (*de lege ferenda*).

Consequently, this is one of the first monographs amid the abundant literature on the International Criminal Court that attempts to examine the breadth and depth of the issues raised in relation to the preconditions for exercising the jurisdiction of the International Criminal Court (Article 12 ICCRSt) and the principle of complementarity, taking into account the 'ubiquitous' factor of international politics as well as contemporary historical data and evidence that are often ignored or overlooked, such as the internal circulars of the ICC Prosecutor's Office.

Undoubtedly, the above co-evaluation provides a panoramic view of the legal issues under consideration, which does not only lead to innovative proposals (such as new criteria for the definition of international crime), but also crucially contributes to the substantiated drawing of conclusions which often contradict the prevalent views of theory and jurisprudence.

Finally, yet importantly, the usefulness of this 'holistic' analysis is particularly demonstrated in the sections regarding Palestine and the concept of the State in international criminal law, immunities and the principle of complementarity. Indeed, the enactment of complementarity for the first time in international criminal law in 1998 during the Rome Conference was the driving force behind the completion of the procedures for the foundation of the International Criminal Court.

The work of Victor Tsilonis, a very promising new scholar, fills a significant gap in the literature and opens up new pathways in the field of Public International Law.

University of Athens, Athens, Greece Nestor Courakis
University of Nicosia, Nicosia, Cyprus

Preface of the Second Edition

Is Humanity on the Verge of Extinction? Polycrisis: Covid-19 pandemic, War in Ukraine, artificial intelligence, natural catastrophes, ecocides, nuclear threat, and the 'new' role of international criminal law

No one could possibly have imagined the torrent of events that have stormed abruptly the apparent serenity of the modern civilised world immediately after the publication of the first edition of this book on the jurisdiction of the International Criminal Court in December 2019. In fact, it was soon proved that we indeed needed new words to describe this series of dark events, leading the Columbia University economic historian Adam Tooze to ingeniously come up with a new term: 'polycrisis'. The prolonged global pandemic of Covid-19 (coined by the abbreviation of the expression 'coronavirus disease of 2019') brought us, rather unexpectedly, back to previous centuries when humanity had to struggle for its very existence fighting against malaria, cholera, bubonic plague, smallpox, influenza and other contagious diseases.

The physical contact became a sort of extravagant habit, while the digital world instantly took the opportunity to step up its presence and influence in order to fill squarely this much-anticipated social vacuum. Zoom, Microsoft Teams and Google Hangouts/Meet meetings became swiftly the new norm, while states and government agencies increased exponentially their efforts to 'utilise' the digital era at its fullest by wiretapping prominent public figures, treating the digital dissemination of (mis)-information as a new exciting weapon and using malware, DDoS, 'zero click' and other, yet publicly unknown, sophisticated digital attacks for critically disrupting operations and services of enemy states.

After the end of the 2-year lockdown period, when it first seemed that humanity was eventually leaving one of its most bizarre chapters in modern history behind, the war in Ukraine erupted like Mount Vesuvius; and while the Vesuvius' eruption ejected 'merely' a cloud of stones, ashes and volcanic gases to a height of 33 km before destroying the Roman cities of Pompeii, Herculaneum, Oplontis and Stabiae, the invasion of Ukraine placed in danger not only Ukraine or Europe but in fact the whole world. Undeniably, the escalation of the conflict, its unending duration and the continuous threats regarding the use of nuclear force heighten daily the devastating possibilities of the war being spread to more states and ultimately lead to a third and possibly last for humanity World War.

Contemporaneously, though, the restless spirit of human ingenuity continued its work in the realm of digital world as if our physical world was meant to last for ever; digital services, run by artificial intelligence like ChatGPT, AI Chat and Dall-E that could arguably assist humans in unsurpassed ways, were triumphantly announced and embraced just before the whole world could be blown to radioactive pieces.

It is striking that when on 6 February 2023 UN Secretary-General António Guterres made one of the darkest ever statements regarding the course of humanity and the war in Ukraine under the solemn title ‘Act decisively before it is too late’, artificial intelligence services were expressing a quite opposing view. In fact, the IOS-based artificial intelligence AI Chat was sufficiently optimistic to answer the question ‘What are the chances that the war in Ukraine will lead to a third world war?’ as follows:

> It is extremely unlikely that the war in Ukraine would lead to a third world war. The war in Ukraine is a regional conflict and the international community has taken strong steps to ensure that it does not escalate into an even larger conflict. Furthermore, the parties involved in the war have no significant interest in escalating the conflict to a world war, since they all understand that they could not gain anything from such an event. Therefore, while anything is possible, the chances of the war in Ukraine leading to a third world war are extremely slim.

Alas, things could never be farther from the truth, although it probably is unfair to judge and evaluate the capabilities of novel artificial intelligence services from one answer alone. Shortly afterwards Chat GPT jumped swiftly to its fourth edition and this provoked technology gurus like Elon Musk to sign a letter calling for a 6-month pause on development of all artificial intelligence technology, but without stopping him apparently from investing heavily in AI development at the same time.

Coincidentally enough, the same day as the above UN Secretary-General António Guterres’ statement (Monday 6 February 2023) was marked by another tragic event. Over 45,000 people were killed and scores more injured by a tremendous earthquake which struck south-eastern Turkey and Syria. And notwithstanding that this environmental catastrophe had nothing to do with the uncontrollable and often illogical human intervention in the environment, it was quite important in terms of international criminal law; the earthquake stopped even momentarily the great possibility of a potential Turkish invasion at the Greek islands of the Aegean Sea as the next big case before the International Criminal Court.

Nonetheless, March 2023 proved to be a historic month for humanity and international criminal law for another, largely unexpected reason: on 17 March 2023, Pre-Trial Chamber II of the International Criminal Court (‘ICC’ or ‘the Court’) issued warrants of arrest for two individuals in the context of the situation in Ukraine: Mr Vladimir Vladimirovich Putin and Ms Maria Alekseyevna Lvova-Belova. Following the Office of the Prosecutor’s applications of 22 February 2023, both persons were *prima facie* regarded as allegedly responsible for the war crimes of unlawful deportation and transfer of children from occupied areas of Ukraine to the Russian Federation pursuant to the provisions of Article 8(2)(a)(vii) and (viii) of the Rome Statute (ICCRst). Consequently, the chilling effect of having the acting head of one of the two greatest nuclear superpowers of the world indicted by the International Criminal Court was publicly met with a 'creepy' feeling; a strange feeling of awe similar to listening that one of NASA's spacecrafts came in close proximity with unidentified objects of extraterrestrial origin in the vicinity of Mars.

And while one was truly tempted to believe that things cannot go any worse, the cruel human-made reality came to place two more abhorrent posters on its window screens; the first one involved Sudan and the second once again Ukraine.

In Sudan, an armed conflict between the Sudanese Armed Forces (SAF) and the paramilitary Rapid Support Forces (RSF) of Sudan officially began on 15 April 2023, with the fighting taking place mostly around the capital city of Khartoum and the Darfur region. In order to realise the size of the conflict, one should also note that the Sudanese Armed Forces (SAF) have about 200,000 active personnel, while the paramilitary Rapid Support Forces (RSF) of Sudan are estimated to number between 70,000–150,000. The latest Sudanese civil war—which has already claimed thousands of lives, caused several thousand more injuries and led to extensive property destruction—broke out shortly after Sudan's ruling military concluded a review of an agreement with Russia to build a navy base on the Red Sea on 11 February 2023 and shortly before the deal was anxiously ratified by Sudan's yet unformed Parliament.

In the occupied territory of Ukraine, the Kakhovka Dam, situated on Ukraine's Dnieper (or Dnipro) river in the Kherson Oblast region, was maliciously breached on 6 June 2023, leading to severe flooding of more than 600 km^2. The massive Soviet-era dam on the Dnipro River was practically separating Russian and Ukrainian forces in southern Ukraine. At the time of this ecocidal incident, the Russian military held control over the dam, having captured it during the initial stages of the Ukraine's invasion. According to some experts and the government of Ukraine, an internal explosion orchestrated by Russia was the reason for the dam's breach. Hence, serious accusations have been pointed towards the Russian military forces, openly endorsing that they have detonated the dam in order to obstruct or postpone an anticipated major Ukrainian counter offence. Conversely, Russian authorities have vehemently denied these claims, attributing the dam's explosion to missiles launched by Ukrainian forces, which allegedly committed a horrendous terrorist act with the aim of cutting off water supplies to Crimea and distracting attention from their already 'faltering' and 'overtly advertised' counter-offensive.

The dam raised the water level of the Dnipro by 16 metres (52.49 feet) and made possible its redirection to the arid Crimean Peninsula, triggering the growth of urban centres and irrigated agriculture. After the Kakhovka Dam's blast, thousands of inhabitants downstream were compelled to evacuate and numerous villages, under both Ukrainian and Russian control, have been swallowed by the floodwaters. Furthermore, the significant loss of water from the reservoir could potentially jeopardise the future critical water provision for the Zaporizhzhia Nuclear Power Plant. While this act is arguably a war crime, it is undeniably an ecocide of the most heinous form and while no side takes 'awkwardly' responsibility of the dam's explosion, we are left being reminded of the maxim 'In war, truth is the first casualty' [often attributed to Aeschylus (fifth century B.C.), Dr Samuel Johnson (1758), Ethel Snowden (1915) and/or Hiram Warren Johnson (1918); in any case, it is spectacularly ironic that the true owner of this proverb is so difficult to ascertain. Nonetheless, Shapiro F R, The Yale Book of Quotations, Yale University Press, Yale (2021), Introduction xvii & p. 565, attributes it categorically to the female writer Ethel Snowden].

Undeniably, all the above stormy developments worldwide lead to the 'eternal question' of international criminal law, i.e., what is or ideally should be exactly the role of international criminal law in our times? Is there a 'new' role for international criminal law in our turbulent world or there is essentially nothing new that international criminal law should offer? It seems that what international criminal law needs to pursue now even harder is 'merely' upholding the original mission of international criminal law to its highest tenable standards, while the deadly fog of war and destruction is being spread worldwide.

In turn that means that the people and institutions involved in international criminal law should provide a reliable and fair international legal framework which ends the impunity even for the strongest persons when they commit egregious international crimes, namely: war crimes, crimes against humanity, genocide and the crime of aggression. Fortunately, it seems that people like the new Prosecutor of the International Criminal Court, Karim Khan KC, and eminent organisations like Eurojust have already realised this by taking unprecedented steps during the ongoing war in Ukraine not only in order to collect, preserve or evaluate evidence, but also to indict key, 'untouchable' public figures. Hence, the ICC Prosecutor applied on 22 February 2023 for the issuance of arrest warrants, while on 23 February 2023 Eurojust announced the commencement of operations of a Core International Crimes Evidence Database and a new International Centre for Prosecution of the Crime of Aggression. Presently, it seems that both the evidence database and the new international centre will act as precursors to the establishment of a new international criminal tribunal which will focus on the prosecution of the crime of aggression. Undeniably, the said concerted actions create a glimpse of hope for international criminal justice and humanity as a whole.

Moreover this also signifies that international criminal law should further examine and analyse the role of new technologies and incidents, ranging from the spread of viruses, ecological catastrophes and the multilayered evolution of digital world, technology and artificial intelligence. Therefore, the second edition of 'The Jurisdiction of the International Criminal Court' contains three new chapters on ecocide, automated lethal weapons and cyber warfare with the explicit aim of providing a new window of thought to the reader regarding their interrelation with international criminal law.

Consequently, I am truly grateful for the research assistance of Marina Cardoso Farias in the fields of ecocide, cyber warfare and automated lethal weapons; Marina is an excellent Brazilian lawyer with a great passion for international criminal law and feel fortunate for her devotion and contribution. Moreover I would like sincerely to thank Marialena Pissa, legal associate at Newlaw law firm, and trainee lawyer Nikolaos-Athanasios Apostolidis for updating all the internet sources of the second edition and the bibliography section. Finally, the last word should be devoted to my dear publisher Springer and its exquisite employees Julia Beier, Laura Hofmann and Leonie Sittner for their unparalleled kindness, professionalism and support throughout the publication of the book's second edition. I am truly thankful for collaborating with them and wish them all the best in their lives and careers; clearly, the publication of this second edition would not have been feasible without their unending support.

As always, the responsibility for any errors or omissions rests solely with me.

In this 25th hour there is still some hope, still an array of light in humanity's iron sky. Strangely enough, the famous Drake's Equation ($N = R^* \times fp \times ne \times fl \times fi \times fc \times L$) offers some solace; in that equation, L is the length of time civilisations release detectable signals into space and Drake believed that a minimum value was 1000 years. So, if that assumption was correct humanity might actually have a considerable amount of chances to reach around 2.936 AD, since 1936 was the year of the first public, high-definition television broadcast by the BBC (*contra* post-Fermi paradox).

The Hague, The Netherlands
8 June 2023

Victor Tsilonis

Contents

Abbreviations

Am Univ Int Law Rev	American University International Law Review
AJIL	American Journal of International Law
Am Soc Int Law Proc	American Society of International Law Proceedings
ASP	Assembly of States Parties
Cardozo J Int Comp Law	Cardozo Journal of International and Comparative Law
Case West Res J Int Law	Case Western Reserve Journal of International Law
COLR	Cork Online Law Review
Colum J Transnatl Law	Columbia Journal of Transnational Law
Duke J Comp Int Law	Duke Journal of Comparative and International Law
Denv J Int Law Policy	Denver Journal of International Law and Policy
ECJ	European Court of Justice
EJIL	European Journal of International Law
Geo J Int Law	Georgetown Journal of International Law
Geo Wash Int Law Rev	George Washington International Law Review
GoJIL	Goettingen Journal of International Law
Harv Int Law J	Harvard International Law Journal
Hum Rights Brief	Human Rights Brief
Hum Rights Law Rev	Human Rights Law Review
HVHRJ	Harvard Human Rights Journal
ICC	International Criminal Court
ICCPE	International Criminal Court for the Protection of the Environment
ICJ	International Court of Justice
ILC	International Law Commission
ILM	International Legal Materials
ILSA J Int Comp Law	International Law Students' Association Journal of International and Comparative Law

Ind Int Comp Law Rev	Indiana International and Comparative Law Review
IMTN	International Military Tribunal of Nuremberg
J Marshall Law Rev	John Marshall Law Review
JICJ	Journal of International Criminal Justice
J Law Soc Challenges	Journal of Law and Social Challenges
LJIL	Leiden Journal of International Law
MJIL	Michigan Journal of International Law
Melb J Int Law	Melbourne Journal of international Law
N Engl J Int Comp Law	New England Journal of International and Comparative law
N Z J Public Int Law	New Zealand Journal of Public and International Law
Penn State Int Law Rev	Penn State International Law Review
ICCRSt	Rome Statute of the International Criminal Court
R.I.D.P.	Revue Internationale de Droit Penale
RGDIP	Revue Générale de Droit International Public
S Calif Interdiscip Law J	Southern California Interdisciplinary Law Journal
SCSL	Special Court for Sierra Leone
SSRN	Social Science Research Network
TJIL	Texas Journal of International Law
Univ Pa Law Rev	University of Pennsylvania Law Review
Univ Colo Law Rev	University of Colorado Law Review
US/USA	United States of America
UK	United Kingdom
Vill Law Rev	Villanova Law Review
Wash Univ Law Rev	Washington University Law Review
Wash Univ Glob Stud Law Rev	Washington University Global Studies Law Review
ZNR	Zeitschrift fű̈r Neuere Rechtsgeschichte

Chapter 1
The Definition of International Crime

Abstract During the early decades of the twentieth century, the term 'international crime' was not conceptually analysed by legal scholars. This trend is exemplified by the *Second Protocol to the Geneva Convention for the Pacific Settlement of International Disputes of 2 October 1924*, which defined aggressive war as a war crime, without explicating the meaning of 'war crime.' A similar approach was taken at the end of World War II and during the Nuremberg trials, where a clear definition for 'international crime' was not provided. The term was first officially defined in the case of *United States of America v. Wilhelm List, et al.*, (also known as the Hostages Trial) by the International Military Tribunal of Nuremberg as "an act universally recognized as criminal, deemed a serious international concern, and for valid reasons, cannot be subjected to the exclusive jurisdiction of the state that would ordinarily control it." This chapter synthesises views of various scholars including Robert Cryer, Hakan Friman, Daryl Robinson and Elizabeth Wilmshurst, Gerhard Werle and Florian Jeßberger, Antonio Cassese, Mahmoud Cherif Bassiouni and Herbert Morays, to propose a novel definition of 'international crime.' The criteria applied in this new definition can have practical implications as it can be used to discern whether a crime is international and hence, if it falls within the scope of an international criminal justice institution. Recognising environmental destruction as a critical international concern, this chapter explores the prerequisites for ecocide to be acknowledged as a new international crime *de lege ferenda*. Therefore, the final section of the chapter, '1.6 Crafting a New Definition of International Crime,' examines not only Boko Haram's kidnapping of hundreds of students but also ecocide. This includes a hypothetical scenario where an oil tanker is maliciously sunk in the South Atlantic Ocean.

1.1 A Holistic Analysis of the International Criminal Law and Jurisdiction of the International Criminal Court

Theoretical but also practical approaches to international criminal law tend to bring home the fact that "law does not exist in a vacuum". On the contrary, intense political pressures often dictate the adoption of legal provisions, opinions, positions and

V. Tsilonis, *The Jurisdiction of the International Criminal Court*,
https://doi.org/10.1007/978-3-031-46138-5_1

'solutions', particularly in the field of international law. Here, whether in the realm of theory or actual international power relations, the various institutions of international criminal justice play an integral role (hybrid courts, international criminal tribunals, the International Criminal Court).

At the same time, the fact that other political, historical and non-legal factors constantly reshape international law, and in particular, international criminal law, compels us to include these in the scope of analysis of the emerging legal issues and cases concerning the jurisdiction of the International Criminal Court (ICC), well aware of the fact that they are usually sidelined or overlooked.

Although, admittedly, this 'holistic' attempt to analyse the aforementioned legal issues has progressively constituted a minor but important stream of thought in the international literature and can also be found, as of October 2013, in the case law of the International Criminal Court (see the official Summary of the landmark ICC Judgment of 11 October 2013 in the Al-Senussi case),[1] academics and scholars generally continue to adopt a one-dimensional approach and examine international criminal law exclusively through the prism of public international law, human rights law or even doctrinal criminal law.[2,3]

The present book attempts a succinct but holistic presentation of the most important issues related to the jurisdiction of the International Criminal Court (ICC), while emphasis is given to contemporary cases (Philippines, Afghanistan, Palestine, Libya etc.). Undoubtedly, this constitutes an attempt to analyse an extremely wide range of complex issues with a high level of difficulty.

The 'holistic' approach sets out to consider, analyse and co-evaluate a wide range of historical, political, geostrategic, international and, obviously, legal factors.[4] The significance of this analysis is demonstrated not only by the chapters on immunities and the principle of complementarity or the cases of Libya and Palestine, but also the evolution of international criminal law itself from a historical perspective; indeed,

---

[1] ICC (2013b).

[2] Tsilonis (2017), pp. 1257–1303.

[3] As Professor William Schabas stated in an interview to the author: "Hence I think that one of the problems with international justice right now, and particularly with the International Criminal Court, is that there is an unavoidable political dimension to it... In Thessaloniki, for example, you assume and accept that all serious crimes will be dealt with in an even manner and this is correct. This is what national justice is needed to do: that every murder that takes place in Thessaloniki will be investigated and prosecuted. But we can't and won't do that at the international level because we make political choices. What I want is to have us acknowledge that these are political choices and then discuss the political values that animate those choices. That is my only point. But I think to pretend that they are not political, which is what we are doing today, leads us into a *cul de sac* and this is a mistake.... Why are we going after the president of Sudan for Darfur and not the president of Israel for Gaza? Because of politics". 'Συνέντευξη με τον καθηγητή Ουίλιαμ Σέιμπας, Διεθνής Προστασία των Ανθρωπίνων Δικαιωμάτων και Πολιτική: Μια Αναπόδραστη Πραγματικότητα' [Tsilonis (2011). Also Intellectum (2010)].

[4] A more thorough analysis of this issue was published in two honourary volumes:

(1) Tsilonis (2016a), pp. 385–404.
(2) Tsilonis (2016b), pp. 1262–1283.

many philosophers have highlighted the importance of history for the acquisition of deeper knowledge.[5]

Inevitably, the overall synthesis and evaluation of all relevant data cannot bring 'absolute results' and thus, the reader of the present book has the opportunity to form his/her own opinion on the degree of influence that these 'non-legal' parameters carry. This does not mean, of course, that the present study does not evaluate the interrelation of all the above factors or does not reach final conclusions on every examined issue. On the contrary, a particular scientific method of co-evaluation of all relevant data necessitates a rather loose connection between them; but drawing direct conclusions in the form of cause and effect is not always possible, as Bernard Rachel pointed out in his monumental critical review of Gottfried Wilhelm Leibniz's *magnum opus*.[6]

Moreover, due to the range of issues examined, the book attempts to engage with a selection of PhD theses on international criminal law. This occurs in the first chapter, concerning the definition of international crime;[7] in the second chapter, regarding the prerequisites for the exercise of the International Criminal Court's jurisdiction and the principle of territoriality;[8] and finally in the fourth and sixth chapter while examining two of the four 'core crimes' where the International Criminal Court (ICC) has jurisdiction, namely the crime of aggression[9] and crimes against humanity.[10] It is the author's sincere hope that the reader will find this fruitful scientific dialogue beneficial, as it attempts to deal with seemingly intractable theoretical issues by proposing novel solutions (in the fourth chapter on crimes against humanity), offer new information and approaches (in the sixth chapter on the crime of aggression), review and criticique the existing discourse on Palestine (regarding the issue of the ICC's *ratione loci*) and, finally, summarise and reformulate theoretical concepts in a distinctive and clear way by introducing a new codification regarding the abstract notion of international crime *de lege ferenda* in the current chapter.

Additionally, particular emphasis is placed on the principle of complementarity—which governs the Rome Statute of the International Criminal Court—, the practical complications surrounding its implementation and the 'awakening hypothesis' of the complementarity principle, which the book introduces for the first time. This refers to the paradoxical non-implementation of the complementarity principle during the

---

[5] "History is philosophy teaching by examples", Dionysius of Halicarnassus; "What experience and history teach is this — that nations and governments have never learned anything from history, or acted upon any lessons they might have drawn from it", George Wilhelm Friedrich Hegel; "World history is the world's court", Friedrich Schiller. See Partington (1997). "If I reveal to you everything that has ever happened, you will know everything that will happen", Confucius in Chalikias S (trans.) (2001).

[6] Monk (2007), pp. 24–25.

[7] Chouliaras (2013).

[8] Vagias (2011).

[9] Pihou (2012).

[10] Naziris (2009).

period from the establishment of the International Criminal Court to the decision on the Al Senussi case (Situation in Libya) on 11 October 2013, when the principle was arguably implemented for the first time, albeit in a distorted way, since it was ruled that Al Senussi should be tried by the State of Libya—despite the country being torn apart by internal armed conflicts.[11] The decision is therefore examined extensively in this chapter, since, along with the decision on the Tomas Lubanga Dyilo case and the cases related to the situation in Kenya, it brings into focus the issue of the non-implementation of the principle of complementarity.

This analysis is essential because, even though much research work and thousands of articles have been written in favour of the principle of complementarity, critique has thus far been scant, while any problems pertaining to the non-implementation of the complementarity principle have not been examined at all. This is because ever since the Rome Conference in 1998, at which the ICC was established, critique has been couched in terms of being either 'for or against' the ICC. Consequently, regardless of whether one agrees or disagrees with the book's final conclusion on the non-implementation of the principle of complementarity, the novelty of this analysis does not lie only in its conclusion (as to the non-application of the principle of complementarity), but mainly in its perspective, which goes beyond 'for or against' arguments and focuses on the fundamental issue of whether this principle has been negated in practice by ICC decisions, internal circulars and the Prosecutor's strategy.

Finally, yet importantly, it should be underlined that issues like the criterion of a case's gravity, the collaboration between States and the ICC via the establishment of domestic laws or the delay in investigations and prosecutions pursuant to Article 16 ICCRSt (an intensely political article that has—thankfully—yet to be put into force) are not examined in this book.

1.2 Unraveling the Complex Nature of International Crimes

The roots of the term "international crime' can arguably be traced back to the Roman era and Cicero who noted that "a pirate is the common foe of the whole world" (*pirata est hostis humani generis).*[12] In the early decades of the twentieth century, legal scholars did not conceptually analyse the term 'international crime'. The Second Protocol to the Geneva Convention for the Pacific Settlement of International Disputes of 2 October 1924 is a key example of this trend: it defines aggressive war as a war crime without elaborating on what exactly the term 'war crime'

[11] ICC (2013a).

[12] The same passage is most often translated as "the pirate is the enemy of humankind". Cicero (1913).

means.[13] As can be expected, the lack of definition of such a crucial legal term did not make a positive contribution to the evolution of international criminal law. Moreover, the fact that even during the Nuremberg trials no definition of this term was introduced speaks for itself. The first definition was eventually introduced a few years later in the landmark case *USA v. Wilhelm List, et. al.* (commonly known as the Hostages Trial). This seminal definition, provided by the United States Military Tribunal at Nuremberg,[14] marked the first time 'international crime' was explicitly delineated in contemporary international case law: "An international crime is such an act universally recognised as criminal, which is considered a grave matter of international concern and for some valid reason cannot be left within the exclusive jurisdiction of the State that would have control over it under ordinary circumstances".[15,16]

The above definition established the following three cumulative characteristics of international crime:

(a) **The universal recognition of an act as an offence.** Thus, for example, the prohibition of alcohol in the United States of America (USA) in the 1930s could never be considered an international crime, because in the vast majority of States worldwide alcohol consumption was fully liberalised and not subject to any legal restrictions, nor, of course, was it considered an offence.
(b) **The exceptionally grave nature of the crime in relation to the damage caused by it**, its widespread commission or the existence of other characteristics which render it an important problem for a significant number of States and, consequently, a great issue of international interest. For instance, the crime of piracy is a distinctive and timeless example of a crime of great international interest.
(c) **The existence of a valid reason which would justify why the offence could not be left within the exclusive jurisdiction of one specific State**, which would under normal circumstances have the legal authority to prosecute its commission, bring it to trial and punish its perpetrator(s).

[13] League of Nations (1925).

[14] Apart from NMT, military tribunals were also created to adjudicate cases of minor significance in the areas under the control of the Allied Forces. The most important of those was the Military Tribunal of the United States of America in Nuremberg, which during the three years following the end of the Nuremberg Trials adjudicated twelve cases in the exact same courtrooms. The USA MT conducted trials according to Article 10 of Allied Control Council Statute, which was similar, but not identical to the NMT Statute. For example, the provision of crimes against peace was broader than the one the Nuremberg Trials were based on, as "initiating intrusions into other countries and aggressive wars against the provisions of International law and Treaties" was added to the existing definition. Intrusion into countries which offered no resistance such as Austria and Czechoslovakia became a crime after this addition. Nonetheless, because the trials were conducted exclusively with the participation of American judges, the international character of these trials has been disputed by some authors. Woetzel (1962), pp. 218–222.

[15] Hostages Trial, US Military Tribunal at Nuremberg (1948).

[16] An indication of the timelessness of this definition is that the renowned Geneva Academy of International Humanitarian Law and Human Rights has adopted it and to this day considers it appropriate for the definition of the term 'international crime', Geneva Academy (2018).

This third characteristic applies when the special circumstances of a crime, which may be connected to the commission of the crime itself, the identity of the perpetrator(s) or other elements of the crime, obstruct the prosecution of the crime by the State that would normally have jurisdiction over it. In such cases, the best solution is thus for the prosecution of the crime and the trial to take place at an international level. For instance, this would theoretically be the case for crimes committed by a State's elected government representatives during their tenure with the complicity of another State's officials, as may occur today in cases of embezzlement of European subsidies, to name but one example.

In addition, it is noteworthy that the aforementioned criterion indirectly promoted the primacy of an international criminal court, which would exercise its jurisdiction over international crimes in lieu of the State; because evidently, it would not be appropriate for the State itself or a national court to determine whether a crime fulfilled all the three criteria set by the 'Hostages Trial'. Therefore the case could not "be left within the exclusive jurisdiction of the state that would have control over it under ordinary circumstances".[17]

Despite its weaknesses—most notably, the prerequisite of the three criteria to be cumulatively met in order for an act to constitute an international crime—the first official definition of the term can be considered exceptionally positive in retrospect. That is because the term 'international crime', despite being included in earlier international texts and conventions, otherwise remained undefined. Hence the first definition given in the 'Hostages Trial' not only provided the foundations for an international discourse on the term, but also guided the evolution of international criminal law, which has reached a peak now that the International Criminal Court exercises jurisdiction over war crimes, crimes against humanity, genocide and, most recently, the crime of aggression.

In contemporary international criminal law theory, various views have been supported regarding the meaning of the term 'international crime', its elements and the criteria defining its relevance to the case at hand.[18] Certainly, this discussion had begun immediately after the Nuremberg Trials and the Hostages Trial. Already in 1950, George Schwarzenberger argued in his monumental essay on international criminal law that "an international crime [. . .] requires the existence of international criminal law. Such a discipline of legal studies does not exist."[19]

Almost four decades later in 1989, the International Association of Criminal Law in Vienna attempted to define international crimes by dividing them into two vast categories:

(a) international crimes *stricto sensu,* i.e., international crimes recognised as such by the international community pursuant to the generally recognised principles of

---

[17] Hostages Trial, US Military Tribunal at Nuremberg (19 February 1948).

[18] The extensive review of the international bibliography found in Athanasios Chouliaras's book is considered quite important for Greek bibliography, although it does not eventually offer a specific view on the definition of an international crime *de lege ferenda.* Chouliaras (2013), pp. 324–386.

[19] Schwarzenberger (1965), pp. 3–36.

international law, which threaten international legal interests (such as the peace and security of the international community)[20] and imply individual criminal liability.[21]

(b) international crimes *lato sensu,* i.e., actions which, though criminalised under a State's domestic law, cannot be efficiently dealt with solely through unilateral actions.[22]

Regarding the above categorisation, Foteini Pazartzi correctly points out that the main distinguishing criterion is the fact that in the first case (the category of international crimes *stricto sensu*), individual criminal liability is directly established at an international level; while in the second case (the category of international crimes *lato sensu)* the criminalisation requirement concerning individual conduct only arises at the level of the states parties,[23] which assume indirectly via international conventions the obligation to criminally prosecute the perpetrators at a national level. Consequently, nowadays, it is exclusively international crimes *sticto sensu* that are the core crimes of the ICC's Rome Statute (ICCRSt), i.e. war crimes, crimes against humanity, the crime of genocide and the crime of aggression,[24] while the list of international crimes *lato sensu* based on the aforementioned distinction is lengthy and disputed, as will be seen below.

This position is essentially supported by Robert Cryer, Hakan Friman, Daryl Robinson and Elizabeth Wilmshurst in the second edition of their volume on international criminal law and procedural criminal law, where they argue that it is probably more accurate and practical to link the term 'international crime' to those crimes which are subject to the jurisdiction of international tribunals or other international/hybrid criminal courts pursuant to international law. These crimes are of course the ones already mentioned: the crime of genocide, crimes against humanity, war crimes and the crime of aggression.[25] The scholars underline that they do not include in the concept of international crime the crimes of piracy, enslavement, torture, terrorism, international drug trafficking and many other crimes, which States are obligated to criminalise and prosecute pursuant to international conventions

[20] As analysed in more detail below, the term 'international community' does not have the meaning one would expect, i.e. the representation of the majority of States; on the contrary, the term skillfully implies the representation of the interests of the most powerful states.

[21] See also Antonopoulos (2003), p. 23.

[22] Triffterer (1987), p. 29, 40.

[23] It must be noted that the term "States Parties" is included 86 times in the Rome Statute of the International Criminal Court (ICCRSt). The same term is often found in many other international conventions, although it is not grammatically correct; Party is an adjective which comes after the noun State in a rather unusual fashion, most probably being a relic of French legal terminology. Thus the correct plural of the term should be States Party, following similar post-noun adjectives in English like "Governor General" and "Notary Public". Nonetheless, because of the fact that it is a widely established term the author has eventually decided to retain the usage of this term.

[24] Pazartzi (2007), pp. 58–61.

[25] Cryer et al. (2010), p. 4.

under national criminal legislation.[26] Nonetheless, at the same time, they acknowledge that many of the above crimes: **(a)** bear a lot of similarities with the four core crimes of international law regarding their suppression; **(b)** are considered by the international community to breach or threaten legal interests, which are protected by public international law, as the Preamble of the ICCRSt[27] also makes apparent; and **(c)** the possibility that some of those crimes that may be subject to the jurisdiction of the ICC in the future, such as the crime of terrorism, torture at a non-state level and drug trafficking, should not be excluded.[28]

Certainly, the four academics' approach to the concept of international crime seems to differ from the one the judges of International Court of Justice (ICJ) Higgins, Kooijmans and Buergenthal adopted. In the well-known case of *Democratic Republic of Congo v. Belgium* in 2000, the three ICJ judges endorsed the view that in the name of effective protection against international crimes "a versatile strategy must be adopted, in which newly-established international tribunals, international legal obligations and domestic courts would all participate",[29] recognising indirectly yet clearly that the concept of international crime should not be interpreted narrowly on the basis of jurisdiction of permanent international courts or international tribunals.

Nonetheless, the analysis of the term 'international crime' was not considered sufficiently important and consequently was not addressed by many scholars after the 'Hostages Trial'.[30] Undoubtedly, the uncertainty surrounding the definition of this term is intensified by academics' work, because of the indiscriminate use of terms such as 'international law crimes', 'international crimes', 'international crimes *largo sensu*', 'international crimes *stricto sensu*', 'transnational crimes', 'international crimes *jus cogens*'[31] and lately 'core crimes'—with the latter now the most widespread term used to refer to the four crimes that come under the ICC's

[26] According to one view there is an important difference between a suppression convention and the Rome Statute of the International Criminal Court (ICCRSt) regarding the classification of an act as an international crime: in the first case, States agree on classification through the ratification of an international convention (formal criterion), while in the second case, the specific criteria set out in the ICCRSt are met, as for example in the case of a widespread or systematic attack carried out in connection with the commission of murder (substantial criterion).

[27] See particularly paras 3, 4 and 9 of the Preamble of the ICCRSt, as well as the phrase "the most serious crimes of concern to the international community as a whole" which is repeated twice in the Preamble (par. 4 and 9) and can be interpreted as a declaration of the fact that the ICCRSt refers only to the most serious international crimes.

[28] Cryer et al. (2010), pp. 26, 20, 5.

[29] Case Concerning the Arrest Warrant of 11 April 2000 2002 ICJ para 5.

[30] See for example Zahar and Sluiter (2007), where no definition of the term 'international crime' is provided.

[31] The principle of *jus cogens* was codified in Article 53 of the Vienna Convention on the Law of Treaties: "A treaty is void if, at the time of its conclusion, it conflicts with a peremptory norm of general international law. For the purposes of the present Convention, a peremptory norm of general international law is a norm accepted and recognized by the international community of States as a whole as a norm from which no derogation is permitted and which can be modified only by a

jurisdiction, i.e. genocide, crimes against humanity, war crimes and the crime of aggression.[32]

Gehrard Werle and Florian Jeßberger set three cumulative conditions for an offence to constitute an international criminal law: **1.** The offence should entail individual responsibility and be subject to punishment. **2.** The violated norm should be part of the body of international law. **3.** The offense should be punishable regardless of whether it has been incorporated into domestic law or not.[33] The criteria set by Werle and Jeßberger can be possibly read under a brighter light if they are also read along with the following two experpts of their book's fourth edition: "International criminal law protects 'peace, security and [the] well-being of the world' as the fundamental values of the international community. The three protected values—peace, security, and the well-being of the world—cannot be strictly separated from one another. World peace and international security, the two values of the international community that lie at the heart of international criminal law, are at the same time the main goals of the United Nations. International criminal law is thus based on a broad concept of peace, which means not only the absence of military conflict between states, but also the conditions within a state. Therefore, a threat to *world* peace can be presumed to result even from massive violations of human rights within *one state*"[34] or by members of "non-state organizations, whose strength and potential for violence corresponds to that of states... Members of such organizations can also commit crimes under international law; despite their lack of connection to a state their conduct can affect the international community as a whole".[35]

Antonio Cassese, one of the founders of contemporary international criminal law, supports a restrictive interpretation of the term 'international crime' in the last edition of his book entitled *International Criminal Law* (2008). In particular, he maintains that "international crimes are breaches of international rules which result in individual criminal liability",[36] in contrast to the breach of those international rules which results in international liability for the State whose officials act as its proxies. Cassese established four criteria which should cumulatively coexist for an act to be characterised as an international crime:

---

subsequent norm of general international law having the same character". Vienna Convention on the Law of Treaties.

It is indicative that Hersch Lauterpacht in 1953 described peremptory norms of international law, not as part of international customary law, but as fundamental principles of international customary law, on which the international public order is founded (*ordre international public*). International Law Commission (1953).

[32] Werle and Jeßberger (2020).

[33] *Ibid.*, para. 101.

[34] *Ibid.*, para. 106.

[35] *Ibid.*, para. 102.

[36] Cassese (2008).

1. The act at hand must constitute a breach of international customary law or at least conventional rules, if these rules codify, stipulate or have contributed to the formulation of international law.[37]
2. The rules breached are intended to protect values that are important to the so-called international community and, therefore, be binding for all States and individuals. Undoubtedly, rules of such importance can be found in the United Nations Charter, the Universal Declaration of Human Rights, the European Convention on Human Rights, the American Convention on Human Rights, the African Statute on Human Rights, the International Covenant on Civil and Political Rights, the International Covenant on Economic, Social and Cultural Rights, the UN Declaration on Principles of International Law concerning Friendly Relationships and Co-operation among States, etc.[38]
3. The existence of a universal interest in the suppression of these crimes. This means that according to international law and under certain circumstances,[39] the alleged perpetrators can be prosecuted and punished by *any* State, regardless of the place in which the crime was committed or the nationality of the victim or perpetrator.[40]
4. Finally, if the perpetrator has acted in an official capacity, e.g. as a *de jure or de facto* state official, the State on whose behalf the crime was committed is barred from invoking the alleged perpetrator's immunity from another State's criminal or civil jurisdiction pursuant to international customary law (although it is generally accepted that if the perpetrator is a head of state, a minister or an active diplomat, then he enjoys absolute personal immunity while carrying out his governmental or diplomatic duties).[41]

On the basis of the four cumulative criteria above, Cassese concludes that international crimes are: war crimes, crimes against humanity, genocide, torture (as a crime that is distinct from those cases in which it could be considered a war crime or a crime against humanity), the crime of aggression, as well as some extreme forms of international terrorism. However, at the same time, he maintains that crimes such as piracy, illegal drug trafficking, illegal gun trade, the smuggling of nuclear and other lethal material, money laundering, slave trade, women and human trafficking or even

---

[37] *Ibid.* 11.

[38] Naziris (2009), p. 16.

[39] Cassese (2008), pp. 21, 29. Cassese neither clarifies nor indicates—even indirectly—what these circumstances are, at this point.

[40] *Ibid.*, 11–12.

[41] *Ibid.* 12; *Regina v. Bartle* (1998) (on appeal from a Divisional Court of the Queen's Bench Division). *Regina v. Evans (1998)* (on appeal from a Divisional Court of the Queen's Bench Division). *Fidel Castro, Audiencia Nacional, Annuario Espanol de Derecho Internacional Privado, (2001)*; *Democratic Republic of the Congo v. Belgium* (2002) ICJ. Pursuant to the existing case law, it is better for the perpetrator to be a diplomat rather than a minister or a prime minister, because then their time in service lasts considerably longer—that is, until retirement.

the crime of illegal racial segregation (apartheid) **are not included** in the concept of international crime.

1.3 Controversies and Conventions in International Crime Classification

Based on the adoption of an extremely restrictive interpretation of the term 'international crime', Cassese justifies his aforementioned conclusion by pointing out *inter alia* that piracy does not infringe upon an international legal interest, but upon the individual interests of States, and that is the reason why the piracy committed throughout past centuries using State crusade fleets was not subject to the universal jurisdiction of States themselves.[42] Of course, even if it is assumed Cassese's position was historically well-founded, it cannot be supported today. This is because rights to property, freedom and security, free movement of people and goods constitute now a set of universally accepted values as indicatively defined in the International Covenant on Civil and Political Rights,[43] the European Convention on Human Rights[44] and the Charter of Fundamental Rights of the EU. [45]
Secondly, concerning crimes such as:

- Drug trafficking
- Illicit arms trading
- Smuggling of nuclear and other lethal material
- Money laundering
- Women and human trafficking
- Racial segregation (apartheid)

Cassese argues that the aforementioned acts are criminalised on the basis of international conventions and not international customary law, while they are commonly committed by individuals or criminal organisations and not by States, obviously overlooking the case of South Africa. Finally, as far as the crime of racial segregation (apartheid) is concerned, he maintains that it does not touch upon a universally accepted value. This, he argues, is because the Convention on the Elimination of all Forms of Racial Discrimination of 1973 may have been ratified by 101 States, but

[42]Cassese (2008), pp. 12, 21.

[43]International Covenant on Civil and Political Rights (1976) (ICCPR) Arts 1 (right to self-determination), 6 (right to life), 9 (right to freedom and security), 12 (right to free movement).

[44]European Covenant on Human Rights (1953) ETS 5 (ECHR) Arts 2 (right of life), 5 (right to freedom and security) and 8 (right to private and family life) ECHR; First Protocol to the ECHR (adopted 4 November 1950, entered into force 3 September 1953) Art. 1 (right to property); Fourth Protocol to the ECHR (adopted 16 September 1963, entered into force 2 May 1968) Art. 2 (right to movement).

[45]*See* for example Charter of Fundamental Rights of the European Union (adopted 18 December 2000, entered into force 1 December 2009) OJ C 326/391, Preamble, Arts 2, 6, 17 and 45.

none could be considered a developed 'Western' State, in Cassese's opinion.[46] However, these arguments are weak, because on the one hand, Cassese seems to classify an act as an international crime if there is a clear 'state element', while on the other he does not accept that racial segregation violates universally accepted human values. Further, he only partly acknowledges the ratification of the Rome Statute by so many States and that the inclusion of racial segregation in art.7(1)(i) ICCRSt as a distinct form of a crime against humanity as well as its definition in art.7(2)(h) ICCRSt may gradually alter the crime's classification.[47]

On the other hand, the world-renowned scholar Cherif Bassiouni, who has probably researched the importance and the role of the definition of international crime more thoroughly than any other eminent scholar, adopted an exceptionally broad interpretation. In the last edition of his book on crimes against humanity, he holds the view that the following characteristics can be found in all international crimes:[48]

(a) The prohibited conduct violates a significant international interest.
(b) The prohibited conduct constitutes an egregious act which infringes upon the commonly shared values of the world community.[49]
(c) The prohibited conduct involves at least two States in its planning, preparation or commission, either because of the diversity of perpetrators and/or victims' nationalities or because the means employed transcend national boundaries.
(d) The effects of the conduct bear upon an internationally protected interest that does not fall within either (a) or (b) above; nonetheless, the conduct's international criminalization is required in order to ensure its prevention, control and suppression, because it is predicated on 'state policy' without which it could not materialise.[50]

Nevertheless, in the second edition of Bassiouni's two-volume work 'Introduction to International Criminal Law', he subdivides this criterion into the following two distinct criteria, thereby extending the criteria list to five in total:

(d1) The conduct offends an internationally protected person or infringes upon an internationally protected legal interest.

04.

---

[46]Cassese (2008), pp. 21, 12–13.

[47]Ibid 13. Cassese notes that "This development could occur if and when cases concerning 'inhumane acts' committed in the context of an institutionalized regime of systematic oppression and domination by one racial group over any other racial group or groups and committed with the intention of maintaining that regime are ever brought before the Court".

[48]Bassiouni (2014), p. 8.

[49]The author's opposition to the use of widely common terms, such as 'international' or 'universal community' is apparent throughout the whole thesis. In this case, the term does not include the huge cultural differences between the people, as they are indicatively outlined in the article of Evans-Pritchard and Dundes Renteln (1995), pp. 1–48.

[50]Bassiouni (2014), pp. 23, 8.

> The conduct infringes upon an internationally protected legal interest, without however the infringement fulfilling the first or second criterion. Nonetheless, it is a conduct which, due to its nature, can only be prevented and confronted successfully through its international criminalisation.[51]

Consequently, one can observe that in his book Bassiouni reintroduces the concept of the 'internationally protected person' into the aforementioned criteria, pursuant to the standards of the International Law Commission, which considered the protection of UN staff to be absolutely essential. At the same time, he rightly removes the notion of 'state policy' and introduces instead the theoretically vague and undefined yet much more appropriate criterion of the successful suppression of the conduct as a result of its international criminalisation.

Based on the five characteristics above, as well as the nature and scope of 281 transnational treaties,[52] Bassiouni argues that all international crimes fulfil at least one of the following fundamental criteria:

(1) International character, i.e. a conduct that either directly or indirectly threatens the peace and security of the international community or is considered atrocious from the perspective of the international community's collective consciousness and its commonly accepted values.
(2) Transnational character, i.e. a conduct that either affects public security and financial interests within at least two States' territory or concerns citizens of at least two nationalities, whether as perpetrators or victims, or takes place in at least two States.
(3) State policy character, i.e. a conduct which partially entails any of the first two elements, while its prevention, control and suppression require international collaboration, because it is based on a state policy, without which it could not be performed.[53] Undoubtedly, the existence of a state policy renders the crime's international criminalisation necessary, since obviously the criminal conduct in question cannot be lawfully suppressed by the respective State's judicial system.

Based on the above, it becomes clear that the crimes committed by the Nazis at the concentration camps fulfil all three criteria, because they were atrocious crimes pursuant to the commonly accepted values of the international community (criterion no. 1), with a transnational character as many victims were of Greek, Polish, French etc. nationality and were transferred to Germany by force (criterion no. 2) and finally, because they were committed as a result of a well-organised state policy (criterion no. 3), which 'decriminalised' and facilitated the criminal activity of millions of ordinary people, who acted 'lawfully' within their national legal frame-

[51] Bassiouni (2013), pp. 142–143.
[52] *Ibid.* 144–145.
[53] Bassiouni (2014), pp. 23, 8–9.

work at the time; they hoarded the victims onto trains or drove those trains or opened the gates of the concentration camps and gas chambers, among other tasks.[54]

Additionally, it becomes apparent that international criminal law does not criminalise actions at an international level solely because they are classified as crimes under almost all States' legal systems. Consequently, rape, abduction, blackmail and homicide *de lege lata* and *de lege ferenda* are not considered international crimes in the first place, because—though they are of course unanimously accepted as morally abhorrent crimes—they lack the international character required for an act to be dealt within the sphere of international law. However, if these actions are committed as part of a crime against humanity or war crime, then they acquire an international character.

1.4 Ecocide: Addressing Environmental Destruction as a Pressing International Concern. A New International Crime *De Lege Ferenda*?

International criminal law typically does not criminalise actions categorised as crimes within state legal systems at the international level. Therefore, criminal actions such as rape, kidnapping, extortion, homicide, and environmental destruction (ecocide) are not *prima facie* considered international crimes; because although they are heinous, they are not inherently international, thus they are not addressed within international criminal law. Nonetheless, if these criminal acts occur as part of a crime against humanity or a war crime (e.g. mass murder of civilians), it is entirely feasible and legally justified to classify them as international crimes.

Ecocide, defined as deliberate environmental destruction, is an international phenomenon with far-reaching repercussions, often impacting multiple states or even continents. According to Bassiouni's *de lege ferenda* definition of an international crime, ecocide could often meet the criteria of an international crime provided that it possesses: (1) an international character (2) a transnational character and (3) a state policy element.

Now let's consider a hypothetical scenario to clarify this point. A multinational shipping company, the primary owner of a subsidiary that officially owns an oil tanker, maliciously sinks it in the middle of the South Atlantic Ocean to claim a hefty insurance indemnity. The resultantcontamination of the South Atlantic Ocean from this tanker's hazardous substance scould lead to a mass die-off of marine species and significant ecocide disturbance. This would directly and indirectly affect many countries with coasts or access to this ocean, such as Argentina, Benin, Brazil, Cameroon, Cape Verde, Equatorial Guinea, Gabon, Gambia, Ghana, Guinea, Guinea-Bissau, Ivory Coast, Liberia, Morocco, Namibia, Nigeria, Senegal, Sierra Leone, South Africa, Suriname, Togo, Uruguay, Venezuela. Countries with direct

[54] Bauman and May (2001), p. 72.

access to both the North and South Atlantic Oceans, such as Sao Tome and Principe, Democratic Republic of Congo, Republic of Congo, Gabon, Equatorial Guinea, and Angola, would also feel these effects.

This intentional sinking of the oil tanker could result in severe ecological consequences, both immediate and long-term. In fact this ecocide would impact greatly not only the said ecosystem but could also potentially devastate the economies of states dependent on the health of the South Atlantic's aquatic ecosystem, in various ways:

1. **Marine Ecosystem Damage:** The primary concern would be the spillage of thousands of tons of oil into the ocean, causing massive harm to marine life such as fish, seabirds, and marine mammals, including dolphins and whales. The heavy crude oil could suffocate marine organisms, block the gills of fish, and coat birds in a toxic layer, critically impeding their ability to fly and insulate themselves. The skin and internal organs of marine mammals might endure severe damage, resulting in significant mortality.
2. **Biodiversity Loss:** The death of these animals and various other marine organisms could substantially disrupt the food chain and the overall biodiversity of the South Atlantic. Predators, having lost their food sources, could struggle to survive, leaving the ecosystem in a state of imbalance for decades at the very least.
3. **Economic Consequences:** Countries along the South Atlantic could be profoundly affected by this ecocide. For instance, countries such as Argentina, Brazil, Namibia, and South Africa, with substantial fishing industries, could experience severe impacts due to a marked decrease in marine life. Coastal tourism, a significant revenue source for many of these countries and others with direct access to the South Atlantic, could also take a considerable hit, especially if the heavy crude oil reaches the coastline, rendering beaches unsuitable for visitors.
4. **Health Risks:** Residents of coastal communities could face severe health risks if they consume seafood contaminated by the oil. They could be confronted with an increased risk of developing various forms of cancer and serious respiratory and skin-related health issues.
5. **Long-Term Environmental Impact:** A significant amount of oil could sink and merge with sediments on the ocean floor, establishing a toxic environment that could persist for decades and devastate the entire benthic (bottom-dwelling) ecosystem. Some components of oil, which do not degrade easily, could remain in the environment for an extended period.
6. **Climate Change:** Oceanic ecosystems play a critical role in regulating the Earth's climate. Plankton, for instance, absorb carbon dioxide from the atmosphere, helping to mitigate the impacts of climate change. However, the damage caused by a massive oil spill to these microscopic organisms could intensify global warming, indirectly projecting potent negative consequences even for states not bordering or with direct access to the South Atlantic Ocean.

Indeed, the extent of the damage and its spread would depend on several factors, including the volume and type of oil spilled, ocean currents, wind conditions, and the effectiveness of the immediate response to contain the spill. Nonetheless, any significant oil spill in the South Atlantic would represent an ecological disaster with far-reaching, long-lasting direct and indirect severe impacts on all of humanity.

In this hypothetical scenario, the intentional sinking of an oil tanker in the South Atlantic Ocean would undeniably have both an international and transnational character, as it would either directly or indirectly threaten the peace and security of the international community and affect public security and financial interests within at least two States' territories.

However, as per the third Bassiouni's criterion, i.e., the state policy character, there could be a significant problem. State policy typically refers to actions or strategies developed and implemented by a government to achieve specific goals, including laws, regulations, decisions, and actions. Clearly, a private corporation's decision to deliberately sink an old oil tanker in the ocean would not initially be part of a state policy unless the tanker belonged to a state company.

Yet, in our globalized modern world where private corporations and multinational giants often surpass states in terms of resources and actual power, it is reasonable to suggest that such actions amount to a 'quasi-state policy'. This adequately satisfies Bassiouni's third criterion of state policy. In other words, by employing this novel term 'quasi-state policy', the author refers to actions or strategies that, while not officially sanctioned by a state, bear a state-like influence or impact due to their scale, scope and/or consequences.

The impact of actions taken by large corporations, such as an oil spill, can indeed have far-reaching consequences similar to state policies. These actions critically affect economies, environments, and societies on a scale comparable to state actions. Consequently, the proposed term 'quasi-state policy' encapsulates corporate policies with state-level impact or actions of state-like significance, as analyzed above.

Consequently, Bassiouni lists 25 categories of international crimes that either infringe upon an important international legal interest; or involve perpetrators and/or victims among whom are the nationals of two or more States; or constitute clear violations of universally accepted values. Hence *de lege ferenda*, his extensive categorisation includes crimes such as the trading of illegal pornography (e.g. child pornography), the forgery and counterfeiting of currency, damage done to submarine cables and the illegal obstruction of international mail services.

It is obvious that Bassiouni follows the original ambitious categorisation of the International Law Commission, which was originally presented in 1991—based on the mandate it had received 13 years earlier to draw up a Code of Crimes against the Peace and Security of Mankind—and included 26 crimes in total as international crimes against the peace and security of mankind.[55]

---

[55] ILC (1991). However, in 1996, the International Law Commission reduced those crimes to twelve and then to just five: the crime of aggression, genocide, crimes against humanity, crimes against the UN and its staff and war crimes. ILC (1996).

In the two-volume work on international criminal law he edited, Bassiouni argues (without, however, offering any additional references that would support his position), that there are 16 international conventions with provisions on terrorism crimes, 23 international conventions with provisions on drug-related crimes and 71 conventions with provisions on armed conflicts (some of which refer to the existing international legal framework, while others do not, with the inescapable result that the provisions of the latter are binding only upon the state parties that have ratified them).[56]

Then, in accordance with the aforementioned criteria, Bassiouni proceeds to list ten characteristics in total as follows. Even if only a single one of these is found in an international convention, Bassiouni considers it adequate to characterise the conduct prohibited by the convention as an international crime:

(1) Explicit or implicit recognition of a prohibited conduct as an international crime or a crime pursuant to international law (in 71 international conventions)
(2) Implicit recognition of the criminal nature of the conduct by requiring that states parties ban, prevent, prosecute or punish the conduct in question (in 190 international conventions)
(3) Criminalisation of the prohibited conduct (in 96 international conventions)
(4) Duty or right to prosecute the prohibited conduct (in 113 international conventions)
(5) Duty or right to punish the prohibited conduct (in 129 international conventions)
(6) Duty or right to extradite the perpetrator (in 74 international conventions)
(7) Duty or right to cooperate on prosecution and punishment, including legal assistance (in 98 international conventions)
(8) Establishment of criminal jurisdiction over the prohibited conduct (in 101 international conventions)
(9) Reference to the establishment of an international criminal court or an international criminal tribunal (in 32 international conventions)
(10) Non-justification of state of necessity because of a superior's orders (in 71 international conventions)[57]

In accordance with these characteristics, it is concluded that the following 27 international crimes are contained in 281 international conventions:

(1) Crime of aggression
(2) Genocide
(3) Crimes against humanity
(4) War crimes

[56] Bassiouni (2013), pp. 24, 141.

[57] Ibid 143, 145–146. Using as indicative examples international legislation on the crime of aggression and for the suppression of illicit drug trafficking, Bassiouni points out that the more 'non-political' an international convention is, the more criminal character it has.

(5) Illegal possession, use, placement and trade of nuclear, chemical or conventional weapons
(6) Nuclear terrorism
(7) Policies of political segregation (apartheid)
(8) Slavery, enslavement practices and human trafficking
(9) Torture and other forms of cruel, inhuman or degrading treatment
(10) Illegal experimentation on humans
(11) Enforced disappearances and extrajudicial executions
(12) Mercenary services
(13) Piracy and illegal acts against the security of navigation at sea and oil extraction platforms
(14) Hijacking and illegal acts against the security of international aviation
(15) Threats and use of violence against internationally protected individuals and UN staff members
(16) Hostage-taking
(17) Use of explosives
(18) Illegal use or obstruction of postal services
(19) Terrorism financing
(20) Illegal drug trafficking and other crimes related to drugs
(21) Organised crime and other related crimes
(22) Destruction and/or theft of national treasures[58]
(23) Illegal acts against specific and internationally protected environmental resources.
(24) International trafficking of indecent material (e.g. paedophile material)
(25) Forgery and counterfeiting
(26) Interception of international submarine cables
(27) Corruption and bribery of foreign officials and civil servants[59]

On the other hand, academics such as Herbert Morays have chosen simpler criteria, starting from the position that the term international crime either refers to transnational crimes that are subject to the jurisdiction of more than one State (e.g. in the case of international drug trafficking or international money laundering) or characterises a conduct which has been deemed illegal at an international level because of an international convention, an international treaty or international customary law.[60]

According to Herbert Morays, while in the past an extremely limited number of crimes were considered to be international crimes (piracy, smuggling, war crimes,

[58] An issue very popular in the media since 2001 after the destruction of Buddha's Statues dated from 6th century BCE by the Taliban in Afghanistan and more recently, after the destruction of cultural world heritage monuments in Mosul and Nimrud by jihadists of the Islamic State in Iraq and Syria (ISIS): The Guardian (2001). US News (2015).

[59] Bassiouni (2013), pp. 24, 144–145.

[60] Morais (2005), pp. 583, 584.

[61] *Ibid.* 584.

crimes against humanity and genocide), particularly after 11 September 2001 the concept of international crime has been substantially expanded and includes crimes such as terrorism and terrorism financing, corruption and cybercrime.[61] Undoubtedly, globalisation, regional integration in Europe and elsewhere, the constant increase in the movement of goods and people at an international level, the overwhelming prevalence of information systems, internet and cloud services in all sectors of human activity (communication, education, science, commerce, services, industry), all have indisputable benefits for our society; however, at the same time, they also greatly contribute to the expansion of international criminal activity.[62]

Morays further posits that a crime can be classified as international if it is based upon an international convention, an international treaty, or international customary law. Clearly, environmental protection and the reversal of global warming are also of great interest to the international community, especially in the past few decades. Global warming or climate change can cause severe environmental destruction to the extent that human actions which exarbecate this alarming global phenomenon could potentially be classified as international crimes, following the relatively straightforward criteria proposed by Herbert Morays. To name but one example, imagine the hypothetical scenario where a group of terrorists were identified as the perpetrators of the 2023 Nova Scotia Wildfires[63] which caused mass evacuations, burning through millions of acres, spreading of the smoke from the fires across large portions of the U.S., affecting air quality for millions as the fires rage on without signs of stopping and suffocating New York City under a thick smog that turned the skies orange and shrouded its skyscrapers as well as the Statue of Liberty.[64] In this instance, this deliberate environmental crime (ecocide) should rightly be classified as an international crime and brought before the proposed International Criminal Court for the Protection of Environment (ICCPE).[65]

Morays finally concludes by suggesting that international crimes can be seen as falling into one of only two categories based on their motivation: **(a)** those committed for economic gain, such as international illicit drug trafficking, abduction, smuggling and human trafficking and **(b)** those committed for ideological or political reasons, such as terrorism, the funding of terrorist activities or the beheading of hostages.[66] However, this is extremely simplistic, to the point where it fails even to accommodate the case of a crime committed for a dual purpose, i.e. for both economic and ideological purposes, as in cases of the abduction and execution of Japanese hostages by the Islamic State of Iraq and Syria (ISIS) organisation.[67]

Following the careful examination of Herbert Morays and M. Cherif Bassiouni's views, certain conclusions can be drawn regarding the classification of a crime as

---

[62] *Ibid.* 585.

[63] CBS News (2023a).

[64] CBS News (2023b).

[65] See Chapter 10 - Ecocide regarding the author's proposal.

[66] Ibid 588.

[67] BBC News (2015a).

international. Notably, Herbert Morays' view criteria for classifying a crime as international are quite broader and simpler than Bassiouni's. Morays attempts to include more crimes under the umbrella of international crime, utilising either the violation of an international convention/treaty or customary international law or the criterion of transnationality. Bassiouni, on the other hand, narrows the scope of international crime, considering the involvement of multiple states (international character criterion), the transnationality element (transnational character criterion) and state policy (state policy criterion) as three cumulative criteria.

On the other hand, other academics who attempted to define and distinguish the term international crime from other crimes of 'international interest' have started out from the term 'transnational crime' and those international conventions which have been characterised as 'suppression conventions'. Neil Boister was one the first scholars who used the term 'suppression conventions',[68] in order to describe those international conventions pursuant to which the contracting states parties were obliged to criminalise and suppress specific actions within their jurisdiction, such as damage to submarine cables,[69] counterfeiting foreign currency,[70] drugs,[71] pornography,[72] human trafficking[73] or illegal disappearance,[74] corruption,[75] hijacking,[76] nuclear terrorism[77] etc.

Regina Menachery Paulose also claims that the Rome Statute for the establishment of an International Criminal Court (ICC) offers a prominent example of the distinction in international criminal law between core crimes (which are included in the ICCRSt) and transnational crimes (which are included in international conventions but not ICCRSt). In other words, Paulose maintains that the core crimes (genocide, crime of aggression, war crimes, crimes against humanity) have been made subject to the ICC's jurisdiction, while transnational crimes have become the main subject of 'suppression conventions', which are essentially criminal conventions with an 'intense transnational character' where the prime goal is the prevention of the criminal activity of individuals and non-state entities more generally.[78]

---

[68] Boister (2002b). Also Boister (1998).

[69] Convention for the Protection of Submarines Telegraph Cables (1888).

[70] International Convention for the Suppression of Counterfeiting Currency (1931).

[71] International Opium Convention (1912). Single Convention on Narcotic Drugs (1975). United Nations Convention against Illicit Traffic in Narcotic Drugs and Psychotropic Substances (1990).

[72] Agreement for the Repression of Obscene Publications (1911).

[73] International Convention for the Suppression of the White Slave Traffic (1951). Also, Convention on the Traffic in Persons and the Exploitation of the Prostitution of Others (1951); Protocol to Prevent, Suppress and Punish Trafficking in Persons, Especially Women and Children, supplementing the United Nations Convention against Transnational Organized Crime (2003).

[74] International Convention for the Protection of All Persons from Enforced Disappearances (2006).

[75] United Nations Convention Against Corruption (2005).

[76] Convention for the Suppression of Unlawful Seizure of Aircraft (1971). Also see Convention for the Suppression of Unlawful Acts against the Safety of Civil Aviation (1973).

[77] International Convention for the Suppression of Acts of Nuclear Terrorism (2007).

[78] Paulose (2012), p. 84.

On the same wavelength, Rodger S. Clark, Robert Cryer, Hakan Friman, Daryl Robinson and Elizabeth Wilmshurst express slightly different positions, even though in general they agree with the aforementioned proposed categorisation. Thus Clark notes somewhat sarcastically that "some or all suppression conventions can be described, at least for educational purposes, as examples of 'transnational' criminal law, separated from the crimes more 'correctly' characterised as 'international', such as genocide and the crime of aggression".[79] Subsequently, he points out that in his opinion transnational crimes are mostly crimes in which international law has an 'interest' rather than crimes 'according to' international law, even though these transnational crimes might not be inherently different from 'international crimes'; therefore, one cannot exclude in advance the probability of a transnational crime being 'upgraded' to an international crime.[80] Finally, he also underlines a jurisdictional criterion for the distinction between transnational and international crimes, as there is nowadays some consensus that international crimes should be subject to the jurisdiction of an international court or at least a hybrid court/tribunal, while transnational crimes should be subject to the domestic jurisdiction of as many countries as possible.[81]

Similarly, Robert Cryer, Hakan Friman, Daryl Robinson and Elizabeth Wilmshurst also claim that transnational crimes include "crimes that are subject to international suppression conventions but for which there is not international criminal jurisdiction yet", as this type of crime—exactly like the core crimes—has real or potential cross-border repercussions and violates fundamental values of the so-called international community.[82]

1.5 Aiming for aComprehensive Codification of International Crimes

Finally, in an International Criminal Law Review paper, Nikolaos Bitzilekis introduces a completely new perspective, claiming that the violation of multiculturalism is of paramount importance in the detection of international crimes.[83] In particular, he supports the view that international crimes may begin as violations of human rights, but they end up drastically affecting the whole of humankind, given that they violate the "the collective art of living in its essential core, i.e. the cultural and ethical diversity as a free creation and promotion of different meanings of life". However,

---

[79] Clark (2010), p. 33.

[80] *Ibid.* 33.

[81] *Ibid.* 34.

[82] Cryer et al. (2010), pp. 20, 334.

[83] Bitzilekis (2015).

he does not offer any specific criteria on the basis of which the violation of multiculturalism could be positively identified.[84]

In any case, it is evident that the scientific dialogue has been quite limited and that the emergence of the term 'international crime' in international law has been non-uniform and *ad hoc*. This helps to explain the ratification of so many conventions and the total lack of legislative cohesion, which has often led to overlapping content. Thus Athanasios Chouliaras justifiably points out in his doctoral thesis that "these general observations lead to the well-founded conclusion that until today there has not been a systematic and universal consideration of the substantial rules of international criminal law, which could also lead to the drafting of an international criminal code".[85]

Nonetheless, the nature of international law itself and the way it operates based on each State's free—at least theoretically—will to accede to conventions and to ratify them accordingly render inevitable this multi-convention overregulation, which in another framework (national or European) could actually be limited as a result of legislative harmonisation and integration practices.

In any case, based on Bassiouni's five aforementioned criteria for a criminal action to be considered an international crime, many of the 27 aforementioned crimes can indeed be considered international, while others can only be considered transnational or partially international. In addition, there are some crimes that have obtained an international character only because it was considered that their prevention and suppression[86] would be best achieved in this way.

Bassiouni himself, though, avoids further categorisation of the 27 international crimes as international, partially international, transnational and 'international' for preventive and suppressive reasons, pointing out that in his view torture does not have an international or transnational character.[87] Moreover, apart from the fact that Bassiouni does not classify these 27 international crimes into further categories, he does not even briefly state what exactly he considers the vague term 'partially international crime' to mean.

At this point, it is worth noting that neither international conventions nor other academic studies proceed to a hierarchical classification of the 27 crimes or international crimes in general, with *jus cogens* crimes being the only exception. Consequently, one could validly assert *ab initio* that all international crimes have the same significance at an international level. However, on the other hand, it is also certain that the importance of the crime of intercepting submarine cables[88] will usually be of less significance than that of the crime of genocide.

Due to the flaws in the classification of the 27 international crimes by Bassiouni and in the existing literature, if one does attempt to put aside the great theoretical

[84] *Ibid*.1051.

[85] Chouliaras (2013), pp. 15, 340.

[86] Bassiouni (2013), pp. 24, 146.

[87] Ibid footnote 36.

[88] On the importance of those unknown to the public cables see Sanger and Schmitt (2015).

Table 1.1 Proposed categorisation of international crimes

International crimes	Transnational crimes	'International' crimes for preventive and suppressive reasons
• Crime of aggression • Genocide • Crimes against humanity • War crimes • Illegal possession, use, storage and trade of nuclear, chemical or conventional weapons • Nuclear terrorism • Policies of political segregation (apartheid) • Slavery, enslavement practices and human trafficking • Illegal experimentation on humans • Torture and other forms of cruel, inhuman or degrading treatment • Piracy and illegal acts against the security of navigation at sea and oil extraction platforms • Hijacking and illegal acts against the security of international aviation • Enforced disappearances and extra-judicial executions • Threats and use of violence against internationally protected individuals and UN staff members • Illegal acts against specific and internationally protected environmental resources	• Mercenary services • Interception of international submarine cables • Corruption and bribery of foreign officials and civil servants • International trafficking of indecent material (e.g. paedophile material) • Illicit drug trafficking and other related crimes • Forgery and counterfeiting	• Hostage-taking • Use of explosives • Illegal use or obstruction of postal services • Terrorism financing • Organised crime and other related crimes • Destruction and/or theft of national treasures

obstacles and distinguish and codify the 27 crimes into distinct categories for the first time, then this can only be achieved within a new theoretical framework. Admittedly, the starting point would be Bassiouni's previous codification, but the outcome will often differ from it substantially. Therefore, the categorisation of the 27 international crimes cannot be based on the four categories introduced by Bassiouni (international crimes; partially international crimes; transnational crimes; 'international' crimes for preventive and suppressive reasons), given that the term 'partially international crimes' is extremely unclear.[89] Hence the new proposed categorisation can only be based on the other three categories.

In other words, the categorisation of the 27 suggested international crimes can only be realised along the lines shown in the Table 1.1. A distinct change in each crime's classification is brought about by the reduction in the number of categories

[89] The author believes that certain terms are incompatible with adverbs like partially. Therefore, it is worth considering that nowhere in the world is there a partially international airport, a partially international player nor a partially international university or scientific union.

from four to three, but also due to the different viewpoint that this book takes as compared with the views of great scholars such as Cassese (e.g. on the crime of racial segregation commonly known as apartheid) and Bassiouni (e.g. on the crime of torture).

However, even after the suggested improvements and radical changes in Bassiouni's original chart (removal of the nebulous category 'partially international crimes', integration of these crimes into the three remaining categories, other changes in crimes' categorisation, etc.), critical elements including the place where a crime is committed *(locus delicti)*, the offenders and/or the victims' nationality, the offenders' motives and other elements of a crime could potentially lead to futher distinctions in accordance with Bassiouni's criteria. Thus, for example, the forgery and counterfeiting of German passports by Spanish counterfeiters would become a transnational crime, while the hostage-taking of French, English, American and Greek tourists by Tunisian terrorists would become an international crime.[90]

For precisely this reason, it is essential to recodify all old and new criteria based on which a crime should be considered as international, regardless of any variations in the aforementioned parameters and without any need to link the criteria to distinct categories (international crimes; transnational crimes; 'international' crimes for preventive and suppressive reasons).

Consequently, based on the analysis in this first chapter and in order to resolve any existing problems concerning the finer points of the categorization of criminal cases according to the various elements of each crime (*locus delicti*, offender's nationality, victim's nationality), a novel codification of the term 'international crime' is introduced.[91]

1.6 Crafting a New Definition of International Crime

Hence, it is proposed that the classification of an act as an international crime could be verified by answering the following, brief questionnaire:

[90]Undoubtedly, the second example is directly related to the last terrorism attack in Tunisia, Tunisia: The Guardian (2015a).

[91]It is noteworthy that the analysis of the term 'international crime' has not been debated sufficiently by academics at an international level, as in the past few years a utilitarian perspective has been adopted according to which international crimes are only those included in the ICCRSt and thus, the analysis of this term is tacitly assumed to be meaningless.

Key Questions

1. Is the conduct under examination wrongful and imputable?
2. Does the conduct under examination violate an internationally recognised human right [as defined in the European Convention on Human Rights (ECHR), the African Charter on Human and Democratic Rights, the American Convention on Human Rights, the International Covenant on Civil and Political Rights, the United Nations Convention on the Rights of the Child etc.] or legal interest(s) protected by international law (i.e. the UN Charter, international conventions or international customary law)?[92]
3. Do the characteristics of the conduct under examination (the manner in which it was committed, the number of perpetrators/victims, the status of the victim/perpetrator, its importance, etc.) constitute a severe violation of internationally recognised human rights or those protected by international law?[93]

Additional Auxillary Questions

4. Does the conduct under examination involve more than one State because of the place in which it was committed, and/or the nationality of the perpetrators and/or victims?
5. Does the conduct under examination involve a perpetrator or an accomplice acting in an official capacity or in a capacity that caused 'quasi state policy' effects?

The first question is essential before we can characterise an act as criminal in the first place. At an international level, it is equally important because it may preclude the prosecution of individuals who were forced to commit crimes involuntarily against their will. Thus, for instance, the answer to the first question, which is also fundamental to every criminal justice system, will exclude the criminal prosecution at an international level of children/juvenile individuals who jointly commit murders, kidnappings or rapes under the influence of drugs (administered to them by force, without their consent).

The second question is extremely important, before we consider whether or not a crime falls within the sphere of international law and should be characterised as an international crime. Nebulous concepts such as 'attracting international interest' or 'international community' need to be avoided at all costs, therefore this book

[92] It must be noted that the term 'right' coming from common law has prevailed in international law over the term 'legal interest' coming from continental law.

[93] This criterion is much clearer from the start, and much easier for the courts to interpret compared to other terms such as 'great moral disapproval' or 'involvement of the international community'.

suggests the adoption of internationally recognised human rights and internationally protected legal interests as crucial criteria. It is well-known that human rights are founded upon a great number of international conventions such as (for example) the ECHR, the Charter of Fundamental Rights of the European Union (CFREU), the African Convention of Human Rights, the American Convention on Human Rights, the International Covenant on Human and Political Rights, the Convention on the Rights of the Child, etc. As far as legal interests protected by international law are concerned, i.e. the UN Charter, international conventions or international customary law, these are indicatively associated with offences such as forgery and currency counterfeiting, damage to submarine cables and illegal obstruction of postal services.

The third question, following the gravity criterion of the Rome Statute, and lately the ECHR,[94] adopts the criterion of a severe violation of an internationally recognised human right or internationally protected legal interest in order to characterise the act under examination as an international crime. And while it certainly goes without saying that genocide will always be genocide, this is not the case for many of the 27 crimes that are considered international crimes and connected to postal services, submarine cables or even hostages and use of explosives, to name but a few examples.

Regarding the two additional auxillary questions—the first on the number of States involved because of the location in which the crime was committed and/or the nationality of the perpetrators and/or the victims; and the second on the involvement of a perpetrator or an accomplice acting in an official capacity or in a capacity that caused 'quasi state policy' effects, the following must be noted. Both criteria have historically, from the very beginning of the discourse on the concept of international crime, been very significant for a number of academics when it comes to the inclusion of a crime within the sphere of international law. However, in my view the globalisation of human society, the increasingly close commercial, business and transnational relations and of course the evolution of international criminal law itself no longer justify the preservation of these criteria for the determination of whether a crime is international or not. Nevertheless, given that these criteria are still considered important by a number of academics, it is suggested that they may be preserved at a second, subsidiary and auxillary level and contribute as indicators for the evaluation of exceptional, borderline cases. In this second edition the phrase "or in a capacity that caused 'quasi state policy' effects" has been added to the second auxillary question in order to address the concerns of the largely outdated characteristics of this criterion and to encapsulate clearly the crime of ecocide too.

---

[94] Art. 17(1)d ICCRSt: "The case is not of sufficient gravity to justify further action by the Court." Moreover Art. 12 of Protocol No 14 to the European Convention of Human Rights states that: "The Court shall declare inadmissible any individual application submitted under Article 34 if it considers that: [. . .] b. the applicant has not suffered a significant disadvantage, unless respect for human rights as defined in the Convention and the Protocols thereto requires an examination of the application on the merits and provided that no case may be rejected on this ground which has not been duly considered by a domestic tribunal."

If the first three questions are answered affirmatively, then an act must be unreservedly considered an international crime *de lege ferenda*. In exceptional, borderline cases, i.e. where it may not be absolutely clear whether the answer to one of the three questions is affirmative or negative (e.g. if the offence is severe or not), the answers to the two additional questions may significantly contribute to the final classification of criminal conduct as an international crime or not.

Thus, according to the above analysis, the mass kidnapping of Nigerian girls by the terrorist organisation Boko Haram constitutes *de lege ferenda* an international crime, **regardless of** the perpetrators' ideological, religious, political or economic motives (i.e. even if it is assumed that their only purpose was to gain illegal economic benefits by receiving excessive ransoms from the mass kidnapping of girls),[95] **regardless of** whether the perpetrators, the victims and the place where the crime was committed concern only one country (Nigeria), **regardless of** the fact that none of the offenders held a state office and **regardless of** whether the act occurred during a non-international/internal armed conflict in which war crimes and/or crimes against humanity were committed according to the press and International Amnesty reports, or not (i.e. even if it was a single act and no armed conflict actually existed).[96]

This is because all three questions in the proposed questionnaire are affirmatively answered. Specifically: **(1)** The act of kidnapping hundreds of girls with the intention of demanding ransom and disrupting the social fabric is ultimately a wrongful and imputable conduct. **(2)** It primarily violates the internationally recognized human right to personal freedom. Lastly, **(3)** its characteristics, including the modus operandi, the number of perpetrators and victims, and the severity of the conduct, amount to a severe violation of personal freedom.[97]

The same principles apply to the previously discussed hypothetical scenario in which an oil tanker is intentionally sunk in the middle of the South Atlantic Ocean, leading to widespread ecocide with immediate implications for multiple states. In this hypothetical situation, all criteria proposed by the author are adequately met, as follows:

(1) The conduct under investigation, namely, the intentional sinking of the tanker, is wrongful and attributable.

---

[95] *The Independent* (2014). See Also *The Guardian* (2015b).

[96] Amnesty International Report (2015), pp. 19–27.

[97] It is easily ascertained *a contrario* how the uncompromising obsession with elements such as the involvement of a perpetrator or accomplice holding a state office would lead to obviously unjust and legally wrong conclusions based not on ICCRSt provisions but on a 'traditional perspective' on international law. Therefore, it is characteristic of this view that the monstrous crimes committed by ISIS against unarmed people would not be subject to the ICC's jurisdiction, even in the cases where the temporal, local or personal jurisdiction perquisites are met (i.e. as regards the hundred murders committed in Paris), because ISIS is not considered a state entity.

(2) The aforementioned conduct violates internationally recognized human rights [e.g., the right to life, the right to respect for private and family life – Articles 2 and 8 ECHR].
(3) The conduct (considering its nature, the number of perpetrators/victims, the status of the victims/perpetrators, its major significance, etc.) constitutes a severe violation of internationally recognized human rights or those protected by international law.
(4) The conduct involves multiple states, as previously analyzed, and encompasses a broad range of nationalities among the perpetrators and victims.
(5) The conduct involves one or more perpetrators whose actions have clearly caused and will continue to result in 'quasi-state policy' effects for numerous states.

In any case, no one can overlook that the core ICC crimes (genocide, crime of aggression, crimes against humanity, war crimes) are much more important than the rest for historical, humanitarian and legal reasons, since a permanent legal institution has already been established for their adjudication. Therefore, as the main purpose of the book is to examine fundamental aspects of the ICC's jurisdiction, only these crimes will be examined in the following chapters. The only exception to this will be the novel crime of ecocide about which a new International Criminal Court for the Protection of the Environment (ICCPE) is eventually proposed in Chapter 10, as being both legally and pragmatically the best legal recourse.

References

Table of Cases

ICC (2013a) Prosecutor v. Saif Al-Islam Gaddafi and Abdullah Al-Senussi Decision on the admissibility of the case against Saif Al-Islam Gaddafi, ICC-01/11-01/11-344-Red
ICC (2013b) The Prosecutor v. Saif Al-Islam Gaddafi and Abdullah Al-Senussi Decision on the Admissibility of the Case Against Mr. Abdullah Al-Senussi, ICC-01/11-01/11, 11 October 2013
ICJ (2002) Democratic Republic of the Congo v. Belgium
Regina v. Bartle and the Commissioner of Police for the Metropolis and others ex Parte Pinochet (1998) (on appeal from a Divisional Court of the Queen's Bench Division)
Regina v. Evans and another and the Commissioner of Police for the Metropolis and others ex Parte Pinochet (on appeal from a Divisional Court of the Queen's Bench Division) (1998)

Books

Antonopoulos K (2003) Individual criminal liability in international law. Sakkoulas
Bassiouni CM (2013) Introduction to international criminal law. Martinus Nijhoff Publishers
Bassiouni CM (2014) Crimes against humanity: historical evolution and contemporary application. CUP

Bauman Z, May T (2001) Thinking sociologically. Blackwell Publishing
Boister N (2002a) Human Rights Protections in the Suppression Conventions
Cassese A (2008) International criminal law. OUP
Chouliaras A (2013) The rise of international criminal justice system. Sakkoulas
Cicero MT (1913) De Officiis. In: Walter Miller (ed) Harvard University Press
Confucius in Chalikias S (trans.) (2001) Confucius Analects Vol. A, Indiktos
Cryer R, Friman H, Robinson D, Wilmshurt E (2010) An introduction to international criminal law and procedure, CUP
Monk R (2007) Wittgenstein. Patakis
Morais HV (2005) Fighting international crime and its financing: the importance of following a coherent global strategy based on the rule of law
Partington A (ed) (1997) Oxford concise dictionary of quotations. OUP
Pazartzi F (2007) Criminal enforcement in international law: international criminal justice in modern times. Sakkoulas
Pihou MA (2012) The concept of aggression in international law. Sakkoulas
Schwarzenberger G (1965) The problem of an international criminal law (1950), reprinted in Mueller G, Wise E (eds) International Criminal Law
Triffterer O (1987) Efforts to Recognise and Codify International Crimes in Rapport General au Colloque Preparatoire du XIV Congres International de Droit Penal, Les Crimes Internationaux et le Droit Penal Interne, Hammamet
Tsilonis V (2016a) International Criminal Justice during the first half of the 20th Century, Essays in Honour of Christophoros D. Argiropoulos, Nomiki Bibliothiki
Tsilonis V (2016b) Crime and Judgement: International Criminal Justice and the Crime of Piracy. In: Gasparinatou M (ed) Essays in Honour of Professor Nestor Kourakis. Sakkoulas
Vagias M (2011) The territorial jurisdiction of the international criminal court: certain contested issues, Ph.D. Thesis. Bynkershoek Publishing
Werle G, Jeßberger F (2020) Principles of international criminal law. Oxford University Press
Woetzel RK (1962) The Nuremberg trials in international law. Stevens & Sons Limited, Plymouth
Zahar A, Sluiter G (2007) International criminal law: a critical restatement. Oxford University Press

Articles/Reports

Amnesty International Report (2015) Our Job is to Shoot, Slaughter and Kill. Amnesty International
Bitzilekis N (2015) The Violation of Mankind's Multiculturalism: Another Approach to the Definition of International Crimes. International Criminal Law Review
Boister N (1998) The Exclusion of Treaty Crimes from the Jurisdiction of the Court. JCSL
Boister N (2002b) Human Rights Protections in the Suppression Conventions. HRL
Clark RS (2010) The International Criminal Law System. In: 17th Annual Australia and New Zealand Society of International Law Conference: The Future of Multilateralism in a Plural World, Convention's Proceedings. N Z J Public Int Law
Evans-Pritchard D, Dundes Renteln A (1995) The Interpretation and Distortion of Culture: A Hmong Marriage by Capture Case in Fresno, California
ILC (1953) Documents of the Fifth Session including the Report of the International Law Commission to the General Assembly
Paulose RM (2012) Beyond the Core: Incorporating Transnational Crimes into the Rome Statute. Cardozo J Int Comp Law

Websites/Web Sources

BBC News (2015a) Profile: Japanese journalist Kenji Goto, https://www.bbc.com/news/world-asia-30978302. Accessed 8 June 2023

BBC News (2015b) Japan out raged at IS 'beheading' of hostage Kenji Goto, http://www.bbc.com/news/world-middle-east-31075769. Accessed 8 June 2023

CBS News (2023a) How did the Canadian wildfires start? A look at what's causing the fires that covered the East Coast in smoke, https://www.cbsnews.com/news/how-did-the-wildfires-in-canada-start-cause-nova-scotia-quebec/. Accessed 20 June 2023

CBS News (2023b) See it in photos: Smoke from Canadian wildfires engulfs NYC in hazy blanket, https://www.cbsnews.com/news/pictures-new-york-city-nyc-smoke-canada-wildfire-haze/. Accessed 20 June 2023

Geneva Academy, Rule of Law in Armed Conflicts Project., http://www.geneva-academy.ch/RULAC/international_criminal_law.php. Accessed 8 June 2023

ILC (1991) Report of the International Law Commission on the work of its forty-third session, http://legal.un.org/ilc/documentation/english/reports/a_46_10.pdf. Accessed 8 June 2023

ILC (1996) Report of the International Law Commission on the work of its forty-eighth session, http://legal.un.org/ilc/documentation/english/reports/a_51_10.pdf. Accessed 8 June 2023

League of Nations (1925) Arbitration, Security and Reduction of Armaments: Protocol for the Pacific Settlement of International Disputes, http://digital.library.northwestern.edu/league/le000016.pdf. Accessed 8 June 2023

Naziris IA (2009) The Crime against Humanity based on Article 7 of the International Criminal Court, Digital Archive of PhD Theses, https://www.didaktorika.gr/eadd/readonline?handle=10442/28846. Accessed 8 June 2023

The Guardian (2001) Harding L, Taliban Blow Apart 2,000 Years of Buddhist history, https://www.theguardian.com/world/2001/mar/03/afghanistan.lukeharding. Accessed 8 June 2023

The Guardian (2015a) Smith D, "School girls Kidnapped by Boko Haram "Brain washed to Fight for Group, http://www.theguardian.com/world/2015/jun/29/schoolgirls-kidnapped-boko-haram-brainwashed-fight-group. Accessed 8 June 2023

The Guardian (2015b) Stephen C, Shaheen K & Tran M, Tunis museum attack: 20 people killed after hostage drama at tourist site, https://www.theguardian.com/world/2015/mar/18/eight-people-killed-in-attack-on-tunisia-bardo-museum. Accessed 8 June 2023

The Independent (2014) Johnston I, Kidnapped Nigerian girls "escape from Boko Haram abductors, http://www.independent.co.uk/news/world/africa/kidnapped-nigerian-girls-escape-from-boko-haram-abductors-9588251.html. Accessed 8 June 2023

The New York Times (2015) Sanger DE & Schmitt E, Russian Ships Near Data Cables Are Too Close for U.S. Comfort, https://www.nytimes.com/2015/10/26/world/europe/russian-presence-near-undersea-cables-concerns-us.html?_r=2. Accessed 8 June 2023

Tsilonis V (2011) International Protection of Human Rights and Politics: An Inescapable Reality, Intellectum, Vol. 07, https://papers.ssrn.com/sol3/Delivery.cfm/SSRN_ID1948998_code1722927.pdf?abstractid=1948998&mirid=1. Accessed 8 June 2023

Tsilonis V (2017) The awakening hypothesis of the complementarity principle. In: Spinellis CD, Theodorakis N, Billis E, Papadimitrakopoulos G (eds) Europe in crisis: crime, criminal justice, and the way forward. Sakkoulas, http://crime-in-crisis.com/en/wp-content/uploads/2017/06/62-VIICTOR-KOURAKIS-FS_Final_Draft_26.4.17.pdf. Accessed 8 June 2023

US News (2015) Shinkman PD, ISIS Destruction of Antiques at Mosul, Nimrud Hides Sinister Moneymaking Scheme. https://www.usnews.com/news/articles/2015/03/09/isis-destruction-of-antiques-at-mosul-nimrud-hides-sinister-moneymaking-scheme. Accessed 8 June 2023

Vienna Convention on the Law of Treaties., https://treaties.un.org/doc/Publication/UNTS/Volume%201155/volume-1155-I-18232-English.pdf. Accessed 8 June 2023

Chapter 2
The Preconditions for the International Criminal Court to Exercise its Jurisdiction

Article 12 of the Rome Statute

Abstract This chapter delves into the essential preconditions for the exercise of the International Criminal Court's (ICC) jurisdiction. These preconditions encompass the aspects of time (temporal jurisdiction or jurisdiction *ratione temporis*), geography (territorial jurisdiction or jurisdiction *ratione loci*), and the nationality of the alleged offender (personal jurisdiction or jurisdiction ratione personae), grounded in the principle of active personality.

The chapter begins by discussing the ICC's temporal jurisdiction, which, as stipulated in Article 126 ICCRSt, commenced on 1 July 2002. This date marks the point from which the ICC's authority to prosecute crimes became effective, following the requisite ratification of the ICCRSt by sixty states.

In examining territorial jurisdiction, the chapter emphasises the universally accepted principle that states possess inherent jurisdiction over criminal offenses committed within their territories. This principle, deeply rooted in state sovereignty, is reflected in Article 12(2)(a) ICCRSt and is a cornerstone of international law, supported by numerous international conventions and bilateral extradition agreements. The chapter further addresses the challenges inherent in Article 12(2) ICCRSt, particularly how the ICC's jurisdiction relies primarily on only two pillars: the principle of territorial jurisdiction and the principle of active personality. This reliance arguably constitutes the Achilles' heel of Article 12(2) ICCRSt.

A significant portion of the chapter is dedicated to exploring the complexities of the ICC's territorial jurisdiction, especially in contexts involving excluded, occupied, and disputed territories. This includes a thorough analysis of how these unique geopolitical scenarios impact the ICC's jurisdiction. Lastly, the chapter offers a comparative analysis of the terms 'crime', 'case', and 'situation' as they pertain to the ICC. Accompanied by critical commentary, the analysis delves into the implications of *ad hoc* acceptance of the ICC's jurisdiction by states not party to the Rome Statute.The chapter aims to provide an in-depth understanding of these foundational aspects, crucial for comprehending the scope and limitations of the ICC's jurisdictional authority.

V. Tsilonis, *The Jurisdiction of the International Criminal Court*,
https://doi.org/10.1007/978-3-031-46138-5_2

2.1 Introduction: The Adoption of the Rome Statute and Article 12 ICCRSt

The United Nations organised an international conference from 16 June to 17 July 1998 to draft and adopt a statute for an international criminal court. Representatives of 160 States participated in the Rome Conference, along with observers from two hundred and fifty non-governmental organisations.[1] The text drafted by the preparatory committee chaired by Adriaan Bos was used as a starting point for the negotiations.[2] The said committee played a central role, as it managed to solve many significant issues and to limit the extent of others, including with regard to the text of the statute of the International Criminal Court, the parameters of the 'complementarity' principle, the relationship between the International Criminal Court and national jurisdictions, etc.[3] Nonetheless, despite the dutiful efforts of the committee, the statute's draft did not only include 116 articles but 1400 additions in brackets[4] and almost 200 points suggesting multiple options on a range of important matters.[5]

The divergence of opinion among the groups of States—which was colourfully reflected from the beginning in large numbers of additions to the draft of the Rome Statute—led to 30 days of tough negotiations and intense disagreement, which extended from the opening of the conference to the adoption of the Rome Statute.

It became clear early on that the participating States were split into two main groups. On the one side, the so-called 'Like-Minded Group' comprised around 60 States and non-governmental organisations that supported the creation of an independent and strong court. Most European States (with the exception of France), Australia and Canada[6] were part of this group, as well as the over whelming majority of the non-governmental organisations whose members participated as observers without the right to vote.[7]

---

[1]Lamprinidi F, "The International Criminal Court: Jurisdiction, Role and Limitations" in Georgoulas S, (ed) Criminology in Greece Today, Kapsimi Athens, p 374.

[2]The importance of the work of the preparatory committee is partly recognised in the preamble of the Rome Statute where gratitude for its work is expressed. Annex I (B) (1998).

[3]Lammers (1998).

[4]I.e. proposed additions to or differentiations of the original text that would be discussed during the conference.

[5]United Nations Diplomatic Conference of Plenipotentiaries on the Establishment of an International Criminal Court (1998) UN Doc. A/CONF.183/SR.9, 122, par. 15 http://legal.un.org/icc/rome/proceedings/E/Rome%20Proceedings_v2_e.pdf last accessed 8 June 2023.

[6]Australia and Canada are two States that have shown a particular interest in the institutions involved in the administering of international justice, and, as a consequence, a great number of lawyers and other specialists have staffed the offices of ad hoc criminal tribunals, as well as those of the international criminal court. During my six-month stay at the Hague in 2004, a common question jokingly asked to all newcomers to the ICTY was: "Are you from Canada or Australia?"

[7]Dousi and Papatolias (2004), p. 21.

The opposing group of dissenting States was known as the 'Non-Aligned Movement'. While its members officially supported the establishment of a court with limited jurisdiction, in essence most of them were opposed to the establishment of an International Criminal Court, because they were worried that it might limit their influence at an international level and/or lead to the prosecution of citizens of theirs acting outside of their territory in accordance with official or unofficial government orders. States like China, India, Israel, Russia and the USA belonged to this group. It is worth noting that even though these States were few in number, they represented over half of the planet's population.

During the negotiations, issues such as the formulation of definitions of crimes over which the ICC would exercise its jurisdiction proved to be relatively unambiguous on the whole.[8] However, the crime of aggression, although included in the International Criminal Court's Statute, was not defined concretely at all. Its definition was deferred to a future conference.[9]

The preconditions for exercising the jurisdiction of the newly founded permanent international criminal court were reflected in Article 12 ICCRSt.[10] However,

---

[8] Of course, this does not mean that there were not any important disagreements. For example, despite the fact that in previous drafts of the Statute the jurisdiction of the court was extended to violations of drug trafficking and trade at an international level under the Convention Against Illicit Traffic in Narcotic Drugs and Psychotropic Substances, 20 December 1988, 28 ILM (1989) 493, as well as to violations of the Convention Against Torture and Other Cruel, Inhuman or Degrading Treatment or Punishment 1465 UNTS (1987) 112, eventually these offences were removed from the final draft of the preparatory committee because of the lack of agreement between the participating States. A similar fate awaited the crime of terrorism, regarding which the wording of Annex I (E) of the Rome Statute is noteworthy: "Regretting that no generally acceptable definition of the crimes of terrorism and drug crimes could be agreed upon for the inclusion, within the jurisdiction of the Court", Annex I (B), Final Act of the United Nations Diplomatic Conference of Plenipotentiaries on the Establishment of an International Criminal Court U.N. Doc. A/CONF.183/13 15 June–17 July 1998) http://legal.un.org/icc/rome/proceedings/E/Rome%20Proceedings_v1_e.pdf last accessed 8 June 2023.

[9] In the final draft of the preparatory committee, three proposed definitions on the crime of aggression or, in other words, the crime against peace, can be found. All three proposed definitions included a large number of parentheses, a fact that rendered their comprehension somewhat like trying to understanding an ancient riddle. The numerous parentheses were placed in a way that left all possible outcomes open and allowed the conclusion of an agreement on this matter. Unfortunately, however, not even this forest of brackets could lead to the adoption of a definition on the crime of aggression. See this very interesting excerpt in the Report of the Preparatory Committee on the Establishment of an International Criminal Court, A/CONF.183/2/Add.1, 14 April 1998, 12-14 https://undocs.org/A/CONF.183/2/Add.1 last accessed 8 June 2023.

[10] Article 12—Preconditions to the exercise of jurisdiction: 1. A State which becomes a Party to this Statute thereby accepts the jurisdiction of the Court with respect to the crimes referred to in article 5. 2. In the case of article 13, paragraph (a) or (c), the Court may exercise its jurisdiction if one or more of the following States are Parties to this Statute or have accepted the jurisdiction of the Court in accordance with paragraph 3: (a) The State on the territory of which the conduct in question occurred or, if the crime was committed on board a vessel or aircraft, the State of registration of that vessel or aircraft; (b) The State of which the person accused of the crime is a national. 3. If the acceptance of a State which is not a Party to this Statute is required under paragraph 2, that State may, by declaration lodged with the Registrar, accept the exercise of jurisdiction by the Court with

because of Article 12's extremely important role, its adoption was the subject of intense dispute,[11] which led to the notorious vote at the end of the Rome Conference.[12] The view which prevailed is reflected in Article 12(2)(a) and (b) ICCRSt: the ICC can exercise its jurisdiction in a case if the State in the territory in which the act took place (or with which the plane or vessel on which it took place is registered) has ratified the Rome Statute; or if the State of which the alleged perpetrator is a citizen has ratified the Rome Statute.[13]

This amounted to a compromise between the diametrically opposed opinions of States like the USA on the one side, and Germany and South Korea on the other. The USA insisted on the consent of the perpetrator's national State as a prerequisite before the ICC could exercise its jurisdiction. They maintained that otherwise, Article 34 of the Vienna Convention on the Law of Treaties, which proclaims that treaties cannot be binding for third, non-contracting parties, would be violated.[14] As the sole exception, they accepted only the extremely rare occurrence of a referral from the UN Security Council.[15] On the other hand, Germany and South Korea suggested directly or indirectly a model of "universal jurisdiction": Germany proposed that State parties must be allowed to transfer to the ICC the jurisdiction they are otherwise entitled to exercise according to existing international law,[16] while South Korea with an elaborate, brilliant provision suggested the ICC exercise direct

---

respect to the crime in question. The accepting State shall cooperate with the Court without any delay or exception in accordance with Part 9.

[11] Williams (1999), p. 329.

[12] Kirsch and Holmes (1999), pp 2, 4.

[13] For a brief, but analytical narration of the work of the Rome Conference on Article 12 ICCRSt, see Vagias (2011), pp. 70–74.

[14] Article 34 - General rule regarding third States: A treaty does not create either obligations or rights for a third State without its consent.

[15] Proposal Submitted by the United States of America, U.N. Doc. A/CONF.183/C.1/L.70,247 http://legal.un.org/docs/?path=../diplomaticconferences/1998_icc/docs/english/vol_2/a_conf183_c1_sr1.pdf&lang=EF last accessed 8 June 2023.

[16] The Jurisdiction of the International Court, an Informal Discussion paper submitted by Germany U.N. Doc. A/AC.249/1998/DP.2, par. 20. One has to point out that it is not absolutely clear in international law which crimes exactly fall within the jurisdiction of States based to the principle of universal jurisdiction. Case Concerning the Arrest Warrant of 11 April 2000 ICJ (2002). *See* Dissenting Opinion of Judge Van den Wyngaert, International Court of Justice (ICJ) https://www.icj-cij.org/files/case-related/121/121-20020214-JUD-01-09-EN.pdf last accessed 8 June 2023. However, it is a fact that both the ICTY and the ICTR in Rule 11B§§ A(ii) and (iii) Rules of Procedure and Evidence, accepted that it is legally possible to transfer cases from those ad hoc criminal tribunals to States based on the principle of universal jurisdiction. See however ICTR (2006). ICTR (2007a, b). It is also indicative that the Appeal Chamber of the ICTR in Bagaragaza Case rejected the Prosecutor's request (as well as the request of the accused himself) for the transfer of the case to Norway with the justification that "Norway's jurisdiction over Mr. Bagaragaza's crimes would be exercised pursuant to legislative provisions dealing with the prosecution of ordinary crimes [. . . while] this provision delimits the Tribunal's authority, allowing it only to refer cases where the state will charge and convict for those international crimes listed in its Statute", 4, par. 16.

jurisdiction over a state party, but with the strict consent either of the perpetrator's national State, or of the State on the territory of which the crime was committed, or of the State where the perpetrator is detained.[17] It must be underlined here that—despite being unclear—South Korea's proposal was similar in essence to the one submitted by Germany, since to the degree that a state party could arrest a suspect, the ICC would be able to exercise its jurisdiction directly, regardless of the location where the crime was committed or of the nationality of the alleged perpetrator. The difference between South Korea's proposal and the German one is rendered purely theoretical if one considers that the ICC cannot adjudicate a case based on the perpetrator's appearance alone and that therefore the cooperation of the ICC with the State in which the perpetrator resides or is being held is always necessary.[18]

Nonetheless, it is a fact that the adoption of Article 12 ICCRSt regarding the requirements for the ICC to exercise its jurisdiction was an integral part of a package that determined the fate of the Statute in the last few hours of the Rome Conference.[19] However, and given that no official conference minutes exist, what exactly took place in the last week of the Conference and especially between the 16 and 17 July 1998 remains open to speculation, notwithstanding the personal and to this day undisputed records compiled by certain participants.[20] Thus matters such as the territorial jurisdiction of the ICC in territories under military occupation have remained unclear from the start.[21] Undoubtedly, however, the adoption of Article 12 ICCRSt was combined with provisions such as those of Articles 98 (on the

[17] Republic of Korea: proposal regarding articles 6 [9], 7 [6], UN Doc. A/CONF.183/C.1/L.6, 227-229, http://legal.un.org/icc/rome/proceedings/E/Rome%20Proceedings_v3_e.pdf, last accessed 8 June 2023.

[18] Schabas (2010), p. 281.

[19] Vagias (2011), pp. 16, 74.

[20] See for instance Kirsch and Robinson (2002), pp. 67–91.

[21] Vagias (2011), pp. 16, 74. Contra Schabas (2010), p. 285.

international obligations of a state party)[22] and 124 ICCRSt (on the possibility of granting a 7-year grace period regarding war crimes).[23,24]

Following the Rome Conference, a Preparatory Committee was in session for the next 4 years with the main goal of drafting the secondary legal texts of the court, i.e. the Rules of Procedure and Evidence[25] as well as the Elements of Crimes.[26] It is noteworthy that while the Rules of Procedure and Evidence of the ad hoc criminal tribunals for the former Yugoslavia and for Rwanda were drafted by the judges themselves, in the ICC's case, the Rules of Procedure and Evidence were drafted by the state party to the Rome Statute, because these States wished to ensure that the system regulating how the ICC works would be as clear and definite as possible.[27]

Eventually, Article 126(1) ICCRSt stipulated that "[t]his Statute shall enter into force on the first day of the month after the 60th day following the date of the deposit of the 60th instrument of ratification, acceptance, approval or accession with the Secretary-General of the United Nations". This provision was eventually fulfilled on 1 July 2002, when the required time period lapsed subsequent to the number of States to have ratified the Rome Statute reaching sixty.

Thus the idea for the establishment of a permanent criminal judicial institution was made reality; the institution could fairly and impartially put on trial and sentence those who committed serious war crimes, crimes against humanity, genocide and eventually the crime of aggression, constituting an important step for the application of the principle of 'international legality', the guarantee of peace and the advocacy of individual freedom.[28] The establishment of a permanent international criminal court

[22] Article 98 Rome Statute - Cooperation with respect to waiver of immunity and consent to surrender: 1. The Court may not proceed with a request for surrender or assistance which would require the requested State to act inconsistently with its obligations under international law with respect to the State or diplomatic immunity of a person or property of a third State, unless the Court can first obtain the cooperation of that third State for the waiver of the immunity. 2. The Court may not proceed with a request for surrender which would require the requested State to act inconsistently with its obligations under international agreements pursuant to which the consent of a sending State is required to surrender a person of that State to the Court, unless the Court can first obtain the cooperation of the sending State for the giving of consent for the surrender.

[23] Article 124 Rome Statute - Transitional Provision: Notwithstanding article 12, paragraphs 1 and 2, a State, on becoming a party to this Statute, may declare that, for a period of seven years after the entry into force of this Statute for the State concerned, it does not accept the jurisdiction of the Court with respect to the category of crimes referred to in article 8 when a crime is alleged to have been committed by its nationals or on its territory. A declaration under this article may be withdrawn at any time. The provisions of this article shall be reviewed at the Review Conference convened in accordance with article 123, paragraph 1.

[24] Vagias (2011), p. 16, 74.

[25] This is the official name of the Code of Criminal Procedure of the International Criminal Court.

[26] A legal text in which the constitutive and the mens rea elements of a crime are analysed at length.

[27] Kirsch (2007), p. 541.

[28] Simeonidou-Kastanidou (2003), p. 402.

came with a jurisdiction that was characterised as "special" in the Greek literature, as it only covers specific crimes as clearly defined today in Articles 5 to 8B ICCRSt.[29]

It is, of course, a matter of fact that global superpowers such as the USA, Russia and China were hostile to the establishment and functioning of the ICC. That is because its role undermines the continuation of the international principle of "legalised hegemony"[30] in the delicate field of criminal law, which had hitherto fallen under the exclusive jurisdiction of national States, but also the exercise of international politics through military power. Moreover, the strictly defined field of international criminal law—which directly or indirectly touches upon many of the State's international activities—is treated by global superpower states as a potential Trojan horse aimed at limiting their international authority through the judicial function of an "independent" and "objective" supranational organisation. Indeed, a good example of this is to be found in the declarations of India, China and the USA that condemn the provisions of Article 12 either because "it made a mockery of the distinction between States parties and States not parties, thus, straying sharply from established international law";[31] or because "it constituted interference in the judicial independence or sovereignty of States";[32] or finally because the adoption of this particular article was one of the main reasons for voting against the Rome Statute.[33] Thus the adoption of Article 12 ICCRSt, which inevitably plays a fundamental part in the functioning of the ICC, proved to be "maybe the hardest compromise throughout all of the negotiations" at the Rome Conference.[34]

2.2 The Territorial Jurisdiction of the ICC

The principle of territorial jurisdiction that is reflected in Article 12(2)(a) ICCRSt is deeply rooted in international law, as well as in the legal orders of almost all States. In other words, it is consistently accepted that a state has indisputable jurisdiction over all criminal offences that are committed in its territory, according to the principle of state sovereignty, and this fact can easily be ascertained from a

[29] Gagas (1999), p. 482.

[30] This particular term was invented by Simpson, who attempts thus to describe the "... existence within an international society of a powerful elite of states whose superior status is recognised by minor powers as a political fact giving rise to the existence of certain constitutional privileges, rights and duties and whose relations with each other are defined by adherence to a rough principle of sovereign equality." Simpson (2004), p. 68.

[31] United Nations Diplomatic Conference of Plenipotentiaries on the Establishment of an International Criminal Court, 9th Plenary Meeting, UN Doc. A/CONF.183/SR.9, 122, par. 15 http://legal.un.org/icc/rome/proceedings/E/Rome%20Proceedings_v2_e.pdf last accessed 8 June 2023.

[32] Ibid 123 par. 37.

[33] Ibid 124 par. 40.

[34] Kirsch and Robinson (2002), p. 83.

significant number of international conventions and bilateral extradition agreements.[35] Thus, a State, always in accordance with the international or bilateral treaties it has signed, either exercises its criminal jurisdiction through its domestic judicial system or uses its discretionary power to delegate criminal jurisdiction to other States or international judicial organisations and authorities.

Consequently, the formulation of the principle of territorial sovereignty in Article 12(2)(a) ICCRSt is in complete agreement with established international law. Therefore, as long as a core crime (genocide, crime of aggression, crimes against humanity, war crimes) is committed by a person in the territory of a state party to the Rome Statute, the ICC has jurisdiction regardless of whether the alleged perpetrator is a national of the State in the territory where the crime was committed or a national of another State. In addition, it is irrelevant to the question of the ICC's jurisdiction whether the alleged perpetrator has been arrested in a state party to the Rome Statute or is located in a State that is not party to the Statute.

Nonetheless, it is important to emphasise that, should the suspect be located in a State that has not ratified the Statute, this State does not in principle have any obligation to cooperate with the ICC and to proceed with the suspect's extradition; unless perhaps the ICC exercises its jurisdiction after a referral from the UN Security Council to the ICC's Prosecutor in accordance with Chapter VII of the Charter of the United Nations of a situation pursuant to Article 13(b) ICCRSt.

A State that has not ratified the Rome Statute is, in principle, under no obligation to comply with the Statute or, in particular, with Article 12(2)(a), which provides for the principle of territorial jurisdiction in the field of international criminal law; acting accordingly, it does not violate Article 34 of the Vienna Convention on the Law of Treaties in any way either. Furthermore, it may seem tempting to argue that the ICC's jurisdiction over a crime committed on the territory of a state party by a national of a state non-party violates the fundamental principle that only states parties to a treaty are bound by its provisions. However, this argument must be rejected since if nothing else the Statute and the ICC's jurisdiction, as established by the Statute, cover the criminal punishment of individuals and not States.[36]

Besides, the nationals of state non-parties to the Statute who commit crimes in the territory of their own State are not in principle subject to the ICC's jurisdiction. Consequently, the aforementioned nationals fall under the ICC's jurisdiction only when it comes to crimes they have committed abroad, and more specifically in the territory of States that are party to the Rome Statute. However, as Antonio Cassese first pointed out, in such cases those citizens would fall under a different jurisdiction one way or another, since territorial jurisdiction is firmly established in international law, along with jurisdiction based on the active and passive personality principles.

---

[35] Williams (1999), p. 39, fns. 6, 7.

[36] For a more thorough review of the matter see Lee (1999), p. 29; Cassese (1999), pp. 144-171, pp 159 and 171.

Thus, "[t]he ICC would simply exercise its jurisdiction in lieu of the territorial state".[37] Hence, at least in principle, the Rome Statute simply authorises the ICC to exercise its jurisdiction as a substitute for a State that is unable or unwilling to exercise its criminal jurisdiction, a fact that does not in itself constitute, of course, a violation of international law.

Nevertheless, the 'Achilles' heel' of Article 12(2) ICCRSt appears to be its almost exclusive reliance[38] on two foundational principles: territorial jurisdiction and the principle of active personality. Territorial jurisdiction determines the Court's authority based on the location of the crime (*locus delicti*), while active personality is based on the nationality of the offender. Notably absent, however, is the ICC's jurisdiction under the principle of passive personality, which would consider the nationality of the victim. Imagine a scenario where UK citizens A, B, C, D, and E, along with their families holding Greek, Italian, and French passports, are killed by a US military drone at the Iraq-Syria border. The drone is operated by a US military officer from a base in Arizona, USA. In this situation, the ICC would confront insurmountable jurisdictional challenges: **(a)** The crime took place on the border between Iraq and Syria, neither of which is a party to the ICC, as neither has ratified the Rome Statute. **(b)** The American drone pilot, based in Arizona, USA, is a national of a state not party to the Rome Statute. Moreover, he is located in a territory of a state that does not recognise the ICC's jurisdiction.

This scenario illustrates the inherent limitations within Article 12(2) ICCRSt, highlighting significant gaps in the ICC's ability to address crimes involving international elements. This is particularly evident in cases where the crime's location and the perpetrator's nationality do not align with states party to the Rome Statute. The victim's nationality, in this context, is rendered ineffectual, offering no basis for ICC jurisdiction. Practically, the only avenue for the ICC to assert jurisdiction in such a scenario would be through a resolution by the UN Security Council.

Furthermore, one cannot ignore the fact that when crimes as hideous as genocide, crimes against humanity, the crime of aggression or war crimes are committed during armed conflicts that are not of an international character, they usually take place with the silent consent or active assistance of a State's national authorities.

Therefore, if a State has not yet accepted the ICC's jurisdiction over crimes committed on its territory by its own nationals, the ICC will be unable to exercise its jurisdiction in the first place, and the only legal recourse will be a referral of the investigation of the "situation" according to Article 13(b) ICCRSt, since in such cases it is not necessary for a State to accept the ICC's jurisdiction for the Court to exercise it.

Admittedly, contrary to initial predictions,[39] there are deficiencies that have not hitherto impeded the ICC in exercising its jurisdiction—such as the

[37] Cassese (2008) VIKTOR, pp. 21, 160.

[38] The only rare exception being the referral of a situation from the UN Security Council under Chapter VII of the Charter and Article 13(b) ICCRSt.

[39] Kaul (2002, vol I), pp. 612–614.

non-establishment in Article 12 ICCRSt of the principle of passive personality, which would allow a State whose nationals are the victims of a crime described in Article 5 ICCRSt (genocide, war crimes, crimes against humanity and, eventually, the crime of aggression) to refer a situation to the ICC.

This of course does not rule out cases arising in the future where the non-establishment of the internationally recognised principle of passive personality in Article 12 ICCRSt causes a legal vacuum. For example, were 500 Dutch soldiers, members of the UN Blue Helmets, to be murdered during a mission in the territory of a State that is not party to the Statute by perpetrators who are nationals of that State, the ICC will not be able to exercise its jurisdiction in principle, unless the Court's Prosecutor is given a relevant order by the UN Security Council pursuant to Article 13(b) ICCRSt and Chapter VII of the UN Charter. It is of course rather self-evident that in such a case the UN Security Council would probably refer the situation to the ICC and that even if its permanent members disagreed, no veto would be invoked by any permanent member state of the Security Council.

Furthermore, it is worth considering a case where an individual suspected of commissioning a crime pursuant to Article 5 ICCRSt is detained by a third State which, however, happens to be party to the ICCRSt. Even though the crime was not committed on the third State's territory or against its citizens—as mooted among others by the Korean representation—,[40] such a case still might not have caused any essential problems for the ICC in exercising its jurisdiction until today. But neither does it allow even for the indirect application of passive personality, since the State whose nationals were victims of the crime might have shown a particular zeal for the arrest of the perpetrator(s), considering that the ICC has no police force of its own and is dependent upon the assistance offered to it by its state parties.[41]

Finally, regarding the crime of aggression, the following three potential outcomes must be highlighted concerning the ICC exercising its jurisdiction after the entry into

[40] United Nations Diplomatic Conference of Plenipotentiaries on the Establishment of an International Criminal Court, 9th Plenary Meeting, UN Doc. A/CONF.183/SR.9, 42, fn 24.

[41] Of course, it cannot be omitted in this chapter that the exercise of the ICC's jurisdiction could thus dangerously escalate tensions in the international relations of neighbouring or non-states, as well as to having unforeseen consequences on international security and peace to such a degree that its omission in the final version of Article 12 ICCRSt is more of an advantage than a disadvantage. See for example the case of Adolph Eichmann, Term Adolf Eichmann, Encyclopedia BRITRANNICA https://www.britannica.com/biography/Adolf-Eichmann last accessed 8 June 2023.

force of Articles 15 bis[42] and 15 ter[43] ICCRSt (a year after the ratification of an approving decision taken after 1 January 2017 by a two-thirds majority of the members of the Assembly of States Parties): (1) the perpetrator is a national of a state party that has ratified the ICCRSt, as well as the new provisions regarding the crime of aggression (2) the perpetrator is a national of a state party that has ratified the ICCRSt, but not the new provisions regarding the crime of aggression (3) the perpetrator is a national of a state party that has not ratified the ICCRSt.

And while the answer is of course obvious with regard to the first case, the second and third demand further analysis. According to Articles 15 bis(4) and (5) ICCRSt, the exercise of the ICC's jurisdiction is limited by the establishment of further preconditions. For the ICC to act upon a crime of aggression—in addition to the general preconditions of Article 12 ICCRSt—the precondition must also be fulfilled

[42] Article 15 bis - Exercise of jurisdiction over the crime of aggression (State referral, proprio motu): 1. The Court may exercise jurisdiction over the crime of aggression in accordance with article 13, paragraphs (a) and (c), subject to the provisions of this article. 2. The Court may exercise jurisdiction only with respect to crimes of aggression committed one year after the ratification or acceptance of the amendments by thirty States Parties. 3. The Court shall exercise jurisdiction over the crime of aggression in accordance with this article, subject to a decision to be taken after 1 January 2017 by the same majority of States Parties as is required for the adoption of an amendment to the Statute. 4. The Court may, in accordance with article 12, exercise jurisdiction over a crime of aggression, arising from an act of aggression committed by a State Party, unless that State Party has previously declared that it does not accept such jurisdiction by lodging a declaration with the Registrar. The withdrawal of such a declaration may be affected at any time and shall be considered by the State Party within three years. 5. In respect of a State that is not a party to this Statute, the Court shall not exercise its jurisdiction over the crime of aggression when committed by that State's nationals or on its territory. 6. Where the Prosecutor concludes that there is a reasonable basis to proceed with an investigation in respect of a crime of aggression, he or she shall first ascertain whether the Security Council has made a determination of an act of aggression committed by the State concerned. The Prosecutor shall notify the Secretary-General of the United Nations of the situation before the Court, including any relevant information and documents. 7. Where the Security Council has made such a determination, the Prosecutor may proceed with the investigation in respect of a crime of aggression. 8. Where no such determination is made within six months after the date of notification, the Prosecutor may proceed with the investigation in respect of a crime of aggression, provided that the Pre-Trial Division has authorized the commencement of the investigation in respect of a crime of aggression in accordance with the procedure contained in article 15, and the Security Council has not decided otherwise in accordance with article 16. 9. A determination of an act of aggression by an organ outside the Court shall be without prejudice to the Court's own findings under this Statute. 10. This article is without prejudice to the provisions relating to the exercise of jurisdiction with respect to other crimes referred to in article 5.

[43] Article 15 ter - Exercise of jurisdiction over the crime of aggression (Security Council referral): 1. The Court may exercise jurisdiction over the crime of aggression in accordance with article 13, paragraph (b), subject to the provisions of this article. 2. The Court may exercise jurisdiction only with respect to crimes of aggression committed one year after the ratification or acceptance of the amendments by thirty States Parties. 3. The Court shall exercise jurisdiction over the crime of aggression in accordance with this article, subject to a decision to be taken after 1 January 2017 by the same majority of States Parties as is required for the adoption of an amendment to the Statute. 4. A determination of an act of aggression by an organ outside the Court shall be without prejudice to the Court's own findings under this Statute. 5. This article is without prejudice to the provisions relating to the exercise of jurisdiction with respect to other crimes referred to in article 5.

that the perpetrator of the crime is necessarily a national of a State that has validated the ICCRSt and has not declared that it does not accept the new provisions on the crime of aggression. The sole exception to the above is a referral for the investigation of the crime of aggression by the UN Security Council pursuant to the provisions of Articles 15 bis(6) to (8) and 13(b) of the ICCRSt.

In any case, in addition to the general preconditions of Article 12 ICCRSt (territorial criterion, criterion of the perpetrator's nationality/principle of active personality), as well as the additional preconditions of Article 15 bis (4) and (5) ICCRSt, it is worth highlighting the general exception of Article 13 (b) ICCRSt. Article 13(b) ICCRSt can be considered a titanium legal spear that penetrates the principle of state sovereignty (and with which the ICC would be equipped). It essentially constitutes the heritage of the ad hoc International Criminal Tribunal for the former Yugoslavia (the ICTY) and the ad hoc International Criminal Tribunal for Rwanda, which from the very beginning were established, functioned and exercised their jurisdiction pursuant to a Resolution by the UN Security Council.[44] Undoubtedly, it is the most effective weapon in the legal arsenal of the ICC, though it can of course only function if the Security Council wills it and, in particular, only if its permanent member states choose to activate it,[45] especially given that pursuant to the provisions of Article 15bis (7) and (9) ICCRSt no other type of determination from any other legal entity, international organization, body or institution (ex. a resolution of political condemnation or moral disdain) is binding for the ICC.

Nonetheless, we observe that in cases with elements of a non-international armed conflict, much like those concerning the regime of Syrian President Bashar al-Assad, it is proven yet again that the opposing geopolitical interests of the Security Council's permanent members, as well as those of the neighbouring States in the area (such as Turkey) may render a resolution by the Security Council (which would ask the ICC's Prosecutor to proceed with an investigation so that the ICC can exercise its jurisdiction) impossible even if a number of crimes that fall within the ICC's jurisdiction are committed over a long period of time and by a number of perpetrators. This fact was heavily criticized early on by the Italian academic, Luigi Condorelli, who poignantly noted that "the final draft offers an inexcusable refuge exactly to those internal armed conflicts which constituted the final push for the negotiations of the Rome Statute".[46]

---

[44] UN Security Council Resolution (1992); UN Security Council Resolution (1994).

[45] Accordingto Article 23 UN Charter, the Security Council consist of 15 members in total, of which five (China, France, Russia, United Kingdom and the United States of America) are permanent. According to Article 27(2) and (3) UN Charter, decisions shall be made by an affirmative vote of nine members, while permanent members have veto rights on all matters which are not procedural in nature. Finally, it is concluded from the combination of Articles 27(3) and 52(3) UN Charter, as well as of Chapter VI on the Pacific Settlement of Disputes, that a member state to the Security Council, if party to a dispute, must abstain from any vote related to said dispute.

[46] Condorelli (1999), pp. 7, 16.

For precisely this reason, if one of the provisions appears to be weaker than the others, then it is none other than the "powerful" provision that establishes the ICC's jurisdiction over a situation pursuant to a Security Council Resolution (Article 13 (b) ICCRSt). That is because, while admittedly in theory this particular provision could render the ICC a kind of permanent and flexible ad hoc international criminal tribunal with indeterminable jurisdiction over time and space (in contrast to the preexisting ad hoc international criminal tribunals for the former Yugoslavia and for Rwanda, the ICTY and the ICTF), the functioning and the consensus among political powers within the Security Council render this "powerful" provision the most unenforced in practice.

2.3 The Acceptance of the ICC's Jurisdiction by State Parties Pursuant to Article 12(1) ICCRSt

It has already been pointed out that the provision of Article 12(2) ICCRSt applies to the ICC's jurisdiction under normal circumstances, from which the ICC can clearly deviate only when the Security Council, under Chapter VII of the UN Charter and pursuant to Article 13(b) ICCRSt, refers to the Prosecutor a situation in which one or more crimes that fall within the ICC's jurisdiction appear to have been committed. For that reason, and for the purpose of determining with maximum precision the extent of the ICC's jurisdiction, Article 12 ICCRSt makes a distinction between the ICC's jurisdiction under normal and exceptional circumstances.

Thus, should a formal written referral according to Article 13(a) ICCRSt, or at least an informal oral referral of a situation[47] according to Article 13(c) ICCRSt be submitted to the ICC's Office of the Prosecutor by a state party[48] then acceptance of the ICC's jurisdiction is required of at least one state party (that is, State in the

[47] The term 'situation' is usually used to refer to an area or a State where it appears that a number of crimes have been committed by an unknown number of perpetrators, i.e. to a number of different events dispersed through time and geographical area that require further investigation. According to the definition of Article 14(1) ICCRSt, Referral of a situation by a State Party: 1. A State Party may refer to the Prosecutor a situation in which one or more crimes within the jurisdiction of the Court appear to have been committed requesting the Prosecutor to investigate the situation for the purpose of determining whether one or more specific persons should be charged with the commission of such crimes.

[48] Article 13 ICCRSt - Exercise of jurisdiction: The Court may exercise its jurisdiction with respect to a crime referred to in article 5 in accordance with the provisions of this Statute if: (a) A situation in which one or more of such crimes appears to have been committed is referred to the Prosecutor by a State Party in accordance with article 14; [...] (c) The Prosecutor has initiated an investigation in respect of such a crime in accordance with article 15.

It goes without saying that the ICC's Prosecutor can begin an investigation *ex proprio motu*, without a referral of any kind by a state party, if an event receives a lot of publicity or if he is otherwise informed of the commission of criminal actions that fall within the ICC's jurisdiction, as for example can happen after receiving a letter from a citizen.

territory of which this particular criminal activity was committed or State of which the accused is a national) for the ICC to be able to exercise its jurisdiction.

Consequently, since one of the States "involved" is already party to the ICCRSt, the ICC has *ipso jure* jurisdiction as long as: (a) the crime is not a war crime and the state party has not lodged a declaration that it does not accept the ICC's jurisdiction with respect to war crimes pursuant to Article 124 ICCRSt; (b) the crime does not fulfill the elements of the crime of aggression or the ICC does not have jurisdiction on that ground;[49] (c) the State has not lodged a declaration with the Registrar that it does not accept the ICC's jurisdiction over the crime of aggression according to the new Article 15 bis(4) ICCRSt;[50] (d) on a practical level, the States "involved" have not managed to activate the proceedings of Article 16 ICCRSt, which provides the Security Council with the authority to request the deferral of an investigation or prosecution for a period of 12 months, subject to indefinite renewal.[51]

Hans Peter Kaul points out regarding the adoption of Article 12 ICCRSt after intense negotiations that "Article 12(2) stipulates the quite conservative jurisdictional precondition that the territorial State or the State of nationality of the accused or both must be States Parties. This is a regression from the universal jurisdiction approach which is generally recognised in customary international law. At the same time, it has long been clear that the principles of territoriality and nationality are internationally undisputed as legitimate bases for criminal jurisdiction".[52]

On the other hand, Schabas points out that the final wording of the provisions of Article 12 ICCRSt gives an important motive to state parties for the ratification of the ICCRSt, since only in this way could they protect their own territory and ensure that the Court will have jurisdiction over the crimes committed there.[53] Given the vast number of States that have ratified the ICCRSt to this day, it is obvious that the ICCRSt has been ratified by a lot of States which were initially believed would not do so, because they suffered from internal conflicts or were often the victims to war crimes and crimes against humanity.[54] The ICC's official website shows that States such as Burundi, Burkina Faso, Colombia, Cambodia, Afghanistan, the Democratic

[49] A thorough analysis of the crime of aggression and the new articles of the Rome Statute can be found in 6th chapter of this book, p 156.

[50] Article 15 bis (4) ICCRSt: The Court may, in accordance with article 12, exercise jurisdiction over a crime of aggression, arising from an act of aggression committed by a State Party, unless that State Party has previously declared that it does not accept such jurisdiction by lodging a declaration with the Registrar. The withdrawal of such a declaration may be affected at any time and shall be considered by the State Party within three years.

[51] Article 16 ICCRSt - Deferral of investigation or prosecution: No investigation or prosecution may be commenced or proceeded with under this Statute for a period of 12 months after the Security Council, in a resolution adopted under Chapter VII of the Charter of the United Nations, has requested the Court to that effect; that request may be renewed by the Council under the same conditions.

[52] Kaul (2002), p. 607.

[53] Schabas (2010a), p. 283.

[54] Glasius (2006), p. 61; Williams (1999), p. 341.

Republic of the Congo, Senegal, Sierra Leone and Djibouti all feature in the large list of States that have accepted the ICC's jurisdiction by ratifying its Statute.[55]

2.4 Contested Issues of the ICC's Territorial Jurisdiction: Excluded, Occupied and Disputed Territories

As Schabas points out, Article 12 ICCRSt may use the term jurisdiction with direct reference to Article 5 ICCRSt ("with respect to the crimes referred to in article 5"), i.e. to the ICC's jurisdiction *ratione materiae*; nonetheless, the content of the article essentially refers to jurisdiction *ratione loci* and *ratione personae*.[56]

2.4.1 The Case of Excluded Territories

With regard to the excluded territories of a state party, it is worth mentioning that until today, two States, Denmark and New Zealand, have made official declarations that exclude the territorial scope of the ICCRSt from certain parts of their country. Specifically, Denmark declared that it does not accept the ICC's jurisdiction over the Faroe Islands and Greenland, while New Zealand explicitly declared the exclusion of the island of Tokelau. Fortunately, Denmark withdrew its problematic declaration in 2006. However, to the degree that the above constitute declarations that limit the obligations of a state party, they are evidently invalid and must not be taken into consideration pursuant to Article 120 ICCRSt.[57]

In spite of the above, i.e. the fact that only Denmark and New Zealand had explicitly advocated the exclusion of territories from the ICC's jurisdiction, on 11 March 2010, the United Kingdom informed the UN Secretary General that it wished for its ratification of the ICCRSt to be extended to the following territories, in which the United Kingdom is responsible for international relations: Anguilla, Bermuda, British Virgin Islands, Cayman Islands, Falkland Islands, Montserrat, Pitcairn, Henderson, Ducie and Oeno Islands, St Helena, Ascension and Tristan da Cunha, Sovereign Base Areas of Akrotiri and Dhekelia, Turks and Caicos Islands. However, there was no mention of the island of Diego Garcia, on which a US Naval Support Facility has been set up and which is widely known today after the mysterious disappearance in 2014 of a Malaysian Airlines aircraft carrying hundreds

[55] List of the States Parties to the Rome Statute https://asp.icc-cpi.int/en_menus/asp/states%20parties/Pages/the%20states%20parties%20to%20the%20rome%20statute.aspx last accessed 8 June 2023.

[56] Schabas (2010a), pp. 40, 283.

[57] Article 120 ICCRSt—Reservations: No reservations may be made to this Statute.

of passengers.[58] However, as already shown, the omission of the island should not be considered as substantive, either from *de lege lata* or *de lege ferenda* view point and therefore, the ICC can also exercise its jurisdiction concerning crimes committed on Diego Garcia.

2.4.2 *The Case of Occupied Territories*

Michail Vagias thoroughly examines this difficult topic in his PhD thesis and subsequent book,[59] distinguishing three main types of cases: (1) both the State with the occupying force and the State with the occupied territory are parties to the ICCRSt; (2) the State with the occupied territory is party to the ICCRSt, but the State with the occupying force is not (3) the State with the occupying force is party to the ICCRSt, but the State with the occupied territory is not.

Regarding occupied territories, no limitations or special conditions are provided for in the ICCRSt that would limit the exercise of the ICC's jurisdiction exclusively in the territories of state parties over which these exercise effective control.[60] Therefore, the ICC's jurisdiction extends to the recognised territory of a state party as a whole, even if parts of it are occupied by another State and the state party does not exercise effective control upon this other State. Consequently, the ICCRSt's ratification by Cyprus, for example, renders the ICC competent *ratione loci* in Northern Cyprus, which has been illegally occupied by Turkey since 1974. Therefore, were crimes against humanity to be committed by Islamist terrorists against American tourists in Northern Cyprus, the ICC could exercise its jurisdiction, even though the USA has not ratified the ICCRSt (that is, despite the lack of *ratione personae* jurisdiction), pursuant to the fact that Cyprus is a state party to the ICCRSt and the ICC has territorial jurisdiction despite the lack of effective control over the territory of Northern Cyprus by the Republic of Cyprus ever since 1974.[61]

What is more, the same could apply for the territory of the Golan Heights, which belong to Syria but have been occupied to this day by Israel, ever since the Six Day War of 1967.[62] Finally, *mutatis mutandis* the same could apply to the Guantanamo Bay detention camp in Cuba, which is located in a territory that Cuba was forced to lease to the USA in 1901 in accordance with the Platt Amendment, which imposed eight conditions that had to be met by Cuba before US military forces would leave

[58] Milanovics (2010); Schabas (2010b).

[59] Vagias (2011), pp. 198–209.

[60] For an analysis of the concept of effective control see Power (2009) http://www.intellectum.org/articles/issues/intellectum6/en/ITL06p033045_Re-engaging%20the%20Gaza%20Debate%20-%20the%20Impact%20of%20Operation%20Cast%20Lead_Susan%20Rose%20Power.pdf last accessed 8 June 2023.

[61] Schabas (2010a), p. 285.

[62] Encyclopedia BRITRANNICA, "Term Six-Day War" https://www.britannica.com/event/Six-Day-War last accessed 8 June 2023.

the island at the end of the Spanish-American War.[63] At this point, however, it must be noted that the ICC's jurisdiction on the aforementioned territories will clearly remain theoretical as long as Cuba and Syria do not ratify the ICCRSt and thus, are not state parties.

Before we move on to the analysis of the matter at hand, it is worth mentioning that the ICCRSt does not include an explicit provision on "occupation" or even mention the term itself for that matter; only footnote 34 on page 13 of the official text of Elements of Crime states that the term "international armed conflict" includes military occupation, and finally: "this footnote also applies to the corresponding element in each crime under Article 8(2)(a) ICCRSt".[64]

It is worth mentioning that the interpretation of the present footnote with regard to the ICC's jurisdiction has not been sufficiently scrutinised in the international literature. This is the main reason why important works, as for example those by Knut Dormann,[65] William Schabas[66] and Cherif Bassiouni,[67] only briefly refer to it, without further commentary.[68]

Nonetheless, in terms of jurisprudence, the ICC's Pre-Trial Chamber I has scrutinised this matter in its decision on the confirmation of charges against Thomas Lubanga Dyilo.[69] In this decision, Pre-Trial Chamber I referred to the lack of an explicit definition of the term "international armed conflict" in the ICCRSt and EoC, as well to footnote 34 of the EoC, thus indirectly but clearly accepting its application not only under Article 8(2)(a) but also under Article 8(2)(b). It then immediately proceeded to mention Article 21 ICCRSt and the possibility of interpreting the ICCRSt through secondary sources of law. In particular, it invoked the text and interpretation of Common Article 2 of the 1949 Genevan Conventions, which also refer to cases of partial or total occupation of a State's territory: "the Convention

[63] The United States, Cuba, and the Platt Amendment, 1901, US Department of State, Office of the Historian https://2001-2009.state.gov/r/pa/ho/time/ip/86557.htm; Rothman (2015) http://time.com/3672066/guantanamo-bay-history/ last accessed 8 June 2023.

[64] Elements of Crimes, footnote 34: The term "international armed conflict" includes military occupation. This footnote also applies to the corresponding element in each crime under article 8 (2) (a).

[65] Dormann et al. (2010), p. 203.

[66] Schabas (2010a), p. 203.

[67] Cherif Bassiouni (2013), p. 169.

[68] Despite Vagias' view, footnote 34 of the Elements of Crimes applies not only to the case of art. 8(2)(a) ICCRSt, as explicitly mentioned, but also to the case of art. 8(2)(b) ICCRSt which refers to "other serious violations of the laws and customs applicable in international armed conflicts". Vagias (2011), p. 198. This view is in agreement with the ICC's jurisprudence as analysed below.

[69] ICC (2007), p. 72.

shall also apply to all cases of partial or total occupation of the territory of a High Contracting Party".[70,71]

Consequently, the ICC's Pre-Trial Chamber I endorsed the decision of the ICTY's Appeal Chamber on the famous Tadić case,[72] which is well-known as the first case on which a first instance judgment was published by the ICTY. In particular, the ICC's Pre-Trial Chamber I fully adopted the ICTY's Appeal Chamber's view with regard to the interpretation of the term 'international armed conflict' and the application of an "overall control" test over a territory.[73]

In particular, the ICC's Pre-Trial Chamber I stated that it "considers an armed conflict to be international in character if it takes place between two or more States; this extends to the partial or total occupation of the territory of another State, whether or not the said occupation meets with armed resistance. In addition, an internal armed conflict that breaks out on the territory of a State may become international—or, depending upon the circumstances, be international in character alongside an internal armed conflict—if (i) another State intervenes in that conflict through its troops (direct intervention), or if (ii) some of the participants in the internal armed conflict act on behalf of that other State (indirect intervention)".[74]

As Vagias notes, the ICC's Pre-Trial Chamber I chose an easy path for the legal foundation of this argument, as the acceptance of the "fact" that the conflict was international because Ituri's occupation automatically overrode any need to prove that groups such as the "Patriotic Forces for the Liberation of Congo" (FPLC) and the "Union of Congolese Patriots" (UPC), acted on behalf of Uganda's government in the area.[75] This was critical because, according to Professor Olympia Bekou, "[i]f the Chamber had adopted the [overall control] test, it would have to prove that the 'Union of Congolese Patriots' acted in effect as Uganda's agent, and thus, to regard a paramilitary group such as the 'Union of Congolese Patriots', as a perpetrator in an 'international armed conflict'. That would indeed be a very interesting interpretation,

[70] Article 2. In addition to the provisions which shall be implemented in peacetime, the present Convention shall apply to all cases of declared war or of any other armed conflict which may arise between two or more of the High Contracting Parties, even if the state of war is not recognized by one of them. The Convention shall also apply to all cases of partial or total occupation of the territory of a High Contracting Party, even if the said occupation meets with no armed resistance. Although one of the Powers in conflict may not be a party to the present Convention, the Powers who are parties thereto shall remain bound by it in their mutual relations. They shall furthermore be bound by the Convention in relation to the said Power, if the latter accepts and applies the provisions thereof.

[71] The Prosecutor v. Thomas Lubanga Dyilo, paras. 72–73.

[72] ICTY (1999).

[73] *The Prosecutor v. Thomas Lubanga Dyilo*, paras. 73–74.

[74] Ibid, para 73. Essentially, this part constitutes a replication of the ICTY Appeal Chamber's decision on Tadić. See *The Prosecutor v. Duško Tadić*, para 34.

[75] Vagias (2011), p. 199.

given that international humanitarian law does not regard (to this day) non-state actors as subjects of the law that governs that type of conflict".[76]

The ICC's judgment regarding the confirmation of charges against Lubanga[77] and the aforementioned analysis indirectly but clearly show that no obstacles exist to the ICC exercising its jurisdiction when: (1) the State with the occupying force as well as the State with the occupied territory are parties to the ICCRSt (2) the State with the occupied territory is a party to the ICCRSt, but the State with the occupying force is not. This is therefore the most appropriate moment to discuss the most problematic of all three possible scenarios, that is when the State with the occupying force is a state party to the ICCRSt, but the State with the occupied territory is not.

It is worth mentioning that this third case is of great academic and practical interest. This is because in the case of the occupation, for example, of Iraq's territory by the USA and its allies, it is not hard to imagine the possibility of, for example, the Polish special forces or the Iraqi ones committing war crimes.[78] Were this to occur, whereas the nationality of the Polish commandos, if discovered, could directly lead to a judicial investigation that may eventually fall under the ICC's jurisdiction pursuant to Article 12(2)(b) ICCRSt,[79] this is not the case for the Iraqi special forces. That is because—as already mentioned—the ICCRSt does not exercise its jurisdiction in accordance with the passive personality principle (jurisdiction based on the victim's nationality), but solely in accordance with the active personality principle (jurisdiction based on the perpetrator's nationality).

What then of the Iraqi perpetrators in this hypothetical situation who commit crimes under Article 5 ICCRSt on Iraqi territory against the occupying forces (which consist of both state parties and state non-parties vis-à-vis the ICCRSt)? Certainly they do not fall under the ICC's jurisdiction for crimes committed against US forces (as the USA has not ratified the ICCRSt) and probably not for crimes committed against the Polish, English or Dutch forces either. The reason for this lies in the first place is their nationality (Article 12(2)(b) ICCRSt) and the fact that the territory (Article 12(2)(a) ICCRSt) cannot be subject to the ICC's jurisdiction. Therefore, in this case, the final judgment on whether the ICC's jurisdiction can be extended ad hoc over an occupied territory when the occupying State is party to the ICCRSt, but the State to which the occupied territory belongs is not, acquires great importance.

I believe that, unfortunately, an ad hoc extension of the ICC's jurisdiction is not possible in this case. A different legal interpretation would not only cause legal uncertainty but, under extreme circumstances, perhaps impel the state parties to the ICCRSt to invade the territory of third States so that the ICC would thus establish ad hoc jurisdiction over crimes committed in territories essentially outside the Court's

[76] Bekou (2008), pp. 347–348; Ambos K, "The first confirmation decision of the International Criminal Court: *Prosecutor v. Thomas Lubanga Dyilo*" https://papers.ssrn.com/sol3/papers.cfm?abstract_id=1972149 last accessed 8 June 2023.

[77] Tsilonis (2010) [in Greek].

[78] See a thorough analysis of their actions in Kyle et al. (2014).

[79] Article 12(2)(b) ICCRSt: ... (b) The State of which the person accused of the crime is a national.

jurisdiction. For instance, following the multiple terror attacks in the centre of Paris on the 13 November 2015, France could have invaded and occupied Palmyra in Syria for the ICC to establish jurisdiction without the interference of the Security Council over the destruction of historical monuments which are considered world heritage,[80] as well as over other crimes committed against civilians there by the Islamic State of Iraq and Syria (ISIS).[81] After all, as already mentioned, the legal possibility of extending the ICC's jurisdiction because a state party is an occupying force in foreign territory is not mentioned or even alluded to anywhere in the ICC's jurisprudence to this day. Finally, this perspective does not seem to be found in international customary law either.[82]

2.4.3 *The ICC's Jurisdiction Over Disputed Territories or Quasi-States: the Case of Palestine*

On 27 December 2008, Israel launched a large-scale military attack on the Gaza Strip under the code name Operation 'Cast Lead', in which its air force, navy and land forces participated. After a week of air bombings, land forces invaded the Gaza Strip on 3 January 2009 and remained there until 18 January 2009.[83] The supposed purpose of the operation was for Israel to stop the rocket attacks against its southern territories as the Gaza Strip, which was to a large degree controlled by Hamas, often provided the launch site for attacks against Israeli residential territories.[84]

The magnitude of the destruction committed in Palestine motivated the organisation of Physicians for Human Rights to appear before the Supreme Court of Israel in order to request the recognition of Israel's humanitarian obligations towards the citizens of the Gaza Strip. In other words, the aforementioned non-governmental organisation believed that the Gaza Strip was under occupation and thus, that Israel was obligated to respect the rules of 'humanitarian' law which regulate the legal

[80] Official UNESCO World Heritage List http://whc.unesco.org/en/list/?delisted=1 last accessed 31 March 2023).

[81] In the international literature, it is referred to either as ISIS or ISIL. The last letter signifies Syria in the first case and Levant in the second. To simply and unify the aforementioned acronyms the abbreviation IS (Islamic State) is also used.

[82] Nonetheless, Vagias boldly puts forward an opposing view in his published PhD thesis, invoking predominantly reasons of political convenience and human rights protection which unfortunately have no legal foundations in the ICCRSt and thus do not convince the author. See Vagias (2011), pp 16, 206–210.

[83] BBC News (2009a); The New York Times, Erlanger (2009).

[84] BBC News (2009b).

status of occupied territories (*Physicians for Human Rights Case et al v Prime Minister et. al.*, 2009).[85,86]

Apart from the appeal of non-profit legal persons before the courts of Israel, international protests worldwide had further consequences. The United Nations Human Rights Council decided to establish an independent international fact-finding mission[87]—the members of which were appointed by the Council's President—to investigate all violations of international human rights law and international humanitarian law "by the occupying Power, Israel, against the Palestinian people throughout the Occupied Palestinian Territory, particularly in the occupied Gaza Strip".[88]

Eventually, the mission completed its work in mid-September 2009 and presented the findings of its investigation by publishing a detailed report of 575 pages.[89] The Goldstone Report concluded that Operation 'Cast Lead' "was directed, at least in part, at a different target: the people of Gaza as a whole. In this respect, the operations were in furtherance of an overall policy aimed at punishing the Gaza population for its resilience and for its apparent support for Hamas, and possibly with the intent of forcing a change in such support".[90]

With regard to international criminal law, the most important matter raised by the Goldstone Report was the possibility of the situation being judicially investigated by the ICC following a referral by the Security Council pursuant to Article 13

[85] Operation 'Cast Lead' was the first ground invasion of "long duration" in the Gaza Strip after the 'Disengagement Plan' which was implemented in September 2005 and according to which Israel vacated all Israeli settlements in Gaza, withdrew its military forces and unilaterally declared an end of the forty-year occupation of the Gaza Strip. See the online archives of the Israeli Ministry of Foreign Affairs regarding the notorious "Disengagement Plan" https://mfa.gov.il/mfa/foreignpolicy/peace/guide/pages/israeli%20disengagement%20plan%2020-jan-2005.aspx last accessed 8 June 2023.

[86] See also Power (2009) http://www.intellectum.org/articles/issues/intellectum6/en/ITL06p033045_Re-engaging%20the%20Gaza%20Debate%20-%20the%20Impact%20of%20Operation%20Cast%20Lead_Susan%20Rose%20Power.pdf. last accessed 8 June 2023.

[87] The Nigerian Ambassador and President of the Council, Martin Ihoeghian Uhomoibhi, appointed former ICTFY chief prosecutor Richard J. Goldstone, to head the independent fact-finding mission. Christine Chinkin, Professor of International Law at the London School of Economics and Political Science, Hina Jilani, former Special Representative of the Secretary-General on Human Rights Defenders and Desmond Travers, a former colonel in the Irish Defence Forces and member of the Board of Directors of the Institute for International Criminal Investigations were also members of this mission.

[88] UNHR Resolution A/HRC/RES/S-9/1 of 12 January 2009 https://unispal.un.org/DPA/DPR/unispal.nsf/0/404E93E166533F828525754E00559E30 last accessed 8 June 2023.

[89] Human Rights in Palestine and Other Occupied Arab Territories: Report of the United Nations Fact Finding Mission on the Gaza Conflict (15 September 2009) https://www.un.org/ruleoflaw/blog/document/human-rights-in-palestine-and-other-occupied-arab-territories-report-of-the-united-nations-fact-finding-mission-on-the-gaza-conflict/ last accessed 8 June 2023. Among the selected "targets" were the Palestinian Legislative Council and the Gaza main prison as well as six policy facilities, a fact that led, along with other events, to the murder of 240 Palestinian police officers in total. See para 32–33 of the Report.

[90] Ibid 523 para 1680–1681.

(b) ICCRSt.[91] This course of action could be pursued should the mission's recommendations for the serious investigation of the alleged crimes both on behalf of Israel and of the Palestinian militants not be followed.[92] The report articulately explained that there were specific reasons behind this recommendation: (1) The judicial system put in place by Israel to deal with allegations of serious wrongdoing by its armed forces personnel did not comply with the universal principles of independence, effectiveness, promptness and impartiality.[93] (2) Israel's "failure" to open prompt, independent and impartial criminal investigations 6 months after the end of military operations constituted a violation of its obligation to investigate allegations of war crimes and other serious violations of international law.[94] (3) The light sentences for settlers and armed forces personnel who are rarely prosecuted and even more rarely convicted. Even if they were to be convicted, the sentences would be very light, since the criminal charges asserted usually do not reflect the degree of gravity of the action. This practice contrasts completely with cases in which Palestinians are accused of crimes against Israelis; a fact that clearly indicates a discriminatory policy against them.[95] (4) The improper and "unprofessional" way in which criminal investigations are carried out, usually making it impossible to prove the charges beyond all reasonable doubt, as well as the fact that the Israeli justice system presents inherently discriminatory features against Palestinians which render the pursuit of justice on their behalf very difficult.[96]

This recommendation was, as expected, rejected by Israel. Nonetheless, for the first time it raised the question of the ICC's jurisdiction in Palestine, and in particular over the latest grand event in the Palestinian drama which unfolded through Operation 'Cast Lead' in Gaza.

Goldstone's recommendation "appeared" to follow the popular view that the only way for the ICC to establish jurisdiction in the case of a State which is not a party of the ICCRSt, and thus has not approved its jurisdiction, would be through a referral from the Security Council. This triggered a great deal of discussion in world politics. The discussion may have had *ab initio* as a starting point the aforementioned and

[91] Article 13(b) ICCRSt: "A situation in which one or more of such crimes appears to have been committed is referred to the Prosecutor by the Security Council acting under Chapter VII of the Charter of the United Nations."

[92] Report of the United Nations Fact Finding Mission on the Gaza Conflict (15 September 2009) paras. 1611–1632, 1763, 1765, 1766. Israel is unfortunately not renowned for the protection of the human rights of Palestinians. See Ballas (2010), where it is stated that none of the 600 complaints concerning the use of torture and ill treatment of Palestinians by Israel's General Security Service (Shin Bet), submitted in the past years by PCATI and a number of other human rights organisations, have resulted in the initiation of criminal investigations against the alleged torturers.

[93] Report of the United Nations Fact Finding Mission on the Gaza Conflict (15 September 2009) paras. 1611–1612.

[94] Ibid para 1620.

[95] Ibid paras. 1622–1626.

[96] Ibid para 1629.

widely known recommendation, but in effect its undue popularity clouded another significantly more groundbreaking recommendation in the Goldstone Report.

Essentially, the Goldstone report promoted the legality of the 21 January 2009 declaration of the Palestinian National Authority which recognises the ICC's jurisdiction over crimes committed in the territory of Palestine from the 1 July 2002 onwards. In other words, the Goldstone Report recognised as legally binding the declaration of the Palestinian National Authority regarding the ICC's jurisdiction, promoting in essence a spillover—teleological interpretation of Article 12(3) ICCRSt according to which the ICC could lawfully approve the recognition of its jurisdiction by the Palestinian National Authority and subsequently consider for the purposes of Article 12(3) Palestine as a State legally represented by the Palestinian National Authority.[97]

Naturally, these discussions soon involved academic circles, since the Palestinian National Authority's decision to accept the ICC's jurisdiction initiated a new round of legal debate in specialised legal journals and web fora[98] on whether the Palestinian National Authority constitutes a State under Article 12(3) ICCRSt and if so, whether the ICC could exercise its jurisdiction accordingly. The discussion, which indirectly related to the ICC's role in world politics, is of great interest, especially if one considers that because of the given geostrategic and geopolitical interests in the UN Security Council, a decision to refer to the ICC potential crimes in the Gaza Strip could be considered until lately only as the stuff of quite exceptional science fiction.

The declaration of the Palestinian National Authority, signed by its Justice Minister Ali Kashan on 21 January 2009 stated that: "[T]he Government of Palestine hereby recognises the jurisdiction of the Court for the purpose of identifying, prosecuting and judging the authors and accomplices of acts committed on the territory of Palestine since 1 July 2002."[99] According to the aforementioned declaration then, which was formally registered in the ICC's Registry,[100] the Palestinian National Authority consented to the exercise of the ICC's jurisdiction over crimes that were committed in Palestine after 1 July 2002, having of course in mind in the

[97] Report of the United Nations Fact Finding Mission on the Gaza Conflict (15 September 2009) para 1632: "The Prosecutor may determine that for the purposes of Article 12, paragraph 3, under customary international law, Palestine qualifies as 'a state'."; para 1767: "1767. To the Prosecutor of the International Criminal Court: With reference to the declaration under article 12 (3) received by the Office of the Prosecutor of the ICC from the Government of Palestine, the Mission considers that accountability for victims and the interests of peace and justice in the region require that the legal determination should be made by the Prosecutor as expeditiously as possible".

[98] Possibly the most important legal discussion is between Yuval Shany, Yaël Ronen and Alain Pellet in 2010, which can be found in the *Oxford Journal of International Criminal Justice* (issues 1, 2 and 4). It continues with Malcom's Shaw study of 2011 in the same journal (issue 1). See also the discussion in the UCLA forum at http://uclalawforum.com/gaza last accessed 8 June 2023.

[99] Palestinian National Authority (2009).

[100] A brief letter sent by the ICC Registrar to the Palestinian National Authority dated 23 January 2009 stated that the registration of the declaration did not signify acceptance of the ICC's jurisdiction. ICC Registrar (2009).

first place the crimes that were committed during Operation 'Cast Lead' in the first three weeks of 2009.

The declaration of the Palestinian National Authority was founded on Article 12(3) ICCRSt.[101] Many considered its acceptance of the ICC's jurisdiction invalid. Firstly, in the case of Palestine, the territorial and national conditions were undoubtedly not fulfilled, since the case did not relate *ab initio* to the territory or the citizens of a state party to the ICCRSt and there was no referral by the UN Security Council to the ICC's Prosecutor for the investigation of the situation.[102] What is more, the justification that Palestine is not an internationally recognised State was put forth, as well as the fact that its acceptance as such would constitute a politicisation of the ICC's role.

Attempting to analyse at length the objections and arguments of international law academics, Ronen at first and subsequently Shany argued that the lack of a declaration of state independence was an important obstacle in considering Palestine as a State that could fall under the ICC's jurisdiction.[103] Nevertheless, Shany's criticism primarily focused on a matter he considered an insurmountable obstacle to recognising Palestine as a State under international criminal law, i.e. the Israeli-Palestinian Interim Agreement on the West Bank and the Gaza Strip known as Oslo II which was signed in 1995 by the Palestinian Liberation Organisation (PLO) and the State of Israel.[104] Pursuant to Article 1 of Annex IV Protocol Concerning Legal Affairs, the criminal jurisdiction of the Palestinian National Authority, which was created pursuant to Oslo II, was limited to "offenses committed by Palestinians and/or non-Israelis in the Territory". The term "Territory", according to Article 1(1) (a), refers to the West Bank and the Gaza Strip, including Eastern Jerusalem, but

---

[101] Article 12(3) ICCRSt - Preconditions to the exercise of jurisdiction: . . . 3. If the acceptance of a State which is not a Party to this Statute is required under paragraph 2, that State may, by declaration lodged with the Registrar, accept the exercise of jurisdiction by the Court with respect to the crime in question. The accepting State shall cooperate with the Court without any delay or exception in accordance with Part 9.

[102] The possibility of Palestinian victims with a double nationality was thoroughly excluded from the discussion as a dangerous parameter which could further complicate the case legally. Nonetheless, as of February 2006, the ICC's Prosecutor has indirectly yet clearly expressed his objection to conducting an investigation into alleged crimes in Iraq and Venezuela among others with reference to the criterion of the victims' double nationality. See OTP Response to Communications Received Concerning Iraq, https://www.icc-cpi.int/NR/rdonlyres/04D143C8-19FB-466C-AB77-4CDB2FDEBEF7/143682/OTP_letter_to_senders_re_Iraq_9_February_2006.pdf last accessed 8 June 2023; OTP Response to Communications Received Concerning Venezuela, https://www.icc-cpi.int/NR/rdonlyres/4E2BC725-6A63-40B8-8CDC-ADBA7BCAA91F/143684/OTP_letter_to_senders_re_Venezuela_9_February_2006.pdf last accessed 8 June 2023.

[103] Ronen (2010), pp. 3, 26; Shany (2010), pp. 329, 337. However, with his 2014 article, Ronen appears to accept that Palestine is an independent State: Ronen (2014), p. 7.

[104] Israeli-Palestinian Interim Agreement ("Oslo II") https://www.jewishvirtuallibrary.org/jsource/Peace/interimtoc.html last accessed 8 June 2023.

excluding Jewish settlements and military locations.[105] The sole exception to the aforementioned general rule of criminal jurisdiction appeared in Article 1(1)(b) which stipulated that the newly established Palestinian National Authority ("the Council") would have criminal jurisdiction over Palestinians and their visitors who have committed offences against Palestinians or their visitors in areas outside the Territory, provided that these offences are not related to Israel's national security. Therefore, according to Oslo II, the criminal jurisdiction of the Palestinian National Authority was significantly limited *ratione personae* and *ratione loci* and—according to Shany—any attempt to circumvent this agreement on behalf of Palestine should have been considered an *ultra vires* act, i.e. an invalid act that evidently exceeds the agreed legal powers of the PNA.[106]

On the other hand, Kai Ambos,[107] Valentina Azarov and Chantal Meloni[108] point out that the so-called Oslo II agreement is not binding for the PNA, not only because it was signed by the PLO and Israel,[109] but mostly because the limits of the ICC's jurisdiction cannot be lawfully determined nor restricted by bilateral state agreements. Besides, in that particular case, pursuant to the bilateral Oslo II agreement it was agreed that the newly established NPA would exercise its jurisdiction over Israeli citizens, without however prohibiting the concession of its jurisdiction to the ICC or another international criminal tribunal.[110]

Furthermore, Alain Pellet argued in an important opinion entitled "The Effects of Palestine's Recognition of the International Criminal Court's Jurisdiction",[111] which was co-signed by a great number of renowned international law specialists,[112] and later in a study in the Journal of International Criminal Justice that the solution to the aforementioned legal question must arise from a teleological and functional interpretation of Article 12 ICCRSt.[113]

---

[105] The Israeli-Palestinian Interim Agreement on the West Bank and the Gaza Strip, Annex IV: Protocol Concerning Legal Affairs https://www.jewishvirtuallibrary.org/jsource/Peace/iaannex4.html last accessed 8 June 2023.

[106] Shany (2010), pp. 329, 341.

[107] Ambos (2014).

[108] Azarov and Meloni (2014). It must be noted, however, that their article criticises Kai Ambos's views in general.

[109] Ronen (2010), pp. 3, 23.

[110] Ambos (2014).

[111] Pellet (2010b)

[112] Co-signed by: Georges Abi-Saab, M. Cherif Bassiouni, Rafaâ Ben Achour, Phon Van den Biesen, Michael Bohlander, Laurence Boisson de Chazournes, Jorge Cardona Llorens, Monique Chemillier-Gendreau, Luigi Condorelli, Benedetto Conforti, Vojin Dimitrijevic, John Dugard, Paula Escarameia, Marina Eudes, Ahmed S. El Kosheri, Salifou Fomba, Mathias Forteau, Francesco Francioni, Zdzislaw W. Galicki, Habib Ghérari, Vera Gowlland-Debbas, Emmanuel Jos, Franck Latty, Ahmed Mahiou, Djamchid Momtaz, Daniel Müller, Jordan Paust, Paolo Picone, Antonio Remiro Brotons, François Rigaux, Hélène Ruiz-Fabri, Jean Salmon, William A. Schabas, Nico Schrijver, Linos-Alexander Sicilianos, Habib Slim, Jean-Marc Sorel, Sandra Szurek, Paul Tavernier, Bérangère Taxil.

[113] Pellet (2010a), p. 981.

In working through the relevant principles of international law, Pellet does not take a stand for or against the existence of a sovereign Palestinian State, although he pointedly states in a footnote that the statehood of the Palestinian National Authority is doubtful in the degree that it can be argued that it does not consider itself a State; nonetheless, it can be argued that the fact that it acts as a State on certain occasions (for example when it made the declaration analysed here) could reinforce the notion of its statehood.[114]

However, the fact that Palestine has today been recognised as a sovereign State by 139 States, i.e. by 71% of UN member states,[115] as well as the fact that it successfully pursued the Palestine 194 campaign for international recognition of the State of Palestine[116] (always under the shadow of the USA veto),[117] thus gaining acceptance as a State from the UN, negates the arguments that the first Oslo Agreement of 1993 renounced whatever statehood it had acquired from 1988 onwards, i.e. when Yasser Arafat proclaimed in Algeria the Palestinian Declaration of Independence. Finally, even if Palestine is not recognised as a State by the UN Security Council, either because it cannot gather enough votes of support or because the USA as a permanent member of the Security Council exercises its veto, Palestine's statehood has been formally recognised by the UN General Assembly.[118] In other words, the UN General Assembly—pursuant among others to Resolution 3210 (XXIX) of 14 October 1974, Resolution 3237 (XXIX) of 22 November 1974, as well as to the pre-existing Resolution 377A (V) of 3 November 1950,[119] which recognises that when the Security Council fails to reach a decision, the UN General Assembly may act if the situation is urgent—recognised in December 2012 with Resolution 67/19[120] the State of Palestine, upgrading its status to "non-member observer state", exactly as it had done in the past with the Vatican.

However, even if Palestine had not obtained "non-member observer state" status through UNGA Resolution 67/19, the view that it has not pursued its status as a State on an international level would not be valid, since it has already been recognised as a

[114]Ibid 983, fn 4.

[115]Official website of the Permanent Observer Mission of the State of Palestine to the UN https://www.ungeneva.org/en/blue-book/missions/non-member-states/state-palestine last accessed 8 June 2023.

[116]The sovereign State of Palestine has also been recognised by the Sahrawi Arab Democratic Republic and the Holy See, neither of which is a member state to the UN. Thus, the aforementioned percentage refers to the 137 UN states which have recognised the sovereign state of Palestine. UNGA (2012); I24news (2015).

[117]The purpose of the campaign was to recognise Palestine as the 194th UN member state https://www.un.org/press/en/2012/ga11317.doc.htm last accessed 8 June 2023.

[118]The New York Times, Ibrahim (1988).

[119]Zimmermann (2013), p. 303.

[120]UNGA (1950); Tomuschat (2008).

State by a large majority of UN member states (as already mentioned), thus, the ICC could theoretically still lawfully exercise its jurisdiction.[121]

Undoubtedly, an investigation of the situation and a case tried by the ICC would be groundbreaking, since it could offer a guide for other similar situations in the future that might be brought before the ICC concerning *inter alia* the alleged illegal occupation of other territories. It is of course widely accepted that the Court cannot play a state role and recognise quasi-states or States under formation as sovereign. The ICC must only adjudicate on whether the preconditions for exercising its jurisdiction exist, according to the interpretation of the term "State" in Article 12 ICCRSt and always in accordance with the purpose and the spirit of the Rome Statute in general.

This case appears to be similar to the Advisory Opinion of 22 July 2010 given to the UN General Assembly by the ICJ regarding Resolution 63/3 of 8 October 2008. Here, the UN General Assembly was cautious enough not to ask the ICJ's opinion on Kosovo's status as a State in international law, but on "whether or not the declaration of independence is in accordance with international law". As the Court noted, in that case the question was "narrow and specific; [...]. It does not ask about the legal consequences of that declaration".[122]

Therefore, in the light of the above-mentioned analysis of the Kosovo case, the question that must now be asked is simply whether Palestine is a State in accordance with the meaning of Article 12(3) ICCRSt, and therefore whether Palestine could indeed make the particular declaration provided for in this provision; and if so, whether the ICC would have to accept the declaration or not.[123]

It is noteworthy that Pierre-Marie Dupuy underlines in his *Collected Courses of the Hague Academy of International Law* the fact that the number of subjects in international law may increase from time to time in line with developments in the international legal order, without this constituting a breach of the generally accepted principle of national sovereignty. Amongst many other examples, he refers to States such as Monaco (and Andorra prior to its 1993 Constitution), whose dependence on their neighbouring States raises serious questions about whether or not there is genuine national sovereignty.[124] In the case of the ICC, such a legal precedent seems to already exist: that of the Cook Islands, which were accepted as a State by the ICC despite being a self-governing legal entity associated with New Zealand. Although the State of the Cook Islands is fully responsible for its internal affairs, New Zealand has retained its competence in external relations following the relevant consultations with the Government of the Cook Islands. The above limitation on the

---

[121] UNGA A/RES/67/19 "Status of Palestine in the United Nations" 4 December 2012 https://digitallibrary.un.org/record/739031 last accessed 8 June 2023.

[122] ICJ (2010), para 51.

[123] This approach is quite common in international law. That is why the texts of many international conventions include phrases such as "for the purposes of this convention". It was also followed by the ICC in order to determine whether the UN has a legal standing in international law. ICJ (1949), pp. 174–220.

[124] Dupuy (2002), pp. 108–112.

exercise of foreign policy was not seen as an impediment to the acceptance of the Cook Islands as a State by the ICC and their accession to its jurisdiction.[125]

In addition, three important international conventions follow the same direction: (1) Art. 44(2) of the Convention on the Rights of Persons with Disabilities, which stipulates that "[r]eferences to 'States Parties' in the present Convention shall apply to such organisations within the limits of their competence";[126] (2) the Agreement establishing the World Trade Organisation;[127] (3) Article XXII of the Convention on International Liability for Damage Caused by Space Objects, where it is provided that "references to States shall be deemed to apply to any international intergovernmental organisation which conducts space activities [...]"[128]

In addition, we must highlight this remark by Advocate General Sir Francis Geoffray Jacobs in the Stardust Marine case at the European Court of Justice (ECJ): "the concept of the State has to be understood in the sense most appropriate to the provisions in question and to their objectives; the Court rightly follows a functional approach, basing its interpretation on the scheme and objective of the provisions within which the concept features".[129]

Similarly, the European Court of Human Rights ruled in *Drozd and Janousek v. France and Spain* that it could exercise its jurisdiction if the Principality of Andorra had lodged a declaration to that effect, authorising the application of the Convention of Human Rights on its territory pursuant to Article 5 of the Statute of the Council of Europe despite Andorra's *sui generis* statehood.[130] To that effect, the ECHR gave consideration to the fact that the spirit of the European Convention on Human Rights favours the broadest possible application of the Convention, so as to achieve the optimal protection of human rights.

On the same wavelength, the International Centre for Settlement of Investment Disputes noted in *Maffesini v. Spain* that since "neither the term 'national of another Contracting State' nor the term 'Contracting State' are defined in the Convention [...] the Tribunal has to answer the following two questions: first, whether or not SODIGA is a State entity for the purpose of determining the jurisdiction of the

[125]Mendes E, "Statehood and Palestine for the Purposes of Article 12(3) of the ICC Statute: a Contrary Perspective" UCLA Forum 44 http://uclalawforum.com/media/background/gaza/2010-03-30_Mendes-Memo.pdf last accessed 8 June 2023.

[126]Convention on the Rights of Persons with Disabilities https://www.un.org/development/desa/disabilities/convention-on-the-rights-of-persons-with-disabilities/convention-on-the-rights-of-persons-with-disabilities-2.html last accessed 8 June 2023.

[127]Agreement establishing the World Trade Organisation https://www.wto.org/english/docs_e/legal_e/04-wto.pdf last accessed 8 June 2023.

[128]Convention on International Liability for Damage Caused by Space Objects https://www.faa.gov/about/office_org/headquarters_offices/ast/media/Conv_International_Liab_Damage.pdf last accessed 8 June 2023.

[129]ECJ (2002).

[130]ECHR (1992) paras. 86–89 https://hudoc.echr.coe.int/eng#{%22itemid%22:[%22001-57774%22]} last accessed 8 June 2023.

Centre and the competence of the Tribunal, and second, whether the actions and omissions complained of by the Claimant are imputable to the State."[131]

Moreover, as has been argued by academics such as Mathias Forteau, the term 'State' has now acquired a certain content in accordance with the context of each dispute,[132] while modern international law perceives the State in the form of a volatile geometric shape, the outline of which depends on the matter under review. Thus the term is included in the category of a general 'concept', whose interpretation depends on the purpose of the provision in which it is found.

All of the above demonstrates how the ICC uses the standing principle of Kompetenz-Kompetenz for the interpretation of the provisions of its Statute and the determination of its jurisdiction.[133] This principle is implicitly included, after all, in Articles 18 and 19 ICCRSt, which stipulate that the Prosecutor must inform the state parties concerned of the initiation of an investigation and that the ICC itself determines whether it has jurisdiction over any case brought before it.[134]

At this point, one certainly cannot overlook the general rules of interpretation of international law, as reflected in the Vienna Convention on the Law of Treaties of 23 May 1969. In particular, Article 31(1) of the Vienna Conventions states that: "A treaty shall be interpreted in good faith in accordance with the ordinary meaning to be given to the terms of the treaty in their context and in the light of its object and purpose."

However, as we have seen, in this case, the term "State" has for each international organisation and court a "variable geometry", that is, a constantly changing definition; a fact which undoubtedly proves that the term "State" does not have such a strictly defined meaning from a legal perspective as one would initially think. In its report on the final draft of the Vienna Convention, the International Law Commission included the following principle as a guideline: "[...] when a comparison of the authentic texts discloses a difference of meaning which the application of Articles

[131] International Centre for Settlement of Investment Disputes, *Emilio Agustín Maffezini and The Kingdom of Spain,* (Washington, D.C.), Case No. Arb/97/7, Decision of the Tribunal on Objections to Jurisdiction, 25 January 2000, para 75 http://www.italaw.com/cases/641 last accessed 8 June 2023.

[132] Forteau (2007), pp. 737, 762–763.

[133] ICTY (1995).

[134] Article 18 - Preliminary rulings regarding admissibility

1. When a situation has been referred to the Court pursuant to article 13 (a) and the Prosecutor has determined that there would be a reasonable basis to commence an investigation, or the Prosecutor initiates an investigation pursuant to articles 13 (c) and 15, the Prosecutor shall notify all States Parties and those States which, taking into account the information available, would normally exercise jurisdiction over the crimes concerned. The Prosecutor may notify such States on a confidential basis and, where the Prosecutor believes it necessary to protect persons, prevent destruction of evidence or prevent the absconding of persons, may limit the scope of the information provided to States.

Article 19 - Challenges to the jurisdiction of the Court or the admissibility of a case

1. The Court shall satisfy itself that it has jurisdiction in any case brought before it. The Court may, on its own motion, determine the admissibility of a case in accordance with article 17.

31 and 32 does not remove, the meaning which best reconciles the texts, having regard to the object and purpose of the treaty, shall be adopted."

Article 12 ICCRSt entitled "Preconditions to the exercise of jurisdiction" clearly stipulates that accession to the ICCRSt in accordance with its first paragraph or by the State in question lodging a declaration of acceptance in accordance with its third paragraph are contingent acts without which the ICC cannot exercise its jurisdiction. In other words, only if one of the above two conditions is fulfilled can the ICC fulfil its mission, namely to prosecute crimes of genocide, aggression, crimes against humanity and war crimes. Therefore, notwithstanding the principle of mutual consent that usually prevails in international law and is a fundamental condition for most international courts exercising jurisdiction,[135] the ICC may exercise its jurisdiction without taking into account the wishes of all parties precisely because of the gravity of the above-mentioned crimes. The fact that the ICC may exercise its jurisdiction after the referral of a case by the UN Security Council pursuant to Article 13 (b) ICCRSt is the final reinforcement of this conclusion. Thus the ICC can justifiably be compared with the European Court of Human Rights (ECtHR), the African Court of Justice and Human Rights (ACJHR)[136] and the Inter-American Court of Human Rights,[137] all of which have the primary objective of protecting human rights in specific parts of the world.

Undoubtedly, Article 12 ICCRSt contains fundamental provisions for regulating a number of crucial issues: (1) how a State accepts the jurisdiction of the ICC and the consequences of this acceptance for the ICC's jurisdiction over certain crimes; (2) which States must accept the jurisdiction of the ICC before it can exercise jurisdiction under normal circumstances (and not in the exceptional case of the Security Council initiating legal proceedings under Article 13 (b) ICCRSt;[138] (3) how a State that has not ratified the ICCRSt may nevertheless choose to accept the jurisdiction of the ICC for a particular case and what the legal consequences of such ad hoc acceptance are.[139]

Furthermore, Article 12 ICCRSt is inextricably linked not only to Article 5 ICCRSt, which refers to crimes that fall within the ICC's jurisdiction, but also to

[135] Including the ICJ, according to Article 36 of its Statute https://www.icj-cij.org/en/statute last accessed 8 June 2023.

[136] See the Court's official website at http://en.african-court.org/ last accessed 8 June 2023.

[137] See the Court's official website at http://www.corteidh.or.cr/index.cfm last accessed 8 June 2023.

[138] Article 13 (b) ICCRSt: A situation in which one or more of such crimes appears to have been committed is referred to the Prosecutor by the Security Council acting under Chapter VII of the Charter of the United Nations.

[139] Kaul (2002), pp. 583–584.

Article 13 ICCRSt[140] (which describes practical ways of establishing jurisdiction),[141] Article 17 ICCRSt (which refers to the principle of complementarity regarding the ICC's jurisdiction with respect to national jurisdictions) and to Article 124 ICCRSt (on a State's right to declare that, for a period of seven years after the entry into force of the Statute, it does not accept the jurisdiction of the Court with respect to war crimes committed by its nationals or on its territory).[142]

The first paragraph of Article 12 ICCRSt includes the crucial rule (as proposed by the Korean delegation during the Rome Conference)[143] that States *ex officio*[144] accept the ICC's jurisdiction over the crime of genocide, crimes against humanity, war crimes and the crime of aggression once they ratify and become party to the ICCRSt. There are nevertheless two possible exceptions to this general rule. A State may, if it considers it appropriate, limit the ICC's jurisdiction (1) in accordance with the aforementioned 7-year exemption in Article 124 ICCRSt pertaining to war crimes, which may apply as soon as a State becomes party to the ICCRSt and makes the requisite declaration; (2) the 'general' exception in Article 121(5) ICCRSt,[145] which theoretically applies to amendments made to the description of any of the crimes within the ICC's jurisdiction, such that each state party can then decide to accept the crimes amended thus as falling under the ICC's jurisdiction or not.

---

[140] Article 12(1) ICCRSt: A State which becomes a Party to this Statute thereby accepts the jurisdiction of the Court with respect to the crimes referred to in article 5.

[141] Article 13 ICCRSt - Exercise of jurisdiction: The Court may exercise its jurisdiction with respect to a crime referred to in article 5 in accordance with the provisions of this Statute if: (a) A situation in which one or more of such crimes appears to have been committed is referred to the Prosecutor by a State Party in accordance with article 14; (b) A situation in which one or more of such crimes appears to have been committed is referred to the Prosecutor by the Security Council acting under Chapter VII of the Charter of the United Nations; or (c) The Prosecutor has initiated an investigation in respect of such a crime in accordance with article 15.

[142] Article 124 ICCRSt - Transitional Provision: Notwithstanding article 12, paragraphs 1 and 2, a State, on becoming a party to this Statute, may declare that, for a period of seven years after the entry into force of this Statute for the State concerned, it does not accept the jurisdiction of the Court with respect to the category of crimes referred to in article 8 when a crime is alleged to have been committed by its nationals or on its territory. A declaration under this article may be withdrawn at any time. The provisions of this article shall be reviewed at the Review Conference convened in accordance with article 123, paragraph 1.

[143] United Nations Diplomatic Conference of Plenipotentiaries on the Establishment of an International Criminal Court Rome, 15 June–17 July 1998, Official Records, UN Doc. A/CONF.183/13, Volume B para 52–54 http://legal.un.org/icc/rome/proceedings/E/Rome%20Proceedings_v2_e.pdf last accessed 8 June 2023.

[144] Kaul (2002), p. 606.

[145] Article 121(5) ICCRSt: Any amendment to articles 5, 6, 7 and 8 of this Statute shall enter into force for those States Parties which have accepted the amendment one year after the deposit of their instruments of ratification or acceptance. In respect of a State Party which has not accepted the amendment, the Court shall not exercise its jurisdiction regarding a crime covered by the amendment when committed by that State Party's nationals or on its territory.

However, it is worth pointing out that today, this exception mainly concerns the amendment of the crime of aggression finally agreed upon at the Kampala Conference in 2010, since the crime of aggression was the only crime that had not been clearly defined from the start and thus essentially did not fall within the ICC's jurisdiction.[146] Consequently, the combination of the provisions of Article 121(4) and (5) ICCRSt clearly shows that even if, for instance, the required seven-eighths of state parties[147] were to accept the amendment of the crime of aggression at some point in the future, this amendment would not apply *ex officio* to all state parties 1 year after ratification or acceptance before the Secretary-General of the United Nations; on the contrary, by not accepting the amendment, an existing state party would be able to indirectly reject the ICC's jurisdiction over a crime of aggression committed previously, or about to be committed in the future, by its nationals or on its territory.[148]

On the other hand, while the provisions of paragraphs 4 and 5 of Article 121 ICCRSt are clear regarding States that have already become parties to the ICCRSt prior to any amendment of Articles 5 to 8 ICCRSt, which define the crimes that fall within the jurisdiction of the ICC, there is ambiguity when it comes to state parties that ratify the ICCRSt after any amendments in the process of being made to Articles 5 to 8 ICCRSt. *De lege ferenda*, of course, it would be legally correct to argue that any nations acceding to the ICCRSt do so based on the provisions in force at the time of their accession. However, the adoption of such a view inevitably leads to the emergence of a potential legal inequality between old and new state parties. Unfortunately, this seems inevitable and cannot be mitigated pursuant to the current provisions of the ICCRSt.

There is, in my view, an even more complex issue regarding new state parties to the ICCRSt that accede during the 1-year time period one between the proposal and ratification or acceptance of an amendment before the United Nations Secretary-General by the required seven-eighths of States. On this matter too, there is a legal vacuum within the ICCRSt that can only be solved by way of intuitive interpretation. In such a case, I believe that the most sound interpretation would simply be to consider new state parties not to have accepted any *outstanding* amendments unless they make an explicit declaration to the contrary, confirming their acceptance of

[146] Article 5 (2) ICCRSt: The Court shall exercise jurisdiction over the crime of aggression once a provision is adopted in accordance with articles 121 and 123 defining the crime and setting out the conditions under which the Court shall exercise jurisdiction with respect to this crime. Such a provision shall be consistent with the relevant provisions of the Charter of the United Nations.

[147] Article 121(4) ICCRSt: Except as provided in paragraph 5, an amendment shall enter into force for all States Parties one year after instruments of ratification or acceptance have been deposited with the Secretary-General of the United Nations by seven-eighths of them.

[148] A more thorough analysis of this issue can be found in the relevant chapter on the crime of aggression. Obviously, a State that does not accept the ICC's jurisdiction over the crime of aggression is primarily interested in the case of its nationals who may be considered perpetrators of the crime of aggression in foreign territories and not in the case of a crime of aggression committed on its territory, since then that State would obviously be the victim of the aggressive behaviour of the forces of an enemy State or States.

those amendments already accepted by at least seven-eighths of state parties. In the absence of such a declaration, the ICC will not be able to exercise its jurisdiction over a crime amended in this manner if committed by the State in question or on its territory. However, from a practical perspective, if the new state party made an explicit declaration in every instance on whether or not it accepts the ongoing amendment then at least its intention may never be legally challenged.[149]

2.5 The ICC's Temporal Jurisdiction: Retrospective Application of the Rome Statute

It is of course well-known that, pursuant to Article 126 ICCRSt, the ICC's temporal jurisdiction was established on "the first day of the month after the 60th day following the date of the deposit of the 60th instrument of ratification, acceptance, approval or accession with the Secretary-General of the United Nations", which made 1 July 2002 its first official day of operation.

With regard to Palestine, the crucial question became whether its territory could fall under the ICC's territorial jurisdiction and, if so, from which point in time. This was the subject of intense debate from December 2008 onwards, when Israel invaded the Gaza Strip under Operation 'Cast Lead'. It would suffice at this point to note that according to the ICC's official press release of 5 January 2015,[150] Palestine submitted a declaration on 1 January 2015[151] under Article 12(3) ICCRSt, stating its acceptance of the ICC's ad hoc jurisdiction over crimes committed after 13 June 2014. This declaration was accepted by the ICC Registry.

Furthermore, only a day later, on 2 January 2015, Palestine acceded to the ICCRSt using a different instrument, as noted in the ICC's official press release of 7 January 2015.[152] As a result the Prosecutor of the ICC opened a preliminary

[149] Obviously, the legal consequences of such a statement and whether such a statement is valid or not is another legal issue. The opposing argument could be the fact that when the new state party validated the ICCRSt, it was certainly well-aware that in the immediate future there would be new, already legally initiated amendments to the ICCRSt.

[150] ICC, Press Release: Palestine declares acceptance of ICC jurisdiction since 13 June 2014, 05/01/2015, ICC-CPI-20150105-PR1080 https://www.icc-cpi.int//Pages/item.aspx?name=pr1080 last accessed 8 June 2023.

[151] Declaration Accepting the Jurisdiction of the International Criminal Court, 31 December 2014 https://www.icc-cpi.int/iccdocs/PIDS/press/Palestine_A_12-3.pdf last accessed 8 June 2023.

[152] Press Release: The State of Palestine accedes to the Rome Statute, 7 January 2015 https://www.icc-cpi.int//Pages/item.aspx?name=pr1082_2 last accessed 8 June 2023.

[153] Press Release: The Prosecutor of the International Criminal Court, Fatou Bensouda, opens a preliminary examination of the situation in Palestine, 16 January 2015 https://www.icc-cpi.int//Pages/item.aspx?name=pr1083 last accessed 8 June 2023.

[154] ICC, "Israel Threatens to Liquidate International Criminal Court (ICC)" (2018); Escritt and Williams (2015).

investigation into the situation in Palestine;[153] members of Israel's government threatened to "liquidate the ICC" and cut its funding.[154] But why would a state sign a declaration accepting the ICC's ad hoc jurisdiction when it had already decided to ratify the ICCRSt and accede to it the next day? As Daphne Richmond-Barak points out the initial legal "paradox" of Palestine's two declarations has a particularly interesting legal explanation.[155]

The logical and legally correct explanation can be found in Article 11(2) ICCRSt where it is stipulated that "if a State becomes a Party to this Statute after its entry into force, the Court may exercise its jurisdiction only with respect to crimes committed after the entry into force of this Statute for that State, unless that State has made a declaration under Article 12, paragraph 3".

The aforementioned differentiation (ad hoc declaration accepting the ICC's jurisdiction as opposed to ratification of the ICCRSt and accession to it) is explained by the provision of Article 126(2) ICCRSt, pursuant to which the ICC cannot conduct a preliminary investigation of crimes committed on Palestinian territory or against Palestinian citizens prior to 1 April 2015. That is because according to Article 126(2) ICCRSt "for each State ratifying, accepting, approving or acceding to this Statute after the deposit of the 60th instrument of ratification, acceptance, approval or accession, the Statute shall enter into force on the first day of the month after the 60th day following the deposit by such State of its instrument of ratification, acceptance, approval or accession". The aforementioned grammatical interpretation of the provision at hand was confirmed in practice by the ICC Prosecutor's Report of 6 November 2014, in which the Prosecutor decided not to further investigate the war crimes that appear to have been committed by Israel military forces on the Mavi Marmara vessel (which had been registered in Comoros), as they were not of sufficient gravity to justify further action by the Court.[156]

Nonetheless, it is important to point out that Article 11(2) ICCRSt allows an acceding State to simultaneously proceed to a declaration accepting the ICC's jurisdiction pursuant to Article 12(3) ICCRSt. This means that when a State decides while ratifying the ICCRSt to simultaneously proceed to a declaration pursuant to Article 12(3) ICCRSt, the ICC is able to investigate a situation that occurred before the state party in question ratified the ICCRSt and even before the specified time in the ad hoc declaration accepting the ICC's jurisdiction concerning "continuing crimes".[157] The same criterion can of course be applied regarding crimes committed after the specified time "insofar as they are sufficiently linked to the situation of crisis referred to the Court as ongoing at the time of the referral".[158]

---

[155] Richemond-Barak (2015).

[156] Situation on Registered Vessels of Comoros, Greece and Cambodia Article 53(1) Report, 06-11-2014 http://www.icc-cpi.int/iccdocs/otp/OTP-COM-Article_53%281%29-Report-06Nov2014Eng.pdf last accessed 8 June 2023; Report on Preliminary Examination Activities 2014 https://www.icc-cpi.int/iccdocs/otp/OTP-Pre-Exam-2014.pdf last accessed 8 June 2023.

[157] Decision (2011).

[158] Ibid 72 para 179.

Therefore, Palestine legally declared that it accepts the ICC's ad hoc jurisdiction over crimes which were committed on its territory during the time period from 13 June 2014 to 1 January 2015.[159] Thus, the ICC could exercise its jurisdiction to investigate alleged crimes committed during Operation 'Protective Edge' in July and August 2014 by Israeli military forces[160]—as long as the ICC considered that the Gaza Strip constitutes Palestinian territory and without of course excluding the submission of charges not only against Israelis, but also against Palestinians.

Nevertheless, it also results from the aforementioned analysis that the ICC is not bound to exercise its temporal jurisdiction (jurisdiction *ratione temporis*) exclusively within the aforementioned time limits, but that—if "continuing crimes" have been committed—it could exercise its jurisdiction before 13 June 2014 as well as after 1 January 2015 "insofar as the contextual elements of the continuing crimes are the same".[161] Therefore, for example, the exercise of the ICC's jurisdiction over the crimes of abduction and murder of the three Israeli teenagers on 12 June 2014, criminal acts to which Israel responded with Operation 'Brother's Keeper'[162] in Gaza, is not automatically excluded by the aforementioned declaration of the Palestinian National Authority (PNA). It is thus evident that even though when a State ratifies the ICCRSt its retroactive effect is ruled out, the same does not apply to a State's ad hoc declaration accepting the ICC's jurisdiction over a particular situation. In the latter case, the retroactive jurisdiction of the ICC is not only fully permissible according to the relevant provisions of the ICCRSt, but may also be extended to a time period before the date declared by the State in question, i.e. in this particular case, before 13 June 2014, to the 12 June 2015, as long as it can be proven that the abduction is itself a continuing crime or part of a series of crimes that constitutes continuing crime.

And while a State's consent for the ICC's ad hoc jurisdiction over a situation could potentially lead us to conclude that via the aforementioned process the ICC establishes a quasi-retroactive power to exercise its jurisdiction, since the interested State's consent constitutes an extremely crucial characteristic that overrules the standard content of a law's retroactive force (as no consent is usually required for a law to have retroactive force). However, it cannot be omitted that the State's consent impinges upon the defence rights of the accused, who of course do not

[159] Declaration Accepting the Jurisdiction of the International Criminal Court, 31 December 2014 https://www.icc-cpi.int/iccdocs/PIDS/press/Palestine_A_12-3.pdf last accessed 8 June 2023.

[160] Patel et al. (2015). This operation, which was the sixth military operation at the Gaza Strip during an eight-year period and lasted a total of 50 days (from 8 July to 26 August 2014), resulted in the deaths of 2220 Palesthinians, 1492 of whom were civilians and 547 children.

[161] Decision Pursuant to Article 15 of the Rome Statute on the Authorisation of an Investigation into the Situation in the Republic of Côte d'Ivoire, ICC-02/11-14 (3 October 2011) 72 para 179. The definition of the term "contextual elements" is provided in page 13 para 27: "27. Under Article 7(1) of the Statute, a crime against humanity involves any of the specified acts that are listed ("underlying acts") when committed as part of a widespread or systematic attack directed against any civilian population, with knowledge of the attack ('contextual elements')."

[162] Kramer (2014).

consent and are not asked to consent to the retroactive force of the ICC's jurisdiction. Therefore, the question that must be answered in my view is whether a State could lawfully under international criminal law violate the fundamental rights of the accused which are inseparably linked to the fundamental legal principle *nullum crimen, nulla poena sine lege* whether the accused are its citizens or not[163] (as in the case of the Palestinian National Authority consenting to the early start of the ICC's jurisdiction over crimes that appear to have been committed by Israeli citizens). I believe that the answer must beyond doubt be *de lege ferenda* negative, since the most fundamental of all principles of criminal law would otherwise be lawfully infringed by the ICCRSt.[164,165]

2.6 The ICC's Jurisdiction Pursuant to the Principle of Active Personality

In the international law case *Lotus*, the ICJ had already declared in 1927 with reference to international law that "[f]ar from laying down a general prohibition to the effect that States may not extend the application of their laws and the jurisdiction of their courts to persons, property and acts outside their territory, it leaves them in this respect a wide measure of discretion which is only limited in certain cases by prohibitive rules; as regards other cases, every State remains free to adopt the principles which it regards as best and most suitable".[166]

---

[163] It is worth mentioning that this fundamental criminal law principle is also stipulated in Article 24 ICCRSt. Article 24 - Non-retroactivity *ratione personae*: 1. No person shall be criminally responsible under this Statute for conduct prior to the entry into force of the Statute. 2. In the event of a change in the law applicable to a given case prior to a final judgement, the law more favourable to the person being investigated, prosecuted or convicted shall apply. Therefore, the aforementioned analysis of the conflict between the legal principles of Articles 12(3) and 24 ICCRSt is of great theoretical and practical interest.

[164] Dana (2009), p. 857. In this extremely interesting study, Dana divides the *nullum crimen nulla poena sine lege* principle into two distinct principles (*nullum crime since lege* and *nulla poena sine lege*), focusing on the second one and adding that this principle definitely has to be interpreted as *nulla poena sine praevia lege poenali*. Moreover, she thoroughly analyses Article 23 ICCRSt, which may constitute some progress in the implementation of international criminal law thus far, but still presents some important problems. Compare also *Cassese* who in the Tadić Case before the ICTFY in 1999 had admitted that even though the *nulla poena sine praevia lege poenali* principle is fundamental for most national criminal legal orders, it is "still inapplicable in international criminal law". ICTY, *The Prosecutor v. Duško Tadić* (Appeal Judgement) IT-94-1-A, International Criminal Tribunal for the former Yugoslavia, 15 July 1999.

[165] On whether this fundamental principle was violated in the Nuremberg and Tokyo Trials see Tsilonis V, 'Η Διεθνής Ποινική Δικαιοσύνη κατά το Πρώτο Μισό του Εικοστού Αιώνα' [International Criminal Justice during the first half of the 20th Century] in Τιμητικός Τόμος Χριστόφορου Δ. Αργυρόπουλου [Essays in Honour of Christophoros D. Argiropoulos] (Criminal Law Practitioners' Association - Nomiki Bibliothiki, Athens 2016), p. 385.

[166] ICJ (1927).

According to Luke Reydams, legal theory has identified seven principles in total, on the basis of which a State can legally exercise its jurisdiction over people, property and acts outside its territory: (1) the principle of territorial sovereignty (2) the principle of active personality (i.e. of the perpetrator's nationality) (3) the principle of passive personality (i.e. of the victim's personality) (4) the principle of the flag state (according to which vessels, aircrafts and embassies registered with a given State are treated as that State's territory) (5) the protective principle (6) the principle of universal jurisdiction (7) the principle of representation. It is notable that for many decades the study of international criminal law equated to the study of the seven aforementioned principles.[167]

As already mentioned, the principles of territorial sovereignty[168] and of active personality are the ones that eventually prevailed in the Rome Conference as the foundations for the ICC's jurisdiction. It is particularly notable that, according to a 2010 report by the international human rights organisations Redress and FIDH, explicit provisions on the applicability of active personality exist in the legal orders of all EU member states as well as of Norway and Switzerland (30 European States in total).[169] Furthermore, the principle of active personality is applicable in Australia[170] and has applied in the USA since 1922, following the Bowman case.[171] Finally, according to Jennifer Zerk's research in Harvard in 2010, States seem to consider the principle of active personality the most legally powerful basis for the immediate exercise of their jurisdiction over crimes committed outside their own territory.[172] It is thus clear that the jurisdiction transferred from the state party to the ICC in accordance with the principle of active personality and Article 12(2)(b) ICCRSt is founded upon a global legal principle that is recognised by both civil and common law States[173] as well as by all international law scholars.

Consequently, if a core crime is committed by a national of a State that is party to the ICCRSt, then the ICC will directly establish jurisdiction, regardless of whether the accused is found in his own State or in the territory of another state party or in the

---

[167] Reydams (2004), pp. 21–22.

[168] In legal theory, the principle of territorial sovereignty has two aspects: a 'subjective aspect' and an 'objective aspect'. Its 'subjective aspect' includes crimes that are physically committed within a state's territorial borders, while its 'objective aspect' includes crimes that take effect within its borders even if the perpetrator performs the act outside of its borders. Colangelo (2009), pp. 769, 792. For instance, the "sabotage" of power lines which took place in November 2015 in the territory of Ukraine, causing a long blackout in the now independent territory of Crimea, is a notable example of the application of the 'objective territorial' principle. Luhn (2015).

[169] Redress-FIDH (2010), pp. 17–18.

[170] Ireland-Piper D, "Extraterritorial Criminal Jurisdiction: Does the Long Arm of the Law Undermine the Rule of Law?" Melbourne Law School Publications https://law.unimelb.edu.au/__data/assets/pdf_file/0007/1687246/Ireland-Piper.pdf last accessed 8 June 2023.

[171] Blakesley and Stigall (2007), pp. 1, 8–13, 20–21. A tragic exception is the 2005 Martinelli case, regarding the crime of child pornography: U.S. Court of Appeals for the Armed Forces (2005).

[172] Zerk (2010), p. 8 https://www.hks.harvard.edu/sites/default/files/centers/mrcbg/programs/cri/files/workingpaper_59_zerk.pdf last accessed 8 June 2023.

[173] Kaul (2002), p. 610.

territory of a state party that is not clearly included in the ICC's jurisdiction according to the principle of territorial sovereignty[174] or even in the territory of a State that does not recognize the ICC's jurisdiction and has not ratified its Statute.

Nonetheless, even this seemingly simple matter of the perpetrator's nationality presents notable theoretical difficulties. Firstly, the principle of active personality under international as well as national law is often connected, as we have seen, with citizenship and not with the term nationality that is used in the ICCRSt. Since the vast majority of modern States have been constructed on the notion of the nation-state, the terms citizenship and nationality are practically identical, but differences between domestic legal orders cannot be excluded;[175] to name but one vivid example according to the interpretive bulletin of the Hellenic Ministry of the Interior, the term "nationality" in the ICCRSt must be interpreted as citizenship, because the term nationality constitutes an attribute without any effect in the area of law. Furthermore, who exactly is a 'citizen' of a State is not always an indisputable matter, despite the fact that international conventions such as the 1954 Convention relating to the Status of Stateless Persons[176] and the 1961 Convention on the Reduction of Statelessness[177] have attempted to solve the matter of statelessness by rendering citizenship a human right. Nonetheless, the matter is in effect how States themselves determine who might become their citizens, how this occurs and under which process. Piper notes that in Australia, for example, permanent residents may not have elective rights or of course Australian nationality, but are nevertheless

[174] As already analysed above with regards to Article 12 ICCRSt.

[175] 'Nationality' is essentially an attribute and constitutes a non-legal connection of a person with a nation. For that reason, those persons who live outside their native country may be called expatriates and/or foreigners. It is possible for foreigners to be a Greek citizens as long as they have Greek citizenship, while the opposite may also be true (a Greek national may be a foreigner if he does not have Greek citizenship. Βλ. Εγκύκλιος του Υπουργείου Εσωτερικών, Φ.82215/18303, Παροχή διευκρινίσεων σχετικά με τον εννοιολογικό προσδιορισμό των όρων «ιθαγένεια», «υπηκοότητα» και «εθνικότητα» 09-07-2013, http://www.ypes.gr/UserFiles/f0ff9297-f516-40ff-a70eeca84e2ec9b9/eggr_f_82215_090713.pdf, last accessed 8 June 2023.

[176] 1954 Convention relating to the Status of Stateless Persons http://www.unhcr.org/ibelong/wp-content/uploads/1954-Convention-relating-to-the-Status-of-Stateless-Persons_ENG.pdf last accessed 8 June 2023.

[177] 1961 Convention on the Reduction of Statelessness http://www.unhcr.org/ibelong/wp-content/uploads/1961-Convention-on-the-reduction-of-Statelessness_ENG.pdf last accessed 8 June 2023.

[178] This creates a number of issues for domestic law, since the Australian Penal Code of 1995, for instance, considers sexual intercourse with a minor under 16 years old or a "young person" with whom a relationship of trust or authority exists a criminal offence. At the same time, the UN Convention on the Rights of the Child considers a child a person under 18 years of age, but on this matter, there is a great lack of cohesion among the penal codes of States, since globally in 2009 the age of legal consent in sexual acts ranged from 12 to 18 years of age. Thus, for example, if a permanent resident of Australia, who is at the same time a citizen of the Philippines, has sexual intercourse with a 12 year-old during his visit to the Philippines, they could be criminally prosecuted in Australia, despite the fact that the act would be legal under Philippine law where the age for legal consent is 12 years old. See World Population Review, Age of Consent by Country

subject to Australian law, even when they are located and act outside the sovereign territory of Australia.[178]

Certainly, according to the explicit phrasing of Article 12(2) ICCRSt, which refers exclusively to the perpetrator's nationality, it is difficult to understand how it could be *mutatis mutandis* considered that a perpetrator falls under the ICC's jurisdiction only because he is a permanent resident of Australia (or Greece etc.), when he is actually a national of Japan (or Russia etc). However, since neither the ICCRSt nor the Rules of Procedure and Evidence include any specific mention of the term 'nationality', the full range of possibilities remain open, including an extremely broad interpretation of the term with regard to the exercise of the ICC's jurisdiction.[179]

An initial interesting matter that might arise in many forms is, I believe, that of the stateless perpetrator. The stateless are, in the vast majority of cases, either persons with no formal nationality or those of a nationality that may no longer exist or nationals of a State that has been dissolved or is no longer recognised as a State, such as for example Somalia. Somalia, of course, has never accepted the ICC's jurisdiction, but were the perpetrator a national of Liberia and in the meantime, because of lengthy conflicts, Liberia ceased to exist as a State, then the matter of the exercise of the ICC's jurisdiction exclusively and only pursuant to Article 12(2)(b) ICCRSt would be doubtful, since it could arguably be maintained that: (a) the alleged perpetrator no longer has an officially recognised nationality (b) the acceptance of the ICC's jurisdiction by the former State ceased to exist since the State was dissolved and ceased to exist according to international law. Consequently, based on the above, the perpetrator in question could not 'automatically' fall under the ICC's jurisdiction pursuant to Article 12(2)(b) ICCRSt without a relevant decision from the ICC that interprets the term 'nationality' and its scope of application.

If we now assume that according to the aforementioned scenario, part of the territory of dissolved Liberia was to be annexed by the State of Guinea and another part by the non-neighbouring State of Guinea-Bissau, then the following could arguably be maintained, according to the specific facts of the case: (a) the alleged perpetrator does not yet officially have any recognised nationality and thus cannot fall under the ICC's jurisdiction according to the principle of active personality of Article 12(2)(b) ICCRSt; (b) the alleged perpetrator is now a national of State (Guinea-Bissau) which does not recognize the ICC's jurisdiction and thus, cannot be put on trial pursuant to Article 12(2)(b) ICCRSt alone (c) the alleged perpetrator is now a national of a State (Guinea) which recognises the jurisdiction of the ICC and thus can be put to trial by the ICC pursuant to Article 12(2)(b) ICCRSt; (d) the acceptance of the ICC's jurisdiction by its former state party no longer exists since the State itself has been dissolved, while the new State (Guinea-Bissau) that annexed

2019 http://worldpopulationreview.com/countries/countries-by-age-of-consent/ last accessed 8 June 2023.

[179] An indication of this is that this matter was not mentioned during the preparatory talks that preceded the establishment of the ICC during the Conference of Rome in 1998 either.

the territory where the perpetrator resides or from which he originates has not recognised the ICC's jurisdiction (e) the acceptance of the ICC's jurisdiction by its former state party no longer exists since the sState itself has been dissolved, while the new State (Guinea) that has annexed the territory where the perpetrator resides or from which he originates has recognised the ICC's jurisdiction, and thus the perpetrator falls under the ICC's jurisdiction because of his nationality (f) the alleged perpetrator declares that, as a free man, he does not accept his new nationality, whichever nationality that might be (i.e. either that of Guinea or Guinea-Bissau); thus the provision of Article 12(2)(b) cannot be applied.

Moreover, a second issue of great interest is the status of refugees, especially in our time when the armed conflicts in the Middle East and Africa, as well as poverty in Asia and Africa, have forced millions of people to move towards Europe and other lands. As already pointed out, neither the ICCRSt nor the Rules of Procedure and Evidence nor the Elements of Crimes, nor even the preliminary documents drawn up during the Rome Conference offer a definition of the term 'nationality', let alone of the specialised issue of 'refugee status'. The 1951 Convention Relating to the Status of Refugees is not particularly enlightening on this issue either, since Article 1(2) implies that a refugee does not lose his nationality merely because of his refugee status.[180] Thus an initial interpretation is that a refugee retains his nationality even after submitting his asylum application. Furthermore, it is rather self-evident that in the case of crimes that fall under international criminal law and are committed prior to one being granted refugee status, it is one's initial nationality that matters. Therefore, the main issue that may arise is what happens if a refugee commits crimes which may fall under the ICC's jurisdiction after applying for asylum in another State.

A notable example is the multiple terrorist attacks that took place in Paris on 13 November 2015, where at least one of the perpetrators appears to have been a Syrian refugee who arrived in France via Greece.[181] Suppose that the passport was found that truly belonged to an individual (Ahmed Almuhamed) who participated in the Paris Attacks and was later arrested; an individual who arrived in France by crossing the borders of Greece eight months previously after disguising himself as a refugee and submitting an asylum application in Greece. In this scenario, the following could be maintained: (1) as a Syrian, the perpetrator could never fall under the ICC's jurisdiction pursuant to Article 12(2)(b) ICCRSt based on his nationality, since Syria has not ratified the ICCRSt (he could of course fall under the ICC's jurisdiction pursuant to Article 12(2)(a) ICCRSt, i.e. based on the principle of territorial jurisdiction, since France is a state party to the ICCRSt). (2) Given that his asylum application was still pending, the perpetrator had not established any

---

[180] 1951 Convention and Protocol Relating to the Status of Refugees http://www.unhcr.org/3b66c2aa10 last accessed 8 June 2023.

[181] Lichfield (2015).

official legal bond to any State other than Syria, from which he appears to come. If, however, his asylum application had been approved, and he was granted refugee status and official travel documents,[182] then it could be presumed that he enjoys all the privileges and rights of a Greek citizen. Therefore, it could be presumed that he would be treated as a Greek citizen who falls under the ICC's jurisdiction pursuant to Article 12(2)(b) ICCRSt,[183] if a broad interpretation of the term 'nationality' were accepted.[184] (3) The news of the participation of this particular individual in the Paris Attacks could immediately lead the Hellenic Ministry of the Interior either to reject the asylum application or to revoke the perpertrator's asylum status if already granted. This would in either case render his original nationality—legal bond with the State he came from (Syria)—the indisputable criterion for establishing the ICC's jurisdiction (pursuant to Article 12(2)(b) ICCRSt). Therefore, based on his nationality, the perpetrator could not be subject to the ICC's jurisdiction (Article 12(2)(b) ICCRSt); again, it is only pursuant to the provision of Article 12(2)(a) ICCRSt—principle of territorial jurisdiction—that he could be subject to the ICC's jurisdiction.[185]

Finally, a third issue which raises a great deal of interest is the case of a perpetrator of dual nationality. If we put to one side the simplest possibilities in this analysis (the perpetrator is a national of two States that have both ratified the ICCRSt and accepted the ICC's jurisdiction or have not ratified the ICCRSt and do not accept the ICC's jurisdiction), it is worth examining the following case: during a secret mission to the borders of Turkey-Syria, C, who is a Greek and US national a member of the US Navy Seals and has permanently resided in the USA since the age of 4, commits the crime of torture against Tajik nationals with a view to discovering the location of an ISIS mountain camp. Reuters publishes relevant pictures that prompt Tajikistan's government to refer the situation to the ICC's Prosecutor pursuant to Article 13(a) ICCRSt. The ICC Prosecutor collects more evidence, including a survivor's testimony, and decides to bring charges against C for the war crime of torture (Article 8(2)(a)(ii) ICCRSt). The Prosecutor establishes the ICC's jurisdiction based on the perpetrator's dual nationality and, in particular, on

[182] Greece does not automatically provide those who have been granted refugee status with a passport; the fee for this process is 85 euros. See the official website of the Greek Asylum Service http://asylo.gov.gr/en/ last accessed 8 June 2023.

[183] Circular of the Ministry of State, Φ.82215/18303 [in Greek].

[184] Such an interpretation would however infringe upon the rights of the accused and the legal principle of *in dubio pro reo*.

[185] In the Tadić case, while discussing Article 4(1) of the Fourth 1949 Geneva Convention for relative to the Protection of Civilian Persons in Time of War, the ICTFY Appeal Court noted that as of 1949 the legal bond of nationality is not considered crucial and that judicial decisions must be mostly based on the substantive links between an individual and a State rather than on formal links. ("the legal bond of nationality was not regarded as crucial and allowance was made for special cases. In the [. . .] case of refugees, the lack of both allegiance to a State and diplomatic protection by this State was regarded as more important than the formal link of nationality" ICTY, *Prosecutor v. Duško Tadić* (Appeal Judgement), IT-94-1-A, 15 July 1999, 5, http://www.refworld.org/docid/40277f504.html last accessed 8 June 2023.

the fact that one of those two nationalities (the Greek one) is linked to a State that has ratified the ICCRSt, namely Greece, because: (1) the exercise of the ICC's jurisdiction is not connected to the nationality of the victims (principle of passive personality) but primarily only to the perpetrator's nationality (dual nationality: Greek and American) or to the territory where the crime was committed (Turkey) according to principles of active personality and territorial sovereignty stipulated in Article 12(2)(a) and (b) ICCRSt; (2) the USA (the perpetrator's first nationality is American) and Turkey (the territory where the crime was committed) have not ratified the ICCRSt and, thus, do not accept the ICC's jurisdiction; (3) because of US involvement, it is anyway practically impossible for the ICC to establish jurisdiction through the UN Security Council (Article 13(2)(b) ICCRSt). However, the USA files an objection against the Court's jurisdiction pursuant to Article 19(2)(c) ICCRSt, claiming that the ICC has no jurisdiction over this particular case since the alleged perpetrator's principal nationality is American and his permanent residence of the last 30 years is the state of Illinois.[186] The accused C files the same objection before the ICC pursuant to Article 19(2)(a) ICCRSt.

In this particular instance, I believe that we must accept that the ICC has jurisdiction over the case, since the alleged perpetrator C holds dual nationality (Greek and American) and thus he is subject to rights and obligations provided for in both States. The fact that the American nationality appears to be his principal nationality and Greek his secondary one is not critical here, since as a dual national he enjoys all the rights that arise from being a national of each country separately, and actually has additional privileges and capabilities at an international level over and above any person who holds only one nationality. Thus, even without a visa, he may invoke the existence of either one or the other nationality in order to visit States that have signed relevant agreements either with the USA or with Greece. International legal theory already appears to agree with this view decades before the establishment of the ICC.[187]

---

[186] Early on, legal theory had accepted that in such case an objection to the ICC's jurisdiction could be filed. Zeidy (2002), pp. 869, 919.

[187] Harvard Draft Convention on Jurisdiction with Respect to Crime, with Comment, Art. 5, reprinted in 29 AJIL Supp. 439 (1935) 533: "Whether, in case of double or multiple nationality, an accused is a national of the State which is attempting to prosecute and punish is a question to be determined by reference to such principles of international law as govern nationality. If international law permits the State to regard the accused as its national, its competence is not impaired or limited by the fact that he is also a national of another State." See also Deen-Racsmány (2001), pp. 606, 611.

2.7 The *Ad Hoc* Acceptance of the ICC's Jurisdiction by a State Non-Party to the Rome Statute

Article 12(3) ICCRSt provides a State that has not ratified the ICCRSt with the rather unusual capability to accept the ICC's jurisdiction ad hoc[188] when it comes to crimes that explicitly fall under its jurisdiction. Such a declaration has to this day never been submitted by a state non-party,[189] and it is indeed difficult to imagine a scenario in which a state non-party that disagrees with the ICC's role in the international legal order would want the ICC to exercise jurisdiction over a situation even for exceptional reasons. Yet the possibility that a state non-party might choose ad hoc to accept the ICC's jurisdiction cannot be ruled out with mathematical certainty. However, should a state non-party submit a written declaration to the ICC Registrar accepting the ICC's jurisdiction over crimes committed on its territory or by its citizens in a particular case *lato sensu*,[190] then according to Article 13 ICCRSt, it must comply with the rules stipulated in detail in Part 9 of the ICCRSt, under the title "International Cooperation and Judicial Assistance". (For instance, following its declaration accepting the Court's ad hoc jurisdiction, a State must comply with Article 89(1) ICCRSt with regards to the arrest and surrender of persons requested by the ICC). However, were the ICC to refuse to exercise its ad hoc jurisdiction (e.g. because its lacks sufficient evidence or because the case is of minor importance), the state non-party is not obligated to comply with the provisions of Part 9 of the ICCRSt.

At this point, it must be noted that after the 1998 Conference of Rome and the adoption of the ICCRSt, the interpretation of the English term crime in question" found in Article 12(3) ICCRSt greatly troubled legal theory as well as signatory States. That is because this particular term is very limited compared to the term "situation" found in Article 14(1) ICCRSt. To begin with, it is worth mentioning that 'situation' is a much broader term than 'case' or 'crime', since it suggests crimes and/or cases that are interconnected in time and space.

What is more, semantically, it is a actually a rather narrow term, although doubtlessly closer to the term "case" in Article 17 ICCRSt, which refers to issues of admissibility for a case that is to be adjudicated by the ICC. According to ICC jurisprudence, a case "comprise[s] specific incidents during which one or more crimes within the jurisdiction of the Court seem to have been committed by one or

---

[188] Article 12(3) ICCRSt: If the acceptance of a State which is not a Party to this Statute is required under paragraph 2, that State may, by declaration lodged with the Registrar, accept the exercise of jurisdiction by the Court with respect to the crime in question. The accepting State shall cooperate with the Court without any delay or exception in accordance with Part 9.

[189] Three state parties appear to have submitted declarations for the ad hoc jurisdiction of the ICC hitherto: Palestine, the Ivory Coast and Ukraine.

[190] The term 'situation' would be more correct here.

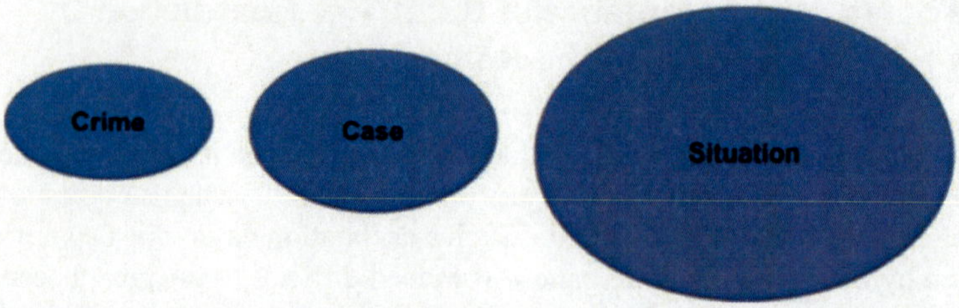

Fig. 2.1 Depiction of the pragmatic relation of the terms 'crime', 'case' and 'situation'

more identified suspects",[191] while legal scholarship has supported the view that "a case must always relate to incident-specific conduct for the purpose of the complementarity provisions of the Rome Statute".[192]

Consequently, if we wanted to schematically present how broad or narrow the aforementioned terms are, we would initially create the following picture (see Fig. 2.1):

According to traditional criminal law theory, whereas the term 'crime' signifies a wrongful act committed by one or more perpetrators against one or more legitimate interests, the term 'case' signifies one or more independent or related crimes committed by one or more perpetrators against one or more legitimate interests. By contrast, the term 'situation' is not found in traditional criminal law or in common law, or for that matter in civil law orders, but only in contemporary international criminal law. According to Article 14(1) ICCRSt, it signifies one or more crimes that are committed by one or more perpetrators against many victims and legitimate interests over a long period of time across a wide territory, and which fall under the ICC's jurisdiction.[193]

Nonetheless, contrary to what one might conclude based on this dogmatically correct analysis of the three terms within the framework in which they were created and have since evolved (the first two in national criminal law, the third one in international criminal law), in the field of international criminal law (where comparisons with national criminal law are often unfitting and unrealistic, as it combines common and civil law traditions) we should *de lege ferenda* portray matters thus (see Fig. 2.2):

As a concept, the scope of the term "crime in question" in Article 13(1) ICCRSt fully matches that of the term "case" in Article 17(1) and (3) ICCRSt, with both

---

[191] Situation in the Democratic Republic of Congo, Decision on the Applications for Participation in the Proceedings of VPRS1, VPRS2, VPRS3, VPRS4, VPRS5 and VPR-6, para 65 https://www.icc-cpi.int/pages/record.aspx?uri=183441 last accessed 8 June 2023.

[192] Rastan (2008), pp. 435, 438.

[193] Article 14 - Referral of a situation by a State Party: 1. A State Party may refer to the Prosecutor a situation in which one or more crimes within the jurisdiction of the Court appear to have been committed requesting the Prosecutor to investigate the situation for the purpose of determining whether one or more specific persons should be charged with the commission of such crimes.

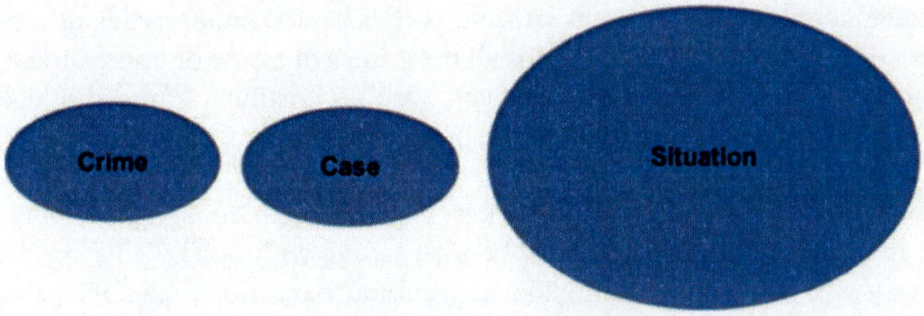

Fig. 2.2 Depiction of the proposed relation of the terms 'crime', 'case' and 'situation'

Fig. 2.3 Depiction of the actual relation of the terms 'crime', 'case' and 'situation'

terms remaining significantly narrower in scope than the term "situation" of Article 13(1) ICCRSt.

Nevertheless, despite the above, the opposite is after all true, since pursuant to Article 44 of the Rules of Procedure and Evidence, the hitherto narrow term "crime in question" of Article 13(1) ICCRSt broadens its scope to equal that of the much wider term "situation", so that matters can in fact be portrayed thus (see Fig. 2.3):

Hans Peter Kaul points out that equating the scope of the narrow term 'crime in question' with that of the much wider term 'situation' commenced on 30 June 2000, when the relevant Preparatory Commission unanimously adopted Article 44 of the Rules of Procedure and Evidence[194] in order to reassure a number of dissenting States concerning the risk of "asymmetric liability".[195] Ruth Wedgwood was perhaps the first to point out that the risk posed by "asymmetric liability" to a State that is not party to the ICC was mainly that if it were to accept the ICC's ad hoc jurisdiction over a particular "crime", it would at the same time face the risk of its own citizens being accused by the ICC for committing the crime, especially if the term was broadly interpreted.[196]

Another threat to the appropriate exercise of the ICC's jurisdiction is that pursuant to the wording of Article 13(1) ICCRSt, a state non-party could declare that it accepts the ICC's jurisdiction **only** over a crime or a series of specific crimes

[194] Report of the Preparatory Commission for the International Criminal Court, Finalized Draft Text of the Rules of Procedure and Evidence, PCNICC/2000/1/Add.1, 2 November 2000 https://www.legal-tools.org/doc/1a75a9/pdf/ last accessed 8 June 2023.

[195] Kaul (2002), p. 611.

[196] Wedgwood (1999), pp. 93, 102–103.

which were committed by citizens of state parties or state non-parties in a case or, more broadly, in a situation; and *not* for all the crimes of a case or, more broadly, of a situation. Such an interpretation, however, would constitute—from a teleological point of view, at least—a distortion of the provision's meaning and purpose and thus cannot be accepted.

Following the above analysis, it is clear, I believe, that *de lege ferenda* the term "crime" in Article 13(1) ICCRSt must be interpreted, within the ICC's special legal order, as a "situation" to ensure the appropriate exercise of the ICC's ad hoc jurisdiction. That is because, as already mentioned, any other interpretation would constitute a distortion of the meaning and purpose of this provision: on the one hand, equating the term "crime" in Article 13(1) ICCRSt with the term's traditional meaning in national criminal law would lead to legal discrepancies and controversial international issues, while on the other hand, the same would be true of equating the term "crime" in Article 13(1) ICCRSt with the extremely broad term "situation" in Article 14(1) ICCRSt. This is precisely what was attempted almost one and a half years after the ICCRSt's adoption in the draft Rules of Procedure and Evidence, which were eventually adopted by the Conference of State Parties in New York on September 2002.[197]

References

Table of Cases

ECHR (1992) Drozd and Janousek v. France and Spain, paras. 86-89 https://hudoc.echr.coe.int/eng#{%22itemid%22:[%22001-57774%22. Accessed 8 June 2023

ICC (2007) The Prosecutor v. Thomas Lubanga Dyilo, Public Redacted Version with Annex I, Decision on the Confirmation of Charges, ICC-01/04-01/06 https://www.icc-cpi.int/pages/record.aspx?uri=247813. Accessed 8 June 2023

ICC Decision on the Applications for Participation in the Proceedings of VPRS1, VPRS2, VPRS3, VPRS4, VPRS5 and VPR-6, para 65. https://www.icc-cpi.int/pages/record.aspx?uri=183441 Accessed 8 June 2023

ICJ (2002) *Democratic Republic of the Congo v. Belgium* https://www.icj-cij.org/files/case-related/121/13743.pdf. Accessed 8 June 2023

ICTR (2006) The Prosecutor v. Michel Bagaragaza, Decision on Rule 11bis Appeal ICTR-2005-86-11bis http://www.worldcourts.com/ictr/eng/decisions/2006.12.13_Prosecutor_v_Bagaragaza.htm. Accessed 8 June 2023

ICTR (2007a) The Prosecutor v. Laurent Bucyibaruta, Decision on the Prosecutor's Request for the Referral of Laurent Bucyibaruta's Indictment to France, ICTR 2005-85-I, http://www.worldcourts.com/ictr/eng/decisions/2007.11.21_Prosecutor_v_Bucyibaruta.htm. Accessed 8 June 2023

ICTR (2007b) The Prosecutor v. Wenceslas Munyeshyaka, Decision on the Prosecutor's Request for the Referral of Wenceslas Munyeshyaka's Indictment to France, ICTR-2005-87-I, http://

[197] ICC (2013).

www.worldcourts.com/ictr/eng/decisions/2007.11.20_Prosecutor_v_Munyeshaka.htm. Accessed 8 June 2023

ICTY (1995) Decision on the Defence Motion For Interlocutory Appeal On Jurisdiction, para 18, https://www.icty.org/x/cases/tadic/acdec/en/51002.htm. Accessed 8 June 2023

ICTY (1999) The Prosecutor v. Duško Tadić, Judgement, IT-94-1-A, http://www.icty.org/x/cases/tadic/acjug/en/tad-aj990715e.pdf. Accessed 8 June 2023

International Centre for Settlement of Investment Disputes (2000) Emilio Agustín Maffezini and The Kingdom of Spain, Case No. Arb/97/7, Decision of the Tribunal on Objections to Jurisdiction, http://www.italaw.com/cases/641. Accessed 8 June 2023

U.S. Court of Appeals for the Armed Forces (2005) United States v. Christopher P. Martinelli, 62 M.J. 52

Books

Bassiouni MC (ed) (2013) Introduction to international criminal law, 2nd edn. Nijhoff M Publishers, Leiden

Cassese A (2008) International criminal law, 2nd edn. OUP, Oxford

Contra Schabas WA (2010) The international criminal court: a commentary on the Rome Statute. Oxford University Press, New York, p 285

Dormann K et al (2010) Elements of war crimes under the Rome Statute of the international criminal court. CUP, Cambridge

Dousi E, Papatolias A (2004) The international criminal court. Athens-Thessaloniki, Sakkoulas

Glasius M (2006) The international criminal court: a global civil society achievement New York: Routledge, London

ICC (2013) Rules of Procedure and Evidence, ICC-PIDS-LT-02-002/13_Eng, 2nd edn. International Criminal Court, The Hague

Kaul HP (2002) Preconditions to the exercise of jurisdiction. In: Cassese A, Gaeta P, Jones JRWD (eds) The Rome Statute of the international criminal court: a commentary, vol I. OUP

Kirsch P & Robinson D (2002) Reaching agreement at the Rome conference. In: Antonio Cassese, Gaeta P, John RWD Jones (eds) The Rome Statute of the international criminal court: a commentary. OUP, Oxford

Kyle C, McEwan S, DeFelice J (2014) American sniper: memorial edition, 2nd edn. Harper Collins, New York

Lammers JG Preface (1998) In Herman von Hebel et al reflection on the International Criminal Court. T.M.C. Asser Press, The Hague

Lamprinidi F (year) The international criminal court: jurisdiction, role and limitations. In: Georgoulas S (ed) Criminology in Greece today. Kapsimi Athens

Lee RS (1999) The Rome conference and its contribution to international law. In: Lee RS (ed) The international criminal court: the making of the Rome Statute. Kluwer Law International, The Hague

Reydams L (2004) Universal jurisdiction: international and municipal legal perspectives. OUP, Oxford

Schabas WA (2010) The international criminal court: a commentary on the Rome Statute. Oxford University Press, New York

Simpson G (2004) Great powers and outlaw states. CUP, Cambridge

Tsilonis V (2010) Thomas Lubanga Dyilo: the unstable step of the International Criminal Court. In: Pitsela A (ed) Criminological quests: honorary volume for Professor Stergios Alexiadis, Sakkoulas Thessaloniki

Tsilonis V (2016) International Criminal Justice during the first half of the 20th Century] in Essays in Honour of Christophoros D. Argiropoulos, Criminal Law Practitioners' Association - Nomiki Bibliothiki, Athens

Williams S (1999) Article 12. In: Triffterer O (ed) Commentary on the Rome Statute of the International Criminal Court, Baden-Baden

Articles/Papers

Ambos K (2014) Palestine, UN Non-Member Observer Status and ICC Jurisdiction, Expert Statement Given at the 'Roundtable on Legal Aspects of the Question of Palestine Convened by the Committee on the Exercise of the Inalienable Rights of the Palestinian People. UNOG 24-25. https://www.ejiltalk.org/palestine-un-non-member-observer-status-and-icc-jurisdiction. Accessed 8 June 2023

Ambos K. The first confirmation decision of the International Criminal Court: Prosecutor v. Thomas Lubanga Dyilo https://papers.ssrn.com/sol3/papers.cfm?abstract_id=1972149. Accessed 8 June 2023

Azarov V, Meloni C (2014) Disentangling the Knots: A Comment on Ambos' 'Palestine, 'Non-Member Observer' Status and ICC Jurisdiction'. https://www.ejiltalk.org/disentangling-the-knots-a-comment-on-ambos-palestine-non-member-observer-status-and-icc-jurisdiction last accessed 8 June 2023

Ballas I (2010) The lack of investigation and punishment of torture in Israel. Intellectum 36 http://www.intellectum.org/articles/issues/intellectum7/en/Irit%20Ballas_The%20lack%20of%20investigation%20of%20torture%20in%20Israel_Intellectum7.pdf. Accessed 8 June 2023

Bekou O (2008) Prosecutor v. Thomas Lubanga Dyilo, Decision on the confirmation of charges. Human Rights Law Rev 8:343

Blakesley CL, Stigall DE (2007) The Myopia of U.S. v. Martinelli: extraterritorial Jurisdiction in the 21st century. Georgetown J Int Law Rev 39:1

Cassese A (1999) The statute of the international criminal court: some preliminary reflection. Eur J Int Law 10:144–171

Colangelo AJ (2009) Double jeopardy and multiple sovereigns: a jurisdictional theory. Wash Univ Law Rev 86

Condorelli L (1999) La Cour Penale Internationale: Un Pas de Geant (Pourvu Qu'il Soit Accompli...). Revue Générale de Droit International Public 103

Dana S (2009) Beyond retroactivity to realizing justice: a theory on the principle of legality in international criminal law sentencing. J Crim Law Criminol 99(4):857

Deen-Racsmány Z (2001) The nationality of the offender and the jurisdiction of the international criminal court. Am J Int Law 95:606, 611

Dupuy PM (2002) L' unité de l' ordre juridique international: cours general de droit international publique. In: Collected Courses of the Hague Academy of International Law vol. 297, Martinus Nijhoff Publishers

Erlanger S (2009) Israel Declares Cease-Fire; Hamas Says It Will Fight On. The New York Times http://www.nytimes.com/2009/01/18/world/middleeast/18mideast.html?hp. Accessed 8 June 2023

Escritt T, Williams D (2015) Israel Lobbies Foreign Powers to Cut ICC Funding, Reuters https://www.reuters.com/article/us-icc-palestinians-israel/israel-lobbies-foreign-powers-to-cut-icc-funding-idUSKBN0KR06720150118. Accessed 8 June 2023

Forteau M (2007) L'État selon le droit International: une figure à géométrie variable? RGDIP 4:737, 762–763

Gagas D (1999) Definitions of the International Criminal Court's Crimes and the Extent of its Jurisdiction. Poiniki Dikaiosini 5

I24news (2015) Vatican upgrades recognition of 'Palestinian state' in new treaty. https://archive.is/20150801162137/http://www.i24news.tv/en/news/israel/politics/71034-150513-netanyahu-government-says-wants-peace-with-palestinians. Accessed 8 June 2023

Ibrahim YM (1988) P.L.O. Proclaims Palestine to Be an Independent State; Hints at Recognizing Israel The New York Times. https://www.nytimes.com/1988/11/15/world/plo-proclaims-palestine-to-be-an-independent-state-hints-at-recognizing-israel.html. Accessed 8 June 2023

ICC Report (2014a) on Preliminary Examination Activities 2014. https://www.icc-cpi.int/iccdocs/otp/OTP-Pre-Exam-2014.pdf. Accessed 8 June 2023

ICC Report (2014b) Situation on Registered Vessels of Comoros. Greece and Cambodia Article 53(1) http://www.icc-cpi.int/iccdocs/otp/OTP-COM-Article_53%281%29-Report-06Nov2014Eng.pdf. Accessed 8 June 2023

Ireland-Piper D. Extraterritorial criminal jurisdiction: does the long arm of the law undermine the rule of law? Melbourne Law School Publications https://law.unimelb.edu.au/__data/assets/pdf_file/0007/1687246/Ireland-Piper.pdf. Accessed 8 June 2023

Israel Threatens to Liquidate International Criminal Court (ICC) (2018) Veterans Today https://www.veteranstoday.com/2015/01/16/israel-threatens-liquidate-international-criminal-court-icc/. Accessed 8 June 2023

Kirsch P (2007) The role of international criminal court in enforcing international criminal court. Am Univ Int Law Rev 22:541

Kirsch P, Holmes JT (1999) The Rome conference on an International Criminal Court: the negotiating process. Am J Int Law 93(2):4

Kramer (2014) T Brother's Keeper' Operation Divides Palestinians, Deutsche Welle. https://www.dw.com/en/brothers-keeper-operation-divides-palestinians/a-17728780. Accessed 8 June 2023

Lichfield J (2015) Paris attacks: Ahmed Almuhamed's passport may have been planted by terrorists. The Independent. http://www.independent.co.uk/news/world/europe/paris-terror-attacks-ahmed-almuhameds-passport-may-have-been-planted-byterrorists-a6735476.html. Accessed 8 June 2023

Luhn A (2015) Crimea declares state of emergency after power lines attacked. The Guardian. https://www.theguardian.com/world/2015/nov/22/crimea-state-of-emergency-power-lines-attacked. Accessed 8 June 2023

Mendes E.. Statehood and Palestine for the Purposes of Article 12(3) of the ICC Statute: a Contrary Perspective UCLA Forum 44. http://uclalawforum.com/media/background/gaza/2010-03-30_Mendes-Memo.pdf. Accessed 8 June 2023

Milanovics M (2010) The territorial scope of the Rome Statute. EJIL http://www.ejiltalk.org/the-territorial-scope-of-the-rome-statute. Accessed 8 June 2023

Patel M, Watson O, Parker Br (2015) Operation protective edge: a war waged on Gaza's children. Defence for Children International Palestine https://issuu.com/dcips/docs/ope.awarwagedonchildren.160415. Accessed 8 June 2023

Pellet A (2010a) The Palestinian Declaration and the Jurisdiction of the International Criminal Court. J Int Crim Just 8

Power S (2009) Re-engaging the Gaza Debate: the impact of operation cast lead. Intellectum Journal. http://www.intellectum.org/articles/issues/intellectum6/en/ITL06p033045_Re-engaging%20the%20Gaza%20Debate%20%20the%20Impact%20of%20Operation%20Cast%20Lead_Susan%20Rose%20Power.pdf. Accessed 8 June 2023

Rastan R (2008) What is a 'Case' for the purpose of the Rome Statute? Crim Law Forum 19: 435, 438

Redress-FIDH (2010) Extraterritorial Jurisdiction in the European Union: A Study of the Laws and Practice in the 27 Member States of the European Union

Report (2000) of the Preparatory Commission for the International Criminal Court, Finalized Draft Text of the Rules of Procedure and Evidence. PCNICC/2000/1/Add.1 https://www.legal-tools.org/doc/1a75a9/pdf/. Accessed 8 June 2023

Richemond-Barak D (2015) Doubly Duty at the ICC. EJIL Analysis. https://www.ejiltalk.org/double-duty-at-the-icc/. Accessed 8 June 2023

Ronen Y (2010) ICC Jurisdiction over Acts Committed in the Gaza Strip: Article 12(3) of the ICC Statute and Non-state Entities. JICJ 8:3

Ronen Y (2014) Israel, palestine and the ICC: territory uncharted but not unknown. JICJ 12

Rothman L (2015) Why US Controls Guantanamo Bay. The Times London. http://time.com/3672066/guantanamo-bay-history/. Accessed 8 June 2023

Schabas W (2010b) Territorial Declarations and the Rome Statute. (PhD Studies). http://humanrightsdoctorate.blogspot.com/2010/08/territorial-declarations-and-rome.html. Accessed 8 June 2023

Shany Y (2010) In defence of functional interpretation of Article 12(3) of the Rome Statute: a response to Yael Ronen. JICJ 8:329

Simeonidou-Kastanidou E (2003) The legal basis and the limits of the international criminal court's jurisdiction. Nomiko Vima 51(3):402

The Preparatory Committee on the Establishment of an International Criminal Court (1998) Report, A/CONF.183/2/Add.1, Available at https://undocs.org/A/CONF.183/2/Add.1

Tomuschat C (2008) Uniting for Peace, UN Audiovisual Library of International Law. http://legal.un.org/avl/pdf/ha/ufp/ufp_e.pdf. Accessed 8 June 2023

United Nations Fact Finding Mission on the Gaza Conflict (2009) Human Rights in Palestine and Other Occupied Arab Territories. Report. https://www.un.org/ruleoflaw/blog/document/human-rights-in-palestine-and-other-occupied-arab-territories-report-of-the-united-nations-fact-finding-mission-on-the-gaza-conflict/. Accessed 8 June 2023

Vagias M (2011) The territorial jurisdiction of the international criminal court: certain contested issues (PhD Thesis). Bynkershoek Publishing, Amsterdam

Wedgwood R (1999) The international criminal court: an American view. EJIL 10(93):102–103

Zeidy E (2002) The principle of complementarity: a new machinery to implement international criminal law. MJIL 23:869, 919

Zerk JA (2010) Extraterritorial Jurisdiction: Lessons for the Business and Human Rights Sphere from Six Regulatory Areas, Working Paper No 59, Harvard Corporate Social Responsibility Initiative. https://www.hks.harvard.edu/sites/default/files/centers/mrcbg/programs/cri/files/workingpaper_59_zerk.pdf. Accessed 8 June 2023

Zimmermann A (2013) Palestine and the International Criminal Court Quo Vadis. JICL 11:303

Websites/Web Sources

Agreement establishing the World Trade Organisation. https://www.wto.org/english/docs_e/legal_e/04-wto.pdf. Accessed 8 June 2023

Annex I (B) (1998) Final Act of the United Nations Diplomatic Conference of Plenipotentiaries on the Establishment of an International Criminal Court (U.N. Doc. A/CONF.183/13) http://legal.un.org/icc/rome/proceedings/E/Rome%20Proceedings_v1_e.pdf. Accessed 8 June 2023

BBC News (2009a) Hamas announces ceasefire in Gaza. http://news.bbc.co.uk/2/hi/7836205.stm. Accessed 8 June 2023

BBC News (2009b) Q&A: Gaza conflict. http://news.bbc.co.uk/2/hi/middle_east/7818022.stm. Accessed 8 June 2023

Circular of the Ministry of State, Φ.82215/18303 [in Greek]

Convention (1951) and Protocol Relating to the Status of Refugees. http://www.unhcr.org/3b66c2aa10. Accessed 8 June 2023

Convention (1954) relating to the Status of Stateless Persons. http://www.unhcr.org/ibelong/wp-content/uploads/1954-Convention-relating-to-the-Status-of-Stateless-Persons_ENG.pdf. Accessed 8 June 2023

Convention (1961) on the Reduction of Statelessness. http://www.unhcr.org/ibelong/wp-content/uploads/1961-Convention-on-the-reduction-of-Statelessness_ENG.pdf. Accessed 8 June 2023

Convention on International Liability for Damage Caused by Space Objects. https://www.faa.gov/about/office_org/headquarters_offices/ast/media/Conv_International_Liab_Damage.pdf. Accessed 8 June 2023

Convention on the Rights of Persons with Disabilities. https://www.un.org/development/desa/disabilities/convention-on-the-rights-of-persons-with-disabilities/convention-on-the-rights-of-persons-with-disabilities-2.html. Accessed 8 June 2023

Decision (2011) Pursuant to Article 15 of the Rome Statute on the Authorisation of an Investigation into the Situation in the Republic of Côte d'Ivoire, ICC-02/11-14 73 para 180 https://www.legal-tools.org/doc/7a6c19/pdf/. Accessed 8 June 2023

Declaration (2014) Accepting the Jurisdiction of the International Criminal Court. https://www.icc-cpi.int/iccdocs/PIDS/press/Palestine_A_12-3.pdf. Accessed 8 June 2023

ECJ (2002) Advocate General Opinion, C-482/99 *France v. European Commmission* ECR I-04397 para 56.

Encyclopedia BRITRANNICA (year) Term Adolf Eichmann., https://www.britannica.com/biography/Adolf-Eichmann. Accessed 8 June 2023

Encyclopedia BRITRANNICA (year) Term Six-Day War. https://www.britannica.com/event/Six-Day-War. Accessed 8 June 2023

Greek Asylum Service. http://asylo.gov.gr/en/. Accessed 8 June 2023

ICC (2015a) Palestine declares acceptance of ICC jurisdiction since 13 June 2014, ICC-CPI-20150105-PR1080. https://www.icc-cpi.int//Pages/item.aspx?name=pr1080. Accessed 8 June 2023

ICC (2015b) The Prosecutor of the International Criminal Court, Fatou Bensouda, opens a preliminary examination of the situation in Palestine. https://www.icc-cpi.int//Pages/item.aspx?name=pr1083. Accessed 8 June 2023

ICC (2015c) The State of Palestine accedes to the Rome Statute. https://www.icc-cpi.int//Pages/item.aspx?name=pr1082_2. Accessed 8 June 2023

ICC Registrar (2009) Letter to the Palestinian National Authority 2009/404/SA/LASS, https://www.icc-cpi.int/NR/rdonlyres/74EEE201-0FED-4481-95D4-C8071087102C/279778/20090123404SALASS2.pdf. Accessed 8 June 2023

ICJ (1927) The Case of the S.S. Lotus, Series-A.- No. 10 https://www.icj-cij.org/files/permanent-court-of-international-justice/serie_A/A_10/30_Lotus_Arret.pdf. Accessed 8 June 2023

ICJ (1949) Reparation for Injuries Suffered in the Service of the United Nations, Advisory Opinion, Reports

ICJ (2010) Accordance with International Law of the Unilateral Declaration of Independence in Respect of Kosovo, Advisory Opinion

ICJ Dissenting Opinion of Judge Van den Wyngaert. https://www.icj-cij.org/files/case-related/121/121-20020214-JUD-01-09-EN.pdf. Accessed 8 June 2023

List of the States Parties to the Rome Statute. https://asp.icc-cpi.int/en_menus/asp/states%20parties/Pages/the%20states%20parties%20to%20the%20rome%20statute.aspx. Accessed 8 June 2023

Official UNESCO World Heritage List. http://whc.unesco.org/en/list/?delisted=1. Accessed 8 June 2023

OTP Response to Communications Received Concerning Iraq. https://www.icc-cpi.int/NR/rdonlyres/04D143C8-19FB-466C-AB77-4CDB2FDEBEF7/143682/OTP_letter_to_senders_re_Iraq_9_February_2006.pdf. Accessed 8 June 2023

OTP Response to Communications Received Concerning Venezuela. https://www.icc-cpi.int/NR/rdonlyres/4E2BC725-6A63-40B8-8CDC-ADBA7BCAA91F/143684/OTP_letter_to_senders_re_Venezuela_9_February_2006.pdf. Accessed 8 June 2023

Palestinian National Authority (2009) Ministry of Justice, Declaration recognising the Jurisdiction of the International Criminal Court. https://www.icc-cpi.int/NR/rdonlyres/74EEE201-0FED-4481-95D4-C8071087102C/279777/20090122PalestinianDeclaration2.pdf. Accessed 8 June 2023

Pellet A (2010b) The Effects of Palestine's Recognition of the International Criminal Court's Jurisdiction. https://www.icc-cpi.int/NR/rdonlyres/D3C77FA6-9DEE-45B1-ACC0-B41706BB41E5/281927/PelletENGCLEAN1.pdf. Accessed 8 June 2023

Permanent Observer Mission of the State of Palestine to the UN. https://www.ungeneva.org/en/blue-book/missions/non-member-states/state-palestine. Accessed 8 June 2023

Proposal (1998) Submitted by the United States of America (U.N. Doc. A/CONF.183/C.1/L.70). http://legal.un.org/docs/?path=../diplomaticconferences/1998_icc/docs/english/vol_2/a_conf183_c1_sr1.pdf&lang=EF. Accessed 8 June 2023

Republic of Korea (1998) Proposal regarding articles 6 [9], 7 [6], UN Doc.A/CONF.183/C.1/L.6, 227-229. http://legal.un.org/icc/rome/proceedings/E/Rome%20Proceedings_v3_e.pdf. Accessed 8 June 2023

The archives of the Israeli Ministry of Foreign Affairs regarding the notorious "Disengagement Plan. https://mfa.gov.il/mfa/foreignpolicy/peace/guide/pages/israeli%20disengagement%20plan%2020-jan-2005.aspx. Accessed 8 June 2023

The Israeli-Palestinian Interim Agreement "Oslo II". https://www.jewishvirtuallibrary.org/jsource/Peace/interimtoc.html. Accessed 8 June 2023

The Israeli-Palestinian Interim Agreement on the West Bank and the Gaza Strip, Annex IV: Protocol Concerning Legal Affairs. https://www.jewishvirtuallibrary.org/jsource/Peace/iaannex4.html. Accessed 8 June 2023

UCLA forum. http://uclalawforum.com/gaza. Accessed 8 June 2023

UN Security Council Resolution (1992) 780/1992, S/RES/780 https://www.nato.int/ifor/un/u921006b.htm Accessed 8 June 2023

UN Security Council Resolution (1994) 955/1994, S/RES/955 http://unscr.com/en/resolutions/doc/955. Accessed 8 June 2023

UNGA (1950) Resolution 377A (V) Uniting for Peace. http://www.un.org/en/sc/repertoire/otherdocs/GAres377A(v).pdf. Accessed 8 June 2023

UNGA (2012) A/RES/67/19 Status of Palestine in the United Nations https://unispal.un.org/DPA/DPR/unispal.nsf/0/19862D03C564FA2C85257ACB004EE69B. Accessed 8 June 2023

UNHR Resolution A/HRC/RES/S-9/1 (2009). https://unispal.un.org/DPA/DPR/unispal.nsf/0/404E93E166533F828525754E00559E30. Accessed 8 June 2023

United Nations. https://www.un.org/press/en/2012/ga11317.doc.htm. Accessed 8 June 2023

United Nations Diplomatic Conference of Plenipotentiaries on the Establishment of an International Criminal Court (1998) UN Doc. A/CONF.183/SR.9, 122, par. 15. http://legal.un.org/icc/rome/proceedings/E/Rome%20Proceedings_v2_e.pdf. Accessed 8 June 2023

US Department of State., The United States, Cuba, and the Platt Amendment, 1901, Office of the Historian. https://2001-2009.state.gov/r/pa/ho/time/ip/86557.htm. Accessed 8 June 2023

World Population Review., Age of Consent by Country 2019 http://worldpopulationreview.com/countries/countries-by-age-of-consent/. Accessed 8 June 2023

Εγκύκλιος του Υπουργείου Εσωτερικών (2013) Φ.82215/18303, Παροχή διευκρινίσεων σχετικά με τον εννοιολογικό προσδιορισμό των όρων «ιθαγένεια», «υπηκοότητα» και «εθνικότητα» http://www.ypes.gr/UserFiles/f0ff9297-f516-40ff-a70eeca84e2ec9b9/eggr_f_82215_090713.pdf, Accessed 8 June 2023

Chapter 3
The Crime of Genocide and the International Criminal Court's Jurisdiction

Abstract Article 6 ICCRSt refers to the "crime of all crimes," namely, genocide. This term was first coined by Polish-Jewish lawyer Raphael Lemkin and subsequently utilised *inter alia* in the jurisprudence of the ICC, ICTY, and ICTR. Despite the international community's commitment to prevent genocide and punish those responsible, multiple instances of genocide have transpired in Asia, Africa, and Europe. Millions of individuals have been slaughtered primarily due to their perceived group identity—be it national, ethnic, racial, religious, or political.

It is significant to note that during the twentieth century, a period marked by unparalleled human evolution, the crime of genocide occurred at least five times: the Pontian Greek and Armenian genocides perpetrated by the Turks, the Jewish and Romani genocides committed by the Nazis during World War II, the Cambodian genocide by Pol Pot's notorious Khmer Rouge regime in the 1970's, the Tutsi genocide in Rwanda by the Hutu in the 1990's, and the Bosnian genocide in which over 8000 people were massacred in Srebrenica by Bosnian Serb forces, arguably the worst atrocity in Europe since World War II.

Furthermore, five additional cases of potential genocide are currently under scrutiny: (1) the Rohingya in Myanmar, a situation under investigation by the ICC (refer to further analysis below), (2) the Nuer and other ethnic groups in South Sudan, (3) the Assyrian Christians and Yazidis in Iraq and Syria, (4) the "anti-Balaka" Christian militias and the Muslim coalition in the Central African Republic, (5) the Darfuris in Sudan.

This chapter focuses on the *mens rea*, i.e., the subjective element, of the crime of genocide and explores the relationship between the prerequisite criterion of "intent and knowledge" in Art. 30(1) ICCRSt and that of the distinct threshold regarding "intent to destroy" in Art. 6 ICCRSt. Furthermore, it critically analyses the four main interpretative approaches that have emerged concerning what it means to destroy a group "in part," beyond the apparent requirement that the destruction must be of substantial magnitude. Lastly, the chapter highlights the promising developments in combating genocide and ICC Chief Prosecutor Fatou Bensouda's innovative legal interpretation of the alleged genocide of the Rohingya in Myanmar, a perspective that is clearly influenced by Michail Vagias's theoretical analysis.

V. Tsilonis, *The Jurisdiction of the International Criminal Court*,
https://doi.org/10.1007/978-3-031-46138-5_3

3.1 The Definition of the Crime of Genocide

Article 6 ICCRSt refers to the "crime of all crimes", *i.e.* to the crime of genocide. This was the term first used in the work of the Polish-Jewish lawyer Raphael Lemkin,[1] and later appeared in the ICC, ICTY and ICTR jurisprudence.[2] However, despite the international community's commitment to prevent genocide and punish its perpetrators, several cases of genocide occurred subsequently in Asia, Africa and Europe. Consequently, millions of people have been murdered solely or primarily on account of their perceived group identity—national, ethnic, racial, religious or political.

In fact, it is noteworthy that the twentieth century, a period marked by an unprecedented level of human progress, was paradoxically marred by the occurrence of the crime of genocide at least five times. These include: the Pontian Greek and Armenian genocide perpetrated by the Turks from 1914 to 1923; the Jewish and Roma genocide orchestrated by the Nazis from 1941 to 1945; the Cambodian genocide executed by Pol Pot's notorious Khmer Rouge regime from 1975 to 1979; the Tutsi genocide in Rwanda committed by the Hutu in 1994; and the Bosnian Muslim/Bosnian Croats genocide where approximately 8000 people were massacred in Srebrenica by the Bosnian Serbs in July 1995, arguably the worst atrocity committed in Europe since World War II.[3]

Moreover, there currently exist five more cases of potential genocidal nature: (1) the Rohingya in Myanmar, a case which is currently under investigation by ICC (see further analysis below) (2) the Nuer and other ethnic groups in South Sudan[4] (3) the Assyrian Christians and Yazidis in Iraq and Syria[5] (4) the Christian militias called "anti-Balaka" and the Muslim coalition in the Central African Republic

[1] Lemkin (1944). An unconventional biography of Lemkin can be found at Sands (2016).

[2] Armed Activities on the Territory of the Congo (New Application: 2000); Democratic Republic of the Congo v. Rwanda (2006), para 26. Kambanda (ICTR-97-23-S); Krstic (IT-98-33-T), Decision (2001a), para 699; ICTY (2001a), para 2; Niyitegeka (ICTR-96-14-A), Decision (2004), para 5.

[3] Tsilonis V, Ibid.., p 128; Schabas (2000), p 12; IT, ICTY (2017), pp. 1597, 1805, 1807-1808, 2465, 2474, http://www.icty.org/case/mladic/4, last accessed 8 June 2023.

[4] Biryabarema (2017), https://www.reuters.com/article/us-southsudan-war/uk-says-killings-in-south-sudan-conflict-amount-to-genocide-idUSKBN17E2TF, last accessed 8 June 2023. Britain's secretary for international development Priti Patel stated *inter alia*: "There are massacres taking place, people's throats are being slit[. . .] villages are being burnt out, there's a scorched-earth policy [. . .] It is tribal, it is absolutely tribal, so on that basis it is genocide."

[5] "Condemning the commission of acts by ISIL (Da'esh) involving murder, kidnapping, hostage-taking, suicide bombings, enslavement, sale into or otherwise forced marriage, trafficking in persons, rape, sexual slavery and other forms of sexual violence, recruitment and use of children, attacks on critical infrastructure, as well as its destruction of cultural heritage, including archaeological sites[...] *Further recognizing* that the commission of such acts which may amount to war crimes, crimes against humanity or genocide, is part of the ideology and strategic objectives of ISIL (Da'esh), and used by ISIL (Da'esh) as a tactic of terrorism[. . .]" Security Council Resolution 2379 (2017), https://undocs.org/en/S/RES/2379(2017), last accessed 8 June 2023. See also First report of the Special Adviser and Head of the United Nations Investigative Team to Promote Accountability

(where it seems that the role of victims and offenders for both side coincide)[6] (5) the Darfuris in Sudan.[7,8]

Just six years after Robert Jackson's Report to the London Conference in 1945,[9] the UN General Assembly adopted Resolution 96(I) in January 1951 and the first international human rights protection treaty within the UN framework entered into force: the Convention on the Prevention and Punishment of the Crime of Genocide.[10] Furthermore, the crime of genocide could not be omitted from the "Draft Code of Offences against the Peace and Security of Mankind",[11] albeit a document that was put on ice indefinitely after 1954.[12] Following the end of the Cold War, the matter of adopting an international convention dealing with crimes against humanity returned to the spotlight. The question of the crime of genocide also arose in this context, despite the 1951 Genocide Convention already having come into force. As early as 1992, the International Law Commission's working group expressed the opinion that genocide should definitely be included in a new international convention,[13] an opinion it retained in the years that followed.[14]

Even though Article 2 of the Genocide Convention included a definition of this crime that was already internationally accepted and had been used by the UN Security Council for the establishment of the international criminal tribunals for the former Yugoslavia and Rwanda (Article 4 ICTY Statute and Article 2 ICTR Statute), it was suggested that this definition could be expanded to encompass political and social groups too.[15] Moreover, a number of delegations maintained that there should be some differentiation regarding the intent requirement, depending on who the alleged perpetrator was: specific intent for those in charge, i.e. those

for Crimes Committed by Da'esh/Islamic State in Iraq and the Levant, S/2018/1031, 16 November 2018, https://digitallibrary.un.org/record/1653330, last accessed 8 June 2023.

[6] Sanders (2017).

[7] See indicatively Power (2014).

[8] Granz 2017).

[9] Jackson (1949), p. 68.

[10] Pursuant to Article XIII of the UNGA Resolution 260 A(III) of 1948, the Genocide Convention came into force on the 12th of January 1951. See United Nations, Treaty Series no 1021 Vol 78, 727.

[11] Draft Code of Offences against the Peace and Security of Mankind (1954).

[12] Draft Code of the Offences Against Peace and the Security of Mankind 1951, Yearbook of the International Law Commission 1951, https://legal.un.org/ilc/texts/instruments/english/commentaries/7_3_1954.pdf, last accessed 8 June 2023 and UNGA Resolution 898 4 December 1954, https://legal.un.org/ilc/texts/instruments/english/draft_articles/7_3_1954.pdf, last accessed 8 June 2023.

[13] ILC Yearbook (1992).

[14] ILC Final Report (1994), p 38. ILC Working Group Report, (1993), p 106.

[15] Report of the ad hoc Committee on the Establishment of an International Criminal Court, No. 22 (A/50/22) (1995) para 60–61, http://www.legal-tools.org/uploads/tx_ltpdb/doc21168.pdf, last accessed 8 June 2023.

making the decisions and plans; and general intent or knowledge for the actual perpetrators of genocidal acts.[16]

Other state delegations made an equally convincing case that the crime of genocide, as defined in the Genocide Convention, reflected customary international law and had already been integrated into the national legal order of many States, while "providing for different definitions of the crime of genocide in the Convention and in the statute could result in the International Court of Justice and the international criminal court rendering conflicting decisions with respect to the same situation under the two respective instruments".[17]

In 1997, the Preparatory Committee[18] chose to reproduce the provision of Article 2 of the Genocide Convention, while it wavered as to whether Article 3 of the Genocide Convention, then included in the draft but within brackets, should be included in the Rome Statute after all.[19] Finally, during the Rome Diplomatic Conference, there was no further discussion about the crime of genocide, as the Organising Committee recommended only the adoption of the definition of Article 2 of the Genocide Convention and all delegations accepted this recommendation,[20]

---

[16] Ibid., para 62.

[17] Ibid., para 61. Certainly, at the time, most of the delegation members were aware of the pending trial before the ICC pursuant to Article IX of the Genocide Convention: Application of the Convention on the Prevention and Punishment of the Crime of Genocide Bosnia and Herzegovina v. Yugoslavia (Serbia and Montenegro) 20 March 1993.

[18] Preparatory Committee (1997), p. 2; Preparatory Committee on The Establishment of An International Criminal Court, Decisions Taken by The Preparatory Committee at its Session Held from 11 to 21 February 1997 A/AC.249/1997/L.52, file:///C:/Users/tsilo/Downloads/A_AC.249_1997_L.5-EN.pdf, last accessed 8 June 2023.

[19] Article III Genocide Convention - The following acts shall be punishable: (a) Genocide; (b) Conspiracy to commit genocide; (c) Direct and public incitement to commit genocide; (d) Attempt to commit genocide; (e) Complicity in genocide.

[20] *Ibid.*, para 2-18 Mr. Van der Wind (the Netherlands) acting as Coordinator, para 19 & 174 the Chairman, para 20 Mr. Kaul (Germany), para 22 Mr. Shukri (Syria), para 24 Mr. Al Awadi (United Arab Emirates), para 26. Mr. Khalid Bin All Abdullah Al-Khalifa (Bahrain), para 28. Mr. Sadi (Jordan), para 29 Mr. Hamdan (Lebanon), para 30. Mr. Dive (Belgium), para 31 Mr. Madani (Saudi Arabia), para 33 Mr. Dhanbri (Tunisia), para 35 Mr. Janda (the Czech Republic), para 44 Mr. S. R. Rao (India), para 49. Mr. Vergne Saboia (Brasil), para 54 Mr. Skibsted (Denmark), para 57 Mr. Mochochoko (Lesotho), para 59 Ms. Daskalopoulou-Livada (Greece), para 64. Mr. Nyasulu (Malawi), para 67 Mr. Fadl (Sudan), para 72 Ms. Li Yanduan (China), para 76. Mr. Choi Tae-hyun (Korea), para 80 Ms. Frankowska (Poland), παρ. 84 Ms. Chatoor (Trinidad and Tobago), para 85 Mr. Al-Humaimidi (Iraq), para 107 Mr. Niyomrerks (Thailand), para 111 Mr. Stigen (Norway), para 113 Mr. Koffi (Ivory Coast), para 116 Mr. de Klerk (South Africa), para 119 Ms. Mekhemar (Egypt), para 121 Mr. Mahmood (Pakistan), para 123 Ms. Flores (Mexico), para 127 Ms. Shahen (Libya), para 132. Ms. Vargas (Colombia), para 135 Mr. Shariat Bagheri (Iran), para 137 Ms. Borek (USA), para 141 Mr. Hersi (Djibouti), para 143 Mr. Effendi (Indonesia), para 145 Mr. Garcia Labajo (Spain), para 150 Mr. Ivan (Romania), para 151 Ms. Diop (Senegal), para 153 Mr. Palihakkara (Sri Lanka), para 157 Mr. Rodriguez Cedeno (Venezuela), para 161 Mr. Politi (Italy), para 166 Ms. Connelly (Irland), para 171 Mr. Guney (Turkey).

save for the Cuban one which insisted on including social and political groups.[21] Thus an historic opportunity to wisely broaden the definition of this crime was missed, in spite of the voices of world-renowned academics who supported such a move.[22] Consequently, the ICC's jurisdiction over the crime of genocide is indissolubly connected with the academic discussion and jurisprudence of international criminal tribunals which refer to the same definition and the same preconditions of exercising jurisdiction.

3.2 Genocide as a Crime Under the Jurisdiction of the International Criminal Court (Article 6 ICCRSt)

Article 6: Genocide

For the purpose of this Statute, "genocide" means any of the following acts committed with intent to destroy, in whole or in part, a national, ethnical, racial or religious group, as such:

(1) *Killing members of the group;*
(2) *Causing serious bodily or mental harm to members of the group;*
(3) *Deliberately inflicting on the group conditions of life calculated to bring about its physical destruction in whole or in part;*
(4) *Imposing measures intended to prevent births within the group;*
(5) *Forcibly transferring children of the group to another group.*

Undoubtedly, genocide is one of the most heinous crimes. Its unceasing commission during the course of written human history led the participant states at the Rome Conference of 1998 to include it under the ICC's jurisdiction at a time when the memory of the genocide against Jews, Roma and other minorities by the Germans during World War II remained a key subject of public debate, including amongst survivors of the concentration camps and their families.

Currently in order for a crime to be classified as genocide and to fall under the ICC's jurisdiction, it must be proven that it meets all constituent elements and the *mens rea* of Article 6 ICCRSt. In this matter, however, it appears that the crime of genocide under Article 6 ICCRSt presents an important particularity, since the very act of interpreting this crime requires an indirect but clear exemption to the provision of Article 21(1)(b) ICCRSt, which explicitly stipulates that applicable treaties and the principles and rules of international law, including the established principles of the international law of armed conflict, are secondary to the ICCRSt. This is because,

---

[21] United Nations Diplomatic Conference of Plenipotentiaries on the Establishment of an International Criminal Court Official Records: Summary records of the plenary meetings and of the meetings of the Committee of the Whole, Third Meeting A/CONF.183/C.1/SR.3 para 100, http://legal.un.org/icc/rome/proceedings /E/Rome%20Proceedings_v2_e.pdf, last accessed 8 June 2023.

[22] Bassiouni (2005), p. 92 fn 208.

in order to correctly interpret the provision of Article 6 on the crime of genocide, it is necessary to first analyse other provisions of the Genocide Convention, as well as other sources of international law,[23] such as the relevant ICJ,[24] ICTY and ICTR[25] jurisprudence.

Admittedly, the working group responsible for drawing up an early draft of the Rome Statute (ICCRSt) had already noted in February 1997 in the official records of its meetings that Article 1 of the Genocide Convention, for instance, would essentially provide the basis in future trials before the ICC for resolving questions such as whether genocide can by definition be committed only in times of war or also in times of peace.[26]

However, it must be noted that even though state delegations paid little attention to Article 6 ICCRSt, some of the problems surrounding its interpretation were thoroughly examined by the Preparatory Committee while drafting the Elements of Crimes. Understandably, this critical text includes plenty of information regarding the *mens rea* of the crime of genocide. Moreover, it places the crime of genocide in a clearly defined framework, which cannot be derived from any other ICCRSt provision.

This framework is important because Article 9(1) ICCRSt[27] explicitly stipulates that the provisions of Elements of Crimes, which had to be adopted by a two-thirds majority of state parties, were to assist the Court in the interpretation and application of Articles 6, 7 and 8, and thus in the assessment of whether a crime meets all the requirements to fall under the *ratione materiae* jurisdiction of the ICC.

Hence, with regard to the provision of Article 6(a) ICCRSt (Killing members of the group), the Elements of Crimes explicitly stipulate the following prerequisites:

---

[23] Article 21 - Applicable law: 1. The Court shall apply: [. . .] (b) In the second place, where appropriate, applicable treaties and the principles and rules of international law, including the established principles of the international law of armed conflict.

[24] For example: ICJ (1999).

[25] See the extended analysis of the jurisprudence of international criminal tribunals that follow hereafter.

[26] Decisions Taken by the Preparatory Committee at its Session Held from 11 to 21 February 1997 A/AC.249/1997/L.5, 12 March 1997, 27, ft 3, http://www.iccnow.org/documents/DecisionsTaken11to21Feb97.pdf, last accessed 8 June 2023.

[27] Article 9 ICCRSt - Elements of Crimes:

(a) Elements of Crimes shall assist the Court in the interpretation and application of articles 6, 7, 8 and 8 *bis*. They shall be adopted by a two-thirds majority of the members of the Assembly of States Parties.
(b) Amendments to the Elements of Crimes may be proposed by:
(a) Any State Party;
(b) The Judges acting by an absolute majority;
(c) The Prosecutor.

Such amendments shall be adopted by a two-thirds majority of the members of the Assembly of States Parties.

(c) The Elements of Crimes and amendments thereto shall be consistent with this Statute.

1. The perpetrator killed one or more persons.
2. Such person or persons belonged to a particular national, ethnical, racial or religious group.
3. The perpetrator intended to destroy, in whole or in part, that national, ethnical, racial or religious group, as such.
4. The conduct took place in the context of a manifest pattern of similar conduct directed against that group or was conduct that could itself effect such destruction.

3.3 The Mens Rea of the Crime of Genocide Under the Rome Statute

To begin with, it is accepted that the *mens rea* of the crime of genocide incorporates the intent to destroy, in whole or in part, a national, ethnical, racial or religious group. Thus, Article 6 ICCRSt includes a more specialised provision in comparison to that of Article 30(1) ICCRSt, which stipulates that "[u]nless otherwise provided, a person shall be criminally responsible and liable for punishment for a crime within the jurisdiction of the Court only if the material elements are committed **with intent and knowledge**".[28]

The definition of genocide provided in Article 6 ICCRSt refers to "acts committed **with intent to destroy**, in whole or in part, a national, ethnical, racial or religious group" (emphasis added). The jurisprudence shows that this is to be interpreted pursuant to Article 30 ICCRSt, including with regard to the existence of specific intent to kill members of the group, inflict serious bodily or mental harm on members of the group, inflict on the group conditions of life calculated to bring about its physical destruction in whole or in part, impose measures intended to prevent births within the group and transfer children of the group to another group.[29] Moreover, it is also to be interpreted as *dolus specialis* with regard to the purpose of the particular acts which cannot be any other but the destruction, in whole or in part, of a protected group.

Thus, in the case against president of Sudan Omar Al Bashir,[30] the ICC noted by majority that any of the aforementioned "five categories of genocidal acts provided for in Article 6 of the Statute must be carried out with 'the intent to destroy, in whole or in part, a national, ethnic, racial or religious group'".[31] Consequently, it observed that the crime of genocide is comprised of two subjective elements: "i. a general subjective element that must cover any genocidal act provided for in article 6(a) to

[28] Emphasis added.

[29] This was a suggestion of the Greek delegation which was ardently accepted and finally included in the definition of the crime of genocide. See Schabas (2009), p. 202.

[30] ICC (2009).

[31] *Ibid.* para 138.

(e) of the Statute, and which consists of article 30 intent and knowledge requirement; and ii. an additional subjective element, normally referred to as '*dolus specialis*' or specific intent, according to which any genocidal acts must be carried out with the 'intent to destroy in whole or in part' the targeted group".[32,33]

Hence, there are two special elements arising from the aforementioned definition of this particular crime's *mens rea*. Firstly, the victims must be members of a particular group (national, ethnic, racial or religious) and must be targeted because of their membership in that group. Secondly, the crimes committed must be part of an overall objective of destroying the group.[34] Only if both these elements exist can such a crime be considered genocide and fall under the ICC's jurisdiction pursuant to Article 6 ICCRSt.

3.3.1 The Intent to Destroy, in Whole or in Part, a National, Ethnic, Racial or Religious Group

Pursuant to Article 6 ICCRSt, genocide may be committed exclusively against any of the four listed groups. National, ethnic, racial and religious groups are those that are clearly protected from acts which are intended to destroy them, in whole or in part.[35] Therefore, according to the explicit wording of Article 6 ICCRSt, political,

---

[32] *Ibid.* para 139. At this point (para 140), the ICC appears to have adopted the ICJ's jurisprudence as reflected in the case of Bosnia and Herzegovina against Serbia and Montenegro, Case Concerning the Application of the Convention on the Prevention and Punishment of the Crime of Genocide, Judgment (No.91) 26 February 2007b, https://www.icj-cij.org/files/case-related/91/091-20070226-JUD-01-00-EN.pdf, last accessed 8 June 2023.

[33] In this judgment, the ICC also made a distinction between the *dolus spedalis* required for the crime of genocide and the *dolus specialis* required for the crime of "persecution (persecutory intent consisting of the intent to discriminate on political, racial, national, ethnic, cultural, religious, gender, or other grounds that are universally recognised as impermissible under international law, against the members of a group, by reason of the identity of the group)", the latter being one of the crimes against humanity listed in Article 7 ICCRSt. In this too, the ICC followed the jurisprudence of the ICJ in the case of *Bosnia and Herzegovina v. Serbia and Montenegro*, as well as that of the ICTY, principally in the case *Kupreškić skic et al*, IT-95-16-T, Judgment of 14 January 2000 para 636, as well as in the cases, Case No. IT-95-10-T, Trial Judgment, 14 December 1999 para 66, 79 and *The Prosecutor v. Krstić*, Case No. IT-98-33-T, Trial Judgment, 2 August 2001 para 550–552, 569, 571.

[34] ICTY (1999).

[35] The view adopted by the famous UNGA Resolution 96(I) in 1946, two years before the adoption of the Convention for the Prevention and Punishment of the Crime of Genocide, was different. This resolution referred to racial, religious, political and other groups, thus leaving a broad scope for the later inclusion of linguistic, ideological, economic, political or other groups through jurisprudence. See General Assembly Resolution 96(I), A/PV.55, 11 December 1946 http://www.un.org/ga/search/view_doc.asp?symbol=A/RES/96(I)&Lang=E&Area=RESOLUTION, last accessed 8 June 2023. The thorniest topic at the time proved to be whether or not to include political groups. Eventually, even though their inclusion was initially approved, the sixth committee of the UNGA

social and professional groups do not fall under the ICC's jurisdiction, since they are not explicitly mentioned in the text.

Admittedly, the traditional legal definition of genocide adopted in Article 6 ICCRSt can be said to fall short of subsequent and more contemporary definitions, such as the one given by Charny: "Genocide in the generic sense means the mass killing of substantial numbers of human beings, when not in the course of military action against the military forces of an avowed enemy, under conditions of the essential defencelessness of the victim."[36] Obviously, even this definition is far from perfect, since it provides a narrow focus exclusively on the instances where mass killings of people have occurred and thus excludes possible cases of mass serious injuries, tortures, exportations etc. Pieter Drost's observation provides a central insight into how such a definition is arrived at: "It does not serve any purpose to limit international protection to particular groups".[37]

Nonetheless, it cannot be easily disputed that the Rome Statute actually fills one of the most important gaps in the Article 6 ICCRSt definition of genocide through Article 7 ICCRSt, which defines crimes against humanity as "any of the following acts when committed as part of a widespread or systematic attack directed against any civilian population".[38] Moreover, Article 7(1)(h) ICCRSt lists the 'persecution' of any identifiable group or collectivity on political, racial, national, ethnic, cultural, religious, gender, or other grounds as a crime that is to be prosecuted by the ICC. In this way, some of the gaps in the ICC's jurisdiction arising from the adoption of the traditional and narrower definition of the crime of genocide are solved through the indirect adoption of wider criteria in Article 7 ICCRSt pertaining to crimes against humanity.

As far as the characteristics of the groups referred to in Article 6 ICCRSt are concerned, it is accepted that the adjectives 'racial', 'ethnic', 'national' and 'religious' are inherently unclear.[39] They have to be clarified as thoroughly as possible to determine which acts satisfy the *mens rea* of the crime of genocide and thus, fall under the ICC's jurisdiction pursuant to Article 6 ICCRSt, instead of Article 7 ICCRSt.

---

decided to remove the term following a joint intervention by Iran, Egypt and Uruguay: UN Doc. A/C.6/SR.128, http://daccess-ods.un.org/access.nsf/Get?Open&DS=A/C.6/SR.128&Lang=E, last accessed 8 June 2023.

[36] Charny (1994), p. 75.

[37] Drost (1959), pp. 122–123.

[38] Article 7(1) ICCRSt.

[39] Especially the first three, since the adjective "religious" has created in practice the less controversy and problems. See Verhoeven (1991), p. 5. Indicative of this is that, for instance, in the ICTY case *The Prosecutor v. Radislav Krstić*, the Indictment stated that the accused intended to "destroy a part of the Bosnian Muslim people as a national, ethnical, or religious group" without any further specifications. In addition, the following excerpt from the judgment of the Trial Chamber against him is also distinctive: "Originally viewed as a religious group, the Bosnian Muslims were recognised as a 'nation' by the Yugoslav Constitution of 1963." ICTY, *Prosecutor v. Radislav Krstić* (Case No. IT-98-33-T) Judgment, 2 August 2001 paras 559, http://www.icty.org/x/cases/krstic/tjug/en/krs-tj010802e.pdf, last accessed 8 June 2023.

Nonetheless, at the same time it is noteworthy that jurisprudentially this matter has often been considered by all sides as undisputed and it has thus prompted relatively little commentary. For instance, in the case of Radislav Krstić, both the Trial Chamber and the Appeal Chamber of the ICTY ruled that Bosnian Muslims essentially constituted a national group, a judicial conclusion that the defence never disputed.[40]

However, in the case of *Clément Kayishema & Obed Ruzindana*, the ICTR adopted a purely subjective criterion for the characterisation of a group of people as a national group, pointing out that a national group could *inter alia* be "a group which distinguishes itself, as such (self-identification); or, a group identified as such by others, including perpetrators of the crimes (identification by others)".[41] Although the judgment explicitly mentions that those 'others' can be the perpetrators themselves, unfortunately it does not specify any other categories of people that could constitute those 'others' as judges of whether a group can fall within the scope of the provision of Article 6 ICCRSt.

The subjective criterion for the determination of a national group was also adopted by the ICTY in the Jelisić judgment, in spite of the admission that the intent of the Genocide Convention was to determine whether there are in fact objective (rather than subjective) criteria for proving the existence of a group.[42] The ICTY's justification, which was *inter alia* based on the amended version of the Indictment of Dragan Nicolić,[43] was that "[a]lthough the objective determination of a religious group still remains possible, to attempt to define a national, ethnical or racial group today using objective and scientifically irreproachable criteria would be a perilous exercise whose result would not necessarily correspond to the perception of the persons concerned by such categorization".[44] The Court went on to express its preference for a negative approach, which "would consist of identifying individuals as not being part of the group to which the perpetrators of the crime consider that they themselves belong and which to them displays specific national, ethnical, racial or religious characteristics".[45]

Following the same subjective line, the ICTR Trial Chamber I ruled in the Bagilishema case that "if a victim was perceived by a perpetrator as belonging to a

[40] ICTY, *Prosecutor v. Radislav Krstić*, paras. 559-560; ICTY (2004b).

[41] ICTR (1999a). Indicative of the difficulty in clearly interpreting and defining the aforementioned terms is that even though the court attempted to briefly define the meaning of religious and racial group, it did not comment on the concept of national group, as well as the distinction between national and ethnic group.

[42] ICTR (2001a).

[43] ICTY, *Prosecutor v. Nicolić* aka "Jenki", 'Review of the Indictment Pursuant to Rule 61 of the Rules of Procedure and Evidence' (Case No. IT-94-1-R61) 20 October 1995 para 27.

[44] *Prosecutor v. Jelisic*, para 70.

[45] *Ibid.* para 71.

protected group, the victim could be considered by the Chamber as a member of the protected group, for the purposes of genocide".[46]

However, already in the Rutaganda case, the ICTR had pointed out that despite the lack of international unanimity as to the exact meaning of the terms national, ethnic, racial and religious group and despite the fact that each of these concepts must be individually assessed in the light of a particular political, social and cultural context,[47] "a subjective definition alone is not enough to determine victim groups, as provided for in the Genocide Convention".[48]

In the same case, the ICTR carefully studied the *travaux preparatoires* of the Genocide Convention. It made clear that certain groups, such as political and economic groups, have been excluded from the protected groups because participation in them is neither permanent nor stable. Therefore, the competent Chamber held that in assessing whether a particular group may be considered as protected from the crime of genocide, it would proceed on a case-by-case basis, "taking into account both the relevant evidence proffered and the political and cultural context as indicated *supra*".[49]

Nonetheless, 5 years after the Rutaganda judgment, ICTR Trial Chamber II made a ruling that essentially reestablished the subjective criterion. Thus, the ICTR ruled that "[i]n accordance with the jurisprudence of the Tribunal, the relevant protected group may be identified by means of the subjective criterion of the stigmatisation of the group, notably by the perpetrators of the crime, on the basis of its perceived national, ethnical, racial or religious characteristics".[50]

The ICTY Appeals Chamber in the Stakić case attempted to clarify and simultaneously limit the influence of the subjective criterion. Thus, the ICTY ruled on appeal that the Krstić and Rutaganda judgments do not suggest that target groups must be defined based solely on the subjective criterion of how perpetrators stigmatise victims, but rather that the subjective criterion is one of the criteria that must be taken into consideration by the Courts, since it is not in itself sufficient to determine which groups are actually protected by the Genocide Convention.[51] To support this conclusion, the Appeals Chamber invoked the ICTR Musema, Bagilishema and Semanza judgments.[52] What is more, the Appeals Chamber clarified that "whether or not a group is subjectively defined is not relevant to whether a group is defined in a positive or a negative way [...] Consequently, when a target

[46]ICTR (2001b). Bagilishema is one of the 12 accused before the ICTR who were acquitted of all charges.

[47]ICTR (1999b).

[48]*Ibid.* para 56.

[49]*Ibid.* para 58.

[50]ICTY (2004a), and further references to the Nikolić Rule 61 Decision para 27; Krstić Trial Judgement para 557; Jelisić Trial Judgement para 70.

[51]ICTY (2006).

[52]Musema Trial Judgement para 162; Semanza Trial Judgement para 317; Bagilishema Trial Judgement para 65.

group is defined in a negative manner (for example non-Serbs), whether the composition of the group is identified on the basis of objective criteria, or a combination of objective and subjective criteria, is immaterial as the group would not be protected under the Genocide Convention".[53]

Consequently, and according to the review of the aforementioned jurisprudence, as well as to the Brdanin and Semanza judgments,[54] it appears best to define a target group in an ad hoc manner, based on subjective as well as objective criteria. This view was followed by both parties to the "Case Concerning the Application of the Convention on the Prevention and Punishment of the Crime of Genocide" before the ICJ, who agreed that international jurisprudence accepts a hybrid subjective-objective approach, while the Court stated that "[t]he issue is not in any event significant on the facts of this case".[55] As for the ICJ's view on the matter of positive and negative approaches to the definition of a protected group: "the drafting history of the Convention confirms that a positive definition must be used [. . .] The rejection of proposals to include within the Convention political groups and cultural genocide also demonstrates that the drafters were giving close attention to the positive identification of groups with specific distinguishing well-established, some said immutable, characteristics. A negatively defined group cannot be seen in that way".[56]

Thus, according to the aforementioned review of the relevant jurisprudence,[57] the execution of a large number of people/members of a national-socialist, neo-fascist political group by anarchist perpetrators, for instance, could never be legally considered as genocide (but primarily as a crime against humanity). Furthermore, the fact that the perpetrators considered the members of the aforementioned group as members of the broader national group of Greeks is irrelevant here, as the shared national identity of the victims is not crucial to the commission of the crime on this particular occasion; the same would apply even if the perpetrators considered their victims 'non-Greeks' (for of course genuine participants in Greek culture could never be racist); this would entail a negative approach, if accepted and also be irrelevant for the legal classification of the crime.

---

[53] ICTR, *Prosecutor v. Stakić* (IT-97-24-A) Appeal Judgment 22 March 2006, para 26.

[54] ICTY, *Prosecutor v. Brdanin* (IT-99-36-T) (Judgment) 1 September 2004 para 684, http://www.icty.org/x/cases/brdanin/tjug/en/brd-tj040901e.pdf, last accessed 8 June 2023; ICTR (2003), last accessed 8 June 2023.

[55] ICJ, *Bosnia and Herzegovina v. Serbia and Montenegro*, Case Concerning the Application of the Convention on the Prevention and Punishment of the Crime of Genocide, Judgment 26 February 2007a para 191, https://www.icj-cij.org/files/case-related/91/091-20070226-JUD-01-00-EN.pdf, last accessed 8 June 2023.

[56] *Ibid.* para 194.

[57] The analysis refers in the first place to the jurisprudence of other international criminal courts on this provision, which has been incorporated unaltered into the ICCRSt and is obviously relevant to the ICC's jurisdiction. However up until 2019 the ICC had yet to publish a single judgment on genocide.

In addition, it is irrelevant whether the perpetrators believe that they are acting with democratic authority, that is, with the authority of an elected or 'socially recognised' majority against a minority group. In other words, even though historically the crime of genocide is usually committed by members of a social majority against members of a minority, it is not legally crucial whether those targeted are a minority or, as in the case of the 1972 genocide in Burundi against the majority Hutu population, a majority.[58]

Thus William Schabas maintains that "the four terms in the Convention not only overlap, they also help to define each other, operating much as four corner posts that delimit an area within which a myriad of groups covered by the Convention find protection"[59] and that accordingly, "there is a danger that a search for autonomous meanings for each of the four terms will weaken the overarching sense of the enumeration as a whole, forcing the jurist into an untenable Procrustes bed".[60] To further support his claim, he refers to the problematic ICTR Akayesu judgment,[61] where the relevant provision for genocide is taken unaltered from the 1948 Genocide Convention and essentially incorporated to the ICCRSt, then applied on a judicial level for the first time.

In that famous judgment, the definitions of the four protected groups are briefly and perhaps not particularly successfully analysed. Thus, ICTR Trial Chamber I draws on the historical ICJ Nottebohm judgment[62] in pointing out firstly that "a national group is defined as a collection of people who are perceived to share a legal bond based on common citizenship, coupled with reciprocity of rights and duties".[63] Subsequently, the Chamber maintained that "[a]n ethnic group is generally defined as a group whose members share a common language or culture",[64] while on the matter of racial groups it noted that "[t]he conventional definition of racial group is based on the hereditary physical traits often identified with a geographical region, irrespective of linguistic, cultural, national or religious factors".[65] Finally, as far as religious groups were concerned, the prevalent opinion was that it is "one whose members share the same religion, denomination or mode of worship".[66]

---

[58] Whitaker (1985); Lemarchand (1991), pp. 70–86.

[59] Schabas (2000), p. 111.

[60] *Ibid.* 112.

[61] ICTR (2003).

[62] ICJ, Nottebohm Case (Lichtenstein v Guatemala) 6 April 1955 (Nottebohm Case (second phase), Judgement, 6 April 1955: I.C. J. Reports 1955, p. 4.), https://www.icj-cij.org/files/case-related/18/018-19550406-JUD-01-00-EN.pdf, last accessed 8 June 2023.

[63] *Prosecutor v. Akayesu*, para 512.

[64] *Ibid.* para 513.

[65] *Ibid.* para 514.

[66] *Ibid.* para 515.

3.3.2 *The Concept of a Group's Partial Destruction as a Prerequisite for the ICC's Jurisdiction*

Furthermore, it is accepted that in order **to commit genocide** that would then fall under the ICC's jurisdiction **it is not necessary to destroy an entire group; its partial destruction would also suffice**. Over the years four main interpretational approaches have emerged for establishing what exactly it means to destroy a group "in part", beyond the self-evident fact that the destruction must of course be of a significant magnitude.

The first and most restrictive interpretation of the term accepts that the result is the destruction of the group in part, while the intent is the destruction of the entire group. This interpretation had been presented as the correct one by the Truman administration in its failed attempt to convince the US Senate to vote for the ratification of the Genocide Convention,[67] but it appears to be founded on incorrect evidence presented by the Assistant Secretary of State Dean Rusk based on a report drafted by Under Secretary of State James Webb.[68] On the same wavelength, in 1950 the creator of the term Raphael Lemkin sent a letter to the US Senate Foreign Relations Committee, highlighting that "the destruction in part must be of a substantial nature so as to affect the entirety".[69,70] However, such an interpretation is not in agreement with the official records of the preparatory meetings for the Genocide Convention when it comes to the wording of Article 2 of the Genocide Convention, which includes the definition of genocide and was included unaltered in Article 6 ICCRSt.

The second interpretation assumes that the phrase "destruction in part" implies the adjective "substantial". This was the interpretation adopted by the USA, when in 1987 the country unexpectedly ratified the Genocide Convention, i.e. only 40 years after its international adoption by numerous other States. In other words, the USA, in order to ratify the Genocide Convention, endorsed the essential meaning of the Article's provision as being "in whole or in substantial part".[71] While the international meaning of a term may only be indicative for national legal orders, it is noteworthy that in the USA, the term "substantial part" has been interpreted as "a part of a group of such numerical significance that the destruction or loss of that part

[67] Truman's attempts to convince the US Senate failed, because a lot of its members feared that the provisions of Article 2 of the Genocide Convention could include cases of murder committed against African Americans, a common phenomenon at the time in the southern states. LeBlanc (1984), pp. 369, 377, https://www.jstor.org/stable/2202281, last accessed 8 June 2023.

[68] *Ibid.* 373.

[69] Schabas WA, "*Genocide in International Criminal Law*", 2nd edn, *Ibid.*, 278 with further references to Raphael Lemkin's work after the end of the Second World War.

[70] Communication by Raphael Lemkin, 2 Executive Sessions of the Senate Foreign Relations Committee, Historical Series 781-805 (1976), p 370.

[71] Genocide Convention Implementation Act of 1987, s. 1093(8), https://www.congress.gov/bill/100th-congress/senate-bill/1851/text, last accessed 8 June 2023.

would cause the destruction of the group as a viable entity within the nation of which such group is a part".[72]

Nonetheless, academics like Jordan Paust have heavily contested *inter alia* the concept of "viable entity", questioning if, to reference but one example, the systematic destruction of 35 million people against the background of a nationwide conspiracy could **not** be considered genocide, given that the remaining five per content of the group (1,842,105 people) was never targeted and could still constitute a viable entity.[73]

On the other hand, a few years later, the International Law Commission, adopting the view of the US legislator up to a point, concluded that "[it] is not necessary to intend to achieve the complete annihilation of a group from every corner of the globe. None the less the crime of genocide by its very nature requires the intention to destroy at least a substantial part of a particular group."[74] Moreover, the Special Rapporteur stated in the relevant report of the Sub-Commission on Prevention of Discrimination and Protection of Minorities that the phrase "'in part' would seem to imply a reasonably significant number, relative to the total of the group as a whole, or else a significant section of a group such as its leadership", suggesting the terms "proportionate scale" and "total numbers" as relevant criteria.[75]

Following the same line of argument the ICC's Preparatory Committee expressed its view in a relevant footnote that the traditional definition of genocide which refers to actions committed with the intent to destroy, in whole or in part a national, ethnical, racial or religious group as such "was understood to refer to the specific intention to destroy more than a small number of individuals who are members of a group".[76]

Similarly, the ICTR ruled in the Kayishema and Ruzindana case that the phrase "in part" marks the intent to murder a significant number of people, who "must

[72] *Ibid.*

[73] Paust (1989), pp. 90, 95–96.

[74] Report of the International Law Commission on the Work of its Forty-Eighth Session 6 May – 26 July 1996, 45, para 8, http://legal.un.org/ilc/documentation/english/reports/a_51_10.pdf, last accessed 8 June 2023. Nevertheless, James Crawford expressed his doubts about the proposed definition of the crime of genocide "requiring the intention to destroy 'at least a substantial part of a particular group', since the word 'substantial' was not contained in the Convention on the Prevention and Punishment of the Crime of Genocide itself. That objective implied that, if the crime of genocide was to exist, a proportion of a particular group had to be targeted." For this reason, he suggested the deletion of the relevant point. See Yearbook of the International Law Commission (1996), 225, http://legal.un.org/docs/?path=../ilc/publications/yearbooks/english/ilc_1996_v1.pdf&lang=EFSRAC, last accessed 8 June 2023.

[75] Whitaker B, *ibid.*, p 16, para 29.

[76] Draft Statute for the International Criminal Court. Part 2. Jurisdiction, Admissibility and Applicable Law, UN Doc. A/AC.249/1998/CRP.8, 2 ft 1, https://www.legal-tools.org/doc/e652fe/pdf/, last accessed 8 June 2023.

targeted due to their membership of the group to satisfy this definition",[77] while the ICTY ruled in the Jelisić case that "the intention to destroy must target at least a substantial part of the group", although not necessarily a "considerable number" of its individual members.[78]

Notwithstanding which, the most enlightening source on the meaning of "substantial part" is a note from the ICTY on the Radislav Krstić Trial Judgment:

> The Trial Chamber is thus left with a margin of discretion in assessing what is destruction "in part" of the group. But it must exercise its discretionary power in a spirit consonant with the object and purpose of the Convention which is to criminalise specified conduct directed against the existence of protected groups, as such. The Trial Chamber is therefore of the opinion that the intent to destroy a group, even if only in part, means seeking to destroy a distinct part of the group as opposed to an accumulation of isolated individuals within it. Although the perpetrators of genocide need not seek to destroy the entire group protected by the Convention, they must view the part of the group they wish to destroy as a distinct entity which must be eliminated as such. A campaign resulting in the killings, in different places spread over a broad geographical area, of a finite number of members of a protected group might not thus qualify as genocide, despite the high total number of casualties, because it would not show an intent by the perpetrators to target the very existence of the group as such. Conversely, the killing of all members of the part of a group located within a small geographical area, although resulting in a lesser number of victims, would qualify as genocide if carried out with the intent to destroy the part of the group as such located in this small geographical area.[79,80]

Nonetheless, it must be noted at this point that while the *mens rea* of the crime of genocide exists only when the crime is committed with the intention to destroy a protected group, in whole or in part, a distinction must be made regarding the individual perpetrator's degree of complicity. In other words, whether the accused may have been involved in only a few murders[81] or other criminal acts and if his actions are directed against the protected group as such rather than against specific individuals.[82]

---

[77] ICTR, *Prosecutor v. Clement Kayishema and Obed Ruzindana*, para 97. This point in the Kayishema and Ruzindana judgment also approves of the ICTR's Baglishema case and of the ICTY's Krstić case.

[78] ICTY, *Prosecutor v. Goran Jelisić*, para 82.

[79] ICTY, *Prosecutor v. Radislav Krstić* (IT-98-33-T), para 590.

[80] The International Law Commission had also pointed out that the "intention must be to destroy a group and not merely one or more individuals who are coincidentally members of a particular group. [. . .] The group itself is the ultimate target or intended victim of this type of massive criminal conduct." See Report of the International Law Commission on the Work of its Forty-Eighth Session fn 45, para 6.

[81] It is the author's opinion that this would apply at least to a few murders and not just one, because in the case of a single murder the intent to commit genocide would be almost impossible to prove beyond the shadow of a doubt before the competent Court. Furthermore, such a perpetrator could never be accused before the ICC for practical reasons, i.e. for reasons relating to the importance of the case itself.

[82] ICTY (2001c), referring to Kayishema Trial Judgement para 99 and ICTR (1998), para 521.

In any case, the ICTR judgment in the Kayishema and Ruzindana case and the ICTY Radislav Krstić trial judgment were adopted in this matter by the ICJ, which in February 2007 issued its decision in the Case Concerning the Application of the Convention on the Prevention and Punishment of the Crime of Genocide (*Bosnia and Herzegovina v. Serbia and Montenegro*).[83] The ICJ referred not only to the Krstić judgment, but also to the Semanza, Kayishema, Bagilishema and Stakić judgments. It then approved the legal interpretation of the term "in part" as implying "substantial part" and deemed this point as "crucial", because according to its learned view the intent to commit genocide must be an intent to destroy at least a substantial part of a protected group. Consequently, according to the ICJ's position, this is required by the nature of the crime of genocide per se, since the purpose is to afford international protection of particular groups from criminal attempts to destroy them, and thus, accordingly, that "part targeted must be significant enough to have an impact on the group as a whole".[84]

The third interpretation adopts a more qualitative than quantitative criterion, legally interpreting the term 'part' in the phrase "in part" as meaning "significant part". In a way, this third proposed interpretation is similar to the concept of "viable entity" adopted by the USA legislator, but instead of evaluating "viability" qualitatively, based on a minimum number below which the group would be unable to survive, it uses a qualitative criterion, investigating whether the extermination a significant subgroup of a specific political, economic, social, cultural or other character could damage the survival of the group as a whole. Which is to say that it sees the concept of "viability" not as a crucial numerical size under which the group is unable to survive, but primarily as a qualitatively significant subgroup of political, economic, social, cultural or other character, the extermination of which could damage the survival of the group as a whole.

Nonetheless, this view cannot be founded on the preparatory works of the Genocide Convention, but only in Whitaker's famous report, where much later on, in the mid-1980s, he claimed that "in part" implies "a reasonably significant number, relative to the total of the group as a whole, or else a significant section of a group such as its leadership".[85] Undoubtedly, the aforementioned passage attempts to introduce two equal criteria: (1) a quantitative criterion that directly relates to the size of the group as a number, since, for instance, pursuant to this, the murder of 50,000 Cypriots in Cyprus would be considered genocide, while this would not be the case for the murder of 50,000 Chinese people, for example, given that the Chinese population totals around 1,394,130,000;[86] and (2) a qualitative criterion, which is connected with the exceptionally significant role that a section of the group might have for the entire group's future survival.

[83] *Bosnia and Herzegovina v. Serbia and Montenegro* (No 91), pp. 198–201.
[84] *Ibid.* 198.
[85] Whitaker B, p. 16, para 19.
[86] See the demographic figures for Cyprus (1,198,427) and China (1,420,062,022) http://worldpopulationreview.com/countries/, last accessed 8 June 2023.

Referring to this report, the Commission of Experts assembled by the UN Security Council in 1992 pursuant to Resolution 780 to investigate violations of international criminal law in the former Yugoslavia[87] agreed that the phrase "in part" includes a qualitative feature as well, beyond the widely accepted quantitative one. Renowned President of the Commission and Emeritus Professor of Law at DePaul University M. Cherif Bassiouni noted that the definition of genocide is flexible enough to include not only the targeting of an entire group, but also even certain parts of it such as its elite or women. Thus, based on the above, all the Bosnians in Sarajevo, for instance, could be considered a protected group, regardless of their nationality or religion.[88]

This conclusion is supported by the 1994 Official Report of the Commission of Experts, which maintained that "destruction of a group in whole or in part does not mean that the group in its entirety must be exterminated. The words 'in whole or in part' were inserted in the text to make it clear that it is not necessary to aim at killing all the members of the group".[89]

Furthermore, the Commission did not hesitate to give specific examples of significant parts of a protected group, whose extermination could amount to genocide: political and administrative leaders, religious leaders, academics, intellectuals and business leaders.[90]

It is noteworthy that this third interpretation which was adopted by the Commission of Experts in its final report in 1994, met with the approval of the ICTY's Prosecutor a few years later,[91] as well as with that of the judges in the cases of

[87] Bassiouni (2001), p. 35.

The Commission worked for two years in total, during which it conducted 35 field investigations and found evidence for the torture of at least 50,000 people and 200,000 deaths, which took place in almost 2000 towns and villages. Nonetheless, and despite the fact that the Commission of Experts received from the Security Council the widest possible mandate since the Nuremberg Trials, it received meagre financial resources and support from the UN during its investigations. In fact, it was primarily funded by private parties and DePaul University! This prompted Bassiouni to write that according to Shakespeare, "a rose by any other name is still a rose. But in the United Nations (UN), a fact-finding mission, notwithstanding its name, is not necessarily a fact-finding mission" (Bassiouni 2001).

[88] Bassiouni (1994), pp. 279, 323.

[89] ICTY (1994).

[90] *Ibid.* para 94. It could however be claimed that in essence these "limited" actions of genocide are rather symbolic, and do not constitute actual corruption. For example, would actions such as Guy Fawkes's attempt to blow up the British Parliament in 1605 amount to genocide, had it been successful?

[91] ICTY (1996), in which the Prosecutor put forth as the initial foundation for his position the Eichmann judgment; ICTY, *Prosecutor v. Jelisić and Cesić* (Case No. IT-95-10-I) Initial Indictment 21 July 1995, 3 para 17, http://www.icty.org/x/cases/jelisic/ind/en/jel-ii950721e.pdf, last accessed 8 June 2023, in which "[i]n May 1992, Goran JELISIC, intending to destroy a substantial or significant part of the Bosnian Muslim people as a national, ethnical, or religious group, systematically killed Muslim detainees at the Laser Bus Co., the Brcko police station and Luka camp"; ICTY, *Prosecutor v. Jelisić and Cesić* (Case No. IT-95-10-I) First Amended Indictment 3 March 1998, 3 para 16, http://www.icty.org/x/cases/jelisic/ind/en/jel-1ai980512e.pdf, last

Sikirica and Jelisić. Nevertheless, the support of the judges for the third interpretation was primarily theoretical since, eventually, it was determined in the first case that the victims did not belong to the elite of the protected group;[92] and in the second that it could not be proven beyond all reasonable doubt that "the choice of victims arose from a precise logic to destroy the most representative figures of the Muslim community in Brcko to the point of threatening the survival of that community".[93] Nonetheless, it was jurisprudentially accepted that genocidal intent "may also consist of the desired destruction of a more limited number of persons selected for the impact that their disappearance would have upon the survival of the group as such".[94]

In the Krstić judgment, the first case in which an international criminal tribunal affirmed that genocide was committed, the Prosecutor managed to convince the court that the young men of military age systematically massacred in Srebrenica[95] were a "significant part" of the Muslim community given that "[t]he Bosnian Serb forces could not have failed to know, by the time they decided to kill all the men, that this selective destruction of the group would have a lasting impact upon the entire group [...] that the combination of those killings with the forcible transfer of the women, children and elderly would inevitably result in the physical disappearance of the Bosnian Muslim population at Srebrenica".[96]

By highlighting the concept of a "significant part", the third interpretation forces us to resort to work through scenarios in order to test its limits. Perhaps the extermination of the political, cultural or religious elite suffices. Thus, for instance, the systematic massacre of ten muftis in a small territory could, along with other criminal acts, amount to genocide. However, it would be more reasonable for someone who fervently wishes to destroy a specific group to turn against its women and children, who could biologically ensure the survival of the group in the future. Consequently, if one was to follow this reasoning, it would not be difficult to arrive at entirely subjective conclusions as to which part of the group is crucial to

---

accessed 8 June 2023; ICTY, *Prosecutor v. Jelisić and Cesić* (Case No. IT-95-10-I) Second Amended Indictment 19 October 1998, 3 para 14, http://www.icty.org/x/cases/jelisic/ind/en/981019.pdf, last accessed 8 June 2023.

[92] ICTY (2001c) para 80, http://www.icty.org/x/cases/sikirica/tjug/en/010903r98bis-e.pdf, last accessed 8 June 2023.

[93] ICTY, *Prosecutor v. Jelisić and Cesić* (Case No. IT-95-10-T) Trial Judgment 14 December 1999 para 93, http://www.icty.org/x/cases/jelisic/tjug/en/jel-tj991214e.pdf, last accessed 8 June 2023.

[94] *Ibid.* para 82 "The character of the attack on the leadership must be viewed in the context of the fate or what happened to the rest of the group. If a group has its leadership exterminated, and at the same time or in the wake of that, has a relatively large number of the members of the group killed or subjected to other heinous acts, for example deported on a large scale or forced to flee, the cluster of violations ought to be considered in its entirety in order to interpret the provisions of the Convention in a spirit consistent with its purpose."

[95] ICTY (2001b): "Within a period of no more than seven days, as many as 7000–8000 men of military age were systematically massacred while the remainder of the Bosnian Muslim population present at Srebrenica, some 25,000 people, were forcibly transferred to Kladanj."

[96] *Ibid.* para 595.

that group's future survival. In any case, it is important to remember that according to the Krstić trial judgment, the massacre of a smaller or larger number of people who amount to a significant part of the group must always be associated with other criminal actions. For instance, in Srebrenica the massacre of men of military age occurred at the same time as the forcible transfer of the rest of the Bosnian Muslim population.[97]

In any case, the second proposed interpretation ("*substantial* part") must not be confused with the third ("*significant* part"). Those who stand behind the third interpretation, which maintains that the term 'part' in the phrase "in part" amounts to a "significant part" of a group, would interpret the selective murder of specific parts of a group as proof of intent to destroy a group in its entirety. That is because they believe that the perpetrator/s of the aforementioned criminal action have determined in advance that the extermination of those significant parts of the group would cause the group existential and irreversible damage. However, the same reasoning could not be applied to the extermination of a "substantial part", as in that case the perpetrators' intent is to destroy a large in number part of the group. This, of course, does not mean that the extermination, for instance, of the religious elite, which can be considered a "significant part", could not also prove the intent to destroy a "substantial part". However, as the ICJ emphasised in its *Bosnia and Herzegovina v Serbia and Montenegro* judgment, which approved of the dictum of the ICTY appeal judgment in the Krstić case, in addition to the quantitative criterion (what percentage of the group as a whole is the targeted part?), the qualitative criterion, i.e. the significance of that part, must also be taken into consideration. Thus, the qualitative criterion cannot stand alone, but must always be combined with the quantitative one.[98]

The **fourth interpretation** of the phrase "in whole or in part" uses the geographic aspect of the alleged criminal action as the principal criterion. That is because the perpetrators' capacity does not extend to a global level, and often not even to a state level, i.e. not even to the entire territory of one State. That is exactly what happened during the civil war in Yugoslavia, where ethnic cleansings took place in many areas, but not throughout the entire territory of the former Yugolsavia. Taking into consideration precisely this aspect of the perpetrators' capacity to commit criminal actions, the ICTY pointed out in the Jelisić trial judgment that "[t]he Prosecution contends, however, that the geographical zone in which an attempt to eliminate the group is made may be limited to the size of a region or even a municipality. The Trial Chamber notes that it is accepted that genocide may be perpetrated in a limited geographic zone. Furthermore, the United Nations General Assembly did not hesitate in characterising the massacres at Sabra and Shatila as genocide [...]"[99,100]

---

[97] *Ibid.*

[98] *Bosnia and Herzegovina v Serbia and Montenegro*, para 200.

[99] *Prosecutor v. Goran Jelisić*, para 83.

[100] With Resolution 37/123, the UN General Assembly characterised the massacres of Palestinians by Israelis in the refugee camps of Sabra and Shatila in 1982 as genocide. It remains an important

In the Krstić case, the ICTY ruled that it is possible for "the killing of all members of the part of a group located within a small geographical area" to amount to genocide "if carried out with the intent to destroy the part of the group as such located in this small geographical area".[101] The judges in the Sikirica case reached the same conclusion, as the ICTY Trial Chamber accepted the Prosecutor's view that "the intent to destroy a multitude of persons belonging to a group may amount to genocide, even where these persons constitute only part of a group within a given geographical area: a country or a region or a single community".[102] The ICJ is also in agreement, as in *Bosnia and Herzegovina v Serbia and Montenegro*, it ruled that "it is widely accepted that genocide may be found to have been committed where the intent is to destroy the group within a geographically limited area".[103] And so are academics such as Nehemiah Robinson, who pointed out early on that the phrase "in part" must include a genocide committed against only a part of a group "either within a country or within a region or within a single community, provided the number is substantial".[104]

3.4 Current and Potentially Emerging Implications: The Rohingya Case

Unfortunately, the twenty-first century has not remained unstained by acts of genocide. At the same time, the ICC has not achieved adequate convictions for genocide. Subsequently, it is vital that the interpretation of the laws be—we could say—revolutionised in order for the ICC to be efficacious.

In an address to the UN Human Rights Council in Geneva, Zeid Ra'ad Al Hussein denounced the "brutal security operation" against the Rohingya in Rakhine state, as "clearly disproportionate" to the insurgent attacks carried out, characterising the

---

resolution, despite the fact that (a) its adoption was preceded by intense debate, (b) the paragraph on genocide was put to vote separately and (c) it has been characterised with reference to the jurisprudence as a resolution of a primarily political nature. There appear to be three aspects that attest to its value: (a) though it is often debated on an international level within the UN, this does not in the slightest minimise the value of resolutions and UNSC decisions; (b) the paragraph on genocide was adopted with a large majority and a notable number of abstentions; abstentions, however, may well simply signify a State's intention to remain neutral in the face of diplomatic pressure and not a negative stance on the matter, perhaps even the opposite; (c) all UN decisions and even the judgments by international courts are of a political nature, but that in itself does not diminish their legal importance. The Situation in the Middle East, GA Res. 37/123, 16 December 1982, Chapter D, https://www.jewishvirtuallibrary.org/un-general-assembly-resolution-37-123-december-1982, last accessed 8 June 2023.

[101] *Prosecutor v. Krstić*, para 590.

[102] *Prosecutor v. Sikirica et al*, para 68.

[103] *Bosnia and Herzegovina v Serbia and Montenegro*, para 199.

[104] Robinson (1960), p. 63.

whole situation as "a textbook example of ethnic cleansing".[105] Following the expulsion of more than 700,000 Rohingya as of August 2017,[106] a 440-page report[107] was published by a UN Human Rights Council fact-finding mission[108] and the ICC Pre-Trial Chamber I handed down its decision confirming that the ICC can exercise its jurisdiction;[109] the ICC Prosecutor Fatou Bensouda then announced the launch of a preliminary investigation into the deportation of hundreds of thousands of Rohingya Muslims from Myanmar into Bangladesh.[110]

Perhaps of even greater significance—both more generally and in relation to genocide specifically—is what appears to be a growing trend for States (especially on the African continent at present) to withdraw from the Rome Statute. The implications of this are that, should the crime of genocide occur in the territory of such States after the time of their withdrawal from the Rome Statute, then it might be legally impermissible for the ICC to prosecute the commission of these and other serious international crimes because of its lack of jurisdiction. Furthermore, since the crime of genocide is often fueled by political undercurrents, the likelihood of any *bona fide* or effective prosecution being brought against the perpetrators of such crimes at the national level is highly unlikely, especially if those responsible for them remain in power.

This fully applies to the case of Omar Al-Bashir, the first sitting president to be indicted by the ICC. Arrest warrants were issued in 2009 and in 2010 pertaining to three counts of genocide, two counts of war crimes and five counts of crimes against humanity. Still, President Al- Bashir is free and has travelled to many African countries without any consequences.[111] Therefore, States that withdraw from the Rome Statute could effectively deprive many victims of their fundamental human right to justice and reparation following the commission of such heinous crimes.

Nor are most States in which the crime of genocide is committed likely to have the necessary capacity and resources to investigate and prosecute such legally challenging crimes. It is a fact that investigations regarding genocide usually constitute extremely time- and money-intensive legal operations that require special knowledge, expertise and a considerable number of jurists and investigators. This is an important reason for agreeing to establish the International Criminal Court in the first place in 1998.

[105] Safi (2017).

[106] Sammers (2018).

[107] UN Human Rights Council, Report of the detailed findings of the Independent International Fact-Finding Mission on Myanmar, A/HRC/39/CRP.2, https://www.ohchr.org/Documents/HRBodies/HRCouncil/FFM-Myanmar/A_HRC_39_CRP.2.pdf, last accessed 8 June 2023.

[108] Safi (2018b).

[109] Decision on the "Prosecution's Request for a Ruling on Jurisdiction under Article 19(3) of the Statute", ICC-RoC46(3)-01/1, https://www.icc-cpi.int/CourtRecords/CR2018_04203.PDF, last accessed 8 June 2023.

[110] Wintour (2018).

[111] Pillai (22 August 2018).

The commission of acts of genocide and denial of international criminal justice could undeniably fuel further regional instability, thereby posing threats to international peace and security.[112] Nonetheless, the horizon is not entirely bleak. In the most recent case of alleged genocide to emerge, against the Rohingya in Myanmar, Pre-Trial Chamber I was convinced by the Prosecutor's novel argument that even though the allegedly coercive acts that forced the Rohingya to flee took place in Myanmar, the deportation offence (included in Art. 7(1)(d) ICCRSt on crimes against humanity) was not fully complete until the refugees entered Bangladesh, a state party to the Rome Statute.[113]

This case is innovative in two respects. First of all, because the ICC Prosecutor has never asked the Court to interpret Article 12(2)(a) ICCRst before[114] and never applied qualified territoriality. Secondly, because it is the first time the Prosecutor has asked for a ruling on jurisdiction under Article 19(3) ICCRSt.[115] Even though such an interpretation of the Rome Statute has also been presented as a violation of Myanmar's sovereignty,[116] the truth is that it constitutes a significant step towards the effectiveness of the International Criminal Court. In any case, as Michael Vagias points out "a strict adherence to the Statute's procedural system might render the Prosecutor's right under Article 19(3) ICCRSt meaningless."[117]

Furthermore, it is important that we specifically comment on Chief Prosecutor's Fatou Bensouda argument, **who likened deportation to "a cross-border shooting", arguing the crime "is not completed until the bullet (fired in one state) strikes and kills the victim (standing in another state)".**[118] She also made an explicit reference to Vagias's theory regarding "subjective territoriality" and "objective territoriality" in support of her view that the ICC has jurisdiction over the case.[119] In particular, Fatou Bensouda pointed out that:

> Commentators agree that States can exercise jurisdiction in relation to crimes that occurred only in part on their territory, including based on "subjective territoriality" (when crimes were commenced on a State's territory, but completed in another) and "objective territoriality" (when crimes were completed on a State's territory, but commenced in another). What

[112] UN, "Global Issues: Peace and Security", https://www.un.org/en/sections/issues-depth/peace-and-security/, last accessed 8 June 2023.

[113] Safi (2018a).

[114] The Prosecutor made reference to objective territoriality in the situation in Afghanistan, public redacted version of 'Request for authorization of an investigation pursuant to article 15', ICC-02/17-7-Conf-Exp, Pre-Trial Chamber, 20 November 2017, fn 49 and in Situation in the Republic of Korea, Article 5 Report, June 2014, para 39.

[115] Vagias (2018).

[116] Agence France-Presse (2018).

[117] Vagias (2018), p. 3.

[118] Application under Regulation 46(3) by the ICC Prosecutor Fatou Bensouda, 'Prosecution's Request for a Ruling on Jurisdiction under Article 19(3) of the Statute' (9 April 2018) 13–14, para 27.

[119] Vagias (2014), pp. 16–22.

is important in both scenarios is States' legitimate interest in conduct which occurs partially on their territory, resulting in their exercise of jurisdiction.[120]

For some, the above simile is absurd and renders the States that are not members of the Rome Statute accountable to the ICC. However, one could argue that as the deportation of Rohingya people to Bangladesh undoubtedly has a significant social impact on Bangladeshis, it is the ICC's duty not only to provide a ruling concerning the Rohingya victims, but also to protect the people of the member state (Bangladesh). In any case, the Pre-Trial Chamber I fully accorded with the Chief Prosecutor's argument, by stating the following:

> In this regard, the Chamber considers that the preconditions for the exercise of the Court's jurisdiction pursuant to article 12(2)(a) of the Statute are, as a minimum, fulfilled if at least one legal element of a crime within the jurisdiction of the Court or part of such crime is committed on the territory of a State-Party.[121]

At a time when it appears as if the ICC is losing its power and efficacy due to the above-mentioned withdrawal or threat of withdrawal of States and the continuous abstention of the most powerful ones (such as US, China, Russia and Israel), the Prosecutor's novel approach arguably constitutes a way of reinforcing the ICC's status via the innovative interpretation of genocide's *actus reus*.

Thus, the ICC is exploring innovative interpretative avenues in order to preserve or even expand its jurisdiction,[122] even over States that have never been or are no longer state parties. If certain factual conditions are met, then no one can exclude the possibility that this might occur for the crime of genocide as well, especially under Art. 6(c) (deliberately inflicting on the group conditions of life calculated to bring about its physical destruction in whole or in part), Art. 6(d) (imposing measures intended to prevent births within the group), and Art. 6(e) (forcibly transferring children of the group to another group).

Finally yet importantly, one should not forget Christopher K. Hall, Daniel D. Ntanda Nsereko and Manuel J. Ventura's inciteful observation that whereas the International Military Tribunal of Nuremberg treated all challenges to its jurisdiction with disdain, in accordance with the Rome Statute the International Criminal Court must determine whether it has jurisdiction over any case before it. Admittedly this rests with the generally accepted principle of the administration of justice, pursuant to which domestic and international courts possess the inherent power to ascertain their own jurisdiction.[123,124]

---

[120] Application under Regulation 46(3) by the ICC Prosecutor Fatou Bensouda, 'Prosecution's Request for a Ruling on Jurisdiction under Article 19(3) of the Statute' (9 April 2018) 15, para 32.

[121] Decision on the "Prosecution's Request for a Ruling on Jurisdiction under Article 19(3) of the Statute", ICC-RoC46(3)-01/1, p. 36, para 64.

[122] Stahn (2005), p. 700.

[123] Hall et al. (2016), p. 852.

[124] It is noteworthy that the ICTY Appeals Chamber decision in Tadic expressly stated its opinion on the issue of a Court's powers: "This power, known as the principle of 'Kompetenz-Kompetenz' in German or 'la compétence de la compétence' in French, is part, and indeed a major part, of the

The same view was justifiably adopted by the ICC at an early stage. Pre-Trial Chamber II held regarding the Situation in Uganda in 2007 that: "[i]t is a well-known and fundamental principle that any judicial body, including any international tribunal, retains the power and the duty to determine the boundaries of its own jurisdiction and competence. Such a power and duty, commonly referred to as 'Kompetenz-Kompetenz' in German and 'la compétence de la compétence' in French, [. . .] is enshrined in article 19, paragraph 1, of the Statute, pursuant to which 'the Court shall satisfy itself that is has jurisdiction in any case brought before it' [. . .]".[125]

Vagias is critical of the Prosecutor's stance, albeit rather ambivalent insofar as most of his analysis constitutes an exemplary writing of the "yes but, no but" type of argumentation. He notes that according to the Appeals Chamber decision in the Situation in the Democratic Republic of the Congo in 2006[126] "it would make little sense to consider and determine for the purposes of jurisdiction the notions of 'deportation' and 'commission in part', prior to an Article 15 procedure designed to resolve precisely the same issues [. . .] From this point of view, the request should be rejected as inadmissible, because it comes at an inopportune or premature procedural moment. This matter should be resolved by a Pre-Trial Chamber, once the Prosecutor files an Article 15 request for authorization, or a request for an arrest warrant in the event of a state or Security Council referral".[127] Nonetheless in his concluding remarks he concedes that "the Prosecutor has made a diligent effort to cautiously establish the Court's jurisdiction over a serious international crime committed in part on state party territory"[128] and that "the Court is essentially called to decide whether the Prosecutor's need to avoid the risk of wasting resources in the investigation of situations beyond ICC jurisdiction may be reconciled with the Statute's procedural scheme concerning jurisdictional determinations".[129]

However, from a legal practitioner's point of view it is difficult to find substantial merits in the interpretation of Article 19(3) ICCRSt as a legal provision with implied restrictions as to its use and scope, especially when one considers the function and

---

incidental or inherent jurisdiction of any judicial or arbitral tribunal, consisting of its 'jurisdiction to determine its own jurisdiction'. It is a necessary component in the exercise of the judicial function and does not need to be expressly provided for in the constitutive documents of those tribunals, although this is often done (see, e.g., Statute of the International Court of Justice, Art. 36, para. 6). But in the words of the International Court of Justice: '[T]his principle, which is accepted by the general international law in the matter of arbitration, assumes particular force when the international tribunal is no longer an arbitral tribunal [. . .] but is an institution which has been pre-established by an international instrument defining its jurisdiction and regulating its operation." (Nottebohm Case (*Liech. v. Guat.*), 1953 I.C.J. Reports 7, 119 (21 March). ICTY (1995).

[125] Situation in Uganda, ICC-02/04-01/05-147, Decision on the Prosecutor's Application that the Pre-Trial Chamber Disregard as Irrelevant the Submission Filed by the Registry on 5 December 2005, Pre-Trial Chamber II, 9 Mar. 2006, paras. 22–23.

[126] Situation in the Democratic Republic of the Congo, Judgment on the Prosecutor's appeal against the decision of Pre-Trial Chamber I entitled ICC (2006).

[127] Vagias (2018), p. 14.

[128] *Ibid.* 21.

[129] *Ibid.* 21.

operation of an international court with pre-trial chambers (unusual for many national jurisdictions based on continental law) and quite an elaborate pre-trial stage with pre-trial hearings, motions and procedures. Hence, given the ambivalence of the legal issue, i.e. the balance between distinct provisions of the Rome Statute which do not expressly collide with each other, as well as the practical implications of a legal analysis that could be considered as valid *or not,* even if its validity would not have any positive impact as already conceded, it is more sound to accept that the provision of Article 19(3) ICCRSt should not be constrained by Articles 13 (ICC's exercise of jurisdiction) and 15 (Prosecutor's investigations *proprio motu*) of the Rome Statute. Instead it should be read 'as it is' and be feasible to be invoked at any stage, even before a proper investigation begins. Again from a procedural point of view the person or the State concerned would not be adversely affected or lose any of the rights stipulated in the provisions of Article 19(2) and (4) ICCRSt, namely to challenge the jurisdiction of the Court *ordinarily* prior to or at the commencement of the trial,[130] *and exceptionally* thereafter.[131]

This interpretation follows implicitly the line of the Appeals Chamber decision in the Situation in the Democratic Republic of the Congo in 2006, where it is clearly stated that "[a]n initial determination of the admissibility of a case cannot be made an integral part of the decision on an application of a warrant of arrest for the reason that article 58 (1) of the Statute lists the substantive prerequisites for the issuance of a warrant of arrest exhaustively. Article 19 (1), second sentence, of the Statute cannot be invoked to make the admissibility of the case an additional substantive prerequisite for the issuance of a warrant of arrest"[132] *(argumentum a contrario).*

3.5 Striving Towards Justice: Reimagining the Interpretation and Prevention of Genocide

Often regarded as "the crime of crimes", genocide strikes at the very core of human existence. It is, therefore, of paramount importance to utilise all legal avenues to ensure that the architects of such crimes are not granted impunity. In this context, there is a compelling need for the Rome Statute and the Elements of Crimes to be interpreted in a flexible manner. This approach should not confine judges and prosecutors to an overly rigid interpretation of the law but should promote *de lege ferenda* interpretive strategies.

As we reflect on the 25th anniversary of the Rome Statute and the 75th anniversary of the Genocide Convention, it is an opportune moment for the ICC to bolster its stature by discovering interpretative pathways that facilitate the appropriate

[130] Art. 19(2) ICCRSt.

[131] Art. 1994) ICCRSt.

[132] Situation in the Democratic Republic of the Congo, Judgment on the Prosecutor's appeal against the decision of Pre-Trial Chamber I entitled ICC (2006). para. 42.

punishment and proof of genocide. Encouragingly, the court appears to have embarked on this journey, as evidenced by Pre-Trial Chamber I's decision in the Rohingya case.

Finally, and critically, regardless of whether individual states—within whose borders acts of genocide are purported to have been committed—remain party to or join the ICC, certain actions maintain enduring significance. These actions encompass the development of mechanisms to prevent genocide, the prompt and effective investigation of alleged acts, the precise validation of the criteria necessary to establish genocide in specific instances, and a realistic assessment of the likelihood of cases alleging the commission of these and other core crimes reaching the ICC.

References

Table of Cases

Democratic Republic of the Congo v. Rwanda (2006) Dissenting Opinion of Judge Koroma, para 26

ICJ (1953) Liech. v. Guat., Nottebohm Case I.C.J. Reports

ICJ (2007a) Bosnia and Herzegovina v. Serbia and Montenegro, Judgment, para 191 https://www.icj-cij.org/files/case-related/91/091-20070226-JUD-01-00-EN.pdf. Accessed 8 June 2023

ICTR (1998) Prosecutor v. Akayesu (Case No. ICTR-96-4-T) Judgment, https://www.refworld.org/cases,ICTR,40278fbb4.html. Accessed 8 June 2023

ICTR (1999a) Prosecutor v. Clement Kayishema and Obed Ruzindana, (Case No. ICTR-95-1-T) Judgment, para 98, http://www.refworld.org/docid/48abd5760.html. Accessed 8 June 2023

ICTR (1999b) Prosecutor v. Georges Anderson Nderubumwe Rutaganda (Case No: ICTR-96-3-T), para 55, http://www.refworld.org/docid/48abd5880.html. Accessed 8 June 2023

ICTR (2001a) Kambanda (ICTR-97-23-S); Krstic (IT-98-33-T), Decision, para 699

ICTR (2001b) Prosecutor v. Ignace Bagilishema (Case No. ICTR-95-1A-T) Judgment, para 65, http://www.refworld.org/docid/48abd5170.html. Accessed 8 June 2023

ICTR (2003) Prosecutor v. Semanza (ICTR-97-20-T) (Trial Judgement and Sentence), para 317 http://www.ictrcaselaw.org/docs/doc37512.pdf. Accessed 8 June 2023

ICTR (2004) Niyitegeka (ICTR-96-14-A), Decision, para 5

ICTY (1995) Prosecutor v. Tadic', IT-94-1-AR72, Decision on the Defence Motion for Interlocutory Appeal on Jurisdiction, Appeals Chamber, 2 Oct. 1995, para. 18,http://www.icty.org/x/cases/tadic/acdec/en/51002.htm. Accessed 8 June 2023

ICTY (1996) Prosecutor v. Karadzić and Mladić (Case Nos. IT-95-18-R61, IT-95-5-R61) Transcript of Hearing of 27 June 1996, http://www.icty.org/x/cases/karadzic/trans/en/960627it.htm. Accessed 8 June 2023

ICTY (1999) Prosecutor v. Goran Jelisić (Case No. IT-95-10-T), Judgment para 66, https://www.icty.org/x/cases/jelisic/tjug/en/. Accessed 8 June 2023

ICTY (2000) Kupreškić skic et al, IT-95-16-T, Judgment, para 636

ICTY (2001a) Jelisic (IT-95-10-A) Dissenting Opinion of Judge Wald, para 2

ICTY (2001b) Prosecutor v. Krstić (Case No. IT-98-33-T) Trial Judgment, para 594, http://www.icty.org/x/cases/krstic/tjug/en/krs-tj010802e.pdf. Accessed 8 June 2023

ICTY (2001c) Prosecutor v. Sikirica et al. (Case No. IT-95-8-T) Judgment on Defence Motions to Acquit 3 September 2001 para 80, http://www.icty.org/x/cases/sikirica/tjug/en/010903r98bis-e.pdf. Accessed 8 June 2023

ICTY (2004a) Prosecutor v. Brdanin (IT-99-36-T) Judgment, para 683, 684, http://www.icty.org/x/cases/brdanin/tjug/en/brd-tj040901e.pdf. Accessed 8 June 2023

ICTY (2004b) Prosecutor v. Radislav Krstić (Case No. IT-98-33-A) Judgment, para 6, http://www.icty.org/x/cases/krstic/acjug/en/krs-aj040419e.pdf. Accessed 8 June 2023

ICTY (2006) Prosecutor v. Stakić (IT-97-24-A) Appeal Judgment, para 25, http://www.refworld.org/docid/47fdfb550.html. Accessed 8 June 2023

ICTY (2017) Prosecutor v. Ratko Mladić, Judgement, Public With Confidential Annex, IT-09-92-T, D116761 - D116145, 1597, 1805, 1807-1808, 2465, 2474, http://www.icty.org/case/mladic/4. Accessed 8 June 2023

The Situation in the Middle East, GA Res. 37/123, (1982). https://www.jewishvirtuallibrary.org/un-general-assembly-resolution-37-123-december-1982, Accessed 8 June 2023

Books

Bassiouni MC (2005) The legislative history of the International Criminal Court: Introduction, analysis and integrated text vol I. Transnational Publishers, New York

Charny IW (1994) Toward a generic definition of genocide. In: Andreopoulos GJ (ed) Genocide, conceptual and historical dimensions. University of Pennsylvania Press, Philadelphia

Drost PN (1959) The crime of state, vol 2: Genocide, A. W. Sijthoff, Leiden

Hall CK, Ntanda Nsereko DD, Ventura MJ (2016) Article 19: Challenges to the jurisdiction of the Court or the admissibility of a case. In: Triffterer O, Ambos K (eds) The Rome Statute of the International Criminal Court: a commentary, C.H. Beck/Hart/Nomos, München/Oxford/Baden-Baden

Lemkin R (1944) Axis rule in occupied Europe: laws of occupation, analysis of government, proposals for redress. Carnegie Endowment for World Peace, Washington DC

Robinson N (1960) The genocide convention: a commentary. World Jewish Congress, New York

Sands P (2016) East West street: on the origins of genocide and crimes against humanity. Weidenfeld and Nickolson, London

Schabas WA (2000) Genocide in international law: the crime of crimes. Cambridge University Press, Cambridge

Schabas WA (2009) Genocide in international criminal law, 2nd edn. Cambridge University Press, Cambridge, p 202

Vagias M (2014) The territorial jurisdiction of the International Criminal Court. CUP, Cambridge

Articles/Papers

Bassiouni MC (1994) The commission of experts established pursuant to security council resolution 780: investigating violations of international humanitarian law in the former Yugoslavia. Crim Law Forum 5:279

Bassiouni MC (2001) Appraising UN justice-related fact-finding missions. Wash Univ J Law Policy 5:35 https://openscholarship.wustl.edu/cgi/viewcontent.cgi?article=1550&context=law_journal_law_policy. Accessed 8 June 2023

Biryabarema E (2017) UK says killings in South Sudan conflict amount to genocide. Available at Reuters. https://www.reuters.com/article/us-southsudan-war/uk-says-killings-in-south-sudan-conflict-amount-to-genocide-idUSKBN17E2TF. Accessed 8 June 2023

Granz M (2017) 5 genocides that are still going on today, (Business Insider, 22 November 2017). https://www.businessinsider.com/genocides-still-going-on-today-bosnia-2017-11#christians-

and-muslims-in-the-central-african-republic-4, https://www.nytimes.com/2016/02/12/opinion/dont-forget-darfur.html?_r=0. Accessed 8 June 2023

Jackson RH (1949) Planning Memorandum distributed to Delegations at Beginning of London Conference, June 1945, Report, United States Representative to the International Conference on Military Trials, U.S. Government Printing Office, Washington DC

LeBlanc LJ (1984) The intent to destroy groups in the genocide convention: the proposed U.-S. understanding. Am J Int Law 78:2. https://www.jstor.org/stable/2202281. Accessed 8 June 2023

Lemarchand R (1991) Burundi: the politics of ethnic Amnesia. In: Fein H (ed) Genocide watch. Yale University Press, New Heaven

Paust JJ (1989) Congress and genocide: they're not going to get away with it. Mich J Int Law 11:90

Pillai P (2018) The African Union, the International Criminal Court, and the International Court of Justice: at the fault lines of international accountability. Am Soc Int Law 22(10) https://www.asil.org/insights/volume/22/issue/10/african-union-international-criminal-court-and-international-court. Accessed 8 June 2023

Safi M (2017) Myanmar treatment of Rohingya looks like "textbook ethnic cleansing, says UN' The Guardian, London, https://www.theguardian.com/world/2017/sep/11/un-myanmars-treatment-of-rohingya-textbo ok-example-of-ethnic-cleansing. Accessed 8 June 2023

Safi M (2018a) ICC says it can prosecute Myanmar for alleged Rohingya crimes. Available at *The Guardian*, London, https://www.theguardian.com/world/2018/sep/06/icc-says-it-can-prosecute-myanmar-for-alleged-rohingya-crimes. Accessed 8 June 2023

Safi M (2018b) Tied to trees and raped: UN report details Rohingya horrors, Available at *The Guardian*, London, https://www.theguardian.com/world/2018/sep/18/tied-to-trees-and-raped-un-report-details-rohingya-horrors. Accessed 8 June 2023

Sammers H (2018) Closed circuit: segregation on the Myanmar train to nowhere, Available at *The Guardian*, London, https://www.theguardian.com/world/2017/sep/11/un-myanmars-treatment-of-rohingya-textbook-example-of-ethnic-cleansing. Accessed 8 June 2023

Sanders L IV (2017) UN warns of genocide in Central African Republic. Deutsche Welle. https://www.dw.com/en/un-warns-of-genocide-in-central-african-republic/a-40002377. Accessed 8 June 2023

Stahn C (2005) Complementarity, amnesties and alternative forms of justice: some interpretative guidelines for the international criminal court. J Int Crim Just 3

Vagias M (2018) International Criminal Courts and Tribunals: The Prosecutor's Request Concerning the Rohingya Deportation to Bangladesh: Certain Procedural Questions. Leiden J Int Law 3

Verhoeven J (1991) Le crime de genocide, originalite et ambigute, Revue Belge de Droit International

Whitaker B (1985) Revised and Updated Report on the Question of the Prevention and Punishment of the Crime of Genocide, UN Doc. E/CN.4/Sub.2/1985/6, para 29, http://undocs.org/en/E/CN.4/Sub.2/1985/6. Accessed 8 June 2023

Wintour P (2018) Myanmar Rohingya crisis: ICC begins inquiry into atrocities *The Guardian*, London, https://www.theguardian.com/world/2018/sep/19/myanmar-rohingya-crisis-icc-begins-investigation-into-atrocities. Accessed 8 June 2023

Websites/Web Sources

Agence France-Presse (2018) MyanmarICC lacks jurisdiction to probe Rohingya crisis, (ABS-CBN News, https://news.abs-cbn.com/overseas/04/13/18/myanmar-says-icc-lacks-jurisdiction-to-probe-rohingya-crisis. Accessed 8 June 2023

Committee on the Establishment of an International Criminal Court (1995) Report, No. 22 (A/50/22) para 60-61, http://www.legal-tools.org/uploads/tx_ltpdb/doc21168.pdf. Accessed 8 June 2023

Draft Code of Offences against the Peace and Security of Mankind (1954). http://legal.un.org/ilc/texts/ instruments/english/draft_articles/7_3_1954.pdf. Accessed 8 June 2023

Draft Code of the Offences Against Peace and the Security of Mankind (1951) Yearbook of the International Law Commission 1951, https://legal.un.org/ilc/texts/instruments/english/commentaries/7_3_1954.pdf. Accessed 8 June 2023

Draft Statute for the International Criminal Court. Part 2. Jurisdiction, Admissibility and Applicable Law, UN Doc. A/AC.249/1998/CRP.8, https://www.legal-tools.org/doc/e652fe/pdf/. Accessed 8 June 2023

General Assembly Resolution 96(I), A/PV.55, 11 December 1946. http://www.un.org/ga/search/view_doc.asp?symbol=A/RES/96(I)&Lang=E&Area=RESOLUTION. Accessed 8 June 2023

Genocide Convention Implementation Act of 1987. https://www.congress.gov/bill/100th-congress/senate-bill/1851/text. Accessed 8 June 2023

ICC (2006) Decision on the Prosecutor's Application for Warrants of Arrest, Article 58', corr. ICC-01/04-169 23-09-2008 1/49 CB PT OA, para. 30, https://www.legal-tools.org/doc/8c20eb/pdf/, Accessed 8 June 2023

ICC (2009) Decision on the Prosecution's Application for a Warrant of Arrest against Omar Hassan Ahmad Al Bashir, ICC-02/05-01/09-3 04-03-2009, https://www.icc-cpi.int/pages/record.aspx?uri=639096. Accessed 8 June 2023

ICJ (1999) Legality of the Use of Force, Yugoslavia v United States, http://www.worldcourts.com/icj/eng/decisions/1999.06.02_use_of_force1.htm. Accessed 8 June 2023

ICJ (2007b) case of Bosnia and Herzegovina against Serbia and Montenegro, Judgment (No.91), https://www.icj-cij.org/files/case-related/91/091-20070226-JUD-01-00-EN.pdf. Accessed 8 June 2023

ICJ Report (1955) Nottebohm Case (Lichtenstein v Guatemala), Judgement, https://www.icj-cij.org/files/case-related/18/018-19550406-JUD-01-00-EN.pdf. Accessed 8 June 2023

ICTY (1994) Final Report of the Commission of Experts" UN Doc. S/1994/674 para 93, http://www.icty.org/x/file/About/OTP/un_commission_of_experts_report1994_en.pdf. Accessed 8 January 2023

ILC Yearbook (1992) UN doc. a/cn.4/ser.a/1992/add.1 55. http://legal.un.org/ilc/publications/yearbooks/english/ilc_1992_v2_p1.pdf. Accessed 8 June 2023

International Law Commission on the Work of its Forty-Eighth Session (1996), Report para 8, http://legal.un.org/ilc/documentation/english/reports/a_51_10.pdf. Accessed 8 June 2023

Power S (2014) Remarks by US Ambassador to the United Nations Samantha Power at the 10th Anniversary of the OSCE's Berlin Conference on Anti-Semitism, https://www.belfercenter.org/publication/remarks-ambassador-samantha-power-10th-anniversary-osces-berlin-conference-anti, last accessed 8 June 2023

Preparatory Committee (1997) Decisions Taken, A/AC.249/1997/L.5, http://www.iccnow.org/documents/DecisionsTaken11to21Feb97.pdf. Accessed 8 June 2023

Preparatory Committee on International Criminal Court Concludes Third Session Press Release (1997) L/2824, http://www.iccnow.org/documents/3PrepCmtConcludes21Feb97.pdf. Accessed 8 June 2023

Preparatory Committee on The Establishment of An International Criminal Court (1997) Decisions Taken by The Preparatory Committee at its Session Held from 11 to 21 February 1997 A/AC.249/1997/L.52, file:///C:/Users/tsilo/Downloads/A_AC.249_1997_L.5-EN.pdf. Accessed 8 June 2023

Security Council Resolution 2379 (2017). https://undocs.org/en/S/RES/2379(2017). Accessed 8 June 2023

Special Adviser and Head of the United Nations Investigative Team (2018) First report, S/2018/1031, https://digitallibrary.un.org/record/1653330. Accessed 8 June 2023

UN Doc. A/C.6/SR.128,. http://daccessods.un.org/access.nsf/Get?Open&DS=A/C.6/SR.128&Lang=E. Accessed 8 June 2023

UN, Global Issues: Peace and Security., https://www.un.org/en/sections/issues-depth/peace-and-security/. Accessed 8 June 2023

UN Human Rights Council., Report of the detailed findings of the Independent International Fact-Finding Mission on Myanmar, A/HRC/39/CRP.2, https://www.ohchr.org/Documents/HRBodies/HRCouncil/FFMMyanmar/A_HRC_39_CRP.2.pdf. Accessed 8 June 2023

UNGA Resolution 898 4 December 1954. https://legal.un.org/ilc/texts/instruments/english/draft_articles/7_3_1954.pdf. Accessed 8 June 2023

United Nations Diplomatic Conference of Plenipotentiaries on the Establishment of an International Criminal Court Official Records., Third Meeting A/CONF.183/C.1/SR.3 para 100, http://legal.un.org/icc/rome/proceedings /E/Rome%20Proceedings_v2_e.pdf. Accessed 8 June 2023

Worldpopulation Website., http://worldpopulationreview.com/countries/. Accessed 8 June 2023

Yearbook of the International Law Commission (1996). http://legal.un.org/docs/?path=../ilc/publications/yearbooks/english/ilc_1996_v1.pdf&lang=EFSRAC. Accessed 8 June 2023

Chapter 4
Crimes Against Humanity Under the ICC's Jurisdiction

Abstract It is an indisputable fact that the history of the human race from the beginning of civilisation to this very day in the 'wondrous' twenty-first century has been tainted many times by detestable and heinous crimes such as mass executions of citizens, enslavement, imprisonment of innocent people, torture, rape, sexual slavery, enforced prostitution, forced pregnancies, enforced sterilizations, persecution of identifiable groups and collectivities, enforced disappearances of persons, implementation of systems of segregation and discrimination on grounds of race (apartheid), deportations of entire populations and other similarly grave actions. The crimes in question are succinctly described today as crimes against humanity. They have been included in the Rome Statute of the International Criminal Court (ICCRSt) since its adoption in 1998. Yet for the most part, they remain unpunished. This is either because States are genuinely unable to prosecute them due to the collapse of their national justice systems or because they are unwilling to intervene on account of government institutions themselves having more often than not abetted, incited or supported criminally punishable actions of such magnitude. This provides the background to the need to establish a permanent institution for the administration of international justice and to the ICC's legitimacy. The present chapter focuses first on the analysis of the critical term "attack"; it then explores the literature on the intriguing interrelation of the overlapping terms "widespread", "systematic", "multiple commission of acts", and "pursuant to or in furtherance of a State or organisational policy", which play a fundamental role in the identification of all types of crimes included in Article 7 ICCRSt (Crimes Against Humanity). Ultimately, Victor Tsilonis proposes a novel interpretation of the terms' interrelation in Article 7 of the ICCRSt.

4.1 Introduction: The Legal Development of Crimes Against Humanity

It is an indisputable fact that the history of the human race from the beginning of civilisation to this very day in the 'wondrous' twenty-first century has been tainted many times by detestable and heinous crimes, such as mass executions of citizens,

V. Tsilonis, *The Jurisdiction of the International Criminal Court*,
https://doi.org/10.1007/978-3-031-46138-5_4

enslavement, imprisonment of innocent people, torture, rape, sexual slavery, enforced prostitution, forced pregnancies, enforced sterilizations, persecution of identifiable groups and collectivities, enforced disappearances of persons, implementation of systems of segregation and discrimination on grounds of race (apartheid), deportations of entire populations and other similarly grave actions. The crimes in question, along with others of equal gravity, are succinctly described today as crimes against humanity. They have been included in the Rome Statute of the International Criminal Court (ICCRSt) since its adoption in 1998. Yet for the most part, they remain unpunished. This is either because States are genuinely unable to prosecute them due to the collapse of national justice systems or they appear to be unwilling to intervene on account of government institutions themselves having more often than not abetted, incited or supported criminally punishable actions of such magnitude. This provides the background to the need to establish a permanent institution for the administration of international justice and to the ICC's legitimacy.[1]

Notably, from a historical viewpoint, even though crimes against humanity were persecuted for the first time in Nuremberg by the International Military Tribunal, the term was indirectly introduced into legal terminology in the early twentieth century, following the crimes committed against the Armenians by the Turks. Three decades already before the Nuremberg Trials, the Joint Declaration of France, Great Britain and Russia of May 1915 clearly stated that "[i]n view of those new crimes of Turkey against humanity and civilization, the Allied governments announce publicly to the Sublime-Porte that they will hold personally responsible [for] these crimes all members of the Ottoman government and those of their agents who are implicated in such massacres".[2]

Following the end of World War II, and specifically during the London Conference, Justice Robert H. Jackson proposed for the first time the use of the term "crimes against humanity" instead of the phrase "persecutions, atrocities and deportations". He did so upon the suggestion of a prominent international jurist who we now know was Sir Hersch Lauterpacht.[3] Following which, crimes against humanity became the third category of crimes in Article VI of the Charter of the International Military Tribunal of Nuremberg. A short time later, in 1954, they were included in Article 2(11) of the Draft Code of Crimes against the Peace and Security of Mankind.[4]

---

[1] Simeonidou-Kastanidou (2003).

[2] Armenian-genocide (1915), http://www.armenian-genocide.org/Affirmation.160/current_category.7/affirmation_detail.html. last accessed 8 June 2023.

[3] Report of Jackson (1949), p. 416.

[4] Draft Code of Crimes against the Peace and Security of Mankind, adopted by the International Law Commission at its sixth session in 1954. http://legal.un.org/docs/?path=../ilc/texts/instruments/english/draft_articles/7_3_1954.pdf&lang=EF. Last accessed 8 June 2023.

At the 1998 Rome Conference, whereas the crime of genocide was incorporated into the Statute of the International Criminal Court without much ado,[5] major differences arose among States as to what would constitute a crime against humanity. These differences were to a great degree unavoidable. During the period between the Nuremberg trials and 1998, the act of genocide had become firmly established as a well-defined crime. By contrast, in 1991 the International Law Commission (ILC) decided to completely abandon the legal term "crime against humanity" in favour of the newly discovered but related term "systematic or mass violations of human rights".[6] This line of thought was adopted a year later by Special Rapporteur Doudou Thiam, who did not include the term "crime against humanity" in the statute for an international criminal court, preferring the new term "systematic or mass violations of human rights" instead. Nonetheless, after 1993, the ILC Working Group revived the term "crimes again humanity", noting that "[i]t seemed inconceivable [to the Working Group] that, at the present stage of development of international law, the international community would move to create an international criminal court without including crimes such as those mentioned above [crimes against humanity], under the Court's jurisdiction".[7]

Furthermore, the UN Security Council itself had further complicated the legal difficulty surrounding the definition of crimes against humanity, since within a period of 18 months it had adopted two different definitions of the term in the Statutes of the International Criminal Tribunal for the former Yugoslavia and that for Rwanda (Articles 5 ICTY and 3 ICTR, respectively).[8] Article 5 ICTY, which was initially adopted by the Security Council in May 1993, referred to crimes committed "in armed conflict, whether international or internal in character, and directed against any civilian population". Article 3 ICTR was slightly different. As of November 1994 it defined crimes against humanity as those committed "as part of a widespread or systematic attack against any civilian population on national, political, ethnic, racial or religious grounds",[9] Meanwhile, in both articles adopted by the Security Council in 1993/94, the crimes themselves remained the same: (1) murder;

[5] Of course, that was because there was already from 1948 a clear and rather indisputable definition in the Convention for the Prevention and Punishment of the Crime of Genocide.

[6] Yearbook of the International Law Commission 1991. UN Doc A/CN.4/SER.A/1991/Add.1 (Part 2), pp. 103–104. http://legal.un.org/ilc/publications/yearbooks/english/ilc_1991_v2_p2.pdf. last accessed 8 June 2023.

[7] The Working Group did not neglect to refer to the inclusion of this term in the Statute for the International Criminal Tribunal for the former Yugoslavia. "Report of the International Law Commission on the Work of its Forty-Fifth Session (3 May – 23 July 1993)" in Yearbook UN Doc. A/CN.4/SER.A/1993Add.1 (Part 2), p. 110, http://legal.un.org/ilc/publications/yearbooks/english/ilc_1993_v2_p2.pdf. last accessed 8 June 2023.

[8] ICTY Statute http://www.icty.org/x/file/Legal%20Library/Statute/statute_sept09_en.pdf. last accessed 8 June 2023.

[9] ICTR Statute (adopted 8 November 1994), http://legal.un.org/avl/pdf/ha/ictr_EF.pdf. last accessed 8 June 2023.

(2) extermination; (3) enslavement; (4) deportation; (5) imprisonment; (6) torture; (7) rape; (8) persecutions on political, racial and religious grounds; (9) other inhumane acts.

Consequently, both on the level of the Ad Hoc Committee and the Preparatory Committee, as well as at the Rome Conference, the enactment of legislation concerning crimes against humanity constituted a great challenge for international legislators, since they had to come up with a new definition. In other words, they had to draft a new article which would take into consideration the contradictions of international law and the different opinions of States.[10] It is noteworthy that even though there was a general consensus on "widespread or systematic attack" as a requirement for identifying the commission of a crime against humanity, the same was not the case with regard to, for instance, the existence of "an element of planning, policy, conspiracy or organization"[11] or the number of victims.

Just as the discipline of human rights deals with significant crimes committed by the State against its citizens, crimes against humanity under the ICC's jurisdiction focus on prosecuting the perpetrators of such crimes as fall under its jurisdiction; although, admittedly, constant attempts are being made to expand the scope of both. At this point, it should be underlined that even though plenty of the historical differences in opinion concerning the definition of crimes against humanity, including for instance the initial precondition of being able to link these crimes with an armed conflict, were addressed during the diplomatic negotiations of the Rome Conference in July 1998, others, such as the role of state policy in the commissioning of a widespread or systematic attack directed against any civilian population, are still in need of an exact legal definition, as we will see later on.

Article 7(1) ICCRSt stipulates that "'crime against humanity' means any of the following acts when committed *as part of a widespread or systematic* attack directed *against any civilian population*, with knowledge of the *attack*".[12] The specific criminal actions are described in brief as follows:

---

[10] However, as pointed out early on, the Rome Statute for the International Criminal Court is not an international criminal code that applies in the direct and immediate manner that domestic criminal law does pursuant to its ratification within a single national legal order. See Simeonidou-Kastanidou (2003), p. 456.

[11] In contrast to war crimes, for which even individual or isolated acts suffice. See Report of the Preparatory Committee on the Establishment of an International Criminal Court Volume I para 85 https://www.legal-tools.org/doc/e75432/pdf/. last accessed 8 June 2023.

[12] Article 7(1) ICCRSt (emphasis added). For the purpose of this Statute, "crime against humanity" means any of the following acts when committed as part of a widespread or systematic attack directed against any civilian population, with knowledge of the attack: (a) Murder; (b) Extermination; (c) Enslavement; (d) Deportation or forcible transfer of population; (e) Imprisonment or other severe deprivation of physical liberty in violation of fundamental rules of international law; (f) Torture; (g) Rape, sexual slavery, enforced prostitution, forced pregnancy, enforced sterilization, or any other form of sexual violence of comparable gravity; (h) Persecution against any identifiable group or collectivity on political, racial, national, ethnic, cultural, religious, gender as defined in paragraph 3, or other grounds that are universally recognized as impermissible under international law, in connection with any act referred to in this paragraph or any crime within

(*1*) Murder; (*2*) Extermination; (*3*) Enslavement; (*4*) Deportation or forcible transfer of population; (*5*) Imprisonment or other severe deprivation of physical liberty; (*6*) Torture; (*7*) Rape, sexual slavery, enforced prostitution, forced pregnancy, enforced sterilization; (*8*) Persecution against any identifiable group or collectivity on political, racial, national, ethnic, cultural, religious, gender or other grounds (*9*) Enforced disappearance of persons; (*10*) The crime of apartheid.

Additionally, the subsequent two paragraphs include a detailed interpretation of the following crucial legal terms: attack, extermination, enslavement, deportation or forcible transfer of population, torture, forced pregnancy, persecution, apartheid, enforced disappearance of persons (in paragraph 2)[13] and gender (in paragraph 3).[14]

---

the jurisdiction of the Court; (i) Enforced disappearance of persons; (j) The crime of apartheid; (k) Other inhumane acts of a similar character intentionally causing great suffering, or serious injury to body or to mental or physical health.

[13] Article 7(2) ICCRSt: For the purpose of paragraph 1:

1. "Attack directed against any civilian population" means a course of conduct involving the multiple commission of acts referred to in paragraph 1 against any civilian population, pursuant to or in furtherance of a State or organizational policy to commit such attack;
2. "Extermination" includes the intentional infliction of conditions of life, inter alia the deprivation of access to food and medicine, calculated to bring about the destruction of part of a population;
3. "Enslavement" means the exercise of any or all of the powers attaching to the right of ownership over a person and includes the exercise of such power in the course of trafficking in persons, in particular women and children;
4. "Deportation or forcible transfer of population" means forced displacement of the persons concerned by expulsion or other coercive acts from the area in which they are lawfully present, without grounds permitted under international law;
5. "Torture" means the intentional infliction of severe pain or suffering, whether physical or mental, upon a person in the custody or under the control of the accused; except that torture shall not include pain or suffering arising only from, inherent in or incidental to, lawful sanctions;
6. "Forced pregnancy" means the unlawful confinement of a woman forcibly made pregnant, with the intent of affecting the ethnic composition of any population or carrying out other grave violations of international law. This definition shall not in any way be interpreted as affecting national laws relating to pregnancy;
7. "Persecution" means the intentional and severe deprivation of fundamental rights contrary to international law by reason of the identity of the group or collectivity;
8. "The crime of apartheid" means inhumane acts of a character similar to those referred to in paragraph 1, committed in the context of an institutionalized regime of systematic oppression and domination by one racial group over any other racial group or groups and committed with the intention of maintaining that regime;
9. "Enforced disappearance of persons" means the arrest, detention or abduction of persons by, or with the authorization, support or acquiescence of, a State or a political organization, followed by a refusal to acknowledge that deprivation of freedom or to give information on the fate or whereabouts of those persons, with the intention of removing them from the protection of the law for a prolonged period of time.

[14] Article 7(3) ICCRSt: For the purpose of this Statute, it is understood that the term "gender" refers to the two sexes, male and female, within the context of society. The term "gender" does not indicate any meaning different from the above.

Given that the detailed presentation of each of the aforementioned issues could constitute the topic of a series of dissertations, we will focus our attention on three key points of Article 7 ICCRSt which are directly linked to the determination of the commission of crimes against humanity under the ICC's jurisdiction. Specifically, we will analyse in detail: (1) the concept of attack, (2) the interpretation of the term "widespread or systematic" and (3) the concept of civilian population. It is worth noting that the aforementioned legal terms ("widespread or systematic"—"-attack"—"civilian population") are all mentioned in the beginning of Article 7 ICCRSt on crimes against humanity and are relevant to all the potential ways of committing crimes against humanity, without exception, as they must necessarily exist for a crime in traditional criminal law to be considered grave enough to fall within the sphere of crimes against humanity.

4.2 The Analysis of the Term "Attack" in the Context of Crimes Against Humanity

The International Criminal Tribunal for the former Yugoslavia (ICTY) ruled in the Đorđević case that according to its statute "in order to constitute a crime against humanity, a crime listed under Article 5 of the Statute must be committed 'in an armed conflict' [. . .] This requirement is specific to the Tribunal; as held by the Appeals Chamber, under customary international law crimes against humanity may also be committed in times of peace".[15]

According to the ICTY's jurisprudence, but primarily according to Article 5 of the ICTY Statute that describes crimes against humanity, an attack as an objective element of the commission of crimes against humanity must necessarily take place during an armed conflict. However, this is not a criterion applied under the ICCRSt, even though the ICC's jurisprudence has not yet adjudicated over this particular issue. That is because: (1) the clear formulation of Article 7 ICCRSt has unlinked the existence of an armed conflict from the commission of an attack; (2) as noted in the aforementioned ICTY judgment, crimes against humanity can be committed according to international customary law both in times of peace and war; (3) the 'records' of the Rome Conference prove that a noteworthy number of States had expressed their conviction that crimes against humanity can be committed even in times of peace.[16]

[15] ICTY (2011a), para 1587 http://www.icty.org/x/cases/djordjevic/tjug/en/110223_djordjevic_judgt_en.pdf last accessed 8 June 2023, which affirms the Appeals Judgment in *The Prosecutor v Tadić* (IT-94-1-A) 15 July 1999 para 251. See also ICTY (2002c), para 86; ICTY (2001a), para 1700.

[16] One of the paradoxes of the Rome Conference is that no official verbatim records were created as is usually the case. However, see Official Records, United Nations Diplomatic Conference of Plenipotentiaries on the Establishment of an International Criminal Court Rome (1998), http://legal.un.org/icc/rome/proceedings/contents.htm last accessed 8 June 2023.

Notably, based on the existing ICTY and ICTR jurisprudence, at first in the Krnojelac case,[17] and later in the Perišić case, ICTY judges pointed out that "an 'attack' may be defined as a course of conduct involving the commission of acts of violence. In the context of crimes against humanity, an 'attack' is distinct from the concept of 'armed conflict' and not limited to the use of armed force. Rather, it may encompass any mistreatment of the civilian population. The attack may precede, outlast or continue during the armed conflict and need not be part of it"[18] according to international customary law.[19]

It is also important that in the Kupreškić et al. case, the competent ICTY Trial Chamber expressed its disapproval regarding the invocation of the Roman law principle *tu quoque* as a line of defence, pointing out that "in international law there is no justification for attacks on civilians carried out either by virtue of the *tu quoque* principle (i.e. the argument whereby the fact that the adversary is committing similar crimes offers a valid defence to a belligerent's crimes) or on the strength of the principle of reprisals".[20] Thus the court ruled that the accused could not rely on the fact that at the time, atrocities by Muslims against Croatian civilians had also been committed.

The same legal reasoning was also followed by the ICTY in the Kunarac et al. case, where it was highlighted that the accused cannot introduce in their defence "evidence of an attack by the other party on the accused's civilian population [...] unless it tends 'to prove or disprove any of the allegations made in the indictment', notably to refute the Prosecutor's assertion that there was a widespread or systematic attack against a civilian population".[21] Consequently, a potential "submission that the other side is responsible for starting the hostilities would not, for instance, disprove that there was an attack against a particular civilian population".[22] On the contrary, any attack against the other side's civilian population is equally illegal and crimes committed as part of this attack could, if all other preconditions are met, amount to crimes against humanity.[23]

On the other hand, the ICTR's jurisprudence especially in the Akayesu and Musema cases was groundbreaking in separating the concept of attack from that of violence. Specifically, the ICTR judges in the Musema case, after initially adopting the legal viewpoint on the definition of the attack of the Akayesu[24] and Rutaganda

[17] ICTY (2002b), para 54; ICTY (2002c), para 86; ICTY (2004d), para 30.

[18] ICTY (2011b), para 82; ICTY (2001a), para 1702; ICTR (2003), para 327.

[19] ICTY (2002a), para 86. http://www.icty.org/x/cases/kunarac/acjug/en/kun-aj020612e.pdf. last accessed 8 June 2023.

[20] ICTY (2000), para 765. http://www.icty.org/x/cases/kupreskic/tjug/en/kup-tj000114e.pdf. last accessed 8 June 2023.

[21] ICTY (2002a), para 88.

[22] ibid.

[23] ibid. para 87.

[24] ICTR (1998), para 581.

cases,[25] ruled that "an attack may also be non-violent in nature, such as imposing a system of apartheid, which is declared a crime against humanity in Article 1 of the Apartheid Convention of 1973, or exerting pressure on the population to act in a particular manner, which may come under the purview of an attack, if orchestrated on a massive scale or in a systematic manner".[26]

4.3 The Analysis of the Terms "Widespread or Systematic" and Their Proposed Interpretations

A number of different ways to interpret the terms "widespread or systematic" has been suggested by legal scholars. According to Damgaard, the term "widespread or systematic", which can be found in Article 7(1) ICCRSt, must be interpreted in light of Article 7(2)(a) ICCRst, which clarifies that the term "attack [. . .] means a course of conduct involving the *multiple commission of acts* referred to in paragraph 1 against any civilian population, *pursuant to* or in furtherance of *a State or organizational policy* to commit such attack".[27] According to this view, the term "widespread or systematic" must be interpreted cumulatively, given that the term "widespread" equates to the term "multiple commissions of acts", and the term "systematic" equates to the phrase "pursuant to or in furtherance of a State or organizational policy".[28] This 'authentic' interpretation of the term "widespread or systematic" in Article 7(1) ICCRSt based on the second paragraph of this same article appears to find jurisprudential foundations on the ICTY Tadić and the ICTR Akayesu judgments, as well as the Nuremberg International Military Tribunal judgment, which clearly stated that "[t]he persecution of the Jews at the hands of the Nazi Government has been proved in the greatest detail before the Tribunal. It is a record of consistent and systematic inhumanity on the greatest scale".[29]

Example 1 *First proposal for the interpretation of the terms "widespread or systematic"*

"widespread" = "multiple commissions of acts";

"systematic" = "pursuant to or in furtherance of a State or organizational policy"

The *second and often prevailing interpretation* sees the terms "widespread" and "systematic" as adjectives characterising the word "attack", as terms with their own distinct definition, which is exactly the case for the terms "multiple commissions of

[25] ICTR (1999), para 70.

[26] ICTR (2000), para 205. http://unictr.irmct.org/sites/unictr.org/files/case-documents/ictr-96-13/trial-judgements/en/000127.pdf. last accessed 8 June 2023.

[27] Damgaard (2008), p. 80.

[28] ibid.

[29] Trial (1947), p. 247. https://www.loc.gov/rr/frd/Military_Law/pdf/NT_Vol-I.pdf. last accessed 8 June 2023.

acts" and "pursuant to or in furtherance of a State or organizational policy". Thus, according to this second proposal, the terms in question are conceptionally unlinked from the terms "multiple commissions of acts" and "pursuant to or in furtherance of a State or organizational policy" of Article 7(2)(a) ICCRSt. Consequently, each of the aforementioned four terms found in the first and second paragraphs of Article 7 ICCRSt becomes its own discrete conceptual entity.

According to Daryl Robinson, who participated in the work of the Rome Conference for the establishment of an international criminal court, the term "widespread" is broader than the term "multiple commissions of acts" just as the term "systematic" is broader than the term "pursuant to or in furtherance of a State or organizational policy". This interpretation is based on Robinson's personal testimony of the Rome Conference, as well as on evidence from negotiations between the delegations of participant States concerning this issue.[30]

Specifically, Robinson points out that "fortunately, a solution was found in order to get past the seemingly irreconcilable difference"[31] between States that wished for a disjunction between the two terms and those who preferred a conjunction. At that time, it was successfully maintained that the potentially overtly broad legal application of the disjunctive term "widespread or systematic" attack would be avoided through the introduction of the first subsection of the second paragraph, which refers to an "attack directed against any civilian population" as "a course of conduct involving the multiple commission of acts [...] pursuant to or in furtherance of a State or organisational policy".

In other words, this is in principle a historical interpretation of the provision, since it is founded on the historical context of the adoption of Article 7 ICCRSt and offers information regarding motives, reasoning and purposes.[32] What is more, Robinson's analysis is based on a teleological interpretation, which examines the purposes of the legislator historically (subjective teleological interpretation).[33]

Example 2 *Second proposal for the interpretation of the terms "widespread or systematic"*

"widespread" $= x_1$
where
"widespread" > "multiple commissions of acts"
"systematic" $= x_2$
where
"systematic" > "pursuant to or in furtherance of a State or organizational policy"
"multiple commissions of acts" $= x_3$
"pursuant to or in furtherance of a State or organizational policy" $= x_4$

[30] Robinson (1999), p. 43.
[31] ibid 47.
[32] Stamatis (2003), pp. 322–324.
[33] ibid 328–331.

(i.e. under which x1, x2, x3 and x4 have their own distinct legal definition and x_1, x_2 are broader than x_3, x_4),

Thus,

$x_1 > x_3$

$x_2 > x_4$

According to Robinson's proposal, the existence of the term "widespread" is not a necessary precondition in all cases. That is because, while doubtlessly the term "widespread" introduces a strict criterion which requires a great number of victims and "massive, frequent, large-scale action", the phrase "a course of conduct involving the multiple commission of acts" introduces a more lenient criterion.[34] Robinson's conclusion here is founded not only in grammar, but also in law, since the multiple commission of a crime may constitute one or more[35] similar criminal acts, while the "widespread commission of a crime" would require, according to Robinson and the current author, at least three.

What is more, according to this view, it is not necessary to prove that the accused personally committed more than one crime in order to be convicted for committing a crime against humanity, but only that the accused is criminally responsible for the commission of one and only one crime (e.g. of rape), as long as this act was committed within the frame of a widespread attack.[36] Certainly, in that case there would probably be an issue of admissibility of the case, i.e. while the accused who appears to have committed a crime against humanity would in principle fall under

[34] The terms "systematic" and "multiple commission of acts" were considered by the delegations to present a significantly lower limit than the "massive, frequent, large-scale action", implied by the term "widespread". Those terms, which are loosely linked with ICTY and ICTR jurisprudence, were chosen to exclude the prosecution of isolated acts. Robinson (1999) fn. 28.

[35] If someone throws a grenade and ten citizens are killed as a consequence of this act, then we have a case of a multiple commission of murder via a single criminal act.

[36] At least, that was the ICTY's opinion on the matter. See the following abstract from the Tadić judgment, ICTY (1997), para 649, (where further references can be found): "A related issue is whether a single act by a perpetrator can constitute a crime against humanity. A tangential issue, not at issue before this Trial Chamber, is whether a single act in and of itself can constitute a crime against humanity. This issue has been the subject of intense debate, with the jurisprudence immediately following the Second World War being mixed. The American tribunals generally supported the proposition that a massive nature was required, while the tribunals in the British Zone came to the opposite conclusion, finding that the mass element was not essential to the definition, in respect of either the number of acts or the number of victims and that "what counted was not the mass aspect, but the link between the act and the cruel and barbarous political system, specifically, the Nazi regime". Clearly, a single act by a perpetrator taken within the context of a widespread or systematic attack against a civilian population entails individual criminal responsibility and an individual perpetrator need not commit numerous offences to be held liable. Although it is correct that isolated, random acts should not be included in the definition of crimes against humanity, that is the purpose of requiring that the acts be directed against a civilian population and thus "[e]ven an isolated act can constitute a crime against humanity if it is the product of a political system based on terror or persecution.". The decision of Trial Chamber I of the International Tribunal in the Vukovar Hospital Decision is a recent recognition of the fact that a single act by a perpetrator can constitute a crime against humanity."

the ICC's jurisdiction, as long as none of the state parties took on the case, his crime ought to have been committed in a particularly detestable manner or on a large scale. Only thus could the case in question pass unscathed the obstacle of Article 17(1) (d) ICCRSt, which introduces a case's gravity as an admissibility criterion, i.e. as a criterion for the *de facto* exercise of the ICC's jurisdiction.[37]

The third proposed interpretation is the one supported by academics such as Rodney Dixon in Triffterer's monumental work[38] or Kai Ambos.[39] According to this view, the second paragraph of Article 7 ICCRSt essentially limits the scope of its first paragraph and of the disjunctive terms "widespread or systematic". In other words, the above view wishes to indirectly introduce through the first subsection of the second paragraph of Article 7 ICCRSt a fundamental limitation to the disjunctive concept "widespread or systematic" in a way that interprets it as cumulative (and thus, subsequently, the concept "widespread *or* systematic" is equated to "widespread *and* systematic").

Example 3 *Third proposal for the interpretation of the terms "widespread or systematic"(essentially transforming the concept from disjunctive to cumulative)*

"multiple commissions of acts" > "widespread"

However, this interpretation leads to

"widespread or systematic" = > "widespread and systematic"

"pursuant to or in furtherance of a State or organisational policy" > "systematic"

with the clarification at this point that the term "pursuant to or in furtherance of a State or organisational policy" is thus rendered wider than the term "systematic" and that their relationship is that of two intersecting circles, since an act can be systematically committed without it however being "pursuant to or in furtherance of a state or organisational policy".[40]

The above can easily be presented in figure (Fig. 4.1)[41]:

Consequently, this third proposal interprets Article 7 ICCRSt as follows: (1) the concept of "multiple commissions of acts" in Article 7(2)(a) ICCRSt is—always within the framework of the ICCRSt—legally broader than the concept of "widespread" in Article 7(1) ICCRSt; (2) the concept of "pursuant to or in furtherance of a State or organisational policy" in Article 7(2)(a) ICCRSt is broader in scope but does not fully encase the concept of "systematic" in Article 7(1) ICCRSt, as their relationship is that of two intersecting circles, because—always according to this

[37] Article 17 ICCRSt - Issues of admissibility: [...] (d) The case is not of sufficient gravity to justify further action by the Court. Also, Robinson (1999), p. 48.

[38] Dixon (1999), pp. 126–127.

[39] Ambos (2001), pp. 406–407.

[40] Naziris (2009), p. 85. In this point, however, a contradiction can be found between this conclusion and the jurisprudence of international criminal tribunals, the accuracy of which is accepted by the writer.

[41] ibid 84.

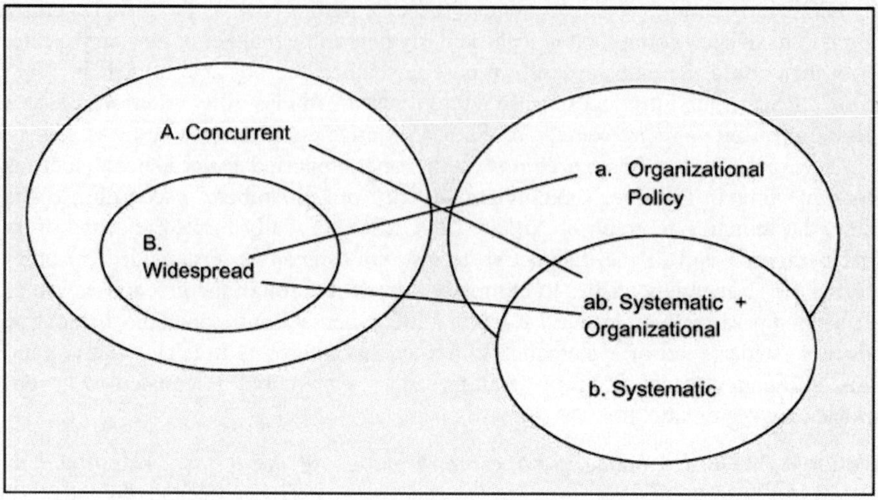

Fig. 4.1 Conceptual correlation of the terms "widespread or systematic"

view—"indeed, systematic acts can be committed even outside a State or organisational policy".[42]

However, this view cannot under any circumstances be accepted, since it does not justify, either jurisprudentially or teleologically, how the legal concept of "multiple commission of acts" could ever be broader than the term "widespread". We then come to the second 'conclusion' of the interpretation in question, i.e. that the concept of "pursuant to or in furtherance of a State or organisational policy" in Article 7(2)(a) ICCRSt is broader in scope, but does not fully encase the concept of "systematic" in Article 7(1) ICCRSt, because "indeed, systematic acts can be committed even outside a State or organisational policy". Cleraly, this is also contrary to the ICTY's jurisprudence (cases Kupreškić et al., Erdemović and Vasiljević),[43] from which it can be explicitly concluded that "typical in each case is the – also extremely large *mutatis mutandis* – number of perpetrators (and of their accomplices)".[44,45]

[42]ibid 85.

[43]ibid 88–89.

[44]ibid 89, 90 where it is stated that "a crime against humanity cannot be committed by one perpetrator". Nonetheless, it is also stated that "It wouldn't be reasonable to exclude from the application scope of the general provision of the crime against humanity attacks of large proportions which are committed with only one action, such as the use of a nuclear bomb against non--combatants." ibid. 91 fn. 207. If we were to accept the aforementioned view, we would have to exclude cases such as the poisoning of a minority city's aqueduct by one perpetrator or the destruction of a village and the extermination of its unarmed residents by a heavily armed militant, commando or helicopter pilot. The ICC's jurisprudence does not support this approach, as already analysed.

[45]As already mentioned, the writer of the present book does not share the view that the fulfillment of the "systematic" criterion must always be connected with the number of perpetrators.

If one accepts as correct the aforementioned jurisprudence,[46] it would be contradictory to believe that the term "systematic" could be considered to include acts committed outside a State or organisational policy, since one would then have to consider the exceptional and unlikely instance (which however has yet to be confirmed jurisprudentially and no one explicitly invokes) of many perpetrators systematically committing a crime against humanity without being organised on a state or other level. Finally the interpretation in question does not in any case take into consideration the ICC Bemba judgment of 15 June 2009, which will be analysed later on.[47]

The fourth interpretation is the one that this book advocates. Undoubtedly, the coexistence within Article 7 ICCRSt of the terms "widespread or systematic" (in the first paragraph), "a course of conduct involving the multiple commission of acts [...]" and "pursuant to or in furtherance of a State or organisational policy" (in the second paragraph) complicates the act of interpretation, an issue that has already been the focus of the work of plenty of academics throughout the world. What is more, it is a fact that most of the mathematically possible options have already been suggested, as we already saw (whether with regard to the 'equivalence' of the terms, the 'dominance' of the terms of the first paragraph over the terms of the second paragraph, or the 'dominance' of the terms of the second paragraph over those of the first).

What new interpretation can be presented after all these years of intense academic discourse on the issue in question? What new interpretation can be suggested when mathematically all the relations between the clashing terms have already been adopted and supported? The writer believes that, as with all complex problems, any attempt to solve this particular intractable matter of interpretation calls for an appropriate starting point, followed by step-by-step clarification and resolution of the problematic issues. Better methodology is also required in this particular case. Such methodology should incorporate the following principles: *(1)* to begin with the analysis of each term separately before proceeding to draw crucial conclusions regarding the interpretation of all the aforementioned terms, which coexist in various Article 7 ICCRSt paragraphs (and not the other way round); *(2)* to take into consideration primarily the recent ICC jurisprudence (Katanga, al-Bashir, Bemba and Ruto judgments), which of course for some of the aforementioned academics would be humanly impossible because of the time at which they expressed their views, but in the cases of some others, the pre-existing ICC jurisprudence has been intentionally or unintentionally ignored; *(3)* to draw justifiable conclusions or justifiably not draw any, if the latter can be deemed tolerable on the present matter.

Regarding the definition of the term "widespread", it was analysed for the first time in the ICC jurisprudence regarding the Court's decision on the confirmation of

[46] Naziris (2009), p. 89 fn 200.

[47] ICC (2009a), para 83. https://www.icc-cpi.int/CourtRecords/CR2009_04528.PDF. last accessed 8 June 2023.

charges against Germain Katanga[48] and on the prosecution's application for a warrant of arrest against Omar Hassan Ahmad Al Bashir.[49] These decisions, which followed the ICTY jurisprudence as reflected in the Kordic and Cerke, Blagojevic and Jokic cases,[50] clarify that even though the terms "widespread" and "systematic" are not explicitly defined in the ICCRSt, the linguistic notion of the term "systematic" excludes random or isolated incidents, as they could not be considered a systemic attacks.[51] What is more, regarding the term "widespread", the Court clarified that it "refers to the large-scale nature of the attack, as well as to the number of victims, while the term 'systematic' pertains to the organised nature of the acts of violence and to the improbability of their random occurrence".[52]

Additionally, and in order to strengthen the aforementioned arguments, it is worth noting that in the most recent case of Ruto, Koshey and Sang,[53] ICC judges pointed out that "[o]n the basis of the material provided to the Chamber, there are substantial grounds to believe that the attack perpetrated was *widespread*. Viewed as a whole, the evidence shows that the attack was massive, frequent, carried out collectively with considerable seriousness and directed against a large number of civilian victims".[54] Further: "[i]n addition, there are substantial grounds to believe that the attack was systematic. An attack is *systematic* when it implies the 'organised nature of the acts of violence and the improbability of their random occurrence'".[55]

Hence, according to the above abstract of the ICC's judgment, one can easily ascertain how similar the interpretation of the terms "widespread" and "systematic" is, *since without reading the rest of the judgment, one could easily presume that the first sentence, which is quoted above verbatim, refers to the analysis of the term "widespread", while the second sentence refers to the term "systematic", even though it is not explicitly included in the second sentence* (Viewed as a whole… civilian victims). Furthermore, it is easy to ascertain that the mention of one term ("widespread") does not negate the existence of the other ("systematic"), since one implies the other, and *vice versa*. Finally one could also arguably endorse the view that if the words "widespread" and "systematic" were removed and gaps left in their stead in the above sentences, one could easily insert the word "systematic" in lieu of the word "widespread" and vice versa.

---

[48] ICC (2008), Pre-Trial Chamber I https://www.icc-cpi.int/CourtRecords/CR2008_05172.PDF. last accessed 8 June 2023.

[49] ICC (2009b), para 81 https://www.icc-cpi.int/pages/record.aspx?uri=639096. last accessed 8 June 2023.

[50] ICTY (2004b), para 94; *The Prosecutor v. Blagojevic and Jokic*. Case No. IT-02-60-T. Trial Judgment, 17 January 2005, para 545–546.

[51] ICC (2009b), para 81. They could however in less common cases be considered widespread attacks.

[52] ibid.

[53] ICC (2012), https://www.icc-cpi.int/CourtRecords/CR2012_01004.PDF. last accessed 8 June 2023.

[54] ibid para 176 (emphasis added).

[55] ibid para 179 (emphasis added).

The close relation of these two terms ("widespread" and "systematic"), which reminds us of the case of twins that are similar in a large degree, is proven beyond doubt by the ICC judges' continued analysis of the terms in question. Thus, firstly regarding a more thorough analysis of the term "widespread" based on the facts of the case, the fulfillment of the criterion of widespread attack

> is demonstrated by the geographical scope of the attack, which covered four different locations in two districts (Uasin Gishu and Nandi) of the Rift Valley Province. Moreover, as recalled in paragraphs 167–172 above, the evidence indicates that in the locations included in the charges presented by the Prosecutor, the amount of burning and destruction of properties, injuries and murders is among the highest in the whole Kenyan territory. As a consequence, the Uasin Gishu and Nandi Districts registered a number of victims which is among the largest of the post-election violence in Kenya. In particular, there are substantial grounds to believe that the violence in the Uasin Gishu District (encompassing Turbo town and the greater Eldoret area) resulted in the death of more than 230 people, the injury to 505 and the displacement of more than 5000 persons. In the Nandi District (encompassing Kapsabet town and Nandi Hills town) at least 7 people were murdered, and a number of houses and business premises were looted and bumt. Thousands of people in Kapsabet and in Nandi Hills were forced to seek refuge at the respective police stations or in IDP camps in the surrounding areas.[56]

Furthermore, the judges of Pre-Trial Chamber II investigated the existence of the criterion of systematic attack, noting that:

> In addition, there are substantial grounds to believe that the attack was systematic... First, the Chamber reiterates that, in the preparatory phase of the attack as well as during its execution, coordinators were in charge of identifying houses belonging to PNU supporters to be attacked in the different target locations. Some of these coordinators were later deployed on the ground to assist the perpetrators and make sure that the selected properties were attacked and burnt down and that PNU supporters were victimized. Second, the evidence shows that the perpetrators approached the target locations simultaneously, in large numbers, and from different directions, by vehicles or on foot, or both. Third, the perpetrators erected roadblocks around such locations with a view toward intercepting PNU supporters attempting to flee, with the aim of eventually killing them. Finally, the evidence indicates that, in the actual implementation of the attack, the physical perpetrators used petrol and other inflammable material to systematically burn down the properties belonging to PNU supporters.[57]

The above long abstracts of the Decision on the Confirmation of Charges in the case of Ruto et al. show the exceptionally close relation or even overlap of the terms "widespread" and "systematic". If, for example, the word "systematic" was erased from the beginning of this abstract and replaced with the word "widespread", one could easily end up being none the wiser regarding the amendment.

According to the decision of the 15 June 2009 in the Bemba case, the content of which the writer is fully in agreement with as far as the analysis of the term "widespread or systematic" is concerned, "the terms 'widespread' and 'systematic' appearing in the chapeau of article 7 of the Statute are presented in the alternative.

---

[56] ibid para 177–178.

[57] ibid para 179.

The Chamber considers that if it finds the attack to be widespread, it needs not consider whether the attack was also systematic. Therefore, the Chamber will confine itself to examining only the requirement that the attack be 'widespread'".[58]

Nonetheless, it must also be underlined that in practice this matter of interpretation may not be so complex or intractable, since to a great degree the terms "widespread" and "systematic" tend to overlap. Therefore, very often, in more than 90% of cases according to the current writer's estimation, when an attack is "widespread" it will also be "systematic", without however mathematically excluding 10% of cases where the two terms will not overlap.

On the matter of these two overlapping terms (widespread and systematic), the ICC's jurisprudence seems to agree. In the Decision on the confirmation of charges in the Katanga case, the judges pointed out that since the Chamber found that the attack was widespread, it was not necessary to consider whether it was also systematic. "However, for the purposes of completeness, the Chamber also notes that there is sufficient evidence to establish substantial grounds to believe that the attack against the civilian population of Bogoro village was also part of a systematic attack against the civilian population, predominately of Hema ethnicity, living in the Ituri region".[59]

In any case, we must not forget that it is the attack itself that must be "widespread or systematic" and not the particular acts allegedly committed by the accused.[60] In addition, according to the ICC jurisprudence in the Bemba case, "*a single act of murder by a perpetrator* may constitute a crime against humanity as long as the legal requirements with regard to the contextual element of crimes against humanity, including the nexus element, are met".[61] Regarding the further clarification of the nexus element, in the same case it was stated that this in practice meant that "[t]he Prosecutor must demonstrate the nexus between the acts of rape and the attack, thus proving that acts of rape were committed by MLC troops as part of a widespread or systematic attack directed against the CAR civilian population from on or about 26 October 2002 to 15 March 2003".[62]

Example 4 *Fourth proposal for the interpretation of the terms "widespread or systematic"*

"widespread" = X1a
"systematic" = X1b
"multiple commission of acts" = X1c
"pursuant to or in furtherance of a State or organisational policy" = X2

[58] ICC (2009a), para 82.

[59] ICC (2008), Pre-Trial Chamber, para 412.

[60] ICTY (2004b), para 94; ICTY (2004a), para 101. ICTY (2002a), para 86 Kunarac et al (IT-96-23/1-A), Judgment, 12 June 2002, para 96.

[61] ICC (2009a), para 151.

[62] ibid. para 164.

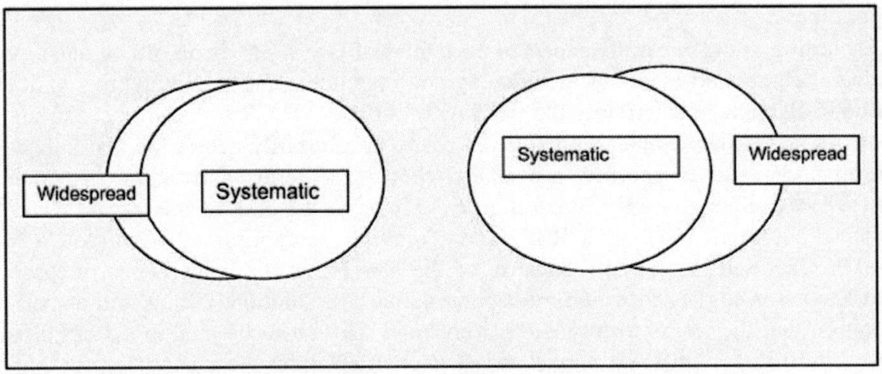

Fig. 4.2 Conceptual Correlation of the terms 'widespread' and 'systematic'

(i.e. where X1a, X1b, X1c and X2 have their own distinct legal content, but the meaning of widespread is considered to resemble to a great degree the meaning of systematic, since in practice, in more than 90% of cases, a widespread attack can be considered to be systematic, and vice versa).

Consequently, and pursuant to the existing ICC jurisprudence, the terms "widespread" and "systematic" are used interchangeably and the presence of at least one of the two is enough to determine that an attack exists in the first place.

Given that: (*a*) the term "multiple commission" introduces a narrower criterion that the term "widespread" and there is significant doubt on how this controversy can be solved and (*b*) in international criminal law the principle of *in dubio pro reo* is in effect, it must be considered that essentially the "multiple commission of acts" in paragraph 2 describes a widespread attack, if, as mentioned above, the meaning of the term "widespread" is wider than the meaning of "multiple commission of acts".

Given that there is in the first place an attack (widespread or systematic = x characteristics + multiple commission of acts), subsequently, it must be investigated whether the distinct criterion of paragraph 2(a) of Article 7 ICCRSt "pursuant to or in furtherance of a State or organisational policy" is fulfilled.

Fact No. 1
There is a great overlap between the two terms of the first paragraph ("widespread" and "systematic") that occurs in at least 90% of cases, if not more (see Fig. 4.2).

Fact No. 2

According to the generally accepted principles of law, a provision of law must be clear, definite and must not include any contradictions. Unfortunately, this is not true in all cases and certainly the wording of Article 7 ICCRSt does not constitute such a model. Nonetheless, one cannot easily or arbitrarily determine that a legal term prevails over another, especially when these terms coexist in the same provision, although partly in conflict, exactly as in the case of the terms "widespread" (Article 7(1) ICCRSt) and "multiple commission" (Article 7(2)(a) ICCRSt). It is precisely because of the above that the coalescence of these two terms is suggested as the most correct and best solution, taking into consideration that the term "widespread" is not only the first to be mentioned but also that, most importantly, it establishes a stricter criterion for the accused's guilt than the term "multiple commission of acts".

Fact No. 3

On the relation of the term "systematic" to the term "multiple commission of acts", these two terms are also extremely closely related and it would be unreasonable to consider that, in the framework of Article 7 ICCRSt on the crimes against humanity, a systematic attack in accordance with the meaning of Article 7(1) ICCRSt could ever take place without that attack involving the multiple commission of acts described in Article 7(2)(a) ICCRSt. It appears, then, that in practice the term "systematic" absolutely includes in its essence the concept of the "multiple commission of acts".

Conclusion

Through the reasoning presented above in Fig. 4.3 the potential contradiction of the legal terms "widespread", "systematic", "multiple commission of acts" and "pursuant to or in furtherance of a State or organisational policy" that coexist within Article 7 ICCRSt is solved in a substantive manner. In addition, the academic discourse on this matter has been given extensive consideration,[63] as has the fair criticism that followed the publication of the ICTY's Kunarac case in 2001, which ignored Article 7(2) ICCRSt and the existence of a State or organisational policy.[64]

[63] Schabas (2008), p. 351; Bassiouni (2011), p. 34-3.

[64] ICTY (2001b), para 27–43. http://www.icty.org/x/cases/kunarac/tjug/en/kun-tj010222e.pdf. last accessed 8 June 2023; ICTY (2002c), http://www.icty.org/x/cases/kunarac/acjug/en/kun-aj020612e.pdf. last accessed 8 June 2023.

<table>
<tr><td colspan="2"><u>The proposed reasoning to pass a judicial judgment according to the 4th proposed interpretation</u>
1. Is the attack against civilians widespread or systematic?
NO YES</td></tr>
<tr><td>If the attack is neither widespread nor systematic, then there is no attack under the meaning of this term with regard to crimes against humanity.
↓</td><td>If the attack is widespread or systematic, then there is, to begin with, an attack according to the first paragraph of Article 7 ICCRSt ("initial attack")
↓</td></tr>
<tr><td>No further discussion is necessary, since there is no attack to begin with, under the framework of Crimes against Humanity (Article 7 ICCRSt).</td><td>Since the preconditions of the first paragraph are fulfilled, because an attack is widespread or systematic, the following question must be answered: Was this attack committed "pursuant to or in furtherance of a State or organisational policy"?
("final attack")</td></tr>
</table>

Fig. 4.3 Analysis of the Proposed Reasoning to Pass a Judicial Judgment according to the fourth Proposed Interpretation

4.4 The Analysis of the Term "Pursuant to or in Furtherance of a State or Organisational Policy"

Article 7(2)(a) ICCRSt explicitly stipulates that an attack directed against any civilian population must be committed "pursuant to or in furtherance of a State or organisational policy". On this point, most academics believe that the application scope of Article 7(2)(a) ICCRSt includes perpetrators who do not act under a State's governance, contrary to how things stood before the ICCRSt's adoption. Moreover, after the ICCRSt's entry into force, the ICTY Appeals Chamber, following a simpler line of legal thought, repeatedly ruled in three cases that international customary law does not require the existence of a "State or organisational policy" as a precondition for the commission of a crime against humanity.[65]

Among the few experts to have expressed a dissenting opinion is M. Cherif Bassiouni, who is not only renowned as the prolific author of scholarly books and articles (including the most important monograph on crimes against humanity),[66] but also served as the president of the preparatory committee of the Rome Conference which was tasked with the completion of Article 7(2) ICCRSt.

Bassiouni points out that "contrary to what some advocates advance, Article 7 does not bring a new development to crimes against humanity, namely its applicability to non-state actors. If that were the case, the mafia, for example, could be charged with such crimes before the ICC, and that is clearly neither the letter nor the spirit of Article 7. The question arose after 9/11 as to whether a group such as al-Qaeda, which operates on a worldwide basis and is capable of inflicting significant harm in more than one state, falls within this category. In the author's opinion, such a group does not qualify for inclusion within the meaning of crimes against humanity as defined in Article 7 [. . .] notwithstanding the international dangers it poses. [. . .] The text [of Article 7(2)(a)] clearly refers to State policy, and the words 'organisational policy' refer to the policy of an organ of the State. The words 'organisational policy' do not refer to the policy of an organisation, but the policy of a State. It does not refer to non-state actors [. . .]".[67]

This interpretation, seen in the light of ordinary interpretative criteria, would be characterised as narrow, since the term "organisational" is interpreted exclusively in the context of a State's organisational policy. Consequently, Bassiouni's interpretation could be considered a creative interpretation which initially interprets the term "organisational" much more broadly than the letter of the law in order to subsequently place it in a much narrower framework than the one established by its formulation.

In any case, the matter of the ICCRSt's interpretation should not be seen only in light of the pre-existing international customary law that eventually led to the Rome Conference of 1998 and the ICCRSt's adoption (will of legislature), but also in light of the scope of the ICCRSt's own provisions, which now exist independently in international criminal law.

In other words, in this particular case, the interpretation of the term at hand is not crucially dependent on an interpretation of the will of the legislature or a review of international customary law concluding that state actors are necessary for the commission of a crime against humanity. On the contrary, Article 7 ICCRSt itself, entitled "Crimes against Humanity", is of the utmost importance as a clear provision of international criminal law (and not of international customary law), as well as in terms of the purpose it serves within international criminal law. Thus, as long as one can arguably assume the existence of widespread, or fairly widespread, agreement

[65] ICTY (2002c), para 98; ICTY (2004a), Judgment para 120; ICTY (2004c), para 98.

[66] Bassiouni (2014).

[67] Bassiouni (2016), pp. 169–170.

on the fact that the purpose of Article 7 ICCRSt is to protect humanity within the ICC's jurisdiction from severe crimes that can be committed against it by ruthless perpetrators, then one must investigate which would be the best possible interpretation, with a view to finding one that would not only respect the wording of this provision but simultaneously serve in the best legally acceptable way possible the purpose of this Article, which is none other than the prevention and suppression of crimes against humanity.

Consequently, William Schabas believes that the term 'organisational' must be interpreted within the context of 'State policy'. The mention of "State or organisational policy" in Article 7(2) ICCRSt must be interpreted broadly enough so that it can include legal entities that act as States, even if they are not officially recognised as such. However, an interpretation of the word "organisational" in a way which would include any group of people convened together for any reason is absurd".[68]

Unfortunately, the aforementioned view cannot be accepted in this book, precisely because such a generalised rejection does not take into consideration the legal interest Article 7 ICCRSt seeks to protect (essentially the legal interest of the human race).

Moreover, this view of Schabas's does not take into consideration that in our uncontrollably capitalistic era, crimes against humanity could easily be committed by private organisations, multinational mercenaries or private military companies or neofascist organisations, to name but a few. Finally, such a strict interpretation of the application scope of Article 7 ICCRSt does not take into consideration or does not attribute sufficient significance to the provisions of Article 12(2)(a) and (b) ICCRSt, which refer to the ICC's jurisdiction and which clearly state that the ICC exercises its jurisdiction with regards to a "State on the territory of which the conduct in question occurred" or a "State of which the person accused of the crime is a national".

Besides, the aforementioned general provisions of Article 12(2)(a) and (b) ICCRSt disconnect the existence of any state representative from the application scope, since the accused may be a rebel, paramilitary, politician or anything else and may have no link to the State. Therefore, the distinction between the perpetrator of crimes against humanity as a perpetrator who is linked to the State and the perpetrators of all the other crimes that fall under the ICC's jurisdiction cannot be accepted.[69]

Certainly, Schabas notes that the greatest problem for the supporters of a broader interpretation is that they cannot explain how they define the term

---

[68] Schabas (2010), p. 152.

[69] It is especially poignant that even the famous Draft Code of Offences against the Peace and Security of Mankind of 1954 mentioned in Article 2(10) (crime of genocide) "acts by the authorities of a State or by private individuals", while Article 2(11) on crimes against humanity adopted a slightly different perspective, maintaining that crimes against humanity can be committed "by the authorities of a State or by private individuals acting at the instigation or with the toleration of such authorities". Draft Code of Offences against the Peace and Security of Mankind, (1954). http://legal.un.org/ilc/texts/instruments/english/draft_articles/7_3_1954.pdf. last accessed 8 June 2023.

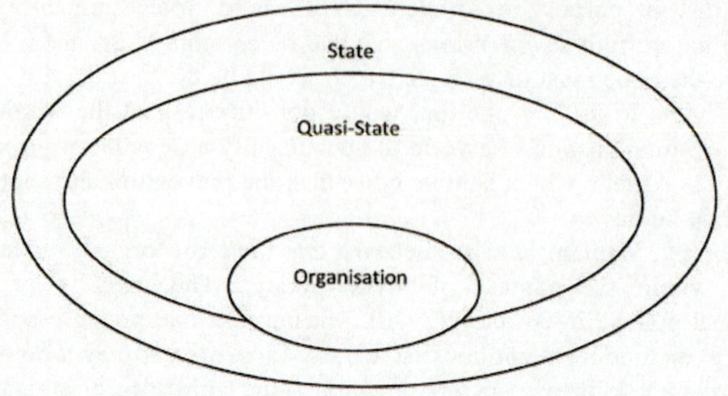

Fig. 4.4 Graphical depiction of the relation of the terms State—Quasi-State (or *De Facto* State)—Organisation

"organisational",[70] contrary to Bassiouni's approach, which offers a legally acceptable interpretation, maintaining that the word State is crucial in helping to define the term "organisational". Almost simultaneously, Schabas himself suggests that the term "organisational" could easily be considered (and here he takes a similar approach to Bassiouni) to refer to cases of quasi-states, examples of which are offerred at various stages in time by Bosnia-Herzegovina, Taiwan, Palestine and the considerable area of Colombia, which was essentially controlled by the FARC.[71]

This view, however, does not appear to be convincing at all, since then the ICCRSt would have included the term "quasi-states", and not the term "organisational". This latter term could under no circumstances be interpreted in a way that would include the concept of a "quasi-state". That is because the term "organisational" is clearly a much narrower concept (see the diagram below), and under no circumstances has it ever been interpreted broadly enough to include quasi-states. At the same time, it could not be harder or even legally unacceptable to attempt to limit in a clearer way the term "organisational", starting from its grammatical interpretation and reviewing its interpretation in other international or not legal documents (see Fig. 4.4).

Thus, one could argue that any organisation with a stable structure and specific stated or unstated aims (as for example the expulsion of immigrants from a State) that are a risk to humanity could fall under Article 7(2)(a) ICCRSt. Consequently, according to the aforementioned definition proposed by the current writer, such an organisation could take many legal forms: it could be a political party or an informal citizen's movement, an association, a company of mercenary troops or even a multinational company.

The criterion to determine whether a legal entity is an organisation in the sense of Article 7 ICCRSt must be operational. In 1997, in the Tadić case, the ICTY judges

---

[70] Schabas (2008), pp. 358–359.
[71] ibid. 359.

agreed on this matter, pointing out that crimes against humanity, as crimes of a collective nature, no longer require a State policy, given that "the law in relation to crimes against humanity has developed to take into account forces which, although not those of the legitimate government, have *de facto* control over, or are able to move freely within, defined territory".[72] The Prosecution, as well as the Defence also agreed on this point.[73] This discussion of course referred to the ICTY's Statute where a nexus between the crime against humanity and an armed conflict was required, and thus, the reference to a non-State force's *de facto* control over a territory is justified. Unlinking the commission of crimes against humanity from armed conflicts renders that criterion of *de facto* control unnecessary.

The recent ICC Decision on the Confirmation of Charges in the Ruto, Koshey and Sang Case (part of the investigation into the situation in Kenya) follows the aforementioned legal reasoning.[74] Claus Kress has actually maintained that this ICC decision supports a teleological interpretation of the provision on crimes against humanity. According to this teleological interpretation, the aim of international criminal law is to promote fundamental human values, and this aim is achieved through a broader interpretation of the term "pursuant to or in furtherance of a state or organisational policy".[75]

As a reasonable consequence of the above, we can accept that:

(a) Such technical know-how and financial and logistical means (funds and equipment) are available today that allow the commission of crimes against humanity, similar to those committed by the Nazis during World War II or several of the parties in the former Yugoslavia, by members of organisations that take various legal forms.
(b) Within the framework of the ICCRSt, crimes against humanity are not connected to the existence of an armed conflict, as was the case in the past pursuant to international customary law or the statutes followed by the international criminal tribunals for the former Yugoslavia and Rwanda (ICTY and ICTR); thus, today the existence of an armed conflict is legally irrelevant to determining whether a crime against humanity has been committed.
(c) The formulation of Article 7(2)(a) ICCRSt undoubtedly refers in a disjunctive manner to a State or an organisation; thus according to the letter of the law, the evolution of international criminal law as seen in light of the ICCRSt, and the generally accepted rules for the interpretation of legal provisions, the removal of the disjunctive "or" and the placement of the term "organisational" within the scope of a State or quasi-state cannot be considered legally correct.

---

[72] ICTY (1997), para 654 http://www.icty.org/x/cases/tadic/tjug/en/tad-tsj70507JT2-e.pdf. last accessed 8 June 2023.

[73] ibid.

[74] ICC (2012), para 24–25 https://www.icc-cpi.int/CourtRecords/CR2012_01004.PDF. last accessed 8 June 2023.

[75] Kress (2010), pp. 855, 861.

References

Table of Cases

ICC (2008) Prosecutor v. Germain Katanga, Decision on the confirmation of charges, ICC-01/04–01/07–717, Pre-Trial Chamber I. https://www.icc-cpi.int/CourtRecords/CR2008_05172.PDF. Accessed 8 June 2023

ICC (2009a) Bemba (ICC-01/05–01/08) Decision pursuant to Article 61(7)(a) and (b) of the Rome Statute on the Charges of the Prosecutor Against Jean-Pierre Bemba Gombo, para. 83. https://www.icc-cpi.int/CourtRecords/CR2009_04528.PDF. Accessed 8 June 2023

ICC (2009b) Decision on the Prosecution's Application for a Warrant of Arrest against Omar Hassan Ahmad Al Bashir, ICC-02/05–01/09–3, para. 81. https://www.icc-cpi.int/pages/record.aspx?uri=639096. Accessed 8 June 2023

ICC (2012) Prosecutor v. Ruto, Koshey and Sang, Decision on the Confirmation of Charges Pursuant to Article 61(7)(a) and (b) of the Rome Statute, ICC-01/09–01/11, https://www.icc-cpi.int/CourtRecords/CR2012_01004.PDF. Accessed 8 June 2023

ICTR (1998) Prosecutor v. Akayesu, Trial Judgment ICTR-96-4-T, para. 581

ICTR (1999) Prosecutor v. Rutaganda, Trial Judgment ICTR-96-3-T, para 70

ICTR (2000) Prosecutor v. Musema Trial Judgment ICTR-96-13-A, para. 205. http://unictr.irmct.org/sites/unictr.org/files/case-documents/ictr-96-13/trial judgements/en/000127.pdf. Accessed 8 June 2023

ICTR (2003) Prosecutor v. Semanza, Trial Judgment ICTR-97-20-T, para. 327

ICTY (1997) Prosecutor v. Tadić, Judgement IT-94-1-T, para. 654. http://www.icty.org/x/cases/tadic/tjug/en/tad-tsj70507JT2-e.pdf. Accessed 8 June 2023

ICTY (2000) Prosecutor v. Kupreškić et al, Trial Judgment IT-95-16-T, para 765. http://www.icty.org/x/cases/kupreskic/tjug/en/kup-tj000114e.pdf. Accessed 8 June 2023

ICTY (2001a) Prosecutor v. Gotovina et al, Judgment IT-06-90-T, para. 1700–1702

ICTY (2001b) *Prosecutor v. Kunarac et al.*, Judgment, Case No. IT-96-23-T & IT-96-23/1-T, para. 27–43. http://www.icty.org/x/cases/kunarac/tjug/en/kun-tj010222e.pdf. Accessed 8 June 2023

ICTY (2002a) Kunarac, Kovac and Vukovic, Appeals Judgement IT-69-23/IT-96-23-1, para. 86

ICTY (2002b) Prosecutor v. Krnojelac, Trial Judgment IT-97-25-T, para. 54

ICTY (2002c) Prosecutor v. Kunarac, Kovac and Vukovic, Judgment IT-96-23/IT-96-23-1, Appeals para. 86, 88, 98

ICTY (2004a) Blaškić, Judgment IT-95-14-A, para. 101, 120

ICTY (2004b) Kordić et al, Judgment IT-95-14/2-A, para. 94

ICTY (2004c) Prosecutor v Kordic and Cerke, Case No. IT-95-14/2-A, Appeals Judgment, para. 94

ICTY (2004d) Prosecutor v. Vasiljević, Trial Judgment IT-98-32-T, para. 30

ICTY (2011a) Prosecutor v. Đorđević, Judgment, IT-05-87/1-T, para. 1587. http://www.icty.org/x/cases/djordjevic/tjug/en/110223_djordjevic_judgt_en.pdf. Accessed 8 June 2023

ICTY (2011b) Prosecutor v. Perišić, Trial Judgment IT-04-81-T, para. 82

Books

Bassiouni MC (2011) Crimes against HumanIty: historical evolution and contemporary application. Cambridge University Press, Cambridge, pp 34–33

Bassiouni MC (2014) Crimes against humanity: historical evolution and contemporary application. Cambridge University Press, Cambridge

Bassiouni MC (2016) Crimes against humanity: historical evolution and contemporary application. Cambridge University Press, Cambridge, pp 169–170

Damgaard C (2008) Individual criminal responsibility for Core international crimes. Springer, Berlin, p 80

Dixon R (1999) Article 7. In: Triffterer O (ed) Commentary on the Rome statute of the international criminal court. Nomos Verlagsgesellschaft, Baden-Baden, pp 126–127

Naziris IA (2009) The crime against humanity based on Article 7 of the international criminal court. Digital Library of the Aristotle University of Thessaloniki, Thessallonik, p 85

Schabas WA (2008) Crimes against humanity: the state plan or policy element. In: Sadat LN, Scharf MP (eds) The theory and practice of international criminal law: essays in honor of M. Cherif Bassiouni. Martinus Nijhoff Publishers, Leiden, pp. 351, 358-359

Schabas WA (2010) The international criminal court: a commentary on the Rome statute. Oxford University Press, Oxford, p 152

Simeonidou-Kastanidou E (2003) The Legal Basis and the Limits of the International Criminal Court's Jurisdiction 51(3) Nomiko Vima 401 [in Greek]

Stamatis K (2003) The foundations of legal reasoning, 6th edn. Sakkoulas, Thessaloniki, pp 322–324, 328-331

Articles/Papers

Ambos K (2001) Verbrechenselemente, sowie Verfarhens- und Beweisregeln des Internationalen Strafgerichtshofs. Neue Juristische Wochenschrift 6:405

Armenian-genocide (1915) France, Great Britain and Russia Joint Declaration. http://www.armenian-genocide.org/Affirmation.160/current_category.7/affirmation_detail.html

Jackson RH (1949) United States representative to the international conference on military trials. US Government Printing Office, Washington DC. Report

Kress C (2010) On the outer limits of crimes against humanity: the concept of organization within the policy requirement: some reflections of the march 2010 ICC Kenya decision. LJIL 23: 855, 861

Robinson D (1999) Defining "crimes against humanity" at the Rome conference. Am J Int Law 93(1):43, 47

Websites/Web Sources

ICTR Statute (1994). http://legal.un.org/avl/pdf/ha/ictr_EF.pdf. Accessed 8 June 2023

ICTY Statute. http://www.icty.org/x/file/Legal%20Library/Statute/statute_sept09_en.pdf. Accessed 8 June 2023

International Law Commission (1954) Draft Code of Crimes against the Peace and Security of Mankind. http://legal.un.org/docs/?path=../ilc/texts/instruments/english/draft_articles/7_3_1954.pdf&lang=EF. Accessed 8 June 2023

International Law Commission (1991) Yearbook UN Doc A/CN.4/SER.A/1991/Add.1. http://legal.un.org/ilc/publications/yearbooks/english/ilc_1991_v2_p2.pdf. Accessed 8 June 2023

International Law Commission (1993) Report on the Work of its Forty-Fifth Session in Yearbook UN Doc. A/CN.4/SER.A/1993Add.1. http://legal.un.org/ilc/publications/yearbooks/english/ilc_1993_v2_p2.pdf. Accessed 8 June 2023

Report of the Preparatory Committee on the Establishment of an International Criminal Court Volume I para 85. https://www.legal-tools.org/doc/e75432/pdf/. Accessed 8 June 2023

Trial (1947) of the Major War Criminals before the International Military Tribunal, Nuremberg, Germany. https://www.loc.gov/rr/frd/Military_Law/pdf/NT_Vol-I.pdf. Accessed 8 June 2023
United Nations Diplomatic Conference of Plenipotentiaries on the Establishment of an International Criminal Court Rome (1998) Official Records. http://legal.un.org/icc/rome/proceedings/contents.htm. Accessed 8 June 2023

Chapter 5
The ICC's Jurisdiction Over War Crimes

Abstract War crimes clearly could not be omitted from the list of crimes that fall under the ICC's jurisdiction. While they have been a matter of concern for humanity since ancient times, the question of international jurisdiction over war crimes was first examined in 1919, when the Commission on the Responsibility of the Authors of the War and on Enforcement of Penalties examined the existing international legal regime and the principles derived from the 1907 Hague Convention. The actual prosecution of war crimes first took place following the end of World War II before the International Military Tribunals of Nuremberg and Tokyo. Despite the fact that, to a greater or lesser degree, war crimes never ceased to interest legal circles and international news services (Korean war, Vietnam war, war in the former Yugoslavia, first and second Iraq wars etc.), public discourse on the commission of war crimes recently peaked following Navi Pillay's publication of the findings of a UN inquiry. According to her report, Syrian President Bashar al-Assad carries great responsibility for the commission of many war crimes on both sides of the conflict, which to this day have led to the death of at least 126,000 people.

The present chapter pays great attention to the analysis and interpretation of the following key terms and phrases of Article 8 ICCRSt: (1) the phrase "unless otherwise provided" and the term "wilful(−ly)" which constitute crucial parameters for the mens rea of war crimes under the ICC's jurisdiction (2) the terms "armed conflict" in conjunction with the phrase "within the established framework of international law" (3) the terms "in particular", "as part of a plan or policy" or "as part of a large-scale commission" and (4) the term "namely". Finally yet importantly, the chapter ends with the examination of the 'phantom' Article 124 ICCRSt which constitutes a notable exception to the ICC's jurisdiction over war crimes.

5.1 Introduction: War Crimes and Two Cases That Do Not Fall Under the ICC's Jurisdiction

War crimes clearly could not be omitted from the list of crimes that fall under the ICC's jurisdiction. While they have been a matter of concern to humanity since ancient times, the question of international jurisdiction over war crimes was first

V. Tsilonis, *The Jurisdiction of the International Criminal Court*,
https://doi.org/10.1007/978-3-031-46138-5_5

examined in 1919, when the Commission on the Responsibility of the Authors of the War and on Enforcement of Penalties examined the existing international legal regime and the principles derived from the 1907 Hague Convention.[1] The actual prosecution of war crimes first took place following the end of World War II before the International Military Tribunals of Nuremberg and Tokyo. While war crimes have never ceased to interest legal circles and international news services (Korean war, Vietnam war, war in the former Yugoslavia, first and second Iraq wars etc.), public discussion of the commission of war crimes recently peaked following Navi Pillay's publication of the findings of a UN inquiry. Accord to her report, the Syrian president Bashar al-Assad carries great responsibility for the commission of many war crimes on both sides of the conflict, which to this day have led to the death of at least 126,000 people.[2]

Notably, when James Leslie Brierly found the prosecution of German war criminals legally pursuant to international law, his main argument was that war crimes should not be prosecuted according to the principles of temporal jurisdiction and that, consequently, jurisdiction must be "exercised without any reference to the location of the crime".[3]

On the other hand, the inclusion of war crimes in the ICCRSt constituted a significant legal step, as their explicit listing was not simply a codification of pre-existing rules of international customary law. On the contrary, it became apparent for the first time that it was necessary to disconnect war crimes from the concept of "international conflict", and thus, the possibility of committing war crimes in civil or "non-international" conflicts was recognised. What is more, although no significant progress was made on the international criminalisation of nuclear[4] and other weapons of mass destruction,[5] the conscripting or enlisting children under the age of

---

[1] The Commission on the Responsibility of the Authors of the War and on Enforcement of Penalties, Recommendation, Report Presented to the Preliminary Peace Conference (1920), pp. 95–154. However, the contemporary term "war crimes" is mentioned only once in the Report: "In this class the Commission has considered acts not strictly war crimes, but acts which provoked the war or accompanied its inception, such, to take outstanding examples, as the invasion of Luxemburg and Belgium", p. 118. There are nevertheless plenty of formulations that come close to the term "war crime": "crimes relating to war" 117, "crimes contrary to the laws and customs of war" 142, "certain acts violating the laws and customs of war to be crimes" 146.

[2] Black (2013), https://www.theguardian.com/world/2013/dec/02/syrian-officials-involved-war-crimes-bashar-al-assad-un-investigators, Last accessed 8 June 2023.

[3] Clapham (1994).

[4] Forbidding the use of nuclear weapons is such a thorny issue that even the ICJ stated that it cannot make a judgment on this particular matter! "[I]n view of the current state of international law, and of the elements of fact at its disposal, the Court cannot conclude definitively whether the threat or use of nuclear weapons would be lawful or unlawful in an extreme circumstance of self-defence, in which the very survival of a State would be at stake", ICC Opinion on the Legality of the Threat or Use of Nuclear Weapons, (8 July 1996) https://www.icj-cij.org/files/case-related/95/095-19960708-ADV-01-00-EN.pdf, last accessed 8 June 2023.

[5] One of the main reasons that India did not sign the ICCRSt. UN Doc. A/CONF.183/SR.9 para 16.

15 years as soldiers[6] and attacks on peacekeeping personnel[7] were included for the first time as war crimes in the ICCRSt under the ICC's jurisdiction.

Further, according to Article 8 ICCRSt, war crimes under the ICC's jurisdiction are split in four general categories: (1) grave breaches of the Geneva Conventions of 12 August 1949 (on international armed conflicts)[8]; (2) other serious violations of the laws and customs applicable in international armed conflict, within the established framework of international law[9]; (3) in the case of an armed conflict not of an international character, serious violations of article 3 common to the four Geneva Conventions of 12 August 1949[10]; (4) other serious violations of the laws and customs applicable in armed conflicts not of an international character, within the established framework of international law.[11]

As analysed in depth later on, the ICC has jurisdiction over war crimes particularly but not exclusively committed within the framework of a plan, a policy or a large-scale commission of such crimes. It is precisely for this reason that pursuant to the ICCRSt war crimes are distinct from crimes against humanity; in contrast to crimes against humanity, war crimes must not necessarily be committed as part of a plan or a policy (or large-scale commission of such crimes).[12]

More specifically, according to Article 8(1) ICCRSt, the ICC has jurisdiction in respect of war crimes committed on the territory of a state party or by citizens of a state party pursuant to the general provisions on jurisdiction (Articles 12(1)-(2)(b)). According to Article 8 ICCRSt, in summary those crimes are: (1) grave breaches of the Geneva Conventions of 12 August 1949; (2) torture or inhuman treatment, including biological experiments; (3) wilfully causing great suffering, or serious injury to body or health; (4) extensive destruction and appropriation of property, not

[6] Article 8(2)(b)(xxvi) ICCRSt: Conscripting or enlisting children under the age of 15 years into the national armed forces or using them to participate actively in hostilities.

Article 8(2)(e)(vii) ICCRSt: Conscripting or enlisting children under the age of 15 years into armed forces or groups or using them to participate actively in hostilities.

This particular war crime was the subject of the first ICC decision in the case of Thomas Lubanga Dyilo, which led to the accused's sentence to 14 years imprisonment. ICC, Prosecutor v Thomas Lubanga Dyilo, Judgment, ICC-01/04-01/06-2842, 14 March 2012, Trial Chamber I http://www.icc-cpi.int/iccdocs/doc/doc1379838.pdf, last accessed 8 June 2023. See also: Tsilonis (2010), p. 1039.

[7] Article 8(2)(b)(iii) ICCRSt: Intentionally directing attacks against personnel, installations, material, units or vehicles involved in a humanitarian assistance or peacekeeping mission in accordance with the Charter of the United Nations, as long as they are entitled to the protection given to civilians or civilian objects under the international law of armed conflict.

[8] Article 8(2)(a) ICCRSt. See also Articles 49 to 52 of the First Convention, 50 to 53 of the Second, 129 to 131 of the Third, and 146 to 149 of the Fourth Geneva Convention (1949), https://www.icrc.org/en/doc/assets/files/publications/icrc-002-0173.pdf&usg=AOvVaw2QEScZEGFSn17zoEBkQhNs, last accessed 8 June 2023.

[9] Article 8(2)(b) ICCRSt.

[10] Article 8(2)(c) ICCRSt.

[11] Article 8(2)(e) ICCRSt.

[12] Triponel and Pearson (2010), pp. 65, 72.

justified by military necessity; (5) compelling a prisoner of war or other protected person to serve in the forces of a hostile Power; (6) wilfully depriving a prisoner of war or other protected person of the rights of fair and regular trial; (7) unlawful deportation or transfer or unlawful confinement; (8) taking of hostages; (9) other serious violations of the laws and customs applicable in international armed conflict, such as:

(9.1) Intentionally directing attacks against the civilian population as such or against individual civilians not taking direct part in hostilities;
(9.2) Intentionally directing attacks against civilian objects, that is, objects which are not military objectives;
(9.3) Intentionally directing attacks against personnel, installations, material, units or vehicles involved in a humanitarian assistance or peacekeeping mission in accordance with the Charter of the United Nations, as long as they are entitled to the protection given to civilians or civilian objects under the international law of armed conflict;
(9.4) Intentionally launching an attack in the knowledge that such attack will cause incidental loss of life or injury to civilians or damage to civilian objects or widespread, long-term and severe damage to the natural environment which would be clearly excessive in relation to the concrete and direct overall military advantage anticipated;
(9.5) Attacking or bombarding, by whatever means, towns, villages, dwellings or buildings which are undefended, and which are not military objectives;
(9.6) Killing or wounding a combatant who, having laid down his arms or having no longer means of defence, has surrendered at discretion;
(9.7) Making improper use of a flag of truce, of the flag or of the military insignia and uniform of the enemy or of the United Nations, as well as of the distinctive emblems of the Geneva Conventions, resulting in death or serious personal injury;
(9.8) The transfer, directly or indirectly, by the Occupying Power of parts of its own civilian population into the territory it occupies, or the deportation or transfer of all or parts of the population of the occupied territory within or outside this territory;
(9.9) Intentionally directing attacks against buildings dedicated to religion, education, art, science or charitable purposes, historic monuments, hospitals and places where the sick and wounded are collected, provided they are not military objectives;
(9.10) Subjecting persons who are in the power of an adverse party to physical mutilation or to medical or scientific experiments of any kind which are neither justified by the medical, dental or hospital treatment of the person concerned nor carried out in his or her interest, and which cause death to or seriously endanger the health of such person or persons;
(9.11) Killing or wounding treacherously individuals belonging to the hostile nation or army;

(9.12) Declaring that no quarter will be given[13];
(9.13) Destroying or seizing the enemy's property unless such destruction or seizure be imperatively demanded by the necessities of war;
(9.14) Declaring abolished, suspended or inadmissible in a court of law the rights and actions of the nationals of the hostile party;
(9.15) Compelling the nationals of the hostile party to take part in the operations of war directed against their own country, even if they were in the belligerent's service before the commencement of the war;
(9.16) Pillaging a town or place, even when taken by assault;
(9.17) Employing poison or poisoned weapons;
(9.18) Employing asphyxiating, poisonous or other gases, and all analogous liquids, materials or devices;
(9.19) Employing bullets which expand or flatten easily in the human body, such as bullets with a hard envelope which does not entirely cover the core or is pierced with incisions;
(9.20) Employing weapons, projectiles and material and methods of warfare which are of a nature to cause superfluous injury or unnecessary suffering or which are inherently indiscriminate in violation of the international law of armed conflict, provided that such weapons, projectiles and material and methods of warfare are the subject of a comprehensive prohibition and are included in an annex to this Statute, by an amendment in accordance with the relevant provisions set forth in articles 121 and 123;
(9.21) Committing outrages upon personal dignity, in particular humiliating and degrading treatment;
(9.22) Committing rape, sexual slavery, enforced prostitution, forced pregnancy, as defined in article 7, paragraph 2 (f), enforced sterilization, or any other form of sexual violence also constituting a grave breach of the Geneva Conventions;
(9.23) Utilising the presence of a civilian or other protected person to render certain points, areas or military forces immune from military operations;
(9.24) Intentionally directing attacks against buildings, material, medical units and transport, and personnel using the distinctive emblems of the Geneva Conventions in conformity with international law;

[13] The roots of this particular provision can be found in Article 23(d) of the 1907 Hague Convention (IV) respecting the Laws and Customs of War on Land and its annex: Regulations concerning the Laws and Customs of War on Land. https://ihl-databases.icrc.org/en/ihl-treaties/hague-conv-iv-1907/regulations-art-23, last accessed 8 June 2023, and is today considered binding for the parties to an international armed conflict. According to the Oxford English Dictionary, this phrase originates from an order by the commander of a victorious army that it "will not quarter (house)" captured enemy combatants. Therefore, none can be taken prisoner and all enemy combatants must be killed. A second, equally prominent, source given for the phrase is Shakespeare Oth. II. iii. 171, where "no quarter" means refusal to enter into an agreement (relations) with an enemy attempting to surrender. "I do not know. Friends all but now, even now, In quarter, and in terms, like bride and groom".

(9.25) Intentionally using starvation of civilians as a method of warfare by depriving them of objects indispensable to their survival, including wilfully impeding relief supplies as provided for under the Geneva Conventions;
(9.26) Conscripting or enlisting children under the age of 15 years into the national armed forces or using them to participate actively in hostilities.

Therefore, the provision at hand excludes from the ICC's jurisdiction cases where the citizen/s of a state non-party (e.g. USA) commit war crimes on US territory or that of another state non-party (e.g. Somalia) against citizens of a state non-party (e.g. China). Moreover, it appears *ab initio* to exclude from the ICC's jurisdiction cases where citizens of a state non-party (e.g. of the USA) commit war crimes on US territory or that of another state non-party (e.g. that of Somalia) against citizens of a state party (e.g. against Greeks). In the latter case, the only circumstances under which the ICC could exercise its jurisdiction would be if the state non-party on the territory of which the crimes appear to have been committed retroactively accepts the ICC's jurisdiction pursuant to Article 12(3) ICCRSt. For the reasons already analysed in the chapter on Palestine, this scenario is not only highly unlikely (since in that case the ICC could exercise its jurisdiction over all the incidents that took place on behalf of either of the involved parties), but also because it presents *de lege ferenda* significant legal issues since the prohibition of the retroactive application of criminal provisions is fundamental to the Western legal tradition.

A general characteristic of Article 8 ICCRSt arises in the context of the two examples above: while more thorough and complete compared to the relevant articles in the statutes of international criminal tribunals, it becomes apparent that, because of its strict formulation, grave cases of war crimes are not included in it, such as for example slavery and forced labour, even though the ICTY has recognised in its jurisprudence that they constitute war crimes.[14]

5.2 The Phrase "Unless Otherwise Provided" and the Term "Wilful(-ly)" in Article 8 ICCRSt As Crucial Parameters for the *Mens Rea* of War Crimes Under the ICC's Jurisdiction

In Article 8, which is by far the lengthiest article in international criminal law at 1600 words, the so-called subsidiary clause of Article 30(1) ICCRSt, "unless otherwise provided" has a special role, especially with regard to the analysis of the adjective "wilful" found in Article 8(2)(a)(i) ICCRSt (wilful killing), and of the adverb "wilfully" found in Article 8(2)(a)(iii) ICCRSt (wilfully causing great suffering), Article 8(2)(a)(vi) ICCRSt (wilfully depriving a prisoner of war or other protected

[14] ICTY (2003a), paras 350–360; ICTY (2003b), paras 250–261.

person of a fair trial) and Article 8(2)(b)(xxv) ICCRSt (wilfully impeding relief supplies).

The analysis and correlation of the two aforementioned terms appear to be very crucial factors for the required *mens rea* of the war crimes that may fall under the ICC's jurisdiction since Article 8 ICCRSt is the only article of those referring to the ICC's core crimes (Art. 5–8B ICCRSt) that explicitly mentions the Court's jurisdiction.

In the international literature, academics like Schabas have maintained that the term "wilful" means intentional. However, Schabas also maintains that the existence of this word does not render the content of this provision's *mens rea* any different than the one included in the general rule of Article 30(1) ICCRSt.[15] Thus, the argument is that the word "wilful" or "wilfully" is without content and that whether it is present or not, the general rule of Article 30(1) ICCRSt must be applied, a rule that, according to both Schabas and the current author, refers only to the first and second class of intent. Based on that legal interpretation, however, Schabas does not address at all the fact that in Article 8(2)(a)(iii) ICCRSt "wilfully causing great suffering, or serious injury to body or health" is listed as a war crime, but the phrase "wilfully causing great suffering" is separated by a comma from the words "or serious injury to body or health".[16]

On the other hand, academics such as Kai Ambos and Knut Dormann have adopted the wiser view that a word or a term within a legal provision always has a particular role to play. Therefore, the term wilful/wilfully cannot be simply ignored; on the contrary, it must be assessed to determine how its presence defines the *mens rea* of the criminal acts it describes.[17]

Thus, it is pointedly noted that "Article 8(2)(a)(i) ICCRSt, which refers to the crime of wilful killing, is a characteristic example of a provision with clear meaning. Indeed, a special *mens rea* is rooted here in the use of the term '*wilful*', which *mens rea*—in view of the unaltered interpretation given to this particular term in the framework of the Geneva Conventions and the First Additional Protocol, which explicitly includes 'recklessness' as the standard of fault required for its application—and includes all standards of fault as well as grave cases of recklessness. In the interests of cohesion, this same broad interpretation of the term 'wilful (ly)' must be adopted for all the provisions in which it is used".[18]

Unfortunately, however, neither view is correct. In the first view adopted by Schabas there are rather obvious reasons for this. We cannot easily ignore terms or transform disjunctive lists into cumulative ones, even though in international criminal law, this is sometimes presented as "correct and necessary". With regard to the second view, admittedly the starting point is correct, but it does not lead to an equally correct conclusion. That is because, even though reference is made to the ICTY's

---

[15] Schabas (2010), p. 214.

[16] ibid 217.

[17] Simeonidou-Kastanidou et al. (2006), pp. 230–231.

[18] ibid, emphasis added.

jurisprudence (Blaskic Judgment), which in the framework of the ICTY and specifically of Article 2 ICTY on grave breaches of the 1949 Geneva Conventions even included forms of negligence regarding the crime's *mens rea* from the perspective of criminal doctrine, it is obvious that the term wilful is similar to purposeful or intentional. In other words, the term means "intentionally". Besides, that is the reason that prominent academics such as Schabas choose to ignore its existence and maintain more or less that its presence or absence does not at all influence the required *mens rea* of the crimes described.

Nonetheless, while no ambiguity or controversy exists as to how other articles of the Statute diverge from the general rule on *mens rea* of Article 30 ICCRSt, there seems to be a problem with divergence when it comes to the Elements of Crimes.

The Preparatory Committee attempted to limit the invocation of Article 32 ICCRSt (mistake of fact or mistake of law) by the future accused. Thus with regard to three types of crimes (improper use of a flag of truce, of the flag or of the military insignia and uniform of the enemy or of the United Nations, as well as of the distinctive emblems of the Geneva Conventions),[19] the Committee replaced the strict criterion of "knowledge" introduced by Article 30 ICCRSt with recklessness through the specification of the aforementioned crimes in the Elements of Crimes.[20]

Thus, with reference to the aforementioned crimes as described in the Elements of Crimes, the subjective but strict criterion of "knowledge" was replaced by the phrase "knew or should have known". This undoubtedly makes the accused's position even more difficult and was one of the causes *sensu lato* of the discussion in legal theory and jurisprudence of how permissible the divergence of the Elements of Crimes from 3 Article 30 ICCRSt is after all. Certainly, it is widely accepted that the far less strict criterion of recklessness introduced by the phrase "knew or should have known" crucially deviates from the criterion of Article 30 ICCRSt, namely that all the material elements of a crime within the ICC's jurisdiction must be committed "with intent and knowledge".[21]

Subsequently, the issue that arises is whether the newly introduced and less (or more) strict criteria that might be provided for in the Elements of Crimes[22] can fall within the scope of the phrase "unless otherwise provided" of Article 30 ICCRSt; or if the Elements of Crime must be considered contrary not only to Article 30 ICCRSt in this respect, but also to Article 9(3)ICCRSt, which clearly stipulates

---

[19] Article 8(2)(b)(vii) -1, Article 8(2)(b)(vii)-2, Article 8(2)(b)(vii)-4 ICCRSt.

[20] Elements of Crimes, Article 8(2)(b)(vii)-1, Article 8(2)(b)(vii)-2, Article 8(2)(b)(vii)-4.

[21] Eser (2002), p. 933.

[22] The Elements of Crimes were adopted pursuant to Article 9(1) ICCRSt by a two-thirds majority of the members of the Assembly of States Parties and may be amended according to Article 9(2) by the same majority. According to Article 9(3) ICCRSt, however, "[t]he Elements of Crimes and amendments thereto shall be consistent with this Statute". It appears that the Elements of Crimes, which until then were unknown to most States as a legal instrument, were a proposal made by the US delegation to assist the Court in the interpretation and application of Articles 6, 7 and 8 ICCRSt. Zimmermann (2003), pp. 19–20.

that "the Elements of Crimes and amendments thereto shall be consistent with this Statute".

Of course, stricter criteria introduced for specific crimes by the Elements of Crimes would not pose such an important problem, at least not from the perspective of criminal justice, *inter alia* since the generally accepted principle of *in dubio pro reo* would apply. The real issue arises through the attempt to introduce less strict criteria of *mens rea* for the crimes that fall under the ICC's jurisdiction, which may be incompatible with Article 30 ICCRSt, considering that Article 51(5) ICCRSt clearly states that "[i]n the event of conflict between the Statute and the Rules of Procedure and Evidence, the Statute shall prevail".

Nonetheless, in the Bemba case, the ICC's Pre-Trial Chamber II took the view that the exception of war crimes in the Elements of Crimes from the standard of Article 30 ICCRSt is permissible. Specifically, the Pre-Trial Chamber ruled that the phrase "unless otherwise provided" in Article 30(1) ICCRSt means that the material elements of a crime must be committed with "intent and knowledge", "unless the Statute **or the Elements of Crimes** require a different standard of fault".[23]

Subsequently, Pre-Trial Chamber II attempted to justify the aforementioned view, using a self-referential argument. It claimed that "this conclusion finds support in paragraph 2 of the General Introduction to the Elements of Crimes which reads: '2. As stated in article 30, unless otherwise provided, a person shall be criminally responsible and liable for punishment for a crime within the jurisdiction of the Court only if the material elements are committed with intent and knowledge. Where no reference is made in the Elements of Crimes to a mental element for any particular conduct, consequence or circumstances listed, it is understood that the relevant mental element, i.e., intent, knowledge or both, set out in article 30 applies.'"[24]

Nevertheless, one cannot easily overlook the fact that the International Criminal Court's Statute includes several clear references to other texts, specifying from the start the matters defined through their provisions—as, for example, in the case of Article 41 (Excusing and disqualification of judges), 46 (Removal from office), 47 (Disciplinary measures) and 50 (Official and working languages) ICCRSt, each of which makes explicit reference to the Rules of Procedure and Evidence. Any further specification or any additional definition for the *mens rea* of the crimes that fall under the ICC's jurisdiction is not one of the matters assigned to the Elements of Crimes.

In any case, this matter is highly controversial in the theory of international criminal law. Academics such as Schabas, Werle, Kelt, Von Hebel and Cassese appear to share the view that exceptions to the general standard of fault of Article 30 ICCRSt are completely possible and permissible with reference to the alterable

---

[23] Emphasis added. ICC (2009a), para 136 https://www.icc-cpi.int/CourtRecords/CR2009_04528.PDF, last accessed 8 June 2023.

[24] ibid para 136, 353.

Elements of Crimes.[25] On the other hand, scholars such as Heller, Ambos and Weigend maintain that according to the spirit of the ICCRSt and the principle of legality, any exceptions to the general standard of fault for the crimes that fall under the ICC's jurisdiction must be based solely on the ICCRSt's own provisions.[26]

This second view wins the support of the author of the present book. Besides, Article 9(1) ICCRSt clearly defines the purpose of the Elements of Crimes, explicitly stating that "Elements of Crimes shall assist the Court in the interpretation and application of articles 6, 7 and 8. They shall be adopted by a two-thirds majority of the members of the Assembly of States Parties". Thus, through the interpretation of the grammatical formulation of Article 9(1) ICCRSt, the subsidiary nature of the Elements of Crimes arises, not only functionally, but also on the level of legal validity as compared with the ICCRSt. After all, the entry into force of the Elements of Crimes did not require the absolute majority of all states parties that the establishment of the ICC did,[27] but a majority of two-thirds of the members of the Assembly of States Parties.[28] Undoubtedly, the Rome Statute constitutes a sort of "Constitution" for the ICC, which is a higher law than any other legal text. Any attempt to indirectly expand or limit the scope of its provisions through the Elements of Crimes cannot be accepted.[29]

---

[25] Schabas (2010), p. 475; Werle (2005), p. 108; Kelt and von Hebel (2001), pp. 29–30; Cassese (2003), p. 176.

[26] Heller (2008), pp. 419, 435–436; Weigend (2004), pp. 319, 327; Ambos (2002), p. 789.

[27] Here of course the phrase "absolute majority of all state parties" refers to the state parties that approved the ICC Statute; those States that eventually decided not to sign at the 1998 Conference of Rome include the USA, China, Israel and Russia.

[28] Article 9 – Elements of Crimes.

(a) Elements of Crimes shall assist the Court in the interpretation and application of articles 6, 7 and 8. They shall be adopted by a two-thirds majority of the members of the Assembly of States Parties.
(b) Amendments to the Elements of Crimes may be proposed by:

1. Any State Party;
2. The judges acting by an absolute majority;
3. The Prosecutor.

Such amendments shall be adopted by a two-thirds majority of the members of the Assembly of States Parties.

(c) The Elements of Crimes and amendments thereto shall be consistent with this Statute.

[29] Indicative of this is the fact that the legislators of the ICCRSt at the Rome Conference rejected a different version of Article 9 ICCRSt, which simply stated that the Elements of Crimes "will be applied" by the ICC. Consequently the present from of Article 9 ICCRSt was adopted, which states that the Elements of Crimes "shall assist the Court in the interpretation and application of articles 6, 7, 8 and 8 bis" and that "the Elements of Crimes and amendments thereto shall be consistent with this Statute" (para 1 & 3). This of course happened in order to more clearly define the role of the ICC and the prominent position of its Statute and to avoid any attempts to override it. Piragoff (1999), p. 529; Kelt and von Hebel (2001), pp. 7, 24.

Furthermore, as already mentioned, the ICCRSt includes provisions for different—either more either less strict—standards of fault, such as the "intent to destroy" required for the commission of the crime of genocide in Article 6 ICCRSt or the "recklessness" required of military commanders for crimes committed by forces under their effective command and control according to Article 28(i) ICCRSt. Therefore, no justification exists for the conclusion that the phrase "unless otherwise provided" in Article 30 ICCRSt refers not only to the Statute itself, but also to provisions of other legal texts that assist the ICC, among which the Elements of Crimes and the Rules of Procedure and Evidence both play prominent roles.

What is more, the analysis of other ICCRSt provisions which use similar terminology is enlightening. Thus, one might notice that Article 31(1) ICCRSt includes the phrase "[i]n addition to other grounds for excluding criminal responsibility provided for in this Statute". In other words, Article 31 ICCRSt on the grounds for excluding criminal responsibility seems to refer only to the Statute, and not to the Elements of Crimes. Nonetheless, some academics, such as Werle, take the exact opposite view on this, highlighting that Article 31(1) ICCRSt explicitly mentions the Statute, and thus, since Article 30 ICCRSt lacks a similarly explicit reference to the ICCRSt, the phrase "unless otherwise provided" does not only refer to provisions of the ICCRSt, but also to the Elements of Crimes.[30]

Further, Article 21 ICCRSt indirectly strengthens this view, since it explicitly states that "the Court shall apply: (a) In the first place, this Statute, Elements of Crimes and its Rules of Procedure and Evidence". In other words, Article 21 ICCRSt gives the same weight to the ICCRSt, the Elements of Crimes and the Rules of Procedure and Evidence, but this simply constitutes an attempt to distinguish the three from other legal texts and sources of international law, since the provisions of Article 9(3) and 51(5) ICCRSt, which explicitly stipulate that the Statute shall prevail over all other legal documents, remain equally valid.

The first phrase of Article 31 ICCRSt simply appears to recognise the existence of other provisions within the ICCRSt that include grounds for excluding criminal responsibility, as for example Article 32 ICCRSt, which refers to mistakes of fact or law. In terms of whether the ICC can recognise grounds for excluding criminal responsibility that are not founded in the ICCRSt, the answer is given in the third paragraph of Article 31 ICCRSt, which states that "the Court may consider a ground for excluding criminal responsibility other than those referred to in paragraph 1 where such a ground is derived from applicable law as set forth in article 21". From this we can conclude that the state delegates of the Rome Conference wanted to imply the application of provisions in texts other than the ICCRSt. Meanwhile, Article 21 ICCRSt (applicable law) stipulates which text prevails when the Court applies provisions other than those in the ICCRSt.

In three types of war crimes (improper use of a flag of truce, of the flag or of the military insignia and uniform of the enemy or of the United Nations, as well as of the

[30] Werle (2005), p. 108.

distinctive emblems of the Geneva Conventions)[31] the strict criterion of "knowledge" stipulated in Article 30 ICCRSt is replaced by recklessness in the Elements of Crimes.[32] It might be concluded *de lege ferenda* that this constitutes an inexcusable divergence from the ICCRSt and should not be taken into consideration by the competent ICC Trial Chambers. Moreover, *de lege ferenda* it must be concluded that any other amendments to the Elements of Crimes must not refer to the *mens rea* of those crimes already defined by the ICCRSt. Finally, as already mentioned, one must not ignore the obvious and legally justified precedence of the ICCRSt over the Elements of Crimes and the Rules of Procedure and Evidence.

5.3 The Terms "Armed Conflict" and "Within the Established Framework of International Law"

The concept of armed conflict is crucial for all four categories of war crimes in Article 8 ICCRSt. The difference between them is that the first two categories—i.e. "grave breaches of the Geneva Conventions of 12 August 1949 (on international armed conflicts)"[33] and "other serious violations of the laws and customs applicable in international armed conflict, within the established framework of international law"[34]—indirectly but clearly require the existence of an international armed conflict as a precondition for their commission, while the next two—i.e. "in the case of an armed conflict not of an international character, serious violations of article 3 common to the four Geneva Conventions of 12 August 1949"[35] and "other serious violations of the laws and customs applicable in armed conflicts not of an international character, within the established framework of international law"[36]—require the existence of an armed conflict that is not of an international character.[37]

Therefore, it appears that the ICC currently has no jurisdiction over the isolated or short use of force. Thus, for instance, the mission to kill Osama Bin Laden in Pakistan[38] could never be considered a war crime—even if Pakistan were a state party to the ICCRSt—, since it was not committed in the context of an international armed conflict or of an armed conflict not of an international character. With regards to what exactly constitutes an armed conflict, this seems to exist when at least one of the two parties believes that it is at war with the other, even if war has not officially

[31] Article 8(2)(b)(vii) -1, 8(2)(b)(vii) -2, 8(2)(b)(vii)-4 ICCRSt.

[32] Elements of Crimes, Article 8(2)(b)(vii)-1, 8(2)(b)(vii)-2, 8(2)(b)(vii)-4.

[33] Article 8(2)(a) ICCRSt.

[34] Article 8(2)(b) ICCRSt.

[35] Article 8(2)(c) ICCRSt.

[36] Article 8(2)(e) ICCRSt.

[37] Sadat (2002), p. 161.

[38] Tsilonis (2011), pp. 7–8, http://www.intellectum.org/en/2011/12/13/terata-stin-omixl/, last accessed 8 June 2023.

been declared. Thus, for instance, the bombing and occupation of Corfu by Italians in 1923 or Japan's invasion of Manchuria in 1931 constituted acts in the context of an armed conflict, even though they were committed without a formal declaration of war. In other words, what is crucial here is what is truly happening and how a State or a party (in an armed conflict not of an international character) interprets a relationship in practice. As pointed out by Kolb and Hyde, if at least one party considers itself in a state of war, even if it has not officially declared that view, then an armed conflict exists.[39]

5.4 The Meaning of the Key Term "In Particular" Within the Context of a Part of a Plan or Policy or a Part of a Large-Scale Commission

Article 8(1) ICCRSt stipulates that the ICC "shall have jurisdiction in respect of war crimes in particular when committed as part of a plan or policy or as part of a large-scale commission of such crimes". Regarding the interpretation of this provision, surprisingly all commentators seem to agree that there is a disjunctive and not a cumulative connection between the terms.[40] In other words, they agree that in order to prove the commission of war crimes, it would suffice to establish that those crimes were committed as part of a plan or policy or as part of a large-scale commission. Of course, the exact definition of the term "in particular" is a key precondition for the determination of those war crimes that could *de lege late* fall under the ICC's jurisdiction.

However, the main issue that arises when it comes to the interpretation of Article 8 ICCRSt is whether the words "in particular" mean that in order for a crime to be classified as a war crime falling under the ICC's jurisdiction, it must not constitute an isolated incident, but must necessarily be committed as part of a plan or policy or as part of a large-scale commission. And while the majority of academics are rather certain that when war crimes have been committed as part of a plan or policy or as part of a large-scale commission, there is no need to examine the criterion of gravity in Article 17(1)(d) ICCRSt, because its fulfilment can be easily and directly ascertained,[41] the exact definition of the words "in particular" still troubles international scholars.

In other words, international scholarship has been troubled by whether the existence of these particular words before the phrase "when committed as part of a plan or policy or as part of a large-scale commission of such crimes" means that war

[39] Kolb and Hyde (2008), pp. 75–76.

[40] That is not the case for the interpretation of Article 7 ICCRSt on crimes against humanity, as analysed in Chap. 4.

[41] Whitten (2012), pp. 503, 505.

crimes under the ICC's jurisdiction are exclusively the ones that are committed as part of a plan or policy or as part of a large-scale commission.[42]

At this point, certain authors maintain that based on the will of the international legislature, the words "in particular" were introduced to the article on war crimes following the efforts made by the American delegation to limit the ICC's jurisdiction over war crimes.[43] Thus the purpose of the words "in particular" was certainly the enactment of a stricter criterion for the exercise of the ICC's jurisdiction.[44]

However, at the same time there were several state party delegations that wished for the ICC to establish its jurisdiction even over isolated war crimes. These delegations pointed out from the start that the fundamental principle of complementarity was sufficient to put a stop to any attempted misuse of power on the part of the ICC. Therefore, as long as national courts adjudicated over isolated incidents of war crimes, there would be no reason for the ICC to intervene. On the contrary, if a strict criterion were introduced from the start establishing the ICC's jurisdiction only over those crimes that are committed as part of a plan or policy or as part of a large-scale commission, then there would be a great danger that isolated war crimes passed over by national courts for political reasons or reasons of national security etc., could not be adjudicated by the ICC either, precisely because they are isolated incidents. Regardless of their gravity, they would be excluded from the ICC's jurisdiction.[45]

Thus isolated war crimes, such as torture, rape, biological experiments with tens or hundreds of victims, would be placed beyond the reach of the law. And if one was to adopt such an interpretation of Article 8 ICCRSt, the criterion of gravity introduced by Article 17(1) ICCRSt would by implication be circumvented too, since an isolated war crime could simply never be adjudicated by the ICC!

Besides, even though the so-called "international community"[46] longed for the USA to become one of the ICC state parties and accepted many more of their

[42] Guan (2010), pp. 703, 715.

[43] Von Hebel and Robinson (1999), p. 105.

[44] ibid 107.

[45] ibid 108.

[46] The current author has criticised the fact that the term "international community" essentially refers to the decisions made by global powers, often just the USA alone. Tsilonis (2009), pp. 271–289; Chomsky (2016).

proposals, the fact remains that eventually the USA never became a state party to the ICC,[47] but on the contrary, enacted special legislation against its jurisdiction.[48]

To sum up, it is clear that such a limited interpretation of Article 8 ICCRSt and of the role of the words "in particular" in this provision can never be accepted. Such a limited interpretation not only contradicts the linguistic nature of the words "in particular" and the role they serve in legal texts, but also it would be capable of causing many legal problems, absurdly limiting the ICC's jurisdiction and creating a loophole that would render the perpetrators of isolated but grave war crimes immune to justice.[49]

On a final note, such an impermissibly limited interpretation does not only contradict the primal purpose of the ICC's establishment (which was to end the impunity of international crimes), but also contradicts even the general rule of interpretation of the ICCRSt, found in Article 10, which stipulates that none of its provisions can be interpreted in a way that would limit or prejudice in any way existing or developing rules of international law for purposes other than those of the Statute[50]; and certainly, such a limited interpretation is not consistent with the ICC's purpose (ending impunity) nor with the rules of international customary law,[51] since international customary law never imposed any limitation on the commission of war crimes, other than that war crimes must be committed in the context of an armed conflict.[52]

---

[47] Lanham (2005), pp. 83–98. Of course, the fact that the USA did not oppose the UNSC Resolution on the situation in Darfur and allowed the referral of the situation in Sudan to the ICC had nothing to do with a change in their stance towards the ICC, but simply served their own interests in Africa. This is verified by the stance they have retained to this day. See for example the 2008 speech of the Bush Administration Legal Adviser John Bellinger where he clarified that: "In a nutshell, I will argue that the United States' fundamental concerns about the ICC have been remarkably consistent across successive Administrations and Congresses controlled by both Democrats and Republicans. And in the absence of significant changes to the Rome Statute to address these concerns, it is unlikely that the United States will become a party to the Rome Statute any time in the foreseeable future. Accordingly, the future of the relationship between the United States and the ICC will be defined mainly by the extent to which the United States and ICC supporters can agree to disagree about the Rome Statute and find constructive and practical ways to work together to advance our shared interest in promoting international criminal justice." Bellinger JB, "The United States and the International Criminal Court: Where We've Been and Where We're Going" (Remarks to the DePaul University College of Law), https://2001-2009.state.gov/s/l/rls/104053.htm, last accessed 8 June 2023.

[48] American Service-Members' Protection Act of 2002 https://2001-2009.state.gov/t/pm/rls/othr/misc/23425.htm, last accessed 8 June 2023.

[49] Whitten (2012), pp. 503–522.

[50] Article 10 ICCRSt: Nothing in this Part shall be interpreted as limiting or prejudicing in any way existing or developing rules of international law for purposes other than this Statute.

[51] "Under customary international law, war crimes do not have to be committed as part of a plan or policy or large-scale set of crimes and it would be illogical and not policy serving to impose a limitation by interpreting the phrase 'in particular' differently than its ordinary meaning." Paust (2010), pp. 681, 701.

[52] Schabas (2010), p. 199.

Moreover, it is worth taking into consideration the fact that equating the words "in particular" with the word "only" or the phrase "only when" is impermissible, even more so if we were to recall that the Preparatory Committee of the Rome Conference had in the past suggested an alternative definition for war crimes which included the word "only" instead of "in particular".[53] And while undoubtedly, *on the one hand*, the adoption of that word would clearly be unsuccessful in solving the matter of interpretation of the point in question and at the same time limit the ICC's jurisdiction over war crimes, *on the other hand,* the decision not to include the word "only" but to include instead the words "in particular" in the text indisputably solves any matter of interpretation that arises not only from the meaning of the words, but also from the legislative process that led to their selection; a legislative process, which appears, according to some authors, to have ended with the presence in Article 8 ICCRSt of the words "in particular". This was in fact crucial to the state parties' acceptance of the whole.[54]

Let us now turn to the somewhat paradoxical (from a legal, but not from a political perspective) approach of the ICC's Prosecution to this particular matter of interpretation. As noted by ICC Chief Prosecutor Luis Moreno Ocampo concerning the situation in Iraq, the words "in particular" found in Article 8(1) ICCRSt do not introduce an absolute condition, but function as a guideline to the ICC that ensures Court will focus on the cases that fulfil its criteria.[55] In other words, the ICC will work almost exclusively on cases of war crimes that appear to have been committed as part of a plan or policy or as part of a large-scale commission of such crimes.

Nonetheless, it is worth mentioning that the aforementioned view of the Prosecution does not necessarily reflect the ICC's position. It is noteworthy one of the first decisions of the Appeals Chamber was very critical towards the Pre-Trial Chamber. Thus it was noted therein that "with respect to war crimes, the requirement of large-scale commission under the Statute is alternative to the requirement of commission as part of a policy. Second, the statutory requirement of either large-scale commission or part of a policy is not absolute but qualified by the expression 'in particular'. Third, the requirement of 'systematic' commission of crimes is not contained in article 8 but only in article 7 on crimes against humanity".[56]

---

[53] ibid 200.

[54] Arsanjani (1999), pp. 22, 33.

[55] Nonetheless, the letter itself reads ambiguously: "For war crimes, a specific gravity threshold is set down in Article 8(1), which states that 'the Court shall have jurisdiction in respect of war crimes in particular when committed as part of a plan or policy or as part of a large-scale commission of such crimes'. This threshold is not an element of the crime, and the words 'in particular' suggest that this is not a strict requirement. It does, however, provide Statute guidance that the Court is intended to focus on situations meeting these requirements. According to the available information, it did not appear that any of the criteria of Article 8(1) were satisfied." Ocampo (2006), http://www.iccnow.org/documents/OTP_letter_to_senders_re_Iraq_9_February_2006.pdf, last accessed 8 June 2023. Benoliel and Perry (2010), pp. 73, 93.

[56] ICC (2006), para. 70 https://www.icc-cpi.int/CourtRecords/CR2006_01807.PDF, last accessed 8 June 2023.

And while, admittedly, the above excerpt is not necessarily sufficiently enlightening, Pre-Trial Chamber II noted in the Bemba case 3 years later that "[i]n the view of the Chamber, the term 'in particular' makes it clear that the existence of a plan, policy or large-scale commission is not a prerequisite for the Court to exercise jurisdiction over war crimes but rather serves as a practical guideline for the Court".[57]

5.5 The Meaning of the Terms "As Part of a Plan or Policy" and "As Part of a Large-Scale Commission"

The definition of the terms "widespread", "systematic" and "multiple commission" has already been thoroughly analysed in the chapter on crimes against humanity. Although the aforementioned terms are closely linked with the terms of Article 8 ICCRSt "part of a plan or policy" and "part of a large-scale commission", their meaning is not the same but does overlap. It goes without saying that the terms of Article 8 ICCRSt "as part of a plan or policy" and "as part of a large-scale commission" have their own separate meaning.

Though this provision is very unclear, it was initially considered a victory for the progressive states that participated in the Rome Conference.[58] And yet: how organised must a perpetrator be in order to be considered part of a plan or policy in the scope of Article 8 ICCRSt? How many people must participate in the planning and execution of this plan or policy in order for a war crime to fall under the ICC's jurisdiction pursuant to Article 8 ICCRSt? What is the minimum number of victims or the geographical extent of the commission of one or more war crimes to fulfil the criterion of a large-scale commission? These are but a few of the most important questions that ICC judges will most certainly be called upon to answer in the next few years, albeit possibly only on an ad hoc basis.

Before the establishment of the ICC, international criminal tribunals or military tribunals exercised their jurisdiction over war crimes only as long as these crimes were committed on a widespread or systematic basis: the Holocaust, war crimes committed on both sides in World War II, ethnic cleansing in the former Yugoslavia, genocide in Rwanda.[59] The statutes of those tribunals did not require the existence of a plan or policy, or of a large-scale commission, because they were established in order to deal with the mass nature of the crimes committed in each case.[60] Consequently, from one perspective and contrary to the nature of the jurisdiction of those tribunals, the Rome Statute of the International Criminal Court leaves open the

[57] ICC (2009b), para 211 https://www.icc-cpi.int/CourtRecords/CR2009_04528.PDF, last accessed 8 June 2023.

[58] Venturini (2001), pp. 95–99.

[59] de Guzman (2012), pp. 18, 23.

[60] ibid.

possibility of the ICC establishing jurisdiction over war crimes of a much lesser gravity.[61]

On the other hand, it is maintained today that even a cyberattack against a civilian communications satellite could be considered a war crime pursuant to Article 8(2)(ii) ICCRSt, especially if it constitutes part of a plan or policy or part of a large-scale commission of such crimes.[62] And it is rather easy to claim for instance, that the existence of a policy can be ascertained as long as other incidents continue to emerge that target a State by sabotaging the communications of neighbouring states. The grand-scale commission of such crimes would require the commission of at least two other similar crimes on a grand scale such as, for example, the destruction of a mobile providers' antennas for an entire city or the demolition of telecommunications towers within a 10-km radius. This follows from the previous analysis, according to which the term "large-scale" requires at least three attacks.

5.6 The Meaning of the Term "Namely"

Another issue that arises in the interpretation of Article 8 ICCRSt is the meaning of the word "namely", which appears several times within this article. In particular, it appears four times in total in the war crimes article of the ICCRSt: (1) in Article 8(2)(a) ICCRSt on grave breaches of the Geneva Conventions of 12 August 1949; (2) in Article 8(2)(b) ICCRSt on "other serious violations of the laws and customs applicable in international armed conflict"; (3) in Article 8(2)(c) ICCRSt on cases of an armed conflict not of an international character and serious violations of article 3 common to the four Geneva Conventions of 12 August 1949; (4) in Article 8(2)(e) ICCRSt on "other serious violations of the laws and customs applicable in armed conflicts not of an international character". Unavoidably, the clear definition of the aforementioned term is key to the establishment of the ICC's jurisdiction in an important number of cases.

Jordan Paust finds this particular matter of interpretation "partially ambiguous",[63] as in his opinion it is not clear whether, for instance, the list of criminal actions that follows this word each time is indicative or exclusive, given that according to international conventions and international customary law, there are many more war crimes than the ones listed in Article 8 ICCRSt; this is also the case for grave (= breaches of the Geneva Conventions of 12 August 1949) or serious (= violations of the laws and customs applicable in armed conflicts not of an international character) war crimes. Nonetheless, Article 22(2) of the Statute may demand for such lists to be interpreted "strictly" and "not be extended by analogy", especially "in case of ambiguity", since that would lead to an interpretation in favour of the accused. On

[61] ibid.

[62] McClure (2012), pp. 431, 436.

[63] Paust (2010), p. 701.

the other hand, it might be the case that Article 22(2) ICCRSt simply demands the strict interpretation of the listed crimes, and not the interpretation of the list itself as an exclusive list of crimes.[64]

At this point, the current author, while recognising the justified queries of other scholars as to the exclusive or indicative nature of the lists in Article 8 ICCRSt, supports their exclusive nature. Despite the fact that, as Paust has already noted, a lot more cases of war crimes could potentially be added to Article 8 ICCRSt, one cannot ignore the fact that the article itself is very long and detailed, and that the way it was drafted resembles articles that exclusively include all the cases they seek to cover. This view is supported by the fact that the word "namely" is followed and defined by the phrase "any of the following acts". In addition, this seems to have been the intent of the international legislators and state delegations.[65]

Moreover, the rule of the strict interpretation of crimes included in Article 22(2) ICCRSt, and the general principle of law *in dubio pro reo* undoubtedly lead to the aforementioned strict interpretation; while the argument that the general rule of interpretation of Article 22(2) ICCRSt only applies to the crimes themselves and not to the individual lists can only be accepted as sophistry, since the word crime in Article 22 ICCRSt refers to the core crimes of the Statute (genocides, crimes against humanity, war crimes and aggression), which are further analysed in their own articles. As a consequence, the application of the general interpretative rule of Article 22(2) ICCRSt, which introduces strict interpretation as a guideline, to Article 8 ICCRSt means nothing other than that obviously all the elements of Article 8 must be interpreted strictly.

5.7 Exceptions to the ICC's Jurisdiction Over War Crimes: The 'Phantom' Article 124 ICCRSt

Long after Article 8 ICCRSt, towards the end of the Statute, comes Article 124 ICCRSt, entitled "Transitional Provision". Its existence is often ignored in the international literature, in part owing to its lack of prominence but especially because neither Article 8 ICCRSt on war crimes nor Article 12 ICCRSt (on the general preconditions for exercising the Court's jurisdiction) indicate or refer to the existence of legal exceptions to the ICC's jurisdiction over war crimes.

Exceptions do however exist and are defined with exceptional clarity in Article 124 ICCRSt, the ICCRSt's "phantom" article. In particular, Article 124 ICCRSt stipulates that notwithstanding Article 12, paragraphs 1 and 2, a State, upon becoming a party to the Statute, may declare that, for a period of 7 years after the Statute's

---

[64] ibid.

[65] Paust JJ, "Commentary on Parts 1 and 2 of the Zutphen Intersessional Draft" in Leila Sadat Wexler (ed) Observations on the Consolidated ICC Text Before the Final Session of the Preparatory Committee, 13bis Nouvelles Etudes Penales, pp. 27, 29.

entry into force in the State concerned, it does not accept the jurisdiction of the Court with respect to war crimes allegedly committed by its nationals or on its territory. A declaration under this article may be withdrawn at any time, although it is debatable whether such a withdrawal could apply retroactively. In other words, even if a state party, in view of a change in government or for another reason, were to withdraw the 7-year exclusion of the ICC's jurisdiction over war crimes relating to its territory or its citizens, the force of this withdrawal could *de lege ferenda* only apply *ex nunc*, with limited practical use.

At this point it must be noted that, prior to the Rome Conference, there was no indication in the work of the Preparatory Committee of any intention to include Article 124 ICCRSt in the Statute. However, the idea of doing so had been mooted at an extremely early stage of the work of the International Law Commission. Thus the ICC may have had direct jurisdiction over the crime of genocide alone, while each State could choose the extent of the ICC's jurisdiction over all other crimes.[66] Nevertheless, at the initiative of France, a rather intense debate broke out during the conference regarding the state parties' right to opt out indefinitely from the ICC's jurisdiction over war crimes and crimes against humanity.[67] This right won the conditional support of the United Kingdom as well, along with that of all five permanent Security Council Members. Thus an additional protocol would provide for a 10-year grace period for States wishing to make use of it.[68] The discussions created an atmosphere that favoured participating States opting out of the jurisdiction of the newly established court as they saw fit. This led to the adoption of Article 124 ICCRSt. Admittedly, considering the intention of the great powers, this result, i.e. Article 124 ICCRSt in its current form, could even be considered a success.

The wording of Article 124 ICCRSt (not least thanks to the work of a member of the UK delegation) expresses the will of the legislature in a manner capable of creating a privileged category of individuals, the citizens of State X or Y, who will be able to commit war crimes for the stated time period of 7 years anywhere in the world without being prosecuted.[69] In the short term, this would mean that citizens of the said State would find themselves in a much more privileged legal position if their State was to ratify the ICCRSt than if it insisted on not ratifying it! In any case, it goes without saying that the ICC cannot, following the expiry of the 7-year period, retrospectively exercise its jurisdiction over war crimes committed on the territory of the state party that made a declaration under Article 124 ICCRSt or over those committed by citizens of that State in their own country (definitely) or anywhere else in the world (probably—according to the current author, this is the correct interpretation).

Fortunately, to this day, only two States have invoked Article 124 ICCRSt and declared that they do not accept the ICC's jurisdiction over war crimes committed by

---

[66] International Law Commission, Final Report (1994), pp. 36–37, 42–43.

[67] Schabas (2010), p. 1193.

[68] ibid 1193.

[69] Wilmshurst (1999), pp. 139–141.

their citizens or in their territory. Those states are France and Colombia. The former withdrew its declaration almost a year before the expiry of the 7-year "grace" period,[70] while Colombia's opt-out period expired on 4 August 2009.

Contrary to William Schabas's prediction that this provision would disappear during the 2010 Review Conference,[71] the 'transitional' provision of Article 124 ICCRSt stands to this day, though contrary to the claims of prominent scholars its existence is not exactly innocent.[72] The ICCRSt has already been ratified by 122 states and gained broad acceptance, despite the backlash it has received from African countries for the great frequency with which it has been put to use in targeting them, as well as from the great powers of our age (USA, Russia, China, Israel, India). The provision continues to exist because the Court hopes that it will tempt these great powers to become state parties to the ICCRSt. However, this hope has yet to be realised, and it is the current author's view that it never will be, given that even if one were to opt out of the ICC's jurisdiction over war crimes, entering the ICCRSt would inevitably signify the acceptance of the Court's jurisdiction over the crime of genocide and over crimes against humanity at the very least. And that is something that does not at all satisfy, let alone please, our planet's great powers.

References

Table of Cases

ICC (2006) Appeals Chamber, Judgement on the Prosecutor's Appeal Against the Decision of Pre-Trial Chamber I Entitled, Decision on the Prosecutor's Application for Warrants of Arrest, Article 58, ICC-01/04, para. 70. https://www.icc-cpi.int/CourtRecords/CR2006_01807.PDF. Accessed 8 June 2023

ICC (2009a) Bemba (ICC-01/05–01/08), Decision Pursuant to Article 61(7)(a) and (b) of the Rome Statute on the Charges of the Prosecutor Against Jean-Pierre Bemba Gombo, para. 136. https://www.icc-cpi.int/CourtRecords/CR2009_04528.PDF. Accessed 8 June 2023

ICC (2009b) Pre-Trial Chamber II, Bemba Decision Pursuant to Article 61(7)(a) and (b) of the Rome Statute on the Charges of the Prosecutor Against Jean-Pierre Bemba Gombo, ICC-01/05-01/08, 15 June 2009, para. 211, https://www.icc-cpi.int/CourtRecords/CR2009_04528.PDF. Accessed 8 June 2023

ICC (2012) The Prosecutor v Thomas Lubanga Dyilo, Judgment, ICC-01/04-01/06-2842, Trial Chamber I. http://www.icc-cpi.int/iccdocs/doc/doc1379838.pdf. Accessed 8 June 2023

ICTY (2003a) The Prosecutor v Kronjelac, Judgment, IT-97-25-T, paras 350–360

ICTY (2003b) The Prosecutor v Naletelic and Martinovic, Judgment IT-98-34-T, paras 250–261

[70] This "grace" period for crimes allegedly committed by French citizens or in French territory expired on 30 June 2009. Its revocation was submitted by the French representative on 13 August 2008, although the document itself is dated 15 June 2008. ibid 1193–1194.

[71] Schabas (2010), pp. 1192, 1994.

[72] ibid 1194.

Articles/Papers

Arsanjani MH (1999) The Rome statute of the international criminal court. Am J Int Law 93:22–43

Benoliel D, Perry R (2010) Israel, Palestine and the ICC. Mich J Int Law 32:73–127

Black I (2013) Bashar al-Assad implicated in Syria war crimes, says UN, The Guardian London https://www.theguardian.com/world/2013/dec/02/syrian-officials-involved-war-crimes-bashar-al-assad-un-investigators. Accessed 8 June 2023

de Guzman M (2012) How serious are international crimes? The gravity problem in international criminal law. Colum J Transnatl Law 51

Guan J (2010) The ICC's jurisdiction over war crimes in internal armed conflicts: an insurmountable obstacle for China's accession? Penn St Int Law Rev 28

Heller KJ (2008) Mistake of legal element, the common law, and article 32 of the Rome statute. J Int Criminal Justice 6

ICCRSt UN Doc. A/CONF.183/SR.9 para. 16

International Law Commission, Final Report (1994)

Lanham K (2005) A Paradox of Prediction: The ICC's Effect on US Humanitarian Policy in The Sudan2 (1) Eyes on the ICC

McClure R (2012) International adjudication options in response to state-sponsored cyberattacks against outer-space satellites. New Eng J Int Comp Law 18

Paust JJ (2010) The international criminal court does not have complete jurisdiction over customary crimes against humanity and war crimes. J Marshall Law Rev 43

Paust JJ Commentary on Parts 1 and 2 of the Zutphen Intersessional Draft. In Wexler LS (ed) Observations on the Consolidated ICC Text Before the Final Session of the Preparatory Committee, 13bis Nouvelles Etudes Penales

Report Presented to the Preliminary Peace Conference, (1920) 14 (1–2) AJIL

Triponel A, Pearson S (2010) African states and the international criminal court: a silent revolution in international criminal law. J Law Soc Challenges 12

Weigend T (2004) The harmonization of general principles of criminal law. Nouvelles Etudes Penale 19

Whitten JH (2012) They're getting away with murder: how the international criminal court can prosecute U.S. private security contractors for the Nisour Square tragedy and why it should. Wash Univ Global Stud Law Rev 11

Books

Ambos K (2002) Der Allgemeine Teil des Völkerstrafrechts. Duncker and Humblot, Berlin

Cassese A (2003) International criminal law. Oxford University Press, Oxford

Chomsky N (2016) Who rules the world? Metropolitan Books/Henry Holt & Co, New York

Clapham A (1994) Brierly's law of nations, 7th edn. Oxford University Press, Oxford

Eser A (2002) Mental elements: mistake of fact and mistake of law. In: Cassese A et al (eds) The Rome statute of the international criminal court: a commentary, vol I. Oxford University Press, New York

Kelt M, von Hebel H (2001) General principles of criminal law and the elements of crimes. In: Lee RS (ed) The international criminal court: elements of crimes and rules of procedure and evidence. New York Transnational Publishers, Ardsley

Kolb R, Hyde R (2008) An introduction to the international law of armed conflicts. Oxford University Press, Oxford

Piragoff DK (1999) Article 30: Mental Element. In: Triffterer O (ed) Commentary on the Rome statute of the international criminal court: Observer's notes, article by article. Nomos, Glashütte

Sadat NN (2002) The international criminal court and the transformation of international justice. Transnational Publishers, Ardsley

Schabas WA (2010) The international criminal court: a commentary on the Rome statute. Oxford University Press, New York

Simeonidou-Kastanidou E et al (2006) Τα Εγκλήματα Πολέμου: οι διεθνείς υποχρεώσεις της Ελλάδας και τα αναγκαία μέτρα προσαρμογής [War Crimes: The International Obligations of Greece and the Necessary Adjustment's Measures]. Nomiki Vivliothiki, Thessaloniki

Tsilonis V (2009) Taming the waves of international criminal justice: the paradox of serving (in) justice through (un)just means and the Saddam Hussein's case. In: Zirk-Sadowski M, Wojciechowski B (eds) Dia-logos (volume 11) multicentrism as an emerging paradigm in legal theory. Peter Lang Publications, New York

Tsilonis V (2010) Thomas Lubanga Dyilo: a wavering step for the international criminal court. In: Pitsela A (ed) Criminological quests: honorary volume for professor Stergios Alexiadis. Sakkoulas, Thessaloniki. [in Greek]

Tsilonis V (2011) Monsters in the Mist, 8 Intellectum 7–8 http://www.intellectum.org/en/2011/12/13/terata-stin-omixl/. Accessed 8 June 2023

Venturini G (2001) War crimes in international armed conflicts. In: Politi M, Nesied G (eds) The Rome statute of the international criminal court: a challenge to impunity. Cambridge University Press, Cambridge

Von Hebel H, Robinson D (1999) Crimes within the jurisdiction of the court. In: Lee RS (ed) The international criminal court: the making of the Rome statute issue, negotiations, results. Kluwer Law International, Alphen aan den Rijn

Werle G (2005) Principles of international criminal law. TMC Asser Press, Den Haag

Wilmshurst E (1999) Jurisdiction of the court. In: Lee RS (ed) The international criminal court: the making of the Rome statute. Kluwer Law International, Alphen Aan Den Rijn

Zimmermann A (2003) International criminal law and the current development of public international law. Duncker & Humblot, Berlin

Websites/Web Sources

American Service-Members' Protection Act of 2002. https://2001-2009.state.gov/t/pm/rls/othr/misc/23425.htm. Accessed 8 June 2023

Bellinger JB The United States and the International Criminal Court: Where We've Been and Where We're Going, Remarks to the DePaul University College of Law, https://2001-2009.state.gov/s/l/rls/104053.htm. Accessed 8 June 2023

Fourth Geneva Convention (1949) Articles 49 to 52 of the First Convention, 50 to 53 of the Second, 129 to 131 of the Third, and 146 to 149 of the of 12 August 1949 https://www.icrc.org/en/doc/assets/files/publications/icrc-002 0173.pdf&usg=AOvVaw2QEScZEGFSn17zoEBkQhNs. Accessed 8 June 2023

ICC (1996) Opinion on the Legality of the Threat or Use of Nuclear Weapons https://www.icj-cij.org/files/case-related/95/095-19960708-ADV-01-00-EN.pdf. Accessed 8 June 2023

Ocampo LM (2006) OTP Letter to Senders for the situation in Iraq. http://www.iccnow.org/documents/OTP_letter_to_senders_re_Iraq_9_February_2006.pdf. Accessed 8 June 2023

Regulations concerning the Laws and Customs of War on Land. https://ihl-databases.icrc.org/en/ihl-treaties/hague-conv-iv-1907/regulations-art-23. Accessed 8 June 2023

Chapter 6
The Crime of Aggression: The Birth of a Crime

Abstract The crime of aggression (The term aggression is different from the word attack. E.g. an act of targeting of the "enemy" can constitute aggression but is not an attack *per se*.) officially emerged for the first time in international criminal law as a crime committed by individuals and not States in August 1945. This coincided with the signing of the London Agreement at the International Military Tribunal in Nuremberg (IMTN). Article 6 of the Nuremberg Statute, which constituted the London Agreement's annex, explicitly referred to "crimes against peace: namely, planning, preparation, initiation or waging of a war of aggression, or a war in violation of international treaties, agreements or assurances, or participation in a common plan or conspiracy for the accomplishment of any of the foregoing."

Yet it is a fact that after the trials and respective convictions at the IMTN and the International Military Tribunal for the Far East (IMTFE), the crime of aggression disappeared from the map of international law primarily for three reasons analysed succinctly by Antonio Cassese.

During the summer of 1998, after a marathon session of negotiations, the crime of aggression was incorporated into the Rome Statute of the International Criminal Court and thus featured among the crimes that fall under the jurisdiction of the ICC. However, it was expressly clarified at the second paragraph of Article 5 (d) ICCRSt that "[t]he Court shall exercise jurisdiction over the crime of aggression once a provision is adopted in accordance with articles 121 and 123 defining the crime and setting out the conditions under which the Court shall exercise jurisdiction with respect to this crime. Such a provision shall be consistent with the relevant provisions of the Charter of the United Nations".

Consequently, Article 121§5 ICCRSt states that "[a]ny amendment to articles 5, 6, 7 and 8 of this Statute shall enter into force for those States Parties which have accepted the amendment 1 year after the deposit of their instruments of ratification or acceptance. In respect of a State Party which has not accepted the amendment, the Court shall not exercise its jurisdiction regarding a crime covered by the amendment when committed by that State Party's nationals or on its territory".

In the Kampala Review Conference in 2010 it was eventually decided that the definition of the crime of aggression will be materialised would be confirmed by the

V. Tsilonis, *The Jurisdiction of the International Criminal Court*,
https://doi.org/10.1007/978-3-031-46138-5_6

addition of Article 8B ICCRSt and concomitantly the removal of the 'vacant' Article 5§2 ICCRSt, which had merely stated that the crime of aggression was to be defined over time. However, the final decision regarding the activation of the ICC's jurisdiction over the crime of aggression was placed on the agenda of the 16th session of the Assembly of States Parties held between 4 and 14 December 2017 in New York pursuant to Articles 15 bis(2) and (3) and 15 ter(2) and (3) ICCRSt. The extremely restrictive approach adopted by the 16th session of Assembly of States Parties casts serious doubts on whether a sui generis, incapacitated crime has been legally established in the place of a true crime.

The term aggression is different from the word attack. E.g. an act of targeting of the "enemy" can constitute aggression but is not an attack *per se*.

6.1 The Right of Declaration of War and the Crime of Aggression: Two Antithetical Notions

The principles derived from the Peace Treaty of Westphalia, i.e. of state sovereignty and state equality, created the belief that States were entitled to wage war whenever they thought it appropriate.[1] However, in the early twentieth century the 1899 and 1907 Hague Regulations—even though they did not prohibit war—encouraged state parties to resort to the Permanent Court of Arbitration in case of a dispute.[2]

Furthermore, a few years later, Article 10 of the Covenant of the League of Nations[3] encouraged Members of the League to "undertake to respect and preserve as against external aggression the territorial integrity and existing political independence of all Members of the League". And Article 11 stated that "Any war or threat of war, whether immediately affecting any of the Members of the League or not, is hereby declared a matter of concern to the whole League, and the League shall take any action that may be deemed wise and effectual to safeguard the peace of nations."[4]

---

[1] Arend and Beck (1993), pp. 11–17, who referred to the views of nineteenth-century English legal expert William Edward Hall regarding States' "right to war".

[2] Laws of War (1900), adopted 29 July 1899, entered into force 4 September 1900, Chapter 2, arts 20–29, for the Permanent Court of Arbitration, http://avalon.law.yale.edu/19th_ce ntury/hague01.asp, last accessed 8 June 2023.

[3] See for further details, Pichou (2012), pp. 10–13.

[4] The Covenant of the League of Nations (1919) (entered into force 10 January 1920) arts 10, 11, http://avalon.law.yale.edu/20th_century/leagcov.asp, last accessed 8 June 2023.

Although other Covenant articles permitted the waging of war under preconditions,[5] the above article could be considered as implying a direct and strict prohibition of war. As such, it prefaced the Kellogg-Briand Pact signed in 1928.[6]

The extremely brief Kellogg-Briand Pact[7] renunciated war as an "instrument of national policy" in two instances,[8] but neither determined which act or action of a State constituted an attack against another State. Moreover, the Pact did not include any penal sanctions in the event that the conditions were transgressed.[9] The only thing it demanded was that "The High Contracting Parties [...] condemn recourse to war for the solution of international controversies, and [...] as an instrument of national policy in their relations with one another."[10] Hence, the Kellogg-Briand Pact was not at all able to deliver on the expectations that its ratification created on an international level, nor essentially to contribute to the establishment of peace. As already mentioned, the fact that the Pact did not include any sanctions in the event of its violation by a state party, nor any reference to possible criminal liabilities, also played a crucial role in the lacklustre outcome above. Thus, although some authors allege that the Kellogg-Briand Pact was invoked during the conflict between China and the Soviet Union in 1929 and during the war between China and Japan in 1931,[11] perhaps its only true value was that "it ended a long period of hard and honest effort by mankind to outlaw war, and at the same time, marked the beginning of a new period of effort towards outlawing aggression."[12]

Furthermore, the Pact's ratification did not prevent Japan's invasion of Manchuria in 1931, Italy's invasion of Abyssinia in 1935 or the coordinated invasion by German and Soviet military forces of Poland shortly before the outbreak of World War II[13] and the later offensive mounted by the Soviet Union in Finland in 1939.[14]

---

[5] See the Hague Regulations of 1907, which make extensive references regarding who is considered as a prisoner of war, belligerent, spy etc., along with their respective rights, basically taking the waging of wars in the future as granted; "Laws of War (1910), adopted 18 October 1907, entered into force 26 January 1910, http://avalon.law.yale.edu/20th_century/hague04.asp, last accessed 8 June 2023.

[6] See Pichou (2012), p. 10. This pact was named after the then US Secretary of State Frank Kellogg and French Minister for Foreign Affairs Aristides Briand, who were its masterminds. It is commonly referred to as the Pact of Paris (Telford Taylor, ibid., 580–581). See the Pact's Preamble, Yale's University digital library "Avalon", http://avalon.law.yale.edu/20th_century/kbpact.asp, last accessed 8 June 2023.

[7] In addition to the Preamble, the Kellogg-Briand Pact included only three articles!

[8] Treaty for Renunciation of War (1929) (adopted 27 August 1928, entered into force 24 July 1929), see the Pact's Preamble and Art. 1, Yale's University digital library "Avalon" http://avalon.law.yale.edu/20th_century/kbpact.asp, last accessed 8 June 2023.

[9] ibid Articles 1–3.

[10] ibid Article 1.

[11] Pichou (2012), pp. 23–24, without any other citations.

[12] Reddi 2008, pp. 655–686, who cites Rifaat AM (659).

[13] Despite the fact that all the aforementioned invading countries had signed the Pact, only the Soviet Union had ratified it.

[14] Term Russo-Finnish War, Encyclopedia BRITRANNICA, https://www.britannica.com/event/Russo-Finnish-War, last accessed 8 June 2023.

Notwithstanding which, the crime of aggression officially emerged for the first time in international criminal law as a crime committed by individuals and not States in August 1945. This coincided with the signing of the London Agreement, which established the International Military Tribunal in Nuremberg (IMTN).[15] Article 6 of the Nuremberg Statute, which constituted the London Agreement's annex, explicitly stated that "The Tribunal established by the Agreement [. . .] shall have the power to try and punish persons who, acting in the interests of the European Axis countries, whether as individuals or as members of organizations, committed any of the following crimes. The following acts, or any of them are crimes coming within the jurisdiction of the Tribunal for which there shall be individual responsibility: (a) Crimes against peace: namely, planning, preparation, initiation or waging of a war of aggression, or a war in violation of international treaties, agreements or assurances, or participation in a common plan or conspiracy for the accomplishment of any of the foregoing."[16]

On 24 October 1945, i.e. just after the end of World War II and shortly before the establishment of the IMTN, the United Nations Charter was signed (UN Charter). In Article 1 of the first chapter of the UN Charter, reference is made to the suppression of belligerent actions as one of the UN's purposes.[17] Entitled "Purposes and Principles", the article states that "The Purposes of the United Nations are: (1) To maintain international peace and security, and to that end: to take effective collective measures for the prevention and removal of threats to the peace, and for the suppression of acts of aggression or other breaches of the peace, and to bring about by peaceful means, and in conformity with the principles of justice and international law, adjustment or settlement of international disputes or situations which might lead to a breach of the peace."[18]

Furthermore, Article 2§4 UN Charter asserts that "[a]ll Members shall refrain in their international relations from the threat or use of force against the territorial integrity or political independence of any state, or in any other manner inconsistent with the Purposes of the United Nations".[19]

---

[15] On 11 December 1946 the UN General Assembly unanimously adopted Resolution 95(I) during its 55th meeting. The Resolution affirmed "the principles of international law recognized by the Charter of the Nuremberg Tribunal and the judgment of the Tribunal". Unusually, with this Resolution the UN General Assembly confirmed a priori the decision of the International Nuremberg Tribunal. Although the political validity of such a statement is indisputable, the legal validity of such a statement is disputed.

[16] See London Agreement (1945), http://avalon.law.yale.edu/imt/imtchart.asp, last accessed 8 June 2023.

[17] It is ironic that over 60 years after the UN established the crime of aggression, one of the cornerstones of the UN Charter has not yet been clarified in international law.

[18] See United Nations Regional Information Centre for Western Europe, https://www.unric.org/en/, last accessed 8 June 2023.

[19] United Nations Charter (1945), adopted 26 June 1945, entered into force 24 October 1945), art 2 (4), https://treaties.un.org/doc/publication/ctc/uncharter.pdf, last accessed 8 June 2023.

Thereafter, in the first article of Chapter VII of the UN Charter, under the general title "Action with Respect to Threats to the Peace, Breaches of the Peace, and Acts of Aggression" (Article 39), it is stated that "The Security Council shall determine the existence of any threat to the peace, breach of the peace, or act of aggression and shall [...] decide what measures shall be taken in accordance with Articles 41 and 42, to maintain or restore international peace and security".[20]

However, today it is generally accepted that there are two exceptions to the general rule of Article 2§4 UN Charter: (1) the inherent right of individual or collective self-defence in case of an armed attack against a member of the United Nations (article 51 UN Charter); and (2) the collective security measures granted by the UN Security Council under Chapter 7 (Articles 9–51 of the UN Charter).

In the case of *United States of America et al v Göering et al*, the IMTN described the crime of aggression as the most heinous crime of all: "War is essentially an evil thing. Its consequences are not confined to the belligerent States alone, but affect the whole world. To initiate a war of aggression, therefore, is not only an international crime; it is the supreme international crime differing only from other war crimes in that it contains within itself the accumulated evil of the whole."[21] Based on this legal view, the IMTN found a total of 12 defendants guilty of the crime of aggression and sentenced them either to death or to incarcerations.[22] Moreover, the IMTN found that Germany had committed acts of aggression against Austria and Czechoslovakia as well as waged wars of aggression against nine states, including Greece.[23] Thus, the International Military Tribunal of Tokyo (IMT) convicted 25 defendants for the commission of the crime of aggression.[24]

Hithertothere have been serious doubts as to whether the crime of aggression was actually a crime according to international law as it stood at the outbreak of World War II,[25] and if so whether it was indeed the most heinous of all.[26] Yet it is a fact that after the trials and respective convictions at the IMTN and the International Military

[20] Ibid.

[21] International Military Tribunal, United States of America et al. v Göering et al (1947), Judgment 30 September-1 October 1946), p. 172.

[22] "Judicial Decisions (1947), p. 172, in 333 etc.

[23] Ibid. 192–213; The other states were Belgium, Yugoslavia, Denmark, Luxemburg, Norway, the Netherlands, Poland and the Soviet Union.

[24] Cassese (2007), p. 842, footnote 2.

[25] Dinstein (2001), p. 109; Röling and Cassese (1992), p. 98. The IMT dedicated a notable part of its decision to this particular crime so as to "manifest" that it had already existed before 1945 and that consequently the fundamental principle nullum crimen nulla poena sine lege certa was not violated.

[26] Schabas points out with emphasis that while Rudolf Hess received a life sentence for the crime of waging of war of aggression, others, like Julius Streicher, were sentenced to death for crimes against humanity. Schabas (2004), pp. 124–141, 125. Additionally, the view of the Presiding Judge of the International Military Tribunal for Tokyo that no one should be sentenced to death for the charge of waging a war of aggression is extremely important. See Tokyo International Military Tribunal, United States of America et al. v Araki et al., Judgment, separate opinion section, (12 November 1948) in Röling and Cuter (1977), p. 478.

Tribunal for the Far East (IMTFE), the crime of aggression disappeared from the map of international law.

According to Cassese, there are three reasons for this:

1. Shortly after the end of World War II it was easy for the heads of defeated states to be criminally punished, given that the violations of the international conventions were so grave that the usual imposition of onerous financial compensation on the defeated States was not considered sufficient on its own; thus it was decided that individual criminal responsibilities should also be attributed to those who played a leading role in the planning and waging of war.
2. Secondly, the UN Charter enacted in 1945 laid out a system of prohibitions and permissions regarding the future use of force. Thus, according to Article 2§4 UN Charter, the use of force was prohibited in international relations and only permitted with the backing of the UN Security Council under Articles 42–49 UN Charter or in case of self-defence according to Article 51 UN Charter. However, even though the prohibition of the use of force was absolutely clear, the cases in which the use of force was eventually permitted were not so clear. In particular, there was disagreement as to whether the use of force was permitted for the purposes of anticipatory defence[27] and if so under which circumstances.[28] Indeed, according to the more appropriate interpretation of Article 51 UN Charter, self-defence is legal when an armed attack by another State is imminent (as in the case of the Six-Day War in 1967, where Israel launched a preventative attack against Egypt), but it is illegal when it aims to prevent a possible attack in the longer term (like in 1981, when Israel destroyed the Osirak nuclear reactor in Iraq and the UN Security Council condemned this action in an unusual manner, namely in the form of Resolution 487/1981).[29] However, as is to be expected, this legal interpretation has yet to be accepted by all States. The resulting legal

[27] In Greek one also comes across the term "defence against imminent attack", which indicates the right legal interpretation of the term but without properly translating the term itself. See the diagram by associate Professor Antonopoulos K, Law School of Democritus University of Thrace, available online, http://www.law.duth.gr/index.php?cid=167&st=1, last accessed 8 June 2023.

[28] Cassese (2007), pp. 843–844.

[29] In the said Resolution it is expressly stated that Iraq—in contrast to Israel—had already joined the Nuclear Non-proliferation Treaty. In addition, it is pointed out that: "in accordance with that Treaty Iraq has accepted IAEA safeguards on all its nuclear activities, and that the Agency has testified that these safeguards have been satisfactorily applied to date[...] 1. Strongly condemns the military attack by Israel in clear violation of the Charter of the United Nations and the norms of international conduct; [...] 4. Fully recognizes the inalienable sovereign right of Iraq, and all other States, especially the developing countries, to establish programmes of technological and nuclear development to develop their economy and industry for peaceful purposes in accordance with their present and future needs and consistent with the internationally accepted objectives of preventing nuclear weapons proliferation; 5. Calls upon Israel urgently to place its nuclear facilities under IAEA safeguards; 6. Considers that Iraq is entitled to appropriate redress for the destruction it has suffered, responsibility for which has been acknowledged by Israel[...]" available online, http://www.un.org/en/ga/search/view_doc.asp?symbol=S/%20%20RES/487(1981), last accessed 8 June 2023.

ambiguity allows States, especially the more powerful ones, to act largely at their discretion. At the same time, it renders the criminalization of aggression problematic, since even in international criminal law legal precision is a requirement for the indictment of individuals.

3. The long period of the Cold War impelled all state parties, regardless of the position they took on the matter, to essentially refrain from backing any firmer legal definition of the crime of aggression for fear that any such definition would eventually be held against them during the protracted political and ideological standoff. Moreover, even the most powerful States felt the need to preserve their freedom of action in the application of the rules of self-defence as much as possible. Hence, it was convenient for all state parties to allow the definition of the crime of aggression to remain pending.[30]

Hence the crime of aggression remained in the darkness for approximately the next three decades, until it momentarily entered the spotlight again in the 1970s. In an *obiter dictum* relating to the decision of the International Court of Justice (ICJ) on the famous case of Barcelona Traction, reference is made to acts of aggression as an example of the state parties' obligation *erga omnes*. It conveys that all States could be held to have a legal interest in the protection of the rights involved.[31] Of course, it should be underlined that the ICJ made the said statement despite the fact that there was no official or commonly accepted definition of the crime of aggression in international theory or practice at that time.

The UN General Assembly tried to some extent to bridge this legal gap in 1974, when it adopted a definition of aggression committed by a State under Resolution 3314.[32] The long-winded text comprised eight articles, the first of which stated that "Aggression is the use of armed force by a State against the sovereignty, territorial integrity or political independence of another State, or in any other manner inconsistent with the Charter of the United Nations [...]".[33]

The definition was never rendered legally binding. It remained an "advisory guide" that had no impact on processes or the way the UN Security Council made decisions thereafter.[34] Nonetheless, the UN Security Council did condemn the actions of a State as aggression a handful of times. Surprisingly, this happened twice in 1985[35]: first in Resolution 573/04-10-1985, where the UN Security Council

[30] Cassese (2007), pp. 843–844.

[31] ICJ (1970), para 33. While there has been a contentious discussion on the issue regarding which recognised international law principles arise today against the background provided by the Westphalia Treaty and how these were applied over the centuries, the above conclusion is one of the points that tends to be accepted.

[32] UNGA Res 3314 (XXIX) (1974), available online, http://www.un.org/en/ga/search/view_doc.asp?symbol=A/%20RES/3314(XXIX), last accessed 8 June 2023.

[33] ibid.

[34] Bassiouni and Ferencz (2013), pp. 313 and 334.

[35] It is a sort of a mystery that both of the two times the UN Security Council decided that the crime of aggression was committed occurred in 1985.

condemned Israel's aerial strike of the Palestine Liberation Organisation's (PLO) facilities in Tunisia,[36] and the second time in the severe wording of Resolution 577/06-12-1985 concerning the invasion of Angola by South Africa's racist regime.[37]

Two years later, in November 1987, the UN General Assembly passed a Resolution entitled "Declaration on the Enhancement of the Effectiveness of the Principle of Refraining from the Threat or Use of Force in International Relations".[38] It reiterated that "All Members shall refrain in their international relations from the threat or use of force against the territorial integrity or political independence of any state, or in any other manner inconsistent with the Purposes of the United Nations."[39]

During the summer of 1998, after a marathon session of negotiations, the crime of aggression was incorporated into the Rome Statute of the International Criminal Court and thus featured among the crimes that fall under the jurisdiction of the ICC. However, it was expressly clarified at the second paragraph of Article 5 (d) ICCRSt that "[t]he Court shall exercise jurisdiction over the crime of aggression once a provision is adopted in accordance with articles 121 and 123 defining the crime and setting out the conditions under which the Court shall exercise jurisdiction with respect to this crime. Such a provision shall be consistent with the relevant provisions of the Charter of the United Nations".

Consequently, Article 121§5 ICCRSt states that "[a]ny amendment to articles 5, 6, 7 and 8 of this Statute shall enter into force for those States Parties which have accepted the amendment one year after the deposit of their instruments of ratification or acceptance. In respect of a State Party which has not accepted the amendment, the Court shall not exercise its jurisdiction regarding a crime covered by the amendment when committed by that State Party's nationals or on its territory".

Then, in the first paragraph of Article 123 ICCRSt it is also stated that "[s]even years after the entry into force of this Statute the Secretary-General of the United Nations shall convene a Review Conference.... [s]uch review may include, but is not limited to, the list of crimes contained in article 5." Finally, in the next two paragraphs of the present article it is made clear that "[a]t any time thereafter, at the request of a State Party and for the purposes set out in paragraph 1, the Secretary-General of the United Nations shall, upon approval by a majority of States Parties, convene a Review Conference. The provisions of article 121, paragraphs 3 to 7, shall apply [...]".

---

[36] The USA abstained from the vote but did not use its veto. UNSC Res 573 (4 October 1985), available online in Israel's Ministry of Foreign Affairs website, https://mfa.gov.il/MFA/ForeignPolicy/MFADocuments/Yearbook7/Pages/95%20Security%20Council%20Resolution%20573%20-1985%2D%2D%20Israel.aspx, last accessed 8 June 2023.

[37] UNSC Res 577 (6 December 1985), available online, https://undocs.org/S/RES/577(1985), last accessed 8 June 2023.

[38] UNGA (1987).

[39] Article 1§1 of this Declaration repeats the exact wording of Article 2§4 of the UN Charter, http://www.un.org/documents/ga/res/42/a42r022.htm, last accessed 8 June 2023.

6.2 The 'Enactment' of the Crime of Aggression Under the Jurisdiction of the ICC

The above provisions were the subject of intense negotiations and heated debate[40] prior to the vote on the Rome Statute in July 1998. The crime of aggression was legislated in the first place as a 'potential crime',[41] as it may have been defined in Article 5(d) ICCRSt as a crime under the jurisdiction of the ICC, but the ICC jurisdiction over the said crime could not materialise without particular provisions being fulfilled at some point in the future.

First, a relevant provision had to be adopted during the Review Conference of the state parties, which would determine the *actus reus* and *mens rea* of the crime and would set the conditions under which the Court could exercise its jurisdiction over this crime. However, the fulfillment of the above provision would not in any way exclude the enactment of a new special model of prosecution for those accused of the crime of aggression. Such a model would fully depart from the standard process of prosecution adopted for all the other crimes under the ICC's jurisdiction.

Second, a provision was required that would qualify as being "consistent with the relevant provisions of the UN Charter". This is a skillfully vague reference to the role of the United Nations and especially of the Security Council. The Security Council is of course a UN organ that comprises 15 state parties (five permanent and 10 elective),[42] and which has principle responsibility for maintaining international peace and security.[43] For this reason, but also given that the most powerful States of our times are amongst its permanent members, the Security Council can define an action as aggression or not and decide upon the employment of measures for the maintenance or restoration of international peace and security pursuant to Articles 41 and 42 of the UN Charter.[44] Nevertheless, because of the lack of a commonly accepted interpretation of the term "aggression" that is legally binding for the Security Council, the whole process remains legally nebulous.

Third, a provision is required to cater for the fact that, pursuant to Article 123 ICCRSt, 7 years must pass after the Rome Statute's entry into force before a Review Conference can take place.

---

[40] Kirsch and Holmes (1999), p. 2.

[41] My own terminology, intended to summarise the legal paradox of "the existence" of a crime in a statute (international convention in this case), the definition of which and its entry into force is to be voted on at some unspecified point in the future. The widely known phrase "the issue was postponed until the Greek calends" sums up this particular situation.

[42] According to the article 23§1 UN Charter the Republic of China, France, Russia, the United Kingdom and the USA are the permanent members of the Council, while the remaining 10 members are elected every 2 years by the General Assembly of the United Nations, according to the provisions of article 23§§1(b) and 2 of the UN Charter, http://www.un.org/en/charter-united-nations/index.html, (last accessed 8 June 2023).

[43] ibid article 24§1.

[44] ibid article 39.

Fourth, a provision is required to further limit the ICC's capabilities such that even if all the above provisions are fulfilled, the ICC could exercise its jurisdiction over the crime of aggression only where the specific state party consents to the amendment of the ICCRSt concerning the jurisdiction of the ICC over the crime of aggression. Otherwise, pursuant to Article 121§5 ICCRSt, the ICC would not have jurisdiction over the crime of aggression if committed by a citizen of a state party that has not ratified the amendment or if committed on the territory of such a State.

A further major issue initially arose with regard to States acceding to the Rome Statute after an amendment had been made to the crime of aggression or the addition of another crime (since one cannot exclude the possibility of the addition of other crimes, be it international drug trafficking,[45] terrorism etc.).

6.3 The Birth of the Crime of Aggression: The Assembly of States Parties in Kampala (2010) and New York (2017)

Eventually, at 00:40 a.m. on Saturday 12 June 2010, shortly after the official conclusion of the Review Conference of the 111 state parties in Kampala (31 May–11 June 2010), it was decided in the presence of state and NGO observers that the definition of the crime of aggression would be confirmed by the addition of Article 8B ICCRSt and the removal of the 'vacant' Article 5§2 ICCRSt, which had merely stated that the crime of aggression was to be defined over time.

Since then a respectable group of 36 states ratified the Kampala amendments on the crime of aggression.[46] Following the crucial work carried out by Ambassador of Liechtenstein Christian Wenaweser, who chaired the negotiations of these amendments in the Assembly's Special Working Group on the Crime of Aggression (2003–2009), served as the President of the Assembly from 2008 to 2011 and also presided over the Review Conference, Liechtenstein became the first state to ratify the Kampala amendments on the crime of aggression.[47] And only 4 years later, in an act of great historical significance, Palestine ratified the amendments to the Rome Statute on the crime of aggression.[48] Consequently the State of Palestine became the

[45] See prime minister of Trinidad and Tobago Arthur Robinson's proposal, during the 44th conference of the UN General Assembly, for the establishment of an international criminal court to combat international drug trafficking. Arnold (2008), p. 34.

[46] The Global Campaign for Ratification and Implementation of the Kampala Amendments on the Crime of Aggression, https://crimeofaggression.info/the-role-of-states/status-of-ratification-and-implementation, last accessed 8 June 2023.

[47] ICC (2012), https://asp.icc-cpi.int/en_menus/asp/press%20releases/press%20releases %202012/Pages/pr793.aspx, last accessed 8 June 2023.

[48] State of Palestine Becomes the Thirtieth State to Ratify the Kampala Amendments on the Crime of Aggression, ICC-ASP-20160629-PR1225, ICC Press Release, 29 June 2016, https://asp.icc-cpi.int/en_menus/asp/press%20 releases/Pages/PR1225.aspx, last accessed 8 June 2023.

30th State to have ratified the Kampala amendments and opened the gates for the ICC's jurisdiction over the crime of aggression after 1 January 2017, subject to a final decision by the Assembly of States Parties (ASP) to activate that jurisdiction.

The decision regarding the activation of the ICC's jurisdiction over the crime of aggression was placed on the agenda of the 16th ASP session held between 4 and 14 December 2017 in New York pursuant to Articles 15 bis(2) and (3) and 15 ter (2) and (3) ICCRst.[49] During that session Panama became the 35th state to ratify the Kampala amendments. After the completion of the turbulent 16th ASP session, only one further state ratified the amendments, such that Ireland became the 36th state to do so thus far.[50] However, quite a few states that should arguably have a great interest in ratifying the amendments and legally fortifying their sovereignty, including Greece,[51] Serbia and Ecuador, have yet to do so due to a profound inadvertence or other largely unknown geopolitical and/or diplomatic reasons.[52]

Apart from the addition of Article 8B, the following additions and amendments have also been made, which render the exercise of the ICC's jurisdiction over the crime of aggression more problematic than over the other crimes, which (as already revealed in the familiar chapter on the prerequisites for the ICC to exercise its jurisdiction) are merely subject to the prerequisites set out in article 12 ICCRSt. Hence, according to the new articles 15 bis and 15 ter ICCRSt[53] under the general title "Exercise of Jurisdiction over the Crime of Aggression", along with the new

---

[49] Kreβ (2018), pp. 1, 7.

[50] The Global Campaign for Ratification and Implementation of the Kampala Amendments on the Crime of Aggression, https://crimeofaggression.info/the-role-of-states/status-of-ratification-and-implementation, last accessed 8 June 2023.

[51] The case of Greece becomes more and more mysteriously paradoxical, especially after reading one of Claus Kreβ's latest papers where it is noted "A similar note of recognition is due to the distinguished delegates Shara Duncan Villalobos from Costa Rica, Vasiliki Krasa from Cyprus, Paivi Kaukoranta from Finland, James Kingston from Ireland and Martha Papadopoulou from Greece for their valuable contributions to the New York, December 2017 negotiations. In the case of Greece, the important role played, over many years, by the distinguished delegate Phani Dascalopoulou-Livada will be remembered." Kreβ (2018), 1, 9, fn. 29.

[52] Ibid.

[53] Rome Statute of the International Criminal Court (adopted 17 July 1998, entered into force 1 July 2002): Exercise of jurisdiction over the crime of aggression (State referral, proprio motu).

(a) The Court may exercise jurisdiction over the crime of aggression in accordance with article 13, paragraphs (a) and (c), subject to the provisions of this article.
(b) The Court may exercise jurisdiction only with respect to crimes of aggression committed 1 year after the ratification or acceptance of the amendments by 30 States Parties.
(c) The Court shall exercise jurisdiction over the crime of aggression in accordance with this article, subject to a decision to be taken after 1 January 2017 by the same majority of States Parties as is required for the adoption of an amendment to the Statute.
(d) The Court may, in accordance with article 12, exercise jurisdiction over a crime of aggression, arising from an act of aggression committed by a State Party, unless that State Party has previously declared that it does not accept such jurisdiction by lodging a declaration with the Registrar. The withdrawal of such a declaration may be affected at any time and shall be considered by the State Party within 3 years.

provision of Article 25§3 bis ICCRSt,[54] the ICC can exercise jurisdiction over the crime of aggression as long as[55]: (a) the actions were committed by a citizen of a state party or by a citizen of a state non-party that has nonetheless made an ad hoc declaration of acceptance of the ICC's jurisdiction; (b) the accused individuals were in a position to exercise effective control over or to direct the political or military action of a State, i.e. they were essentially political or military leaders; (c) the actions were committed 1 year after the ratification or acceptance of the amendments by 30 state parties; (d) a positive decision had been taken by the Assembly of State Parties after 1 January 2017 by a two-thirds majority of state parties; (e) a state party has not previously declared that it does not accept such jurisdiction by lodging a declaration with the Registrar, which remains in force and has not been called off;

(e) In respect of a State that is not a party to this Statute, the Court shall not exercise its jurisdiction over the crime of aggression when committed by that State's nationals or on its territory.
(f) Where the Prosecutor concludes that there is a reasonable basis to proceed with an investigation in respect of a crime of aggression, he or she shall first ascertain whether the Security Council has made a determination of an act of aggression committed by the State concerned. The Prosecutor shall notify the Secretary-General of the United Nations of the situation before the Court, including any relevant information and documents.
(g) Where the Security Council has made such a determination, the Prosecutor may proceed with the investigation in respect of a crime of aggression.
(h) Where no such determination is made within 6 months after the date of notification, the Prosecutor may proceed with the investigation in respect of a crime of aggression, provided that the Pre-Trial Division has authorized the commencement of the investigation in respect of a crime of aggression in accordance with the procedure contained in article 15, and the Security Council has not decided otherwise in accordance with article16.
(i) A determination of an act of aggression by an organ outside the Court shall be without prejudice to the Court's own findings under this Statute.
(j) This article is without prejudice to the provisions relating to the exercise of jurisdiction with respect to other crimes referred to in article 5.

[54] ibid Article 25§3 bis ICCRS: In respect of the crime of aggression, the provisions of this article shall apply only to persons in a position effectively to exercise control over or to direct the political or military action of a State.

[55] Ibid., Article 15 *bis;* Article 15 *ter*: **Exercise of jurisdiction over the crime of aggression (Security Council referral)**

(a) The Court may exercise jurisdiction over the crime of aggression in accordance with article 13, paragraph (b), subject to the provisions of this article.
(b) The Court may exercise jurisdiction only with respect to crimes of aggression committed 1 year after the ratification or acceptance of the amendments by 30 States Parties.
(c) The Court shall exercise jurisdiction over the crime of aggression in accordance with this article, subject to a decision to be taken after 1 January 2017 by the same majority of States Parties as is required for the adoption of an amendment to the Statute.
(d) A determination of an act of aggression by an organ outside the Court shall be without prejudice to the Court's own findings under this Statute.
(e) This article is without prejudice to the provisions relating to the exercise of jurisdiction with respect to other crimes referred to in article 5.

(f) and the Security Council has not decided otherwise in accordance with Article 16 ICCRSt.[56,57]

Moreover, the Security Council has an exceptional capacity to refer a situation to the ICC, usually one involving a state non-party under Article 13(b) ICCRSt and pursuant to Chapter VII of the UN Charter. Under Chapter VII of the UN Charter, the non-acceptance of the crime of aggression by a state party should not *de lege ferenda* constitute an obstacle to the exercise of ICC's jurisdiction, assuming there exists a relevant Security Council Resolution.[58]

---

[56] Ibid., see also Article 16 ICCRSt: **Deferral of investigation or prosecution**

No investigation or prosecution may be commenced or proceeded with under this Statute for a period of 12 months after the Security Council, in a resolution adopted under Chapter VII of the Charter of the United Nations, has requested that the Court do so; that request may be renewed by the Council under the same conditions.

[57] Additions and amendments have also been made to article 8 bis of the Elements of Crimes: Introduction

1. It isunderstood that any of the acts referred to in article 8 bis, paragraph 2, qualify as an act of aggression. 2. There is no requirement to prove that the perpetrator has made a legal evaluation as to whether the use of armed force was inconsistent with the Charter of the United Nations. 3. The term "manifest" is an objective qualification. 4. There is no requirement to prove that the perpetrator has made a legal evaluation as to the "manifest" nature of the violation of the Charter of the United Nations.

Elements

1. The perpetrator planned, prepared, initiated or executed an act of aggression. 2. The perpetrator was a person in a position effectively to exercise control over or to direct the political or military action of the State which committed the act of aggression. 3. The act of aggression—the use of armed force by a State against the sovereignty, territorial integrity or political independence of another State, or in any other manner inconsistent with the Charter of the United Nations—was committed. 4. The perpetrator was aware of the factual circumstances that established that such a use of armed force was inconsistent with the Charter of the United Nations. 5. The act of aggression, by its character, gravity and scale, constituted a manifest violation of the Charter of the United Nations. 6. The perpetrator was aware of the factual circumstances that established such a manifest violation of the Charter of the United Nations.

[58] Annex III (2010), https://bit.ly/2yTLxO2, last accessed 8 June 2023, pp. 47, 55. The Working Group on the Crime of Aggression held eight meetings on 1, 4, and 7 to 9 June 2010. H.R.H. Prince Zeid Ra'ad Zeid Al-Hussein (Jordan) served as Chair of the Working Group...

1. It is understood that the Court may exercise jurisdiction over the crime of aggression on the basis of a Security Council referral in accordance with article 13 (b) of the Statute once the amendment on aggression [is adopted by the Review Conference/has entered into force].
2. It is understood that the Court shall exercise jurisdiction over the crime of aggression on the basis of a Security Council referral in accordance with article 13 (b) of the Statute irrespective of whether the State concerned has accepted the Court's jurisdiction in this regard.

Jurisdiction *ratione temporis*

3. It is understood, in accordance with article 11, paragraph 1, of the Statute, that the Court has jurisdiction only with respect to crimes of aggression committed after the amendment [has been adopted by the Review Conference/has entered into force].
4. It is understood, in accordance with article 11, paragraph 2, of the Statute, that in case of article 13, paragraph (a) or (c), the Court may exercise its jurisdiction only with respect to crimes of

During the process before the ASP's New York session at the end of December 2017 to facilitate the activation decision, the contrasting views among state parties became overtly apparent. Already in March 2017, Canada, Colombia, France, Japan, Norway and the UK disseminated a paper promoting a "restrictive position", while states including Liechtenstein, Argentina, Botswana, Samoa, Slovenia and Switzerland also submitted their views endorsing a "more permissive position".[59]

Nonetheless in the very late hours of the New York Assembly Session, the drama reached its peak in a manner not dissimilar to what had happened in the previous ASP Conference in Kampala in 2010. France and the UK demanded that all state parties accept the "restrictive position"[60] as part of the ASP resolution accompanying the activation decision of the crime of aggression. Understandably the vigorous position of two of the world's most powerful states created a situation 'between a rock and a hard place' for many participating state parties. Certainly, from a legal perspective it would have been feasible for the ASP to adopt a distinctly less stringent text that was much more compatible with the Rome Statute. But as we have seen already, international law and international politics quite often become entangled. Consequently, the state parties never considered opposing the views of France the UK on this issue. Quite a large number of state parties supported a "more

---

aggression committed after the entry into force of the amendment for that State, unless that State has made a declaration under article 12, paragraph 3.

Domestic jurisdiction over the crime of aggression

4 *bis*. It is understood that the amendments address the definition of the crime of aggression and the conditions under which the Court shall exercise jurisdiction with respect to this crime for the purpose of this Statute only. The amendments shall, in accordance with article 10 of the Rome Statute, not be interpreted as limiting or prejudicing in any way existing or developing rules of international law for purposes other than this Statute. The amendments shall therefore not be interpreted as creating the right or obligation to exercise domestic jurisdiction with respect to an act of aggression committed by another State. *[The paragraphs below are only relevant in case the amendments are adopted in accordance with the amendment procedure set out in article 121, paragraph 5, of the Rome Statute:]*

Acceptance of the amendment on the crime of aggression

5. *[Acceptance by the victim State not required where the aggressor State has accepted jurisdiction]* It is understood that article 121, paragraph 5, second sentence, of the Statute does not prevent the Court from exercising jurisdiction in respect of an act of aggression committed by a State Party that has accepted the amendment on aggression.

6. [***Alternative 1 – "positive" understanding:*** *jurisdiction without acceptance by the aggressor State]* It is understood that article 121, paragraph 5, second sentence, of the Statute does not prevent the Court from exercising jurisdiction in respect of an act of aggression committed against a State Party that has accepted the amendment.

[***Alternative 2 – "negative" understanding:*** *no jurisdiction without acceptance by aggressor State]* It is understood that article 121, paragraph 5, second sentence, of the Statute prevents the Court from exercising jurisdiction in respect of an act of aggression committed by any State that has not accepted the amendment.

[59] Kreβ (2018), pp. 1, 9.

[60] The restrictive position was also supported by certain sections of academia. For an eloquent and concise example see Akande and Tzanakopoulos (2012), p. 58.

permissive position" but were left with the tough choice between either accepting a resolution that essentially constituted an amendment to the Kampala amendment, or losing the window of opportunity for activating the Court's jurisdiction over the crime of aggression until a future ASP Conference.[61]

At this point the two Vice Presidents of the Assembly proposed a draft resolution to be considered by the delegations of all state parties. Crucially, the "Draft resolution proposed by the Vice Presidents" reflected the French and British position as follows:

The Assembly of States Parties:

2. Confirms that, in accordance with the Rome Statute, the amendments to the Statute regarding the crime of aggression adopted at the Kampala Review Conference enter into force for those States Parties which have accepted the amendments 1 year after the deposit of their instruments of ratification or acceptance and that in case of a State referral or proprio motu investigation the Court shall not exercise its jurisdiction regarding a crime of aggression when committed by a national or on the territory of a State Party that has not ratified or accepted these amendments[62];

However, the 'unconditional surrender' to the position of France and the UK was sugarcoated as follows:

3. Reaffirms paragraph 1 of article 40 and paragraph 1 of article 119 of the Rome Statute in relation to the judicial independence of the judges of the Court;

Although this provision seemed to be no more than a statement of the obvious fact that the Court is the competent judicial body that will independently apply the legal provisions of the Rome Statute, France (with the support of the UK) nevertheless insisted on moving it to the Preamble. When Switzerland disagreed, "the almost incredible possibility loomed large that the century-long journey towards providing for an international criminal jurisdiction over the crime of aggression would ultimately derail"[63] because of a technicality. At this critical moment, the delegates from South Africa, Samoa and Portugal contributed to preventing the collapse of the negotiations. Finally, Vice President Sergio Ugalde from Costa Rica, after finding that the French proposal could not pass, asked one last time whether the Vice Presidents' proposal met with consensus among the participants. Following a moment of great suspense, the aforementioned Vice Presidents' proposal was eventually adopted.[64]

---

[61] Kreβ (2018), p. 11.

[62] ICC 2017 of an activation decision presented by delegations, sub. A, p. 28, http://bit.ly/2ToDjHb. last accessed 31 March 2023).

[63] Kreβ (2018), p. 12.

[64] Ibid.

Table 6.1 In which cases will ICC have jurisdiction over the crime of aggression?

	Victim State *has* ratified the amendments	Victim State *has not* ratified the amendments
Aggressor state has ratified the Rome statute and accepted the crime of aggression amendments	ICC jurisdiction: YES	ICC jurisdiction: YES
Aggressor state has ratified the Rome statute and not opted out	ICC jurisdiction: NO	ICC jurisdiction: NO
Aggressor state has not ratified and not opted out	ICC jurisdiction: NO	ICC jurisdiction: NO
Aggressor state has ratified and opted out	ICC jurisdiction: NO	ICC jurisdiction: NO
Aggressor state has not ratified and opted out	ICC jurisdiction: NO	ICC jurisdiction: NO

Table 6.1 reflects clearly to what extent and to which states the crime of aggression applies today, contrary to the wishes of most participating states[65]:

6.4 Conclusion: The Birth of the Crime of Aggression or the Birth of an Incapacitated Crime?

It is still doubtful and open to interpretation whether the latest amendments essentially mean that the new state parties will be obliged to accept new amendments pertaining to the crime of aggression, whereas the old state parties are able to take advantage of the positive provision of Article 121§5 ICCRSt and remain beyond the scope of the ICC's jurisdiction where the crime of aggression is concerned, assuming they make the relevant declaration.[66]

Though the crime of aggression is now in full force, the new provisions do not take into proper consideration contemporary technological advancements, especially with regard to the technological evolution of computer science and the World Wide Web.[67]

[65] ICC 2017 of an activation decision presented by delegations, sub. A, ibid. p. 22.

[66] Article 121:. . . . 5. Any amendment to articles 5, 6, 7 and 8 of this Statute shall enter into force for those States Parties which have accepted the amendment 1 year after the deposit of their instruments of ratification or acceptance. In respect of a State Party which has not accepted the amendment, the Court shall not exercise its jurisdiction regarding a crime covered by the amendment when committed by that State Party's nationals or on its territory.

[67] For example, the Stuxnet virus which attacked Iran's nuclear facilities because of the actions of other States' secret services. Falliere et al. (2011) https://www.symantec.com/content/en/us/enterprise/media/security_response/whitepapers/w32_stuxnet_dossier.pdf, last accessed 8 June 2023. At the beginning of 2011 a New York Times article confirmed the suspicions that the Stuxnet virus came from the equally well-prepared and well-resourced American-Israeli operation. Broad et al. (2011), https://www.nytimes.com/2011/01/16/world/middleeast/16stuxnet.html, last accessed

Moreover, the new model of referral for the crime of aggression lacks cohesion both with regard to referral itself and the jurisdiction of the ICC. Depending on the crime that is alleged to have been committed, this model will work against the ICC administration because of both the increase in complexity that the model of referral introduces and the reduction in the authority of the Court that results from a justified distrust of the new model. Unfortunately, this problem has emerged because of the paralysing process of determining the crime of aggression and the political compromises that were required for it to be recognised as a crime in the first place.

This is not only because the *ratione temporis* jurisdiction is distinct from all other crimes over which the ICC has jurisdiction ("one year after the ratification or acceptance of the amendments by thirty States Parties", whichever occurs later). It is also because it is expressly stated that the ICC will not exercise its jurisdiction over a crime of aggression committed by citizens of a State that has not ratified/accepted the ICC Statute or on the territory of such a State (Article15 bis §5 ICCRSt) unless the case is referred by the Security Council. In such cases it makes no difference whether or not a State has accepted the jurisdiction of the Court for this crime. Finally, following the resolution adopted at the New York Assembly of States Parties in 2017, even if the crime of aggression takes place in the territory of a state that has ratified the Rome Statute (and hence has become a state party), no protection will be afforded to that State. Thus the crime of aggression has been turned into a 'boutique crime' normally enforceable exclusively between States that have ratified the Rome Statute and crime of aggression amendments with a view to being protected against its possible commission by other States; other States who will be beyond the scope of the ICC's jurisdiction for the crime of aggression either because they never ratified the Rome Statute or have not accepted the crime of aggression amendments. And the only exception to this is a referral by the Security Council which is very unlikely to occur for reasons already explained.

Finally yet importantly, the status of the Security Council referral to the ICC means that a "two-speed crime" is introduced which impregnably seals the international system of legalised domination, which essentially involves two classes of State.[68] The first category applies to all States that are non-permanent members of the Security Council, and consequently their citizens too; it will be legally possible for these to come under the ICC's jurisdiction even without having accepted it or even if they have accepted its jurisdiction over all crimes apart from the crime of aggression, since pursuant to Chapter VII of the UN Charter a Security Council referral can overturn any opt-out ratification or no ratification at all. The second category applies to the five permanent members of the Security Council, namely the USA, the United Kingdom, France, Russia and the Republic of China. On the basis of the above-mentioned provisions and analysis, their citizens will have the legal advantage never to fall under the jurisdiction of the ICC for any alleged commission

8 June 2023; Sanger (2009), https://www.nytimes.com/2009/01/11/washington/11iran.html, last accessed 8 June 2023.

[68] Simpson (2004), p. 71.

of a crime of aggression at any time, since their States will, as permanent members of the Security Council, veto any Security Council referral to the ICC of a case concerning a former Head of State, chief of armed forces or some other influential individual of theirs (minister, general etc.).

References

Table of Cases

ICJ (1970) Belgium v. Spain, Case Concerning the Barcelona Traction, Light and Power Company, Limited Judgment, Second Phase, ICJ Rep. 50, para 33

Books

Arend AC, Beck RJ (1993) International law and the use of force: beyond the UN chapter paradigm. Routledge, West Sussex

Arnold R (2008) Law enforcement within the framework of peace support operations. Martinus Nijhoff Publishers, Leiden

Bassiouni MC, Ferencz BB (2013) The crime against peace. In: Bassiouni MC (ed) Introduction to international criminal law. Martinus Nijhoff Publishers, Leiden

Dinstein Y (2001) War, aggression and self-defense, 3rd edn. Cambridge University Press, Cambridge

Pichou MA (2012) The notion of aggression in international law. Sakoulas, Thessaloniki

Röling RVA, Cassese A (1992) The Tokyo trial and beyond. Polity Press, Cambridge

Röling RVA, Cuter C (1977) The Tokyo judgment, volume B. APA University of Amsterdam, Amsterdam

Schabas WA (2004) The unfinished work of defining aggression: how many times must the Cannoballs Fly before they are forever banned? In: McGoldrick D, Rowe P, Donnelly P (eds) The permanent international criminal court. Hart Publishing, Oxford

Simpson G (2004) Great powers and Outlaw states. Cambridge University Press, Cambridge

Articles/Papers

Akande D, Tzanakopoulos A (2012) The crime of aggression in the ICC and state responsibility. Harv Int Law J 58

Broad WJ, Markoff J, Sanger DE (2011) Israeli Test on Worm Called Crucial in Iran Nuclear Delay' New York Times, https://www.nytimes.com/2011/01/16/world/middleeast/16stuxnet.html. Accessed 8 June 2023

Cassese A (2007) On some problematical aspects of the crime of aggression. Leiden J Int Law 20: 841–849

Judicial Decisions (1947) International military tribunal (Nuremberg), judgment and sentences. AJIL 41

Kirsch P, Holmes JT (1999) The Rome conference on an international criminal court: the negotiating process. AJIL 93

Kreβ C (2018) On the activation of ICC jurisdiction over the crime of aggression. J Int Criminal Justice 16:1–17

Reddi VJ (2008) The ICC and the crime of aggression: a need to reconcile the prerogatives of the SC, the ICC and the ICJ. Int Criminal Law Rev 8:655–686

Sanger DE (2009) U.S. Rejected Aid for Israeli Raid on Iranian Nuclear Site, New York Times, New York, https://www.nytimes.com/2009/01/11/washington/11iran.html. Accessed 8 June 2023

UNGA (1987) Declaration on the Enhancement of the Effectiveness of the Principle of Refraining from the Threat or Use of Force in International Relations A/RES/42/22 73rd plenary meeting 42/22

United States of America et al v Göering et al (1947) Judgment international military tribunal. AJIL 41

Websites/Web Sources

Annex III (2010) Report of the Working Group on the Crime of Aggression, Attachment III: Understandings regarding the Amendments to the Rome Statute of the International Criminal Court on the Crime of Aggression, Referrals by the Security Council, RC-11, https://bit.ly/2yTLxO2. Accessed 8 June 2023

Article 23§§1(b) & 2 of the UN Charter, http://www.un.org/en/charter-united-nations/index.html. Accessed 8 June 2023

Falliere N, Murchu LO, Chien E (2011) Symantec Security Response: W32. Stuxnet Dossier, https://www.symantec.com/content/en/us/enterprise/media/security_response/whitepapers/w32_stuxnet_dossier.pdf. Accessed 8 June 2023

ICC (2012) Crime of Aggression: First Ratification of the Amendments, ICC-ASP-20120509-PR793, New York, ICC Press Release, https://asp.icc-cpi.int/en_menus/asp/press%20releases/press%20releases%202012/Pages/pr793.aspx. Accessed 8 June 2023

ICC (2017) Report on the Facilitation on the Activation of the Jurisdiction of the International Criminal Court over the Crime of Aggression (ICC-ASP/16/24), Annex III Elements of an activation decision presented by delegations, sub. A

Law School of Democritus University of Thrace, Professor Konstantinos Antonopoulos, http://www.law.duth.gr/index.php?cid=167&st=1. Accessed 8 June 2023

Laws of War (1900) Pacific Settlement of International Disputes (Hague I), Chapter 2, arts 20–29, for the Permanent Court of Arbitration, http://avalon.law.yale.edu/19th_century/hague01.asp. Accessed 8 June 2023

Laws of War (1910) Laws and Customs of War on Land (Hague IV), http://avalon.law.yale.edu/20th_century/hague04.asp. Accessed 8 June 2023

London Agreement (1945) Yale University digital library "Avalon", http://avalon.law.yale.edu/imt/imtchart.asp. Accessed 8 June 2023

State of Palestine (2016) ICC-ASP-20160629-PR1225, ICC Press Release, https://asp.icc-cpi.int/en_menus/asp/press%20releases/Pages/PR1225.aspx. Accessed 8 June 2023

Term Russo-Finnish War, Encyclopedia BRITRANNICA, https://www.britannica.com/event/Russo-Finnish-War. Accessed 8 June 2023

The Covenant of the League of Nations (1919) arts 10, 11, http://avalon.law.yale.edu/20th_century/leagcov.asp. Accessed 8 June 2023

The Global Campaign for Ratification and Implementation of the Kampala Amendments on the Crime of Aggression, https://crimeofaggression.info/the-role-of-states/status-of-ratification-and-implementation. Accessed 8 June 2023

The Pact's Preamble, Yale's University digital library "Avalon" http://avalon.law.yale.edu/20th_century/kbpact.asp. Accessed 8 June 2023

Treaty for Renunciation of War (1929) (Kellogg-Briand Pact), Yale's University digital library "Avalon", http://avalon.law.yale.edu/20th_century/kbpact.asp. Accessed 8 June 2023

UNGA Res 3314 (XXIX) (1974). http://www.un.org/en/ga/search/view_doc.asp?symbol=A/%20RES/3314(XXIX). Accessed 8 June 2023

United Nations Charter (1945) art 2 (4), https://treaties.un.org/doc/publication/ctc/uncharter.pdf. Accessed 8 June 2023

United Nations Regional Information Centre for Western Europe, https://www.unric.org/en/. Accessed 8 June 2023

UNSC Res 573 (1985). https://mfa.gov.il/MFA/ForeignPolicy/MFADocuments/Yearbook7/Pages/95%20Security%20Council%20Resolution%20573%20-1985%2D%2D%20Israel.aspx. Accessed 8 June 2023

UNSC Res 577 (1985), https://undocs.org/S/RES/577(1985). Accessed 8 June 2023

Chapter 7
Immunities Under Art. 27 ICCRSt and the ICC's Jurisdiction

Abstract Diplomatic immunity, as well as the immunity of individuals that either used to or still do hold an official capacity is a matter of great importance in the ICCRSt, addressed in Article 27 ICCRSt.

Article 27 ICCRSt consists of two paragraphs, each of which serves different aims, and is often misunderstood. The first paragraph of Article 27 ICCRSt originates from earlier legal texts, such as the Charter of the International Military Tribunal of Nuremberg, the International Military Tribunal for the Far East Charter, the Convention on the Prevention and Punishment of the Crime of Genocide and from the ICTY and ICTR Statutes. It stipulates that official capacity as a Head of State or Government, a member of a government or parliament, an elected representative or a government official shall in no case exempt a person from criminal responsibility under this Statute, nor shall it, in and of itself, constitute a ground for reduction of sentence. On the other hand, the second paragraph of Article 27 ICCRSt constitutes and indirect but obvious waiver, of their states parties' right to invoke the immunity of their Head of State before the ICC, pursuant to international customary law.

Additionally, and in a sense contrary to Article 27 ICCRSt, Article 98 ICCRSt with the lengthy title "Cooperation with respect to waiver of immunity and consent to surrender" stipulates in its first paragraph that the ICC "may not proceed with a request for surrender or assistance which would require the requested State to act inconsistently with its obligations under international law with respect to the State or diplomatic immunity of a person or property of a third State, unless the Court can first obtain the cooperation of that third State for the waiver of the immunity".

The present chapter through an intriguing analysis of the interrelation between Articles 27 and 98 ICCRSt, as well as the Chad, Malawi, Jordan and Belarus cases advances the necessity of a calm and lege artis analysis of immunity in international criminal law.

V. Tsilonis, *The Jurisdiction of the International Criminal Court*,
https://doi.org/10.1007/978-3-031-46138-5_7

7.1 Introduction: On Article 27 ICCRSt, "Irrelevance of Official Capacity"

Diplomatic immunity, as well as the immunity of individuals who either used to or still do hold an official capacity, is a matter of great importance in the Rome Statute, addressed in Article 27 ICCRSt.[1]

Article 27 ICCRSt consists of two paragraphs, each of which serves different aims and is often misunderstood. The first paragraph of Article 27 ICCRSt originates from earlier legal texts, such as the Charter of the International Military Tribunal of Nuremberg,[2] the International Military Tribunal for the Far East Charter,[3] the Convention on the Prevention and Punishment of the Crime of Genocide and from the ICTY[4] and ICTR[5] Statutes. It stipulates that official capacity as a Head of State or Government, a member of a government or parliament, an elected representative or a government official shall in no case exempt a person from criminal responsibility under this Statute, nor shall it, in and of itself, constitute a ground for reduction of sentence. On the other hand, the second paragraph of Article 27 ICCRSt constitutes an indirect but obvious waiver of states parties' right to invoke the immunity of their Head of State before the ICC, pursuant to international customary law.

---

[1] Article 27—Irrelevance of official capacity: 1. This Statute shall apply equally to all persons without any distinction based on official capacity. In particular, official capacity as a Head of State or Government, a member of a Government or parliament, an elected representative or a government official shall in no case exempt a person from criminal responsibility under this Statute, nor shall it, in and of itself, constitute a ground for reduction of sentence.

2. Immunities or special procedural rules which may attach to the official capacity of a person, whether under national or international law, shall not bar the Court from exercising its jurisdiction over such a person.

[2] Article 7: The official position of defendants, whether as Heads of State or responsible officials in Government Departments, shall not be considered as freeing them from responsibility or mitigating punishment. Charter of the International Military Tribunal—Annex to the Agreement for the prosecution and punishment of the major war criminals of the European Axis ("London Agreement"), https://www.refworld.org/cgi-bin/texis/vtx/rwmain?docid=3ae6b39614, last accessed 8 June 2023.

[3] Article 6—Responsibility of accused: Neither the official position, at any time, of an accused, nor the fact that an accused acted pursuant to order of his government or of a superior shall, of itself, be sufficient to free such accused from responsibility for any crime with which he is charged, but such circumstances may be considered in mitigation of punishment if the Tribunal determines that justice so requires. International Military Tribunal for the Far East Charter (IMTFE Charter), http://www.un.org/en/genocideprevention/documents/atrocity-crimes/Doc.3_1946%20Tokyo%20Charter.pdf, last accessed 8 June 2023.

[4] Article 7—Individual criminal responsibility: [...]2. The official position of any accused person, whether as Head of State or Government or as a responsible Government official, shall not relieve such person of criminal responsibility nor mitigate punishment. Updated Statute of the International Criminal Tribunal for the Former Yugoslavia, as amended by Resolution 1877/7-07-2009, https://www.un.org/ruleoflaw/blog/document/updated-statute-of-the-international-criminal-tribunal-for-the-former-yugoslavia/, last accessed 8 June 2023.

[5] Article 6 of the ICTR Statute is identical to Article 7 of the ICTY Statute.

7.2 The Relationship Between Article 27 ICCRSt and Article 98 ICCRSt: Cooperation with Respect to Waiver of Immunity and Consent to Surrender

Additionally, and in a sense contrary to Article 27 ICCRSt, Article 98 ICCRSt with the lengthy title "Cooperation with respect to waiver of immunity and consent to surrender" stipulates in its first paragraph that the ICC "may not proceed with a request for surrender or assistance which would require the requested State to act inconsistently with its obligations under international law with respect to the State or diplomatic immunity of a person or property of a third State, unless the Court can first obtain the cooperation of that third State for the waiver of the immunity".

Moreover, the second paragraph of this Article, which is almost identical to the first, stipulates that "[t]he Court may not proceed with a request for surrender which would require the requested State to act inconsistently with its obligations under international agreements pursuant to which the consent of a sending State is required to surrender a person of that State to the Court, unless the Court can first obtain the cooperation of the sending State for the giving of consent for the surrender".

Undoubtedly, during the course of time Article 98 ICCRSt has proven to be one of the most controversial ICCRSt articles, even though initially there were no signs that this would be so; its text was drafted from scratch during the Rome Conference without attracting much attention from the vast majority of participants.[6] Nonetheless, the provisions introduced to the ICCRSt by this article are in practice particularly significant for the ICC's jurisprudence, since many states parties allow the presence of foreign military forces on their territory through agreements widely known as "Status of Forces Agreements" (SOFAs), and their provisions on immunity fall under the scope of the article in question. However, as already pointed out, those bilateral agreements cannot limit the ICC's jurisdiction, and must be considered, according to the correct legal interpretation, null and void.

Consequently, Article 98 ICCRSt settles any potential conflict between the legal provisions of the ICCRSt and those of bilateral SOFAs or of other similar agreements, providing for the higher legal force of those provisions of the ICCRSt that require a state party to arrest and surrender a person following the Court's request. Thus, almost inevitably, the aforementioned provision was used by the legal departments of States such as the USA as a Trojan horse against the ICC. It is indicative that, after the ICCRSt's entry into force in July 2002, US State Department lawyers depended on Article 98 ICCRSt, and in particular on the provision of its second paragraph, to limit the ICC's jurisdiction initially through provisions introduced in the Rules of Procedure and Evidence and later through a global campaign to draw up bilateral agreements under the title "Bilateral Non-Surrender Agreements".[7]

[6] Kreβ and Prost (2008), Commentary 1604.

[7] Schabas (2010), p 1037.

7.3 The Non-Compliance of the African Union with the ICC's Request for the Arrest and Surrender of Sudan's Sitting President Al-Bashir

In addition to Bilateral Non-Surrender Agreements and SOFAs, the thorny issue of the conflict between Article 27 and 98 ICCRSt also arose lately, following the African Union's decision not to comply with the ICC's arrest warrant against Sudan's sitting president, Omar Al-Bashir,[8] and subsequent decisions against the Republic of Chad[9] and Malawi—both states parties to the ICCRSt—in December 2011.[10]

On 31 March 2005, the UN Security Council (UNSC) adopted Resolution 1593 (2005), with which it referred the situation in Darfur, Sudan to the ICC, urging "all States and concerned regional and other international organizations to cooperate fully".[11]

Nonetheless, and in spite of the UNSC inviting the African Union to closely cooperate with the ICC through Resolution 1593,[12] the relationship between the institutions was anything but harmonious. Already in July 2008, many months before the issuance of the arrest warrant for President Al-Bashir in March 2009, the African Union adopted a formal communiqué that stressed "the need for international justice to be conducted in a transparent and fair manner, in order to avoid any perception of double standard"[13]; expressed "concern at the threat that such development may pose to efforts aimed at promoting the rule of law and stability, as well as building strong national institutions in Africa"[14]; and requested the UNSC[15] to defer the process initiated by the ICC for a year,[16] pursuant to Article 16 ICCRSt.[17]

---

[8] ICC (2009d).

[9] ICC (2011c).

[10] ICC (2011a).

[11] UNSC Resolution 1593 (2005).

[12] ibid.

[13] African Union, Peace & Security Council Communiqué, PSC/Min/Comm. (CXLII) para. 7, http://www.iccnow.org/documents/AU_142-communique-eng.pdf, last accessed 8 June 2023.

[14] ibid.

[15] In Resolution 1828 (2008), the UNSC appears to at least take into consideration the existence of this particular request by the African Union, formally including it in the text of its Resolution and expressing its intention to "consider these matters further". UNSC Resolution 1828 (2008).

[16] African Union, Peace & Security Council Communiqué, PSC/Min/Comm. (CXLII) para. 7, http://www.iccnow.org/documents/AU_142-communique-eng.pdf, last accessed 8 June 2023, p 175, para. 11.

[17] Article 16—Deferral of investigation or prosecution: No investigation or prosecution may be commenced or proceeded with under this Statute for a period of 12 months after the Security Council, in a resolution adopted under Chap. VII of the Charter of the United Nations, has requested the Court to that effect; that request may be renewed by the Council under the same conditions.

Nonetheless, on 4 March 2009, almost 4 years after UNSC Resolution 1593 (2005) and 8 months after the African Union communiqué, the ICC's Pre-Trial Chamber I adopted its Decision on the Prosecution's Application for a Warrant of Arrest against Omar Hassan Ahmad Al Bashir, in which it stated that "without prejudice to a further determination of the matter pursuant to article 19 of the Statute, the Chamber considers that the current position of Omar Al-Bashir as Head of a state which is not a party to the Statute, has no effect on the Court's jurisdiction over the present case".[18]

Pursuant to this decision, the ICC twice conveyed to all state parties, in accordance with Article 27 ICCRSt, a request for cooperation in the arrest and surrender of Al-Bashir: once on 6 March 2009[19] and a second time on 21 July 2010.[20] In the interim, the Thirteenth Ordinary Session of the Assembly of the African Union was held, in which most of the states to which the request was addressed participated, that is: (a) states geographically bordering Sudan; (b) states on the same continent as Sudan; and (c) states traditionally maintaining close trade relations with Sudan.

The decision adopted regarding the African Union's stance towards the ICC[21] commenced with the Assembly's "deep concern at the indictment issued by the Pre-Trial Chamber of the ICC against President Omar Hassan Ahmed El Bashir of the Republic of The Sudan"[22] and "the unfortunate consequences that the indictment has had on the delicate peace processes underway in Sudan".[23] Thus it was decided that "the AU Member States shall not cooperate pursuant to the provisions of Article 98 of the Rome Statute of the ICC relating to immunities, for the arrest and surrender of President Omar El Bashir of The Sudan".[24]

Notwithstanding the African Union's indirect critique of neo-colonialist practices in the area of international law, its position is founded on a reasonable—at least in the first place—legal argument, which calls for further investigation and analysis. In other words, the African Union's position appears to be founded on the higher legal force given by Article 98(1) ICCRSt to rules of international customary law, and pointedly to those on state or diplomatic immunities, over the provisions of the ICCRSt, which allow the Court to request a State (often, a state party) to surrender a person or otherwise cooperate with the Court.

Unquestionably, the African Union's stance not only reveals the conflict between Articles 27 and 98(1) ICCRSt, but also implies a deeper conflict between

[18] Emphasis added. Situation in Darfur, Sudan, ICC (2009b), Public Redacted Version, para. 41.

[19] Request to All States Parties to the Rome Statute for the Arrest and Surrender of Omar Hassan Ahmad Al Bashir, Situation in Darfur (ICC-02/05-01/09-7 1/6 EO PT), Registry, 6 March 2009.

[20] Supplementary Request to All States Parties to the Rome Statute for the Arrest and Surrender of Omar Hassan Ahmad Al Bashir, Situation in Darfur (ICC-02/05-01/09-96 1/6 RH PT) Registry 12 July 2010.

[21] ICC (2009c).

[22] ibid., para 2.

[23] ibid., para 3.

[24] ibid., para 10.

fundamental principles, which can be found in Article 27 ICCRSt. Developments of recent decades in international law reveal an effort to promote principles and concepts, such as those of *ius cogens* and *erga omnes*, as well as a confrontational approach to phenomena of impunity and doctrines, such as that of immunity, which are indirectly but clearly considered an important obstacle to be overcome through international justice and the protection of human rights. On the other hand, the retention of immunities reflects the traditional principles of international law, such as the principle of national sovereignty and the promotion of permanent and stable relations between sovereign States. The complete abolishment of such immunities would cause unavoidable backlash that would not be easy to overcome from a legal perspective.

Consequently, it should not surprise us that Al-Bashir attended the inauguration ceremony of Chad's Head of State, Idriss Deby Itno, in 2011[25] as well as the summit of the Common Market for Eastern and Southern Africa (COMESA), which was held in Malawi in October of the same year. It was Al-Bashir's participation in the two aforementioned summits that gave Pre-Trial Chamber I the opportunity (which, as we will see below, it squandered) to formulate and express in depth its legal opinion on the matter of the apparent *de facto* conflict between Articles 27 and 98(1) ICCRSt and to properly reply to the completely reasonable objections of the African Union.

In its first decision on the state party of Malawi (the reasoning of which was used word foreword in its second decision on Chad), the ICC pointed out that the two African states violated the obligations they had assumed by signing the ICCRSt. That was because the authorities of both Malawi and Chad, despite receiving a warning from the Registry prior to the visit of Omar Al Bashir, decided neither to respond to the Court nor to arrest the suspect.[26]

In other words, the ICC underlines that the violation of ICCRSt obligations by the two States was the result of those State's decision to pointedly ignore the Court's request and not to reply to it i.e. regardless of whether their legal argumentation of the application of Article 98(1) ICCRSt was indeed well-founded or not. Consequently, the violation of Malawi's and Chad's obligations was found to be procedural rather than substantive, as it did not relate to the actual or supposed existence of a right, but to the form of its manifestation.

On this matter, the ICC pointed out that the two States did not respect its sole authority to decide whether immunities are applicable in a particular case, as

---

[25] The Decision does not mention this summit at all. Instead in para 3: "The Registry informed the Chamber in its 'Report on the second visit of Omar Al Bashir to Chad' dated 9 August 2011 ('First Report of the Registry') that, according to media reports, Omar Al Bashir had visited the Republic of Chad on 7 and 8 August 2011 for the purposes of attending the inauguration ceremony of Chad's Head of State, Idriss Deby Itno.", https://www.icc-cpi.int/CourtRecords/CR2012_04203.PDF, last accessed 8 June 2023.

[26] Corrigendum to the Decision Pursuant to Article 87(7) of the Rome Statute on the Failure by the Republic of Malawi to Comply with the Cooperation Requests Issued by the Court with Respect to the Arrest and Surrender of Omar Hassan Ahmad Al Bashir (ICC 2011b, para 10).

pursuant to Article 119(1) ICCRSt "[a]ny dispute concerning the judicial functions of the Court shall be settled by the decision of the Court", while pursuant to Rule 195(1) of the Rules of Procedure and Evidence a state party must notify the Court that a request for surrender or assistance raises a problem of execution and provide any relevant information.[27]

7.4 Criticism of the ICC Decision on Chad and Malawi and Other Relevant Cases

The ICC's Pre-Trial Chamber I could and potentially should have stopped the analysis of this legal issue there, or it would have at least be in the interest of its prestige and credibility to do so. However, the competent ICC Chamber, recognising that the legal issues at hand were exceptionally important, essentially decided to proceed with their unnecessary examination. Of course, had it proceeded with a substantive and in-depth examination of the legal issues that arose, then the unnecessary legal analysis would as *obiter dictum* (and not as *ratio decidendi*) obviously be of significant value among the ICC's jurisprudence. However, as we will find out, this decision did not advance the ICC's prestige, nor did it promote international criminal justice among the global community;[28] on the contrary, it provided another opportunity for justified criticism and damaged the ICC's reputation.

Thus, Pre-Trial Chamber I summarised at first the arguments presented by the two state parties. It then pointed out that the two state parties:

1. accorded Al-Bashir, as the sitting President of Sudan, immunity from arrest in line with established principles of customary law and Article 98(1) ICCRSt.
2. as member states of the African Union, aligned with its decisions and did not execute the warrant of arrest for Al-Bashir, pursuant to Article 98(1) ICCRSt.[29]

Unfortunately, the highly subjective and mistaken opinion of the competent ICC Chamber is apparent early on in the body of its decision against the Republic of Malawi, especially where the Court points out that it "has already rejected such an argument"[30] at the time of the issuance of its first warrant of arrest against Omar Al-Bashir, when it decided that "the current position of Omar Al-Bashir as Head of a

[27] Section V. Cooperation under article 98, Rule 195—Provision of Information

1. When a requested State notifies the Court that a request for surrender or assistance raises a problem of execution in respect of article 98, the requested State shall provide any information relevant to assist the Court in the application of article 98. Any concerned third State or sending State may provide additional information to assist the Court.

[28] A term through which the author attempts to imply all the recognised States in the world, and not simply the seven to ten states implied by the common but "misty" term "international community".

[29] ICC (2011a).

[30] ibid., para 14. Admittedly, the two arguments presented are so closely linked that one could reasonably argue that they are actually one.

State which is not a party to the Statute, has no effect on the Court's jurisdiction over the present case"[31] pursuant to Article 27 ICCRSt. Consequently, the ICC, persisting with the same reasoning, declared through Pre-Trial Chamber I that the argument presented cannot under any circumstances be accepted, namely that "international law affords immunity to Heads of States in respect of proceedings before international courts".[32]

At this point, it is worth mentioning that in the Court's March 2009 decision, which accepted the prosecution's application for a warrant of arrest against Al Bashir, Pre-Trial Chamber I had provided four justifications for its decision. The **first** (incomplete, self-referential and unconvincing) justification was that "according to the Preamble of the Statute, one of the core goals of the Statute is to put an end to impunity for the perpetrators of the most serious crimes of concern to the international community as a whole".[33]

The **second** (equally unconvincing) justification was a direct reproduction of the first and second paragraphs of Article 27 ICCRSt. In particular, the Court reproduced word for word the provision of Article 27 ICCRSt, splitting its two paragraphs into three parts, without any analysis or comment, while the phrase "in particular" was the only one missing from the beginning of the second sentence of the first paragraph of Article 27 ICCRSt, thus making the reproduction a little less obvious.[34]

The **third** justification was admittedly more important and noteworthy, albeit indirect and allusive: a reference to Article 21 ICCRSt[35] was made as well as to the fact that, pursuant to this article, the ICC does not apply sources of law other than the Statute and the Rules of Procedure and Evidence unless a lacuna exists that cannot be filled by the application of the criteria of interpretation provided in Articles 31 and 32 of the Vienna Convention on the Law of the Treaties and the provision of Article 21(3) ICCRSt.[36] As a consequence, this reference to Article 21 ICCRSt implies that even if international law provides for the immunity of Heads of States, this legal

[31] ICC (2009a), para. 41; ICC (2011a).

[32] ICC (2011a).

[33] ICC (2009a), para. 42.

[34] ibid., para 43.

[35] Article 21—Applicable law: 1. The Court shall apply: (a) In the first place, this Statute, Elements of Crimes and its Rules of Procedure and Evidence; (b) In the second place, where appropriate, applicable treaties and the principles and rules of international law, including the established principles of the international law of armed conflict; (c) Failing that, general principles of law derived by the Court from national laws of legal systems of the world including, as appropriate, the national laws of States that would normally exercise jurisdiction over the crime, provided that those principles are not inconsistent with this Statute and with international law and internationally recognized norms and standards.

2. The Court may apply principles and rules of law as interpreted in its previous decisions.

3. The application and interpretation of law pursuant to this article must be consistent with internationally recognized human rights and be without any adverse distinction founded on grounds such as gender as defined in article 7, paragraph 3, age, race, colour, language, religion or belief, political or other opinion, national, ethnic or social origin, wealth, birth or other status.

[36] ICC (2009a), para. 44.

principle is not included in Article 27 ICCRSt and thus cannot be invoked by the accused before the ICC.[37]

Finally, the **fourth** justification was that, as the Court clarified in its 5 February 2009 "Decision on Application under Rule 103", the UN Security Council had accepted, by referring the Darfur situation to the Court pursuant to article 13 (b) ICCRSt, that "the investigation into the said situation, as well as any prosecution arising therefrom, will take place in accordance with the statutory framework provided for in the Statute, the Elements of Crimes and the Rules as a whole".[38] Thus, the ICC appears to indirectly promote an interpretation of Article 27-(2) ICCRSt, according to which the application of the provision in question includes even the Heads of States that have not signed the said Statute. This appears to be only because the formulation of this provision does not exclude such an interpretation, without taking into consideration at all that the ICCRSt is an international convention between states, the interpretation of which is regulated by the Vienna Convention on the Law of the Treaties and its Article 34, which clearly stipulates that "a treaty does not create either obligations or rights for a third State without its consent". Consequently, this justification also appears to be unconvincing, as one must assume that when the UN Security Council referred the situation in Darfur to the ICC "as appropriate and in accordance with the Rome Statute", it obviously meant that Article 34 of the Vienna Convention, as well as principles of customary law which provide for the immunity of Heads of States, must also be respected by the Court.

At this point, it is worth mentioning that the ICC does not invoke in its decision the perhaps more convincing opinion that the UN Security Council withdrew Al-Bashir's immunity through its referral and thus, that there is no issue surrounding the application of Article 27(2) ICCRSt. In other words, the ICC could potentially invoke more soundly the relevant decisions in the Taylor case by the Special Court for Sierra Leone[39] and in the Milosevic case by the ICTY,[40] which support the theory of "implied withdrawal of immunity". However, even those two decisions are unsound, as they both wrongly maintain that the provisions of their Statutes which regulate the matter of official capacity within the framework of their special role and jurisdiction also regulate the matter of immunities for Heads of States, prime ministers and other officials pursuant to international law. In this particular case, i.e. with regards to the drafting of the ICCRSt, based on which the ICC is called to exercise its jurisdiction and administer justice, this argument is further weakened by the fact that when the Security Council refers a situation to the ICC pursuant to the ICCRSt, it does so without being able to amend in any way its provisions on the crimes described (jurisdiction *ratione materiae*) or on the territorial and temporal limits of its jurisdiction or any other ICCRSt provisions of less importance.

[37] ibid.

[38] ibid., para 45; ICC, Decision on Application under Rule 103 (ICC-01/05-185), para. 31.

[39] SCSL (2004).

[40] ICTY (2001b), para 26–34.

Therefore, similarly, when the Security Council refers a situation to the ICC, this referral cannot amend the general rule on immunities, as stipulated in Article 27-(2) ICCRSt, and applied in practice through Article 98 ICCRSt, which regulates the ICC's requests to state parties for the surrender of an accused person or for assistance in a case. Consequently, the argument is completely false that the obstacle of immunity of Article 98(1) ICCRSt could be overcome should the Security Council, pursuant to Chap. 7 of the UN Charter, but deviating from the ICCRSt, order all states to arrest or surrender a sitting Head of a third State found in their territory.[41]

What is more, ICC judges, despite recognising the inherent conflict between Article 27(2) and 98(1) ICCRSt, again presented four arguments to justify their aforementioned position:

(a) Immunity for Heads of State before international courts has been rejected time and time again since World War I,[42] while the ICTY has repeatedly stated that "individuals are personally responsible, whatever their official position, even if they are heads of State" since Article 7(2) of its Statute and Article 6(2) of the Statute of the International Criminal Tribunal for Rwanda "are indisputably declaratory of customary international law".[43]
(b) There has been an increase in Head of State prosecutions by international courts in the last decade. While only one international prosecution of a Head of State (that of Slobodan Milosevic) had been initiated when the judgment in the "Arrest Warrant Case" was rendered in February 2002, international prosecutions against Charles Taylor, Muammar Gaddafi, Laurent Gbagbo and Omar Al-Bashir followed, a fact that proves that initiating international prosecutions against Heads of State have gained widespread recognition as accepted practice.[44]
(c) By ratifying the ICCRSt and pursuant to Article 27(2) ICCRSt, 120 States have renounced any claim to immunity for their Heads of State.[45]
(d) All ICCRSt state parties have entrusted the ICC with exercising its jurisdiction over the most heinous crimes of international concern, and thus it would be inconsistent for one of them to entrust the Court with this mandate and then refuse to surrender a Head of State accused of genocide, war crimes and/or crimes against humanity. After all, when acting on the Court's behalf, state parties are instruments for the enforcement of the *jus puniendi* of the international community, which has entrusted the prosecution of the most serious

[41] Contra Dire Tilde, "The ICC Decisions on Chad and Malawi: On Cooperation, Immunities, and Article 98" (2013) JICJ 11199, 208, where she points out that "In particular, in cases of Security Council referrals, the Security Council could decide that all states have an obligation to cooperate with the ICC in the arrest and surrender of suspects such that states would have the obligation to arrest and surrender heads of state notwithstanding the AU interpretation of Article 98(1)."

[42] ICC (2011a).

[43] ICTY (2001a), para 28; ICTY (1998), para. 140.

[44] ICC (2011a).

[45] ibid., para 40.

crimes to the ICC's jurisdiction when States fail to prosecute their perpetrators. In addition, the interpretation of Article 98(1) ICCRSt proposed by the African Union, combined with Article 27(2) ICCRSt would disable the ICC and contradict the establishment of international criminal justice, as promoted by the ICCRSt (*argumentum a contrario*).[46]

Unfortunately, those four arguments do not provide a sufficient, convincing or satisfactory justification either, and thus, it would have been wiser for the Court to have stopped analysing the procedural violations committed by the two state parties. That is because, by stating that it has already rejected the argument of immunity, Pre-Trial Chamber I essentially avoids expressing an opinion on the real legal issue that arises through the invocation of Article 98(1) ICCRSt.[47] In other words, its analysis appears to be wrong from the start, since its starting point is also wrong: the matter is not, as the Court itself declares, whether the ICC can exercise its jurisdiction over a Head of State, but the application scope of Article 98(1) ICCRSt and how its provisions relate to those of Article 27 ICCRSt.

Because, admittedly, the sources of law, the legal precedents and the jurisprudence of other courts invoked by Pre-Trial Chamber I do not sufficiently support the opinion that a state party to the ICCRSt is obliged to arrest and surrender to the ICC an official leading a State that has decided not to become a state party to the ICCRSt. It is noteworthy that the sources referenced in the decision refer principally to the general issue of the jurisdiction of international criminal tribunals over Heads of State, and not to a State's duty to cooperate with the Courts for their arrest and surrender. For example, the extract of the ICJ decision invoked by Pre-Trial Chamber I, in which it is pointedly noted that "immunity does not mean impunity",[48] does not mention at all a State's obligation to arrest and surrender to an international court an official, let alone a sitting Head of a State, such as Al-Bashir, who enjoys immunity pursuant to international law. In addition, even though the ICJ refers to Article 27 ICCRSt, it does not refer to Article 98(1) ICCRSt or to the conflict between the two.

Similarly, those ICTY decisions on the Milosevic[49] and Furundzija[50] cases, as well as the relevant SCSL decisions in the Taylor case,[51] exclusively refer to the matter of immunity when invoked by the accused as a defence against the jurisdiction of an international tribunal in the scope of a trial.

Therefore, Pre-Trial Chamber I appears to willingly or inadvertently confuse the nonexistence of immunity as an exception to the ICC's jurisdiction pursuant to

[46] ibid., para 41–46.

[47] ibid., para 14.

[48] ICJ (2002), Case Concerning the Arrest Warrant of 11 April 2000 (DRC v. Belgium) Judgment 14 February 2002, ICJ Reports 3, para. 48, https://www.icj-cij.org/files/case-related/121/121-20020214-JUD-01-00-EN.pdf, last accessed 8 June 2023.

[49] ICTY (2001b), para. 34.

[50] ICTY (1998).

[51] Taylor Case, Decision on Immunity from Jurisdiction, para. 140.

Article 27 ICCRSt, with the matter of immunity as a condition for the cooperation of a state party with the ICC according to Article 98 ICCRSt. Namely, the competent ICC Chamber appears to confuse the limits of the Court's jurisdiction *ratione personae* as summarised in Article 27(2) ICCRSt, with the measures required for the effective exercise of its jurisdiction in practice.

This type of examination of the aforementioned prickly legal issue makes it seem as if Pre-Trial Chamber I considers Article 98(1) ICCRSt as essentially nonexistent within the framework of the Rome Statute. In other words, an article that must necessarily be concealed under the peculiar legal veil of Article 27(2) ICCRSt, but also under all the other ICCRSt provisions. However, this unacceptable judgment cannot abolish the provision of Article 98(1) ICCRSt. Consequently, this provision continues to exist and so does the ICC's supreme duty to respect and interpret all ICCRSt provisions in an appropriate, thorough and non-misleading way; i.e., even those which limit from a practical point of view its jurisdiction.

As a consequence, this particularly significant mistake of the ICC, i.e. equating the nonexistence of immunity as a defence against the Court's jurisdiction pursuant to Article 27(2) ICCRSt, with the existence of immunity as a term for the cooperation of a state party before it proceeds with the arrest of a suspect pursuant to Article 98(1) ICCRSt, is dangerous not only because it constitutes a *contra legem* interpretation of an ICCRSt provision, but also because it could be used as grounds for criticism of and opposition (already from the African Union and its members states, but potentially from others as well) to the ICC as an institution that serves as a cover for the policy of the most powerful States on the planet, and that does not even respect its own Statute.

Following the decisions against Chad and Malawi, further similar decisions were issued. In December 2017 a decision was issued against Jordan[52] because the State of Jordan did not cooperate with the ICC notwithstanding that "[o]n 21 February 2017, acting on the basis of media reports of Omar Al-Bashir's expected travel to Jordan in order to participate in the 28th Arab League Summit in Amman on 29 March 2017, the Registry transmitted to Jordan a note verbale inviting it to provide information regarding the visit and renewing the request to cooperate with the Court in the arrest and surrender of Omar Al-Bashir, in the event that he enters Jordanian territory".[53] The State of Jordan argued that Omar Al Bashir "enjoyed sovereign immunity as a sitting Head of State under the rules of customary international law and that that immunity had not been waived by Sudan nor by the Security Council of the United Nations in its resolution 1593(2005)."[54] Consequently, the State of Jordan invoked articles 98(1) and 27(2) ICCRSt so as to conclude that according to this view a state party should not "waive the immunity of a third State

[52] ICC (2017).

[53] ibid., para. 5, p 4.

[54] ibid., para. 7, pp. 4–5.

and act inconsistently with its obligations under the rules of general international law on the immunity of a third State".[55]

Moreover, Jordan highlighted that "[w]hile it would be open to the Council to exercise its Chap. VII powers to suspend the customary and conventional obligations of States to respect the immunity of a foreign Head of State, it has not done so in the present case".[56] Nonetheless, the Court rejected Jordan's argument since according to the majority opinion "Sudan cannot claim, vis-à-vis the Court, Omar Al-Bashir's immunity as Head of State: Sudan has the obligation to arrest him and surrender him to the Court." Second, the "immunities of Omar Al-Bashir as Head of State do not apply vis-à-vis States Parties to the Statute when they execute a request for arrest and surrender issued by the Court in the exercise of its jurisdiction in the situation in Darfur."[57] Consequently, it was ruled that article 98(1) ICCRSt is not applicable to the arrest of Bashir and his surrender to the ICC; "no immunity needs to be waived and States Parties can execute the Court's request for arrest and surrender of Omar Al-Bashir without violating Sudan's rights under international law. Therefore, States Parties, including Jordan, have the obligation to execute the Court's request for cooperation and arrest Omar Al-Bashir and surrender him to the Court."[58] Although this decision was appealed by Jordan, the ICC has understandably and quite expectedly maintained its firm stance on this legal issue. Thus in December 2018, a request for cooperation to Belarus was likewise sent.[59]

7.5 The Necessity of a Calm and Legally Correct Analysis of Immunity in International Criminal Law

Undoubtedly, in the wake of this legally incorrect position of the ICC, the opinion indirectly but clearly arises that if the African Union's position was adopted then the Statute would be devalued, since this position would lead to an obviously impossible result pursuant to Article 32 (b) of the Vienna Convention.[60] This view, however, is also incorrect for three reasons: (1) the application of Article 32 of the Vienna Convention requires that the general rules of interpretation of Article 31 of the

[55] ibid.

[56] ibid., para. 16, p 7.

[57] ibid., para 39, p 15.

[58] Ibid.

[59] ICC (2018).

[60] Article 32—Supplementary means of interpretation: Recourse may be had to supplementary means of interpretation, including the preparatory work of the treaty and the circumstances of its conclusion, in order to confirm the meaning resulting from the application of article 31, or to determine the meaning when the interpretation according to article 31: (a) Leaves the meaning ambiguous or obscure; or (b) Leads to a result which is manifestly absurd or unreasonable.

Vienna Convention would have led to an impossible or unreasonable conclusion.[61] Nowhere in the decisions against Malawi and Chad did the ICC adopt an interpretation of Article 98 (1) ICCRSt that led to an impossible or unreasonable conclusion. Thus, it is impossible to reasonably draw the conclusion that the correct interpretation of Article 98(1) ICCRSt demands the application of Article 32 of the Vienna Convention, which refers to supplementary means of interpretation, and not that of Article 31 of the Vienna Convention, which refers to general rules of interpretation, precisely because the application of the latter would lead to an unreasonable dead-end. (2) Even if one was to adopt the view that the African Union's proposed interpretation of the provision of Article 98(1) ICCRSt, which is based on the general rule of interpretation of Article 31 of the Vienna Convention, would lead to an exceptionally difficult interpretation/"conclusion", that does not in any case mean that an entire article or even a paragraph of an article of an international convention must not be applied, but, on the contrary, the judge is obligated to examine other means of interpretation, such as for example the minutes of the conference that led to the drafting of the provision at hand. (3) In particular, in this case, the interpretation of Article 98(1) ICCRSt proposed as correct by the States of the African Union, even if adopted as a whole, would not render the ICCRSt devoid of meaning and essence, since the ICCRSt is not a Statute created with the exclusive aim of prosecuting Heads of State and those who enjoy diplomatic immunity. Such a conclusion is not only excessively wide in its scope, but also ignores the historical trajectory of the ICC to this day, i.e. the decisions already published in the cases of Kony,[62] Thomas Lubanga Dyilo,[63] Ntaganda[64] and others in which the matter of diplomatic or functional immunity does not arise.

It is apparent, then, that based on the above one must further examine the legal position adopted by the African Union, before rejecting or adopting it. What is more, one must also examine any other possible, reasonable and legally acceptable interpretations, before eventually deciding on the most correct one. A crucial point here

[61] Article 31—General rule of interpretation:

(a) A treaty shall be interpreted in good faith in accordance with the ordinary meaning to be given to the terms of the treaty in their context and in the light of its object and purpose.
(b) The context for the purpose of the interpretation of a treaty shall comprise, in addition to the text, including its preamble and annexes: (a) Any agreement relating to the treaty which was made between all the parties in connexion with the conclusion of the treaty; (b) Any instrument which was made by one or more parties in connexion with the conclusion of the treaty and accepted by the other parties as an instrument related to the treaty.
(c) There shall be taken into account, together with the context: (a) Any subsequent agreement between the parties regarding the interpretation of the treaty or the application of its provisions; (b) Any subsequent practice in the application of the treaty which establishes the agreement of the parties regarding its interpretation; (c) Any relevant rules of international law applicable in the relations between the parties.
(d) A special meaning shall be given to a term if it is established that the parties so intended.

[62] ICC (2005).

[63] ICC (2012).

[64] ICC (2006).

appears to be the way one decides on the most correct interpretation for Article 98(1) ICCRSt. According to Article 31 of the Vienna Convention, Article 98-(1) ICCRSt must be interpreted "in good faith, in accordance with the ordinary meaning to be given to the terms of the treaty in their context and in the light of its object and purpose". In addition, pursuant to Article 31(3)(c) of the Vienna Convention, the correct interpretation of Article 98(1) ICCRSt must take into consideration "any relevant rules of international law applicable in the relations between the parties", such as those that refer to the immunity of Heads of State, foreign ministers and other officials.[65]

That is because there may be several acceptable interpretations of the provision of Article 98(1) ICCRSt, but, nonetheless, the ICC must adopt the best possible one, thus giving credence to its work and role. Undoubtedly, academic writing can also significantly aid the Court in the matter of selecting the correct interpretation of Article 98(1) ICCRSt. Already in 2004, before the UNSC's referral of the situation in Darfur to the ICC, Dapo Akande attempted to analyse the complex relation of Article 98 ICCRSt with Article 27 ICCRSt, and to interpret their provisions.[66]

Akande then maintained that the provision of Article 98(1) ICCRSt can only be applied to the officials of state non-parties to the Statute, because if the opposite was true, the Statute would lose its purpose.[67] Admittedly, however, if the interpretation of the term "third states" in Article 98 ICCRSt was "states that have not ratified the ICCRSt", then the matter would be rendered simple enough and would be easily solved.

Secondly, Akande maintains that, pursuant to Article 27 ICCRSt, an accused's immunity is not only withdrawn before the ICC itself, but also before all of its states parties, because of the cooperative relationship that exists between them and the Court. That is because, by ratifying the ICCRSt and in particular Article 27 ICCRSt, state parties waived the immunity of their officials not only within the scope of Article 27 ICCRSt, hence, with regard to the invocation of immunity during the pre-trial and trial stage of a case, but also indirectly within the framework of a cooperation request for surrender or assistance from the Court towards a state party. To strengthen this legal argument, Akande invoked the relevant national legislation of a large number of state parties, such as the United Kingdom, Canada, Malta, Ireland, Samoa and South Africa.[68] This second position is of course of limited value, since of the 120 ICCRSt state parties, only five are actually included in this list (as the reference to the legislation of South Africa appears to be incorrect), while the vast majority of national legislation of the state parties to the Statute do not introduce any distinction between citizens of state parties and citizens of state non-parties.

What is more, this second position of Akande ignores the meaning and purpose of Article 27 ICCRSt, which refers to the objection of immunity that could be invoked

[65] Article 31 of the Vienna Convention.

[66] Akande (2004), p 407.

[67] ibid., p. 424.

[68] ibid., p. 425.

in its absence by a Head of State before the ICC. Article 27 ICCRSt, however, under no circumstances refers to bilateral relations between state parties nor to the cooperative relationship between the ICC and its state parties. Besides, pursuant to Article 13 ICCRSt, the ICC's jurisdiction is not influenced by the accused's nationality, as long as the exercise of its jurisdiction is initiated lawfully, either after the referral of a situation to the Prosecutor by a state party, within which one or more ICCRSt crimes have been committed, or after the referral of a situation to the ICC by the Security Council, or after a *proprio motu* investigation by the Prosecutor in accordance with Article 15 ICCRSt.[69]

In any case, it is certain that this first article by Akande on the conflict between Articles 27 and 98 ICCRSt concurs with the African Union's view that Article 98(1) ICCRSt affords protection to the officials of States that have not ratified the ICCRSt, and thus, that the President of Sudan, Omar Al-Bashir, could never be lawfully arrested within the territory of a state party, given that Sudan has not ratified the ICCRSt.

Contrary to the above, 5 years later, in an article of 2009 Dapo Akande adopted a different view, maintaining that, following the UNSC referral of the situation in Darfur, Sudan must be considered in this particular case as a state party to ICCRSt![70]

In addition to all the other reasons as to why this conclusion is unfounded, it is a fact that when the Security Council refers a case to the ICC, the ICC can only adjudicate over a case pursuant to Article 13 (b) ICCRSt; nothing more and nothing less. And while it is extremely doubtful whether in such a case the ICC's jurisdiction could be considered to necessarily include a withdrawal of immunity pursuant to Article 27 ICCRSt,[71] it is certain that none of the grounds for the exercise of the ICC's jurisdiction, including the referral of a situation by the Security Council, can negate the application of Article 98(1) ICCRSt, since this provision does not relate to the role of the ICC but to the conduct of its member states.

This conclusion is also supported by UNSC Resolution 1593 for Sudan and 1970 for Libya, through which the Security Council imposed certain legal obligations on both Libya and Sudan without, however, fictitiously considering them state parties to the ICCRSt. Besides, in this case the Security Council could not under any circumstances have excluded from the ICC's jurisdiction the citizens of other States that are not party to the ICCRSt and who operated in the same area, regardless of whether this provision is problematic in the first place. Additionally, it is noteworthy that while paragraph 5 of Resolution 1593 introduces an obligation for Sudan to

[69] Article 13—Exercise of jurisdiction: The Court may exercise its jurisdiction with respect to a crime referred to in article 5 in accordance with the provisions of this Statute if: (a) A situation in which one or more of such crimes appears to have been committed is referred to the Prosecutor by a State Party in accordance with article 14; (b) A situation in which one or more of such crimes appears to have been committed is referred to the Prosecutor by the Security Council acting under Chap. VII of the Charter of the United Nations; or (c) The Prosecutor has initiated an investigation in respect of such a crime in accordance with article 15.

[70] Akande (2009), pp. 333, 340–342.

[71] Tladi (2013), pp. 199, 212.

cooperate with the ICC, this obligation is not, according to the text, existent for all states, or at least for all ICCRSt state parties. The obligation to cooperate is founded upon Article 98 ICCRSt.

Consequently, we return again to the analysis of Article 98 ICCRSt. Undoubtedly, according to the grammatical interpretation, the ICC cannot request the cooperation of one or more States, if such a request requires them to violate their obligations with respect to the State or diplomatic immunity. Thus, with regard to the arrest of Al-Bashir, the ICC could not lawfully insist on its request for surrender from Malawi and Chad at the time he was in those two States, considering that according to international customary law, the Head of a State enjoys complete or absolute immunity, i.e. whether acting in an official or personal capacity.[72]

Nonetheless, it is crucial at this point to clarify whether the term "diplomatic immunity" in Article 98(1) ICCRSt is a synonym for the term "state immunity". In the Arrest Warrant case, the ICJ equated the immunity enjoyed by diplomats and consular agents with the one enjoyed by high-ranking state officials, by stating that *"diplomatic and consular agents, certain holders of high-ranking office in a State, such as the Head of State, Head of Government and Minister for Foreign Affairs, enjoy immunities from jurisdiction in other States, both civil and criminal"*.[73]

Furthermore, the ICJ pointed out that a high-ranking state official, such as a Minister for Foreign Affairs, a Prime Minister or a Head of State, is *"recognised under international law as representative of the State solely by virtue of his or her office"*,[74] and that therefore an individual who falls within one of the above categories enjoys full immunity from criminal jurisdiction, both for acts performed in an "official" capacity, and for those claimed to have been performed in a "private capacity", whether before or after his or her period in office, since his or her arrest in another State would clearly prevent him or her from exercising the functions of his or her office.[75]

Finally, the ICJ rejected the argument presented by Belgium that the immunities accorded to the aforementioned individuals can in no case protect them where they are suspected of having committed war crimes or crimes against humanity,[76] and that despite the House of Lords Pinochet Decision of 24 March 1999 (United Kingdom) and the Court of Cassation Qaddafi decision of 13 March 2001 (France).[77] In conclusion, the ICJ noted: "The Court has carefully examined State practice, including national legislation and those few decisions of national higher courts, such as the House of Lords or the French Court of Cassation. It has been unable to deduce from this practice that there exists under customary international law any form of exception to the rule according immunity from criminal jurisdiction

[72] ICC (2009a).

[73] ibid., para 51.

[74] ibid., para 53.

[75] ibid., para 54–55.

[76] ibid., para 56.

[77] ibid.

and inviolability to incumbent Ministers for Foreign Affairs, where they are suspected of having committed war crimes or crimes against humanity."[78]

This same view was repeated by the ICJ a few years later in the Case Concerning Certain Questions of Mutual Assistance in Criminal Matters. In this judgment, the ICJ appeared to suggest that diplomatic immunity is similar to the immunity enjoyed by Heads of State, since "the rule of customary international law reflected in Article 29 of the Vienna Convention on Diplomatic Relations, while addressed to diplomatic agents, is necessarily applicable to Heads of State",[79] and, further, "[t]his provision translates into positive obligations for the receiving State as regards the actions of its own authorities, and into obligations of prevention as regards possible acts by individuals".[80]

The same conclusion is also drawn by Judge ad hoc Yusouf in his Separate Opinion,[81] where he notes that "the customary validity of the immunity of a Head of State abroad has been recognised by several conventions" directly or indirectly,[82] such as Article 21 (1) of the Convention on Special Missions, Article 3 (2) of the Draft Articles on Jurisdictional Immunities of States and Their Property, Article 29 of the Vienna Convention on Diplomatic Relations, and Article 1 of the resolution of the Institut de droit international of 26 August 2001. With regard to the widely known international Vienna Convention on Diplomatic Relations, it may directly refer only to diplomatic agents, but it would be unreasonable to assume that diplomatic agents enjoy a higher level of protection than Heads of State, who are by definition the highest representatives of the States that they lead.[83]

Consequently, different views such as the dissenting opinion of Judge ad hoc Van den Wyngaert in the Arrest Warrant case, where she maintained that "there are fundamental differences between the circumstances of diplomatic agents, Heads of State and Foreign Ministers",[84] cannot be seriously taken into consideration since, even if we were to accept that diplomatic immunity and state immunity are closely linked but still fundamentally different,[85] they offer no solution to the following three crucial issues:

[78] ibid., para 58.

[79] ICJ, Case Concerning Certain Questions of Mutual Assistance in Criminal Matters (Djibouti v. France) Judgment 4 June 2008, ICJ Reports of Judgements, Advisory Opinions and orders (2008) para 174, https://www.icj-cij.org/files/case-related/136/136-20080604-JUD-01-00-EN.pdf, last accessed 8 June 2023.

[80] ibid.

[81] Separate Opinion of Judge ad hoc Yusouf, https://www.icj-cij.org/files/case-related/136/136-20080604-JUD-01-09-EN.pdf, last accessed 8 June 2023.

[82] ibid., para 37.

[83] ibid.

[84] ICJ, Dissenting Opinion of Judge Van den Wyngaert, para. 15, https://www.icj-cij.org/files/case-related/121/121-20020214-JUD-01-09-EN.pdf, last accessed 8 June 2023.

[85] Brownlie (2003), p. 323.

1. Where exactly the difference lies between the legal status of diplomatic agents, Heads of States and Ministers for Foreign Affairs.
2. Why it is not unfounded to consider that a diplomatic agent, who is undoubtedly of a lower rank than a Minister of Foreign Affairs, a Prime Minister or a Head of State, enjoys higher protection of immunity than his or her superiors in rank.
3. Whether the core of the principle of immunity or, in other words, the reason behind its existence internationally, lies in the nature of the office held and the role one performs for his or her State or in other facts, such as for instance the fact that any State has the right to approve or to reject the credentials of diplomatic agents of third States who enter its territory.

References

Table of Cases

ICC (2005) Prosecutor v. Joseph Kony and Vincent Otti (ICC-02/04-01/05). https://www.icc-cpi.int/uganda/kony. Accessed 8 June 2023

ICC (2006) Prosecutor v. Bosco Ntaganda (ICC-01/04-02/06). https://www.icc-cpi.int/drc/ntaganda. Accessed 8 June 2023

ICC (2009a) Decision on the Prosecution's application for a warrant of arrest against Omar Hassan Ahmad Al Bashir, ICC-02/05-01/09-3. https://www.icc-cpi.int/pages/record.aspx?uri=639096. Accessed 8 June 2023

ICC (2009b) Prosecutor v. Omar Hassan Ahmad Al Bashir, Decision on the Prosecution's Application for a Warrant of Arrest against Omar Hassan Ahmad Al Bashir, ICC-02/05-01/09-3. https://www.icc-cpi.int/CourtRecords/CR2009_01517.PDF. Accessed 8 June 2023

ICC (2011a) Decision Pursuant to the Article 87(7) on the Failure of the Republic of Malawi to Comply with the Cooperation Requests Issued by the Court with Respect to the Arrest and Surrender of Omar Hassan Ahmed Al-Bashir, Al-Bashir (ICC-02/05-01/09), Pre-Trial Chamber I. https://www.legal-tools.org/doc/476812/pdf/. Accessed 8 June 2023

ICC (2011b) ICC-02/05-01/09-139-Corr, Pre-Trial Chamber. https://www.legaltools.org/doc/476812/pdf/. Accessed 8 June 2023

ICC (2012) Prosecutor v. Thomas Lubanga Dyilo, Judgment pursuant to Article 74 of the Statute (ICC-01/04-01/06-2842) Trial Chamber I. https://www.icc-cpi.int/pages/record.aspx?uri=1379838. Accessed 8 June 2023

ICC (2017) Decision under article 87(7) of the Rome Statute on the non-compliance by Jordan with the request by the Court for the arrest and surrender or Omar Al-Bashir, ICC-02/05-01/09-309. https://www.icc-cpi.int/Pages/record.aspx?docNo=ICC-02/05-01/09-309&ln=fr. Accessed 8 June 2023

ICC (2018) Request to the Republic of Belarus for Cooperation in the Arrest and Surrender of Omar Hassan Ahmad Al-Bashir, ICC-02/05-01/09. https://www.icc-cpi.int/Pages/record.aspx?docNo=ICC-02/05-01/09-395. Accessed 8 June 2023

ICJ (2002) DRC v. Belgium, Judgment para 48. https://www.icj-cij.org/files/case-related/121/121-20020214-JUD-01-00-EN.pdf. Accessed 8 June 2023

ICTY (1998) Prosecutor v. Anton Furundzija (IT-95-17/1-T), Trial Chamber, Judgment

ICTY (2001a) Prosecutor v. Slobodan Milosevic, Decision on Preliminary Motions, para 28. http://www.icty.org/x/cases/slobodan_milosevic/tdec/en/1110873516829.htm. Accessed 8 June 2023

ICTY (2001b) Prosecutor v. Slobodan Milosevic, Decision on Preliminary Motions, para 34. http://www.icty.org/x/cases/slobodan_milosevic/tdec/en/1110873516829.htm. Accessed 8 June 2023

SCSL (2004) Prosecutor v. Taylor (SCSL-03-01-I-059) (Appeals Chamber), Decision on Immunity from Jurisdiction, Special Court for Sierra Leone. http://www.worldcourts.com/scsl/eng/decisions/2004.05.31_Prosecutor_v_Taylor.pdf. Accessed 8 June 2023

Books

Brownlie I (2003) Principles of public international law. OUP

Kreβ C, Prost K (2008) Article 98 in Triffterer, Commentary

Schabas WA (2010) The International Criminal Court: a commentary on the Rome Statute. OUP

Articles/Papers

Akande D (2004) International law immunities and the International Criminal Court. AJIL 98:407

Akande D (2009) The Legal Nature of the Security Council Referrals to the ICC and its Impact on Al Bashir's Immunities. JICJ 7:333

Tladi D (2013) The ICC Decisions on Chad and Malawi on Cooperation, Immunities, and Article 98. JICJ 11:199

Websites/Web Sources

ICC (2009c) Decision on the Meeting of African States Parties to the Rome Statute of the International Criminal Court (ICC), Doc. Assembly/AU/13(XIII), Assembly/AU/Dec.245 (XIII), Rev.1. https://au.int/sites/default/files/decisions/9560assembly_en_1_3_july_2009_auc_thirteenth_ordinary_session_decisions_declarations_message_congratulations_motion_0.pdf. Accessed 8 June 2023

ICC (2009d) Warrant of Arrest for Omar Hassan Ahmad Al Bashir (ICC-02/05-01/09-1) Pre-Trial Chamber I. https://www.icc-cpi.int/CourtRecords/CR2009_01514.PDF. Accessed 8 June 2023

ICC (2011c) Decision Pursuant to Article 87(7) of the Rome Statute on the Failure by the Republic of Chad to Comply with the Cooperation Requests Issued by the Court with Respect to the Arrest and Surrender of Omar Hassan Ahmad Al Bashir, Al-Bashir (ICC-02/05-01/09), Pre-Trial Chamber I. https://www.icc-cpi.int/CourtRecords/CR2012_04203.PDF. Accessed 8 June 2023

ICJ Dissenting Opinion of Judge Van den Wyngaert, para 15. https://www.icj-cij.org/files/case-related/121/121-20020214-JUD-01-09-EN.pdf. Accessed 8 June 2023

ICJ Reports of Judgements (2008) Djibouti v. France, Judgment 4 June 2008, ICJ Advisory Opinions and orders, para 174. https://www.icj-cij.org/files/case-related/136/136-20080604-JUD-01-00-EN.pdf. Accessed 8 June 2023

UNSC Resolution 1593 (2005) UNSC Doc. SC/RES/1593. https://www.icc-cpi.int/NR/rdonlyres/85FEBD1A-29F8-4EC4-9566-48EDF55CC587/283244/N0529273.pdf. Accessed 8 June 2023

UNSC Resolution 1828 (2008) UNSC Doc. SC/RES/1828. https://www.legal-tools.org/doc/cf90b5/pdf/. Accessed 8 June 2023

Chapter 8 The ICC's Jurisdiction Following a Security Council's Referral of a Situation Concerning Citizens of States Non-Parties to the ICC: the Situation in Sudan and Libya (Art. 25 UN Charter & 13(b) ICCRSt)

Abstract The general obligation of states parties to cooperate, enshrined in Article 86 ICCRSt, also applies to states non-parties to the Rome Statute, when referred to the ICC pursuant to Article 13 (b) ICCRSt. In particular, Article 86 ICCRSt, under the title "General Obligation to Cooperate", is the first Article of Part 9 on "International Cooperation and Judicial Assistance" and stipulates that: "States Parties shall, in accordance with the provisions of this Statute, cooperate fully with the Court in its investigation and prosecution of crimes within the jurisdiction of the Court." This obligation of cooperation in Article 86 ICCRSt is also enshrined in UNSC Resolutions through which the UNSC, pursuant to Article 13 (b) ICCRSt, refers states nonparties to the ICC, thus establishing the ICC's jurisdiction over them. It is a fact that the establishment of a permanent and international system of criminal justice over international crimes appears to have as its main goal the elimination of impunity concerning the crime of genocide, war crimes, crimes against humanity as well as the crime of aggression.

The Security Council also issued Resolutions 1593 (2005) and 1970 (2011); the former referred the situation in Darfur (Sudan) to the ICC, and the latter, the situation in Libya. Both resolutions are thoroughly reviewed in this chapter and a few important conclusions are drawn from the Security Council's position regarding the true application of international criminal justice.

8.1 The ICC's Jurisdiction Over Citizens and Territories of States that Have Not Ratified the Rome Statute of the ICC

Pursuant to Article 12 ICCRSt, the Court may exercise its jurisdiction only if *one or more of the States on the territory of which the conduct in question occurred or of which the accused is a national*:

1. are Parties to the Statute or;
2. have accepted the Court's jurisdiction pursuant to paragraph 3.

V. Tsilonis, *The Jurisdiction of the International Criminal Court*,
https://doi.org/10.1007/978-3-031-46138-5_8

Nonetheless, pursuant to Article 13 ICCRSt, the ICC's jurisdiction can be exercised over states non-parties to the Rome Statutes. In particular, Article 13 ICCRSt stipulates that the Court may exercise its jurisdiction with respect to the crime of genocide, war crimes, crimes against humanity and the crime of aggression referred to in Article 5 in accordance with the provisions of this Statute if:

(a) a situation in which one or more of such crimes appears to have been committed is referred to the Prosecutor by a state party in accordance with article 14;
(b) a situation in which one or more of such crimes appears to have been committed is referred to the Prosecutor by the Security Council acting under Chap. VII of the Charter of the United Nations; or
(c) the Prosecutor has initiated an investigation in respect of such a crime in accordance with article 15.[1]

8.2 The Application of Jurisdiction Pursuant to Article 13 ICCRSt

In practice, the ICC applied Article 13 (a) ICCRSt when initiating an investigation concerning the Democratic Republic of Congo, the Central African Republic and Uganda, i.e. it did so following a request to investigate the situation submitted by the States themselves ("self-referral", for more on which, see Chap. 9 on the complementarity principle).

In addition, it applied Article 13 (b) ICCRSt, when the UNSC first referred the situation in Darfur (Sudan) to the ICC, and later the situation in Libya. In both cases, arrest warrants were issued for sitting Heads of States and high-ranking officials, i.e. among others against the Sudanese President Omar Hassan Ahmad Al-Bashir and the now deceased Libyan leader Muammar Gaddafi.

What is more, in applying Article 13 (c) ICCRSt, Pre-Trial Chamber II charged the ICC Prosecutor to initiate an investigation into the situation in Kenya. It was the first time the Prosecutor initiated an investigation *proprio motu*, without a previous referral from a state party of the UN Security Council.[2] With an impartiality not often found in international criminal law, the Prosecutor brought not only government officials but also rebel leaders to accountability before international criminal justice.

The ICC Prosecutor has also publicly announced that he is examining at least nine more cases in four continents, including in Afghanistan, Colombia, Georgia, Guinea, Honduras, the Republic of Korea, Nigeria and Palestine.

Nonetheless, while the scope of the Court and the role it plays in deterring international crime are constantly growing, so are the challenges and difficulties it faces. From a political perspective, it faces significant criticism from States and their leaders. Even though such criticisms do not recognise the fact that the vast majority

[1] Article 13 ICCRSt.

[2] Later, Article 13 (c) ICCRSt was also applied to the situation in the Ivory Coast.

of cases examined by the Court have been referred to it either by interested state parties themselves or by the UN Security Council, the fact remains that they are damaging to the Court's status and having a negative influence on public opinion and international cooperation.

8.3 The ICC's Jurisdiction Pursuant to Article 13 (b) ICCRSt Read Together with Article 25 UN Charter

As an exception to the preconditions described in Article 12 ICCRSt, the ICC may exercise its jurisdiction following the referral of a situation from the UNSC pursuant to Article 13 (b) ICCRSt. In particular, the jurisdiction of the ICC is established in this case if the Security Council, acting under Chap. VII of the Charter of the United Nations, refers to the Prosecutor a situation in which one or more such crimes appear to have been committed.

This particular provision clearly aims to extend the ICC's jurisdiction to crimes committed outside the territory of a state party or by citizens of a State that has not ratified the Statute. Consequently, one must examine the legal basis for the obligation of states non-parties to the Rome Statute to "fully cooperate" with the ICC, as per the UNSC's request.

It is generally well-known that Article 2(4) of the Charter of the United Nations prohibits the use of force by all member states: "*[a]ll Members shall refrain in their international relations from the threat or use of force against the territorial integrity or political independence of any state, or in any other manner inconsistent with the Purposes of the United Nations.*"[3] Consequently, Article 2(4) UN Charter aims not only to prohibit the unilateral use of force, but also to establish through the Security Council a system of "central control" over the threat or actual use of force. Thus the Security Council will be able to intervene in accordance with the powers awarded to it by Chap. VII of the UN Charter. The brief and inclusive prohibition of Article 2(4) is considered to enshrine a *jus cogens* rule of international customary law.[4]

It is widely accepted that the Security Council, acting under Chap. VII of the UN Charter, may enforce legal obligations on member states to the UN in accordance with Article 25 UN Charter. In particular, according to Article 25 UN Charter: "The Members of the United Nations agree to accept and carry out the decisions of the Security Council in accordance with the present Charter."

Consequently, if a State is not a party to the ICCRSt but is a member of the UN, then pursuant to Article 25 UN Charter it is obligated to carry out the decisions of the

[3] UN Charter (1945), adopted 26 June 1945, entered into force 24 October 1945.

[4] Hatzikonstantinou (2005), p 74. Nonetheless, even this interpretation of Article 2(4) UN Charter has been the subject of many discussions and not only on what constitutes threat or actual use of force, but also on the meaning of a State's territorial integrity.

Security Council and, consequently, in the present case, to comply with the referral to the ICC Prosecutor pursuant to Article 13 (b) ICCRSt. In other words, if a State is not party to the ICC but is a member of the UN, the ICC's jurisdiction appears to be adequately founded in Article 25 UN Charter, read together with Article 13 ICCRSt, as long as the Security Council, acting under Chap. VII of the UN Charter, refers a situation to the Prosecutor in which one or more crimes within the jurisdiction of the Court appear to have been committed.

This interpretation accords with the traditional principles of *pacta sunt servanda* and *pacta tertiis nec nocent nec prosunt*,[5] according to which a State has a legal obligation to comply with the treaties and conventions it has ratified. However, no obligation or right is created for a State by a convention to which it is not a party.[6]

Nonetheless, in the hypothetical scenario where a State is not party to the ICCRSt nor a member of the UN, a legal obstacle would arise, since the Security Council cannot enforce legal obligations on this State, at least not pursuant to Article 25 UN Charter. Considering, however, that almost all states are members of the UN, this hypothesis is in principal theoretical,[7] without of course excluding the possibility for it to become real in the future. In such an unlikely instance, however, the Security Council may legally be unable to enforce its will pursuant to Article 25 UN Charter read together with Article 13(b) ICCRSt, but, in practice, it has the ability to take all measures necessary to ensure the cooperation of a dissenting State.

On the other hand, the possibility of a state withdrawing from the UN also appears to be completely hypothetical, as ***first***, it has never happened to this day, with the exception of Indonesia's withdrawal in 1965;[8] ***second***, no express provision is made in the Charter concerning whether or how a member can legally withdraw from the UN; and ***third*** and most importantly, a unilateral withdrawal from the UN that is not founded on any Charter provision could not in any case exclude a State's responsibility or negate the obligations that arise during its time as a UN member.

Therefore, in accordance with the principle of *pacta sunt servanda*, a state could not exclude its responsibility to accept and carry out UNSC Resolutions under Chap. VII of the UN Charter by deciding to withdraw from the UN. I believe the

---

[5] Sangroula (2010).

[6] Articles 35–36 of the Vienna Convention on the Law of Treaties.

[7] Today, only Taiwan, Western Sahara, Kosovo, Cook Islands, Niue, the Holy See and Palestine are not members of the UN, although the latter two have been awarded observer status.

[8] During the Indonesia–Malaysia confrontation, and in response to the election of Malaysia as a non-permanent member of the United Nations Security Council, in a letter dated 20 January 1965, Indonesia informed the UN Secretary-General that it had decided to withdraw from the UN. However, following the overthrow of President Sukarno, in a telegram dated 19 September 1966, the new government notified the Secretary-General of its decision "to resume full cooperation with the United Nations and to resume participation in its activities starting with the twenty-first session of the General Assembly". On 28 September 1966, the United Nations General Assembly took note of the decision of the Government of Indonesia and the President invited the representatives of that country to take their seats in the Assembly. See Yearbook of the United Nations 1966, p 1070.

same would be true should a State be expelled from the organisation pursuant to Article 6 UN Charter.[9]

What is more, it is noted that the ICC may demand a State's cooperation pursuant to Article 13 (b) ICCRSt and in particular in accordance with Article 93(1) ICCRSt,[10] which is exceptionally wide in scope and applies only to state parties.[11] Nonetheless, the ICC cannot demand the cooperation of a state party beyond the scope of the ICCRSt's provisions concerning the arrest and surrender of a person, while on the other hand any objections brought forth by a State must also be founded on the ICCRSt. Thus a State can essentially postpone or deny a request for arrest and surrender based on the provisions of Article 89(2),[12] 93(3) [13] and (4),[14] 94 [15] and 95 [16] ICCRSt. Those provisions largely apply to cases that have been referred to the ICC but for which a criminal investigation has also been initiated on a national level.

---

[9] Article 6 UN Charter: A Member of the United Nations which has persistently violated the Principles contained in the present Charter may be expelled from the Organization by the General Assembly upon the recommendation of the Security Council.

[10] Article 93—Other forms of cooperation

1. States Parties shall, in accordance with the provisions of this Part and under procedures of national law, comply with requests by the Court to provide the following assistance in relation to investigations or prosecutions:

(a) The identification and whereabouts of persons or the location of items;
(b) The taking of evidence, including testimony under oath, and the production of evidence, including expert opinions and reports necessary to the Court;
(c) The questioning of any person being investigated or prosecuted;
(d) The service of documents, including judicial documents;
(e) Facilitating the voluntary appearance of persons as witnesses or experts before the Court;
(f) The temporary transfer of persons as provided in paragraph 7;
(g) The examination of places or sites, including the exhumation and examination of grave sites;
(h) The execution of searches and seizures;
(i) The provision of records and documents, including official records and documents;
(j) The protection of victims and witnesses and the preservation of evidence;
(k) The identification, tracing and freezing or seizure of proceeds, property and assets and instrumentalities of crimes for the purpose of eventual forfeiture, without prejudice to the rights of bona fide third parties; and
(l) Any other type of assistance which is not prohibited by the law of the requested State, with a view to facilitating the investigation and prosecution of crimes within the jurisdiction of the Court.

[11] Cryer et al. (2010), p 511; Schabas (2010), p 973.

[12] Refers to the case where the person sought for surrender brings a challenge before a national court on the basis of the principle of ne bis in idem.

[13] Refers to the case where execution of a particular measure of assistance is prohibited in the requested State on the basis of an existing fundamental legal principle of general application.

[14] Refers to the case where the request concerns the production of any documents or disclosure of evidence which relates to the requested State's national security.

[15] Refers to the case where the immediate execution of a request would interfere with an ongoing investigation or prosecution of a case different from that to which the request relates. In such a case, the requested State may postpone the execution of the request for a period of time agreed upon with the Court.

8.4 The ICC's Jurisdiction in the Situation in Sudan and Libya (Article 13 (b) ICCRSt): the Referral of States Non-Parties to the ICC Through UNSC Resolutions

The general obligation of state parties to cooperate, enshrined in Article 86 ICCRSt, also applies to state non-parties to the Rome Statute, when referred to the ICC pursuant to Article 13 (b) ICCRSt. In particular, Article 86 ICCRSt, under the title "General Obligation to Cooperate", is the first Article of Part 9 on "International Cooperation and Judicial Assistance" and stipulates that: "States Parties shall, in accordance with the provisions of this Statute, cooperate fully with the Court in its investigation and prosecution of crimes within the jurisdiction of the Court." This obligation of cooperation in Article 86 ICCRSt is also enshrined in UNSC Resolutions through which the UNSC, pursuant to Article 13 (b) ICCRSt, refers states non-parties to the ICC, thus establishing the ICC's jurisdiction over them.

It is a fact that the establishment of a permanent and international system of criminal justice over international crimes appears to have as its main goal the elimination of impunity concerning the crime of genocide, war crimes, crimes against humanity as well as the crime of aggression.

The Security Council also issued Resolutions 1593 (2005) and 1970 (2011); the former referred the situation in Darfur (Sudan) to the ICC, and the latter, the situation in Libya.

With regard to the referral of situations by the Security Council to the ICC and the extension of the ICC's jurisdiction over state non-parties to the ICC, three legal issues arise from the application of Article 13 (b) to the situations in Sudan and Libya, and are worthy of further examination:

1. The validity of the referrals to the ICC pursuant to Article 13 (b) ICCRSt, given the exceptions to the ICC's jurisdiction established by those same referrals.
2. The legal status of states non-parties to the Rome Statute, which fall under the ICC's jurisdiction pursuant to Article 13 (b) ICCRSt. Should those States be considered state parties to the Rome Statute, following their referral to the ICC by the Security Council? Or, put slightly differently, is the extension of the ICC's jurisdiction over them lawful?
3. The duration of the ICC's jurisdiction over state non-parties to the Statute pursuant to a UNSC Resolution.

[16] Refers to the case where there is an admissibility challenge under consideration by the Court pursuant to Article 18 or 19 ICCRSt.

8.4.1 The ICC's Jurisdiction in the Al-Bashir Case (Darfur Situation): UNSC Resolution 1593

Sudan is not a state party to the Rome Statute. Though it signed the Statute in 2002, the State has not ratified it to this day.

In this case, in order to establish the ICC's jurisdiction over war crimes and crimes against humanity committed in Sudan, the UN Security Council referred the situation in Darfur to the ICC in March 2005, acting under Chap. VII of the UNC Charter and Articles 25 UN Charter and 13 (b) ICCRSt. Consequently, in accordance with the aforementioned UNSC Resolution, the ICC established its jurisdiction over the situation in Darfur and was able to investigate accusations on grave violations of international humanitarian law and international human rights law. Simultaneously, the Security Council demanded Sudan's full cooperation with the ICC, even though Sudan is not a state party to its Statute.

In particular, according to Resolution 1593 (2005):

> The Security Council,
>
> [...]
>
> Acting under Chapter VII of the Charter of the United Nations,
>
> [...]
>
> 2. Decides that the Government of Sudan and all other parties to the conflict in Darfur, shall cooperate fully with and provide any necessary assistance to the Court and the Prosecutor pursuant to this resolution and, while recognizing that States not party to the Rome Statute have no obligation under the Statute, urges all States and concerned regional and other international organizations to cooperate fully.[17]

Consequently, the Sudanese government, as a member of the UN, was compelled to cooperate with the ICC pursuant to the aforementioned UNSC Resolution. Nonetheless, the position adopted by the Sudanese Council of Ministers was utterly negative, since it deemed that the UNSC Resolution, which *inter alia* permitted the arrest of Sudanese citizens accused of crimes against civilians in the Western Sudanese area of Darfur, violated Sudan's state sovereignty and administration of justice. The day after UNSC Resolution 1593 (2005), Sudanese President Omar Al-Bashir rushed to assure his citizens that he would not surrender any of them to the International Criminal Court; shortly thereafter, according to deputy spokeswoman Marie Okabe, Sudan expelled ten humanitarian groups from Darfur and seized the agencies' assets; the aid groups affected included Oxfam, Solidarities and Mercy Corps.[18] What is more, in September 2012 Al-Bashir continued to follow his standard policy of defying both Resolution 1593 and the arrest warrant issued for him by the ICC, stating that he planned to participate in the UN General Assembly in

---

[17] UNSC Resolution 1593 (2005).

[18] CNN (2009).

New York, since the USA had not ratified the ICCRSt either and was therefore under no obligation to execute the arrest warrant for him.[19]

In addition to the backlash from the Sudanese government, Resolution 1593 was also strongly criticised among UN members, for whom the most controversial aspect of referral was operative paragraph 6. In particular, according to this paragraph, the Security Council "[d]ecides that nationals, current or former officials or personnel from a contributing State outside Sudan which is not a party to the Rome Statute of the International Criminal Court shall be subject to the exclusive jurisdiction of that contributing State for all alleged acts or omissions arising out of or related to operations in Sudan established or authorized by the Council or the African Union, unless such exclusive jurisdiction has been expressly waived by that contributing State".[20]

This paragraph was thought to negate the purpose of Resolution 1593 (2005) and impinge upon its credibility, as in effect, the Resolution states that a state non-party to the Rome Statute is under an obligation to cooperate fully with the ICC, pursuant to Article 13 (b) ICCRSt, but at the same time, in accordance with paragraph 6, the citizens of such a State, for example the citizens of the USA, are excluded from the ICC's jurisdiction for crimes committed in the state non-party over which the ICC's jurisdiction is established with this Resolution (on Sudan), and fall under the exclusive jurisdiction of their own State.

The day Resolution 1593 was adopted, a number of state delegations expressed their doubts about operative paragraph 6. The representative of France, Jean-Marc De La Sablière, initially stated that "France welcomes the historic resolution"[21] as "[f]or the first time, the Security Council has referred a situation to the International Criminal Court"[22] and that "[t]o achieve that result, my country was prepared to recognize [...] a jurisdictional immunity vis-à-vis the International Criminal Court for certain nationals or personnel of States not parties to the Rome Statute".[23] However, he later underlined that "the jurisdictional immunity provided for in the text we have just adopted obviously cannot run counter to other international obligations of States and will be subject, where appropriate, to the interpretation of the courts of my country".[24]

The representative of the Philippines, Lauro Baja, and of Tanzania, Augustine Mahiga, of Argentina, César Mayoral, and of Brazil, Ronaldo Mota Sardenberg, who also served as President to the UNSC at the time, were of the same opinion. In particular, the representative of the Philippines stated *inter alia*: "Any further impasse—any further inaction—on the part of the Council [...] would have reduced

[19] Eventually, he decided not to attend the UN General Assembly. Deen (2013); Sudan Tribune (2013).

[20] UNSC Resolution 1593 (2005) para. 6.

[21] Security Council (2005), 60th year: 5158th meeting, Thursday, 31 March 2005.

[22] ibid.

[23] ibid.

[24] ibid.

this august body to a nadir of irrelevance with regard to ending impunity and responding to the protection of human rights and humanitarian law. [...] We do, however, share the concerns of some delegations about the manner in which resolution 1593 (2005) was arrived at. Once again, fault lines in the Council and potential veto threats prevented the emergence of a strong, robust and clear signal from this body—which the Council badly needs these days. Perhaps that is the reason why the call for Security Council reform grows louder as the days go by. [...] Operative paragraph 6 of the resolution is killing its credibility—softly, perhaps, but killing it nevertheless. We may ask whether the Security Council has the prerogative to mandate the limitation of the jurisdiction of the ICC under the Rome Statute once the exercise of its jurisdiction has advanced. Operative paragraph 6 subtly subsumed the independence of the ICC into the political and diplomatic vagaries of the Security Council. Nevertheless, that eventuality may well be worth the sacrifice if impunity is, indeed, ended in Darfur [...]".[25]

On the other hand, the representative of Tanzania, Augustine Mahiga stated: "We are therefore unable to accept that the resolution should in any way be interpreted as seeking to circumvent the jurisdiction of the Court".[26] César Mayoral, the representative of Argentina, took the same stance: "The Argentine Republic voted in favour of this resolution on the basis of the report submitted to the Security Council by the High Commissioner for Human Rights, which stated clearly that serious violations of human rights and crimes against humanity had been committed and verified in Darfur. [...] we regret that we had to adopt a text that establishes an exception to the jurisdiction of the Court. It is our hope that this will not become standard practice. We would like to make it clear that the exception provided for in paragraph 6 should be limited exclusively to those nationals or members of the armed forces of a State that is not party to the Rome Statute that are participating in peacekeeping operations established or authorized by the Security Council.[27] Finally, we wish to establish clearly that we are against any position or agreement which generically would exclude the nationals of a State from the jurisdiction of the Court, because that would affect the basis for such jurisdiction and thwart the letter and the spirit of the Rome Statute".[28]

Finally, the position adopted by the UNSC President and representative of Brazil was thorough and fully justified.

> Brazil is in favour of the referral of the situation in Darfur to the International Criminal Court (ICC). Nevertheless, Brazil was not able to join those members that voted in favour of the resolution. [...] The maintenance of international peace and the fight against impunity cannot be viewed as conflicting objectives. Brazil reiterates that the ICC provides all the necessary checks and balances to prevent possible abuses and politically motivated misuse

[25] ibid., p. 6.

[26] ibid., p. 9.

[27] This was of course wishful thinking on behalf of Argentina, or in the best-case scenario, an interpretation that could potentially be used by the ICC in the unlikely event that a case of a citizen of a state non-party to the ICCRSt was brought before it.

[28] UNSC (2005), 5158th meeting.

> of its jurisdiction. Thus, efforts to secure broader immunities from the jurisdiction of the Court are both unwarranted and unhelpful, in our view. [...] For those reasons, Brazil abstained in the voting on the resolution on the referral. As recommended by the report of the International Commission of Inquiry, the ICC remains the only acceptable instance of criminal law for dealing with the issue of accountability in the Sudan. We have exhaustively negotiated a text that could better reflect both the concerns of countries non-parties to the Rome Statute, as well as the commitments of those countries that have ratified that instrument. For the sake of the referral, Brazil painstakingly agreed during the negotiations upon provisions that presented a serious level of difficulty for my Government, such as the exemption from jurisdiction for nationals of those countries not parties to the Statute [...] To go further would constitute an inadequate and risky interference of the Council in the constitutional basis of an independent judicial body and a position inconsistent with the principles we have defended in the past on this issue. The text just approved contains a preambular paragraph through which the Council takes note of the existence of agreements referred to in article 98-2 of the Rome Statute. My delegation has difficulty in supporting a reference that not only does not favour the fight against impunity but also stresses a provision whose application has been a highly controversial issue. We understand that it would be a contradiction to mention, in the very text of a referral by the Council to the ICC, measures that limit the jurisdictional activity of the Court. In addition, Brazil also was not in a position to support operative paragraph 6, through which the Council recognizes the existence of exclusive jurisdiction, a legal exception that is inconsistent in international law. These are substantial issues that, in our view, will not contribute to strengthening the role of the ICC—which is our aspiration. Brazil has consistently rejected initiatives aimed at extending exemptions of certain categories of individuals from ICC jurisdiction, and we maintain our position to prevent efforts that may have the effect of dismantling the achievements reached in the field of international criminal justice. Both the acceleration and the format of negotiations during the last few days have prevented some delegations from balancing the clear objective of referral to the ICC against the hindrances imposed thereon. Insurmountable constraints thus prevented Brazil from voting in favour of a proposal that we have always understood would be the appropriate instrument to help curb violence and end impunity in Darfur.[29]

Nonetheless, there were also those who viewed the Resolution positively, such as the representatives of Greece, Mr. Vassilakis, and Denmark, Ms. Loj. In particular, Mr. Vassilakakis stated *inter alia*:

> When we address issues in which moderation is given top priority, we achieve positive results. It is in that spirit that we voted in favour of the resolution. We believe that it strengthens the authority of the Security Council in its efforts to promote peace, security, international justice and law in all societies, particularly those in conflict. The resolution also strengthens the authority of the International Criminal Court, which will have the chance to prove itself and show what it can do. The resolution creates certain exceptions for the specific case of the Sudan for countries not parties to the Statute of the International Criminal Court. That will create certain problems of interpretation regarding the application of the principle of exclusive international jurisdiction. In our view, the resolution does not infringe on that principle, which is firmly rooted in the Statute of the Court and in other international

[29] ibid., p. 11. However, neither the UNSC President and Brazilian representative nor any other representative invoked the provision of Article 16 ICCRSt (Deferral of investigation or prosecution). Contrary to the provision of Article 98 ICCRSt (Cooperation with respect to waiver of immunity and consent to surrender), which is only included in the Darfur referral, this provision is included in both the UNSC referral of the situation in Darfur and that of the one in Libya.

> agreements. Despite that, we preferred to vote in favour rather than to allow violations of humanitarian law to go unpunished.[30]

Rather optimistically, the representative of Denmark Ms. Loj stated that her country's interpretation of operative paragraph 6 on exclusive jurisdiction is that "it does not affect the universal jurisdiction of Member States in areas such as war crimes, torture and terrorism. As regards the formulation regarding the existence of the agreements referred to in article 98, paragraph 2, of the Rome Statute, Denmark would like to stress that that reference is purely factual; it is merely referring to the existence of such agreements. Thus, the reference in no way impinges on the integrity of the Rome Statute".[31]

To conclude, it is apparent that the situation in Sudan raised questions regarding the credibility of the Security Council, as well as the role and influence of international diplomacy on international criminal justice. It is also worth noting that even though Sudan signed the Rome Statute on 8 September 2000, it later withdrew its support towards the Court. Nonetheless, the ICC has jurisdiction over this particular situation given that the Security Council adopted Resolution 1593 (2005), which referred the situation in Darfur to the ICC Prosecutor for investigation. This referral specifically but unlawfully excludes from the ICC's jurisdiction citizens of state non-parties to the ICC who were in Sudan at the time. It is obvious that this paragraph was included to protect mostly American citizens working in Sudan for the UN, non-governmental organisations such as CHF International or the secret services. This is also the reason why the USA, although it opposed the ICC's establishment and jurisdiction from the start, chose to abstain from the vote that led to the adoption of this Resolution, instead of voting against, which would in itself have been enough to block the Resolution. Undoubtedly, this also signifies a shift in the USA's stance, given that up to this point, the country maintained an exceptionally hostile attitude towards the ICC.

On the other hand, however, the arrest warrant for Sudan's President, Omar Al-Bashir, and the wording of Resolution 1593 (2005) turned African States, who until recently had supported the ICC, against it, and strengthened the arguments of those who see the ICC as an instrument of modern-day imperialism. It is worth mentioning that pursuant to this Resolution, the ICC issued two arrest warrants, prior to the one against Al-Bashir, both Sudanese nationals: Minister of State for the Interior Ahmad Harun, and alleged leader of the Janjaweed Militia Ali Kushayb. However, in both cases, the government of Sudan refused to cooperate and did not surrender either person. It is the author's opinion that the investigation initiated by the ICC Prosecutor is focused on the government of Sudan, and not on the rebels, because international power cells wish *for certain reasons* to see a change of the governing power in Sudan. Whether that is because Sudan buys its weapons systems from China, while exporting 7% of the oil used by China today, and because the USA would like to overthrow the Sudanese government to thwart the relationship

[30] ibid., p. 9.

[31] ibid., p. 6.

between China and Sudan, or because of other geopolitical reasons is beyond the scope of the present study.

8.4.2 The ICC's Jurisdiction Over the Situation in Libya: UNSC Resolution 1970

Libya is also a state non-party to the Rome Statute and the scene of the second situation which the UN Security Council referred to the ICC pursuant to Article 13 (b) ICCRSt, demanding its full cooperation with the Court through Resolution 1970 (2011).

According to UNSC Resolution 1970 (2011), the Security Council "[d]ecides that the Libyan authorities shall cooperate fully with and provide any necessary assistance to the Court and the Prosecutor pursuant to this resolution and, while recognizing that States not party to the Rome Statute have no obligation under the Statute, urges all States and concerned regional and other international organizations to cooperate fully with the Court and the Prosecutor".[32]

Nonetheless, and despite the ICC's request to the National Transitional Council of Libya to arrest and surrender Saif Al-Islam Gaddafi and Abdullah Al-Senussi to the Court to stand trial in the Hague[33] in accordance with the arrest warrant issued for them,[34] the Council refused to surrender either person, standing by its view that Gaddafi's son and the high-ranking official in his former regime had to stand trial in Libya.[35]

The refusal of the National Transitional Council of Libya inevitably raised questions about whether and under which conditions a State that has not ratified the ICCRSt is obligated to comply with it, as well as with the relevant Security Council recommendations.

It is noteworthy that on 23 November 2011, the day after the termination of the case against Muammar Mohammed Abu Minyar Gaddafi and a couple of days after his son's arrest by Libyan authorities, the ICC issued a press release on the case against Saif Al-Islam Gaddafi and Al-Senussi, emphasising *first* that the arrest warrant for the two was still pending, *second* that the Libyan authorities had an obligation to fully cooperate with the ICC, and *third* that if they wished to try

---

[32] UNSC Resolution 1970 (2011).

[33] ICC (2011b), Pre-Trial Chamber I, Request to the Libyan Arab Jamahiriya for the arrest and surrender of Muammar Mohammed Abu Minyar Gaddafi, Saif Al-Islam Gaddafi and Abdullah Al-Senussi (ICC-01/11-01/11) 4 July 2011, https://www.icc-cpi.int/CourtRecords/CR2011_08694.PDF, last accessed 8 June 2023.

[34] ICC (2011a).

[35] 'Gaddafi Son's Libya Trial to Be Delayed by Five Months: Official' Reuters (London, 9 September 2012), https://www.reuters.com/article/us-libya-saif-trial/gaddafi-sons-libya-trial-to-be-delayed-by-five-months-official-idUSBRE8880F720120909, last accessed 8 June 2023.

Gaddafi's son in Libya, they had to submit a challenge of admissibility of the case before Pre-Trial Chamber I in accordance with Articles 17 and 19 ICCRSt.[36]

This press release is indicative of the ICC's view that, following Resolution 1970, Libya constituted a *de facto* state party to the ICCRSt. Therefore, the National Transitional Council of Libya was under an obligation to execute the arrest warrant for Saif Al-Islam Gaddafi. In any case, it was under an obligation to act as a state party of the ICC within the framework of this particular case (or any other case to arise in the future pursuant to the UNSC referral); and to invoke all ICCRSt provisions that could potentially prevent the ICC from trying the case, such as for instance the principle of complementarity.

Nonetheless, the fact that the State of Libya (like for example the USA, China, Russia, Turkey etc.) has not ratified the ICCRSt, as well as the fact that the ICC's jurisdiction over the situation in Libya was established through UNSC Resolution 1970, raised the following crucial legal question: is the legal obligation of Libya to fully cooperate with the ICC founded on UNSC Resolution 1970 or on the ICCRSt, despite the fact that Libya has neither signed nor ratified the latter?

This question is of exceptional importance, since, if one considers the ICCRSt as the legal basis for Libya's obligation, then it becomes obvious that the State of Libya has all the rights and obligations of a state party to the ICCRSt. Thus Libya could, for instance, invoke Article 17(1)(a) ICCRSt and claim that the ICC should determine the case to be inadmissible, as "[it] is being investigated [...] by a State which has jurisdiction over it" (principle of complementarity).

On the contrary, were one to conclude that Libya's obligation to fully cooperate with the ICC is founded on UNSC Resolution 1970, then that means that its obligation is absolute or even "unconditional", since Libya, as a state non-party to the ICCRSt, would not in this case be able to invoke any ICCRSt provision that could release it from its obligation to surrender Saif Al-Islam Gaddafi. If that is the case, then it is apparent that UNSC Resolution 1970 is a *sui generis* order against which no legal argument can stand.

To conclude, the situation in Libya was much more pointed than previous situations in Kenya and Sudan when it comes to raising major issues regarding:

(a) The limits of the ICC's jurisdiction over state non-parties to its Statute and the legal basis on which their obligation to cooperate with the Court is founded (ICCRSt or UNSC Resolution?)
(b) The principle of complementarity, according to which the ICC's jurisdiction is complementary to national courts (Preamble, Articles 1 & 17 ICCRSt)
(c) The misuse of the provisions according to which the Security Council can refer a case to the ICC, while making a distinction between the ICC's jurisdiction over Libyan and non-Libyan perpetrators, i.e. essentially, between nationals of Libya and nationals of the USA (since the vast majority of NATO member states, save for the USA and Turkey, have ratified the ICCRSt). That is because operative

[36] This press release is no longer available on the ICC's official website.

paragraph 6 of Resolution 1970, much like in the case of Sudan, stated that "nationals, current or former officials or personnel from a State outside the Libyan Arab Jamahiriya which is not a party to the Rome Statute of the International Criminal Court shall be subject to the exclusive jurisdiction of that State for all alleged acts or omissions arising out of or related to operations in the Libyan Arab Jamahiriya established or authorized by the Council, unless such exclusive jurisdiction has been expressly waived by the State".

8.5 Comparing the Content of the Two Resolutions: the Omission of Article 98(2) ICCRSt in the Second Resolution Regarding Libya

At this point, it must be emphasised that Resolution 1593 (2005) on the situation in Darfur (Sudan), by referring in its preamble to the existence of Article 98 (2) ICCRSt, significantly contrasted with Resolution 1970 (2011) on the situation in Libya.[37]

In particular, the preamble of Resolution 1593 (2005) rather cleverly mentions "the existence of agreements referred to in Article 98-2 of the Rome Statute". According to Article 98 (2) ICCRSt, "the Court may not proceed with a request for surrender which would require the requested State to act inconsistently with its obligations under international agreements pursuant to which the consent of a sending State is required to surrender a person of that State to the Court, unless the Court can first obtain the cooperation of the sending State for the giving of consent for the surrender".

Incidentally, such agreements had mostly been signed between the USA and dozens of States, as part of a well-designed policy of the USA to limit the ICC's jurisdiction. Associated discussions even raised the need early on for legal protection for people working for international organisations or as mercenaries.[38]

However, it seems that because of the inclusion of operative paragraph 6 on the exclusion of the ICC's jurisdiction in Resolution 1970, even the USA deemed further reference to Article 98(2) ICCRSt unnecessary.

Nonetheless, the preceding operative paragraph 5 of Resolution 1970 can only be seen as a legal farce. This paragraph, which cannot be found in the previous Resolution 1593 (2005) on Darfur (Sudan), states that:

> [...] the Libyan authorities shall cooperate fully with and provide any necessary assistance to the Court and the Prosecutor pursuant to this resolution and, **while recognizing that States not party to the Rome Statute have no obligation under the Statute, [the UNSC] urges**

[37] "Taking note of the existence of agreements referred to in Article 98-2 of the Rome Statute". UNSC Resolution 1593 (2005), p 1.

[38] Scheffer (2005), p 333.

all States and concerned regional and other international organizations to cooperate fully with the Court and the Prosecutor. [emphasis added][39]

8.6 The Temporal Jurisdiction of the ICC Pursuant to Article 13 (b) ICCRSt

The question of the temporal limitation of the ICC's jurisdiction over the cases it undertakes pursuant to a referral by the Security Council, in accordance with Article 13 (b) ICCRSt, remains open. Consequently, the referrals of the situation in Sudan and in Libya determine the starting point for the Court's jurisdiction but not its end. Indeed:

1. Resolution 1593 (2005) referring the situation in Libya to the ICC states that the Security Council "[d]ecides to refer the situation in Darfur since 1 July 2002 to the Prosecutor of the International Criminal Court".
2. Resolution 1970 (2011) referring the situation in Libya to the ICC states that the Security Council "[d]ecides to refer the situation in the Libyan Arab Jamahiriya since 15 February 2011 to the Prosecutor of the International Criminal Court".

Thus, even though the aforementioned excerpts specifically determine the starting time for the ICC's jurisdiction over the situation at hand, no mention, direct or indirect, is made to this day of its end point.[40]

It is worth noting that UNSC Resolution 1593, issued on 31 March 2005, referred the situation in Darfur "since 1 July 2002" to the ICC; pursuant to which the first arrest warrant against the President of Sudan, Omar Al-Bashir, for war crimes and crimes against humanity was issued in March 2009, i.e. 7 years after the entry into force of the Rome Statute and 4 years after the adoption of the Resolution.

Thus, through the adoption of the arrest warrant, ICC Pre-Trial Chamber I indirectly but clearly ruled that the ICC's jurisdiction *ratione temporis* over a state non-party pursuant to the aforementioned Resolution was "continuous", i.e. it even applied to actions committed a long time after its adoption, but also after its specified starting point. It must be noted that in the aforementioned situation, the ICC, without directly determining the temporal limits of its jurisdiction,[41] found that they extended to 14 July 2008, when the Prosecutor submitted the application for the arrest warrant against the President of Sudan. Paragraph 37 of the relevant decision states: "In relation to the jurisdiction *ratione loci* and *ratione temporis*, the Chamber recalls that the 31 March 2005 referral by the Security Council pursuant to article 13 (b) of the Statute and the 1 June 2005 Prosecution's decision to open an investigation pursuant to article 53(1) of the Statute define the territorial and temporal parameters

[39] UNSC Resolution 1970 (2011), para. 5.

[40] Schabas (2010), p 298.

[41] See also ICC (2009a).

of the Darfur situation encompassing the territory of the region of Darfur in Sudan [...] since 1 July 2002."[42]

It could therefore be argued that, since a situation is referred to the ICC by the Security Council, pursuant to Article 13 (b) ICCRSt and under Chap. VII of the UN Charter (Article 25 UN Charter), its "expiration point", if unstated, would be the moment when the grounds for the adoption of Chap. VII measures, i.e. "any threat to the peace, breach of the peace, or act of aggression",[43] cease to exist. Therefore, it is for the ICC to determine whether this particular threat to the peace, breach of the peace or act of aggression has ceased to exist, which means that the temporal parameters of the ICC's jurisdiction over a state non-party are potentially very broad and unclear.

Regarding the continuation of the ICC's jurisdiction following the issuance of the arrest warrants in question, it must be noted that, pursuant to UNSC Resolutions 1593 (2005) for Sudan and 1970 (2011) for Libya, arrest warrants against Ahmad Muhammad Harun, Ali Muhammad Ali Abd-Al-Rahman and the President of Sudan, Omar Hassan Ahmad Al Bashir, as well as against Saif al-Islam Gaddafi and Abdullah Al-Senussi of Libya may have been issued, but have yet to be executed. Therefore, one could argue that after those arrest warrants were issued, the validity if the Resolutions, and thus, the jurisdiction of the ICC is extended until their execution, i.e. until the accused "fully cooperate with the ICC".

However, this matter is obviously relevant to the application of the Resolutions in practice and not to the temporal parameters of the ICC's jurisdiction, which *de lege ferenda* must start on the day of the adoption of a Resolution by the Security Council and expire on the date a situation ceases to exist. This is the conclusion that emerges if one considers that in any other case, i.e. if the ICC's jurisdiction was to begin many years before the adoption of a UNSC Resolution, there could well be an impermissible retroactive application of a legal provision against a State that had chosen not to become party to the ICCRSt.[44] With regards to the expiration of the ICC's jurisdiction, that would necessarily have to remain in the Court's discretion, given that *inter alia*: (1) when a Resolution is adopted by the Security Council, the situation is still in progress; (2) such a situation, as for example a civil armed conflict, can be long-lasting.

On the other hand, one could argue that the referral of a situation to the ICC without an expiration date is legally problematic. The only solution to such a problem is the adoption of a new Resolution that could extend the duration of the first, although the use of a veto is always a concern during the adoption of UNSC

[42] ICC (2009b).

[43] Article 39 UN Charter.

[44] However, for practical reasons only, one could potentially allow for the ICC's temporal jurisdiction to begin a few days or even a few weeks before the adoption of a Resolution. Of course, from a strictly legal perspective even this view constitutes an impermissible retroactive application of the law, which could however be justified by force majeure concerns, given that it is humanly impossible to call a Security Council meeting within a few minutes or hours from the moment governments and state delegations are informed of a certain event.

Resolutions. In conclusion, one could also argue that the rules in place for the ad hoc referral of a situation to the ICC by a state non-party to the ICCRSt could also apply to UNSC referrals.

8.7 The ICC's Jurisdiction Pursuant to Article 13 (b) ICCRSt and the Principle of Complementarity

The State's obligation to cooperate with the ICC is linked to the principle of complementarity, according to which national courts are in the first place competent to adjudicate a case, with the ICC adjudicating a case as an *ultimum refugium* court only when "the State is unwilling or unable genuinely to carry out the investigation or prosecution" (Article 17(1)(a) ICCRSt).[45]

Nonetheless, at the same time, unlawfully and contrary to the purpose of this paragraph, the UN Security Council attempted to limit the ICC's jurisdiction, since in operative paragraph 6 of Resolution 1970, it decided that "nationals, current or former officials or personnel from a State outside the Libyan Arab Jamahiriya which is not a party to the Rome Statute of the International Criminal Court shall be subject to the exclusive jurisdiction of that State for all alleged acts or omissions arising out of or related to operations in the Libyan Arab Jamahiriya established or authorized by the Council, unless such exclusive jurisdiction has been expressly waived by the State". It is noteworthy that the same legal means to exclude certain persons from the ICC's jurisdiction was followed in Resolution 1693, which referred to the situation in Darfur.

In addition to the obvious misuse of the role and rights of the Security Council as stipulated in the ICCRSt, the aforementioned provision is problematic for other reasons as well. The Geneva Conventions impose on their contracting parties an obligation to "search for persons alleged to have committed, or to have ordered to be committed, such grave breaches, and shall bring such persons, regardless of their nationality, before its own courts".[46]

Given, then, that the Geneva Conventions are rightly recognised as substantive for international humanitarian law and, thus, as conventions that introduce *jus cogens* rules, any contrary provision found either in another international convention or in a Security Council Resolution must be considered void and inactive *ex tunc*.

---

[45] It is widely accepted that the principle of complementarity applies in cases when both the person and the charges brought before the ICC are the exact same as those brought before national courts.

[46] The First Geneva Convention for the Amelioration of the Condition of the Wounded and Sick in Armed Forces in the Field (1949) Article 49; the Second Geneva Convention for the Amelioration of the Condition of Wounded, Sick and Shipwrecked Members of Armed Forces at Sea (1949) Article 50; the Third Geneva Convention relative to the Treatment of Prisoners of War (1949) Article 129; the Fourth Geneva Convention relative to the Protection of Civilian Persons in Time of War (1949) Article 146.

Even the invocation of Article 103 UN Charter would not be sufficient to circumvent this state of affairs, as the article in question stipulates that "[i]n the event of a conflict between the obligations of the Members of the United Nations under the present Charter and their obligations under any other international agreement, their obligations under the present Charter shall prevail". Article 103 UN Charter cannot therefore prevail over *jus cogens* international law rules; also the exercise of UNSC powers in this way, i.e. introducing clear exceptions to the ICC's jurisdiction, is (1) a clear violation of the ICCRSt (and of *jus cogens* international law rules that one could argue are part of it); (2) completely circumvents the role of the Security Council as stipulated in Article 13 (b) ICCRSt;[47] and (3) is without doubt a misuse of power.

For these reasons, we must not be at all surprised by the statements of state representatives on the aforementioned issue during the discussions in the Security Council concerning Resolution 1593. The discussion that took place during this meeting is exceptionally important for four reasons:

1. First, because the situation in Darfur (Sudan) is the first situation to be referred to the ICC by the Security Council.
2. Second, because this referral was the first to include a provision aimed solely at unlawfully limiting the ICC's jurisdiction, a provision later included unaltered in the UNSC referral of the situation in Libya.
3. Third, because despite the adoption of this provision that unlawfully limits the ICC's jurisdiction, great powers such as the USA and China, who traditionally oppose the existence and role of the ICC, abstained from the vote in the case of Sudan;[48] but later, in the case of Libya, voted in favour of the referral—both because of the urgency of the situation and because their fears evaporated in light of the results of the Sudan referral.[49]
4. Fourth and most important of all for the purposes of the current analysis, because, as one can easily ascertain, the discussion concerning Resolution 1593 on the situation in Darfur (Sudan) was a thorough and multifaceted analysis by state representatives of the ICC's jurisdiction and attempts at obtaining exemptions from it. The depth of this discussion vastly differs from the brief discussion that took place the day that Resolution 1970 on the situation in Libya was adopted.[50]

Nonetheless, it is worth recalling at this point that even though operative paragraph 6 of Resolution 1970 unlawfully limits the ICC's jurisdiction, the previous paragraph 5 includes a special and explicit mention of the international organisations and

[47] Since the purpose of Article 13 (b) ICCRSt is to allow the ICC, after the adoption of a relevant UNSC Resolution, to exercise its jurisdiction over citizens of state non-parties to the Rome Statute, even for crimes committed on the territory of a state non-party. Derbal (2008), pp. 3–4.

[48] UNSC (2005), 5158th meeting.

[49] Security Council (2011), 66th year: 6491st meeting, Saturday, 26 February 2011.

[50] ibid. Undoubtedly, this discussion is much briefer because of the stance of powerful states on the matter of Libya and the urgency with which it was introduced for discussion in the Security Council.

neighbouring states involved that have no obligation under the ICCRSt to cooperate with the Court and the Prosecutor.[51]

This fact, in addition to the aforementioned analysis, reveals the hypocrisy of the Security Council, which on the one hand, wishes to present itself as a supporter of the administration of international criminal justice and a protector of human rights, while on the other (and despite criticism from some of its members) excludes from the Court's jurisdiction those individuals who are citizens of States that are in possession of great global power but have not even ratified the Rome Statute!

8.8 Final Conclusions on the Role of the Security Council in the Cases of Sudan and Libya

We studied extensively the role of the Security Council in the first referrals of situations in Sudan and Libya to the ICC under Chap. VII of the UN Charter. However, the Security Council's reasoning behind the two Resolutions it adopted does not accord with international law principles. On the contrary, by selectively exercising its powers, the Security Council attempted to lay the foundations for a new hegemonic justice on an international level, under which the sovereign's subjects would be made an example of, while his enforcers will remain "lawfully" unpunished, protected by an unprecedented legal labyrinth of exceptions, which will introduce once more the old principle of victor's justice.

This fact is of course extremely harmful to the ICC's credibility in a way that is beyond the Court's control, and in any case constitutes an approach that it should neither approve of nor share. In an ideal world, the ICC's Prosecutor and judges would find the UNSC Resolution in question invalid in part, i.e. at least with regard to those provisions that introduce selective exceptions to the ICC's jurisdiction over situations in state non-parties to the ICCRSt and their own citizens.

What is more, in the ideal world of *de lege ferenda*, the ICC Prosecutor and judges would initially examine thoroughly the reasons behind the Security Council's arbitrariness, as well as the crucial events and circumstances that led to the adoption of Resolutions with selective and arbitrary provisions. Subsequently, they would proceed with the judicial investigation of those events, prosecuting suspects who are citizens of the hegemonic powers that the aforementioned provisions seek to protect.

---

[51] The terminology used here includes the Prosecutor, as he is one of the Organs of the Court. Article 34 ICCRSt—Organs of the Court: The Court shall be composed of the following organs:

1. The Presidency;
2. An Appeals Division, a Trial Division and a Pre-Trial Division;
3. The Office of the Prosecutor;
4. The Registry.

If, however, the adoption of the Rome Statute is the *Magna Carta* of international criminal law, then I am afraid that we must wait a while before we can see a sitting global leader and his followers stand trial.

References

Books

Cryer R et al (2010) An introduction to international criminal law and procedure. CUP

Hatzikonstantinou K (2005) Preemptive war or the misrepresentation of reason. Papazisi Publications

Schabas WA (2010) The International Criminal Court: a commentary on the Rome Statute. CUP

Articles/Papers

Deen T (2013) Sudan's "Wanted" President Skips U.N. General Assembly. Available at IPSnews, http://www.ipsnews.net/2013/09/Sudans-Wanted-President-Skips-U-N-General-Assembly/. Accessed 8 June 2023

Derbal A (2008) The ICC's involvement in the situation in darfur: not a threat to Peace University of Notre Dame, Center for Civil and Human Rights, Working Paper No. 1, pp 3–4

Gaddafi Son's Libya Trial to Be Delayed by Five Months, Available at Reuters, London, https://www.reuters.com/article/us-libya-saif-trial/gaddafi-sons-libya-trial-to-be-delayed-by-five-months-official-idUSBRE8880F720120909. Accessed 8 June 2023

Sangroula Y (2010) International Treaties: features and importance from international law perspective 2. https://doi.org/10.2139/ssrn.2359978. Accessed 8 June 2023

Scheffer D (2005) Article 98(2) of the Rome Statute: America's Original Intent. JICJ 3:333. https://www.researchgate.net/publication/30955411_Article_982_of_the_Rome_Statute_America's_Original_Intent. Accessed 8 June 2023

Websites/Web Sources

CNN (2009) Sudan orders aid agency expulsions, http://edition.cnn.com/2009/WORLD/africa/03/04/sudan.expel/. Accessed 8 June 2023

ICC (2009a) Bahr Idriss Abu Garda, Decision on the Prosecutor's Application under Article 58 (Public Redacted version), ICC-02/05-02/09, para 2, https://www.icc-cpi.int/CourtRecords/CR2009_03857.PDF. Accessed 8 June 2023

ICC (2009b) Decision on the Prosecution's Application for a Warrant of Arrest against Omar Hassan Ahmad Al Bashir (Public Redacted Version), ICC-02/05-01/09, para. 37, https://www.icc-cpi.int/CourtRecords/CR2009_01517.PDF. Accessed 8 June 2023

ICC (2011a) Pre-Trial Chamber I, Warrant of Arrest for Saif Al-Islam Gaddafi (ICC-01/11), https://www.icc-cpi.int/CourtRecords/CR2011_08353.PDF. Accessed 8 June 2023

ICC (2011b) Pre-Trial Chamber I, (ICC-01/11-01/11), https://www.icc-cpi.int/CourtRecords/CR2011_08694.PDF. Accessed 8 June 2023

Security Council (2005), New York (S/PV.5158), https://digitallibrary.un.org/record/544860?ln=en. Accessed 8 June 2023

Security Council (2011) New York (S/PV.6491), http://www.un.org/en/ga/search/view_doc.asp?symbol=S/PV.6491. Accessed 8 June 2023

Sudan Tribune (2013) Sudanese President challenges US to deny his visa request or arrest him. http://www.sudantribune.com/spip.php?article48143. Accessed 8 June 2023

UN Charter (1945) Article 2(4), http://www.un.org/en/sections/un-charter/un-charter-full-text/. Accessed 8 June 2023

UNSC (2005) S/PV.5158. http://www.un.org/ga/search/view_doc.asp?symbol=S/PV.5158. Accessed 8 June 2023

UNSC Resolution 1593 (2005) UNSC Doc. SC/RES/1593, https://www.icc-cpi.int/nr/rdonlyres/85febd1a-29f8-4ec4-9566-48edf55cc587/283244/n0529273.pdf. Accessed 8 June 2023

UNSC Resolution 1970 (2011) UNSC Doc. SC/RES/1970, http://unscr.com/en/resolutions/doc/1970. Accessed 8 June 2023

Chapter 9
The Awakening Hypothesis of the Complementarity Principle

Abstract The principle of complementarity described in the ICC Rome Statute is often taken for granted in the legal analysis of international criminal law and its jurisprudence. Indeed, apart from William Schabas and his monumental paper "'Complementarity in Practice': Some Uncomplimentary Thoughts", very few have ever questioned it. However, closer examination proves that the complementarity principle was a mere shadow without any flesh and bones whatsoever, at least—arguably—until the Abdullah Al-Senussi case. Hence, the 'awakening hypothesis' of the complementarity principle first examines the myth of the complementarity principle and the fact that it was never actually enforced until October 2013. Thereafter analysis follows of the reasoning of the two Abdullah Al-Senussi judgments (Pre-Trial and Appeals Chamber). Finally, Victor Tsilonis'awakening hypothesis regarding the complementarity principle raises the question of whether the Al-Senussi case truly represents the first instance of enforcing this principle. This consideration does not overlook the fact that, since these two judgments the ICC Prosecutor at that time, Fatou Bensouda, consistently affirmed the Court's adherence to the complementarity principle, at least rhetorically.

9.1 Introduction

It is considered essential for any true legal system to function on fundamental principles, which are reflected in the first place in its legislation. Some of these principles may be of the utmost importance, others less so; nonetheless they are all considered to be inviolable and perform a legitimizing function *par excellence*—apart from in the case of specific exceptions that may be prescribed in existing provisions or arise during the evolution of case law. This concluding chapter addresses significant issues concerning the application of the complementarity principle contained in the sixth and tenth paragraphs of the Preamble and in Article

V. Tsilonis, *The Jurisdiction of the International Criminal Court*,
https://doi.org/10.1007/978-3-031-46138-5_9

1 ICCRSt; and especially—albeit indirectly—in Article 17 ICCRSt entitled "Issues of admissibility"[1] as well as indirectly in Article 20(3) ICCRSt (*ne bis in idem*).[2]

The complementarity principle means that the jurisdiction of the ICC is activated only in the form of a reserve parachute in case the original 'parachute', i.e. the national jurisdiction, fails to perform its duty effectively and directly.[3,4] In other words, the ICC's impetus to act can be halted by the states parties' judicial systems, so long as the latter demonstrate the characteristics of a functional legal system and adequate willingness to prosecute war crimes, genocide, crimes against humanity and, possibly, the crime of aggression.[5]

[1] The forerunner of Article 17 ICCRSt was an article which was approved by the International Law Commission and entitled "Issues of admissibility". Draft Statute for an International Criminal Court, 1994: Article 35—Issues of admissibility: The Court may, on application by the accused or at the request of an interested State at any time prior to the commencement of the trial, or of its own motion, decide, having regard to the purposes of this Statute set out in the preamble, that a case before it is inadmissible on the ground that the crime in question: (a) has been duly investigated by a State with jurisdiction over it, and the decision of that State not to proceed to a prosecution is apparently well-founded; (b) is under investigation by a State which has or may have jurisdiction over it, and there is no reason for the Court to take any further action for the time being with respect to the crime; or (c) is not of such gravity to justify further action by the Court. http://legal.un.org/ilc/texts/instruments/english/draft%20articles/7_4_1994.pdf, last accessed 8 June 2023.

[2] Article 20 ICCRSt—Ne bis in idem… **3.** No person who has been tried by another court for conduct also proscribed under article 6. 7 or 8 shall be tried by the Court with respect to the same conduct unless the proceedings in the other court: (a) Were for the purpose of shielding the person concerned from criminal responsibility for crimes within the jurisdiction of the Court: or (b) Otherwise were not conducted independently or impartially in accordance with the norms of due process recognized by international law and were conducted in a manner which, in the circumstances, was inconsistent with an intent to bring the person concerned to justice.

[3] Although the Article 17 ICCRSt refers to the case of "a state" (state party, according to this author's view) being "unwilling" or "unable" but not inactive, this phrasing has not been interpreted to mean that a case is inadmissible before the ICC when a state is inactive, without being unwilling or unable, as a strictly grammatical interpretation of Article 17 ICCRSt would imply. In the case of Lubanga the Pre-Trial Chamber I noted that: The first part of the test relates to national investigations, prosecutions and trials concerning the case at hand insofar as such case would be admissible only if those States with jurisdiction over it have remained inactive in relation to that case or are unwilling or unable, within the meaning of article 17 (1) (a) to (c), 2 and 3 of the Statute. ICC, Decision concerning Pre-Trial Chamber I's Decision of 10 February 2006 and the Incorporation of Documents into the Record of the Case against Mr. Thomas Lubanga Dyilo, ICC-01/04-01/06-8-US-Corr 09-03-2006, ibid. p 19, para 29, (emphasis added).

[4] Kastanidou-Symeonidou (2003), p 452.

[5] After the 2010 Kampala conference, only 15 states eventually followed the path set out by Liechtenstein and ratified the articles 8bis, 15bis and 15ter which activate the ICC jurisdiction on the crime of aggression. See official list of states: https://treaties.un.org/Pages/ViewDetails.aspx?src=TREATY&mtdsg_no=XVIII-10-b&chapter=18&lang=en, last accessed 8 June 2023. According to the data provided by the official campaign launched for the ratification of the amendment, 36 states including Greece are currently examining the ratification of the crime of aggression: http://crimeofaggression.info/the-role-of-states/status-of-ratification-and-implementation/, last accessed 8 June 2023. Press release 09-05-2012: https://asp.icc-cpi.int/en_menus/asp/press%20releases/press%20releases%202012/Pages/pr793.aspx, last accessed 8 June 2023. The ICC can exert its jurisdiction for the crime of aggression as soon as 30 states parties ratify the

In effect, however, the complementarity principle had yet to be applied until recently, namely in the recent decision on the case against Al-Senussi in October 2013. It is a fact that even since the first ICC case, which concerned the recruitment of minors as soldiers by Thomas Lubanga Dyilo, the competent ICC Trial Chamber (following the Office of the Prosecutor's submission) has ruled against the application of the complementarity principle so that the Thomas Lubanga Dyilo trial could proceed in the first place.[6,7]

9.2 About the Principle of Complementarity and Its Relation to ICC Jurisdiction

Undoubtedly, the complementarity principle has constituted a novel concept for international criminal law[8] ever since it was formulated in Rome in 1998 during the final drafting of the ICC Rome Statute.[9] Up until then—as the decisions of earlier international criminal tribunals (predominantly the ICTY and ICTR) show—any responses to international crimes had limited temporal and territorial jurisdiction that

amendment and a two-thirds majority decision of states parties is taken at a Review Conference no sooner than 1 January 2017. However, until the amendment is accepted by seven-eighths of states parties, the ICC will be unable to exercise its jurisdiction regarding a crime of aggression committed by citizens of a state party which has not accepted the amendment or committed on the territory of such a state party. See Articles 15ter (2) and (3), 121 (3), (5) and (6), https://www.icc-cpi.int/nr/rdonlyres/add16852-aee9-4757-abe7-9cdc7cf02886/283503/romestatuteng1.pdf, last accessed 8 June 2023.

[6] Tsilonis (2010), pp. 1039–1057.

[7] The whole debate in the 2010 Review Conference of the Rome Statute in Kampala, as well as the stocktaking exercise that took place during the Conference in question had no practical impact whatsoever on the ICC policy change at that time nor, as evidently proven today, 3 years later. For an extremely optimistic review see Bergsmo et al. (2010), p 791–811.

[8] Although its ideological roots may be traced back to Article 6 in the London Agreement of 8 August 1945 (which led to the founding of IMT), http://avalon.law.yale.edu/imt/imtchart.asp, last accessed 8 June 2023, where it is stated: "Nothing in this Agreement shall prejudice the jurisdiction or the powers of any national or occupation court established or to be established in any allied territory or in Germany for the trial of war criminals." However, the IMT tried only 22 of the accused due to the allies' lack of political will and lack of resources and not because of the "role of criminal jurisdiction". See contra Zeidy (2003), p 869.

[9] The final text of paragraph 6 in the Preamble derives largely from the "Dominican Republic: Proposal Regarding the Preamble", which initially referred to the fact that the Statute's states parties were "Being prepared to strengthen the United Nations system harmoniously with a permanent international criminal court which, complementary to national jurisdictions, will have jurisdiction over those crimes which are of concern to international society as a whole." Dominican Republic: Proposal Regarding the Preamble, UN Doc. A/CONF.183/C.1/L.52, 203, https://www.dropbox.com/s/z1gc07v13ofb34o/Proposal%20Submitted%20by%20the%20Dominican%20Republic.pdf?dl=0, last accessed 8 June 2023.

was exerted on the basis of the 'reverse' principle of primacy over national jurisdictions.[10,11]

The complementarity principle was initially included in the ICC Rome Statute three times: (a) verbally in a way that resembles *reductio ad absurdum* the sixth paragraph of the Preamble of the ICC Rome Statute,[12] (b) expressly in the tenth paragraph of the Preamble of ICC Rome Statute,[13] and (c) expressly in Article 1 ICCRSt, where it is mentioned that the ICC "shall be supplementary to the national criminal courts' jurisdictions". Nonetheless, no clear definition of the unprecedented complementarity principle is indicated in any of the aforementioned passages, therefore its practical application is regulated: (1) in Article 17 ICCRSt entitled "Issues of admissibility",[14] (2) indirectly in Article 20(3) ICCRSt, which refers to the fundamental legal principle *ne bis in idem*.[15] This has been accepted by the ICC Appeals Chamber, which acknowledged the existence of the complementarity principle in Article 17 ICCRSt in subsections (a) and (b) of Article 17(1) ICCRSt.[16]

---

[10] Article 9 (2) ICTY Statute and Article 8 (2) ICTR Statute, where it is expressly stated that "the International Tribunal shall have primacy over national jurisdictions".

[11] On the contrary, Article 1 (2) and (3) of the Special Court for Sierra Leone (SCSL) Statute similarly recognizes the complementarity principle: Article 1—Competence of the Special Court: [...] **2.** Any transgressions by peacekeepers and related personnel present in Sierra Leone pursuant to the Status of Mission Agreement in force between the United Nations and the Government of Sierra Leone or agreements between Sierra Leone and other Governments [...] shall be within the primary jurisdiction of the sending State. **3.** In the event the sending State is unwilling or unable genuinely to carry out an investigation or prosecution, the Court may, if authorized by the Security Council on the proposal of any State, exercise jurisdiction over such persons, http://www.rscsl.org/Documents/scsl-statute.pdf, last accessed 8 June 2023.

[12] "Recalling that it is the duty of every State to exercise its criminal jurisdiction over those responsible for international crimes", paragraph 6 of the ICCRSt Preamble.

[13] "Emphasizing that the international Criminal Court established under this Statute shall be complementary to national criminal jurisdictions", paragraph 10 of the ICCRSt Preamble.

[14] Article 17 ICCRSt—Issues of Admissibility: 1. Having regard to para 10 of the Preamble and article 1, the Court shall determine that a case is inadmissible where: (a) The case is being investigated or prosecuted by a State which has jurisdiction over it, unless the State is unwilling or unable genuinely to carry out the investigation or prosecution; (b) The case has been investigated by a State which has jurisdiction over it and the State has decided not to prosecute the person concerned, unless the decision resulted from the unwillingness or inability of the State genuinely to prosecute; (c) The person concerned has already been tried for conduct which is the subject of the complaint, and a trial by the Court is not permitted under Article 20, para 3; (d) The case is not of sufficient gravity to justify further action by the Court.

[15] Article 20 ICCRSt Ne bis in idem: No person who has been tried by another court for conduct also proscribed under article 6, 7 or 8 shall be tried by the Court with respect to the same conduct unless the proceedings in the other court: (a) Were for the purpose of shielding the person concerned from criminal responsibility for crimes within the jurisdiction of the Court: or (b) Otherwise were not conducted independently or impartially in accordance with the norms of due process recognized by international law and were conducted in a manner which, in the circumstances, was inconsistent with an intent to bring the person concerned to justice.

[16] The Statute itself imposes obstacles upon the Court's exercising jurisdiction, as stated in Article 17, referring firstly to complementarity (Article 17(1)(a) to (b)), secondly to ne bis in idem principle

Nevertheless, it is clearly indicated that the complementarity principle also includes—in addition to subsections (a) and (b)—a third subsection (c) in Article 17(1) ICCRSt, which summarily refers to the principle *ne bis in idem* (which is further analysed in Article 20 ICCRSt). All three subsections regulate the ICC's power to evaluate the judicial authorities' jurisdiction over the primary State in regard to its own officially supplementary jurisdiction. Consequently, the first subsection of Article 17(1) ICCRSt refers to cases under investigation or prosecution by a State which has jurisdiction over them; the second subsection of Article 17(1) ICCRSt refers to cases that have been investigated by a State having jurisdiction over them, *but* has ruled against prosecution; and the third subsection of Article 17(1) ICCRSt refers to cases of a State that has already tried the accused in question for the conduct that constitutes the specific subject of the charges.[17]

However, according to another, slightly different view, the issues of admissibility involve backing down from exerting jurisdiction. In other words, the ICC may have jurisdiction over one case but, for reasons exemplified in Article 17 ICCRSt the ICC, finally decide it has no right to exert it.[18] Hence, following this train of thought, one could argue that if Articles 11–15 ICCRSt refer to the ICC's *original jurisdiction*, then Article 17 ICCRSt regulates the ICC's *eventual jurisdiction*.

Consequently, Article 17(1) ICCRSt includes three *ab initio* identifiable standards[19] which regulate the ICC's *final jurisdiction*: (1) the first two subsections involve the application or not of the complementarity principle, following certain actions and decisions of a member state's judicial system; (2) the third subsection involves the application of the fundamental principle *ne bis in idem*; and (3) the fourth and final subsection involves the evaluation of the case's gravity.

Although Article 17(1) ICCRSt sets the criteria that must be examined (first, complementarity, second, *ne bis in idem* and third, the gravity standard), it does not expressly clarify in which order the criteria are to be examined. However, it seems that the Prosecutor selected the reverse order, examining the gravity standard first. This can be proven by a letter sent at the beginning of 2006 concerning the situation in Iraq, where it is mentioned: "Taking into account all the considerations, the situation did not appear to meet the required threshold of the Statute. In light of the conclusion reached on gravity, it was unnecessary to reach a conclusion on

(Articles 17(1)(c), 20) and thirdly to the sufficient gravity of the crime (Article 17(1)(d)). The existence of any of the aforementioned obstacles, listed in article 17, makes the case inadmissible. ICC, Prosecutor v. Thomas Lubanga Dyilo, Judgment on the Appeal of Mr. Thomas Lubanga Dyilo against the Decision on the Defence Challenge to the Jurisdiction of the Court pursuant to Article 19 (2)(a) of the Statute of 3 October 2006, ICC–01/04–01/06–772, 14 December 2006, para. 23, http://www.icc-cpi.int/iccdocs/doc/doc243774.pdf, last accessed 8 June 2023.

[17] Rastan (2010), pp. 84, fn 2.

[18] Schabas (2010), p 340.

[19] See previous analysis for the indirect connection between complementarity and ne bis in idem principle.

complementarity."[20] However, Pre-Trial Chamber I had a different opinion, since it considered the issue of whether or not the complementarity principle was to be applied in Thomas Lubanga Dyilo's case as "the first part of the examination of admissibility"[21] and the gravity standard as "the second part of the examination of admissibility".[22]

Nevertheless, although the issues of admissibility raised on the basis of ICC Rome Statute are directly linked to the determination of situations where there is reasonable basis to proceed with an investigation,[23] Article 17 ICCRSt is essentially triggered only when an individual case has been considered. According to ICC case law, a case comprises "specific incidents during which one or more crimes within the jurisdiction of the Court seem to have been committed by one or more identified suspects",[24] while it has also been argued by academics that "a case must always be linked to an incident-specific conduct for the purpose of the complementarity provisions of the Rome Statute".[25]

Based on a narrow interpretation of the Article 17(1) (a) ICCRSt provision, it has been widely argued that the complementarity principle should be applied in any case when any State investigates a criminal case, i.e. regardless or whether or not it has ratified the Rome Statute.[26] This view, which adheres to the strictest grammatical interpretation of Article 17(1)(a) ICCRSt, construes "the case [. . .] investigated or

---

[20]Letter of Prosecutor, 9 February 2006, http://www.iccnow.org/documents/OTP_letter_to_senders_re_Iraq_9_February_2006.pdf, last accessed 8 June 2023.

[21]Pre-Trial Chamber I drew a legal distinction between the terms "situation" and "case" as follows: "The Chamber considers that the Statute, the Rules of Procedure and Evidence and the Regulations of the Court draw a distinction between situations and cases in terms of the different kinds of proceedings, initiated by any organ of the Court, that they entail. **Situations**, which are generally defined in terms of temporal, territorial and in some cases personal parameters, such as the situation in the territory of the Democratic Republic of the Congo since 1 July 2002, entail the proceedings envisaged in the Statute to determine whether a particular situation should give rise to a criminal investigation as well as the investigation as such. Cases, which comprise specific incidents during which one or more crimes within the jurisdiction of the Court seem to have been committed by one or more identified suspects, entail proceedings that take place after the issuance of a warrant of arrest or a summons to appear." ICC, Situation in the Democratic Republic of Congo, Decision on the Applications for Participation in the Proceedings of VPRS1, VPRS2, VPRS3, VPRS4, VPRS5 and VPRS6, para 65, (emphasis added), http://www.icc-cpi.int/iccdocs/doc/doc183441.pdf, last accessed 8 June 2023.

ICC, Decision concerning Pre-Trial Chamber I's Decision of 10 February 2006 and the Incorporation of Documents into the Record of the Case against Mr. Thomas Lubanga Dyilo, ICC-01/04-01/06-8-US-Corr 09-03-2006, 20, para. 30, http://www.icc-cpi.int/iccdocs/doc/doc236260.PDF, last accessed 8 June 2023.

[22]ibid. 19, para 29 and 24, para 41.

[23]Arts 15 (3) and 53 (1) ICCRSt.

[24]Situation in the Democratic Republic of Congo, Decision on the Applications for Participation in the Proceedings of VPRS1, VPRS2, VPRS3, VPRS4, VPRS5 and VPR-6, para 65, (emphasis added), http://www.icc-cpi.int/iccdocs/doc/doc183441.pdf, last accessed 8 June 2023.

[25]Rastan (2008), p 438.

[26]Schabas (2010), pp. 340–341.

prosecuted by a State which has jurisdiction over it" not as a case being investigated or prosecuted by a state party of the Rome Statute, but potentially as a case being investigated or prosecuted by any State in the world, i.e. even by a State which is not a member of the UN. But in this case, the question is whether or not such an interpretation could substantially damage the ICC to the extent that any leading State could employ the Rome Statute provisions to advance their own national interests, while abstaining from the Rome Statute's ratification and opposing the ICC's legal function.

However, it is evident that when the international legislators drafted the Rome Statute, they actually intended via Article 17 to give priority to the States that would ratify the Statute and not every State in the world. This conclusion is supported by four distinct views: (1) *the historical point of view*, i.e. referencing previous examples of the international criminal tribunals (especially the ICTY and ICTR, where the reverse principle of primacy was in force); (2) *the functional point of view* (since such a wide interpretation could severely complicate the jurisdictional issues and largely obstruct the ICC's work);[27] (3) *the general interpretive point of view* (since Article 17 ICCRSt has not been interpreted by the ICC in its strictest grammatical sense, as demonstrated by the fact that the ICC can try a case even when a State does not investigate it despite being neither unwilling nor unable to do so); and (4) *the teleological point of view* (since the content and principles of the Rome Statute dialectically determine how the Court's relationship to the states parties develops).

9.3 The Complementarity Principle 'In Practice'

In addition to the foregoing analysis of the complementarity principle, we must consider the way the principle has been addressed by the Office of the Prosecutor and judges of ICC.

A typical example is Luis Moreno Ocampo who, upon being sworn in as Chief Prosecutor of the ICC in June 2003, stated:

> Interdependence is also requested by the complementary nature of the Court. The Court is complementary to national systems. This means that whenever there is genuine State action, the Court cannot and will not intervene. As a consequence of complementarity, the number of cases that reach the Court should not be a measure of its efficiency. On the contrary, the absence of trials before this Court, as a consequence of the regular functioning of national institutions, would be a major success. For this reason, the first task of the Office of the Prosecutor will be to establish links with prosecutors and judges from all over the world. They continue to bear primary responsibility for investigating and prosecuting the crimes within the jurisdiction of the Court [. . .][28]

[27] Benvenuti (1999), pp. 21–50; Holmes (1999), p 67.

[28] Moreno-Ocampo (2003).

Nevertheless, 3 months later, on September 2003, in the official document entitled "Paper on Some Policy Issues Before the Office of the Prosecutor"[29] (the finalized version was completed after a public meeting that took place on 17 and 18 June in The Hague), the first official position of the Office of the Prosecutor of the ICC was publicised regarding the application of the complementarity principle.

This paper, which came to the attention of the academic community only several years after its publication,[30] raises the following issues concerning the application of the complementarity principle.

9.4 National Jurisdictions and the Office of the ICC Prosecutor: the Selection of Jurisdiction

It is explicitly stated on the second page of the paper that "national investigations and prosecutions, where they can be undertaken, will normally be the most effective and efficient means of bringing offenders to justice; States themselves will normally have the best access to evidence and witnesses. To the extent possible the Prosecutor will encourage States to initiate their own proceedings".[31] Yet in the next paragraph of the same page one reads: "Close co-operation between the Office of the Prosecutor and all parties concerned will be needed to determine which forum may be the most appropriate to take jurisdiction in certain cases, in particular where there are many States with concurrent jurisdiction, and where the Prosecutor is already investigating certain cases within a given situation."[32]

This raises the question about the way the Court's competency will be determined in order to exert jurisdiction in the aforementioned 'certain cases'. The question is answered in the second paragraph of the third page of the paper.

[29] ICC-OTP, Paper on Some Policy Issues Before the Office of the Prosecutor, http://www.icc-cpi.int/nr/rdonlyres/1fa7c4c6-de5f-42b7-8b25-60aa962ed8b6/143594/030905policy_paper.pdf, last accessed 8 June 2023.

[30] Schabas (2008b), pp. 5–33.

[31] ICC-OTP, Paper on Some Policy Issues Before the Office of the Prosecutor, p. 2, http://www.icc-cpi.int/nr/rdonlyres/1fa7c4c6-de5f-42b7-8b25-60aa962ed8b6/143594/030905policy_paper.pdf, last accessed 8 June 2023.

[32] ibid. It should be remembered here that the term 'situation' used in the ICC Rome Statute refers to the investigation of a case in a wider or narrower geographical region, which could include one part of a single State (e.g. Sudan) or territories of several States.

9.5 The Two-Tiered Approach to Cases by the Office of the Prosecutor

Following a reference to the ICC's limited resources, in the second paragraph of the third page of the paper it is stated that "the Office will function with a two-tiered approach to combat impunity. On the one hand it will initiate prosecutions of the leaders who bear most responsibility for the crimes. On the other hand it will encourage national prosecutions, where possible, for the lower-ranking perpetrators, or work with the international community to ensure that the offenders are brought to justice by some other means".[33]

The use of the phrase 'some other means', via which lower-ranking perpetrators will be brought to justice, is nebulous but not of crucial significance. Nonetheless, the two-tiered approach to cases that the Office of the Prosecutor adopts from the outset is of great importance and constitutes *the first evidence of this scholar's awakening hypothesis of the complementarity principle.* The introduction of a two-tiered system facilitates the distinction between higher-ranking and lower-ranking perpetrators, according to which the higher-ranking perpetrators will come under the ICC's jurisdiction and the lower-ranking perpetrators under that of the national courts.

However, the aforementioned strategy adopted by the Office of the Prosecutor, which was largely accepted by the ICC up to October 2013, manifests the 'reverse' interpretation and practical application of the complementarity principle, which collides with the historical, grammatical, teleological or any other sincere and objective interpretation of the principle as described in the Preamble and Articles 1, 17 and indirectly 20 of the ICC Rome Statute. At this point, it must be clarified that the grounds on which the Office of the Prosecutor distinguishes between major and minor cases, so that the major ones can initially be investigated by the Office of the Prosecutor and the rest by the state parties, are in no way related to the gravity of a case (Article 17 (1)(d) ICCRSt), to which no direct or indirect reference is made; hence any subsequent invocation could only be considered a sophism.[34]

[33] ibid, 3.

[34] There is a reference to the gravity criterion on page 7 of the Paper, where it is stated that "Article 17, dealing with admissibility, adds to the complementarity grounds one related to the gravity of a case. It states that the Court (which includes the Office of the Prosecutor) shall determine that a case is inadmissible where 'the case is not of sufficient gravity to justify further action by the Court'. The concept of gravity should not be exclusively attached to the act that constitutes the crime but also to the degree of participation in its commission". ibid, 4.

9.6 The Complementary Nature of the ICC

Nevertheless, it must be noted that on the fourth page of the paper entitled "The Complementary Nature of the Court", efforts are made to mitigate or even circumvent the aforementioned conclusions. This is initially achieved through the repetition of the statement that the absence of trials would constitute a major success *for the* ICC, and then—after an explicit reference both to the principle of complementarity and the 'fact' that the ICC, in contrast to the ICTY and ICTR, is not intended to replace national courts—through the statement that the ICC should operate when national authorities/courts are unwilling or unable to conduct investigations and prosecutions.[35] Furthermore, it is noted in the paper that the Prosecutor must first assess whether national systems are already exercising or could exercise jurisdiction with respect to particular crimes that come under the jurisdiction of the Court.[36]

Nevertheless, the fifth page of the paper stipulates that the Court and an incapacitated state party may agree that "a consensual division of labour is the most logical and effective approach",[37] given that "groups bitterly divided by conflict may oppose prosecutions at each others' hands and yet agree to a prosecution by a Court perceived as neutral and impartial. There may also be cases where a third State has extra-territorial jurisdiction, but all interested parties agree that the Court has developed superior evidence and expertise relating to that situation, making the Court the more effective forum. In such cases there will be no question of 'unwillingness' or 'inability' under article 17″.[38]

Moreover, Article 17 ICCRSt neither foresees nor implies that: (1) there is a possibility of an internal agreement between the Court and a state party concerning jurisdiction issues and especially the investigation/trial of a case; (2) there are assignments of judicial investigation and trial processes between the Court and a state party by means of an unofficial or official agreement of both parties; (3) the state parties will permit the ICC to exercise jurisdiction, since the ICC is considered objective and neutral;[39] or (4) the state parties will permit the ICC to exercise jurisdiction on the basis that the ICC has developed advanced know-how when it comes to collecting evidence and trying certain cases.

---

[35] ibid.

[36] ibid.

[37] ibid, 5.

[38] ICC-OTP, Paper on Some Policy Issues Before the Office of the Prosecutor, 5, http://www.icc-cpi.int/nr/rdonlyres/1fa7c4c6-de5f-42b7-8b25-60aa962ed8b6/143594/030905policy_paper.pdf, last accessed 8 June 2023.

[39] Of course, this has no application either in law or in reality, since in recent years there have been objections made concerning what is perceived to be a "prejudiced court" by several States and the African Union, which consists of 54 States.

9.7 The Hypothesis of the Complementarity Principle as a Dead Letter

The attitude of the Office of the Prosecutor—including the *ab initio* position it expressed in 2003 and its manifest intention to exercise its powers *ultra vires* between 2003 and now—reflects an arbitrary interpretation of the complementarity principle. As William Schabas, who has profound knowledge of the ICC legal framework and relevant political processes, emphasises: "Yet from the beginning of the work of the International Criminal Court, the main efforts appear to have been aimed at attracting cases for prosecution rather than insisting that States fulfil their obligations."[40]

It is noteworthy that before Luis Moreno Ocampo took up office as the first ICC Prosecutor, the Office of the Prosecutor—which had already commenced its operations without a head of office[41]—had assigned specialists to undertake a study on the legal issue of complementarity. The paper, written by 12 acclaimed jurists, attempted to lay the foundations for the interpretation of the complementarity principle as a dead letter rather than a substantive principle. The 12 renowned jurists attempted—by defining and using terms such as 'partnership', 'vigilance', 'dialogue with States' and 'division of labour'—to demarcate the desire of the ICC for a new 'productive' relationship with the state parties.

For instance, it is mentioned in the paper that the term partnership "highlights the fact that the relationship with States that are genuinely investigating and prosecuting can and should be a positive, constructive one. The Prosecutor can [. . .] encourage the State concerned to initiate national proceedings [. . .] and possibly provide advice and certain forms of assistance to facilitate national efforts. There may also be situations where the Office of the Prosecutor (OTP) and the State concerned agree that a consensual division of labour is in the best interests of justice; for example, where a conflict-torn State is unable to carry out effective proceedings against persons most responsible."[42]

Furthermore, 'vigilance' was defined—with reference to the principle of the ICC's partnership with state parties—mostly in terms of the Prosecutor's duty to gather information and data in order to verify that national procedures are genuinely carried out. Should the latter prove not to be the case then the Prosecutor must be poised to take follow-up steps, leading if necessary to an exercise of jurisdiction.[43]

Moreover, apart from the initial definition of partnership, which in cases established as being inadmissible under the Statute is considered as the "consensual division of labour" between the Office of the Prosecutor and the ICC, another legal dissonance emanates from the legal text.

[40] Schabas (2008b), p 6.

[41] The specialists' study was conducted following the decision of the Director of the ICC Common Services at the time, Bruno Cathala. See: Cassese A et al. (2009).

[42] ibid, 3–4.

[43] ibid, 4.

In paragraph 9 entitled "Judicial Institutions", the 12 specialists argued that while Article 17 ICCRSt states that a case is inadmissible when "the case is being investigated or prosecuted by a State which has jurisdiction over it",[44] the OTP should as a matter of policy[45] "be prepared to adopt a similar approach as in respect of ICTY, the ICTR, hybrid tribunals as the Sierra Leone Special Court, courts and tribunals of UN administered territories and other such courts"![46]

Nevertheless, the adjudication of the 12 jurists on this issue, which is related to the complementarity principle, is apparently political and not legal. However, on a legal basis: (1) it is unjustified; (2) it proceeds to an overtly broad interpretation that equates *ad hoc* criminal tribunals with states parties, clearly contradicting the preparatory proceedings that led to the enactment of the ICC Rome Statute, or the ICC Rome Statute itself or any other legal document; and (3) it gives priority to tribunals rather than to the ICC, whether those that exist and function today or those that may be created in the future. Nonetheless, ad hoc or hybrid tribunals have a temporally and regionally restricted jurisdiction and their efficacy in all this—including their judicial priority over the ICC, which is equivalent to that typically possessed by states parties (and which by the way the 12 jurists practically negate with their analysis later on)—is not based on the ICC Rome Statute, cannot be legally substantiated and cannot be reconciled with the ICC's enacted jurisdiction.

Furthermore, the third and likely most significant dissonance arises in the fourth chapter of the paper, under the title "Special Issues" and the imaginative subtitle "Uncontested Admissibility and Consensual Sharing of Labour".[47] Undeniably, an ambitious goal of this chapter is to highlight those cases where the admissibility issue of a case brought before the ICC would undisputedly be positively judged, given that "none of the criteria of Article 17(1)(a)-(c) are satisfied" and "thus, even if a challenge were raised, the outcome would be clear".[48]

Therefore, bearing in mind the aforementioned context, the next page of the paper and particularly paragraph 61 entitled "Appropriate Circumstances for Burden-sharing" includes the following remarks:

> There may also be situations where *the appropriate course of action is for a State concerned not to exercise jurisdiction*, in order to facilitate admissibility before the ICC. Voluntary acceptance of ICC admissibility does not necessarily presuppose or entail neither a loss of national credibility nor a lack of commitment to the fight against impunity *(sic)*.[49]

Consequently, as far as the legal opinion of the 12 jurists is concerned, the voluntary inaction of a state party does not seem to constitute a violation of the ICC Rome

[44] Article 17(1)(a) ICCRSt.

[45] Cassese A et al. (2009).

[46] ibid, 5.

[47] ibid, 18 para 59. The title of the official text is "Special Issues" and the subtitle "Uncontested Admissibility and Consensual Division of Labour".

[48] ibid.

[49] ibid, 19 para 61 (emphasis added).

Statute or infringement of the complementarity principle.[50] Strangely, however, the most problematic part is not found in the above-mentioned text, but in the extended explanatory annotation that accompanies it:

> Article 17 determines the admissibility consequences arising when a state investigates or prosecutes, but does not expressly compel states to act. However, it is stated in the paragraph 6 of the Preamble that exercising criminal jurisdiction is the States' 'duty'. Although the Preamble as such does not create any legal obligations, the Statute provisions can be interpreted in the light of the Preamble. The duty to "exercise criminal jurisdiction" should be interpreted according to the common principle "*aut dedere aut judicaire*", and for that reason it is met through the extradition and surrender, since those are the legal proceedings that lead to prosecution. Nevertheless, as noted below, the reference to a duty reflects also the *spirit* of the Statute, i.e. that the States will be responsible for the investigation and prosecution. That is essential for the effective function of the ICC. In the cases described here, refusing to exercise jurisdiction against prosecution before the ICC is a measure taken in order to improve the efficiency of the performance of justice, and therefore is in line with the letter and the spirit of the Rome Statute and other international commitments regarding the basic crimes. This can be discerned from the failure to prosecute [a State] due to its indifference or its willingness to protect the offenders, which can be correctly considered inconsistent to the struggle against impunity.[51]

On the basis of the above analysis, the useful footnote included, the 12 internationally acclaimed jurists invoke the common international law principle of *aut dedere aut judicaire*—which, incidentally, is not expressly stated anywhere in the ICC Rome Statute—,[52] and thus provide an innovative interpretation of the complementarity principle, through which a State acts lawfully when it refuses to exercise its jurisdiction as a matter of first priority and in accordance with the complementarity principle itself.

---

[50] Shortly afterwards the ICC case law opposed the unofficial entry of the term 'inaction' in the Statute. See ICC, Decision concerning Pre-Trial Chamber I's Decision of 10 February 2006 and the Incorporation of Documents into the Record of the Case against Mr. Thomas Lubanga Dyilo, ICC-01/04-01/06-8-US-Corr 09-03-2006, para. 29, www.worldcourts.com/icc/eng/decisions/2006.02.24_Prosecutor_v_Lubanga.pdf, last accessed 8 June 2023.

[51] Cassese A et al. (2009), ibid, 42, p. 19, n 24.

[52] It is highly dubious whether the "aut dedere aut judicaire" principle constitutes an active principle of International Criminal Law included in Article 21(1)(b) ICCRSt today, i.e. after an initial ICC recommendation and subsequent ICTY, ICTR and SCSL recommendations.

Article 21—Applicable law. 1. The Court shall apply: (a) in the first place, this Statute. Elements of Crimes and its Rules of Procedure and Evidence; (b) in the second place, where appropriate, applicable treaties and the principles and rules of international law, including the established principles of the international law of armed conflict…

In any case, none of the twelve eminent legal scientists cited any such legal source in the study in question, nor did they make any reference to Article 21 ICCRSt!

9.8 The Issue of Voluntary Referrals

This analysis points towards the newly introduced version of complementarity—or the 'non-complementarity' principle—which was whole heartedly embraced by the first Prosecutor Luis Moreno Ocampo through the systematic promotion of the 'self-referral' system.[53] According to this new interpretation, certain states that were members of the ICC but also torn by conflict and serious domestic problems could be 'encouraged' under Article 14 ICCRSt to remit a case that fell under their jurisdiction to the Office of the Prosecutor.[54]

A characteristic incident took place in September 2003. The Office of the Prosecutor initially stated in the Annex to the "Paper on Some Policy Issues before the Office of the Prosecutor: Referrals and Communications" that "in the light of the complementarity regime set out in the Statute and the central role accorded to it in the general policy of the Office, the Prosecutor will generally seek to alert the relevant State of the possibility of taking action itself very early in the process".[55] However, he quickly demonstrated his preference for the self-referral of state parties on the grounds that when the State, "of its own volition, has requested the exercise of the Court's jurisdiction, the Prosecutor can be confident that the national authorities will assist the investigation, will accord the privileges and immunities necessary for the investigation, and will be anxious to provide if possible and appropriate the necessary level of protection to investigators and witnesses".[56]

In other words, despite the fact that the interested States were parties to the ICC Rome Statute and, according to Article 15(1) ICCRSt, the Prosecutor had the uncontested right to initiate investigations *proprio motu* on the basis of information on crimes that were within the jurisdiction of the Court,[57] the Prosecutor adopted the policy of inviting and welcoming voluntary referrals by states that were then experiencing civil war or conflict.[58] Certainly, if this particular method *de lege*

[53] In his study included in the Essays in Honor of Bassiouni CM, Schabas W, mordantly reveals: "Luis Moreno Ocampo has essentially solicited such referrals from the states concerned". Schabas (2008a), p. 361.

[54] Article 14 Referral of a situation by a State Party: (1) A State Party may refer to the Prosecutor a situation in which one or more crimes within the jurisdiction of the Court appear to have been committed requesting the Prosecutor to investigate the situation for the purpose of determining whether one or more specific persons should be charged with the commission of such crimes. (2) As far as possible, a referral shall specify the relevant circumstances and be accompanied by such supporting documentation as is available to the State referring the situation.

[55] Annex to the "Paper on some policy issues before the Office of the Prosecutor": Referrals and Communications, p. 4, https://www.icc-cpi.int/itemsdocuments/20160915_otp-policy_case-selection_eng.pdf, last accessed 8 June 2023.

[56] ibid, 5.

[57] Article 15 Prosecutor: 1. The Prosecutor may initiate investigations proprio motu on the basis of information on crimes within the jurisdiction of the Court.

[58] Office of the Prosecutor, "Report on the Activities Performed During the First Three Years" (June 2003 to June 2006), 12 September 2006, p. 7.

ferenda continues to gain ground then it will inadvertently distort the complementarity principle, which is allegedly a milestone achievement of the ICC Rome Statute.

From a legal point of view it is evident that the *proprio motu* procedure is included among the inalienable rights of the Office of the Prosecutor, given that, according to the provisions of Article 12(2)(a) and (b) ICC Rome Statute, the conduct in question will have occurred in a state party's territory (or if the crime was committed on board a vessel or aircraft, then one registered with the State in question) or involved a state party national.[59] However, it seems that this legal path was not selected by the Prosecutor due to political reasons. In other words, the Office of the Prosecutor believed that international diplomacy called for the abandonment of the *proprio motu* procedure, since its use could provoke speculation about the Court's potential victimisation of certain states, when in fact there have been many situations throughout the world where the ICC's jurisdiction could have been exerted following a *proprio motu* inquiry by the Prosecutor. The risk of searing criticism from discontented State(s) aimed at the ICC for its arbitrary selection of cases was clear. Such an attack against the ICC would damage its credibility and add new problems to the already existing and unavoidable difficulties surrounding its initial operation.[60]

Nevertheless, in the "Report on the Activities Performed During the First Three Years" covering the operations of the Office of the Prosecutor from 2003 to 2006, the Prosecutor himself attributed the sidelining of *proprio motu* inquiries and the legally controversial selection of voluntary referrals to the fact that this policy would increase "the likelihood of important cooperation and support on the ground".[61] The line of argument clearly draws on practical and manifestly non-legal reasoning. In the same report, he attempted to analyse the relationship between the right of *proprio motu* inquiry and the self-referral system, claiming that "while *proprio motu* power is a critical aspect of the Office's independence, the Prosecutor adopted the policy of inviting and welcoming voluntary referrals by territorial states as a first step in triggering the jurisdiction of the Court. This policy resulted in referrals for what would become the Court's first two situations: Northern Uganda and the DRC."[62]

[59] Article 12—Preconditions to the exercise of jurisdiction: 1. A State which becomes a Party to this Statute thereby accepts the jurisdiction of the Court with respect to the crimes referred to in article 5.

2. In the case of Article 13, para (a) or (c), the Court may exercise its jurisdiction if one or more of the following States are Parties to this Statute or have accepted the jurisdiction of the Court in accordance with para 3: (a) The State on the territory of which the conduct in question occurred or, if the crime was committed on board a vessel or aircraft, the State of registration of that vessel or aircraft; (b) the State of which the person accused of the crime is a national.

[60] See Office of the Prosecutor, Report on the Activities Performed During the First Three Years (June 2003–June 2006), pp. 2, 5, https://www.icc-cpi.int/nr/rdonlyres/d76a5d89-fb64-47a9-9821-725747378ab2/143680/otp_3yearreport20060914_english.pdf, last accessed 8 June 2023.

[61] ibid, 2.

[62] ibid, 7.

This view of the legitimacy of the self-referral system was soon imparted to the competent ICC judicial authorities. Therefore, in the case of Thomas Lubanga Dyilo, Pre-Trial Chamber I essentially verified the Office of the Prosecutor's view that the self-referral system is in agreement with the complementarity principle.[63] Having ruled already that the term 'case' suggests "specific incidents during which one or more crimes within the jurisdiction of the Court seem to have been committed by one or more identified suspects",[64] Pre-Trial Chamber I confirmed that on 19 March 2005, Thomas Lubanga Dyilo was arrested and detained by the DRC authorities on charges of genocide and crimes against humanity (pursuant to Articles 144 and 166–169 respectively).[65]

In this case, Pre-Trial Chamber I fully adopted the Office of the Prosecutor's views and ruled that "when the President of the DRC sent the letter of referral to the Office of the Prosecutor on 3 March 2004, it appears that the DRC was indeed unable to undertake the investigation and prosecution of the crimes falling within the jurisdiction of the Court committed in the situation in the territory of DRC since 1 July 2002. In the Chamber's view, this is why the self-referral of the DRC appears consistent with the ultimate purpose of the complementarity regime, according to which the Court by no means replaces national criminal jurisdictions, but it is complementary to them."[66]

All of the above occurred despite the fact that on 22 February 2006—when the ruling in question was handed down by Pre-Trial Chamber I—a higher criminal court in Bunia (Tribunal de Grande Instance) had already indicted Thomas Lubanga Dyilo on charges of genocide and crimes against humanity, and there was generally no sign of unwillingness or incapacity on the part of the State when it came to having jurisdiction over the case in accordance with Article 17(1)(a) ICCRSt.

In the meantime, the Office of the Prosecutor's campaign for the infringement of the complementarity principle through 'self-referrals' quickly brought its first results. In December 2003, the Ugandan government took the first step when it

[63] ICC, Decision concerning Pre-Trial Chamber I's Decision of 10 February 2006 and the Incorporation of Documents into the Record of the Case against Mr. Thomas Lubanga Dyilo, ICC-01/04–01/06–8-Corr 17-03-2006, http://www.icc-cpi.int/iccdocs/doc/doc236260.PDF, last accessed 8 June 2023.

[64] As mentioned before, the Pre-Trial Chamber I has distinguished between the legal terms "situation" and "case". Situation in the Democratic Republic of Congo, Decision on the Applications for Participation in the Proceedings of VPRS1, VPRS2, VPRS3, VPRS4, VPRS5 and VPRS6, para 65, (emphasis added), http://www.icc-cpi.int/iccdocs/doc/doc183441.pdf, last accessed 8 June 2023.

[65] Decision concerning Pre-Trial Chamber I's Decision of 10 February 2006 and the Incorporation of Documents into the Record of the Case against Mr. Thomas Lubanga Dyilo, para 33. Oddly enough, para 36 mentions that "Therefore, in the Chamber's view, the Prosecution's general statement that the DRC national judicial system continues to be unable in the sense of article 17 (1) (a) to (c) and (3), of the Statute does not wholly correspond to the reality any longer." Nonetheless, even this ICC recorded evaluation could not lead to any change to the decision concerning the admissibility issue!

[66] ibid, para 35.

reported on the Northern Uganda situation to the ICC.[67] Refuting his previous statements, the Prosecutor 'clarified' that "the scope of the referral encompasses all crimes committed in Northern Uganda in the context of the ongoing conflict involving the LRA",[68] whereas in the initial press release for journalists there was only talk of "locating and arresting the LRA leadership".[69] Nonetheless, it must be pointed out that Uganda's self-referral led to the issue of five warrants of arrest, four of which remain active but unexecuted, while the fifth warrant of arrest against Raska Lukwiya will remain forever unexecuted after his death in 2006.[70] Judging by these five sealed warrants of arrest issued in July 2005, Uganda's self-referral does not seem to have had the expected results—at least as far as the criterion of ICC's caseload is concerned.

In March 2004, the Democratic Republic of Congo (DRC) reported on the situation in Ituri to the ICC. However, in the Ugandan case, the government had already sent an official letter to the ICC in May 2004 via its legal adviser, in which it was stated *inter alia* that "the Government of Uganda has been unable to arrest [. . .] persons who may bear the greatest responsibility" for the relevant crimes; that "the ICC is the most appropriate and effective forum for the investigation and prosecution of those bearing the greatest responsibility" for those crimes; and that the Government of Uganda "has not conducted and does not intend to conduct national proceedings in relation to the persons most responsible".[71] By contrast, in the DRC government's letter jurisdiction was simply assigned to the ICC without explicit reference to incapacity and/or unwillingness (elements that were both mentioned more or less explicitly in the aforementioned letter from Uganda).[72]

Finally, in a letter to the ICC Prosecutor of July 2012, Mali's Minister of Justice Malick Coulibaly wished to incorporate his country into the renowned club of states attempting to use self-referral to override the complementarity principle and willingly submit to ICC jurisdiction. In his succinct letter he states: "According to the Article of ICC Rome Statute, the State of Mali, as a contracting State to the Rome Statute, has the honour to report to you the most serious crimes committed on its grounds since January 2012, to the extent that the Mali courts cannot prosecute or

[67] See Zeidy (2005), pp. 83–120.

[68] ICC, Decision to Convene a Status Conference on the Investigation in the Situation in Uganda in Relation to the Application of Article 53, paras 4–5, http://www.icc-cpi.int/iccdocs/doc/doc97225.pdf, last accessed 8 June 2023.

[69] President of Uganda Refers Situation Concerning the Lord's Resistance Army (LRA) to the ICC, https://www.icc-cpi.int/pages/item.aspx?name=president+of+uganda+refers+situation+concerning+the+lord_s+resistance+army+_lra_+to+the+icc, last accessed 8 June 2023.

[70] See official website of ICC on the Uganda situation, https://www.icc-cpi.int/uganda, last accessed 8 June 2023.

[71] ICC, Warrant of Arrest for Joseph Kony issued on 8 July 2005 as amended on 27 September 2005, ICC-02/04–01/05–53, 11 para. 37, http://www.icc-cpi.int/iccdocs/doc/doc97185.pdf, last accessed 8 June 2023, with reference to "A Letter about Jurisdiction". This letter also refers to four other warrants of arrest issued in secret concerning the situation in Uganda on 8 July 2005.

[72] Schabas (2008b), p. 19.

judge the offenders."[73] Nevertheless, this unlawful, in the current author's opinion, self-referral case of the State of Mali simultaneously leaves some room for a 'return to legitimacy', since the phrase 'to the extent that' can be interpreted in many ways, including with reference to new incidents as they emerge.

9.9 The Pre-Trial Chamber Decision on the Al-Senussi Case (11 October 2013)

At the end of June 2011, Pre-Trial Chamber I issued warrants of arrest for Muammar Gaddafi, Saif Al Islam Gaddafi and Al-Senussi for crimes against humanity, murder and the persecution of recognizable groups or communities for political, racial, national, ethnic, religious or gender reasons (Article 7(1)(a) and (h) ICCRSt).[74] According to the indictment, the crimes in question were committed in Benghazi between 15 February and 28 February 2011. Given that Libya is not an ICC state party, Al-Senussi is a Libyan citizen and the alleged crimes were perpetrated on Libyan territory against Libyan citizens, the warrant of arrest could only be issued after the Security Council referred the situation in Libya to the ICC.[75]

Almost two whole years later, in April 2013, Libya appealed the admissibility of the case against Al-Senussi by making reference to Article 8 ICCRSt,[76] and subsequently all the parties involved (the State of Libya, the Office of the Prosecutor, the Legal Representative of the Victims and the Counsel for the Defense of Al-Senussi) submitted written statements setting out their views. Libya's submission of responses, admissibility challenge and final submissions took until 26 September 2013.[77] The State claimed that not only had it initiated the investigation of the crimes purportedly committed by Al-Senussi, but it had also provided substantial evidence, thus demonstrating the ability and willingness of its judicial authorities to conclude the investigation and run the suspect's trial in Libya. As far as the similarities between the ICC case and those conducted by Libya are concerned, Libya has claimed that the subject matter of its investigations is much broader than the ICC's. However, they deal with the same crimes as those outlined in the ICC

[73] Referral letter by the Government of Mali, 13 July 2012, http://www.icc-cpi.int/NR/rdonlyres/A245A47F-BFD1-45B6-891C-3BCB5B173F57/0/ReferralLetterMali130712.pdf, last accessed 8 June 2023.

[74] ICC, Pre-Trial Chamber I, "Warrant of Arrest for Abdullah Al-Senussi", ICC-01/11-01/11-4, 27 June 2011, http://www.icc-cpi.int/iccdocs/doc/doc1101360.pdf, last accessed 8 June 2023.

[75] UN Security Council Resolution 1970/26-02-2011 "Peace and Security in Africa", para 4, https://undocs.org/S/RES/1970(2011), last accessed 8 June 2023.

[76] Application on behalf of the Government of Libya relating to Abdullah Al-Senussi pursuant to Article 19 ICCRSt, ICC-01/11-01/11-307-Red2, 03-04-2013, https://www.icc-cpi.int/CourtRecords/CR2013_02635.PDF, last accessed 8 June 2023.

[77] ICC, Decision on the Admissibility of the Case Against Abdullah Al-Senussi, ICC-01/11-01/11-466 Red, pp. 8–9, http://www.icc-cpi.int/iccdocs/doc/doc1663102.pdf, last accessed 8 June 2023.

indictment, which occurred between the 1980s and 20 October 2011, when Muammar Gaddafi was killed, i.e. several months after the attacks against civilians in February 2011, in connection with which Al-Senussi stands accused by the ICC. Libya therefore argued that its own charges against Al-Senussi were sufficient to raise the admissibility challenge before the ICC.[78]

Furthermore, Libya described in detail the requisite infrastructure. A renovated courtroom complex and a prison facility were to be used for the trial proceedings and the assistance of the UN, the European Union and other countries to be called upon so that issues of transitional justice could be handled effectively. Libya highlighted that Al-Senussi was in safe and secure government-controlled custody in Libya, and that the necessary evidence and testimony had already been collected. Given that the issue of infrastructure had already been resolved, there is no evidence that Libya was either unable or unwilling to carry out a genuine investigation.[79]

On this basis, Libya requested that Pre-Trial Chamber I declare the case against Al-Senussi inadmissible before the Court or, alternatively, consider implementing complementarity by declaring the case inadmissible, subject to the fulfillment of certain conditions by Libya.[80] Libya was essentially requesting the ICC to implement the complementarity principle for the very first time. Not only had it not been implemented up until then; on the contrary—as we have seen—there had been successive attempts to infringe upon it, even before the ICC was officially founded.

In mid-October 2013 Pre-Trial Chamber I issued a lengthy ruling. Based on the existing Appeals Chamber case law concerning the interpretation of Article 17 ICCRSt,[81] Pre-Trial Chamber I drew attention to two crucial questions concerning whether a case is admissible before the Court: (a) whether, at the time of the proceedings in respect of a challenge to the admissibility of a case, there is an ongoing investigation or prosecution of the case at the national level and (b) whether the State is unwilling or unable genuinely to carry out such investigation or prosecution.[82]

It is evident that the first question concerns the assessment of whether or not Libya's judicial investigation relates to the 'same case', i.e. the same person and the same criminal conduct.[83] On this matter Pre-Trial Chamber I highlighted that the

[78] ibid, 9–13.

[79] ibid, 12–13.

[80] ibid, 14.

[81] ICC, Prosecutor v. Germain Katanga and Mathieu Ngudjolo Chui, "Judgment on the Appeal of Mr. Germain Katanga against the Oral Decision of Trial Chamber II of 12 June 2009 on the Admissibility of the Case", 25 September 2009, ICC-01/04-01/07-1497, paras. 1 and 75–79, http://www.icc-cpi.int/iccdocs/doc/doc746819.pdf, last accessed 8 June 2023. Also see ICC, Pre-Trial Chamber I, "Decision requesting further submissions on issues related to the admissibility of the case against Saif Al-Islam Gaddafi", 7 December 2012, ICC-01/11–01/11–239, para. 6.

[82] ICC, Decision on the Admissibility of the Case Against Abdullah Al-Senussi, ICC-01/11–01/11–466 Red, 15, http://www.icc-cpi.int/iccdocs/doc/doc1663102.pdf, last accessed 8 June 2023.

[83] The term "conduct" is used in the official English text of the Decision; an analysis of its argumentation and interpretation with reference to all state parties is also presented, ibid, 18–31.

Appeals Chamber had already ruled, by broadly interpreting the term, that the conduct subject to the national investigation should be *substantially* the same conduct alleged in the proceedings before the Court.[84] As far as the definition of the phrase "substantially the same conduct" is concerned, Pre-Trial Chamber I highlighted that this varies and depends on the concrete facts and circumstances of the case[85] and, therefore, requires case-by-case analysis.[86,87]

In the proceedings before the Court, Pre-Trial Chamber I considered Al-Senussi's alleged conduct as set out in the warrant of arrest issued against him and in conjunction with the Article 58 Decision (i.e. the decision about the warrant of arrest for Al-Senussi),[88] and compared this to the criminal conduct that was the subject of the legal proceedings in Libya, as described by Libya in its admissibility challenge.

The present case before the Court concerns the individual criminal responsibility of Al-Senussi for killings and acts of persecution, the victims of which were targeted due to their political opposition to Gaddafi's regime. The crimes were allegedly committed directly by Al-Senussi or through the Libyan Security Forces during the repression of the demonstrations that took place in Benghazi from 15 February 2011 to at least 20 February 2011, as part of a policy orchestrated at the highest level of the Libyan government to deter and quell the revolution against the Gaddafi regime throughout Libya.[89]

Pre-Trial Chamber I recalled that the previous decision concerning Article 58 ICCRSt includes a list with specific 'incidents' or 'events'.[90] Nevertheless,

---

[84] ibid, 32.

[85] The term "facts and circumstances of the case" is used in the official English text of the Decision, ibid, 34.

[86] The term "a case-by-case analysis" is used in the official English text of the Decision, ibid, 34, where a special reference to the May 2013 decision is made, concerning the admissibility of Saif Al Islam Gaddafi. The term is repeated at page 40, para 78. See ICC, Decision on the Admissibility of the Case against Saif Al-Islam Gaddafi, ICC-01/11-01/11-344-Red, 31-05-2013, p. 32, para. 77, http://www.icc-cpi.int/iccdocs/doc/doc1599307.pdf, last accessed 8 June 2023. Also see ICTR, Prosecutor v. Ntagerura et al., Case No. ICTR-99-46-A, Appeals Chamber Judgement, 7 July 2006, para. 23. ICTR, Prosecutor v. Ntakirutimana, Cases Nos. ICTR-96-10-A and ICTR-96-17-A, Appeals Chamber Judgement, 13 December 2004, paras. 73–74. ICTY, Prosecutor v. Kupreskic et al., Case No. IT-95-16-A, Appeals Chamber Judgement, 23 October 2001; ICTY, Prosecutor v. Blaskic, Case No. IT-95-14-A, Appeals Chamber Judgement, 29 July 2004; ICTY, Prosecutor v. Kvocka et al., Case No. IT-98-30/1-A, Appeals Chamber Judgment, 25 February 2005.

[87] A swift reading of the cases brought before the ICC today suffices to show that they are significantly different, as far as the description of the true conduct parameters used in court for each suspect or each of the accused is concerned, and proves that different cases cannot necessarily be considered equal when it comes to the alleged wide or narrow interpretation of the conduct, ibid. 41, para 75.

[88] ICC, Decision on the Admissibility of the Case Against Abdullah Al-Senussi, ICC-01/11-01/11-466 Red, 36, para. 68, http://www.icc-cpi.int/iccdocs/doc/doc1663102.pdf, last accessed 8 June 2023.

[89] ibid, 36–38.

[90] ibid, 45, para 78.

"since, as in the case against Mr. Gaddafi, the conduct that is alleged in the criminal proceedings against Mr. Al-Senussi is not shaped by the 'incidents' mentioned in the Article 58 Decision (for the issue of a Warrant of Arrest for Al-Senussi), it is not required that domestic proceedings concern each of those 'events' at the national level in order for the Chamber to be satisfied that Libya is investigating or prosecuting Mr. Al-Senussi for substantially the same conduct that is alleged in the proceedings before this Court."[91] Consequently, as these 'events' constitute basic indicative examples of Al-Senussi's alleged conduct, the proceedings before the national authorities do not need to make reference to each 'incident' separately in the indictment.[92] Thus, the fact that the file of the national judicial proceedings may or may not include enough of these 'incidents' (especially those marked as extremely violent or typical of the criminal actions attributed to the accused) constitutes a critical indicator of whether or not the case investigated by the ICC and simultaneously by the national judicial authorities is the same.[93]

---

[91] ibid, 45, para 79.

[92] The Article 58 Decision (concerning the issue of the warrant of arrest for Al-Senussi) includes, inter alia, the following incidents that occurred in Benghazi during 15–20 February 2011: (**1**) the arrest by the Security Forces on 15 February 2011 of a lawyer who was organising a protest against Gaddafi regime scheduled for 17 February 2011 (para 43); (**2**) the arrest of several authors, writers and alleged dissidents (including that of the Libyan author Idriss Al-Mismari) between 15 and 17 February 2011 (para 43 and 44); (**3**) the attack by the Security Forces on demonstrators with tear gas and live ammunition, following the gathering of an increasing number of demonstrators in the area of Birka, in A1 Fatah street and Jamal Abdun Naser street on 16 February 2011, causing the death of at least three civilian demonstrators (para 36(i); (**4**) the attack, on the same day, by forces loyal to Muammar Gaddafi on civilian demonstrators who were hit with sticks and dispersed (para 52); (**5**) the event of 17 February 2011 at the Juliyana Bridge, when Security Forces armed with machineguns barricaded the street to stop the demonstrators, opened fire for a significant period of time on the unarmed demonstrators, causing a large number of injuries and deaths among the demonstrators, and arrested those demonstrators that were not shot and were not able to flee (para 36 (ii) and 53); (**6**) the attack, on the same day, carried out by the Security Forces who fired with live ammunition on unarmed demonstrators, who had gathered near the High Court in the centre of Benghazi to protest against the arrest of the individual who had been organizing the forthcoming protest against Gaddafi regime (para 50); (**7**) the killing and seriously injuries, still on 17 February 2011, perpetrated by the Security Forces on a number of other demonstrators in different areas of the town (para 36(iii) and 52) and the attacks by the Security Forces continuing throughout the night (para 53); (**8**) the killing and seriously injuring by the Security Forces on 18 February 2011 of a number of civilians while participating in the funeral procession for the demonstrators killed the day before (para 36(iv) and 54); (**9**) the killing by the Security Forces of at least 60 demonstrators on 20 February 2011 (para 36(vi)). Furthermore, the Article 58 Decision refers to protesters subjected to torture (para 46) and the abduction and subsequent torture of family members of alleged dissidents (para 47). ICC, Decision on the "Prosecutor's Application Pursuant to Article 58 as to Muammar Mohammed Abu Minyar Gaddafi, Saif Al-Islam Gaddafi and Abdullah Al-Senussi", ICC-01/11–12, 27-06-2011, http://www.icc-cpi.int/iccdocs/doc/doc1099314.pdf, last accessed 8 June 2023.

[93] ICC, Decision on the Admissibility of the Case Against Abdullah Al-Senussi, ICC-01/11-01/11-466 Red, 8–9, http://www.icc-cpi.int/iccdocs/doc/doc1663102.pdf, last accessed 8 June 2023, 45, para. 78.

The competent ICC Pre-Trial Chamber ruled that the evidence submitted by the Libyan authorities proved that the judicial proceedings against Al-Senussi were ongoing. The Libyan authorities examined witnesses repeatedly, collected documents such as medical reports, death certificates and written orders, requested the victims to present evidence of their allegations, submitted requests for any additional information concerning this particular case to external sources (other states and international organizations) and did not neglect to seek any evidence potentially favourable to the accused.[94]

Moreover, Pre-Trial Chamber I deemed that "the evidence relied upon by Libya for the purposes of the Admissibility Challenge demonstrates the taking of identifiable, concrete and progressive investigative steps in relation to Mr. Al-Senussi's criminal responsibility [. . .] with a view to clarifying and ascertaining, inter alia, the following relevant factual aspects":[95]

(1) the existence of a policy conceived by the highest level of the State government to deter and quell the demonstrations against the Gaddafi regime through "recruitment and arming of mercenaries and supporters for the repression" of the demonstrations[96]
(2) the mobilisation of militia and transfer of equipment, recruitment of missionaries, incitement of civilians to kill protesters, provision of supplies to the Security Forces and other arrangements for the repression of the demonstrations, including the role of Al-Senussi himself and his alleged accomplices in these activities
(3) Al-Senussi's command over the Security Forces and his presence in Benghazi immediately after the outbreak of the revolution in order to control the situation
(4) the numerous attacks on civilian demonstrators by the Security Forces in many areas of Benghazi between 15 and 20 February 2011, causing serious injuries to countless civilians or their death, as well as similar attacks conducted by them in the whole state throughout the period of the repression of the revolution against the Gaddafi's regime
(5) Al-Senussi's direct involvement in the shooting of the civilian demonstrators in Benghazi between 15 and 20 February 2011
(6) the arrest of journalists, activists and civilians demonstrating against the Gaddafi regime and the role of Al-Senussi and his alleged accomplices in some of these events
(7) instances of detention and torture of civilian dissidents.[97]

Subsequently, Pre-Trial Chamber I reached the conclusion *ab initio* that the judicial investigations of the Libyan authorities do pertain to the relevant factual aspects of Al-Senussi's alleged criminal conduct and that, therefore, Libya has in fact initiated

[94] ibid, 46–82, para 81–157.
[95] ibid, 83–84, para 162.
[96] ibid, 49, para 86.
[97] ibid, 83–85, para 162.

a national judicial procedure that includes the same case brought before the Court, according to the proper interpretation of the Article 17(1)(a) ICCRSt.[98]

In other words, the ICC responded positively to the first crucial question of whether or not there is an ongoing national judicial investigation or criminal prosecution during the ICC proceedings.

As far as the second question was concerned, i.e. whether or not a State is unwilling or unable to carry out such an important judicial investigation or criminal prosecution, Pre-Trial Chamber I recalled that the State challenging the admissibility of a case carries the burden of proof for "all aspects of the Admissibility Challenge to the extent required by the concrete circumstances of the case".[99] However, the Pre-Trial Chamber acknowledged that a test of Libya's potential unwillingness or incapability could be conducted only if serious doubts existed about the true nature of the national judicial proceedings. Libya may bear the burden of proof for the Admissibility Challenge, but each party's allegations must still be evidentially substantiated in order to be lawfully submitted.

Subsequently, Pre-Trial Chamber I gave *"holistic"*[100] consideration to a wide range of allegations introduced by the parties and which were found to be evidentially substantiated and pertinent to the case. The relevant data included the quantity and quality of the collected evidence; the scope of the investigations into Al-Senussi's case as well as the methodology used and the resources made available; the recent transfer of the cases of Al-Senussi and thirty of those co-accused to the Accusation Chamber; analysis of specific judicial proceedings conducted against other Gaddafi regime officials in Libya; and the recent efforts to resolve the Libyan judicial system's problems using international assistance. Furthermore, Pre-Trial Chamber I took into consideration the severe problems of Libya after the civil war:[101] the absence of witness protection programmes; the significant

[98] ibid, 86, para 164. The court indicated that although a number of criminal acts inflicted on civilians because of their political opposition to Gaddafi's regime constitute the crime of "persecution" in accordance with article 7(l)(h) of the Statute, the fact that the political aspect is aggravated according to articles 27 and 28 of the Libyan Criminal Code further characterises the murders and inhuman acts committed by Al-Senussi. ibid, 86–87, para 166. Also see Decision on the Admissibility of the Case against Saif Al-Islam Gaddafi, ICC-01/11-01/11-344-Red, 31-05-2013, 46, para 111 http://www.icc-cpi.int/iccdocs/doc/doc1599307.pdf, last accessed 8 June 2023.

[99] The decision states "all aspects of the Admissibility Challenge to the extent required by the concrete circumstances of the case", Decision on the Admissibility of the Case Against Abdullah Al-Senussi, 15, para. 27.

[100] (Emphasis added). It is probably the first time that this term is included in the case law of the ICC, albeit in the official summary of the lengthy decision. See Summary of the Decision on the admissibility of the case against Mr. Abdullah Al-Senussi, 5, https://thenewlibyareport.files.wordpress.com/2014/05/english-summary.pdf, last accessed 8 June 2023.

[101] ICC Judge Christine Van den Wyngaert highlighted in a separate declaration that she was extremely shocked to hear about the abduction and liberation of the Libyan Prime Minister Ali Zeidan on 10 October 2013, as well as the general security levels in Libya, since their deterioration could dramatically affect Libya's ability to carry out proceedings against Al-Senussi. Furthermore, before the Decision was issued, she would have preferred to have received the views of all interested parties concerning whether the current security situation in Libya is safe enough for the

difficulties that local authorities faced in their effort to maintain security in certain prisons; and the absence of legal representation for Al-Senussi.

The holistic examination of the above did not result in any negative indications concerning the judicial proceedings in Libya against Al-Senussi. In other words, the judicial investigation of the case in Libya was not deemed to have been conducted in order to protect the accused from the implications of his criminal acts, a move that would have clearly suggested the notion of 'unwillingness' under Article 17(2)(a) ICCRSt.[102] Furthermore, it was decided that the judicial proceedings conducted on a national level did not involve any unjustified delay, which would certainly have undermined any genuine intention to bring Al-Senussi to justice pursuant to Article 17(2)(b) ICCRSt. In addition, Pre-Trial Chamber I reached the conclusion that the judicial investigations concerning Al-Senussi had been conducted in an impartial and independent way and with the intention to bring the person in question before the court and, consequently, there was no issue concerning the application of cumulative requirements pursuant to Article 17(2)(c) ICCRSt.

Moreover, the fact that Al-Senussi had no legal representation at this stage did not constitute 'unwillingness' pursuant to Article 17(2) ICCRSt, since it was not an indication of Libya's unwillingness to bring Al-Senussi before the court, but rather a consequence of the state of the country after the civil war and the overthrow of Gaddafi's regime. Hence, following a strictly grammatical interpretation of the provision, Pre-Trial Chamber I concluded that Libya was not unwilling to put Al-Senussi on trial, simply because Al-Senussi had no legal representation in Libya. Besides, regrettably the scope of Article 17 ICC Rome Statute does not cover human rights issues surrounding the 'fair trial' principle or the prohibition of death penalty, both matters that would lead to Al-Senussi having to remain in The Hague and to be brought before the ICC.[103]

---

trial of Abdullah Al-Senussi to proceed there. See Declaration of Judge Christine Van den Wyngaert, available online, http://www.icc-cpi.int/iccdocs/doc/doc1663117.PDF, last accessed 8 June 2023.

[102] Article 17—Issues of admissibility: 2. In order to determine unwillingness in a particular case, the Court shall consider, having regard to the principles of due process recognized by international law, whether one or more of the following exist, as applicable: (a) The proceedings were or are being undertaken or the national decision was made for the purpose of shielding the person concerned from criminal responsibility for crimes within the jurisdiction of the Court referred to in article 5; (b) There has been an unjustified delay in the proceedings which in the circumstances is inconsistent with an intent to bring the person concerned to justice; (c) The proceedings were not or are not being conducted independently or impartially, and they were or are being conducted in a manner which, in the circumstances, is inconsistent with an intent to bring the person concerned to justice.

[103] The Defence highlighted in a previous paper the swift trials that took place in Libya against higher officers of the Gaddafi regime, which concluded in death sentences being handed down to the accused and carried out. Defence Application on behalf of Abdullah Al-Senussi for Leave to Reply to the "Libyan Government's Response to 'Defence Application on behalf of Mr. Abdullah Al-Senussi concerning Libya's Announcement of Trial Date in August 2013'" and Defence Request for this Application and the Defence Application of 10 July 2013 to be decided on an

As far as Libya's *ability* to investigate the case and prosecute Al-Senussi was concerned, the ICC Pre-Trial Chamber I first examined the possibility that Libya "is not able to obtain the accused", due to a total or substantial collapse or unavailability of its national judicial system pursuant to Article 17(3) ICCRSt.[104] Certainly in the case of Al-Senussi, who was already in custody in Libya, such a claim could not be validly supported. Consequently, Pre-Trial Chamber I continued to examine Libya's ability to "obtain the necessary evidence and testimony" pursuant to Article 17-(3) ICCRSt, by taking into consideration the data collected by the Libyan authorities and the stage that the national judicial proceedings had reached by then. Undisputedly, the lack of a dedicated witness protection programme and the fact that certain prisons still fell outside the jurisdiction of the Libyan Ministry of Justice were deemed to be negative factors. Nevertheless, in Al-Senussi's case Libya presented substantial evidence, which included several witness and victim testimonies,[105] as well as documents such as orders, medical records and flight records.

For these reasons Pre-Trial Chamber I concluded that, following an overall assessment of all factors, Libya is neither unable to conduct judicial proceedings in Al-Senussi's case **nor** otherwise unable to "carry out its proceedings" due to a total or substantial collapse or unavailability of its national judicial system.[106] In an attempt to set apart Al-Senussi's case from Saif Al Islam Gaddafi's case, where continuous attempts to find him legal representation had failed, it must be stressed that in Al-Senussi's case there had been several Libyan lawyers who wished to represent him in the national judicial proceedings, despite the fact that none of them managed to visit him or be granted the requisite power of attorney.

Concomitantly, in accordance with the aforementioned legal analysis, Pre-Trial Chamber I—after its first decision, in which the ICC was considered the competent judicial body to rule on this case—decided on 11 October 2013 that because of the fact that the Al-Senussi case was today under judicial investigation by Libya's criminal system and Libya was willing and able to carry out its investigation, the case was inadmissible pursuant to Article 17(1)(a) ICCRSt and did not fall under ICC jurisdiction due to the complementarity principle.

However, at the end of its decision, the Court highlighted the Prosecutor's right to appeal the decision pursuant to Article 19(10) ICCRSt when "he or she is fully satisfied that new facts have arisen that negate the basis on which the case had previously been found inadmissible" pursuant to Article 17 ICCRSt. Nonetheless,

---

urgent basis, ICC-01/11-01/11-398, para 10, http://www.icc-cpi.int/iccdocs/doc/doc1631011.pdf, last accessed 8 June 2023.

[104] Article 12—Issues of Admissibility: 3. in order to determine inability in a particular case, the Court shall consider whether, due to a total or substantial collapse or unavailability of its national judicial system, the State is unable to obtain the accused or the necessary evidence and testimony or otherwise unable to carry out its proceedings.

[105] It is noteworthy that at least one of the witnesses testified while detained, and that several potential witnesses continue to be detained today in Al Hadba prison, which operates under the supervision of the present Libyan government, i.e. the National Transitional Council.

[106] Article 17 (3) ICCRSt.

given the cumulative requirements of Article 19 ICCRSt, as well as the 5-day period provided for in 154(1) Rule of Procedure and Evidence to submit the request, this did not occur and is not likely to occur in the future.

To sum up, if one considers the conclusions of the *awakening hypothesis of the complementarity principle*, one should feel content about this *prima facie* positive development in favour of the complementarity principle's application for the first time in the ICC history. On the other hand, it could be argued that political tendentiousness, international diplomatic considerations and the refusal of Libya's National Transitional Council over a period of 2 years to deliver Al-Senussi to the ICC ultimately led to a judicial compromise, pursuant to the aforementioned report of the 12 jurists and the Office of the Prosecutor's Paper on Policy Issues in 2003. Following this line of argument, it remains the case that the complementarity principle functions as a dead letter and cannot be overturned by the awakening hypothesis.

Thus what had up to this point been the single case of Saif Al Islam Gaddafi and Abdullah Al-Senussi[107] was split in two. The more important and notorious Gaddafi was brought before the ICC and the less famous Al-Senussi before the Libyan judicial authorities. One of the three main reasons given in the Decision on the Admissibility of the Case against Saif Al Islam Gaddafi for deciding that the ICC should try him was that "the Chamber has noted a practical impediment to the progress of domestic proceedings against Mr. Gaddafi as Libya has not shown whether and how it will overcome the existing difficulties in securing a lawyer for the suspect."[108] However, the insuperable problems that Al-Senussi experienced communicating with his lawyers were not considered equally significant,[109] as reflected in the different judicial outcomes and jurisdictions (ICC's jurisdiction over Gaddafi case and Libya's jurisdiction over Al-Senussi case).

Nonetheless, on 17 October 2013, Al-Senussi's Defense Team (which included Professor William Schabas) filed a request for the review and suspension of the case by virtue of its admissibility in line with Articles 19(6), 82(1)(a), 82(3), 83(2)

[107] See the ICC's official website, Prosecutor v. Saif Al-Islam Gaddafi, formerly The Prosecutor v. Muammar Mohammed Abuminyar Gaddafi, Saif Al-Islam Gaddafi and Abdullah Al-Senussi, ICC-01/11–01/11, https://www.icc-cpi.int/libya/gaddafi, last accessed 8 June 2023. Following the murder of Muammar Mohammed Abu Minyar Gaddafi (commonly known as Colonel Gaddafi) by insurgents on 20 October 2011, the case inevitably continued against the two-remaining accused.

[108] ICC, Decision on the admissibility of the case against Saif Al-Islam Gaddafi), ICC-01/11–01/11–344-Red, International Criminal Court (ICC) (31 May 2013) 89, para 215, http://www.icc-cpi.int/iccdocs/doc/doc1599307.pdf, last accessed 8 June 2023.

[109] Although it is also highlighted in the Decision that the Pre-Trial Chamber I "is mindful that the Defence ability to raise certain factual matters may have been prejudiced by the absence of direct contacts with Mr. Al-Senussi, since a visit to Mr. Al-Senussi by his counsel has not taken place despite the Chamber's order to this effect". ibid, 110, para 219.

(a) ICCRSt, Articles 154(1) and 156 Rules of Procedure and Evidence and 64 Regulation of the Court.[110,111]

In its appeal, the Defence argued that the Appeals Chamber must suspend the decision of 11 October 2013, because if Libya was to proceed to conduct and complete the trial proceedings in line with this decision, it "would defeat the purpose of the appeal", thus creating an irreversible situation.[112] Therefore, the Defence argued that "it is essential that the Admissibility Decision is suspended to prevent Libya from relying on the Decision to try and sentence Mr. Al-Senussi before the Appeals Chamber has finally determined whether Libya can indeed try him".[113]

The Defence argued that Libya is "unable and unwilling genuinely to conduct fair trial proceedings"[114] and that, consequently, Pre-Trial Chamber I had erred in finding that his case was inadmissible before the ICC. Were this to pave the way for establishing that Article 17 ICCRSt does in fact include respect for human rights and the fair trial principle, then it would be evident that Al-Senussi could not be tried in Libya. From this perspective it would seem that the Defence was attempting to implant the fair trial criterion within the interpretational framework of Article 17 ICCRSt. However, the scope of Article 17 seems much more restricted and refers to cases where a State attempts to use judicial proceedings taking place on its territory as a shield to protect the accused, and not to cases where the accused faces the infringement of his human rights and of his rights as the accused or faces the death penalty (in Al-Senussi's case all of the above apply).

Therefore, the fact that Al-Senussi "has been detained in Libya for nearly 13 months without access to any lawyer despite his repeated requests to see a lawyer"[115] or that "he has been interrogated in detention in violation of his rights under Libyan law without any lawyer being present"[116] or that "he is cut-off from the world and has been denied family visits and telephone calls"[117] or even that "his ICC Defense team has been prevented by the Libyan authorities from having any contact with him despite the Pre-Trial Chamber's orders to this effect"[118] do not *stricto sensu* raise issues under Article 17 ICCRSt.[119]

---

[110] Public censored document, ICC, Appeal on behalf of Abdullah Al-Senussi against Pre-Trial Chamber I's 'Decision on the admissibility of the case against Abdullah Al-Senussi', and Request for Suspensive Effect, ICC-01/11-01/11-468-Red 17-10-2013, http://www.icc-cpi.int/iccdocs/doc/doc1666694.pdf, last accessed 8 June 2023.

[111] It is noteworthy that the OPCV was against the Libyan request not to bring Al-Senussi before the ICC. ibid, 99–100, paras 195–198.

[112] ibi, 6–7.

[113] ibid, 8.

[114] ibid, 10.

[115] ibid, 11.

[116] ibid, 11.

[117] ibid, 11.

[118] ibid, 11.

[119] "[T]he Chamber emphasizes that alleged violations of the procedural rights of the accused are not per se grounds for a finding of unwillingness or inability under article 17 of the Statute. In order

Nevertheless, what ultimately emerged from the appeal as an absolutely crucial issue was the suspension of the Admissibility Decision, since the acceptance of this request would result in Al-Senussi sustaining the position of the accused as it was prior to the Admissibility Decision. Furthermore, "*the Appeals Chamber could then find that the immediate surrender of Mr. Al-Senussi to The Hague during the appellate proceedings is justified in light of the appeal against the postponement of the surrender order and to ensure a secure and privileged setting for communications between Mr. Al-Senussi and his Counsel, given that Libya has not permitted him to have any such contact with his Counsel in Libya. In the Defence's submission such a finding would serve to protect Mr. Al-Senussi's fundamental rights, taking into account that the failure to do so could not be corrected or reversed at any later stage.*"[120]

Undoubtedly, though, the unhindered communication of Al-Senussi with his Defence Team is of utmost importance for one further reason: it could constitute a significant source of new information, not only about the issue of the possible inability or unwillingness of Libya to bring his case before the domestic courts, but first and foremost about the whole situation in Libya. Finally but importantly, it is clear that although the fair trial principle and the protection of Al-Senussi's fundamental rights as a human being and the accused do not seem to fall *ab initio* into Article 17 ICCRSt, an alternative interpretational approach could possibly be *teleologically* accepted, given that both (on the one hand, a state's unwillingness and inability to bring a case to court and, on the other, the infringement of the fair trial principle and the fundamental rights of the accused) lead to exactly the same outcome: harsh criticism of the ICC, the failure of international criminal justice and the rescission of any attempt to put an end to impunity in a legally proper, fair and civilized way.

Nonetheless, on 24 July 2014, the ICC Appeals Chamber confirmed the Pre-Trial Chamber's decision that Al-Senussi should stand trial in Libya. Although the Appeals Chamber rejected the Defence's arguments, the ICC judges seemed to be cautiously adopting for the first time what has already been coined 'positive

---

to have a bearing on the Chamber's determination, any such alleged violation must be linked to one of the scenarios provided for in article 17(2) or (3) of the Statute. In particular, as far as the State's alleged unwillingness is concerned, the Chamber is of the view that, depending on the specific circumstances, certain violations of the procedural rights of the accused may be relevant to the assessment of the independence and impartiality of the national proceedings that the Chamber is required to make, having regard to the principles of due process recognized under international law, under article 17(2)(c) of the Statute. However, this latter provision, identifying two cumulative requirements, provides for a finding of unwillingness only when the manner in which the proceedings are being conducted, together with indicating a lack of independence and impartiality, is to be considered, in the circumstances, inconsistent with the intent to bring the person to justice." Decision on the Admissibility of the Case Against Abdullah Al-Senussi, 117–118, para 235 and fn. 541 where there is an extremely interesting analysis on the different phrasing of Article 17 (2) (c) ICCRSt and Article 9(ii) Rules of Procedure and Evidence (cumulative phrasing in the first, disjunctive phrasing in the second).

[120] ibid, 13.

complementarity';[121] that is, whether a trial according 'minimised rights' to the accused could fall foul of Article 17's 'unwilling' or 'unable' criteria:

> Taking into account the text, context and object and purpose of the provision, this determination is not one that involves an assessment of whether the due process rights of a suspect have been breached per se. In particular, the concept of proceedings "being conducted in a manner which, in the circumstances, is inconsistent with an intent to bring the person concerned to justice" should generally be understood as referring to proceedings which will lead to a suspect evading justice, in the sense of not appropriately being tried genuinely to establish his or her criminal responsibility, in the equivalent of sham proceedings that are concerned with that person's protection.
>
> However, there may be circumstances, depending on the facts of the individual case, whereby violations of the rights of the suspect are so egregious that the proceedings can no longer be regarded as being capable of providing any genuine form of justice to the suspect so that they should be deemed, in those circumstances, to be "inconsistent with an intent to bring the person to justice".[122]

According to Yvonne McDermott Rees, the second paragraph seems to suggest that the ICC left open a more expansive interpretation of the complementarity clause, such that it would include unfairness to the accused. Conversely, however, the Appeals Chamber refused to accept additional evidence from the Defence, which purported to show that the authorities had mistreated the accused in custody for the purposes of obtaining a confession from him.[123]

9.10 The Awakening Hypothesis of Actual Complementarity

Although legal theory generally suggests otherwise, all provisions and principles may not be equal in the practical application of the law. And if this can be reasonably and lawfully true on the basis of the hierarchy of laws, it can also occur in a 'paradoxical' way, even within the same legal framework and despite the fact that no issue of conflict of laws arises, where the 'weighing' of different laws is largely inevitable.

Nevertheless, a legally enacted principle as an actual dead letter—i.e. totally inapplicable or applied in a manner that is contrary to its expressly defined context—constitutes a rare phenomenon in advanced judicial systems operating within a democratic society. Undeniably, such an exceptionally rare anomaly brings confusion and awkwardness to jurists, since referring to it expressly as such in studies and

[121] Heller (2006); Burke-White (2008), pp. 59–85; Carnero Rojo (2005), pp. 829–869.

[122] ICC, Judgment on the Appeal of Mr. Abdullah Al-Senussi against the Decision of Pre-Trial Chamber I on 11 October 2013 on the Admissibility of the Case against Abdullah Al-Senussi, 3–4, para 2–3, http://www.icc-cpi.int/iccdocs/doc/doc1807073.pdf, last accessed 8 June 2023.

[123] McDermott Rees (2014).

monographs casts serious doubts on the judicial system within which it is supposed to exist and 'operate'. Thus, this principle passes its 'legal life' as a dead letter and the judicial system within which it 'exists' continues to operate in a manner inconsistent with the officially proclaimed approach and despite its inherent weakness or, better yet, anomaly.

The complementarity principle of the ICCRSt has until very recently constituted a dead letter, but is now arguably beginning to be filled with some life as a result of the decision against Al-Senussi.[124]

The present application of the complementarity principle constitutes proof of the awakening hypothesis of the complementarity principle; on one level, a hypothesis that presents the case of an expressly formulated principle which has been substantially non-existent within its legal framework for many years, and only after the publication of a judgment begins to fulfill its express purpose. Furthermore, on a second level, the complementarity principle's awakening shows the paradox of principles with different legal force, although, theoretically, they all have the same nominal force within their formulated legal framework.

The ICC decisions against Al-Senussi in October 2013 and July 2014 indicate that complementarity has ceased being a principle 'in trance'. Of course, the question of which prevails—the awakening hypothesis of complementarity principle or the hypothesis of complementarity principle as a dead letter (since, if one accepts that the decisions were the result of a political arrangement to bring Gaddafi's son before The Hague and Al-Senussi before Libya, then once again the complementarity principle was still not applied)—will only be resolved by future decisions of the ICC. Although the flaring up of the civil war in Libya and the recent sentencing of Al-Senussi to death[125] provide no cause for optimistism about the awakening of the complementarity principle,[126] ultimately, history will decide which hypothesis triumphs.

Lately, the principle of complementarity has finally started to emerge as a core factor in determining the ICC's jurisdiction. The Chief Prosecutor Ms. Bensouda has invoked the principle of complementarity in the situation between Russia and Georgia in the Ossetia region.[127] Moreover, following the threats of certain African

[124] It is noteworthy here that while the complementarity concept constitutes a loan from quantum mechanics to legal science (since the term complementarity is used to express the paradox of wave-particle duality in the scientific field of quantum mechanics), the new term of the awakening hypothesis that this study attempts to introduce constitutes a loan from the science of philology, scholars of which were asked to aid the author in the description of this paradoxical phenomenon: a legal principle remains empty for several years and suddenly it starts to 'fill' or 'fill up', to take a form.

[125] BBC News (2015b).

[126] The last episode of the civil unrest and war being the bombing of a Greek oil tanker. "Greek Oil Tanker Bombed in Libyan Port of Derna", BBC (2015a); Joffe (2014).

[127] Situation in Georgia, Public Document with Confidential, EX PARTE, Annexes A, B, C, D.2, E.3, E.7, E.9, F, H and Public Annexes 1, D.1, E.1, E.2, E.4, E.5, E.6, E.8,G, I, J, ICC-01/15-4 13-10-2015 1/160 EO PT, 132–133, 150–151, https://www.icc-cpi.int/CourtRecords/CR2015_19375.PDF, last accessed 8 June 2023.

states (initially Burundi, Gambia and South Africa) to withdraw from the Rome Statute,[128,129] Chief Prosecutor Ms. Bensouda has once more referred to the principle of complementarity as a core principle of the ICC's jurisdiction and has more extensively focused on the principle's application in the latest Office of The Prosecutor's Report on Preliminary Examination Activities 2016.[130] The author of this chapter hopes that its informal dissemination to academics, ICC staff and members of the International Criminal Court Bar Association has *inter alia* assisted in the late recognition of the significance of the principle of complementarity as well.[131] Certainly, it remains to be seen to what extent this core principle of the Rome Statute will be truly revived and obtain the status that international legislators had initially envisaged for it, which was neither 'passive', 'positive', 'proactive' or 'radical' complementarity but simple, actual complementarity.[132]

References

Table of Cases

ICC (2006a) Decision ICC-01/04-01/06-8-Corr. http://www.icc-cpi.int/iccdocs/doc/doc236260.PDF. Accessed 8 June 2023

ICC (2006b) Prosecutor v. Thomas Lubanga Dyilo, ICC–01/04–01/06-772, 14 December 2006, para 23. http://www.icc-cpi.int/iccdocs/doc/doc243774.pdf. Accessed 8 June 2023

ICC (2009) Appeals Chamber, Prosecutor v. Germain Katanga and Mathieu Ngudjolo Chui, Judgment on the Appeal of Mr. Germain Katanga against the Oral Decision of Trial Chamber II of 12 June 2009 on the Admissibility of the Case", ICC-01/04-01/07-1497, paras. 1. http://www.icc-cpi.int/iccdocs/doc/doc746819.pdf. Accessed 8 June 2023

[128] But see also "ASP President welcomes the revocation of South Africa's withdrawal from the Rome Statute", 11 March 2017, https://www.icc-cpi.int/Pages/item.aspx?name=pr1285, last accessed 8 June 2023.

[129] Statement of the President of the Assembly of States Parties on the process of withdrawal from the Rome Statute by Burundi, 18 October 2016, https://www.icc-cpi.int/Pages/item.aspx?name=pr1244, last accessed 8 June 2023; President of the Assembly regrets withdrawal of any State Party from the Rome Statute and reaffirms the Court's fight against impunity, 22 October 2016, https://www.icc-cpi.int/Pages/item.aspx?name=pr1248, last accessed 8 June 2023, 10 April 2017; Press Conference by the President of the Assembly on withdrawal from the Rome Statute, 15:00 (GMT) in Dakar, 24 October 2016, https://www.icc-cpi.int/Pages/item.aspx?name=ma206, last accessed 8 June 2023.

[130] The Office of the Prosecutor, Report on Preliminary Examination Activities 2016, pp. 2–3, 5, 48–49, 72.

[131] The latest explicit referral to the complementarity principle can be found in the Statement of the Prosecutor of the International Criminal Court, Ms. Fatou Bensouda, regarding the situation in the Kasaï provinces, Democratic Republic of the Congo, 31 March 2017, https://www.icc-cpi.int/Pages/item.aspx?name=170331-otp-stat, last accessed 8 June 2023.

[132] For a concise analysis of passive, positive, proactive and radical complementarity with further bibliographical references see the MA thesis of Karanikola (2017).

ICC (2011a) Decision on the "Prosecutor's Application Pursuant to Article 58 as to Muammar Mohammed Abu Minyar Gaddafi, Saif Al-Islam Gaddafi and Abdullah Al-Senussi", ICC-01/11-12. http://www.icc-cpi.int/iccdocs/doc/doc1099314.pdf. Accessed 8 June 2023

ICC (2011b) Prosecutor v. Saif Al-Islam Gaddafi, formerly The Prosecutor v. Muammar Mohammed Abuminyar Gaddafi, Saif Al-Islam Gaddafi and Abdullah Al-Senussi, ICC-01/11-01/11. https://www.icc-cpi.int/libya/gaddafi. Accessed 8 June 2023

ICC (2013a) Decision on the Admissibility of the Case against Saif Al-Islam Gaddafi, ICC-01/11-01/11-344-Red, para 77. http://www.icc-cpi.int/iccdocs/doc/doc1599307.pdf. Accessed 8 June 2023

ICC (2013b) Judgment on the Appeal of Mr Abdullah Al-Senussi against the Decision of Pre-Trial Chamber I on the Admissibility of the Case against Abdullah Al-Senussi, http://www.icc-cpi.int/iccdocs/doc/doc1807073.pdf. Accessed 8 June 2023

ICC, Decision on the Admissibility of the Case Against Abdullah Al-Senussi, ICC-01/11-01/11-466 Red, 36, para 68. http://www.icc-cpi.int/iccdocs/doc/doc1663102.pdf. Accessed 8 June 2023

ICC, Decision on the Applications for Participation in the Proceedings of VPRS1, VPRS2, VPRS3, VPRS4, VPRS5 and VPRS6, para 65. http://www.icc-cpi.int/iccdocs/doc/doc183441.pdf. Accessed 8 June 2023

ICC, Situation in the Democratic Republic of Congo, Decision on the Applications for Participation in the Proceedings of VPRS1, VPRS2, VPRS3, VPRS4, VPRS5 and VPR-6, http://www.icc-cpi.int/iccdocs/doc/doc183441.pdf. Accessed 8 June 2023

ICC, Summary of the Decision on the admissibility of the case against Mr Abdullah Al-Senussi, 5 https://thenewlibyareport.files.wordpress.com/2014/05/english-summary.pdf. Accessed 8 June 2023

ICTR (2004) Prosecutor v. Ntakirutimana, Cases Nos. ICTR-96-10-A and ICTR-96-17-A, Appeals Chamber Judgement

ICTR (2006) Prosecutor v. Ntagerura et al, Case No. ICTR-99-46-A, Appeals Chamber Judgement

ICTY (2001) Prosecutor v. Kupreskic et al, Case No. IT-95-16-A, Appeals Chamber Judgement

ICTY (2004) Prosecutor v. Blaskic, Case No. IT-95-14-A, Appeals Chamber Judgement

ICTY (2005) Prosecutor v. Kvocka et al., Case No. IT-98-30/1-A, Appeals Chamber Judgment

Books

Schabas WA (2008a) Crimes against humanity. In: Sadat LN, Scharf MP (eds) The theory and practice of international criminal law: essays in Honor of Cherif M. Bassiouni. Koninklijke Brill NV, Leiden

Schabas WA (2010) The International Criminal Court: a commentary on the Rome Statute. Oxford University Press, New York

Tsilonis V (2010) Thomas Lubanga Dyilo: the unstable step of the International Criminal Court? In: Pitsela A (ed) Criminological quests: treatises in the Honour of Emeritus Professor Stergios Alexiadis. Sakkoulas, Thessaloniki

Articles/Papers

Benvenuti P (1999) Complementarity of the International Criminal Court to National Jurisdictions. In: Latanza & Schabas (ed) Essays, vol I

Bergsmo M, Bekou O, Jones A (2010) Complementarity after Kampala: capacity building and the ICC's legal tools. GoJIL 2:791

Burke-White WW (2008) Implementing a policy of positive complementarity in the Rome system of justice. Crim Law Forum 19:59–85

Carnero Rojo E (2005) The role of fair trial considerations in the complementarity regime of the International Criminal Court: from 'no peace without justice' to 'no peace with victor's justice'? Leiden J Int Law 18(4):829

Cassese A et al (2009) Informal expert paper: the principle of complementarity in practice. 3 ICC-01/04-01/07-1008-AnxA 30-03-2009. https://www.legal-tools.org/doc/90915d/pdf/. Accessed 8 June 2023

Heller KJ (2006) The shadow side of complementarity: the effect of Article 17 of the Rome Statute on national due process. Crim Law Forum 17:255. https://papers.ssrn.com/sol3/papers.cfm?abstract_id=907404. Accessed 8 June 2023

Holmes JT (1999) The principle of complementarity. In: Lee RS (ed) The International Criminal Court: the making of the Rome Statute. Kluwer Law International, The Hague

ICC, Annex to the Paper on some policy issues before the Office of the Prosecutor: Referrals and Communications, https://www.icc-cpi.int/itemsdocuments/20160915_otp-policy_case-selection_eng.pdf. Accessed 8 June 2023

ICC-OTP, Paper on Some Policy Issues Before the Office of the Prosecutor, http://www.icc-cpi.int/nr/rdonlyres/1fa7c4c6-de5f-42b7-8b25-60aa962ed8b6/143594/030905policy_paper.pdf. Accessed 8 June 2023

Joffe G (2014) Libya air strikes: Conflict linked to Wider Middle East. Available at BBC, https://www.bbc.com/news/world-africa-28948948. Accessed 8 June 2023

Karanikola V (2017) The principle of complementarity: a comparative analysis of the jurisprudence among the ad hoc Criminal Tribunal for the Former Yugoslavia. International Criminal Tribunal for Rwanda and the International Criminal Court, 117–122, Pandemos Digital Library of Panteion University. http://pandemos.panteion.gr/getfile.php?uri=http://localhost:8080/fedora/objects/iid:18184/datastreams/PDF1/content&mimetype=application%2Fpdf&filename=12PMS_DIE_EUR_SPO_KaranikolaVa.pdf. Accessed 8 June 2023

Kastanidou-Symeonidou E (2003) Legitimizing basis and ICC jurisdiction limit. NoB 51:452

McDermott Rees Y (2014) Towards positive complementarity? Available at: Phd in Human Rights Blog, http://humanrightsdoctorate.blogspot.gr/2014_07_01_archive.html. Accessed 8 June 2023

Rastan R (2008) What is a 'case' for the purpose of the Rome Statute? CrimLF 19:435

Rastan R (2010) Complementarity: contest or collaboration. In: Bergsmo M (ed) Complementarity and the exercise of universal jurisdiction for core international crimes. Torkel Opsahl Academic Epublisher, Oslo

Schabas WA (2008b) Complementarity in practice': some uncomplimentary thoughts. CrimLF 19:5

Zeidy E (2003) The principle of complementarity: a new machinery to implement international criminal law. MJIL 23:869

Zeidy ME (2005) The Ugandan Government Triggers the first test of the complementarity principle: an assessment of the first state's party referral to the ICC. IntlCLR 5:83–120

Websites/Web Sources

BBC News (2015a) Greek Oil Tanker Bombed in Libyan Port of Derna. http://www.bbc.com/news/world-africa-30681904. Accessed 8 June 2023

BBC News (2015b) Profile: Abdullah al-Senussi. http://www.bbc.com/news/world-middle-east-17414121. Accessed 8 June 2023

Crime of Aggression, Status of ratification and implementation. http://crimeofaggression.info/the-role-of-states/status-of-ratification-and-implementation/. Accessed 8 June 2023

Dominican Republic: Proposal Regarding the Preamble, UN Doc. A/CONF.183/C.1/L.52, 203. https://www.dropbox.com/s/z1gc07v13ofb34o/Proposal%20Submitted%20by%20the%20Dominican%20Republic.pdf?dl=0. Accessed 8 June 2023

ICC (1994) Draft Statute 1994: Article 35. http://legal.un.org/ilc/texts/instruments/english/draft%20articles/7_4_1994.pdf. Accessed 8 June 2023

ICC (2005) Warrant of Arrest for Joseph Kony issued on 8 July 2005 as amended on 27 September 2005, ICC-02/04-01/05-53, 11 para 37. http://www.icc-cpi.int/iccdocs/doc/doc97185.pdf. Accessed 8 June 2023

ICC (2006) Office of the Prosecutor, Report on the Activities Performed During the First Three Years. https://www.icc-cpi.int/nr/rdonlyres/d76a5d89-fb64-47a9-9821-725747378ab2/143680/otp_3yearreport20060914_english.pdf. Accessed 8 June 2023

ICC (2011) Pre-Trial Chamber I, Warrant of Arrest for Abdullah Al-Senussi, ICC-01/11-01/11-4. http://www.icc-cpi.int/iccdocs/doc/doc1101360.pdf. Accessed 8 June 2023

ICC (2012) Referral letter by the Government of Mali. http://www.icccpi.int/NR/rdonlyres/A245A47F-BFD1-45B6891C3BCB5B173F57/0/ReferralLetterMali130712.pdf. Accessed 8 June 2023

ICC (2013c) Application on behalf of the Government of Libya relating to Abdullah Al-Senussi pursuant to Article 19 ICCRSt, ICC-01/11-01/11-307-Red2. https://www.icc-cpi.int/CourtRecords/CR2013_02635.PDF. Accessed 8 June 2023

ICC (2013d) Defence Application on behalf of Abdullah Al-Senussi for Leave to Reply to the Libyan Government's Response to 'Defence Application on behalf of Mr. Abdullah Al-Senussi concerning Libya's Announcement of Trial Date in August 2013, ICC-01/11-01/11-398, para 10. http://www.icc-cpi.int/iccdocs/doc/doc1631011.pdf. Accessed 8 June 2023

ICC (2015) Situation in Georgia, Public Document with Confidential. https://www.icc-cpi.int/CourtRecords/CR2015_19375.PDF. Accessed 8 June 2023

ICC (2016a) President of the Assembly regrets withdrawal of any State Party from the Rome Statute. https://www.icc-cpi.int/Pages/item.aspx?name=pr1248. Accessed 8 June 2023

ICC (2016b) Press Conference by the President of the Assembly. https://www.icc-cpi.int/Pages/item.aspx?name=ma206. Accessed 8 June 2023

ICC (2016c) Statement of the President of the Assembly of States Parties on the process of withdrawal from the Rome Statute by Burundi. https://www.icc-cpi.int/Pages/item.aspx?name=pr1244. Accessed 8 June 2023

ICC (2017a) ASP President welcomes the revocation of South Africa's withdrawal from the Rome Statute. https://www.icc-cpi.int/Pages/item.aspx?name=pr1285. Accessed 8 June 2023

ICC (2017b) Statement of the Prosecutor of the International Criminal Court, Ms Fatou Bensouda. https://www.icc-cpi.int/Pages/item.aspx?name=170331-otp-stat. Accessed 8 June 2023

ICC. https://www.icc-cpi.int/nr/rdonlyres/add16852-aee9-4757-abe79cdc7cf02886/283503/romestatuteng1.pdf. Accessed 8 June 2023

ICC, Decision to Convene a Status Conference on the Investigation in the Situation in Uganda in Relation to the Application of Article 53, paras 4–5. http://www.icc-cpi.int/iccdocs/doc/doc97225.pdf. Accessed 8 June 2023

ICC, Declaration of Judge Christine Van den Wyngaert. http://www.icc-cpi.int/iccdocs/doc/doc1663117.PDF. Accessed 8 June 2023

ICC, President of Uganda Refers Situation Concerning the Lord's Resistance Army (LRA) to the ICC. https://www.icccpi.int/pages/item.aspx?name=president+of+uganda+refers+situation+concerning+the+lord_s+resistance+army+_lra_+to+the+icc. Accessed 8 June 2023

ICC, Situation in the Democratic Republic of Congo, Decision on the Applications for Participation in the Proceedings of VPRS1, VPRS2, VPRS3, VPRS4, VPRS5 and VPRS6, para 65. http://www.icc-cpi.int/iccdocs/doc/doc183441.pdf. Accessed 8 June 2023

Letter of Prosecutor (2006). http://www.iccnow.org/documents/OTP_letter_to_senders_re_Iraq_9_February_2006.pdf. Accessed 8 June 2023

London Agreement of 8 August 1945. http://avalon.law.yale.edu/imt/imtchart.asp. Accessed 8 June 2023

Moreno-Ocampo L (2003) Statement made at the ceremony for the solemn undertaking of the Chief Prosecutor of the ICC. https://www.icc-cpi.int%2FNR%2Frdonlyres%2FD7572226-264A-4B6B-85E3-2673648B4896%2F143585%2F030616_moreno_ocampo_english.pdf&usg=AOvVaw3lMglPOBu9BI3Qb_944hds. Accessed 8 June 2023

Official website of ICC on the Uganda situation. https://www.icc-cpi.int/uganda. Accessed 8 June 2023

Press release (2012). https://asp.icc-cpi.int/en_menus/asp/press%20releases/press%20releases%202012/Pages/pr793.aspx. Accessed 8 June 2023

Special Court for Sierra Leone (SCSL). http://www.rscsl.org/Documents/scsl-statute.pdf. Accessed 8 June 2023

UN Security Council Resolution 1970/26-02-2011 "Peace and Security in Africa", para 4, https://undocs.org/S/RES/1970(2011). Accessed 8 June 2023

United Nations Treaty Collection. https://treaties.un.org/Pages/ViewDetails.aspx?src=TREATY&mtdsg_no=XVIII-10-b&chapter=18&lang=en. Accessed 8 June 2023

Chapter 10
Ecocide: The Emergence of a New Crime Within the Jurisdiction of the International Criminal Court?

Abstract The Chernobyl Nuclear Disaster (1986), the Exxon Valdez Oil Spill (1989), and the Kakhovka Dam destruction (2023) epitomise infamous ecocides, overshadowing countless lesser-known yet equally significant ecocidal incidents. The critical role of a healthy environment in ensuring human survival and progress underscores the necessity of addressing ecocide as a potential threat to human civilisation's long-term survival. In response to this growing concern, in June 2021 an Independent Expert Panel, initiated by Stop Ecocide in June 2021, comprising 12 specialists, proposed a legal definition of ecocide. Nevertheless, this definition garnered criticism from various quarters, including prominent academics and legal experts such as Kevin Jon Heller, Kai Ambos, Michael Karnavas, and Matthew Gillett. Subsequently, alternative definitions emerged from different groups, notably the Promise Institute for Human Rights (UCLA) Group of Experts and scholars, including Matthew Gillett. This chapter scrutinises the discussions around the undeniable need for a redefined concept of ecocide. It illustrates that while the other proposed definitions of ecocide may be more in accordance with legal principles (*de lege artis*), there is substantial room for improvement. Not only should the definition of ecocide be more explicit, but it should also contain as few lacunas as possible to anticipate any future occurrences. In this vein, Victor Tsilonis proposes an innovative definition of ecocide, aiming to fill existing gaps in the legal understanding of this crime. The chapter concludes that considering the International Criminal Court's constraints in terms of financial, structural, and human resources, as well as its mandate prescribed by the Rome Statute and overseen by the Assembly of States-Parties, a compelling case can be made for the establishment of a new, specialised international legal institution: the International Criminal Court for the Protection of Environment" (ICCPE). This proposed institution would be specifically tailored to tackle the complex and thus far neglected crime of ecocide, providing a dedicated framework for addressing environmental destruction on an international scale.

V. Tsilonis, *The Jurisdiction of the International Criminal Court*,
https://doi.org/10.1007/978-3-031-46138-5_10

10.1 Introduction: Ecocides in the Last Fifty Years, the Explosion of Kakhovka Dam and the Pursuit of Global Environmental Preservation

Over the last few decades, people have been inundated with increasingly alarming news about environmental catastrophes, including the Chernobyl Nuclear Disaster (1986), the Exxon Valdez Oil Spill (1989), the Kuwait Oil Fires (1991), the Amazon Rainforest Fires (1995), the Indian Ocean Earthquake and Tsunami (2004), Hurricane Katrina (2005), the Deepwater Horizon Oil Spill (2010), the Fukushima Daiichi Nuclear Disaster (2011), the Australian Bushfires (2019–2020), and most recently, the Nova Scotia Wildfires (2023). Moreover, since the beginning of the war in Ukraine in 2022, there has been a marked rise in news about worrying environmental issues. These reports initially culminated in growing fears of an imminent nuclear catastrophe at the Zaporizhzhia Nuclear Power Plant[1] but have so far resulted in the 'mere' destruction of the Kakhovka Dam.[2]

On the first week of February 2022, a giant trawler shed 100,000 dead fish into the Atlantic Ocean off the French coast, creating a shocking image that even possibly a skilled artist could not imagine before.[3] In the same week, almost 6300 barrels of oil leaked into the Cayambe Coca reserve in the Ecuadorian Amazon and polluted the Coca River, an important source for indigenous communities in the area.[4] Contemporaneously, it is at least hopeful to acknowledge that there have been a lot of movements in the past few years to recognise ecocide as a new international crime—especially from countries severely affected by climate change and NGOs with a particular focus on the protection of environment.

Nonetheless, no one was actually expecting soon an ecocide that would have both elements of a war crime and be one of the greatest ecocides at the same time. And this was the ecocidal explosion of the Kakhovka dam in Ukraine on 6 June 2023. The dam, prior to its partial destruction, was a significant civil structure that was built during Soviet times. It stood 30 m tall, stretched for 3.2 km, and created the vast 2155 sq km (832 sq mile) Kakhovka reservoir, which was fully capable of withholding 18 cubic kilometres (4.3 cubic miles) of water, i.e., a volume roughly equivalent to the Great Salt Lake in the U.S.[5] It served as the power source for the Kakhovka hydroelectric plant, a significant energy generator. The reservoir was critically used to supply vast amounts of water to local communities, support farming, and provide critical cooling for the Zaporizhzhia nuclear power plant.

[1] Euronews (2023a), last accessed 10 June 2023.

[2] The Guardian (2023a), last accessed 10 June 2023. Also Euronews (2023b).

[3] The Guardian (2022a).

[4] Al Jazeera (2022), last accessed 20 June 2023.

[5] Reuters (2023).

After tis malicious breach severe flooding of over 600 square kilometers consequently occurred.[6]

The huge Soviet-era dam on the Dnipro River was practically separating Russian and Ukrainian forces in southern Ukraine. At the time of this ecocidal act, the Russian military held control over the dam, having captured it during the initial stages of the Ukraine's invasion. Ukrainian President Volodymyr Zelenskiy accused Russian forces of blowing up the Kakhovka Hydroelectric Power Station internally and argued that Russia should be held to account for this 'terrorist attack', which was orchestrated in order to obstruct or postpone an anticipated major Ukrainian counter offence.[7] Conversely, Russian authorities have vehemently denied these claims, attributing the dam's explosion to HIMARS missiles launched by Ukrainian forces, which allegedly committed a horrendous terrorist act with the explicit aim of cutting off the water supply of Crimea.[8] Moreover, the dam's explosion aimed at distracting attention from the Ukrainian 'faltering' and 'overtly advertised' counter-offensive.

Concerns of utmost seriousness have been raised that the diminished reservoir might leave three vital areas in Ukraine's agricultural heartland lacking essential water resources. Numerous canals are fed by this reservoir, each playing a key role in watering vast areas of farmland. The North Crimean canal, supplying water to western Kherson and then flowing to Crimea, and the Kakhovsky canal, responsible for hydrating a majority of the agricultural fields in the Kherson region before reaching Zaporizhzhia, are the most crucial canals.

The dam raised the water level of the Dnipro by 16 m (52.49 feet) and made possible its redirection to the arid Crimean Peninsula, triggering the growth of urban centres and irrigated agriculture. After the Kakhovka Dam's blast, thousands of inhabitants downstream were compelled to evacuate, and numerous villages, under both Ukrainian and Russian control, have been swallowed by the floodwaters. Furthermore, a few hours after the collapse of the dam, an adviser to the Ukrainian president stated to the press that "a global ecological disaster" was under way, while on 8 June 2023 Ukrainian President Volodymyr Zelenskiy highlighted that 50,000 hectares of forest were flooded and that 20,000 animals and 10,000 birds were "under threat of imminent death".[9,10]

Additionally, the reservoir's significant water loss can potentially jeopardize the future critical water provision for the Zaporizhzhia Nuclear Power Plant. The cooling systems for Europe's largest nuclear plant are supplied with water from the Kakhovka reservoir. If the dam falls below 12.7 m, i.e., the lowest level at which water can still be pumped upstream to Zaporizhzhia Nuclear Power Plant, there currently exist no other alternative water sources to keep the nuclear plant cool enough to function.

---

[6] Le Monde with AFP (2023).

[7] Reuters (2023).

[8] The dam supplied Crimea with 85% of its water needs, Reuters (2023).

[9] The Guardian (2023a), accessed 10 June 2023.

[10] Le Monde (2023).

Apart from potentially constituting a war crime, the dam's destruction clearly represents an ecocide of the most heinous form. As no side assumes responsibility—a process that is notably fraught—we are left with a sobering reminder of the proverb: "In war, truth is the first casualty".[11]

10.2 A Potential War Crime? The Destruction of Nova Kakhovka Dam

Pursuant to the provision of Article 8(2)(b)(iv) ICCRSt, a war crime can be committed if one intentionally launches "an attack in the knowledge that such attack will cause incidental loss of life or injury to civilians or damage to civilian objects or widespread, long-term and severe damage to the natural environment which would be clearly excessive in relation to the concrete and direct overall military advantage anticipated".

Mathew Gillett takes for granted that the destruction of Kakhovka dam was caused by the Russian forces;[12] and while this possibility cannot and should not be excluded it is equally clear that the possibility of the dam having been hit by Western missiles launched by the Ukrainian armed forces should not be excluded either at this point.[13] On other hand learned academics like Marco Milanovic have justifiably abstained from taking any such 'small detail' for granted. Milanovic references *jus in bello* (or international humanitarian law in politically correct terms) stipulations that pertain to 'attacks'. There is ambiguity about whether such an attack has occurred, according to Art. 49(1) of the Additional Protocol I to the Geneva Conventions, which characterises an attack as any violent act against the opposing force, whether it is offensive or defensive. If, as per Russia's assertion, the dam suffered damage from Ukrainian artillery fire, this would be considered an attack under Art. 49(2) of the Additional Protocol I to the Geneva Conventions, because this provision applies to all attacks, no matter where they take place, even on national territories temporarily occupied by an enemy. However, if the dam's critical damage was secretly instigated by Russia, it is less clear whether this event would

---

[11] Often attributed to Aeschylus (5th Century B.C.), Dr Samuel Johnson (1758), Ethel Snowden (1915), Hiram Warren Johnson (1918). The 2021 edition of the Yale Dictionary of Quotations attributes it "safely" to Ethel Snowden (wife of labour politician Philip Snowden) about whom there is unquestionable published evidence that she indeed wrote it in 1915, following maybe the footsteps of many female thinkers whose wisdom has been falsely credited to less intelligent men. In any case, it is spectacularly ironic that the true owner of this proverb is so difficult to ascertain. Shapiro (2021), p. 565.

[12] Gillet (2023).

[13] In fact, a layman observing the initial pictures of the aftermath of the explosion in Guardian might be inclined to think the opposite, i.e., that the theory of the dam being hit by missiles appears quite plausible. This is because there are two enormous holes on the left and right sides of the dam, while a significant portion remains intact at its center.

constitute an ‘attack’ under international humanitarian law. And this is the case because *jus in bello* generally does not classify the destruction of one’s own dam as an attack.[14] For instance, if Ukraine deliberately destroyed a dam under its management to inundate a region and halt the progress of Russian forces, this would not be considered an attack under *jus in bello*, even if there were significant civilian casualties. Likewise, from Russia’s perspective, the Nova Kakhovka dam precisely fits this scenario, given that it was under their control, regardless of the fact that, objectively, the dam and the entire territory belongs to the sovereign state of Ukraine.[15]

So to sum up, in the case of the destruction of the Nova Kakhovka dam it seems *prima facie* much more plausible that it could amount to an attack if it was conducted by the Ukrainian forces **but not** if it was conducted by Russian forces, because the sabotage of objects belonging to the sphere of control of one adversary does not constitute an attack.[16] Nonetheless, if according to the concrete facts of the case that may be revealed in the future or a novel interpretation of *jus in bello* provisions, this action could be validly regarded as an attack, then one should examine the rules on distinction, proportionality and precautions.

Consequently, the first question is whether the dam served as a military target, thereby relinquishing its protection as a civilian structure. Pursuant to Article 52(2) of Additional Protocol I of the Geneva Conventions, “*military objectives are confined to those structures which, by their character, location, objective, or utilization, contribute effectively to military operations and whose complete or partial obliteration, seizure, or neutralization, under the existing circumstances, provides a tangible military benefit.*” This criterion consists of two aspects, both of which should be satisfied. A dam, inherently, is not a military objective *per se*, although it could potentially become one by its “*character, location, objective or utilisation*”.

The Nova Kakhovka dam’s unique ‘nature as a hydroelectric power station is crucial. It produces a significant amount of energy—nearly 2000 MW at full capacity. This electricity could be utilised wholly or at least partly for military operations, including powering military installations and facilities, communication systems, or other critical infrastructure. Thus, the dam’s intrinsic nature might be seen as making an effective contribution to ongoing military actions in the region.

Secondly, the dam’s ‘location’ could also render it a military objective. Positioned strategically on the Dnieper River, control over the dam could influence the dynamics of power in the region which is under heavy military conflict. This location could afford a military advantage in terms of controlling water and energy resources, affecting transportation routes, deviating or postponing attacks and military operations etc.

[14] Schmitt (2022).

[15] Milanovic (2023).

[16] Schmitt (2022).

Thirdly, considering its 'purpose' or 'use', the dam might also serve as a military objective. If, for instance, it were exploited for the transport of military goods or personnel, or if the energy it generated were primarily used to support military facilities, it would certainly be classified as a military objective. The existence of the road on top of the Nova Kakhovka dam could further complicate its potential classification as a military objective. This road could indeed facilitate or have facilitated the movement of military equipment and personnel, serving as a significant strategic asset in these times of conflict. If the dam's road was being used to transport military hardware or troops, it could potentially fulfil the 'purpose' or 'use' criteria under Article 52(2) of Additional Protocol I of the Geneva Conventions.

Nonetheless, it's worth reiterating that the identification of a structure as a military objective must be context-specific and consider the actual use of the structure at the time. The mere presence of a road on a dam doesn't inherently qualify the dam as a military objective. However, if there's evidence that the road is actively facilitating military actions, its status could shift accordingly.

However, it's important to note that, based on the principles of distinction and proportionality in international humanitarian law, even if the Nova Kakhovka dam could be regarded as a military objective, any attack should avoid or at least minimise harm to civilians and civilian objects. Consequently, a thorough assessment of the potential civilian harm caused by its destruction would be required before any military action.

So the primary inquiry here is if the dam was making "an effective contribution to military operations." For instance, the path atop the Nova Kakhovka dam could be used for the transport of military apparatuses or provisions; moreover, the electricity produced by the Kakhovka Hydroelectric Station could power military installations. Based on the publicly revealed facts thus far, it does not likely that to be the case in this situation, but no such scenario should be excluded.

Regarding the second aspect, in theory, the demolition of a dam can offer "a tangible military benefit", such as impeding enemy maneuverability within the impacted region. Again, both aspects of the test must be met—if the dam was not contributing effectively to military operations, it would not qualify as a military target, even if its demolition offered a theoretical military benefit.

10.3 Ecocide and the Search for a Legal Definition

Ecocide, broadly speaking, refers to actions that lead to long-term damage to the environment. The term was originally used in the '70s following the use of defoliant agents in Indochina. However, it has since become an object of thoughtful reflection and a landmark in attempts to establish an indisputable legal definition.

Most recently, in June 2021, an Independent Expert Panel chaired by jurists Philippe Sands and Dior Fall Sow came up with a latest definition of ecocide. According to the experts' panel, "ecocide" means *"unlawful or wanton acts committed with knowledge that there is a substantial likelihood of severe and either widespread or long-term damage to the environment caused by those acts".*[17]

This definition was intended to serve as a basis for an amendment of the Rome Statute (ICCRSt), which could potentially include ecocide as the Court's fifth (5th) core crime. Additionally, at the 2019 Assembly of States Parties (ASP) the States of Vanuatu and Maldives called for the inclusion of ecocide within the Rome Statute.[18] Moreover, the same proposal received support from other states (Belgium, Finland, Bangladesh and Samoa) at the Assembly of States Parties in 2020 and 2021.[19] More recently the recognition of ecocide as an international crime has also gained support within France, the UK and the European Union. Nevertheless, there is still a long—and in some respects questionable—legal road ahead before this landmark amendment to the Rome Statute can be achieved.

This chapter analyses the crime of ecocide, from its theoretical definition to its potentially actual exercise of jurisdiction. It highlights the difficulties in reaching a consensus on a legal definition for ecocide and focuses on the anthropocentric versus ecocentric debate, which lies within the current anthropocentric crimes of the Rome Statute (war crimes, crimes against humanity, genocide, crime of aggression) and the newly proposed crime of ecocide. "It then proceeds to analyze the current ICCRSt framework to determine where and whether ecocide could fit in, as well as the new proposed definition of ecocide and the new proposals to amend the Rome Statute accordingly. Finally, the chapter proposes the establishment of a new International Criminal Court for the Protection of Environment (ICCPE), which will exercise jurisdiction specifically over the crime of ecocide and be much more effective in protecting the environment as a whole.

Since the term "ecocide" was first used to refer to the use of defoliant agents such as "Agent Orange" during the Vietnam War,[20] scholars and practitioners have been trying to agree on a legal definition for the crime. The one consensus seems to be that ecocide relates to the destruction of the environment, but the extent of this destruction, the role the environment plays at the crime (a protected good in itself or a tool for human development?) and the exact contours of the crime still are under discussion.

The issue of ecocide started to gain attention during the 1972 UN Stockholm Conference on the Human Environment[21]—where the term was used by the Swedish Prime Minister—and several definitions have emerged since then.

Still in the '70s, Professor Richard Falk proposed the criminalisation of ecocide to the UN. In this occasion, he defined ecocide as:

---

[17] Independent Expert Panel for the Legal Definition of Ecocide (2021).

[18] Government of the Republic of Vanuatu (2019); Stop Ecocide International (2019), last accessed 20 June 2023.

[19] ICC ASP (2022).

[20] Chiarini (2022), p. 3. Similarly, Chiarini (2021), p. 2. See also Weisberg (1970).

[21] Chiarini (2022), pp. 4–9. Also, Chiarini (2021), pp. 3–4.

> [a]ny of the following acts committed with the intent to destroy, in whole or in part, a human ecosystem:
>
> (a) The use of weapons of mass destruction, whether nuclear, bacteriological, chemical or other;
> (b) The use of chemical herbicides to defoliate and deforest natural forests for military purposes;
> (c) The use of bombs and artillery in such quantity, density or size as to impair the quality of the soil or to enhance the prospect of diseases dangerous to human beings, animals or crops;
> (d) The use of bulldozing equipment to destroy large tracts of forest or cropland for military purposes;
> (e) The use of techniques designed to increase or decrease rainfall or otherwise modify weather as a weapon of war;
> (f) The forcible removal of human beings or animals from their habitual places of habitation to expedite the pursuit of military or industrial objectives.[22]

Falk's proposal, especially in its operative clause, is similar to the definition of genocide. This is explained by the fact that when Falk proposed this definition within the context of a draft convention on the crime of ecocide, in 1973, there was also an ongoing proposal to add ecocide into the 1948 Genocide Convention.[23]

These proposals did not go forward. Likewise, the International Law Commissions had originally included environmental harm in its *Draft Code of Crimes Against the Peace and Security of Mankind*,[24] but it was not incorporated in its final version. First, the commission considered including "acts causing serious damage to the environment" under Article 26, but as need for intent was part of the discussion, this was changed to "wilful and severe damage to the environment", only to exclude it altogether in the end.[25]

In 2010, environmental activist and lawyer Polly Higgins proposed the following definition of ecocide:

> the extensive destruction, damage to or loss of ecosystem(s) of a given territory, whether by human agency or by other causes, to such an extent that peaceful enjoyment by the inhabitants of that territory has been severely diminished.[26]

This definition was at the centre of the ecocide debate until recently, especially due to Higgins's activism for the recognition of ecocide as an international crime. However, there was little consensus about it, which changed when the *Stop Ecocide Foundation* convened an Independent Expert Panel for the Legal Definition of Ecocide.[27] This panel presented a new and more robust definition for the crime, which is further explored in session 3. The main problem with finding a legal

[22] Falk (1973), p. 93.
[23] Chiarini (2022), pp. 5–8.
[24] Higgins et al. (2013), p. 251.
[25] *Ibid.*
[26] Higgins (2016). Also Stop Ecocide International (2023), accessed 20 June 2023.
[27] Independent Expert Panel for the Legal Definition of Ecocide (2021).

definition for the crime is the lack of consensus regarding most of its elements.[28] That is, whether responsibility for ecocide should be objective or subjective; whether only natural persons should be held accountable or companies as well; or whether intent is necessary.

10.4 The Anthropocentric v. Ecocentric Debate

Most importantly, these definitions do not seem to agree on the nature of the crime itself: whether it should protect the environment as a means for human existence (and adopt an anthropocentric approach) or protect the environment *per se* (and adopt an ecocentric approach).

The approach taken in defining ecocide can have practical concerns in its application. Taking the two environmental-related news mentioned above as an example, the difference between an anthropocentric and an ecocentric approach would change how (and if) these conducts would be eventually prosecuted. In the example of the giant trawler shedding 100,000 dead fish into the Atlantic Ocean off the French coast, only an ecocentric approach would likely incur in prosecuting the crime. The mass discharge of fish, caused by a tear in the vessels' net, is said to impact not only the fish population itself but also its predators (such as dolphins).[29] Despite being a conduct that greatly impacts on a whole ecosystem, there is no direct impact on humans, which means that an anthropocentric approach would not cover the conduct as a crime.

Similarly, in the example of the barrels of oil leaked into the Cayambe Coca reserve, an anthropocentric approach would only prosecute the crime of ecocide insofar as the pollution of the Coca River's banks directly impacts the communities living in the area.[30] Locals have been reported to take part of a clean-up crew and say that *"no one can bathe normally in the river, nor drink from here, there is no fish, there is nothing,"*.[31] However, an ecocentric approach would aim to protect the region's rainforests and its wildlife in itself. As Heller and Lawrence[32] point out, this approach would allow to protect the environment regardless of the use it may have to human beings. The main tension perhaps is that, while an anthropocentric approach is closer to the international legal system developed post World War II (with human dignity at its centre) an ecocentric approach offers a rupture of this system, but a rupture that is close to contemporary movements to protect the environment.[33]

---

[28] Dissenha and Farias (2021), p. 313.

[29] The Guardian (2022a).

[30] Al Jazeera (2022).

[31] Al Jazeera (2022).

[32] Lawrence and Heller (2007), p. 5.

[33] Dissenha and Farias (2021), p. 313.

Looking at the examples of definitions above, it is likely that proposed definitions of ecocide involve an anthropocentric approach at some point. Falk's definition explicitly mentions the destruction of a "human ecosystem". Higgins's definition only criminalises harming the environment "to such an extent that peaceful enjoyment by the inhabitants of that territory has been severely diminished". Whenever the definition seemingly only includes harm to the environment, such as Article 26 of the *Draft Code of Crimes Against the Peace and Security of Mankind*, it is likely that additional provisions include some form of anthropocentric element, such as a proportionality test. This is the case with the legal definition presented by the Independent Expert Panel, as seen below.

10.5 Ecocide Within the Current Framework of the ICC

Currently, ecocide finds its closer match within the ICCRSt as a war crime. However, ecocide might be approached within the current ICC framework through other crimes such as crimes against humanity and the crime of genocide, albeit through an anthropocentric approach.

As a war crime, Article 8 (2) (b) (iv) criminalises the severe damage to the environment in the following manner:

> Article 8
>
> War Crimes
>
> [...]
>
> 2. For the purpose of this Statute, "war crimes" means:
>
> [...]
>
> (b) Other serious violations of the laws and customs applicable in international armed conflict, within the established framework of international law, namely, any of the following acts:
>
> [...]
>
> (iv) Intentionally launching an attack in the knowledge that such attack will cause incidental loss of life or injury to civilians or damage to civilian objects *or widespread, long-term and severe damage to the natural environment which would be clearly excessive in relation to the concrete and direct overall military advantage anticipated*; (emphasis added)

There are a couple of considerations regarding this provision. First, although Article 8 (2) (b) (iv) does not mention the term "ecocide", the provision itself is similar to the idea of ecocide most scholars and advocated had in the 70s, especially Falk's definition of ecocide mentioned above.[34] It is also close to an ecocentric definition of ecocide, insofar as its phrasing gives the idea that the mere "damage to the natural environment" would be enough to constitute a war crime, regardless of

[34] Falk (1973).

the effects of such damage to humans. Lawrence and Heller note that this interpretation is possible due to the use of the disjunctive "or".[35] However, the application of this provision is extremely limited. As part of Article 8 (2) (b) ICCRSt, the conduct must take place in the context of and be associated with an international armed conflict in order to constitute a crime.[36] That is to say, if a widespread, long-term and severe damage to the natural environment occurs during peace time, or during a non-international armed conflict, the ICC has no jurisdiction over it. The damage to the environment must also be "clearly excessive in relation to the concrete and direct overall military advantage anticipated". Finally, terms such as "widespread, long term and severe damage" may also be difficult to be defined in practice.[37] Thus, although the ICCRSt does incorporate a provision that is close to the idea of ecocide, Article 8 (2) (b) (iv) still addresses environmental harm in a much narrower way than what is envisioned by advocates of the criminalisation of ecocide.[38]

Alternatively, ecocide could be criminalised through already existing core crimes within the ICC framework, such as genocide and crimes against humanity. This would necessarily imply adopting an anthropocentric approach, as both crimes have human beings at its centre. It is nevertheless a possibility to protect the environment, even if only as a tool for humans.

Regarding the crime of genocide, there is a link between the two crimes. Chiarini notes[39] that, in the 70s and 80s, there were proposals to include ecocide into the 1948 Genocide Convention. On one of these occasions, UN Special Rapporteur on the Prevention and Punishment of the Crime of Genocide Nicodème Ruhashyankiko compared the crime of ecocide to the crime of genocide.[40] Similarly, Crook and Short[41] argue that ecocide can be a method of genocide, given that environmental destruction threatens the existence of a group. An example of this can be seen in the Situation in Darfur, where Pre-Trial Chamber I lists the contamination of wells and water pumps as one of the ways in which the targeted groups were attacked.[42] On the other hand, ecocide within Article 6 ICCRSt can only be prosecuted as an instrument of genocide. Given that the crime of genocide requires the *dolus especialis* to "destroy, in whole or in part, a national, ethnical, racial or religious group, as such", the primary intention of the perpetrator would necessarily have to be destroying any of the protected groups as such, not harming the environment. The destruction of the environment would therefore only be instrumental and its protection *per se* secondary.

---

[35] Lawrence and Heller (2007).

[36] Article 8 (2) (b) (iv) - Elements of Crimes.

[37] Drumbl (1998), p. 126.

[38] Cassese (2003), pp. 60–61.

[39] Chiarini (2022), pp. 3–7; See also Chiarini (2021), p. 5.

[40] Ruhashyankiko (1978).

[41] Crook and Short (2014).

[42] Second Warrant of Arrest for Omar Hassan Ahmad Al Bashir, ICC-02/05-01/09-9, https://www.icc-cpi.int/CourtRecords/CR2010_04825.PDFZ, last accessed 8 June 2023.

Regarding crimes against humanity, this would be the less restrictive approach to prosecute ecocide within the current ICCRSt framework, as it would be applicable during peace time and would not require a *dolus specialis*. Currently, none of the specific acts listed in Article 7 (1) have any connection to the environment. But the open clause of Article 7 (1) (k)—which criminalises "Other inhumane acts of a similar character intentionally causing great suffering, or serious injury to body or to mental or physical health."—, could be used for prosecuting ecocide. As long as the conduct is similar in nature and gravity to other crimes against humanity, the destruction of the environment could be criminalised (e.g. deforestation or the contamination of rivers and other resources that are essential to populations). This of course is also a very anthropocentric conception of ecocide, which would still fall short in protecting the environment in itself or recognising the climate and ecological emergency.

Insofar as the current ICCRSt framework is still very limited in its protection of the environment, the Court may still prioritise cases in which its core crimes are committed along with the destruction of the environment. As an example, in 2016 the Office of the Prosecutor issued a Policy Paper on Case Selection and Prioritisation[43] that demonstrated concern for the environment by "giving particular consideration" to prosecuting crimes "committed by means of, or that result in, *inter alia*, the destruction of the environment, the illegal exploitation of natural resources or the illegal dispossession of land". This could serve as an alternative while State Parties consider and support amendments to the Statute.

10.6 Examining the Independent Expert Panel's Proposed Ecocide Definition: Legal and Practical Concerns

In June 2021, an Independent Expert Panel convened by *Stop Ecocide* and composed with 12 specialists presented a proposal for a legal definition of ecocide. The panel proposed the inclusion of Article 8 *ter* to the ICCRSt:

Article 8 ter
Ecocide

1. For the purpose of this Statute, "ecocide" means unlawful or wanton acts committed with knowledge that there is a substantial likelihood of severe and either widespread or long-term damage to the environment being caused by those acts.
2. For the purpose of paragraph 1:
   a. "Wanton" means with reckless disregard for damage which would be clearly excessive in relation to the social and economic benefits anticipated;
   b. "Severe" means damage which involves very serious adverse changes, disruption or harm to any element of the environment, including grave impacts on human life or natural, cultural or economic resources;

[43] Office of the Prosecutor (2016).

c. "Widespread" means damage which extends beyond a limited geographic area, crosses state boundaries, or is suffered by an entire ecosystem or species or a large number of human beings;
d. "Long-term" means damage which is irreversible or which cannot be redressed through natural recovery within a reasonable period of time;
e. "Environment" means the earth, its biosphere, cryosphere, lithosphere, hydrosphere and atmosphere, as well as outer space.[44]

Article 8 *ter* is based on the structure of Article 7 ICCRSt (on crimes against humanity) and influenced by Article 8 (2) (b) (iv) ICCRSt, which criminalises the destruction of the environment during international armed conflicts.[45] The main influences from Article 8 (2) (b) (iv) are the use of terms "widespread", "long term" and "severe" to describe the prohibited damage, the use of a proportionality test and the use of endangerment liability (as opposed to a requirement for materialisation of harm).[46] Additionally, the panel proposed a new preambular paragraph 2 *bis*:

> Concerned that the environment is daily threatened by severe destruction and deterioration, gravely endangering natural and human systems worldwide.[47]

According to the panel, the formulation of this paragraph is based on the ICJ's phrasing in its Advisory Opinion on the Legality of Use of Nuclear Weapons (1996),[48] in which the Court recognised that "the environment is under daily threat" and that "environment is not an abstraction but represents the living space, the quality of life and the very health of human beings, including generations unborn' and further confirmed that that 'the general obligation of States' to ensure protection of the environment forms a part of the corpus of international law".[49]

These proposed amendments were surely the product of many discussions and careful consideration by the panel. However, there are still some important considerations to be made regarding this definition of ecocide as well as its elements, as they may pose some legal and practical concerns.

First, the use of the phrasing "severe *and* widespread *or* long-term". The panel was caught between using a conjunctive (widespread, long-lasting *and* severe), like Article 8 (2) (b) (iv) of the ICCRSt and using a disjunctive (widespread, long lasting *or* severe), like the 1976 Convention on the Prohibition of Military or any other Hostile Use of Environmental Modification Techniques. Eventually, the panel decided to go for a mid-point between both, where the test applied would not be too low nor too high. However, this mixed approach may pose difficult interpretative problems.[50] Moreover, the cumulative element of "severe" and "widespread or long term" may be reductant or impose an unnecessary additional test. The test already

[44] Independent Expert Panel for the Legal Definition of Ecocide (2021).

[45] *Ibid.*

[46] *Ibid.*

[47] *Ibid.*

[48] *Ibid.*

[49] See ICJ (1996), p. 226.

[50] Ambos (2021).

defines "severe" as "damage which involves very serious adverse changes, disruption or harm to any element[51] of the environment, including grave impacts on human life or natural, cultural or economic resources."[52] This test would likely include acts that were considered "widespread" (understood by the panel by "damage which extends beyond a limited geographic area, crosses state boundaries, or is suffered by an entire ecosystem or species or a large number of human being") or long-term ("understood as damage which is irreversible or which cannot be redressed through natural recovery within a reasonable period of time").[53] Thus, the inclusion of a cumulative "severe" test would put an unnecessary weight into the consideration of the act as a crime.

Second, the use of the expression "substantial likelihood" in the beginning of the definition. By criminalising not acts that damage the environment, but those acts merely committed with "knowledge that there is a substantial likelihood of severe and either widespread or long-term damage to the environment being caused by those acts",[54] the definition opens itself to the possibility of an inchoate offence. This is on purpose: the proposal adds that it uses an "endangerment liability, rather than a requirement for materialisation of harm."[55] A person that knowingly acts in a way that is substantially likely that a damage to the environment occurs but does not incur in any damage may still be liable under this definition. As an analogy, this would be almost an attempted murder to the environment.

Third, the panel introduces the concept of "wanton acts" and proposes that omission is equally criminalised, both of which do not fit within the current ICCRSt framework. Wanton, for the panel, means "with reckless disregard for damage which would be clearly excessive in relation to the social and economic benefits anticipated".[56] The panel also "proposes a *mens rea* of recklessness or *dolus eventualis*".[57] This concept of recklessness/*dolus eventualis*, however, is highly controversial,[58] especially considering Article 30 ICCRSt's condition that a person is only liable if the material elements of a crime are committed with "intent and knowledge". Similarly, the panel proposes that the conduct "includes an act or omission".[59]

[51] The panel also notes that "any element" "is ntended to make it clear that it is enough to affect any element encompassed by the definition of the environment, that is, 'the earth, its biosphere, cryosphere, lithosphere, hydrosphere and atmosphere, as well as outer space".

[52] Independent Expert Panel for the Legal Definition of Ecocide (2021).

[53] *Ibid.*

[54] *Ibid.*

[55] *Ibid.*

[56] *Ibid.*

[57] *Ibid.*

[58] War Crimes Research Office (2010); Decision on the confirmation of charges, ICC-01/04-01/06-803-tE, https://www.icc-cpi.int/CourtRecords/CR2007_02360.PDF, last accessed 8 June 2023; Decision Pursuant to Article 61(7)(a) and (b) of the Rome Statute on the Charges of the Prosecutor Against Jean-Pierre Bemba Gombo, ICC-01/05-01/08-424, https://www.icc-cpi.int/pages/record.aspx?uri=699541, last accessed 8 June 2023.

[59] Independent Expert Panel for the Legal Definition of Ecocide (2021).

However, omission is not contemplated within any of the modes of individual criminal responsibility under Article 25 ICCRSt, and at most can be included through an interpretation of Article 28, regarding command responsibility. Thus, some of the elements presented in this proposal do not completely fit within the ICCRSt framework, which would either involve a larger change in the Statute, or difficulties in its interpretation.

Finally, concerning the ecocentric/anthropocentric approach, the proposed definition adds some anthropocentric elements that led it to criticism. The proposed Article 8 *ter* involves a proportionality test when defining a "wanton" act as *"reckless disregard for damage which would be clearly excessive in relation to the social and economic benefits anticipated"*, for example. Adopting an anthropocentric approach could mean that the panel's proposal is not enough to protect the environment in the way advocates for the criminalisation of ecocide envisioned. Minkova[60] notes that this anthropocentric element may "significantly obstruct the application of Article 8 *ter* if adopted at the ICC". Similarly, Heller argues that a workable definition of ecocide would exclude any trace of anthropocentrism (besides changing the *mens rea* to negligence).

10.7 Proposals for Amending the Rome Statute to Include Ecocide

Although academics already discussed the possibility of incorporating ecocide into the Rome Statute as the Court's 5th core crime, it was not until very recently that there was some movement in that sense. In 2019, during the 18th Session of the ASP, the small island States of Vanuatu and Maldives stressed the need to criminalise acts that would amount to ecocide.[61] The proposal came from an understandable concern that both nations are at risk of ceasing to exist due to climate change. Support for the proposal followed shortly. At the 19th Session of the ASP, Belgium and Finland also raised the criminalisation of ecocide.[62] In the same Session, Vanuatu, along with the Stop Ecocide Foundation and the Institute for Environmental Security hosted a side event dedicated to the crime of ecocide,[63] and received the support of the States of

[60] Minkova (2021).

[61] Government of the Republic of Vanuatu (2019), last accessed 20 June 2023.

[62] "Intervention enregistrée de Mme la Vice-Première Ministre et Ministre des Affaires étrangères Sophie Wilmès à l'occasion du Débat général de la 19è session de l'Assemblée des Etats parties au Statut de Rome de la Cour pénale internationale", General Debate of the 18th Session of the Assembly of States Parties to the Rome Statute of the International Criminal Court, 22 December 2020, The Hague, https://static1.squarespace.com/static/5ca2608ab914493c64ef1f6d/t/5fe1e759b356721fce380f27/1608640346408/GD.BEL.14.12+(2).pdf, last accessed 08 June 2023. Also ICC ASP (2022).

[63] PILPG Lawyering Justice Blog (2020).

Samoa Bangladesh. Moreover, States like the United Kingdom[64] and Chile,[65] as well as the European Union have demonstrated their intention of promoting the recognition of ecocide as a crime at the ICC.

However, the current support for this new amendment is not enough to envision ecocide as the ICC's 5th core crime anytime soon. Under Article 121 (3) ICCRSt, "the adoption of an amendment at a meeting of the Assembly of States Parties or at a Review Conference on which consensus cannot be reached shall require a two-thirds majority of States Parties." As much as Maldives and Vanuatu's proposal has been receiving some support from the States mentioned above, this does not come near the two-thirds majority of States Parties required.

Additionally, even if the proposal gets enough support and the crime of ecocide is incorporated into the ICCRSt as a new crime, the ICC would not have jurisdiction over all of its State Parties concerning the crime. As explained in Chaps. 2 and 6, Article 121 (5) ICCRSt prescribes that "[a]ny amendment to articles 5, 6, 7 and 8 of this Statute shall enter into force for those States Parties which have accepted the amendment one year after the deposit of their instruments of ratification or acceptance. In respect of a State Party which has not accepted the amendment, the Court shall not exercise its jurisdiction regarding a crime covered by the amendment when committed by that State Party's nationals or on its territory". Thus, it is unlikely that States who could see their nationals being prosecuted for ecocide accept its amendment into the Statute, limiting the Court's jurisdiction over the crime. The Court's jurisdiction would also be limited in the one year after these States ratify the amendment.

The proposal supported by the Stop Ecocide Foundation is to include ecocide as a crime by creating another provision, Article 8 *ter*.[66] But another alternative would be to amend the ICCRSt's Article 7 and include ecocide as a form of crime against humanity. There are two key considerations to be made here. The first is that this would mean an amendment to Article 7 of the ICCRSt, which means that Article 121 (3) and (5) would equally apply and there would be a need of a similar acceptance amongst State parties for it to be approved. A similar procedure took place when a Swiss proposal to recognise the starvation of civilians in non-international armed conflicts as a war crime was unanimously adopted.[67] The second consideration is that recognising ecocide as a crime against humanity would inherently require an anthropocentric approach to the crime. Crimes against humanity under the ICCRSt necessarily require a "widespread or systematic attack directed against any civilian population [...]". Thus, environmental harm would only amount to an international crime when there was an established link between such harm and the well-being of civilians. While this is far from what environmental activists have in mind when discussing the criminalisation of ecocide, such an approach would

[64] United Kingdom, Environment Bill 2021, paragraph 287.

[65] Chile, Camara de Diputados, Resolución n° 1620 (2021).

[66] Independent Expert Panel for the Legal Definition of Ecocide (2021).

[67] Switzerland, Federal Department of Foreign Affairs (2019). *Also* Opinio Juris (2019).

perhaps incur in more acceptance of the crime, especially from States that fear a definition of ecocide that is too open. In this scenario, ecocide would fall into the same threshold as other crimes that are already part of the ICCSt system.

10.8 Beyond the ICC and Kierkegaardian Leaps: Advocating for a New International Criminal Court for the Protection of the Environment (ICCPE)

In his exquisite article "How democracies die, fast and slow" John Keane[68] notes that "the slowest form of democide – caused by the destruction of the living planetary environments in which humans dwell – should be the most worrying for democrats of all persuasions everywhere... As if Earth's revenge against its human destroyers, environmental shocks are sometimes marked by frightening quantum qualities that display a will of their own". Moreover Keane points out that while "disasters can bring out the best in citizens", we should not forget Thucydides' memorable work "History of the Peloponnesian War" (431 BC),[69] where it was vividly and quite early depicted how the typhus plague did not 'merely' kill nearly a third of the citizens of democratic Athens but also provoked political havoc, proving that environmental catastrophes can destroy the foundations of democracy.

In line with Keane, Rafi Youatt underlines how "obvious, perhaps, is how each crisis is connected to a deeply rooted, hydra-headed anthropocentrism",[70] because "anthropocentric ideas and practices nonetheless matter greatly in both the crisis of democracy and the crisis of the planet". Youatt argues that both the planet and democracy are in peril due to deeply rooted anthropocentrism, which views humans as superior and central. This anthropocentrism, Youatt claims, results in political injustice and ecological destruction. The author dismisses the idea that extending more rights to nonhuman nature can solve the problem. Instead, Youatt suggests we need to redefine what it means to be human and conceive politics as a process intertwined with the nonhuman world. The paper[71] criticises the narrow view of anthropocentrism that disregards the political qualities of most of the natural world and emphasises the need to recognize the interconnectedness between humans and nature. The author proposes that democracy, if it is to survive and evolve, must be less anthropocentric and more aware of its ecological embeddedness. Eventually Youatt suggests that the human, in political and democratic contexts, should be seen as an ecologically embedded being rather than an exclusively rational, liberal subject.[72]

---

[68] Keane (2023).

[69] Thucydides (431 BC).

[70] Youatt (2023).

[71] *Ibid.*

[72] *Ibid.*

Furthermore, Ferenc Laczó raises in his article "How democracies transform, fast and slow"[73] an important theoretical construction against "the *adagissimo* version of democide via the despoliation of our planet and ecological shock"[74] advanced by John Keane. Laczó critiques John Keane's interpretation of democracy in his book "The New Despotism." because he disagrees with Keane's binary categorisation of political regimes as democracies and despotic states; instead Laczó argues that such a black-and-white view fails to observe the complex modern realities of today's varied authoritarian and democratic systems of governance. Consequently he expresses concern about the blurring of personal and political in the era of digital surveillance and the potential inadequacy of democracy in addressing urgent issues like climate change. Laczó critiques Keane's idealistic opposition of democracy and power and suggests a more pragmatic view, based upon the urgent need to treat democracy as a historical and empirical problem, which should be resolved through collective self-restraint.[75]

Similar to Ferenc Laczó's harsh critique regarding John Keane's views, many scholars and experts have been equally or even more harsh criticisers of the International Experts Panel (IEP) proposed definition of ecocide. Kevin Jon Heller[76] was eagerly awaiting for the proposed definition only to become sceptical after reading it *inter alia* because the commentary failed to described in many respects the *mens rea* of ecocide and did not explain why the IEP did not opt ecocide to be a crime against humanity. Darryl Robinson highlighted "why combining international criminal law (ICL) with international environmental law (IEL) raises fascinating novel challenges that are not initially evident to those of us trained in ICL", as well as why "there is no elegant 'magic bullet' solution".[77]

Kai Ambos has stressed[78] that the IEP proposal to introduce ecocide as a fifth core international crime, alongside genocide, crimes against humanity, war crimes, and the crime of aggression, lacked robust reasoning and practical guidance. Although intended to protect the environment, the proposal did not provide empirical data to support its effectiveness, while it remained unclear whether serious environmental crimes could equate to genocide. Moreover, the proposal's structure mimicked that of crimes against humanity, but extended it to peace times and expanded its applicability. Finally, the practical application posed great interpretive challenges, prompting doubts about the necessity of a new, stand-alone core crime for environmental protection.

Tarini Mehta has pointed out[79] that a strong case exists for the adoption of ecocide as a strict liability offense under international criminal law. She argues

---

[73] Laczó (2023).

[74] *Ibid.*

[75] *Ibid.*

[76] Heller (2021).

[77] Robinson (2021).

[78] Ambos (2021).

[79] Mehta (2020).

this would impose a more stringent duty of care on corporations whose activities cause environmental harm, thereby deterring and holding accountable those who degrade the environment. This approach, already advocated by several commentators, challenges the traditional fault-based liability under international law. Despite existing legal frameworks, Mehta supports a shift from a 'polluter pays' principle to a 'polluter no longer pollutes' system, which could offer a preventative justice solution. As the rate of biodiversity loss and environmental degradation continues to increase while "over half of the global GDP – amounting to around US$44 trillion – is moderately or highly dependent on ecosystem services",[80] Mehta vehemently endorses that evolving the law to meet these challenges is not just beneficial but absolutely essential. Recognising ecocide as a crime at national, regional, and international levels, she concludes, could be a vital step towards the protection of the environment.

Michael Karnavas has perhaps written the most colourful account[81] of a great set of raised objections ranging from the Stop Ecocide pamphlet's graphic design to more serious issues including the proposed term 'ecocide' *per se*, the drafting process, the impracticability of having a fifth crime within the Rome Statute, the ICC judges' ability to assess complex environmental crimes, the singularities of the damage threshold in ecocide, the adoption of the term ecocide per se, the critical flaws of the *mens rea* description and the utterly problematic *actus reus* description. To sum up Michael Karnavas' mixed views, while he is generally in favour "of drafting a concise and well-founded definition of crimes against the environment in times of peace/non-armed conflict situations" he concurrently considers "the initiative as unrealistic, the definition replete with flaws, and the commentary remarkably wanting".

Similarly, Matthew Gillett seems to have taken great inspiration from Charles Dickens' classic novel 'The Tale of Two Cities' in his two-part article published in Opinio Juris.[82] Titled 'A Tale of Two Definitions: Fortifying Four Key Elements of the Proposed Crime of Ecocide,' Gillett enumerates several suggested flaws of the ecocide definition proposed by the Independent Expert Panel's ("IEP") in 2021.

The first flaw he advances is the absence of enumerated acts that should be considered as ecocides, since this lack is in deep contrast "with the structure of all existing crimes under the Rome Statute". According to the author this is a fatal flaw since it violates the principle of legality and the findings of the European Court on Human Rights in *Kokkinakis v Greece* decision[83] as well as the relevant findings of the United Nations Working Group on Arbitrary Detention that criminal laws should be "formulated with sufficient precision" because imprecise offences do not allow

[80] World Economic Forum (2020), p. 8.

[81] Karnavas (2021).

[82] Gillett (2023a, b).

[83] ECHR, *Kokkinakis v Greece* (1993).

individuals to regulate their conduct accordingly, jeopardize the exercise of their fundamental rights and "are likely to result in arbitrary deprivation of liberty".[84]

Hence in his book "Prosecuting Environmental Harm Before The International Criminal Court" he suggests the following definition:

> Ecocide means wilfully committing any of the following acts and thereby causing severe damage to the natural environment that is also widespread or long-term:
>
> a) killing, harming, or removing protected flora or fauna;
> b) destroying or damaging ecosystems or wild animal habitats;
> c) destroying or damaging natural heritage;
> d) trafficking or dumping hazardous substances;
> e) releasing, emitting, or introducing harmful quantities of substances or energy into the air, water, or soil;
> f) causing or contributing to the large-scale emissions of greenhouse gases or the destruction of greenhouse gas sinks or reservoirs;
> g) any other acts of a similar character, where those acts involve unsustainable harm to the natural environment.
>
> 2. Irrespective of whether it qualifies as any of the acts listed in paragraph 1, conduct shall not be considered ecocide if it is both (a) strictly in accordance with international law, particularly international environmental law, and (b) authorized by a competent national authority.
>
> 3. In order to fulfil the definition in paragraph 1, the damage to the natural environment must be severe, while also being either widespread or long-term (or both). Consequently, in all cases the anticipated damage must be severe, but no one of the qualifiers can be significant enough on its own to satisfy the definition of ecocide. Moreover, the severe, widespread, and/or long-term nature of the harm may be established on the totality of the conduct at issue, which may include multiple underlying acts.
>
> 4. The terms of paragraph 1 shall be interpreted in accordance with international law, particularly environmental law.[85]

There are several objections to the above definition and its underlying rationale. Firstly, Gillett assumes from the beginning and throughout his two-part article that the International Criminal Court (ICC) is unquestionably the most suitable legal institution for prosecuting ecocide. However, he does not give adequate consideration to the practical and inherent limitations of the ICC, including its limited human resources, financial constraints, existing trial workload, projected future trials (such as the situation in Ukraine), and overall legal capacity. These factors are of significant importance and must be thoroughly taken into account before reaching by leaps and bounds the unwavering conclusion that the International Criminal Court is indeed the most appropriate legal institution for trying ecocide (see the last section of the Ecocide Chapter in this book).

Moreover, the provisions of paragraph 2(a) and (b) of Gillett's proposed definition pose significant problems. The author suggests that "conduct shall not be considered ecocide if it is **both (a)** strictly in accordance with international law, particularly international environmental law, **and (b)** authorized by a competent national authority." (emphasis added). The reasoning behind this caveat is unclear,

---

[84] Human Rights Council (2021), p. 9, para. 55.

[85] Gillett (2022), p. 350.

but it appears that the author assumes that most or all states are democratic, uncorrupted, and genuinely concerned about the environment. Consequently, the authorisation of a project by a competent legal authority is viewed in conjunction with a vague referral to international law as a valid safeguard for both the environment and the actor who proceeds with a conduct based on an 'untouchable' authorisation from a competent state authority. Unfortunately, this reasoning does not align at all with reality.

To name but one latest example, the fact that Japan intends to release approximately 1.3 millions of tons of water with tritium[86] from the destroyed Fukushima[87] Daiichi nuclear power plant has raised significant environmental concerns from neighbouring states, environmental organisations and individuals-active members of the civil society. Admittedly, before the Japanese state being able to release such an enormous amount of 'treated' water which would be sufficient to fill about 500 Olympic-sized swimming pools, it had to get first authorisation from the competent Japanese authority and then also permission from the International Atomic Energy Agency[88] in accordance with international law. Nonetheless, given the grave potential consequences of such an action as well as the adverse reactions from a wide range of actors (individuals, organisations and states) it still highly questionable whether such an act could amount to actual ecocide, despite all granted permissions. However, according to Gillett's proposed definition such an action could never amount to ecocide.

Moreover, Gillett's proposed definition includes significantly fewer protections than the definition put forward by the Promise Institute for Human Rights (UCLA) Group of Experts, where Gillett served as a specialist. In paragraph 2 of the Promise Institute for Human Rights (UCLA) Group of Experts' definition it was expressly stated that a *conduct should not be regarded ecocide "if it is (a) lawful under national law, (b) lawful under international law, and (c) employs appropriate available measures to prevent, mitigate, and abate harms"*.[89] The necessity of this third safeguarding component stems from the fact that a significant amount of activities remain insufficiently governed by both national regulations and international law. As an illustration, the release of greenhouse gases (GHG) by private entities often goes unrestricted by both domestic and international legislations too. Hence, this third threshold embodies a fundamental precept of environmental law, which emphasises the requirement to undertake relevant, easily implementable steps for harm prevention, mitigation, or alleviation. The term 'appropriate' underlines that these measures should be financially and technologically feasible, with special consideration for the distinct circumstances of developing nations. Considering that ecocide is proposed as a grave international offense, this clause should necessitate an

---

[86] McCurry (2023).

[87] The Guardian (2023b).

[88] IAEA (2023).

[89] Promise Institute for Human Rights (UCLA) Group of Experts, Proposed Definition of Ecocide, 9 April 2021, accessed 8 June 2023, p. 2.

extreme degree of individual blame and a severe lapse because "*[t]he provision should not be interpreted in a manner that includes simple negligence, strict liability, or strict retrospective evaluations with hindsight. Any of those possibilities would be inconsistent with international criminal liability and would also inhibit support from states*".[90] The Promise Institute for Human Rights (UCLA) Group of Experts finally remarked that despite requiring a stringent standard, this clause would not lack substance, as there are, unfortunately, numerous cases today that showcase a conscious disregard and failure to adopt even basic mitigation measures.[91]

Furthermore, it is indisputable that Gillett takes this leap well after the publication of his aforementioned textbook where in stark contrast with his latest two-part article in Opinio Juris he candidly states that "[*i]nstead of exclusively trying to adjust the ICC's provisions and principles to try to cover environmental harm, there is considerable merit in developing a purpose-designed international court for the environment (ICE), able to address and provide legal redress for all major forms of serious environmental harm threatening the planet, while doing so efficiently and through fair but flexible proceedings*". [Gillett M, Prosecuting Environmental Harm Before the International Criminal Court, Cambridge (Cambridge, 2022) p. 354] Consequently, to leap contrary to your previous view that in fact a new International Criminal Court for the Protections of Environment (ICCPE) is a much more suitable option constitutes a wrongful application of the leap that Kierkegaard first thought of.

Being too harsh on academics who put forth their best efforts to produce scholarly work, while simultaneously failing to adequately address other crucial aspects, creates an imbalanced critique. For example, taking the International Criminal Court's suitability for trying ecocide as a given fact is problematic. This perspective overlooks the ICC's current challenges and inherent limitations. It also fails to properly consider the sources primarily cited. For instance, Michael Karnavas' article eloquently presents complex issues of environmental crimes, including requisite expertise, ongoing long-term damage, and international judges' potential inability to assess expert evidence, while Darryl Robinson duly notes that the "ICC is already over-loaded with the crimes currently under its jurisdiction", hence it "would handle very few ecocide cases in the decades to come".[92]

This hasty approach to critique brings to mind Wystan Hugh Auden's poem 'Leap Before you Look,' which was inspired by Kierkegaard's work 'Leap of Faith': "Much can be said for social savoir-faire,// But to rejoice when no one else is there// Is even harder than it is to weep;// No one is watching, but you have to leap".[93]

[90] *Ibid.* p. 7.

[91] *Ibid.*, p. 7.

[92] Robinson (2021) (accessed 12 September 2023).

[93] Auden (1989), pp. 29–30.

10.9 A Novel Definition on Ecocide for the New International Criminal Court for the Protection of the Environment (ICCPE)

Following the above literature review and examination of the criticism raised against the definition of ecocide advanced by the International Experts Panel, my proposed definition on ecocide is the following:

1. In alignment with the Statute of the International Criminal Court for the Protection of the Environment, 'ecocide' is any intentional act, whether lawful or unlawful, directly or indirectly committed by any agent, which is capable of causing significant degradation, harm, or disruption to the natural environment and ecosystems, potentially resulting in irreversible, near-irreversible or hardly-reversible consequences. This can either directly impact at least one sovereign state or have a cumulative, persistent, long-term impact upon the environment. The criminal actions encompassed by this definition primarily include:

   a) Engaging in activities that could result in the death, harm, or displacement of protected or unprotected fauna or flora from their natural habitats within the ecosystem.
   b) Undertaking activities that could cause destruction or significant harm to the ecosystem supporting various living organisms, such as overfishing or the introduction of invasive species.
   c) Initiating the release, emission, or disposal of hazardous substances, waste, or analogous materials that can significantly harm or degrade the natural environment or the living organisms within it.
   d) Provoking or directly or indirectly causing the emission of greenhouse gases, including both large-scale and cumulative, smaller-scale emissions.
   e) Engaging in large-scale deforestation or activities that lead to land degradation, regardless of their legal status.
   f) Engaging in the production, disposal, or mismanagement of materials that result in significant environmental pollution, including but not limited to plastic waste, heavy metals, and radioactive substances.
   g) Overexploiting natural resources, including but not limited to water, soil, minerals, and biological resources.
   h) Any other actions or omissions that meet the conditions stated in the aforementioned cases, including cumulative actions over time that result in significant environmental harm or serious ecosystem disruption.

2. If from the aforementioned restrictive acts or omissions, damage or destruction to the natural environment occurs, or if death, harm, or displacement of fauna or flora takes place, this would be deemed an aggravating circumstance and would be duly taken into account when determining the imposed sentence, in accordance with the principles outlined in Article [...] of the International Criminal

Court for the Protection of the Environment, which align with Article 78, paragraphs 1 and 3 of the Rome Statute of the International Criminal Court.

3. For the purposes outlined in paragraph 1 of this article:

   a) The term 'intentional act' indicates the possession of knowledge regarding the fundamental nature of an action or omission that has the potential to cause the intended outcome, while simultaneously accepting the likelihood of such a result (dolus eventualis). *Dolus eventualis* refers to a situation where an individual, although not necessarily desiring the specific outcome, accepts the possibility of it occurring and proceeds with the action or omission.
   b) The term 'act' is used in a broad sense within this definition, encompassing both actions and omissions.
   c) The term 'serious' denotes the infliction of irreversible or extremely challenging to reverse consequences related to the destruction or harm to the natural environment, with impacts affecting the lives of humans or the living organisms within an ecosystem.
   d) The phrase "affecting at least one state" implies the causation of damage that extends to, at a minimum, one state or a specific part thereof, without necessarily excluding the possibility of detrimental consequences spreading to other states.
   e) The term 'long-term nature' refers to the non-reversible or difficult to reverse outcome resulting from ecocide, taking into consideration the time required for the restoration of environmental impacts.
   f) The term 'natural environment' encompasses the entirety of the Earth's biosphere, lithosphere, cryosphere, hydrosphere, atmosphere, as well as the space that interacts with the Earth, with particular emphasis on the significance of the Milky Way galaxy.

The explicit aim of the above definition is to capture a wide range of criminal actions that pose significant threats to the environment and emphasise their potential long-term consequences. It seeks to address activities that can harm ecosystems, biodiversity, and the overall health of the planet, while creating a concrete definition with sufficient *de lege artis* precision, which would have the least potential loopholes.

10.10 Towards a New International Criminal Court for the Protection of Environment (ICCPE): A Distinct Rationale for a Distinct Crime

An alternative would be to create a new international criminal jurisdiction altogether. As seen above, the main issue with trying to incorporate ecocide within the ICCRSt framework is that a definition of ecocide that is workable and effective in protecting the environment may be at odds with the logic of the Rome Statute itself. Thus, a new tribunal would allow for both an ecocentric approach of the crime and the incorporation of additional elements (*mens rea*, criminal of liability of corporations) that would be more effective in protecting the environment. Additionally, this would have the advantage of not overwhelming even more the ICC, which is already struggling to undertake more cases even with its existing thresholds and jurisdictional limitations.

The crime of ecocide is inherently different from the current core crimes of the ICC. First, while crimes under the current ICCRSt. framework are inserted under an anthropocentric logic, a workable legal definition of ecocide would need to operate under an ecocentric logic. Second, the ICCRSt. already has its own framework regarding elements of its crimes such as criminal liability, *mens rea*, or the exclusive prosecution of natural persons. While this framework makes sense under the current ICCRSt. logic, it is likely that the same logic would be at odds with the protection of the environment through the prosecution of ecocide. Thus, creating a new court for ecocide would be the most logical alternative for establishing international jurisdiction over the crime.

The first advantage of this new jurisdiction would be that drafters would be free to completely adopt an ecocentric approach to ecocide. The ICC, on the other hand, works inherently in an anthropocentric logic,[94] which makes the incorporation of an ecocentric definition of ecocide within its framework unlikely and perhaps even at odds with it.

Similarly, this new jurisdiction would be free to decide upon elements such as criminal liability and *mens rea* in a way that would effectively work towards prosecuting ecocide. This could include recklessness/*dolus eventualis* and omission, for example, which, as explained above, does not exist in the ICCSt framework.

Thus, it would be possible to criminalise negligent acts that incurred in the destruction of the environment, which is usually how environmental catastrophes take place. Additionally, there would not be a need to balance between environmental damage and the benefits of such damage to humans, or even to establish a direct link between the environmental damage and its effects on humans.

Another possibility under a new International Criminal Court for the Protection of the Environment (ICCPE) would be to put also corporations into trial and establish corporate criminal liability. The ICC holds exclusively jurisdiction over natural persons,[95] so it is unable to go after corporations that are often behind widespread and/or long-term environmental destructions.[96] Consequently, in order to establish international criminal liability for corporations would only be practically feasible and legally permissible via the creation of a new international criminal jurisdiction altogether.

---

[94] Dissenha and Farias (2021), p. 313.

[95] ICCRSt, art 25.

[96] Bekou (2021).

10.11 Assessing the ICC's Capacity to Undertake a New Core Crime Within a New Jurisdiction

A great advantage to this would be that the ICC would not be even more overwhelmed with the establishment of another international crime. This comes from a concern that the Court, which already can't handle a large number of cases, gets even more busy by trying to accommodate ecocide. Either that or the Court would get even more selective of its cases, risking that ecocide is only officially criminalised, without the crime being effectively prosecuted. A new court, focused on ecocide, would be more equipped to deal with these cases.

The ICC has been facing budgetary challenges, which impacts its work. The approved budget of the ICC for 2022 amounted to nearly €155 million.[97] However, this is considerably less than the 9.5 per cent increased proposed by the Committee on Budget and Finance (amounting to €162.35 million in total).[98] The proposed budget considered the increase in activities of the Court, for example the number of active trials within the Court (which was expected to double),[99] raising concerns over how tight the ICC's budget is at the moment. This affects the ICC throughout its several divisions. For example: i) the OTP is understaffed, directly impacting its work[100] and potentially affecting its reputation;[101] ii) budget constraints for additional training required by the OTP to meet its needs;[102] iii) Delays in mission and case management operations by the Victims and Witnesses Section could potentially expose key individuals to life-threatening risks;[103] iv) Victims Participation and Reparations Section is currently unable to *"carry out its mandate at an acceptable level regarding any additional activity such as victim representation under article 15(3) or pre-trial proceedings in a new case".*[104]

In addition, external factors might impact the ICC's financial situation even more, such as State-Parties failing to meet their financial obligations on time or unexpected new situations and cases. For instance, in May 2020, the ICC Committee on Budget and Finance (CBF) declared that *"€70.45 million was outstanding for all years, including contributions for the host State loan"*,[105] which represented 47% of the budget of that year.[106] The CBF also noted that the timely payment of contributions

---

[97] ICC, Resolution ICC-ASP/20/Res.1 (2021).

[98] ICC, Resolution ICC-ASP/20/10 (2021).

[99] *Ibid.*, para 15.

[100] Independent Expert Review of the International Criminal Court and the Rome Statute System (2020).

[101] ICC, Resolution ICC-ASP/20/10 (2021).

[102] Independent Expert Review of the International Criminal Court and the Rome Statute System (2020).

[103] ICC, Resolution ICC-ASP/20/10 (2021).

[104] *Ibid*, para. 496.

[105] ICC, Resolution ICC-ASP/18/5 (2020).

[106] *Ibid.*

by State Parties is essential for the Court to meet its financial obligations and to ensure its core activities and operations.[107] The opening of additional investigations and/or cases might spread this already limited budget even more thin. The opening of investigations regarding the Situation in Ukraine in 2022, for example, adds considerably more resources that were not foreseen in the ICC's budget. It is worth noting that the new ICC Prosecutor, Karim Khan, had already made difficult strategic choices as his office *"has spread itself too thin"*.[108] This unforeseen situation led Prosecutor Khan to call, in more than one occasion, for additional budget and resources to conduct these investigations.[109]

If the existing material jurisdiction of the ICC is enough to overwhelm its staff and budget, a new crime would likely be more than the ICC can handle in the near future. An overwhelmed Court must make difficult decisions regarding which cases to proceed. In the case of ICC, the Court considers a gravity threshold, and the OTP has more and more added to its balance the likelihood of a future conviction. Cases involving ecocide, which even with a workable definition would involve complicate considerations (regarding the degree of intent, the type of criminal responsibility, whether a nexus is necessary between the environmental damage and its impact on humans, etc), would be likely set aside for (understandable) strategic reasons.

Thus, a new international court would be more suitable to prosecute the crime of ecocide. It would focus its resources and attention solely in cases concerning ecocide. Most importantly, cases of ecocide would have a better prospect of proceeding in a specific jurisdiction than at the ICC, where the Court is already struggling to handle existing investigations and prosecutions even with its limited material jurisdiction.

10.12 The Feasibility of a New Permanent International Criminal Court for the Protection of the Environment (ICCPE)

This would not be the first time a new international criminal jurisdiction is created to deal with a specific issue. Rather, there were several international criminal jurisdictions established for specific purposes. Besides the ICTY and the ICTR, there was also the establishment of the Special Tribunal for Lebanon, the Extraordinary Chambers in the Courts of Cambodia or The Special Court for Sierra Leone, all tasked with prosecuting specific crimes in specific circumstances. Additionally, prominent legal scholars started advocating towards the creation of a special tribunal for the punishment of the crime of aggression against Ukraine in March 2022. A new tribunal focused on environmental crimes would add to this list, and its support could

[107] *Ibid,* paras 37 and 40.

[108] Anderson (2021).

[109] ICC, Statement of ICC Prosecutor (2022). *Also* ICC, Statement of ICC Prosecutor (2022).

be built from the current momentum—where the environment finally takes a central role in the political agenda.

When the International Criminal Tribunal for the Former Yugoslavia and the International Criminal Tribunal were created by the United Nations Security Council (UNSC), there was not a permanent international criminal jurisdiction like the ICC. The prospects of such a jurisdiction were dim before the 90s, mostly due to the tensions of the Cold War.[110] Soon after the creation of the ICTR, however, the UNSC allegedly reached what former US permanent representative to the UN called "tribunal fatigue".[111] In essence, this meant that the hypothesis of new *ad hoc* tribunals were scratched by the UNSC due to the logistics and political support necessary, further supporting the creating of a permanent jurisdiction such as the ICC.[112]

This, however, does not mean that the creation of the ICC (intended to serve as a permanent international criminal jurisdiction) would prevent the creation of other types of jurisdictions to prosecute international crimes. Apart from the ICTY and the ICTR, there are other examples such as the Extraordinary Chambers in the Courts of Cambodia, the Special Court for Sierra Leone, the Special Tribunal for Lebanon and the Kosovo Specialist Chambers and Specialist Prosecutor's Office. All these jurisdictions prosecuted international crimes at the same time as the ICC, demonstrating the possibility of other international criminal jurisdictions to be established for different purposes.

Most recently, a group of academics and practitioners issued a statement *"calling for the creation of a Special Tribunal for the Punishment of the Crime of Aggression Against Ukraine"* during an event hosted by the think-tank Chatham House.[113] The idea was backed by Ukraine.[114] It also comes as a response for the ICC's lack of jurisdiction over the crime of aggression[115] if the aggression is committed by a State that does not recognise the ICC's jurisdiction (such as Russia) and the situation is not referred by the UNSC. The proposal received understandable criticism involving its logistics and matters of selective justice.[116] It nevertheless received the support of names such as ILC member Dapo Akande and Ben Ferencz, former Prosecutor for the Nuremberg Military Tribunal.

This support demonstrates that even the costs and logistic issues associated with the creation of international tribunals are not enough to deem it impossible, if political will is present. Similarly, it is possible to envision a special jurisdiction

[110] Schabas (2006), p. 11.

[111] Scheffer (1996).

[112] Cassese (2002), pp. 15–16.

[113] Chatham House (2022), last accessed 20 June 2023.

[114] The Guardian (2022b).

[115] However, it is worth noting that the OTP declared that it has jurisdiction to investigate acts of genocide, crimes against humanity and war crimes committed in the territory of Ukraine. *See*: ICC, Statement of ICC Prosecutor (2022).

[116] Opinio Juris (2022).

for the crime of ecocide. Ideally, this would be of a permanent nature, an International Criminal Court for the Protection of the Environment (ICCPE). As far as support and political will is concerned, the environment and climate change are increasingly part of the agenda for States. With the right of amount of support and advocacy, this idea does not seem too far-fetched. Rather, it makes sense due to the especial nature of the crime and legitimate concerns for the protection of the environment.

References

Table of Cases

ECHR, *Kokkinakis v Greece (1993). https://hudoc.echr.coe.int/eng?i=001-57827.* Accessed 8 June 2023

Human Rights Council, Working Group on Arbitrary Detention, Opinions adopted by the Working Group on Arbitrary Detention at its ninety-second session, 15–19 November 2021, *Opinion No. 75/2021 concerning Ros Sokhet (Cambodia),* p. 9, para. 55. https://www.ohchr.org/sites/default/files/2022-03/A_HRC_WGAD_75_2021_Cambodia_AEV.pdf. Accessed 8 June 2023

ICJ, Legality of the Threat or Use of Nuclear Weapons (Advisory Opinion) 1996 ICJ Reports

Situation in the Central African Republic, Decision Pursuant to Article 61(7)(a) and (b) of the Rome Statute on the Charges of the Prosecutor Against Jean-Pierre Bemba Gombo, ICC-01/05-01/08, 15 June 2009

Situation in the Democratic Republic of the Congo, Decision on the confirmation of charges, ICC-01/04-01/06, 29 January 2007

Books

Auden WH (1989) The Dyer's hand and other essays. Vintage

Cassese A (2002) From Nuremberg to Rome: International Military Tribunals to the International Criminal Court

Cassese A (2003) International criminal law. Oxford

Higgins P (2016) Eradicating ecocide: exposing the corporate and political practices destroying the planet and proposing the laws to eradicate ecocide. Shepheard-Walwyn

Schabas WA(2006) The UN International Criminal Tribunals: The Former Yugoslavia, Rwanda and Sierra Leone

Shapiro FR (2021) The Yale book of quotations. Yale University Press

Thucydides, "*History of the Peloponnesian War*" (431 B.C.). https://www.gutenberg.org/files/7142/7142-h/7142-h.htm. Accessed 8 June 2023

Articles/Collective Book Chapters

Chiarini G (2021) Ecocide and international criminal court procedural issues: additional amendments to the "Stop Ecocide Proposal". CCJHR Working Paper Series N° 15
Chiarini G (2022) Ecocide: from the Vietnam war to international criminal jurisdiction? Procedural issues in-between environmental sciences, climate change and law. COLR 21(1):1–34
Crook M, Short D (2014) Marx, Lemkin and the genocide–ecocide nexus. Int J Hum Rights 298
Dissenha RC, Farias MC (2021) Criminalização do ecocídio: qual a contribuição do Estatuto de Roma. Revista Brasileira de Ciências Criminais 183:313
Drumbl M (1998) Waging war against the world: the need to move from war crimes to environmental crimes. Fordham Int Law J 122
Falk RA (1973) Environmental Warfare and Ecocide – facts, appraisal, and proposals
Gillett M (2023a) A tale of two definitions: fortifying four key elements of the proposed crime of ecocide (Part I), Opinio Juris, 20-06-2023. http://opiniojuris.org/2023/06/20/a-tale-of-two-definitions-fortifying-four-key-elements-of-the-proposed-crime-of-ecocide-part-i/
Gillett M (2023b) A tale of two definitions: fortifying four key elements of the proposed crime of ecocide (Part II), Opinio Juris, 20-06-2023. http://opiniojuris.org/2023/06/20/a-tale-of-two-definitions-fortifying-four-key-elements-of-the-proposed-crime-of-ecocide-part-ii/
Higgins P, Short D, South N (2013) Protecting the planet: a proposal for a law of ecocide. Crime Law Soc Change 59:251
Independent Expert Review of the International Criminal Court and the Rome Statute System, Final Report (2020)
Lawrence JC, Heller KJ (2007) The first ecocentric environmental war crime: the limits of Article 8(2)(b)(iv) of the Rome Statute
Milanovic M (2023) The destruction of the Nova Kakhovka Dam and international humanitarian law: some preliminary thoughts. https://www.ejiltalk.org/thedestruction-of-the-nova-kakhovka-dam-and-international-humanitarian-law-some-preliminary-thoughts/. Accessed 8 June 2023
Minkova LG (2021) The fifth international crime: reflections on the definition of "ecocide". J Genocide Res 2
Ruhashyankiko N (1978) Study of the question of the prevention and punishment of the crime of genocide
Scheffer DJ (1996) International judicial intervention. Foreign Policy 102
Schmitt M (2022) Attacking dams – Part II: The 1977 Additional Protocols, February. https://lieber.westpoint.edu/attacking-dams-part-ii-1977-additional-protocols/. Accessed 8 June 2023
War Crimes Research Office (2010) Modes of liability and the mental element analyzing the early jurisprudence of the International Criminal Court. Am Univ Wash Coll Law
Weisberg B (1970) Ecocide in Indochina: the ecology of war. Canfield Press

Websites/Web Sources

Al Jazeera, "Ecuador's Amazon residents seething after new oil spill", 03 February 2022. https://www.aljazeera.com/news/2022/2/3/oil-everywhere-ecuador-amazonians-seethe-over-new-spill. Accessed 8 June 2023
Ambos K, Protecting the Environment through International Criminal Law? EJIL: Talk!, 29 June 2021. https://www.ejiltalk.org/protecting-the-environment-through-international-criminal-law/. Accessed 8 June 2023
Anderson JH, "The ICC in times of budget crunch", December 2021. https://www.justiceinfo.net/en/85475-icc-times-budget-crunch.html. Accessed 8 June 2023

Bekou O, Side-event on "Ecocide: From Amazonia to Oceania to the Hague. Bringing voices together towards a common goal", No Peace Without Justice, 16 December 2021. https://www.youtube.com/watch?v=mEFfyE91brg&t=2790s. Accessed 8 June 2023

Chatham House, "A Criminal tribunal for aggression in Ukraine", March 2022. https://www.chathamhouse.org/events/all/research-event/criminal-tribunal-aggression-ukraine. Accessed 8 June 2023

Decision on the confirmation of charges, ICC-01/04-01/06-803-tE. https://www.icc-cpi.int/CourtRecords/CR2007_02360.PDF. Accessed 8 June 2023

Decision Pursuant to Article 61(7)(a) and (b) of the Rome Statute on the Charges of the Prosecutor Against Jean-Pierre Bemba Gombo, ICC-01/05-01/08-424. https://www.icc-cpi.int/pages/record.aspx?uri=699541. Accessed 8 June 2023

Euronews (2023a) Ukraine's Zaporizhzhia Nuclear Plant Shuts Down Last Reactor in Face of Flooding Threat, 10 June 2023. https://www.euronews.com/2023/06/10/ukraines-zaporizhzhia-nuclear-plant-shuts-down-last-reactor-in-face-of-flooding-threat. Accessed 8 June 2023

Euronews (2023b) UN Aid Chief says Ukraine Faces 'Hugely Worse' Humanitarian Situation after the Dam Rupture, 10 June 2023. https://www.euronews.com/2023/06/10/un-aid-chief-says-ukraine-faces-hugely-worse-humanitarian-situation-after-the-dam-rupture. Accessed 10 June 2023

Eurozine, 14 April 2023. https://www.eurozine.com/how-democracies-transform-fast-and-slow/. Accessed 8 June 2023

General Debate of the 18th Session of the Assembly of States Parties to the Rome Statute of the International Criminal Court, 22 December 2020. https://static1.squarespace.com/static/5ca2608ab914493c64ef1f6d/t/5fe1e759b356721fce380f27/1608640346408/GD.BEL.14.12+(2).pdf. Accessed 8 June 2023

Gillet M (2023) "The Kakhovka Dam and Ecocide – A Convergence of International Criminal Law, International Humanitarian Law, International Environmental Law, and International Human Rights Law?", 3 July 2023, Verfassungsblog. https://verfassungsblog.de/the-kakhovka-dam-and-ecocide/. Accessed 12 Sept 2023

Government of the Republic of Vanuatu, Statement by H. E. John H. Licht, General Debate of the 18th Assembly of States Parties to the Rome Statute of the International Criminal Court, 2-7 December 2019. https://asp.icc-cpi.int/sites/asp/files/asp_docs/ASP18/GD.VAN.2.12.pdf. Accessed 8 June 2023

Heller KJ, Skeptical Thoughts on the Proposed Crime of "Ecocide" (That Isn't). http://opiniojuris.org/2021/06/23/skeptical-thoughts-on-the-proposed-crime-of-ecocide-that-isnt/, Opinio Juris, 23 June 2021. Accessed 8 June 2023

IAEA, "IAEA Finds Japan's Plans to Release Treated Water into the Sea at Fukushima Consistent with International Safety Standards". https://www.iaea.org/newscenter/pressreleases/iaea-finds-japans-plans-to-release-treated-water-into-the-sea-at-fukushima-consistent-with-international-safety-standards. Accessed 12 Sept 2023

ICC ASP, "Finland: H. E. Mr. Pekka Haavisto, Minister of Foreign Affairs", 06 December 2022. https://www.youtube.com/watch?v=RDyepTLExaA. Accessed 8 June 2023

ICC Assembly of Party States, Proposed Programme Budget for 2022 of the International Criminal Court (Resolution ICC-ASP/20/10), 16 August 2021. https://asp.icc-cpi.int/sites/default/files/iccdocs/asp_docs/ASP20/ICC-ASP-20-10-ENG.pdf. Accessed 8 June 2023

Independent Expert Panel for the Legal Definition of Ecocide, Commentary and Core Text, "Stop Ecocide Foundation", June 2021. https://static1.squarespace.com/static/5ca2608ab914493c64ef1f6d/t/60d7479cf8e7e5461534dd07/1624721314430/SE+Foundation+Commentary+and+core+text+revised+%281%29.pdf. Accessed 8 June 2023

Karim AA Khan QC, Statement of ICC Prosecutor on the Situation in Ukraine: "I have decided to proceed with opening an investigation", February 2022. https://www.icc-cpi.int/news/statement-icc-prosecutor-karim-aa-khan-qc-situation-ukraine-i-have-decided-proceed-opening. Accessed 8 June 2023

Karim AA Khan QC, Statement of ICC Prosecutor on the Situation in Ukraine: "Receipt of Referrals from 39 States Parties and the Opening of an Investigation", March 2022. https://www.icc-cpi.int/news/statement-icc-prosecutor-karim-aa-khan-qc-situation-ukraine-receipt-referrals-39-states. Accessed 8 June 2023

Karnavas M, Ecocide: Environmental Crime of Crimes or Ill-Conceived Concept?, Opinio Juris, 29 July 2021. http://opiniojuris.org/2021/07/29/ecocide-environmental-crime-of-crimes-or-ill-conceived-concept/. Accessed 8 June 2023

Keane J, How Democracies Die, Fast and Slow, Eurozine, 21 February 2023. https://www.eurozine.com/how-democracies-die-fast-and-slow/?complete=true&type=card. Accessed 8 June 2023

Laczó F (2023) How Democracies Transform, Fast and Slow: a Response to John Keane

Le Monde, Galland F, War in Ukraine: The destruction of the Kakhovka dam marks a turning point in 21st-century wars, 8 June 2023. https://www.lemonde.fr/en/opinion/article/2023/06/08/war-in-ukraine-the-destruction-of-the-kakhovka-dam-marks-a-turning-point-in-21st-century-wars_6030458_23.html?utm_source=flipboard&utm_content=LeMonde_en%2Fmagazine%2FInternational. Accessed 10 June 2023

Le Monde with AFP, Kakhovka dam breach: Flooding extends over 600 square kilometers, residents evacuated, 8 June 2023. https://www.lemonde.fr/en/international/article/2023/06/08/kakhovka-dam-breach-flooding-extends-over-600-square-kilometers_6030492_4.html. Accessed 10 June 2023

McCurry J, "Fukushima: Japan insists release of 1.3m tonnes of 'treated' water is safe", The Guardian. https://www.theguardian.com/environment/2023/feb/15/fukushima-japan-insists-release-of-treated-water-is-safe-nuclear-disaster. Accessed 12 Sept 2023

Mehta T, Symposium Exploring the Crime of Ecocide: Accountability for Environmental Destruction–Ecocide in National and International Law (Part II) The Way Forward, Opinio Juris, 25 September 2020. http://opiniojuris.org/2020/09/25/symposium-exploring-the-crime-of-ecocide-accountability-for-environmental-destruction-ecocide-in-national-and-international-law-part-ii-the-way-forward/. Accessed 8 June 2023

Office of the Prosecutor, Policy paper on case selection and prioritisation, 15 September 2016. https://www.icc-cpi.int/itemsdocuments/20160915_otp-policy_case-selection_eng.pdf, last accessed 8 June 2023

Opinio Juris, Kevin Jon Heller, "The Rome Statute's Flawed Amendment Regime — Starvation in NIAC Edition", 07 December 2019. http://opiniojuris.org/2019/12/07/the-rome-statutes-flawed-amendment-regime-starvation-in-niac-edition/. Accessed 8 June 2023

Opinio Juris, Heller KJ, "Creating a Special Tribunal for Aggression Against Ukraine Is a Bad Idea", 07 March 2022. https://opiniojuris.org/2022/03/07/creating-a-special-tribunal-for-aggression-against-ukraine-is-a-bad-idea/. Accessed 8 June 2023

PILPG Lawyering Justice Blog, Jefferies I, "ASP side event: ecocide as an international crime: key considerations", 11 December 2020. https://www.publicinternationallawandpolicygroup.org/lawyering-justice-blog/2020/12/11/asp19-side-event-ecocide-as-an-international-crime-key-considerations. Accessed 8 June 2023

Report of the Committee on Budget and Finance on the work of its thirty-fourth session (Resolution ICC-ASP/18/5), 24 August 2020. https://asp.icc-cpi.int/sites/asp/files/asp_docs/ASP19/ICC-ASP-19-5-ENG-CBF34%20Report-Final.pdf. Accessed 8 June 2023

Resolution ICC-ASP/20/Res.1, 09 December 2021. https://asp.icc-cpi.int/sites/asp/files/asp_docs/ASP20/ICC-ASP-20-Res1-AV-ENG.pdf. Accessed 8 June 2023

Reuters, Faulconbridge G, "Nova Kakhovka dam breach: what do we know so far", 7 June 2023. https://www.reuters.com/world/europe/what-is-kakhovka-dam-ukraine-what-happened-2023-06-07/. Accessed 8 June 2023

Robinson D, Your Guide to Ecocide: Part 1, Opinio Juris, 16 July 2021. http://opiniojuris.org/2021/07/16/your-guide-to-ecocide-part-1/. Accessed 8 June 2023

Second Warrant of Arrest for Omar Hassan Ahmad Al Bashir, ICC-02/05-01/09-9. https://www.icc-cpi.int/CourtRecords/CR2010_04825.PDFZ. Accessed 8 June 2023

Stop Ecocide International (2019) "Sovereign States Call on ICC to Seriously Consider Ecocide Crime". https://www.stopecocide.earth/newsletter-summary/sovereign-states-call-on-icc-to-seriously-consider-ecocide-crime-. Accessed 8 June 2023

Stop Ecocide International, Higgins P. https://www.stopecocide.earth/polly-higgins. Accessed 8 June 2023

Switzerland, Federal Department of Foreign Affairs, "Swiss initiative: intentional starvation of civilians in civil wars is now a war crime", 06 December 2019. https://www.admin.ch/gov/en/start/documentation/media-releases.msg-id-77442.html. Accessed 8 June 2023

The Guardian (2022a) "Shock in France after giant trawler sheds 100,000 dead fish off coast", 05 February 2022. https://www.theguardian.com/environment/2022/feb/05/shock-in-france-after-giant-trawler-sheds-100000-dead-fish-off-coast. Accessed 8 June 2023

The Guardian (2022b) Wintour P, "Ukraine backs international tribunal plan to try Putin for crime of aggression", 04 March 2022. https://www.theguardian.com/world/2022/mar/04/ukraine-backs-plan-for-international-tribunal-to-try-putin-for-of-aggression. Accessed 8 June 2023

The Guardian (2023a) Beaumont P, Symons H, Scruton P, Swan L, Kirk A and Morresi E, "A Visual Guide to the Collapse of Ukraine's Nova Kakhovka Dam", 9 June 2023. https://www.theguardian.com/world/2023/jun/09/visual-guide-ukraine-nova-kakhovka-dam-collapse. Accessed 8 June 2023

The Guardian (2023b) "Fukushima". https://www.theguardian.com/environment/fukushima. Accessed 12 Sept 2023

World Economic Forum (2020) Nature Risk Rising: Why the Crisis Engulfing Nature Matters for Business and the Economy. https://www3.weforum.org/docs/WEF_New_Nature_Economy_Report_2020.pdf. Accessed 8 June 2023

Youatt R, Anthropocentrism and Democracy in Planetary Times: a Response to John Keane, Eurozine, 12 April 2023. https://www.eurozine.com/anthropocentrism-and-democracy-in-planetary-times/. Accessed 8 June 2023

Gillett M, Prosecuting Environmental Harm Before the International Criminal Court, Cambridge University Press (Cambridge, 2022)

Chapter 11
Lethal Autonomous Weapons, Drones and Robots: To What Extent Their Usage Infringes Upon Established Principles of International Criminal Law?

Abstract In this chapter, Victor Tsilonis explores the complex interplay between technology, warfare, and international law, focusing particularly on lethal autonomous weapons (LAWS). These advanced weapons systems, growing increasingly prevalent, pose intricate challenges for international criminal law and humanitarian law, especially in attributing individual criminal responsibility. Tsilonis underscores a critical concern: the inadequacy of existing legal frameworks in addressing the distinctive implications of LAWS, leading to serious risks of impunity and diminished accountability.

In the debate surrounding LAWS, Tsilonis contends that while calls for an outright ban are well-intentioned, they may be unrealistic. Instead, he advocates for the establishment of comprehensive 'ground rules' to govern the use of LAWS and calls for the adaptation and evolution of legal frameworks to ensure robust individual accountability. To this end, Tsilonis proposes the introduction of Article 8 tris to the ICC Rome Statute: Liability for Crimes under the ICC Jurisdiction Committed Using Lethal Autonomous Weapons (LAWS).

This chapter provides a thought-provoking analysis of the formidable legal and ethical dilemmas presented by emerging military technologies. It is an essential read for anyone interested in the dynamic realm of modern warfare and the urgent need for international criminal law and international legal standards to adapt to rapid technological advancements.

Initially used predominantly in counter-terrorism operations, the usage of drones has become increasingly more common in modern warfare. The 2022 conflict between Ukraine and Russia has seen the most intense use of drones in modern warfare.[1] It is expected that Ukraine expands its drone fleet even more.[2] The same trend is true for

[1] "Seven (Initial) Drone Warfare Lessons from Ukraine", Modern War Institute, 12 May 2022, https://mwi.usma.edu/seven-initial-drone-warfare-lessons-from-ukraine/, last accessed 8 June 2023.

[2] "Ukraine sent dozens of 'dronations' to build army of drones", BBC, 08 July 2022, https://www.bbc.co.uk/news/technology-62048403, last accessed 8 June 2023. *Also* "Ukraine's military in push to develop high-tech 'Army of Drones'", Al Jazeera, 15 July 2022, https://www.aljazeera.com/

V. Tsilonis, *The Jurisdiction of the International Criminal Court*,
https://doi.org/10.1007/978-3-031-46138-5_11

other kinds of lethal autonomous weapons (LAWs or AWs)[3] and robotic technology that operate without an onboard human presence.

Considering this trend, this chapter focuses on these new technologies and to what extend does their usage may be at odds with established principles of international criminal law (as well as norms of *jus ad bellum* and *jus in bellum*). It also dives into the issue of liability, since the remote operation or (in the case of highly autonomous devices) no operation, can lead to jurisdictional issues for the ICC. Finally, and having in mind the advances in this kind of technology, this section explores the possibility of conflicts conducted solely by automated devices—and seeks to establish some ground rules.

It is important first to define the objects of this section. Firstly, LAWS are here understood as weapon systems that, once activated, can select and engage targets without further human intervention. They raise far-reaching concerns about the protection of life during war and peace, which exponentially surpass the concerns regarding the use of drones thus far. Drones, in their turn, are unmanned aerial vehicles. Although several types of drones can be remotely piloted, this chapter focuses on the more advanced automated drones that enjoy autonomy with little or no room for human intervention. The same is true for the types of robots that this section examines—those without a human operator behind it at all times. Considering that LAWs is usually utilised as an umbrella term, covering both drones and other types of robots, this chapter will often refer to all these categories as such.

11.1 The Fundamental Principles of International Criminal Law and the Utilisation of LAWS (or AWS)

It is quite understandable that if the usage of either LAWS, drones or robots ever infringes upon principles international criminal law, this could be in the context of crimes already falling under the material jurisdiction of the ICC, i.e. exclusively crimes against humanity, genocide, crime of aggression, and, most likely, war crimes. This section aims to explore to which extent the usage of these devices (LAWS or AWS) may go against norms of international criminal law and even norms of *jus ad bellum* and *jus in bellum*.[4]

In the case of the crime of genocide and crimes against humanity, the usage of autonomous devices may infringe upon principles of international criminal law only insofar as they constitute a means to commit one of these crimes. For example, if

news/2022/7/15/ukraines-military-in-push-to-develop-high-tech-army-of-drones, last accessed 8 June 2023.

[3] Also known as "autonomous weapon systems" (AWS).

[4] Jus ad bellum refers to the norms applicable before engaging in war and relates to the conditions under which States may resort to the used of armed force against another State. Jus in bellum, in its turn, refers to the norms applicable during war and the conduct of parties during hostilities.

drones are somehow programmed to target a specific national, ethnic, racial or religious group and the one behind its programming and operation does so with the intention to destroy this group, in whole or in part (genocide).[5] Or if LAWS are utilised as part of a widespread or systematic attack directed against any civilian population and the operator of these devices has knowledge of the attack (crimes against humanity),[6] provided that these LAWS are used to commit one of the acts referred to by Art. 7(1) ICCRSt.

Regarding the crime of aggression, a state can recur to the use of automated devices such as drones and other LAWS/robots to use illegal force (or threaten the use of force) against another state, thus infringing upon *jus ad bellum* norms incorporated by the ICC.[7] It would be possible that the use of automated weapons amounted to the crime of aggression, but this must be analysed on a case-by-case basis. A clear example of the illegal use of these devices would be an intensive use of drone strikes on another State's territory without an authorisation by the UN Security Council or which did not constitute self-defence.[8] But what about a single drone strike?[9] Or in cases such as Pakistan, which have given the US consent to use drones against non-state actors and subsequently withdrawn its consent?[10] These examples, while not exhaustive, demonstrate a few of many grey areas concerning the use of force that could render the use of automated devices a crime of aggression. However, similar to the case of crimes against humanity or genocide, the use of drones in itself would not constitute a crime of aggression *de lege lata*, given the extremely limited scope of the ICC's jurisdiction regarding the said crime. Rather, it would be considered as a means to commit the crime. Additionally, Heyns et al.[11] note that even if the use of drones can be considered lawful as a matter of *jus ad bellum* (i.e. the prohibition on the use of force by a State), it might still be unlawful in the context of an armed conflict, going against norms of *jus in bellum*.

Finally, the use of these devices is more closely related to war crimes, as they may (but not necessarily do) go against established principles of international criminal law. In the context of war crimes, the main problem with the usage of LAWs, drones and robots is how they can infringe upon principles of *jus in bellum* also established by international criminal law, such as the fundamental principles of distinction and/or proportionality.

---

[5] Chapter 3 for the exact definition and elements of the crime of genocide.

[6] Chapter 4 for the exact definitions and elements of crimes against humanity.

[7] Chapter 6 for the exact definition and elements of the crime of aggression.

[8] Casey-Maslen (2018), p. 602.

[9] Casey-Maslen (2018), p. 602. The author believes that there is "a strong argument" that this may be the case, referring to UNGA Resolution 3314 (XXIX) and the 1988 case of Israeli commandos killing a single Palestine Liberation Organization member was considered an aggression by the UNSC.

[10] There could also be questions regarding who is entitled to give such consent and if the consent was valid (e.g. Yemen, Somalia). Heyns (2016), p. 797.

[11] Heyns (2016), p. 79.

The principle of distinction guarantees that parties of a conflict always distinguish between civilians and combatants. This norm of customary international law prohibits attacks from being directed against civilians.[12] It was considered by the ICJ on its Advisory Opinion on Nuclear Weapons[13] as one of the "cardinal principles" encapsulating international humanitarian law. Dinstein[14] has also referred to it as *"the most basic norm of the law of international armed conflict"*. Clearly, the prohibition of the use of inherently indiscriminate weapons, which this section also explores, is derived from this core principle of international humanitarian law. The principle of proportionality, in its turn, prohibits launching attacks which *"may be expected to cause incidental loss of civilian life, injury to civilians, damage to civilian objects, or a combination thereof, which would be excessive in relation to the concrete and direct military advantage anticipated"*.[15]

The ICC Statute has incorporated these principles, especially within Art. 8(2)(b) ICCRSt and its provisions. For instance, it incorporates the principle of distinction by criminalising attacks against civilians not taking part of hostilities, civilian objects, humanitarian personnel and their materials, combatants *hors de combat* or targets that are not military objectives.[16] It also incorporates the principle of proportionality under Art. 8(2)(b)(iv) ICCRSt by prohibiting attacks causing damage *"which would be clearly excessive in relation to the concrete and direct overall military advantage anticipated"*.

Regarding the principle of distinction, the problem main question is whether these systems would be able to distinguish not only between civilians and combatants *per se*, but also consider more complicated issues regarding this principle. For example, distinguishing a regular combatant from one that is *hors de combat*, identifying medical staff as well as armoured vehicles/personnel from the Red Cross, or refrain from attacking a combatant that has expressed the intention to surrender.[17]

Stemming from the principle of distinction, customary international humanitarian law also prohibits the use of inherently indiscriminate weapons. In the context of international criminal law, the ICTY in *Martić* found that *"a direct attack against civilians can be inferred from the indiscriminate weapon used."*[18] The ICRC has

[12] ICRC, IHL Database – Customary IHL, "Rule 1. The Principle of Distinction between Civilians and Combatants", https://ihl-databases.icrc.org/customary-ihl/eng/docs/v1_rul_rule1, last accessed 08 June 2023.

[13] Legality of the Threat or Use of Nuclear Weapons (Advisory Opinion) 1996 ICJ Reports 1996, 226, p. 257.

[14] Dinstein (2005).

[15] ICRC, IHL Database – Customary IHL, "Rule 14. Proportionality in Attack" https://ihl-databases.icrc.org/customary-ihl/eng/docs/v1_rul_rule14, last accessed 04 July 2022.

[16] Art. 2(b)(i)-(iii),(iv)-(vI), ICCRSt.

[17] van den Boogaard (2016), p. 12.

[18] ICTY (2008) (confirming the Trial Chamber's finding).

noted that certain LAWS would be inherently indiscriminate and thus prohibited.[19] However, this would be the case with LAWS *"whose effects, in their normal or expected circumstances of use, could not be sufficiently understood, predicted and explained."*[20] On the same note, the ICRC recommends States to expressly rule out unpredictable autonomous weapon systems.[21]

A lot of the mistakes involved in the usage of these devices (LAWS or AWS) may result in wrongfully targeting civilians was seen with the use of drones for unlawful targeting and killing of people suspected of being terrorists.[22] There are two main issues seen in this practice: **1)** suspected terrorist(s), who might not have any 'opportunity' for a fair trial, but instead receive an arbitrary death sentence executed summarily by a flying robot (a drone) operated by military personnel; **2)** as it is quite often the case because of the distance the drone is operated and multiple field parameters, mistakes are quite usual—wrong people are unjustly targeted, wrong people are killed instead of those intended to be targeted and many innocent people (women and children) lose their life in the course of the drone attacks, along with the 'rightfully' targeted people. Nonetheless, despite the harsh criticism and multitude of deadly mistakes, as well as the grave dangers and the humanitarian and human rights implications involving the use of drones in the context of counter-terrorism operations, States have been incrementally expanding their utilisation. There is plausible danger that this arbitrary practice could also be used in the near future for other kind of killings as well (espionage, political conspiracies, attempted dictatorship, among others).

However, it should be noted that, although the use LAWS, drones and automated robots *may* go against the principle of distinction, this is not the same as saying that their use will *always* go against this principle.

First, a lot of these devices are sufficiently accurate in order not to be considered "inherently indiscriminate". Casey-Maslen[23] compares the accuracy of Hellfire missiles and Paveway II bombs (commonly associated with armed drones of the Predator and Reaper variants) with rockets used during World War II and bombs used in Indochina to illustrate this. Depending on the model, weather conditions, and distance, the circular error probable[24] of the Hellfire missile system and Paveway II laser-guided bombs ranges from about 6m to less than 10m.[25] In comparison, German V-2 rockets had a CEP of about 17km and conventional bombs used in

[19] ICRC (2021), p. 7.

[20] *Idem.*

[21] ICRC (2021), p. 1.

[22] Boyle (2013), p. 1, on the myth of drone effectiveness. *Also* Ogunfolu and Fagbemi (2015), pp. 106, 109 and 116–117.

[23] Casey-Maslen (2018).

[24] Also known as 'CEP', it is a measure of the precision of a weapon system. CEP refers to the radius of a circle (stemming from the target) where at least half of the missiles are expected to land.

[25] Casey-Maslen (2018), pp. 221–222.

Indochina *"are said to have had a CEP of 130-140 metres and laser-guided bombs, 22 metres."*[26]

Secondly, the use of these devices might not be considered "inherently indiscriminate" or infringing upon the principle of distinction when used in areas composed solely of legitimate targets. In the ICTY *Martić* case, the Trial Chamber found that: *"the M-87 Orkan is an indiscriminate weapon, the use of which in densely populated civilian areas, such as Zagreb, will result in the infliction of severe casualties."*[27] Hence it considered the use of these cluster munitions a war crime insofar as they were used in densely populated civilian areas. It is quite possible that this finding would have been different if a weapon system similar or not to M-87 Orkan had been used in areas where there were no civilians or other protected persons or objects in the vicinity, but instead existed there only military personnel and equipment, like in the case of a military base's bombardment.

Regarding the principle of proportionality, its definition points to considerations that would already be quite difficult for a human to conclude with certainty, let alone an automated system. Who is a civilian or what is a civilian object? What is the military advantage anticipated? What would constitute an excess? And what would happen if an artificial intelligence military system (LAWS/AWS) took a wrong decision with severe/deadly consequences? Who should be criminally responsible, the manufacturer, the seller, the commander-in-charge or all of them? Van den Boogaard[28] points to elements of the proportionality equation that put in question the ability of autonomous weapons systems to properly analyse: **i)** distinction (i.e. the possibility of algorithms of recognising valid military targets); **ii)** determining the expected military advantage (i.e. identifying a military objective as well as the possibility of collateral damage and conducting a context-driven analysis of this objective); **iii)** applying a "reasonable judgment"[29] in terms of the proportionality equation.

While artificial intelligence may eventually develop itself to make decisions based on different types of scenarios that may take place in armed conflict (perhaps even developing a sophisticated system that identifies combatants *hors de combat* and develops an accurate calculation of military objectives), it is difficult to envision that a software will be capable in the near future of taking into account all of the scenarios that may take place during conflict and to make decisions that would already be complicated from the point of view of a human. Thus, it is likely that autonomous systems may infringe upon the principle of proportionality, and consequently infringe upon established principles of international criminal law.

---

[26] *Ibid.*, pp. 222–223.

[27] ICTY (2007).

[28] van den Boogaard (2016).

[29] The author makes reference to the concept of reasonableness used in the *Galić* Trial Judgement at the ICTY, where the Trial Chamber found that *"in determining whether an attack was proportionate it is necessary to examine whether a reasonably well-informed person in the circumstances of the actual perpetrator, making reasonable use of the information available to him or her, could have expected excessive civilian casualties to result from the attack"*. ICTY (2003).

However, it should be noted again that there might be occasions (even if exceptional ones) in which automated systems won't have issues regarding distinction or proportionality (for example, if LAWS/AWS are used in areas away from civilians or civilian objects and can target solely legitimate targets). Thus, in this case, the use of these weapons *per se* does not infringe upon principles of international humanitarian law nor international criminal law.

There is also the distant possibility of criminalising these weapons through Art. 8 (2)(b)(xx) ICCRSt of the Rome Statute. This provision criminalises, in the context of international armed conflicts:

> Employing weapons, projectiles and material and methods of warfare which are of a nature to cause superfluous injury or unnecessary suffering or which are inherently indiscriminate in violation of the international law of armed conflict, provided that such weapons, projectiles and material and methods of warfare are the subject of a comprehensive prohibition and are included in an annex to this Statute, by an amendment in accordance with the relevant provisions set forth in articles 121 and 123;

However, there are a few issues regarding the actual implementation of this provision for LAWS/AWS, drones and automated robots. As already mentioned above, the first issue is that these devices are not necessarily "inherently indiscriminate", despite worries about their accuracy. Secondly, while the ICRC has expressed serious concerns regarding LAWS and even recommend States to expressly rule out unpredictable autonomous weapon systems,[30] there is no kind of prohibition on their use. Thirdly, there would still be the need for an amendment pursuant to articles 121 and 123 of the ICCRSt. for the use of these devices to be criminalised. And thus far, there have been no amendments of this kind. Additionally, this condition might render Art. 8(2)(b)(xx) ICCRSt inoperable. States would still be free to deviate from this legal requirement,[31] i.e. any future amendment of Art. 8(2)(b)(xx) ICCRSt, because such an amendment would only apply to those States that accept it under Art. 121(5) ICCRSt.

Overall, it can be argued that while the use of LAWS, drones, or other automated robots do not infringe upon established principles of international criminal law *per se*, the way they are programmed and used may quite possibly do so. This is especially the case in the context of armed conflicts, where the use of automated weapons has the potential to also go against *jus in bellum* core principles such as the principle of distinction and the principle of proportionality. Thus, while the use of these devices is not considered an international crime in itself, they may be used to commit crimes against humanity, genocide, and the crime of aggression, and its usage may lead to a war crime.

---

[30] ICRC (2021), p. 1.

[31] Cottier and Krivanek (2015), pp. 467–468.

11.2 Assessing Liability in the Use of Autonomous Weapons at the ICCand a Novel Article for Addressing the Lacuna

The integration of Lethal Autonomous Weapons (LAWS), drones, and other automated robots into military operations poses unique challenges in international criminal law, particularly concerning liability under the jurisdiction of the International Criminal Court (ICC). The remote or fully automated operation of these devices complicates the establishment of individual criminal responsibility. This section explores potential legal avenues for holding responsible those who operate, command, or even programme these devices. It emphasises the necessity of ensuring human accountability to prevent impunity for crimes committed using such technologies. The ICC's jurisdiction extends solely over natural persons, making the accountability of fully autonomous weapon systems currently unfeasible. This situation is reminiscent of medieval animal trials, albeit with the crucial difference that animals lack human-level intelligence. A key challenge in attributing liability to LAWS is the requirement of both *actus reus* and *mens rea* in criminal law. The latter is particularly problematic for automated devices, which lack mental states and the capacity for intent. To establish individual criminal responsibility, it is essential to trace the criminal conduct to one or more individuals. However, the increasing autonomy of these weapon systems risks obscuring this traceability, complicating the establishment of individual liability. This issue is particularly acute when multiple individuals are involved in the operation of an LAW, making it difficult to pinpoint specific decisions or actions leading to an attack. Even if one considers the use of LAWS, drones and/or other automated robots an international crime under the jurisdiction of the ICC, there is an additional issue regarding liability. Due to its remote operation (or no operation at all, in the case of fully automated devices), establishing individual criminal responsibility might prove itself a significant legal challenge. One could imagine legal solutions such as holding criminally responsible those who have somewhat operated these devices, political and/or criminal leaders, or even those who programmed these devices. This section considers the above options and concludes that, regardless of the legal solution(s) adopted, it is important not to disregard the issue of creating human responsibility behind in order not to allow for these kinds of crimes to be committed under full protection of the law.

The ICC only has jurisdiction over natural persons.[32] Thus, the possibility of holding a fully autonomous weapon system, drone, or robot accountable is yet unthinkable (and might even one remind of the animal trials in the medieval times, although admittedly animals do not possess human-level intelligence). An additional issue relating to liability and LAWS relies on the fact that a crime consists essentially of two elements: *actus reus* and *mens rea*,[33] the latter of which represents an issue

[32] ICCRSt. Article 25(1).

[33] Art. 30 (1), ICCRSt: *"Unless otherwise provided, a person shall be criminally responsible and liable for punishment for a crime within the jurisdiction of the Court only if the material elements are committed with intent and knowledge."*

when talking about automated devices, that do not possess a mental state nor are they capable of intent.[34]

Thus, in order to establish individual criminal responsibility, the criminal conduct in question must be traced to an individual (or multiple individuals). The main danger with the increasing use of autonomous weapons (as well as the increasing autonomy of its systems) is that this traceability may become undermined and establishing individual liability may not be possible.[35] This is especially tricky if there are multiple people involved in the employment of an LAW: there might be a difficulty in tracing decisions made by individuals during the course of time that led to an attack, understanding in how these decisions interacted, or establishing how these decisions and consequences correspond to the provisions related to criminal liability at the ICCRSt.[36]

The ICCRSt established several types of individual criminal responsibility under art. 25, along with command responsibility under article 28. These may give an indication of those individuals that could eventually be held liable for attacks and casualties committed by autonomous devices: operators (if any), political/military leaders or even the ones behind the programming of these devices. However, as seen below, the modes of liability established by the ICCRSt do not properly address situations involving LAWS.

First, a person may be criminally responsible and liable for punishment under art. 25(3)(a) if that person: *"Commits such a crime, whether as an individual, jointly with another person or through another person, regardless of whether that person is criminally responsible"*. This provision, which entails principal liability, does not necessarily require that the accused is present at the crime scene, nor that the perpetrator physically carries out the attack.[37] The Lubanga Trial Chamber concluded that the commission of a crime jointly with another person has two elements: i) *"the existence of an agreement or common plan between two or more persons that, if implemented, will result in the commission of a crime;"* and ii) *"hat the accused provided an essential contribution to the common plan that resulted in the commission of the relevant crime."*[38]

This mode of liability could entail *prima facie* responsibility for operators, their commanders and those who are also part of a team responsible for drones such as intelligence officers and video analysts that assists a drone's movements.[39] However, while this scenario is conceivable in the case of LAWS used recently that involve a large team of operators (such as Predator drones),[40] it may not be as simple in the case of fully autonomous weapons. A truly fully autonomous weapon may act

[34] HRW, IHRC (2015), p. 2.

[35] Boulain et al. (2021), p. 45.

[36] *Idem.*

[37] ICC (2012); ICC (2007).

[38] ICC (2012), para. 1006.

[39] Casey-Maslen (2018), p. 244.

[40] *Idem.*

independently and beyond any common plan between those employing it. Additionally, there would be no "essential contribution to the common plan" if a LAW was to independently carry on an attack that mistakenly targeted civilians or combatants *hors de combat*, or even if a partially autonomous system lost signal and was unable to receive further instructions from its operators and the team responsible for it.[41]

A second possibility is the mode of aiding and abetting under art. 25(3)(c), ICCRSt. This provision allows for the criminal responsibility of those who *"[f]or the purpose of facilitating the commission of such a crime, aids, abets or otherwise assists in its commission or its attempted commission, including providing the means for its commission"*. Under this mode of liability, it is possible for an individual to be held responsible as an accessory to the commission of the crime, and there is no need to share the same purpose as the perpetrator. Rather, the individual must merely have a knowledge that their acts will assist the principal perpetrator in the commission of its acts.[42] This could be applicable to those who are responsible for LAWS as part of a larger operation and deploy it in a certain area.[43] In theory, this would also allow for those who programme or design those weapons to be held responsible. (see the recent case.[44] Designer responsibility has already been envisioned in the context of autonomous vehicles that may result in (sometimes fatal) accidents (e.g. Tesla vehicles).[45] However, there are several issues with this mode of liability in the context of LAWS. First, this mode of liability presupposes that there is a principal perpetrator. As mentioned above, the LAW itself would lack the *mens rea* in order to be considered a principal and it would be difficult to point other individuals as principle perpetrators if a system acts autonomously and unexpectedly. Second, in the case of developers, they may not meet the necessary *actus reus* and *mens rea* in order to amount to a crime and their conduct (i.e. designing the autonomous weapon system) may precede the existence of an armed conflict.[46]

Another conceivable scenario is entailing command responsibility to military leaders. Art. 28 ICCRSt permits the responsibility of commanders and other superiors in the following manner:

[41] HRW, IHRC (2015), p. 19.

[42] Ambos (2015), p. 979. Also ICTY (1998).

[43] Casey-Maslen (2018), p. 245.

[44] Boulain et al. (2021), p. 48. See also Nordic Monitor (2022).

[45] Casey-Maslen (2018), p. 231.

[46] Boulain et al. (2021), p. 48.

(a) A military commander or person effectively acting as a military commander shall be criminally responsible for crimes within the jurisdiction of the Court committed by forces under his or her effective command and control, or effective authority and control as the case may be, as a result of his or her failure to exercise control properly over such forces, where:

   (i) That military commander or person either knew or, owing to the circumstances at the time, should have known that the forces were committing or about to commit such crimes; and
   (ii) That military commander or person failed to take all necessary and reasonable measures within his or her power to prevent or repress their commission or to submit the matter to the competent authorities for investigation and prosecution.

In the context of autonomous weapons, a commander could in theory be held criminally responsible if they knew, or should have known (i.e. if a similar device had previously done something similar) that a LAW under its responsibility was committing or about to commit a crime, and if they failed to take all necessary and reasonable measures to stop it.[47]

However, this provision is not exactly suited for human-robot relations, but rather to human relations within a context of subordination. It is difficult to ascertain whether it would be possible to recognise LAWS as "forces under his or her effective command and control". The Human Rights Watch (HRW) and the International Human Rights Clinic (IHRC) further demonstrate[48] some challenges in applying this provision: i) the commission of a crime committed might be debatable in itself, as the "subordinate" (LAW) is not capable of having *mens rea*, one of the constitutive elements of a crime; ii) the element of knowledge might be difficult to prove, as fully autonomous systems may not communicate its target beforehand, or in time; iii) it is not possible to conceive "investigation and prosecution" for a robot, meaning responsibility could only arise in respect of the failure to act (which may not be possible either as LAWS may make decisions in a millisecond); iv) the element of "effective control" might also be put into question in cases of fully autonomous systems or due to the possibility of technical or communication issues.

Consequently, there inevitably exists a significant gap in terms of the current ICCRSt framework and the possibility of establishing individual criminal responsibility for the use of LAWS that could amount to an international crime. The ICCRSt could be ill-suited to apply to fully autonomous systems. Additionally, its modes of liability and its definition of intent and knowledge[49] arguably does not encompass recklessness,[50] besides expressly forbidding analogies.[51] Addressing the identified gap in the ICCRSt framework is imperative to establish criminal responsibility for individuals orchestrating attacks using LAWS. Failure to do so may allow for the

---

[47] HRW, IHRC (2015), p. 21.

[48] HRW, IHRC (2015).

[49] ICCRSt, Art. 30.

[50] Chapter 5 and the discussion on recklessness.

[51] ICCRSt, art. 22(2): *"The definition of a crime shall be strictly construed and shall not be extended by analogy. In case of ambiguity, the definition shall be interpreted in favour of the person being investigated, prosecuted or convicted."*

utilization of these devices in committing international crimes with impunity, shielded by the current limitations of the law. This gap underscores the urgent need for legal adaptation in response to the rapidly evolving and challenging technological landscape of autonomous systems. Such legal reforms are essential to ensure accountability for those employing LAWS and to prevent the potential misuse of these technologies in the perpetration of international crimes. Prompt and decisive action is necessary to adapt our legal frameworks to these advancements, thereby safeguarding the principles of international criminal justice and upholding accountability in an era of technological complexity. In light of the complex challenges and legal ambiguities outlined above, particularly concerning the liability issues associated with the use of Autonomous Weapon Systems at the ICC, the subsequent draft article is proposed to address these specific lacunae. This article aims to provide a clear legal framework, ensuring that the evolving landscape of autonomous weaponry is comprehensively covered under international criminal law.

Article 8 tris ICCRSt:

Liability for Crimes under the ICC Jurisdiction Committed Using Lethal Autonomous Weapons (LAWS)

1. Definition of Lethal Autonomous Weapons (LAWS): For the purposes of this Statute, a Lethal Autonomous Weapons (LAWS) is defined as a weapon system that, once activated, can autonomously select and engage targets without further human intervention.
2. Criminal Liability for the Use of LAWS:

   (a) Principal Liability (complementing Art. 25(3)(a) ICCRSt): An individual shall be criminally responsible and liable for punishment for war crimes, crimes against humanity, genocide and the crime of aggression committed through the use of one or more LAWS if that individual:

      (i) Programs, activates, or employs LAWS with the intent for it to commit a crime under the jurisdiction of the Court.
      (ii) Knowingly provides essential technological or operational support for the specific criminal use of the LAWS.

   (b) Command Responsibility (complementing Art. 28 ICCRSt): A military commander or person effectively acting as a military commander shall be criminally responsible for crimes committed by one or more LAWS under their effective command and control, where:

      (i) They knew or, owing to the circumstances at the time, should have known that the LAWS were being used or was about to be used to commit such crimes.
      (ii) They failed to take all necessary and reasonable measures within their power to prevent or repress their commission or to submit the matter to the competent authorities for investigation and prosecution.

3. Liability of Heads of Corporate Entities:

   (a) Heads, Chief Executives, Members of the Executive Council, and other competent superiors of corporate entities involved in the design, manufacture, programming, or sale of LAWS can be held accountable for their use in the commission of crimes under the Court's jurisdiction, pursuant to the applied personae materiae principle.

(b) Liability arises where it can be established that the entity acted with knowledge that the LAWS would be used for criminal purposes, or where due diligence to prevent such use was grossly inadequate.

4. Shared Responsibility: In cases where multiple actors contribute to the commission of a crime through the use of LAWS, each actor's contribution shall be evaluated based on their intent, knowledge, and the extent of their involvement in the crime's commission.
5. Implementation by the Office of the Prosecutor: Following the adoption of the above or a similarly drafted article, the Office of the Prosecutor will develop and adopt specialised investigative techniques and legal strategies to effectively prosecute crimes involving the use of LAWS.

11.3 Navigating the Future of Warfare: Establishing Ethical and Legal Boundaries for Lethal Autonomous Weapons

The challenge of assigning responsibility for the deployment of Lethal Autonomous Weapon Systems (LAWS) underscores significant concerns about their use. Human Rights Watch (HRW) and the International Human Rights Clinic (IHRC) advocate for a total prohibition of fully autonomous weapons, arguing that such a ban would effectively bridge existing gaps in liability.[52] The International Committee of the Red Cross (ICRC) also recommends prohibiting unpredictable autonomous weapon systems,[53] which could address liability issues and prevent violations of humanitarian and international criminal law principles.

Nevertheless, the practicality of a total ban on LAWS is debatable. Countries including Israel, Russia, South Korea, and Turkey have reportedly deployed weapons with autonomous features, while nations like Australia, the UK, China, and the USA are substantially investing in their advancement.[54] Despite over 30 countries and the Non-Aligned Movement advocating for a ban,[55] major powers such as the USA, China, and Russia have resisted such initiatives.[56]

The increasing use of these technologies, as seen in the 2022 Russia-Ukraine conflict,[57] raises concerns about their potential use in biological and chemical

[52] HRW, IHRC (2015).

[53] ICRC (2021), p. 7.

[54] Trager (2022), last accessed 08 June 2023. Regarding the former exemple, the author argues that whether the autonomous mode of these systems was active is disputed.

[55] HRW (2020), last accessed 08 June 2023.

[56] Trager (2022), last accessed 08 June 2023.

[57] Beaubien (2022), last accessed 08 June 2023; Stashevskyi and Bajak (2022), last accessed 08 June 2023.

warfare.[58] As these systems become more sophisticated,[59] future warfares dominated by lethal autonomous weapons (LAWS) become a conceivable and in fact quite expected future reality. In this evolving inescapable situation, establishing foundational rules is critical. The Convention on Certain Conventional Weapons (CCW) set up an informal Group of Governmental Experts (GGE) to deliberate on the implications of LAWS. In 2019, the GGE outlined guiding principles, including ensuring human accountability and oversight, prohibiting LAWS that contravene international humanitarian law (IHL) standards, and prioritising civilian safety throughout the design, development, testing, and deployment stages.[60]

In 2019, the GGE formulated a set of guiding principles on LAWs, which include: i) maintaining human/State responsibility for decisions on the use of weapons systems; ii) ensuring that a human operator or commander exercises judgement over the operational context; iii) prohibiting the use of LAWs that are inherently against principles and norms of IHL (such as inherently indiscriminate weapons or those that cause superfluous injury or unnecessary suffering) and iv) taking into account the risk of civilian casualties during the whole process of design, development, testing and deployment of these weapons, taking precautions to help minimalize the risk of incidental loss of life, injuries to civilians and destruction of civilian objects.[61]

The idea of imposing a limit on technology that could be used for causing human casualties is not new. Asimov's Three Laws of Robotics, based on the work of the famous science fiction author Isaac Asimov, already addressed this issue in the 1950s. Namely, the fact that *"[a] robot may not injure a human being or allow a human being to come to harm"* and, arguably, the second law *that "a robot must obey the orders given it by human beings except where such orders would conflict with the First Law"*.[62]

On the same note, the idea of warfare completely led by LAWs does not necessarily go against norms of IHL and ICL. Furthermore, the total automation of warfare, although it may appear at first glance to be in conflict with international humanitarian and international criminal law norms, does not inherently violate them. Hitoshi Nasu and Colonel Korpela of the United States Military Academy argue that the use of LAWs might bring "significant humanitarian benefits" by mitigating the risk of human error, verifying military targets, and lessening reduce the use of high explosives (along with its casualties).[63]

Thus, as fully autonomous weapon systems continue to be developed and deployed, it is imperative that states reach a consensus on key guidelines. These rules should strive to minimise civilian casualties and adhere to the established

[58] Bozkurt (2022), last accessed 08 June 2023.

[59] Koetsier (2021), last accessed 08 June 2023.

[60] Geneva Internet Platform (2023).

[61] *Idem.*

[62] Asimov (2008), p. 38 (first edition: Gnome Press, 1950).

[63] Nasu and Korpela (2022), last accessed 08 June 2023.

principles of international criminal law and international humanitarian law. Importantly, states must also confront the issue of criminal liability for the misuse of these systems to avert an accountability gap that would allow the irresponsible use of LAWS with legal impunity. Establishing these guidelines is not merely a legal requirement; it represents a moral obligation to steer the future of warfare towards a more regulated and humane path.

References

Table of Cases

ICC (2007) *Prosecutor v. Lubanga,* Decision on the Confirmation of Charges, , ICC-01/04-01/06-803-tem, para. 330
ICC (2012) *Prosecutor v. Lubanga,* Judgment pursuant to Article 74 of the Statute, ICC-01/04-01/06-284, paras 1003, 1005
ICJ (1996) Legality of the Threat or Use of Nuclear Weapons (Advisory Opinion) ICJ Reports
ICTY (1998) *Prosecutor v. Furundžija,* Judgement, IT-95-17/1-T, para. 236
ICTY (2003) Prosecutor v. Stanislav Galić, Judgement IT-98-29-T, para. 58
ICTY (2007) *Prosecutor v. Milan Martić*, Trial Judgment T-95-11-T, para. 463
ICTY (2008) Prosecutor v. Milan Martić, Appeals Judgment IT-95-11-A, para. 251

Books

Ambos K (2015) Article 25. In: Triffterer O, Ambos K (eds) Rome Statute of the International Criminal Court: a commentary. OUP, p 979
Asimov I (2008) I ROBOT, 1st edn. Gnome Press, p 38
Boulain V, Bruun L, Goussac N (2021) Autonomous weapon systems and international humanitarian law: identifying limits and the required type and degree of human-machine interaction. SIPRI, p 45
Casey-Maslen S (2018) Autonomous weapons systems and international criminal law. In: Casey-Maslen S, Homayoun Nejad M, Stauffer H, Weizmann N (eds) Drones and other unmanned weapons systems under international law. Brill | Nijhoff, Boston
Cottier M, Krivanek D (2015) In: Triffterer O, Ambos K (eds) Rome Statute of the International Criminal Court: a commentary. OUP, pp 467–468
Dinstein Y (2005) Collateral damage and the principle of proportionality. In: Wippman D, Evangelista M (eds) New wars, new laws? Applying laws of war in 21st century conflicts. Transnational Publishers, New York

Articles/Papers

Beaubien J (2022) In the Russia-Ukraine war, drones are one of the most powerful weapons. Available at NPR. https://www.npr.org/2022/07/30/1114024870/russia-ukraine-war-drones?t=1660772417059
Boyle M (2013) The costs and consequences of drone warfare. Int Aff 89(1):I

Bozkurt A (2022) Russia accused Turkey of planning to equip Bayraktar drones with biological/chemical weapons. Available at Nordic Monitor. https://nordicmonitor.com/2022/09/russia-accused-turkey-of-planning-to-equip-bayraktar-drones-with-bio-chemical-weapons/

Heyns C, Akande D et al (2016) The international law framework regulating the use of armed drones. ICLQ 65:791

ICRC (2021) Position on Autonomous Weapon Systems and Background Paper. p 7

Kallenborn Z (2022) Seven (initial) drone warfare lessons from Ukraine. Modern War Institute. https://mwi.usma.edu/seven-initial-drone-warfare-lessons-from-ukraine/

Koetsier J (2021) Autonomous drones achieve most sophisticated level of 3D aerial autonomy to date. Available at Forbes. https://www.forbes.com/sites/johnkoetsier/2021/05/29/autonomous-drones-achieve-most-sophisticated-level-of-3d-aerial-autonomy-to-date/?sh=7da76f386531

Nasu H, Korpela C (2022) Stop the "Stop the Killer Robot" debate: why we need artificial intelligence in future battlefields. Available at Council on Foreign Relations. https://www.cfr.org/blog/stop-stop-killer-robot-debate-why-we-need-artificial-intelligence-future-battlefields

Ogunfolu A, Fagbemi O (2015) I have a drone: the implications of American drone policy for Africa and international humanitarian law. Afr J Int Comp Law 23(1):106, 109 and 116–117

Stashevskyi O, Bajak F (2022) In Ukraine war, a race to acquire smarter, deadlier drones. Available at AP News. https://apnews.com/article/russia-ukraine-kyiv-technology-17a364a50a9d7861c59ea423c7491458

Trager R (2022) Killer robots are here—and we need to regulate them. Available at Foreign Policy. https://foreignpolicy.com/2022/05/11/killer-robots-lethal-autonomous-weapons-systems-ukraine-libya-regulation/

van den Boogaard J (17 March 2016) Proportionality and autonomous weapons systems. J Int Humanit Leg Stud (2015) issue 2. Forthcoming Amsterdam Center for International Law No. 2016-07, Amsterdam Law School Research Paper No. 2016-17. Available at SSRN: https://ssrn.com/abstract=2748997

Websites/Web Sources

Al Jazeera (2022) Ukraine's military in push to develop high-tech 'Army of Drones'. https://www.aljazeera.com/news/2022/7/15/ukraines-military-in-push-to-develop-high-tech-army-of-drones. Accessed 8 June 2023

BBC (2022) Ukraine sent dozens of 'dronations' to build army of drones. https://www.bbc.co.uk/news/technology-62048403. Accessed 8 June 2023

Geneva Internet Platform, GGE on lethal autonomous weapons systems. https://dig.watch/processes/gge-laws. Accessed 8 June 2023

HRW (2020) Stopping killer robots, country positions on banning fully autonomous weapons and retaining human control. https://www.hrw.org/report/2020/08/10/stopping-killer-robots/country-positions-banning-fully-autonomous-weapons-and

HRW, IHRC (2015) Mind the gap: the lack of accountability for killer robots, p 2. Accessed 8 June 2023

ICRC Database Customary IHL Rule 1. The principle of distinction between civilians and combatants. https://ihl-databases.icrc.org/en/customary-ihl/v1/rule1. Accessed 8 June 2023

ICRC Database Customary IHL Rule 14. Proportionality in attack. https://ihl-databases.icrc.org/customary-ihl/eng/docs/v1_rul_rule14. Accessed 8 June 2023

Nordic Monitor, Russia accused Turkey of planning to equip Bayraktar drones with biological/chemical weapons, 12 September 2022. https://nordicmonitor.com/2022/09/russia-accused-turkey-of-planning-to-equip-bayraktar-drones-with-bio-chemical-weapons/. Accessed 8 June 2023

Chapter 12
Cyber Warfare: International Criminal Law in the Digital Era

Abstract This chapter delves into the complex and rapidly-evolving field of cyber warfare and the consequential legal challenges. Victor Tsilonis critically examines the International Criminal Court's (ICC) jurisdiction over crimes committed in cyberspace, particularly focusing on *ratione loci* (territorial jurisdiction) aspect. Emphasising the inherently transnational nature of cyber crimes, the chapter explores the difficulty of pinning down the 'territory' in which such crimes occur. It delves into the concept of "déterritorialisation" and questions traditional territorial jurisdiction. It studies the ICC's broad interpretation of territoriality and how this approach can encompass cybercrimes originating from multiple territories. The chapter also introduces the 'ubiquity doctrine', a novel legal approach that extends beyond traditional territorial jurisdiction, addressing crimes with cross-border impacts. An elaborate hypothetical scenario of a state-sponsored hacker group operation is presented to elucidate the multifaceted *loci delicti* associated with cyber warfare. The chapter concludes by asserting the necessity of a case-by-case basis assessment for the ICC's jurisdiction over cybercrimes. It posits that the Court's jurisdiction might only be excluded under a certain combination of conditions that dissociate the crime from any State-Party to the Rome Statute. This analysis sets a crucial step in understanding the legal intricacies involved in global cyber warfare and the crucial role of international criminal law.

12.1 Cyber Warfare: A New Battlefield and a New Facet of International Criminal Law

In addition to LAWs or AWs, another trend, i.e., cyber warfare, is becoming increasingly more and more dominant in modern warfare, with the inevitable daring challenge of bringing international humanitarian law and international criminal law more swiftly into the digital era and the largely unwritten rules of conduct of cyber warfare.

This modern trend requires international criminal law to be revisited in light of the novel specificities of cyber warfare. For this reason, this chapter focuses on the issue of cyber warfare and the applicability of international criminal law. First, it looks

V. Tsilonis, *The Jurisdiction of the International Criminal Court*,
https://doi.org/10.1007/978-3-031-46138-5_12

into the definition of cyber warfare and cyberattacks in the context of international criminal law, as well as how and/or when cyberattacks may be characterised as war crimes pursuant to the Rome Statute (ICCRSt). Then, it turns to examine indicatively challenges that the exercise of the ICC's jurisdiction over cyberattacks may bring, both concerning the establishment of its jurisdiction and critical issues of liability.

12.2 A Brief Account of the History of Cyber Warfare

Certainly, the use of cyberattacks against a State is not new. Even though the attribution of the 'first' state-sponsored cyberattack can be extremely challenging and in fact might remain eternally unknown due to the covert nature of cyber warfare and the difficulty in attributing cyberattacks to specific actors, one of the most notable early instances often referenced as a potential state-sponsored cyberattack is 'Moonlight Maze'. Moonlight Maze was the name of a US government investigation in 1999 into a constant and massive data breach of classified information. It is one of the earliest known instances of organised, state-sponsored cyber espionage, 'following' the much more unknown 'Solar Sunrise' incident.[1] It seems that all first started in 1996 and affected Wright Patterson Air Force Base, National Aeronautics and Space Administration (NASA), the US Pentagon, weapon laboratories, military contractors, universities, academics, the US Department of Energy, and numerous other American government agencies; however this espionage cyber-warfare operation remained admirably unnoticed until March 1998 at best.[2,3,4]

The investigators claimed that if all the information stolen was printed out and stacked into a pile of documents, it would reach approximately the height of 507 meters.[5] The Moonlight Maze investigation revealed that gigantic amounts of data were being exfiltrated from the research files not only of the Wright Patterson Air Force base, but also from a large number of computers in the Defense network, the national nuclear laboratories of the Energy Department, numerous US government agencies and even civilians (academics and contractors). The FBI case file was eloquently named "Moonlight Maze," since the IT security specialists could not shed light on what was happening other than reporting that the data was being sent

---

[1] The Solar Sunrise cyberattack occurred in 1998, while Moonlight Maze was investigated in 1999 but most probably started in 1996! Consequently, the word 'following' has been put into brackets. Gragido and Pirc (2011), pp. 161–164.

[2] Doman (2016).

[3] Other accounts endorse the view that Moonlight Maze was revealed in 1999, the same year the Moonlight Maze investigations officially began. *See also* Clarke and Knake (2010), p. 56.

[4] Michael Vatis, the director of the FBI National Infrastructure Protection Center, stated that the cyberattacks appeared to have originated in Russia although the evidence was scarce for such a bold statement. Gragido and Pirc (2011), p. 165, with further reference.

[5] The Independent (2020).

through a long series of stops in many countries before ending up 'somewhere'.[6] For this purpose an extensive network of proxy servers working in various universities and libraries in the United States, as well as at least one server in England, were utilised by the attacker in a way that even in 2017 Kaspersky highlighted its importance and connection with modern threats like "Turla".[7] Moreover, they could not stop the data from being stolen in a daily basis. Every time new defenses were put in place the attacker would overcome them. Then suddenly one day, the attacks stopped. Or, possibly, the attacker(s) started attacking in a way security experts could not find out any more.[8] Undeniably, Moonlight Maze raised quite early concerns about Russian state-sponsored involvement, although concrete proof of state-sponsorship was never established.[9]

Shortly after the 'Solar Sunrise' and 'Moonlight Maze' yearslong cyberattacks, another prolonged cyber attack of espionage nature was revealed by the courageous Shawn Carpenter. These cyberattacks were collectively called 'Titan Rain' and targeted once more various American government agencies, including NASA, the US Pentagon, military contractors, civilian academics, and the US Department of Energy. Carpenter, a network analyst at Sandia National Laboratories whose work was focused on Lockheed Martin and other aerospace corporations, embarked on a mission to establish attribution of foreign entities engaged in exploring, compromising, exploiting, and extracting data from networks like Sandia's. After months of travel and research, he meticulously tracked a group of alleged Chinese cyber spies, monitored their communications and gathered evidence on their activities.

They aimed to access sensitive data within restricted network environments, while taking precautions to remain undetected, hide their presence and cover their tracks. While the US government remained silent about Titan Rain, high-ranking officials acknowledged the seriousness of the breaches identified by Carpenter. The FBI conducted investigations into the possibility of state-sponsored attacks by the People's Republic of China, although attribution remained always a subject of speculation and debate. Nevertheless, it is noteworthy that the activities associated with the People's Liberation Army's cyber warfare units expanded beyond Titan Rain, with further incidents observed in Germany and the United Kingdom in 2007.[10]

The next major chapter of cyber warfare belongs unequivocally to Stuxnet. The infamous Stuxnet computer worm was secretly utilised since 2005 to damage and postpone the Iranian nuclear program but was first uncovered in 2010.[11] Stuxnet was a highly sophisticated computer worm and arguably the first piece of malware

[6] Clarke and Knake (2010), p. 56.

[7] Pankov (2017).

[8] Clarke and Knake (2010), p. 63.

[9] *Contra* Rid and Buchanan (2014), p. 11, who note the existence of "a reasonable level of certainty".

[10] Gragido and Pirc (2011), pp. 166–170.

[11] Reuters (2013). *See* also Wrissbrodt (2013), pp. 351–352.

designed not just to disrupt or steal information from information technology systems, but to cause physical damage to specific industrial systems. Its primary target was Iran's nuclear program. Specifically, Stuxnet worm was designed to attack Siemens programmable logic controllers (PLC) used to control processes in Iran's uranium enrichment facilities. Consequently, the Stuxnet worm was programmed to alter the speed of frequency converter drives used in uranium enrichment: it would increase and decrease the speed of centrifuges used to enrich uranium, causing them to spin too quickly or too slowly. This not only damaged the centrifuges themselves but also negatively affected the uranium enrichment process. A report by the Institute for Science and International Security suggested that Stuxnet might have damaged up to 2000 centrifuges at the Natanz enrichment plant in Iran.[12]

As a result, Stuxnet also caused significant delays in Iran's nuclear program, setting it back actually by years. Although no nation officially claimed responsibility, there exists a longstanding consensus among many cybersecurity and global affairs experts that it was developed jointly by American and Israeli intelligence services.[13] Following the unprecedented success of the Stuxnet computer worm and the assassination of two Iranian nuclear scientists by Israel in 2010 and at least another two in 2011–2012,[14,15] plans for a 'traditional' Israeli and/or US military attack were halted as not being necessary any more.[16]

The cyberattack on Estonia's government websites, which required even NATO and the US to send security experts to Estonia, took place quite early on April 2007.[17] It was arguably the first time that eminent American newspaper The New York Times ever used the word "cyberwar",[18] following the BBC,[19] The Guardian[20] and other major English media[21] rhetoric. The cyberattacks took place following the removal of a bronze statue of a World War II-era Soviet soldier from a central park to a less prominent place in Tallinn.[22] These attacks were hyperbolically compared to naval blockades where one state's "ports are shut to the sea"[23] by another state. The bulk of the cyberattacks used a technique called "distributed denial-of-service" (Ddos) attack. By flooding the country's websites with vast amounts of unnecessary data, the attackers successfully clogged not only the

[12] Zetter (2014), p. 8.

[13] The Guardian (2011).

[14] The Guardian (2012a).

[15] The Guardian (2012b).

[16] The Guardian (2011).

[17] Weissbrodt (2013), pp. 349–350.

[18] The New York Times (2007).

[19] BBC News (2007).

[20] The Guardian (2007).

[21] *See* indicatively Sydney Morning Herald (2007).

[22] Herzog (2011), p. 49.

[23] The New York Times (2007).

country's servers, but also its routers and switches, i.e., the specialised electronic devices directing traffic on the network. In order to multiply the cyberattack's negative effects, the hackers infiltrated computers around the world with malware known as bots and banded them together in networks to perform the cyber assaults unknowingly like 'zombies'; it is estimated that perhaps around one million computers from all over the world were 'recruited' for the execution of the said cyberattack.[24] Estonia blamed Russia for playing a crucial part in the cyber warfare.[25]

Moreover, in 2008 Georgia's technological venture of laying submarine cables in order to link its national internet infrastructure with Western Europe sparked another incident of serious cyberattacks. The volatile relations with Russia were exacerbated, because it was considered that the completion of the project would greatly reduce Georgia's dependence on Russian infrastructure and fortify Georgia's political sovereignty. As the project neared its completion in July 2008, a prominent cyber assault was directed towards the website of Georgia's president, Mikheil Saakashvili. An orchestrated distributed denial-of-service attack bombarded the site with an overwhelming volume of ICMP, TCP, and HTTP requests, resulting in more than a day-long shutdown. This event marked the onset of a formidable series of cyberattacks that would persist over the following weeks.

As Russia commenced its territorial incursion into Georgia on 8 August 2008 another denial-of-service assault coincided with the physical invasion. During that time, a significant portion of Georgian internet traffic was channeled through Russia, rendering Georgia susceptible to Russian cyber espionage and digital offensives. For the second time in the same summer, a host of Georgian websites, including the presidential website, the Ministry of Defense and the Ministry of Foreign Affairs websites, as well as several news portals, were targeted. Subsequently, a number of high-profile financial institutions, crucial to Georgia's economy, fell also prey to cyberattacks. The attackers not only orchestrated distributed denial-of-service attacks but also took over and vandalised several websites with Russian propaganda. Simultaneously, the digital infrastructure in nations including Turkey and Ukraine, which also facilitated internet connectivity to Georgia, was reported to have been targeted.[26] The denial-of-service attacks and website vandalisations persisted through August 2008. Eventually Georgia, with the aid of Internet Service Providers (ISPs), was able to block the sources of these attacks and restore its digital infrastructure. Given the concurrent timing of the digital and physical invasions, there was a widespread conjecture about Russian involvement in these cyberattacks.[27] Moreover in 2009 was Kyrgyzstan's turn to be knocked offline. A critical denial-of-

[24] *Ibid.*

[25] BBC News (2007).

[26] DiMaggio (2022), pp. 36–37.

[27] *Ibid.*

service attack hit the country's two main ISPs, accounting for nearly 80 percent of the country's bandwidth.[28]

Consequently in 2014 NATO acknowledged that a serious electronic attack against one of its members could trigger the alliance's Article 5 collective defense clause, which allows members to take military action against the aggressor "on a case by case basis".[29]

Moreover, it came as no surprise—in fact one could argue that it was quite late[30]—when in June 2016 NATO Secretary General Jens Stoltenberg publicly announced that just like air, sea, land, and space, cyberspace was now officially considered a potential battlefield by the world's biggest military alliance, i.e., essentially a fifth military operational domain.[31]

During that Press Conference and particularly during the "Questions and Answers" session Jens Stoltenberg highlighted inter alia that:

> Cyber defense is part of collective defense. Most crises and conflicts today have a cyber dimension, so treating cyber as an operational domain would enable us to better protect our missions and operations. . .This is about. . .also to help and assist nations in defending their cyber networks, and since it's very hard to imagine a military conflict today without a cyber dimension. . .[and] all possible conflicts we can foresee in the future. . .One of the challenges when we speak about cyber is that it's not always easy to tell exactly who is attacking you. So, everything related to attribution is one of the issues which are high on our agenda, and we are developing capabilities to be better able to attribute different kinds of cyber attacks.[32]

Indisputably this late recognition of cyberspace as a military operational domain constituted solid truth that the concept of cyber warfare had already evolved and most probably would continue to evolve beyond the complete grasp of academics, generals and military experts.[33] Sharma vividly describes cyber warfare as "an elephant assessed by a group of blind people, with every one drawing different meanings based upon their perceptions",[34] while the truth is that cyber warfare is not a potent force multiplier, but in fact "cyber war is a new form of warfare and, rather than cyber war merely being an enhancement of traditional operations, traditional operations will be force multipliers of cyber war"[35] in the future. And this is the case because cyber warfare constitutes a revolution in military affairs which will inevitably change the world order as all previous revolutions in military affairs have done in the past.[36]

---

[28] The New York Times (2009).

[29] NATO Press Release (2014) 120, Wales Summit Declaration.

[30] *See* Czosseck and Geers (eds.) (2009).

[31] NATO, Press Conference (14 June 2016).

[32] *Ibid.*

[33] Ranger (2016).

[34] Sharma (2009), p. 4.

[35] *Ibid.*

[36] *Ibid.*, p. 5.

Consequently, it was rather expected that less than a month before the 2022 Russian invasion of Ukraine, several Ukrainian government websites would be hacked. Several websites including those of the Ministry of Defence, the Ministry of Foreign Affairs, and the Cabinet of Ministers were temporarily down, and a message appeared "warning Ukrainians to 'prepare for the worst'".[37] Following that, after the official beginning of the conflict between Ukraine and Russia, a series of cyberattacks have been reported, including attacks on Ukraine's digital infrastructure (affecting financial services and energy), an attack targeting KA-SAT,[38] and attacks into Ukrainian radio and TV networks in order to display fake news.[39]

Hence, it comes as no surprise that the most powerful states have placed high on their agenda the cyber warfare. To name but few indicative examples, China has placed a national focus on expertise in cyber warfare (as well as space) in its revised conscription laws.[40] United States of America has also publicly placed a high priority on cyber warfare capabilities pursuant to the U.S. Department of Defense Cyber Strategy released in 2018, where it is outlined the US's intention to defend the state, its people and way of life from cyberattacks.[41] Likewise the United Kingdom has expressed its commitment to enhance its cyber capabilities. "The Integrated Review of Security, Defence, Development and Foreign Policy" in 2021 emphasized the importance of cyber capabilities for national security.[42] To the same vein France has also stressed the importance of cyber defense. The Strategic Review on Cyber Defense, published in 2018, highlights the necessity of investing in cyber capabilities for national defense.[43] Finally Germany released officially earlier than other states in 2016 "The Cybersecurity Strategy for Germany", which outlines the country's focus on strengthening its cyber defense.[44]

Finally, if one had to choose between the last most prominent cyber attacks that affected critically states, enterprises and organisations that would be he SolarWinds cyberattack.

---

[37] BBC News (2022).

[38] A telecommunications satellite providing broadband internet access.

[39] European Parliament (2022). *See also* CSO (2022).

[40] The Guardian (2023).

[41] U.S. Department of Defense, Summary of the 2018 Department of Defense Cyber Strategy, <https://media.defense.gov/2018/Sep/18/2002041658/-1/-1/1/CYBER_STRATEGY_SUMMARY_FINAL.PDF> accessed 8 June 2023.

[42] HM Government (2021).

[43] French Ministry of the Armed Forces, Strategic Review on Cyber Defense (2018). *See also* Italian Institute for International Political Studies, The French Strategic Review of Cyber Defense, 2 May 2018, <https://www.ispionline.it/en/publication/french-strategic-review-cyber-defense-20376> last accessed 8 June 2023.

[44] Federal Ministry of the Interior, Building and Community, Cybersecurity Strategy for Germany (2016) <https://www.enisa.europa.eu/topics/national-cyber-security-strategies/ncss-map/national-cyber-security-strategies-interactive-map/strategies/cyber-security-strategy-for-germany/@@download_version/5f3c65fe954c4d33ad6a9242cd5bb448/file_en> accessed 8 June 2023.

The SolarWinds cyberattack was a major cybersecurity breach discovered in December 2020. It served as an example of a supply chain attack in which the perpetrators targeted software from the IT management company SolarWinds. The attackers, members of the state-sponsored hacker group Nobelium—also responsible for the Sunburst backdoor and Teardrop malware[45]—infiltrated the software development pipeline for SolarWinds' Orion software platform. This platform is widely utilized by state agencies, organizations, enterprises, and institutions to manage their IT networks.

Initially, the attackers compromised a Microsoft employee's computer[46] and subsequently introduced malicious code into the Orion platform updates. This maneuver effectively created a digital Trojan horse that went undetected for several months. The covert backdoor, which was secretively engineered by the Trojan horse, allowed them unprecedented access to potentially tens of thousands of SolarWinds' customers. This pool of customers included numerous U.S. federal agencies and Fortune 500 companies that had installed the Orion software.

According to an official statement from Microsoft, the illicit cyber activity primarily targeted IT companies (57%), followed by government agencies (20%).[47] A smaller percentage of targets included non-governmental organizations, think tanks, and financial services. Furthermore, Microsoft indicated that the activity was primarily focused on U.S. interests (about 45%), the U.K. (about 10%), with lesser numbers from Germany and Canada. In total, 36 states were targeted worldwide.[48]

The extent of the damage was significant, as the attackers gained access to sensitive data, disrupted operations, and even sabotaged systems. This attack is considered one of the most significant cybersecurity incidents to date due to its sophistication and high-profile targets. Following this cyberattack, there were substantial repercussions for SolarWinds and the broader tech and cybersecurity industry. The incident illuminated vulnerabilities in software supply chains and incited discussions about improving network security to guard against similar types of attacks in the future.[49]

---

[45] Microsoft Security Response Center (2021a).

[46] Wired (2021).

[47] Microsoft Security Response Center (2021b).

[48] *Ibid.*

[49] Zetter (2023).

12.3 The Tallinn Manuals

It is important to note that this chapter should mention the Tallinn Manuals and predominantly to Tallinn Manual 2.0.[50] Although these instruments are non-binding both regarding the ICC and States, there is no doubt of their importance in providing a prima facie essential guidance on the interpretation of international humanitarian law norms to the cyberspace.[51] For this reason, the said chapter turns often to the Tallinn Manuals—especially the Tallinn Manual 2.0—as an auxiliary source of interpretation.

The Tallinn Manual 1.0 was created by an international group of experts in international law and cyber security who were convened by the NATO Cooperative Cyber Defence Centre of Excellence (CCDCOE) in Tallinn, Estonia. The project was led by Professor Schmitt M N of the United States Naval War College and involved a team of over 20 legal experts from various countries. The Tallinn Manual 1.0 was published in 2013 and was purported to be arguably the first comprehensive analysis of how international law, including the law of armed conflict, applied to cyber warfare. The manual was intended to provide guidance to governments, military leaders, and other stakeholders on the legal framework for cyber operations in the context of armed conflict. It covered a range of topics, including sovereignty, due diligence, the use of force, and the law of armed conflict. Its publication was a significant event in the development of international law in the cyber domain. It provided a comprehensive analysis of how existing international legal principles applied to cyber warfare and helped clarifying some of the existing legal ambiguities.

However, as the cyber threat landscape continued to evolve, it became clear that a second edition of the Tallinn Manual was needed. The Tallinn Manual 2.0, published in 2017, expanded its scope in order to cover a wider range of cyber operations beyond those related to armed conflict. The manual examined how international law applied to issues such as cyber espionage, cybercrime, and protection of critical infrastructures.

Moreover, the Tallinn Manual 2.0 attempted to address some of the criticisms of its first edition. Hence, it has been argued that Tallinn Manual 2.0 was developed through a more transparent and inclusive process, with broader participation from legal experts worldwide. It also incorporated a more diverse range of perspectives, including those from non-Western countries, while providing updated guidance on the interpretation of international law to the rapidly evolving landscape of cyber operations. Thus, Tallinn Manual 2.0 expanded its analysis and provided a much more comprehensive guidance on the legal framework for cyber operations regarding a broader range of contexts.

---

[50] Schmitt (2017), (hereinafter 'Tallinn Manual 2.0').

[51] Trahan (2021).

12.4 Cyber Warfare and Cyberattacks in the Context of International Criminal Law

This section explores how cyberwarfare can be included within international criminal law. Firstly, it defines the closely related terms of cyber warfare, cyberattacks, cybercrimes, and other related terms such as cyber espionage and then analyses how cyberattacks could potentially fall under crimes under the ICCRSt. Following that, this section analyses how cyberattacks could be considered war crimes under article 8 of the ICCRSt by looking at its constitutive elements.

Michael Vagias validly points out that while "the Rome Statute establishing the International Criminal Court (ICC) was adopted in 1998 and entered into force in 2002",[52] the first legislative attempts to address internet criminality at national level had already taken place since the 80's and onwards in many states, including the United Kingdom, the United States of America, Australia and Canada [US, Computer Fraud and Abuse Act, aka CFAA, (1986), UK, Computer Misuse Act (1990), Australia, Cyber Crime Act (2001), Canada, Act to Amend the Criminal Code and to make consequential amendments to other Acts (2001)].[53,54]

While it is quite understandably that the Rome Statute was shaped through a protracted and diplomatically stressful process that left virtually no room for the discussion of contemporary technological developments,[55] it is equally important to note that the coming of the digital era did not invade the thoughts of ICC officials for many years. Hence, it is quite characteristic that even in the Strategic Plan (2016–2018) of the Office of the Prosecutor[56] the focus on the digital era rests solely on the adaptation of "the Office's investigative and prosecutorial capabilities and network to the scientific and technological environment in which it operates".[57]

In other words while the Strategic Plan 2016–2018 acknowledges the need of "understanding and shaping how future technology can assist it to execute its mandate",[58] its focus is placed one-dimensionally on the need to utilise more new digital technologies for "the identification, collection and presentation of evidence through technology",[59] with only a final and somewhat vague referral to the immediate need of gaining "insight into new possibilities and threats coming from technological evolution".[60] Nonetheless, even in that final sentence the possibility

[52] Vagias (2016), p. 203.

[53] *Ibid.*, p. 203.

[54] Australian Government, Cyber Crime Act (2001); Government of Canada, An Act to amend the Criminal Code (organized crime and law enforcement) and to make consequential amendments to other Acts (2001).

[55] *See* Chap. 1 of the book.

[56] Office of the Prosecutor, Strategic Plan 2016–2018.

[57] *Ibid.*, p. 23.

[58] *Ibid.*, para. 60, p. 23.

[59] *Ibid.*, para. 60.

[60] *Ibid.*, para. 61.

of war crimes, crimes against humanity and genocide to be conducted via the digital world is totally overlooked, since the word 'threats' implies dangers that may arise out of the use of novel technologies against the Court and the Office of the Prosecutor *per se*.

Likewise the Office of the Prosecutor's Strategic Plan 2019–2021 notes merely that "[t]he Office will also continue to interact with Internet Service Providers to identify possibilities to preserve online, publicly accessible information that is relevant for its investigations and prosecutions".[61] Hence, even in this next publicly available Strategic Plan, the only referral made to the digital era is about digital information which could be linked to 'situations'[62] and consequently should be preserved.

Although commonly referred inextricably, cyber warfare, cyberattacks, cybercrimes, and other related terms (e.g., cyber espionage) constitute different acts/concepts with distinct legal consequences. However, it is worth noting that these concepts are more and more interrelated, and a single act may constitute more than one of the above terms.[63]

Cybercrime is a broader term used to define illegal activity committed through or facilitated by computer-based means, such as a PC, a network or a hardware device.[64] Cyberattack has been defined by the *Talinn Manual 2.0* as *"a cyber operation, whether offensive or defensive, that is reasonably expected to cause injury or death to persons or damage or destruction to objects"*.[65] Finally, cyber warfare can be understood as the use of cyberattacks that either occur in the context of armed conflict or whose effects are equivalent to those of a conventional armed attack.[66] In this sense, it is important to note that cyber warfare will always meet the conditions of a cyberattack, even though the opposite is not true.[67] Therefore, by focusing the analysis on cyber warfare, this section will equally analyse issues that may arise within the context of cyberattacks.

Outside the context of an armed conflict, cyberattacks may also amount to international crimes under the ICC jurisdiction. For example, cyber-operations may be used to perpetrate crimes against humanity or genocide.[68] The

[61] Office of the Prosecutor, Strategic Plan 2019–2021.

[62] *See* Chap. 1 of the book for the distinction between a 'situation' and a 'case' within the legal realm of the International Criminal Court.

[63] Faga (2017).

[64] Hathaway et al. (2012), p. 834.

[65] Schmitt (2017), p. 126.

[66] Hathaway et al. (2012), pp. 836–837. It is worth noting, however, that this term *"is virtually non-existent in official documents and it lacks international acceptability"*. *See* Faga (2017), p. 9.

[67] Hathaway et al. (2012), p. 837.

[68] Trahan (2021).

characterisation of a cyber operation as either a crime against humanity or genocide would evidently depend on the contextual elements of each core crime.[69]

To name but one example, a cyberattack would amount to a crime against humanity if it was committed "as part of a widespread or systematic attack against a civilian population",[70] provided that its perpetrator had knowledge of this.[71] Additionally, a cyberattack should result in one or more of the acts listed under art. 7 (1) of the ICCRSt (e.g., murder, extermination, or torture). In this context, Trahan[72] gives the example of a cyber-operation that leads to a dam's system being infiltrated, opening its gates, and flooding a city with major loss of life. In this example (and if the attack met the contextual elements of crimes against humanity), Trahan[73] suggests that this could lead to the crime against humanity of murder (art. 7(1)(a), ICCRSt), or persecution if the attack was directed against members of a particular protected group (art. 7(1)(h), ICCRSt). Additionally, the act listed under art. 7(1)(k) ICCRSt (i.e., "*Other inhumane acts of a similar character intentionally causing great suffering, or serious injury to body or to mental or physical health*") might be interpreted to encompass particularly serious cyberattacks.[74]

Similarly, a cyberattack could be considered genocide if it is conducted *"with the intent to destroy, in whole or in part, a national, ethnical, racial or religious group, as such"*.[75] Again, this cyberattack should result in one of the acts listed under Article 6 ICCRSt (e.g., killing members of the group, causing serious bodily or mental harm, etc.), meaning this would likely be a cyberattack with kinetic effects. It is important to note, however, that in the case of the crime of genocide its most important element remains its *dolus specialis,* i.e., the intent to destroy (in whole or in part) one of the protected groups. Thus, if the above example of the cyberattack on a dam system happened with the requisite *dolus specialis* of the perpetrator, this could amount to genocide. Trahan[76] also mentions the concept of cyber-enabled genocide, such as using cyber technology to monitor protected groups or using cyber means to incite genocide (and the killing itself occuring physically).

Finally, a cyberattack could—at least theoretically—also amount to a crime of aggression. Weissbrodt[77] suggests that, although it is not explicitly mentioned in the definition of aggression, it still could be argued that certain cyberattacks could amount to aggression, as long as the Prosecution could establish the existence of a State action behind it which rose to the level of use of armed force (provided that

[69] *See* Chaps. 3 and 4 for the exact definition and elements of the crime of genocide and crimes against humanity, respectively.

[70] ICCRSt, art. 7 (1).

[71] *Ibid.*

[72] Trahan (2021), p. 1157.

[73] *Ibid.*

[74] Trahan (2021), p. 1158.

[75] ICCRSt, art. 6.

[76] Trahan (2021), pp. 1158–1160.

[77] Wrissbrodt (2013), p. 369.

there is jurisdiction over the crime). However, Ambos[78] rejects this possibility, arguing that "a computer network attack (CNA) would hardly amount to a crime of aggression". Ambos[79] lists three reasons for this: **i)** the fact that art. 8*bis* ICCRSt does not encompass conduct by non-state actors (who are usually behind cyberattacks); **ii)** the fact that only exceptionally an attack of this kind would be considered aggression within the meaning of art. 8*bis* ICCRSt (2); and **iii)** the fact that a cyberattack would hardly qualify as a "manifest violation of the Charter of the United Nations", which constitutes the threshold set by art. 8*bis* (1) ICCRSt.

Thus, it is likely that cyberattacks end up within the exercise of the ICC's jurisdiction as war crimes, and within the context of cyber warfare. The remainder of this section explores this possibility, which also must comply with the contextual elements of war crimes (i.e., the existence of a link to an armed conflict), as well as its physical elements (i.e., a cyberattack that falls within one of the crimes listed under art. 8 of the ICCRSt). As it is explained below, the way cyber warfare is conducted could pose particularly difficult challenges for the ICC.

12.5 Cyberattacks as War Crimes: Existence and Link to an Armed Conflict

As explained in Chap. 5, the use of the terms 'armed conflict' and "within the established framework of international law" under Article 8 ICCRSt demonstrate that the ICC currently has no jurisdiction over the isolated or short use of force.[80] Thus, the existence of an armed conflict (either an international armed conflict or a non-international armed conflict) is absolutely essential. Additionally, the ICC's Elements of Crimes lists as an element for every war crime the fact that the conduct should have taken *"place in the context of and was associated with"* an armed conflict.[81] This means that the existence of an armed conflict is not enough, it is also necessary that there exists an active link between the conduct and the conflict itself.[82]

In the context of international criminal law, in order to determine the existence of an armed conflict for the purpose of establishing a war crime, courts may take into consideration factors including: **i)** the employment of armed force;[83] **ii)** its attribution to one of the parties to the conflict;[84] or **iii)** the fact that at least one of the parties

[78] Ambos (2016).

[79] *Ibid.*

[80] *See* Sect. 5.3.

[81] Article 8 ICCRSt - Elements of Crimes.

[82] *See also* Trahan (2021), p. 1154.

[83] Ambos (2014), pp. 164–183. *See also The Prosecutor v. Duško Tadić* Decision on the Defence Motion for Interlocutory Appeal on Jurisdiction, IT-94-1-AR, 02 October 1995, para. 70.

[84] *Ibid.*

considers itself in a state of war (regardless of the existence of an official declaration or not).[85]

Authors like Ambos[86] and Hathaway et al.[87] distinguish two scenarios in which cyberattacks can be linked to armed conflict. The first is the occurrence of a cyberattack in the context of an already existing armed conflict. The second is the possibility of a cyberattack initiating an armed conflict. Both possibilities have different legal thresholds, which are examined below.

The first scenario is less controversial, as the threshold for the existence of an armed conflict has already been met through already prior recourse to conventional armed force.[88] As the existence of an armed conflict has already been established in this scenario, the only thing left to verify would be a link between the cyberattack itself and one of the parties to the conflict.

A more complicated scenario would be if a cyberattack were to initiate an armed conflict. The above-mentioned three criteria used to determine the existence of an armed conflict refers to the use of armed force, an essential element. Thus, this cyberattack would need to meet a threshold to amount to an armed force. While this has never happened thus far,[89] it is not difficult to envision happening in the future.[90] In order to measure this, Ambos[91] suggests following the *effects approach*—i.e., examining the actual effects of a cyberattack rather than the means used to commit it. Should a cyberattack produce (kinetic) effects similar to the damage caused by a traditional physical attack, it will be much more likely considered as the use of armed force,[92] and potentially give rise to an armed conflict.

One example of a cyberattack that could produce kinetic effects akin to a physical attack and potentially give rise to an armed conflict is an attack on a state's critical infrastructure. Critical infrastructure, such as power grids, water treatment plants, and transportation systems, are central to the proper functioning of modern society. If these systems were seriously disrupted or disabled by a cyberattack, the effects could be similar to a physical attack, such as a bombing or a missile strike. Hence, if a cyberattack successfully targeted a power grid, it could cause widespread power outages and disrupt the functioning of essential services. Hospitals, communication systems, and transportation systems could be critically affected, causing harm to people and infrastructure. The effects of such an attack could correspond to those of a physical attack, and it could potentially lead to an armed conflict if the targeted country believed that the attack was carried out by another state and constituted an

[85] Kolb and Hyde (2008).

[86] Ambos (2016).

[87] Hathaway et al. (2012).

[88] Ambos (2016), pp. 157–158.

[89] Hathaway et al. (2012), p. 850.

[90] For instance, Germany has recognised that armed hostilities may be "totally conducted by using cyber means". *See* Federal Government of Germany (2021), p. 7. *See also* Ambos (2016), fn. 34.

[91] Ambos (2016), pp. 158–159.

[92] *Ibid. See also* Trahan (2021), fn. 34.

armed attack. Thus, cyberattacks targeting critical infrastructure could be justifiably considered as comparable to traditional uses of force and could potentially give rise to armed conflict.

12.6 Cyberattacks That Could Amount to War Crimes

Although article 8 ICCRSt has never been used in the context of cyber warfare, there is no impediment to its applicability in the context of cyberattacks. On the contrary, the ICJ in the *Legality of the Threat or Use of Nuclear Weapons* case has emphasized that IHL norms are applicable to *"all forms of warfare and to all kinds of weapons, those of the past, those of the present and those of the future"*.[93] Similarly, the Talinn Manual 2.0, under Rule 80, mentions that the IHL norms are applicable to cyber operations executed in the context of an armed conflict.[94]

As such, the principles of distinction and proportionality[95] are equally applicable to cyber operations. Regarding the principle of distinction, rule 94 of the Tallinn Manual 2.0 states that the civilian population *"shall not be the object of cyberattack"*, whereas rule 105 prohibits *"to employ means or methods of cyber warfare that are indiscriminate by nature"*. The Tallinn Manual 2.0 also refers to the principle of proportionality under rule 113, under which *"[a] cyber attack that may be expected to cause incidental loss of civilian life, injury to civilians, damage to civilian objects, or a combination thereof, which would be excessive in relation to the concrete and direct military advantage anticipated is prohibited."*

Should a cyber operation breach rules of IHL, this could amount to war crimes and incur on individual criminal responsibility,[96] including under article 8 of the ICCRSt. It is not hard to imagine a scenario in which a cyberattack leads to the actus reus (i.e., objective elements) of Article 8 crimes such as intentionally directing attacks against the civilian population (art. 8(2)(b)(i), or 8(2)(e)(i), ICCRSt.) or civilian objects (art. 8(2)(b)(ii), ICCRSt.), provided that the contextual elements described above, as well as subjective elements (*mens rea*) are also present.

---

[93] *See Legality of the Threat or Use of Nuclear Weapons* (Advisory Opinion) 1996 ICJ Reports. 226, p. 257, para. 86.

[94] Tallinn Manual 2.0, Rule 80.

[95] *See* section: 'Lethal Autonomous Weapons, Drones and Robots: to what extent their usage infringes upon established principles of international criminal law?' above for the definition of the principles of distinction and proportionality.

[96] *See also* Tallinn Manual 2.0, rule 84: 'Cyber operations may amount to war crimes and thus give rise to individual criminal responsibility under international law'.

12.7 Inducing Others Via the Web to Commit War Crimes or Other Crimes of the Rome Statute

Vagias uses as a theoretical scenario the 'case' of an influential Russian blogger based in Moscow, who is accused of encouraging individuals to perpetrate a genocide against Georgians in South Ossetia via articles and posts in English at a Russian-hosted website. According to the facts of that 'case' the ICC Prosecutor is seeking the issuance of an arrest warrant for the Russian blogger, who went shortly to The Netherlands, under the charge of inciting genocide pursuant to Article 25(3)e ICCRSt. Admittedly, if that had indeed happened, the competent Pre-Trial Chamber would then have been tasked with determining whether the specific crime fell under the Court's territorial jurisdiction before issuing an arrest warrant. More specifically, the Court would have to clarify the extent online incitement was committed on the territory of a State Party in order then to establish jurisdiction pursuant to Article12 ICCRSt.[97]

Following the war in Ukraine more realistic 'cases' have potentially emerged. To name but one example, Russian bloggers and writers may incite Russian soldiers, members of the Wagner paramilitary group and military commanders to commit war crimes and/or crimes against humanity during the fiercely fought prolonged conflict (e.g.: see Table 12.1 which shows the blogger's nationality, age, country of residence, server's location, place where the incited crime was committed, the incited crime and the ICC's jurisdiction pursuant to Art. 25 and 26 ICCRSt). The authors of the said texts may reside permanently in Russia, China, South Africa, Brazil and India and 'utilise' web domains hosted by servers located in Russia, China, South Africa, Brazil and India. Finally the true age of the aforementioned is under debate, but it is rumoured that their age range widely from 16 to 86 years old. Pursuant to Article 25(3) ICCRSt a person is criminally responsible and liable for punishment for a crime within the jurisdiction of the Court if "(b) he/she orders, solicits or induces the commission of such a crime which in fact occurs or is attempted;.... (d) In any other way contributes to the commission or attempted commission of such a crime by a group of persons acting with a common purpose". Furthermore, pursuant to Article 26 ICCRSt entitled "Exclusion of jurisdiction over persons under eighteen" It is expressly stated that the ICC has no jurisdiction over persons who were under the age of 18 at the time the crime was committed, as in most national jurisdictions, a person is considered an adult at the age of 18.

[97] Vagias (2016), p. 534.

Table 12.1 The case of hackers inciting members of the Russian forces via their posts and websites to commit war crimes and crimes against humanity

Blogger ID and nationality	Country of residence	Server location	Place where the incited crime was committed	Current age	Crime incited	Jurisdiction pursuant to Articles 25 and 26 ICCRSt
B001 Russian	Russia	Russia	Ukraine (occupied territory)	18	War crimes	Debatable, maybe criminally responsible, maybe not. (Questions to be considered: was he over 18 when the alleged crime was committed? What is the critical time to be considered, the time the article was published and disseminated or the time the actual crime took place?)
B002 Chinese	China	Russia	Ukraine (occupied territory)	34	War crimes and crimes against humanity	Yes, criminally responsible
B003 Russian and South African	South Africa	China	Ukraine (occupied territory)	45	Crimes against humanity	Yes, criminally responsible
B004 Brazilian officially but of Russian origin	Brazil	India	Ukraine (occupied territory)	56	War crimes	Yes, criminally responsible
B005 Russian	India	South Africa	Ukraine (occupied territory)	17	Crimes against humanity	No, not criminally responsible
B006 Russian	Russia	Brazil	Russia (Belgorod)	85	War crimes and crimes against humanity	Yes, criminally responsible

12.8 Exercising ICC's Territorial Jurisdiction Over Cyberattacks and Crimes Committed Via the Web: Challenges of the Digital Era

Adding to the difficulties of establishing cyberattacks as war crimes in the context of cyber warfare, the ICC is expected to find significant challenges when trying to establish its jurisdiction over crimes committed through cyberspace. First, the ICC will need to establish whether it has territorial jurisdiction (i.e., jurisdiction *ratione loci*) over the crime—which can be particularly hard if one considers that the cyberspace quite often involves multiple state territories. However, in practice this might not be so difficult as it *prima facie* may seem, since it is now widely accepted that a crime committed via the web can have simultaneously multiple places of crime (*loci delicti*).

Moreover, if one draws a parallel with the use of LAWs or AWs, the fact that these attacks are operated remotely, will potentially incur additional difficulties in establishing individual criminal responsibility, with the added challenge of the likelihood the authors of the cyberattack(s) in question remain anonymous within the indiscernible web clouds.

The first challenge the ICC may face when establishing its jurisdiction is regarding its territorial jurisdiction (i.e., jurisdiction *ratione loci*) over acts committed through cyberspace.

Article 12 ICCRSt under the title 'Preconditions to the Exercise of Jurisdiction" and specifically the provision of 12(2)(a) ICCRst explicitly states that the Court has territorial jurisdiction when *"The State on the territory of which the conduct in question occurred or, if the crime was committed on board a vessel or aircraft, the State of registration of that vessel or aircraft"* is a state party to the Rome Statute (ICCRSt).

The term 'territory' in this article poses some important questions regarding the cyberspace.[98] How will the ICC interpret territoriality in the cyberspace? And if there is a link between the conduct that took place on the cyberspace and a territory, would this be sufficient? Neither the Rome Statute or the Rules of Procedure and Evidence or the Elements of Crimes, make any specific referral to the notion of 'qualified territoriality' (subjective or objective territoriality) or the establishment of jurisdiction (based on the location of the commencement or of the results of a crime, respectively) or 'ubiquity'. Indisputably, this last lack of referral to ubiquity creates *prima facie* an important lacuna, since ubiquity is a notion closely linked with crimes committed within or via the digital world. (jurisdiction over a crime if any part thereof has been committed on the territory of a State Party).

[98] The other possibilities for the ICC to have jurisdiction are either if the crime is committed by a national of a State-Party, or if the case has been referred to the ICC by the UNSC through a resolution, but this is often not the case.

An issue on the establishment of territorial jurisdiction in the cyberspace is referred to by Chaumette[99] as *"déterritorialisation"* (i.e., the fact that cyberspace is not a tangible space geographically located that could amount to the common concept of State territory, but rather a universal and virtual reality that is difficult to grasp).[100] On that note, however, Chaumette[101] concludes that, although cyberspace could be seen as aiming to avoid any connecting territory (in the usual sense of the word), there would always be a connecting link to a territory, for instance the State where the computer in which the cyberattack was initiated is, the State where the targeted system is located, or the State where the central servers are.[102]

The following question then relates to this connecting link to a territory. Often, cyberattacks take its material form in multiple territories. In the example above, a cyberattack could be initiated in State A, target (and even produce effects) in State B and have its central servers in State C (or even go through servers located in multiple States). This could make the analysis of where the "conduct in question" (in the sense of article 12(2)(a), ICCRSt) took place in a State-Party extremely difficult.[103]

In the Situation in the People's Republic of Bangladesh/Republic of the Union of Myanmar, the ICC adopted a broader interpretation of the principle of territoriality.[104] In doing so, Pre-Trial Chamber III held that the word 'conduct' is to be read in a factual sense, *"capturing the actus reus element underlying a crime subject to the jurisdiction ratione materiae of the court"*.[105]

In addition, Pre-Trial Chamber III also found that, under customary international law, States may assert territorial criminal jurisdiction (even if part of the conduct takes place outside its territory), *"as long as there is a link with their territory."*[106]

In the case of Myanmar/Bangladesh, the Chamber found that this link was present as the crime in question (deportation, under article 7(1)(d), ICCRSt) essentially implied the crossing of the Myanmar/Bangladesh border as one of its elements,

[99] Chaumette (2018).

[100] *Ibid.*, p. 4.

[101] *Ibid.*, pp. 4–5.

[102] *Ibid.*

[103] *See also* Trahan (2021).

[104] *Situation in the People's Republic of Bangladesh/Republic of the Union of Myanmar,* Decision Pursuant to Article 15 of the Rome Statute on the Authorisation of an Investigation into the Situation in the People's Republic of Bangladesh/Republic of the Union of Myanmar, ICC-01/19, 14 November 2019. *Situation in the People's Republic of Bangladesh/Republic of the Union of Myanmar*, Decision on the Prosecution's Request for a Ruling on Jurisdiction under Article 19(3) of the Statute, ICC-RoC46(3)-01/18, 06 September 2018.

[105] *Situation in the People's Republic of Bangladesh/Republic of the Union of Myanmar,* Decision Pursuant to Article 15 of the Rome Statute on the Authorisation of an Investigation into the Situation in the People's Republic of Bangladesh/Republic of the Union of Myanmar, ICC-01/19, 14 November 2019, para. 46.

[106] *Ibid.,* para. 54.

thus having one of its constituting elements taking place in a State-Party (i.e., Bangladesh).[107]

Another way of tackling this challenge is through the ubiquity doctrine. The ubiquity or 'effects doctrine', is a concept that extends beyond traditional territorial jurisdiction in order to take properly into account real situations where the application of traditional legal views regarding territorial jurisdiction would be practically insufficient and/or create critical loopholes for the actual conferment of justice. It is especially relevant in the context of international or transnational crimes or 'mere' crimes with cross-border impacts.

To name but one example in the case of state-sponsored group of hackers who conduct secretly cyber warfare, it is possible that the members of the group may operate simultaneously from various global locations (Moscow, Zurich, London etc.) via the utilisation of 'zombie computers' in multiple locations (Athens, New York, Berlin etc.) with the explicit aim of inflicting serious harm to the civilian infrastructure of various states (Belgium, France, The Netherlands etc.). Consequently, in the above case, it would be *de lege ferenda* correct to endorse the view that the places of crime, i.e., the *loci delicti,* are simultaneously: **1.** Russia, Switzerland and the United Kingdom (states linked to the group's physical operation) **2.** Greece, United States of America and Germany (states linked to the physical existence of 'zombie computers') **3.** Belgium, France and The Netherlands ('target' states) [e.g.: see Table 12.2 which shows the *loci delicti* of the State-sponsored hacker group operations, the states were 'zombie computers' are located, the places where VPN are located and the states that have been targeted].

Moreover, if we added up to the above scenario the possibility that the hackers' group utilised also VPN servers based in Denmark, Austria and Iceland in order to mask further their illicit cyber warfare activities, then the table would be further expanded as follows (see Table 12.2):

Table 12.2 outlines the four sets of *loci delicti* related to the above case scenario of a state-sponsored group of hackers conducting covert cyber warfare against other states. The first set consists of the states linked to the group's physical operations (Russia, Switzerland, and the United Kingdom). The second set includes the physical locations of the 'zombie computers' used by the state-sponsored hackers' group (Greece, the United States, and Germany). The third set includes the states where the vpn servers are located (Austria, Denmark, Iceland). Finally, the fourth set includes the target states of the cyberattacks, (Belgium, France and The Netherlands).

In simple terms, according to the principle of ubiquity a crime is considered to have occurred in every jurisdiction where any component of the crime took place, or where the effects of the crime are materialised. For instance, if an individual in state A commits a cybercrime that has significant effects on individuals or systems in state B, then under the principle of ubiquity, state B has also jurisdiction over the crime, even though the primary act was commenced and carried out in state A. Thus far the ubiquity doctrine has been applied in various ways across jurisdictions. It is

[107] *Ibid.,* para. 62.

Table 12.2 The case of State-sponsored hacker group operations making cyber warfare

Loci Delicti	States where hackers operate from	States with 'zombie computers'	States where VPN servers are located	States being targeted
1. Russia	State-sponsored hacker group operations			
2. Switzerland	State-sponsored hacker group operations			
3. United Kingdom	State-sponsored hacker group operations			
4. Greece		Physical existence of 'zombie computers'		
5. United States		Physical existence of 'zombie computers'		
6. Germany		Physical existence of 'zombie computers'		
7. Belgium				Target of cyber warfare
8. France				Target of cyber warfare
9. The Netherlands				Target of cyber warfare
10. Austria			Location of VPN servers	
11. Denmark			Location of VPN servers	
12. Iceland			Location of VPN servers	

particularly relevant in the context of international law and has been used in cases related to terrorism, cybercrime, drug trafficking, and other forms of organised crime.

The application of the principle of ubiquity is supported by the application of the provisions of Article 21(1)(b) and (c) ICCRSt, which explicitly state that the Court shall apply "where appropriate, applicable treaties and the principles and rules of international law, including the established principles of the international law of armed conflict; (c) Failing that, general principles of law derived by the Court from national laws of legal systems of the world. . .provided that those principles are not inconsistent with this Statute. . .".

Given the aforementioned legal analysis as well as the said case scenario, the critical question of whether the ICC might exercise its jurisdiction *ratione loci* will likely be assessed on a case-by-case basis. Clearly, in forming its assessment, the Court will closely look at whether any of the *actus reus* elements of the crime in question took place in, or had a link with, the territory of a State-Party. However, given the multiplicity of locations, it seems quite possible that in most cases the Court will be able to establish and exercise its *ratione loci* jurisdiction, as the two tables above demonstrate.

Consequently, it seems that the only case the ICC jurisdiction will be excluded is only if the following three conditions are cumulatively met: **1)** the perpetrators are nationals of a state that has not ratified the Rome Statute (ICCRSt) **2)** all multiple places directly or indirectly involved for the conduct of the cyber warfare are located in states which have not ratified the Rome Statute and **3)** the harm/damage eventually caused affects a state or states which have not ratified the Rome Statute.

Hence, if Russian and Chinese hackers operated in Iran and Syria for the purpose of conducting cyber warfare via servers located in India, Israel, Pakistan and North Korea with the explicit aim of causing serious damage to nuclear plants based in the United States of America, all the said three conditions would cumulatively be met because: **1)** Neither China nor Russia are states-parties to the Rome Statute (ICCRSt) **2)** Iran and Syria, i.e., the two states the hackers operate from, have not ratified the ICCRSt **3)** None of India, Israel, Pakistan and North Korea, i.e., the states where the servers are located, are states-parties, since they have not ratified the ICCRSt **4)** United States of America, i.e., the state where the nuclear plant is located, has not ratified the ICCRSt too. Nonetheless if the nuclear plant was adjacent to Canada, then it could arguably be found that the court has *rationae loci* jurisdiction, because Canada is a longstanding state-party and the harm/damage caused to it too suffices in order the gravity threshold to be duly met.

References

Table of Cases

ICJ (1996) Legality of the Threat or Use of Nuclear Weapons (Advisory Opinion) 1996 ICJ Reports. 226, p. 257

Prosecutor v. Duško Tadić (1995) Decision on the Defence Motion for Interlocutory Appeal on Jurisdiction, IT-94-1-AR

Situation in the People's Republic of Bangladesh/Republic of the Union of Myanmar (2018), Decision on the Prosecution's Request for a Ruling on Jurisdiction under Article 19(3) of the Statute, ICC-RoC46(3)-01/18

Situation in the People's Republic of Bangladesh/Republic of the Union of Myanmar (2019) Decision Pursuant to Article 15 of the Rome Statute on the Authorisation of an Investigation into the Situation in the People's Republic of Bangladesh/Republic of the Union of Myanmar, ICC-01/19

Books

Ambos K (2014) Treatise of international criminal law. Volume II: the crimes and sentencing. OUP

Clarke RA, Knake RK (2010) The next threat to national security and what to do about it. Harper Collins

Czosseck C, Geers K (eds) (2009) The virtual battlefield: perspectives on cyber warfare. IOS Press

DiMaggio J (2022) The art of cyberwarfare: an investigator's guide to espionage, ransomware, and organized cybercrime. No Starch Press

Gragido W, Pirc J (2011) Cybercrime and espionage: an analysis of subversive multi-vector threats. Syngress

Kolb R, Hyde R (2008) An introduction to the international law of armed conflicts. OUP

Schmitt MN (2017) Tallinn Manual 2.0 on the international law applicable to cyber operations. CUP

Zetter K (2014) Countdown to zero day: Stuxnet and the launch of the world's first digital weapon. Crown Publishing Group

Zetter K (2023) The untold story of the boldest supply-chain hack ever. Wired. https://www.wired.com/story/the-untold-story-of-solarwinds-the-boldest-supply-chain-hack-ever/. Accessed 8 June 2023

Articles/Papers

Ambos K (2016) Individual criminal responsibility for cyber aggression. J Confl Secur Law 21(3): 495

Chaumette AL (2018) International criminal responsibility of individuals in case of cyberattacks. Int Crim Law Rev 18:1

Faga HP (2017) The implications of transnational cyber threats in international humanitarian law: analysing the distinction between cybercrime, cyber attack and cyber warfare in the 21st century. Baltic J Law Polit 10(1):1

Hathaway OA et al (2012) The law of cyberattack. Calif Law Rev 100:817

Herzog S (2011) Revisiting the Estonian cyber attacks: digital threats and multinational responses. J Strateg Secur 4(2):49

Rid T, Buchanan B (2014) Attributing cyber attacks. J Strateg Stud:1–36. https://doi.org/10.1080/01402390.2014.977382

Sharma A (2009) Cyber wars: a paradigm shift from means to ends. In: Czosseck C, Geers K (eds) The virtual battlefield: perspectives on cyber warfare. IOS Press

Trahan J (2021) The criminalization of cyber-operations under the Rome Statute. J Int Crim Justice 19:1133

Vagias M (2016) The territorial jurisdiction of the ICC for core crimes committed through the internet. J Confl Secur Law 21(3):523

Weissbrodt D (2013) Cyber-conflict, cybercrime and cyber-espionage. Minn J Int Law 22:347

Websites/Web Sources

Australian Government, CyberCrime Act (2001). https://www.legislation.gov.au/Details/C2004C01213. Accessed 8 June 2023

BBC News (2007) Estonia Hit by Moscow Cyber War. http://news.bbc.co.uk/2/hi/europe/6665145.stm. Accessed 8 June 2023

BBC News (2022) Ukraine cyberattack: Russia to blame for hack, says Kyiv. https://www.bbc.com/news/world-europe-5999253. Accessed 8 June 2023

CSO (2022) Russia-linked cyberattacks on Ukraine: a timeline. https://www.csoonline.com/article/3647072/a-timeline-of-russian-linked-cyberattacks-on-ukraine.html?page=3. Accessed 8 June 2023

Doman C (2016) The first cyber espionage attacks: how operation moonlight maze made history, medium. https://medium.com/@chris_doman/the-first-sophistiated-cyberattacks-how-operation-moonlight-maze-made-history-2adb12cc43f7. Accessed 8 June 2023

Federal Government of Germany (2016) Federal Ministry of the Interior, Building and Community, Cybersecurity Strategy for Germany (2016). https://www.enisa.europa.eu/topics/national-cyber-security-strategies/ncss-map/national-cyber-security-strategies-interactive-map/strategies/cyber-security-strategy-for-germany/@@download_version/5f3c65fe954c4d33ad6a9242cd5bb448/file_en. Accessed 8 June 2023

Federal Government of Germany (2021) On the application of international law in cyberspace - position paper. https://www.auswaertiges-amt.de/blob/2446304/32e7b2498e10b74fb17204c54665bdf0/on-the-application-of-international-law-in-cyberspace-data.pdf. Accessed 8 June 2023

French Ministry of the Armed Forces, Strategic Review on Cyber Defense (2018). Italian Institute for International Political Studies, The French Strategic Review of Cyber Defense. https://www.ispionline.it/en/publication/french-strategic-review-cyber-defense-20376. Accessed 8 June 2023

Government of Canada, Justice Laws website, An Act to amend the Criminal Code. https://laws-lois.justice.gc.ca/PDF/2001_32.pdf. Accessed 8 June 2023

HM Government (2021) Global Britain in a competitive age: the integrated review of security, defence, development and foreign policy. https://www.google.com/url?sa=i&rct=j&q=&esrc=s&source=web&cd=&ved=0CAIQw7AJahcKEwjg1vyktdH_AhUAAAAAHQAAAAAQAg&url=https%3A%2F%2Fassets.publishing.service.gov.uk%2Fgovernment%2Fuploads%2Fsystem%2Fuploads%2Fattachment_data%2Ffile%2F975077%2FGlobal_Britain_in_a_Competitive_Age-_the_Integrated_Review_of_Security__Defence__Development_and_Foreign_Policy.pdf&psig=AOvVaw21MYbJ9Ho9mLt1bwdpUYbp&ust=1687335648229476&opi=89978449. Accessed 8 June 2023

International Criminal Court (2015) Office of the Prosecutor, Strategic Plan 2016-2018' Strategic Goal 4, paras 58–61. https://www.icc-cpi.int/sites/default/files/iccdocs/otp/070715-OTP_Strategic_Plan_2016-2018.pdf. Accessed 8 June 2023

International Criminal Court (2019) Office of the Prosecutor, Strategic Plan 2019-2021, para. 55, p. 30. https://www.icc-cpi.int/sites/default/files/itemsDocuments/20190726-strategic-plan-eng.pdf. Accessed 8 June 2023

Microsoft Security Response Center (2021a) Nobelium Resource Center. https://msrc.microsoft.com/blog/2020/12/december-21st-2020-solorigate-resource-center/. Accessed 8 June 2023

Microsoft Security Response Center (2021b) New Nobelium Activity. https://msrc.microsoft.com/blog/2021/06/new-nobelium-activity/. Accessed 8 June 2023

NATO (2016) Press Conference: NATO Secretary General Jens Stoltenberg following the North Atlantic Council meeting at the level of NATO Defence Ministers. https://www.nato.int/cps/en/natohq/opinions_132349.htm?selectedLocale=en. Accessed 8 June 2023

NATO, Press Release (2014) 120: Wales Summit Declaration Issued by the Heads of State and Government participating in the meeting of the North Atlantic Council in Wales. https://www.nato.int/cps/en/natohq/official_texts_112964.htm. Accessed 8 June 2023

Pankov N (2017) Moonlight maze: lessons from history. Kaspersky Daily. https://www.kaspersky.com/blog/moonlight-maze-the-lessons/6713/. Accessed 8 June 2023

Ranger S (2016) Cyberwarfare comes of age: the internet is now officially a battlefield. ZDNet. https://www.zdnet.com/article/cyberwarfare-comes-of-age-the-internet-is-now-officially-a-battlefield/. Accessed 8 June 2023

Reuters (2013) Researchers say Stuxnet was deployed against Iran in 2007. https://www.reuters.com/article/us-cyberwar-stuxnet-idUSBRE91P0PP20130226. Accessed 8 June 2023

The Guardian (2007) Traynor, Ian, Russia accused of unleashing cyberwar to disable Estonia. https://www.guardian.co.uk/world/2007/may/17/topstories3.russia. Accessed 8 June 2023

The Guardian (2011) Ewen MacAskill, Stuxnet Cyberworm Heads off US Strike on Iran. https://www.theguardian.com/world/2011/jan/16/stuxnet-cyberworm-us-strike-iran. Accessed 8 June 2023

The Guardian (2012a) James Meikle, Iran: Timeline of Attacks. https://www.theguardian.com/world/2012/jan/11/secret-war-iran-timeline-attacks Accessed 8 June 2023

The Guardian (2012b) Mehdi Hasan, Iran's nuclear scientists are not being assassinated. https://www.theguardian.com/commentisfree/2012/jan/16/iran-scientists-state-sponsored-murder. Accessed 8 June 2023

The Guardian (2023) China revises military conscription laws in space warfare push. https://www.theguardian.com/world/2023/may/02/china-revises-military-peoples-liberation-army-conscription-laws-space-cyberwarfare. Accessed 8 June 2023

The Independent (2020) Fox B, Riechmann D, Baldor L & Brien MO, Hack may have exposed deep US secrets; damage yet unknown. https://www.independent.co.uk/news/hack-may-have-exposed-deep-us-secrets-damage-yet-unknown-hackers-hackers-donald-trump-government-us-b1774648.html. Accessed 8 June 2023

The New York Times (2007) Landler M & Markoff J, Digital Fears Emerge After Data Siege in Estonia. https://www.nytimes.com/2007/05/29/technology/29estonia.html. Accessed 8 June 2023

The New York Times (2009) Mackey R, Are 'Cyber-Militias' Attacking Kyrgyzstan? https://archive.nytimes.com/thelede.blogs.nytimes.com/2009/02/05/are-cyber-militias-attacking-kyrgyzstan/. Accessed 8 June 2023

The Sydney Herald Morning (2007) Estonia urges firm EU, NATO response to new form of warfare: cyberattacks. https://www.smh.com.au/national/estonia-urges-firm-eu-nato-response-to-new-form-of-warfare-cyberattacks-20070516-gdq5iu.html. Accessed 8 June 2023

Think Tank European Parliament (2022) Russia's War on Ukraine: Timeline of Cyberattacks. https://www.europarl.europa.eu/thinktank/en/document/EPRS_BRI(2022)733549. Accessed 8 June 2023

Wired (2021) Goodin D, SolarWinds Hackers Continue Assault With a New Microsoft Breach. https://www.wired.com/story/solarwinds-hackers-continue-assault-new-microsoft-breach/. Accessed 8 June 2023

Index

V. Tsilonis, *The Jurisdiction of the International Criminal Court*,
https://doi.org/10.1007/978-3-031-46138-5

B

C